Foundations of Economic Evolution

Dedicated to Peer Otto

NEW HORIZONS IN INSTITUTIONAL AND EVOLUTIONARY ECONOMICS

Series Editor: Geoffrey M. Hodgson
Research Professor, University of Hertfordshire Business School, UK

Economics today is at a crossroads. New ideas and approaches are challenging the largely static and equilibrium-oriented models that used to dominate mainstream economics. The study of economic institutions – long neglected in the economics textbooks – has returned to the forefront of theoretical and empirical investigation.

This challenging and interdisciplinary series publishes leading works at the forefront of institutional and evolutionary theory and focuses on cutting-edge analyses of modern socio-economic systems. The aim is to understand both the institutional structures of modern economies and the processes of economic evolution and development. Contributions will be from all forms of evolutionary and institutional economics, as well as from Post-Keynesian, Austrian and other schools. The overriding aim is to understand the processes of institutional transformation and economic change.

Titles in the series include:

Property Rights, Consumption and the Market Process
David Emanuel Andersson

The Evolution of Path Dependence
Edited by Lars Magnusson and Jan Ottosson

Economics, Culture and Social Theory
William A. Jackson

Deep Complexity and the Social Sciences
Experience, Modelling and Operationality
Robert Delorme

Creative Industries and Economic Evolution
Jason Potts

Institutional Variety in East Asia
Formal and Informal Patterns of Coordination
Edited by Werner Pascha, Cornelia Storz and Markus Taube

Capitalism and Democracy
A Fragile Alliance
Theo van de Klundert

Foundations of Economic Evolution
A Treatise on the Natural Philosophy of Economics
Carsten Herrmann-Pillath

Foundations of Economic Evolution

A Treatise on the Natural Philosophy of Economics

Carsten Herrmann-Pillath

Academic Director, East–West Centre for Business Studies and Cultural Science,
Frankfurt School of Finance and Management, Germany

Edward Elgar
Cheltenham, UK • Northampton, MA, USA

Published by
Edward Elgar Publishing Limited
The Lypiatts
15 Lansdown Road
Cheltenham
Glos GL50 2JA
UK

Edward Elgar Publishing, Inc.
William Pratt House
9 Dewey Court
Northampton
Massachusetts 01060
USA

A catalogue record for this book
is available from the British Library

Library of Congress Control Number: 2013936170

This book is available electronically in the ElgarOnline.com
Economics Subject Collection, E-ISBN 978 1 78254 836 2

MIX
Paper from
responsible sources
FSC® C013056

ISBN 978 1 84720 474 5

Printed and bound in Great Britain by T.J. International Ltd, Padstow

Contents

List of Figures

Preface

This book aims at providing a philosophical framework for the naturalistic turn in economics that is currently taking place. By this, I am referring to the fact that the sciences play an increasing role in economics, in the shape of new disciplines such as neuroeconomics, the diffusion of experimental methods and the further emphasis on empirical methods while becoming nonchalant over the axiomatic foundations. However, I believe that the need for a philosophical foundation arises from the fact that the underlying theories of economics are not yet built on naturalistic foundations. One of the central difficulties relates with the perennial problem of the social sciences and their philosophy: How to account for the human capacity of meaning and autonomy against what would be perceived as a reductionist enterprise in which all human action would be subsumed under causal laws which are the domain of the sciences. My book submits a proposal of how to solve this problem.

This proposal is based on one single and simple idea, which, on the surface, seems radically reductionist: Knowledge is a physical phenomenon. I trace the aforementioned difficulties back to one of the greatest errors in the intellectual history of humankind, Cartesian substance dualism. I argue that this still haunts the social sciences and economics in assigning a special place to the 'mental' in their theories. In economics, this is reflected in the fact that in the foundations of economics, knowledge is mostly treated as a mental state of individuals. So, many problems in economics are actually ill-posed problems of the coordination of those individualized mental states: This is why, for example, the problem of expectations has been of prime importance in the development of macroeconomics in the twentieth century. The question of the nature of knowledge is dividing many streams of economic thought, such as the opposition between 'Austrian' views of the market process as opposed to a 'neoclassical' one. I argue that these troubles evaporate if we recognize a fundamental ontological fact: Knowledge is a physical state of the world, just as other physical states of the world. This view translates into what might be seen as a naïve, pre-scientific attitude towards economic phenomena. So, for example, I approach prices as material objects, such as price tags, or markets as material settings, such as marketplaces or computer–based auction sites. 'Knowledge' emerges in processes when physical objects interact causally with other physical objects, in particular, human beings, their brains and their bodies. That being said, we need to recognize the special properties knowledge has. There are many physical phenomena with very different properties: Compare a mechanical lever with superconductivity. Treating knowledge as physical does not preclude the possibility that knowledge has emergent properties which makes it special among the zoo of physical phenomena. So, my approach to naturalism is not just plain and simple materialism: I go for emergentist naturalism.

If I were to identify classical thinkers in economics who already thought in these lines, I name Hayek, Veblen and Georgescu-Roegen (which may appear to be a strange combination for many readers).

- From Hayek, I take two fundamental ideas. The first idea is to build the conceptual foundations of economics on the Philosophy of Mind, of which Hayek developed his own version in his book 'The Sensory Order'. Economics remains incomplete without a proper scientific conception of mental phenomena. The other idea is the notion of distributed knowledge: Human knowledge is impossible without the interaction between minds; for Hayek, knowledge is dispersed about a multiplicity of entities which are not identical with a single human brain. These two ideas were essential for Hayek's understanding of markets as knowledge generating and processing systems.
- From Veblen, I also adopt two ideas. The first idea is that human behaviour is based on an interactive system of bodily states (his 'instincts') which are embedded into systems of social rules ('institutions'); the institutions are embodied in those individual states (his 'habits of thought'), and they evolve. The second idea is that in the context of the economy, institutional and technological evolutions are independent processes, which are intermediated via markets. Technology is a separate domain, and human behaviour differs across the domains, driven by peculiar combinations of motivational forces (epitomized in his figures of the 'engineer' and the 'captain of industry').
- From Georgescu-Roegen, I take one great idea. This is that economics as a science remains fatally incomplete if we do not explicitly include the energetic transformations that drive economic activity into the definition of its object. All economic activity is a physical process and therefore obeys physical laws. Therefore, the most universal laws of physics need to be part and parcel of the foundations of economics, which is Thermodynamics (materially, and not just in formal terms). This also means that the human economy is part and parcel of the encompassing 'economy of nature', namely the ecology of the Earth System.

Taken together, the intellectual legacy of these three authors defines the setting of my naturalistic approach to economics. Indeed, this book is not a big intellectual feat; it does not harbour great theories or complicated mathematics. I pursue the humble task to put the ideas of many others together. Facing the disciplinary fragmentation across the sciences, and between the sciences and the human studies, this may not be a mean achievement, but it is still a far cry from presenting a fully-fledged theory. Therefore, I do not claim to present a new theory in economics. I am doing Natural Philosophy at the gates of economics, waiting for entry. However, I pose a challenge to economics as it stands: I prompt economists to take the naturalistic turn of their discipline to the end, which I define as consilience between economics and the other sciences. The foundations of economics cannot be grounded within economics, but need to be discovered in this theatre of consilience.

With 'Natural Philosophy' I refer to an outmoded branch in philosophy which was still vigorous in the nineteenth century, and is regarded to be defunct today because of the unfolding of the great theories of sciences since then. Yet, Natural Philosophy is often done by scientists themselves, less by professional philosophers. I revive this tradition for a simple reason. Establishing a naturalistic framework for economics requires to build a synthesis between different disciplines in the sciences (such as physics and biology), and to relate these to topics which are specific to the social sciences (such as institutions). I think that the different disciplines themselves cannot offer such a framework, which would otherwise result either into reductionism or into maintaining disciplinary boundaries as they stand. So, Natural Philosophy is the intellectual activity to achieve conceptual integration by means of reflecting upon those disciplinary–specific approaches and their cross–disciplinary integration. For example, I do Natural Philosophy when I reflect upon the meaning of 'individual' in economics, drawing on philosophical approaches and on the rich discussion of this concept in biology.

I rely on two nineteenth century philosophers who did Natural Philosophy, Hegel and Peirce, with Peirce at the centre. In many respects, Peirce builds on Hegel, even though he often distances himself from Hegel. Hegel is of prime importance for my approach to economics because he introduced a conception of mind which is strictly externalist on the one hand, but at the same time explains human autonomy and freedom. Externalism means that mind is the expression of subjective processes in their recurrent interactions with the external world, and that mental activities are impossible without these externalizations. This idea also defines Peirce's pragmat(ic)ism: The 'mental' is action in the world. According to Hegel, the great paradox of human existence is that freedom is impossible without interdependence between human individuals, exactly because without the 'social' human life would remain entangled in biological causalities. As I will argue in this book, this Hegelian approach results into a fundamental shift in the conceptualization of core economic ideas, such as the notion of 'subjective preferences': There cannot be purely 'subjective' preferences independent from actual choices done in a social context, and only actual choices constitute preferences. Action and interaction result in what Hegel calls 'objective spirit'. Institutions are part and parcel of objective spirit. Hegel's ideas therefore prepare the ground for applying modern theories of the extended mind on economics, radically questioning the assumption of the identity between brain and mind, which, for example, underlies contemporary neuroeconomics and its efforts to reduce subjective utilities to a neuronal substrate.

However, Hegel was a Pre-Darwinian thinker, so his ideas still bear the mark of teleology and historical determinism. A few decades later, Peirce could build on two scientific revolutions of his times, Darwin's theory and Thermodynamics. Still, his philosophical views retain many elements of Hegelian thinking. Therefore, what I am going to do in this book is to establish Peircian metaphysics for economics.

This does not imply literally following Peirce in all respects. Peirce himself vacillated between a thoroughly naturalistic view and a panpsychistic view of mind and matter. I think that these questions can be resolved today, as there are important contributions to Peirce exegesis that strengthen the naturalistic interpretation. In this interpretation, I regard three ideas as essential, apart from approaching mind as a process of externalized interaction.

- The first idea is to view the world as being fundamentally random, and to approach knowledge as a phenomenon that emerges from interactions in the world; that means, knowledge evolves, and being a part of the world, this implies that the world evolves.
- The second idea is that a proper understanding of evolution requires a complex notion of causality harking back to Aristotle, especially with regard to the notion of final causality; against the background of Darwinian Theory this does not imply teleology, but directionality of change. The essential contribution of Thermodynamics is the insight that forces of directionality and the random nature of the world do not stay in contradiction.
- The third idea is that the evolution of knowledge builds on the emergence and evolution of signs, understood as physical phenomena; this establishes the analytical stance of semiotics, which can be applied on different levels of generality, reaching from ontology to questions that are specific to domains such as economics.

What are the implications of this approach for economics, ultimately? As I pinpointed previously, this is to approach 'the economy' as a physical system. Markets are material phenomena. That means, for example, technological knowledge is causally conjoined states of brains as neuronal systems and artefacts, prices are material entities such as price tags or numbers on a computer screen, or markets are market places that are constituted by networked physical interactions between biological individuals, constituting a geography of human interactions. The naturalistic approach to markets means that markets are a particular kind of artefact that has emerged from the evolution of human material civilization. Economics is the specialized study of those artefacts. That means, for example, economics investigates into the emergence of certain new artefacts that are essential for the economy, such as money or firms, and what this emergence implies for the patterns of interactions in the economy, and how these consequences affect the embedded functionings of the economy in the larger ecological structures of the Earth System. In this view, economics is not defined by a certain set of analytical principles, but, in line with the other sciences, by means of reference to a peculiar object. Chemists study chemical substances, biologists study forms of life, psychologists study individual human cognitive and affective systems, and economists study markets as cultural artefacts that are peculiar to the social organization of the human species.

This is the outlook of the Natural Philosophy of Economics. The book had a gestation period of a quarter of a century; some of the essential ideas go back to my 1988 PhD thesis where I elaborated on a combination between economics, general systems theory and China studies to explore the on-going changes in the Chinese economy. At that time, this meant leveraging the marginality of my economic thinking, as China was far from being the 'economic miracle' of today. However, China played an essential role for this early research as well as for further developments, as I thought (and many observers agree today) that the Chinese experience can only be fully understood in economics if economics proper also undergoes an intellectual transformation. From these days onwards, Chinese friends have accompanied my intellectual development until today, and ultimately this book has firstly been presented to the public in two lecture series at Chinese universities: I am indebted to Feng Xingyuan, Hu Biliang and Wang Dingding. At the time of my PhD and early Postdoctoral research, I was happy to receive the intellectual and academic support of German scholars who stood firmly in the tradition of the 'Freiburg School', in particular my supervisor at University of Cologne, Gernot Gutmann, the Marburg scholars, Alfred Schüller, Ulrich Fehl and Hans-Günther Krüsselberg, and Dieter Cassel, my mentor in the early years of my first professorship in Chinese Economic Studies at University of Duisburg (today Duisburg-Essen). Without their support, paving the way for a career in academia in spite of very heterodox leanings, I would not have been able to continue with my work. Early tenure provided the desired space for intellectual freedom and autonomy.

Some of these early ideas were also published in the now defunct 'Journal of Social and Evolutionary Systems'; at that time I was extremely grateful to the editor, Paul Levinson, to see my contributions together with contributions of leading thinkers in the field. But these publications remained irrelevant for economics. Since that time, my intellectual mentor in Evolutionary Economics has always been Ulrich Witt, until most recently

Director of the Evolutionary Economics Unit at the Max-Planck-Institute of Economics at Jena. Ulrich Witt pursued a naturalization program of his own design, and we do not agree on every point. But our efforts are clearly based on a deeply shared commitment to the same intellectual goals, and it was always immensely gratifying to enjoy his intellectual openness and creativity.

In 2002, I launched the first attempt at creating a new synthesis for economics based on evolutionary science. This was supported by Birger Priddat, a leading economist–philosopher in Germany who always ventured into territories beyond standard economics. My book 'Grundzüge der Evolutionsökonomik' (included in one of his edited book series) is a precursor to the current book, but has an entirely different structure and is lacking the philosophical focus, thematically as well as in terms of highlighting certain essential principles. That book was also very radical in trying to establish evolutionary principles of writing via an online version that allowed readers to activate links and to post comments. However, written in German, it was a complete failure, since the German audience was not yet fully aware of the potential of online writing.

In 2010, I published another book ('The Economics of Identity and Creativity') that sketches many ideas of the current book 'in a nutshell', and which was written on invitation by John Hartley, a leading scholar in the field of Cultural Studies. In 2008, John Hartley invited me to take part in the inauguration of a network of scholars working on the new program of 'Cultural Science' which is Cultural Studies, naturalized. His support and the acclaim by these colleagues working in as different fields as archaeology, economics and media studies gave a great boost to my confidence that I was struggling ahead on the right track.

I had already started to work seriously on an English book with the same scope as the 'Grundzüge' in 2007. Since then, I developed many new ideas which partly even go back to my early interest as a student in relating linguistics and economics. One major activity was to explore the notion of 'performativity'; I was extremely lucky to receive Professor Masahiko Aoki's encouragement, as I had already applied his approach in my early work of the late 1980s. This is reflected in the pivotal role that Aoki's theory of institutions plays in this book. My work on performativity was published in a series of three papers in the 'Journal of Economic Methodology' between 2010 and 2013, and I enjoyed the support of the editor, John Davis, whose thoughts on 'identity economics' also influenced me deeply. Another sort of intellectual breakthrough in the recent years was the discovery of the philosophy of Charles Sanders Peirce. One of the intellectual leaders in Biosemiotics, Stanley Salthe, opened my eyes to the connection between semiotics and evolutionary theory, and I was lucky to even co-author a paper with him. Relating Peirce with Evolutionary Economics is certainly exposing the 'heterodox' nature of my work even more pronouncedly, and so it was essential to me that Professor Don Ross, a leading philosopher of economics, expressed his encouragement. Don Ross is another core intellectual source of my work, especially regarding the externalist approach to mind and its application on neuroeconomics and behavioural economics. Finally, I am grateful to Geoffrey Hodgson for his continuing support in writing this book and for including it in his edited series at Edward Elgar.

Recently, I have also received intellectual stimulus from a few young scholars, which deserves mentioning as the attraction of conventional economics has grown in recent years, given the conditions of the academic labour market. There is a tragic note about the fact that even I myself advise my PhD students to avoid the topics that I deem to be the most important ones, as this does not help to maximize future academic employment opportunities. Above all, I am deeply indebted to Christian Hederer who read all the chapters of the book and made many invaluable proposals of improvement. In 2010, I was also lucky to get into touch with two French young scholars, Frédéric Basso and Olivier Oullier, working in the field of economics and the brain sciences; their thinking about Hayek helped me a to envisage cross-disciplinary linkages in these fields. Finally, it was in 2011 that I met with Ivan Boldyrev, a young Russian scholar who introduced me, the German, into Hegel's thinking, which was a veritable discovery.

It is easy to see that my work has also proceeded outside the mainstream channels of academic communication today. The 'Natural Philosophy of Economics' is nothing that fits into mainstream conferences, and there are even very few specialist fora. Therefore, I was happy to enjoy the intellectual hospitality of the Committee for Evolutionary Economics that was launched 20 years ago by Ulrich Witt as a part of the formal structure of the German 'Verein für Socialpolitik', the German association for academic economics. Especially, I mention Kurt Dopfer who always managed to connect unconventional economics with international collaboration and contributed important edited volumes to the intellectual endeavour of Evolutionary Economics; he has always been open to invite me to contribute.

☯

Now, let me briefly overview the gist of my argument. The eight chapters of the book are divided into three parts implicitly. The first three chapters, 'Ontology', 'Causation' and 'Evolution' deal with fundamental aspects of science and develop the 'Peircian metaphysics'. The four chapters on 'Individuals', 'Networks', 'Institutions' and 'Technology' elaborate on the four fundamental elements that make up the core phenomenon economics deal with, and which is treated in the final part with Chapter Eight, 'Markets'. This architecture of the book is simple and means to construct the fundamentals of markets reaching back to the roots, so, starting out from ontology, then moving to the concept of causation (causation in economics must match with foundational ontological notions of causation) and ending up with the theory of evolution in the first part, we look at constitutive elements of markets in the second part. Here, individuals are the most fundamental constituents, reflecting the individualistic stance of economics. Yet, individuals are approached as complex systems that are themselves made up by interactions between networks, institutions and technology. Those three constituents are mutually connected, but are phenomena with an autonomous analytical status. 'Networks' refer to the patterns of interactions between human individuals which are the backbone of their extended minds, 'institutions' refer to the special patterns of regularities in these networks, and 'technology' refers to the artefacts that emerge in networked interactions and which undergird their further evolution.

Chapter One presents ontological foundations of a naturalistic approach to economics. I argue that these foundations need full consideration in economics because consilience across different scientific disciplines is only possible on the basis of universal impossibility theorems, that is propositions about what is impossible in the world (such as, for example, the impossibility of a *perpetuum mobile*). Following Hayek, I put one impossibility theorem at the centre of my argument, the impossibility to reduce mind on brain by means of mental operations that are brain processes in turn. This theorem belongs to the general class of Gödelian impossibility theorems in mathematics, logics and science. Based on this, I introduce the 'Principle of Bimodality', which results into four aspectual modes to approach the world: On the one hand, there is the duality of observer independent versus observer relative facts (a distinction that I borrow from Searle), and we have the distinction between the matterenergy mode and the semiotic mode, which is essential for the Peircian view.

I relate these four modes to the Aristotelian conception of causality, concentrating on the three modes of efficient causality, formal causality and final causality, which I combine into the fundamental analytical tool of this book, the Peircian semiotic triad. The semiotic triad is a meta-principle for arranging different explanatory hypotheses in analysing complex evolving systems; in these systems, selective forces operate on the emergence of functions which is driven by the interaction between efficient causal processes and emergent semiotic intermediations. In terms of general ontology, I treat this semiotic triad as a 'physical inference device', which is the basic pattern in which knowledge is constituted as a physical phenomenon. I refer this approach to recent theories of information in physics, such as Frieden's notion of 'Extreme Physical Information'. This is possible if we realize that the relationship between observers and objects is fundamental for general ontology, once we approach 'observers' as physical processes generating information, which accumulates into physically embodied knowledge, and not simply and naively as human observers. I conclude the chapter with a reflection upon the implications for economics, in particular the conceptualization of markets in the four modes.

Chapter Two presents more detail on the analysis of causal processes through which knowledge emerges. For this, the relationship between observer and object is essential. I approach this relationship in terms of the foundational theory of Thermodynamics. This leads back to Georgescu-Roegen, but presents an alternative view that avoids his misunderstandings of Statistical Thermodynamics. To the contrary, the relationship between Classical Thermodynamics and Statistical Thermodynamics is central for developing a physical approach to knowledge. The chapter spans a wide range of aspects, reaching from the analysis of randomness and regularity to the analysis of the Earth System. The common thread is the Maximum Entropy approach in Non-Equilibrium Thermodynamics which states that open physical systems far from equilibrium will tend towards states in which entropy production in the system–environment ensemble is maximal. This approach has been recently applied on the analysis of the Earth System, thus having important implications for locating the analysis of the economy in the context of general ecology. These applications help to reinstate Georgescu-Roegen's argument why economics needs to be based on Thermodynamics. However, Chapter Two leads to this conclusion by means of reflecting upon the fundamental notion of causation in the context of the observer–object interaction: Then, the role of the biosphere in driving the Earth System towards maximum entropy production states roots in the fact that the biosphere is a system of accumulating information aka knowledge.

Retracing the argument of this chapter backwardly, this conclusion is reached via the analysis of a special kind of structure, which are functions; functions emerge from the interaction of the semiotic and the matterenergy mode in processes of observation. Observations result in information relative to a purpose, which in turn is established by evolutionary forces of selection. This notion of observation is universal: Bees observe flowers in their causal interactions with them, but we can also state more generally, that certain types of causal interactions are physical observations; these are causal interactions which lead to emergent information in terms of emergent constraints on possible states of the world. I develop a general thermodynamic approach to this idea, based on the analysis of the fundamental categories of energy, entropy and work against the background of the formal definitions of randomness vs. regularity. Then we can understand the peculiar physical nature of the Earth System as reflecting the Thermodynamics of knowledge. I establish a simple relationship between three general principles, of which the most general is the Second Law of Thermodynamics, which, in considering the duality of observer and object, relates with the more specific Principles of Maximum Power (Lotka), Maximum Entropy (Jaynes) and Maximum Entropy Production. On the level of applied research, these principles relate with concepts such as the 'Constructal Law' in the analysis of physical flow systems which manifest emergent order, hence accumulation of information aka knowledge.

Chapter Three turns to the analysis of evolution, which focuses on the fact that selective forces only operate on the level of populations of physical inference devices, such that functions evolve on the population level, but materialize on the level of the single individuals. I present a generalized theory of evolution which is based on the Thermodynamics of knowledge, therefore retains important elements of the original Darwinian paradigm, but leaves aside more recent specifications in the so-called 'synthesis' with population genetics. Most fundamentally, evolution is seen as a process that manifests the Second Law, and does not work against it. This is because the accumulation of information reflects a growing gap between realized and possible states of the evolving systems, thus increasing information quantities, resulting from the growing impact of constraints which embody knowledge accumulated by past selection. This most general idea of evolution is a framework for recent theories of 'inclusive inheritance', which allow the building of a more detailed version of Hayek's ideas about the interaction between biological and cultural evolution. This view can draw on extended research on a generic formal framework for analysing selection, that is Price's equation, which I report in the interpretation by Steven Frank. Frank's approach is essential because it relates back to generic theories about the generation of physical information from stochastic interactions between observers and objects.

Based on this universal theory of evolution, I present a few more specific hypotheses which are of special significance for the subsequent chapters. Following Stephen Gould, I regard exaptation as a fundamental process in the evolution of novelties in selection. Exaptation expresses the difference between fitness and adaptation in evolutionary processes far from equilibrium. Fitness results in being a conserved quantity in evolution, that is, represents a zero-sum game on one level of analysis; this is established by the Red Queen Principle which follows from the status of the fitness term as indicating relative fitness. However, resulting from Red Queen races, exaptations emerge which improves adaptation in terms of the realizations of functions relative to the environment. This expresses the more fundamental fact that evolution is a frequency–dependent process. One important aspect of this is another fundamental principle, the Handicap Principle, which refers to signal selection, that is the semiotic mode in the Peircian framework. The Handicap principle is another driver of the emergence of adaptations via exaptations, because it establishes a fundamental functional dualism between the adaptive and the signalling (aka semiotic) functions of phenotypical properties. This framework allows integrating more specific hypotheses about generic properties of evolutionary processes that relate with thermodynamic aspects of energetic transformations, such as the role of size and complexity and the phenomenon of scaling laws.

These three chapters establish the basis of what Ulrich Witt has called the 'hypothesis of ontological continuity' of evolution. The next four chapters develop the components of the foundations of economic evolution.

Chapter Four sketches a naturalistic theory of the individual. The naturalistic theory of the individual accepts the fact that individuals are demarcated by the physical boundaries of the body, but it rejects the idea that knowledge is contained within those boundaries. The naturalistic theory of the individual relates with recent theories on distributed cognition, the extended mind and distributed agency which have been emerging in the Cognitive Sciences and the Philosophy of Mind, thus reaching back to the ideas presented in Chapter One. Further, the naturalistic theory of the individual claims that all hypotheses on human individuals need to be based on evolutionary explanations and must not be introduced axiomatically, as it is done in most of economic theorizing. In this framework, minds are systems of material signs which relate to human brains as neuronal systems, and which allow for the emergence of individuals as intentional systems, hence actors. This reinstates the Hegelian idea that the human individual, a 'person', is established inter–subjectively; however, this is interpreted naturalistically as physical interactions involving material signs. These physical interactions centre on human brains as physical systems of a special kind, that is neuronal systems. Neuronal systems are energetically 'expensive', which reflects the basic physical relationship between energy transformations and information processing. Therefore, in the early evolution of human brains the interaction between energetic transformations, brain growth and the capacity to cooperate in human groups in order to harness energy sources was a driving force of the emergence of particular capacities of human brains, such as the capacity to imitate actions of others.

Based on recent brain research, I develop a basic model of brain semiosis in terms of physical interactions between brains and show some of the principled implications for foundational categories in economics; in particular, the notions of agency and preferences. Agency is seen as a property of individuals which results from identity: identity establishes personhood and is embedded into human groups, both synchronically as confluence of population–level processes of social categorizations and diachronically as narratives that distinguish individuals relative to others. Preferences are seen as evolutionary phenomena. Preferences are not 'inside' the individuals, but are the actions taken (thus vindicating the Revealed Preference approach in a modified, naturalistic sense). In a Hegelian way, the actions taken as being recognized by others are the sources of individual knowledge about reasons for choice. I present a theory of wants and needs that relates to the co-evolution of biological determinants and cultural determinants of human agency, which operationalizes these Hegelian insights into the notion of individual preferences.

Chapter Five explores networks. Networks are the patterns of physical interactions between human individuals, mediated by signs as physical artefacts: As such, networks are the backbone of human extended minds. I posit the basic idea that networks correspond to knowledge structures in terms of their evolving structural constraints on expanding set of possible interactions. This view, as has been shown seminally by Jason Potts, has far-reaching consequences for economics which normally assumes that 'imperfections' of market networks hamper information processing. Network theory states that only 'imperfections', that is constraints on possible sets of interactions, can lead to sustainable knowledge evolution (thus avoiding a 'complexity catastrophe' à la Kauffman). Network evolution strikes a balance between the need to grow the capacity for storing knowledge and the need to preserve the capacity of evolvability, that is generating new information. My theory of networks partly continues with the vigorous research on networks in sociology and physics, which has shown that there are universal properties of networks that allow for the application of mathematical concepts cross–disciplinary. On the other hand, my approach differs from these views in making the role of artefacts explicit, that is signs, thus adopting a bimodal approach to network analysis (which is currently only done in the context of Actor–Network Theory in sociology), and in approaching network interactions in three dimensions, namely transaction, perception and communication (which is mostly practised in the context of research on Complex Adaptive Systems).

One central concern of the chapter is to show how network structure emerges from certain biological constraints on human group formation, and to analyse the flow of innovations enabling network interactions in groups with increasing scale. These constraints reflect past forces of selection, and the flow on innovations results from emergent capacities on the network level. In other words, emergent network structure determines network evolvability. Constraints imply the fundamental categorization of network structures into small groups, tribes and large groups, which correspond to distinct social formations in human societies. These network structures provide the setting for the unfolding of different dynamics of information generation and transmission; these dynamics mostly result from the fundamental mechanism of information externalities in network triads with three dimensions. I show how these dynamics result in a number of distinct network phenomena, which are reflected in three basic concepts specific to the analysis of human networks: Trust, power and status. I draw on the rich literature on social capital in sociology and economics to render these concepts empirically operational.

Power is the central category in the analysis of institutions which I present in *Chapter Six*. This is because institutions are a special kind of network regularity which results from the possibility of sanctions, ultimately rooted in the brute fact of human violence. I eschew efficiency based economic theories of institutions in favour of power–based theories which argue that human institutions evolve to contain the detrimental effects of violence on the gains of cooperation in human groups, thus viewing the secular decline of levels of violence in human societies as a major aspect of institutional evolution (as shown by Steven Pinker recently). This approach is only gaining ground recently in economics, too, such as in the theory on institutions proposed by North, Wallis and Weingast. Institutional evolution is driven by recurrent solutions to the fundamental dilemma that on the one hand enforcement builds most effectively in specialization of coercive powers, which, however, creates the possibility of unilateral defection from cooperation. I propose that the unfolding of this dilemma is shaped by specific forms of group selection in the human species, thus harking back to the fundamental categories of evolutionary analysis as developed in Chapter Three: Institutions play a pivotal rule here because, if working, they partly align individual interests and create conditions for convergent strategies in equilibrium selection in strategic interactions, thus fostering group–level cooperation that enhances relative collective powers in inter–group competition. The solutions of the 'specialization dilemma' in the governance of violence are strongly influenced by the cognitive dynamics of institutions.

The chapter develops basic elements of a theory of cognition and institutions, distinguishing between the different elementary cognitive processes of induction, analogy and deduction, and different mechanisms to anchor institutions in creating commitments (that is self–policing enforcements), such as self–interest and emotions. As a consequence, institutional evolution is strongly path–dependent and manifests the interaction between institutions and ideas, approached in terms of the history of human civilization. I show how the different group structures in network evolution played together in the unfolding of ever–growing network connectivity through civilizational change, with the emergence of agriculture and empires being the evolutionary stage in which the phenomenon of 'institution' emerged in full shape. This evolutionary novelty of institutions roots in the fundamental property of performativity. In applying this notion, I combine recent research on performativity in economic sociology with John Searle's theory of institutions, and I analyse the dynamics by means of a game theoretic conceptual framework developed by Masahiko Aoki. This theory shows how institutions emerge from the causal interactions between signs that emerge in human interactions, taken as physical entities, and neuronal structures which determine behavioural dispositions. So, I can show how performativity also relates with the function of institutions in human distributed cognition. The chapter presents an application of the theory on the primordial institution of the phenomenon of markets, the emergence of money.

Chapter Seven focuses on technology. Technology is an essential aspect of institutions, as institutions rely on technologies of power, that is means of violence, techniques of communication and so forth. Economics neglects the material aspects of technology which are essential for understanding its partial autonomy as an evolutionary domain, which means the artefactual. One cannot simply approach technology in terms of the means–ends relationship, with technology only representing the means. Technological evolution also includes the evolution of technologically determined wants, which renders the means–ends relationship endogenous. Technology is not simply a 'tool', because technology co-determines cognition. On a most fundamental level, all technologies build on measurements in their functionings, such that they obtain the role of physical inference devices; this provides the bases for their role in human distributed cognition. Thus, technology is an essential element in the human extended mind. This holds on the micro–level as well as on macroscopic scales.

On the macro–level, I analyse technology against the background of the general conceptualization of the Earth System. The upshot is an energetic theory of economic growth, which has been developed in much detail recently by Robert Ayres and collaborators, and which establishes the pivotal connection between the physics of knowledge and economics. I argue that the relationship between knowledge growth and energy is based on the fundamental thermodynamic concepts developed in Chapter Two; especially, I argue that economic growth is the expression of the Maximum Power Principle (in terms of extensions proposed by Geraat Vermeij). In this context, it is important to recognize the fact that technological change on the secular scale has always been strongly driven by military factors, thus establishing a deep connection between technological and institutional evolution. I illustrate this point by means of what is certainly one of the most important stages in human history, the Industrial Revolution, as compared to developments in China. This interaction between institutions and technology converges in the emergence of different production regimes, which in turn relate with phase transitions in the evolution of global network connectivity of human societies, reaching from primordial group structures to large scale groups of agricultural societies and eventually to the modern globalized societies.

These macro–level phenomena root in certain basic characteristics of technology on the micro–level, which I relate to the concept of performativity, again. Technology as a structure of knowledge is distributed across producers and users of technology, therefore is embodied in interactions between them. As a consequence, technology also relates with particular patterns of social organization, both in the economy and in other domains, in particular, the military. Then, the process of technological creativity is also seen as a population–level phenomenon and cannot be simply reduced to the creative actions of individuals. On this level, we can analyse technological evolution in terms of generic concepts of evolutionary theory.

Chapter Eight closes the argument of the book. I analyse markets as artefacts, against the background of the ideas and hypotheses developed so far. In doing this, I enter the realm of economics proper, but try to be a simple as possible. So, my argument refers to economics as it is conceived today in terms of the basics, undergraduate level, so to say. In the previous chapters, we have already gained important insights into certain basics, such as the revision of the theory of preferences in Chapter Four, the role of network imperfections in Chapter Five (thus questioning 'perfect markets' as reference points for 'idealizations' in economics, as discussed in Chapter One) or the energetic theory of growth in Chapter Seven. Chapter Eight starts with a methodological reflection upon the role of economics in analysing the economy: I argue that economics as a science is special in having a performative function relative to its object, markets. The intellectual evolution of economics is part and parcel of the evolution of markets. In concentrating on markets, I propose a narrow delineation of the disciplinary boundaries of economics. This can be traced back to the results of Chapter Six: The artefact of money is essential for the emergence of markets, as it allows the obstacles to the unfolding of specialization processes that result from the asset specificity of market opportunities to be overcome. Money enables distinct patterns of network interaction in large groups, which differs fundamentally from social exchange in small groups and tribes. However, these emergent patterns build on all the interaction capabilities that are created on those different levels, an insight which connects with social capital research on markets. The artefact of money enables the emergence of other artefacts, in particular, prices, which implies that absolute prices are theoretically more basic than relative prices.

This naturalistic view of markets draws on the important recent theory proposed by Hans-Christoph Binswanger who established a connection between the monetary conception of the market and the energetic theory of economic growth. The intermediating variable is the creation of credit, which leverages the fundamental network pattern of trust by means of artefacts that allow for its quantification and fungibility. The creation of credit enables the expansion of energetic throughputs via entrepreneurial investments aiming at the generation of pecuniary profits, motivated by the endogenous expansion of wants. The mechanisms of market competition are analysed on Veblenian terms, harking back to evolutionary principles as established in Chapter Three, in particular the Red Queen Principle and the Handicap Principle. This means, in a nutshell, that relative status plays an important role in explain both entrepreneurial actions and consumer demand, as posited by Veblen and already stated by Adam Smith much earlier. Further, markets are performative in an essential way, as market valuations are performative, referring to both the particular valuations, which ultimately build on mutual expectations in network dynamics (I draw on the recent notion of 'social network markets'), and to the institutions that govern valuations (such as accounting methods and standards).

Taken together, the proposed theory of markets entails a number of radical consequences for economics as it stands. In particular, the interpretation of prices as artefacts implies that the standard supply and demand approach to prices is misleading; the concept of equilibrium is substituted by the concept of market clearing, and the determination of prices is explained by other factors. Most generally, prices are institutions. This holds especially for two core prices in markets, the interest rate and the wage rate. I generalize Stiglitz' theory of credit rationing, ultimately going back to Keynes' treatment of long-term expectations; I extend on Akerlof's treatment of wage determination in firms and argue that wages are institutional solutions by which the market clearing function of wages is balanced with the incentive function of wages within organizations which connects with sets of norms governing perceptions of fairness and other dimensions of valuation.

☯

To summarize, this book develops a naturalistic approach to economics which treats the economy as an evolving physical system of knowledge which is governed by fundamental functions of harnessing and dissipating energy, and which is shaped by patterns of distributed cognition in human groups, building on social interactions mediated by evolving sign systems and technological artefacts. The artefact of money is essential to establish the analytical autonomy of the domain of economics. Thus my Natural Philosophy of Economics is Aristotelian, distinguishing between generic social exchange and exchange where money and the motivation for money is pivotal (chrematistics). However, I leave the Aristotelian ethical valuation of this distinction aside, interpreting naturalism in economics as a scientific approach that aims at establishing truthful propositions about reality.

On a most fundamental level, I interpret the human economy as a natural phenomenon by which the Earth System increases its capacity to dissipate energy and thus to achieve states that are further away from equilibrium. This deeper physical aspect of the economy is becoming more and more visible in the phenomenon of Global Warming. This book does not provide an answer to solving these challenges to the human species and the survival and entire ecosystems. However, it is obvious that responses need to be multi–dimensional, affecting all aspects of human behaviour and social interaction that have been scrutinized in this book. Ultimately, I think that the solution can only be found by philosophy, in terms of the creation of values and beliefs which define the human species in a new way, akin to the rise of human civilization during the emergence and growth of agricultural empires, the Jasperian 'axis time' when geniuses such as Confucius and Socrates shaped the ways human civilization evolved until today. We need to perform our identities as human beings differently.

1. Ontology

> Indian chief, watching smoke signals at the horizon: 'What's going on there?' Warrior: 'Smoke on the horizon, great chief!' Chief: 'That's what I see, you idiot! But what do the signs tell us?' Warrior: 'That there is smoke at the horizon.' Chief (angry): 'You want a blow with my tomahawk?' Warrior: 'It's not my fault, that there is smoke at the horizon telling us there is smoke at the horizon.' (Morris and Goscinny, 1962, Lucky Luke, La Caravane, own translation)

1.1. THE NATURALISTIC TURN IN ECONOMICS AND THE PHYSICAL NATURE OF KNOWLEDGE

1.1.1. The changing nature of economics

Over the last three decades economics has been in the course of being naturalized. The emergent naturalism of economics is reflected in two trends. The first is increasing cross–disciplinary research on human behaviour, such as in psychology and the neurosciences. The second is the adoption of methodological approaches of the sciences, in particular the experiment and the laboratory; this is also changing the social fabric of economics, following similar phenomena in the sciences (Doing 2008). Modern economics is becoming a cooperative venture that requires investment into laboratory devices or in large–scale compilation of comparative data on natural experiments (see for example recent progress in 'genoeconomics', Beauchamp et al. 2011); it is aiming at the collective accumulation of empirical results designed for testing competing hypotheses, and it is no longer defined by a small number of fundamental axioms.

The rise of naturalism goes hand in hand with an increasing focus on economic evolution. Whereas in the past, reference to 'evolution' highlighted the borderline between mainstream and heterodox approaches to economics, today evolution is seen as one of the defining features of the economy (for instance Krugman 1996; Smith 2003; North 2005). Research into evolution is complex and thus requires methodological pluralism, which is increasingly evident in on-going economic research (Davis 2006). This renders old methodological fault lines obsolete, such as the distinction between 'evolutionary economics' and '(mainstream) economics'. The economy is an 'evolving complex system' (Arthur et al. 1997), with a recurrent flow of technological, institutional and behavioural novelties. Our task is to understand this system, also having in mind improvements of our actions within that system, such as new approaches in economic policies or new strategies in business. Evolution, complexity and economics are no longer propositions that stay in tension with each other (Durlauf 2012).

1.1.2. The meaning of 'naturalism'

In this chapter, I am going to provide a few ontological foundations of naturalism, without aiming at a fully-fledged systematics. This is necessary for our topic since naturalism continues to stand in tension with certain fundamental principles of economics as they have been stated in the first decades of the 20th century. These principles defined economics as an interpretive science, or a *Geisteswissenschaft*. By this I refer to the fact that the mathematical principles of economics, in particular the notions of utility and rationality, were not seen as being descriptors of reality (for the continuing relevance of this position, see Gul and Pesendorfer 2008); instead, they are treated as purely formal criteria for the generation of hypotheses that can be tested empirically. In practice, economists mostly followed Friedman's (1953) instrumentalism in applying those principles, even though there had been clear statements of the interpretive character of economics (for example von Mises 1949). In spite of the fact that instrumentalism was debunked by philosophers of science working in the field of economics, building on general refutations of instrumentalism in the philosophy of science (Popper 1983: 111ff; Hausman 1992: 162ff; Caldwell 1994: Chapter 8) it factually remained a guiding principle of economic research, arguing that the economy is far too complex to be grasped by the sort of theorizing that would directly identify and generalize over empirical regularities. A black box approach to essential elements was deemed as being reasonable and powerful to reduce this complexity. However, this means that economic theories mainly adopted an interpretive stance, in the sense of Max Weber's (1985: 1ff) notion of the social sciences.

In this view, most of economics falls into the domain of *Geisteswissenschaften*, which is especially true for fields such as game theory. Yet, this stance contradicts the tendency to import theoretical tools from the sciences, in particular physics (Mirowski 1988). In a nutshell, economics evolved as a mathematized *Geisteswissenschaft*, but did not fully transform itself into a *Naturwissenschaft*. This is recognized by scientists critically reflecting upon the peculiar methodological characteristics of economics (for example Wilson 1998: 216ff; Roehner 2002: Chapter 1; for penetrating observations on scientism in economics, see Mirowski 1988, McCloskey 1994); in the philosophy of economics, the problem was mainly reflected in the Popperian strand of thought which pointed out that economics fails to meet strict criteria of falsification (Redman 1993: 116ff). Post–Popperian fallibilism was therefore highly welcomed by economists, who interpreted the Lakatosian description of how science works in a normative way, thus legitimizing their practice (Hands 1993); then, the distinction between the core principles of a particular scientific discipline and different layers of more specific hypotheses, especially in the so-called ‘protective belt’, was received as a recommendation to stick to the core principles, as long as they prove to be sufficiently powerful in the generation of hypotheses, which is certainly a proven feature of economics as it stands. Economics presents itself as a ‘progressive research programme’, and challenging theories and paradigms do not seem to be in sight. This situation prevails in spite of the fact that in many areas many instances of falsification of central hypotheses of economics have been accumulating over decades, such as the so called ‘anomalies’ of rationality in human behaviour.

So, the question is whether the naturalistic turn in economic practice and reasoning can be put into a larger context in order to enable a more systematic consideration of the foundations of the discipline. In this chapter, I build on a strict notion of naturalism which has been developed in the analytical Philosophy of Mind (for a survey, see Papineau 2009b). This broadens the scope of the term substantially, as it obtains the status of a principled approach to ontology, that is our basic assumptions about the status of ‘reality’. Then, naturalism means to adopt the principle of causal closure of the world: All physical effects result from physical causes, and there are no exogenous causes. Especially, naturalism adopts the monistic approach to the mind/brain distinction, and hence rejects the Cartesian substance dualism, in open or disguised form. Naturalism in this sense would question the dichotomy between *Geisteswissenschaften* and *Naturwissenschaften* in the first place. This is because firstly, the principle of physical closure seems to imply reductionism, as all mental phenomena would be seen as physical events; secondly, because the human mind would be seen as a neuronally embodied computational system without any special ontological status; and thirdly, because it seems to preclude any sort of methodological autonomy of the *Geisteswissenschaften*, such as for example that constituted by hermeneutics. One of my tasks in this chapter is to show that this view is wrong. Naturalism does not preclude emergentism, even in the context of physics (Bunge 1977: 97f; Laughlin 2005). Quite the opposite, it is naturalism which entails the conception of economics as ‘novelty-embracing, anti-reductionist evolutionary economics’ (Hodgson 1999: 127ff). In the sciences, this view is especially shared by non-reductionist approaches to biology, which are part and parcel of modern mainstream biology (for example Mayr 1982: 73ff; Maynard Smith and Száthmary 1995).

So, I claim that the tension between the *Geisteswissenschaften* nature of economic theory and the emerging *Naturwissenschaften* spirit of its research practice can be resolved in adopting a fully-fledged naturalistic perspective based on philosophical considerations. I speculate that the deeper reason for this tension lies in the creative powers of reality and its potential to generate ontological novelty.

1.1.3. Natural Philosophy: Hegel and Peirce

In order to achieve this aim of a philosophical reconstruction of the foundations of economics, I embark on doing 'natural philosophy'. Natural Philosophy was an important part of philosophy in the nineteenth century but came to be eclipsed by the rapid growth of the sciences as an independent enterprise. In a sense, philosophy of science is a descendant of Natural Philosophy, but only as being understood as philosophical reflection about the sciences. Yet, today the borderlines between philosophy of science and 'natural philosophy in the closet' are blurring again. One of the major reasons is the fact that philosophers of science recognized decades ago that the original idea to develop universal principles of scientific activities is doomed to fail because it is impossible to define observational languages independently from the theories in question, even obtaining one single and unified observational language for all sciences (Stegmüller 1973). Consequently, over the recent decades we could observe the emergence of disciplinary philosophies of the different sciences. The reason lies in the fact that the different sciences have peculiar conceptual frameworks which seem to be irreducible to other disciplines, such as the distinct notion of probability in quantum physics (Bub 2006), molecular shape in chemistry (Ramsey 2000) or the species concept in biology (Ghiselin 1997). This development indicates the continuing need for a meta–philosophy that scrutinizes structural principles of the world constituted by those disciplinary differences; so, the question is, what do those disciplinary differences reveal about the structure of the world? This is Natural Philosophy, as it is evident that the answer to this question cannot be provided by any of those disciplines alone, as long as we do not have an encompassing 'Theory of Everything' (Barrow 1995). Then, the different disciplines would relate to Natural Philosophy as a universal frame of reference, thus enabling cross– and trans–disciplinary research. So, in closing this chapter I will argue that Natural Philosophy is the epistemic activity by which we can achieve consilience of the different sciences (Wilson 1998).

My use of the term 'natural philosophy' is close to the nineteenth century legacy. I regard the sciences as a major source of philosophical insight and treat them as central references for both ontology and epistemology. However, the sciences are incomplete as sources of our knowledge. This results from the incompleteness of the entire endeavour of science, but also from more principled constraints on the growth of scientific knowledge. These constraints result from the complexity of the phenomena in question (Popper 1982), but also from the inherent limits to the growth of knowledge generating activities, even including economic constraints (Rescher 1999).

Therefore, it is necessary to reflect upon certain fundamentals in a philosophical mode, if only as a default mode of thinking. This especially refers to the fundamentals of ontology and epistemology: Ontology deals with our fundamental assumptions about the structure of reality, epistemology deals with our capacities to approach the world as knowing subjects. In a naturalistic approach, these fundamentals have to be distilled from the most recent results of the sciences, but this distillation needs to work on the grounds of meta-theoretical principles which can only be established by means of philosophical reflection (for a related approach by economist–philosophers, see Ladyman and Ross 2007).

I mainly draw on two 'classical' philosophers in order to build those foundations, Hegel and Peirce. Peirce often debunked Hegel as a source of his own thought (for instance Peirce 1992: 256, 1998: 143ff), but actually picked up many of the latter's core ideas. Both concur in regarding the sciences as an essential source of philosophical insight: Hegel was an avid reader of the most recent contributions to the sciences, and commented widely upon it (Westphal 2008; Ferrini 2009); Peirce, after all, was a practicing scientist throughout his life. Both believed, however, that there is a specifically 'mental' aspect of reality. One of my central arguments in this chapter, which is fundamental for the entire book, is that the conception of the 'mental' is crucial for laying the foundations of economics as an evolutionary science, approached in terms of naturalism. The main difference between Hegel and Peirce lies in the circumstance that Hegel is a pre-Darwinian thinker, whereas Peirce drew on the two fundamental innovations of 19th century sciences, Evolutionary Theory and Thermodynamics.

From Hegel I borrow his idea of 'spirit', and in particular of 'objective spirit' (compare Boldyrev and Herrmann-Pillath 2012 for a more detailed discussion). Hegel's philosophy stood at the root of the distinction between *Naturwissenschaften* and *Geisteswissenschaften*, in particular in Dilthey's original approach to this duality (for an overview, see Forster 2008). Today, we can lend an entirely new interpretation to Hegel's conception of 'spirit' which builds on the sciences. The human mind is seen as a phenomenon of distributed cognition, hence rejecting the brain/mind identity hypothesis (Crisafi and Gallagher 2010). This implies that specific human behavioural features, such as culture and meaning, emerge from complex physical systems of distributed cognition, also dubbed the 'extended mind' along the lines firstly pointed out by Clark and Chalmers (1998) (for a critical evaluation, see Sprevak 2009). This approach is in fact familiar to economists as it implicitly underlies much of Hayek's work (in particular going back to his analysis of the 'Sensory Order' (Hayek 1952). Today, Hegel's approach is mostly misunderstood as positing a sort of panpsychism, that is extending the mind to the universe. However, as the troubles with translating the Hegelian 'Geist' into 'spirit', and not 'mind', already show, this would be very misleading. Just as in modern notions of distributed cognition, the Hegelian spirit relies on its external expressions and creations to evolve its own complexity, especially in terms of different levels of consciousness. Hegel clearly rejects any sort of substance dualism, but avows emergentism, which is formally specified in his dialectics (Westphal 2008). In the Hegelian view, mind as spirit is made up by the different phenomena that I will deal with in this book, in particular by human institutions. In spite of the 20th century ideological clash between followers of Hegel and liberal thinkers, this idea is also clearly expressed by Hayek (for example Hayek 1973: 17): Hayek adopted the view that human mind is made up by many elements which are external to the human organism, and which he subsumed under the heading of 'culture'. More specifically, Hayek argued that human knowledge is not only manifested in human thought, but also human institutions or in economic phenomena such as prices.

From Peirce I borrow the notion of 'signs', hence semiotics, seen in the larger context of his philosophy. Peirce elaborated on a comprehensive philosophical cosmology, in which the mental was seen as primordial category. In my view, this position needs to be re-interpreted in the light of modern science (which certainly would have met with acclaim by the scientist Peirce). Then, the 'mental' would refer to the role of information in the physical evolution of the universe (for an overview, see von Baeyer 2003). Peircian semiotics presents a thorough analysis of this evolution of information, of which human knowledge is just one manifestation (Peirce 1998: 410ff). This is the particular aspect in which philosophy becomes directly relevant for the sciences, because the Peircian system builds on a much more complex notion of causality, fully receiving Aristotelian analysis (Peirce 1998: 314ff). The bedrock of naturalism, the assumption of causal closure, adopts a different meaning when considering this rich conception of causality (which in modern science is mostly present in Complex Systems Theory, see Ellis 2008). Peirce's views ultimately relate back to Hegel, even though he is distancing himself from the latter; both Hegel and Peirce firstly define the 'mental' in terms of its expressions (reflecting a broad intellectual movement in the 19th century, see Taylor 1985), and secondly analyse the mental process in terms of a triadic conceptual structure. Ultimately, this convergence between the two thinkers can be traced back to shared references to Aristotle, especially in the context of thinking about the directionality of change.

1.1.4. The Aristotelian notion of causal explanation

Indeed, Aristotle can certainly be counted as one of the first naturalistic thinkers. However, his ideas about causal explanation differ substantially from modern views, which more or less follow the 'covering law' concept that was firstly introduced by Hempel (for an overview on this and the subsequent ramifications, see Stegmüller 1983). This approach follows the example of Newtonian Mechanics: In causal laws, individual events are seen as being connected via causal relations that have the status of laws, that is general propositions. If we add the idea of a temporal sequence between these events which inheres the Arrow of Time as a fundamental cosmological principle, this results into the Aristotelian notion of 'efficient causality' (which is actually a medieval conceptual translation of the original Greek sources).

Aristotle was concerned with the proper response to 'Why' questions and he argued that the mere identification of an efficient–causal process is not sufficient to achieve a full response to those questions (cf Falcon 2012). Fully-fledged explanations of natural phenomena always refer to four kinds of causes:

- Material causes identify the substance out of which a phenomenon is formed, such as the rock out of which a mountain is formed;
- Formal causes refer to the shape of phenomena, such as the structural and configurational characteristics of the mountain;
- Efficient causes point towards the sequence of changes in the world by which the mountain came into existence in its current shape;
- Final causes refer to the directionality of the forces that determine the changes towards a particular shape of the mountain.

In the original treatment of these causes, reference was often made to processes which involve human action, such as the formation of a statue. In this case, the four causes would converge on a teleological explanation. In these explanations, the formal and the final causes directly connect with human design and intentions. So, for example, the material cause of a statue is the bronze out of which is made, the formal cause is the shape of the statue, the efficient cause is the originator of the action that results into the statue, that is the artist, and the final cause is the purpose of making the statue. It is interesting to notice that Aristotle refers to efficient causes, in this example, as the 'art' of bronze–casting, that is, not just to the sequence of actions. This implies reference to regularities in terms of the knowledge needed to achieve the realization of the artist's design. Hence, we see how the distinction between sequences of individual events and general regularities, which is essential to the covering law interpretation of efficient causation, already inheres to the Aristotelian notion.

Now, Aristotle did not argue that teleological explanations of this sort also apply on nature in general. But he argued that there are important kinds of phenomena for which formal and final causes are primordial, relative to material and efficient causes. This is life. Properties of living systems can only be fully explained by referring to the generative process by which they come into existence, and by the purpose those properties have in the context of these systems. Then, a formal cause is implicit in the fact that the generation of a rabbit requires the existence of rabbits which reproduce themselves, hence represent the fully developed shape of rabbits; a final cause is implicit to the functions that the different properties of rabbits have in the whole system called 'rabbit', including the role of rabbits in their ecological niche, and the purposes of these properties, of which the most general is survival. If we rethink this Aristotelian view in terms of modern concepts, we can translate this statement into the propositions, firstly, that the generation of rabbits presupposes the existence of the (genetic) information that is involved in the ontogeny of single rabbits, and secondly, that this information refers to general functions of rabbit–properties in ensuring survival and reproduction. Hence, we realize that the Aristotelian notion of causality is directly pertinent to the analysis of evolution (for a related thought, see Gould 2002: 1207). So, taking the example of the mountain, on first sight this was not congenial to Aristotle, as he did not claim that all phenomena in nature need reference to final causes in order to reach a full explanation. The question is whether the explanation of mountains requires reference to evolutionary processes; if so, final and formal causality would apply in any attempt for an explanation (such as geological evolutions, along the lines of extending the evolutionary paradigm even towards physics in general, see for example Smolin 1997; Chaisson 2001).

Peirce explicitly referred to Aristotle, but was able to build on the new science of evolution that was created by Charles Darwin at his times. In Short's (2007: Chapters 4 and 5) detailed analysis of the role of final causation in Peirce's thinking the fundamental difference appears to be the idea that randomness is an essential feature of the world and also constitutive for the manifestation of finality. Peirce concentrated on what might be regarded to be the most general core of the Aristotelian approach: final–causal explanations refer to a certain type of end-state that results without directional forces working on the sequences of singular events. For example, consider the dispersion of a liquid in a solution. On the one hand, there is a sequence of efficient causes that underlies the physical process that results in mixing; but at the same time, we cannot claim that those forces themselves have the direction towards this end-state. The end-state materializes because it is the most probable state, given the constraints under which the physical process operates. Therefore, Short proposes to distinguish between 'mechanistical' and 'anisotropic' processes: mechanistical processes relate to sequences of individual events, governed by regularities, and anisotropic processes refer to types of events, in which certain states are favoured for reasons that do not directly refer to the individual events assigned to the states.

Peirce had realized that both Thermodynamics and Darwinian Theory constitute prime examples for those anisotropic processes. In Thermodynamics, certain states are favoured because they are the most probable ones, such as the mixing of liquids in a solution, and in Darwinian Theory, certain states are favoured as they are selected for some general purposes, which ultimately refer to the most universal purposes of reproduction and survival. In both cases, we need to refer to certain modes of explanation which are different from the regularities that govern the sequences of singular events (for a related view, see Hull et al. 2001). These are the final and formal causes of Aristotle. For example, as we shall see in the next chapter, in the context of Statistical Mechanics, the definition of the state space of a physical system can be regarded as a formal cause in explaining the outcomes of applying the laws of Thermodynamics, and the implied probabilities of states as the final causes.

Now, coming back to the relationship between Hegel and Peirce, we can argue that this more complex notion of causality boils down to the role of concepts in causal explanations. This follows from the distinction between singular events and types of events, as a type of event relates with a concept. In Peirce's philosophy, these concepts are the 'signs'. In the context of modern scientific language, this seems confusing at first sight, but is actually easy to understand if we refer back to the notion of 'information' that I already alluded to. I argue that the Peircian concept of signs allows for embarking on an evolutionary approach to information. Two simple ideas are sufficient, considering the following. Firstly, if we say that we obtain information about something unknown, this means that this information increases the probability of a particular possible state of this unknown; then, this information is a 'sign' of this unknown phenomenon. In fact, all our knowledge about the world builds on signs in this sense; we probe into the world by means of some actions (such as a physical experiment), and we receive signs which indicate certain properties of the underlying reality (for a corresponding view in the brain sciences, see Friston and Stephan 2006). Secondly, given the fact that the information that we gain is driven by our actions, the meaning given to these signs is not entirely determined by the underlying reality, but by the purposes of our action; hence, we interpret reality, and do not simply reproduce it. In other words, information is always relative to the receiver of information. Peirce's philosophy offers the appropriate conceptual framework to deal with these essential aspects of information.

1.1.5. The Principle of Bimodality

Based on Hegel and Peirce, I restate the dualism of *Geisteswissenschaften* and *Naturwissenschaften* as the 'Principle of Bimodality'. This is aspectual dualism in a monistic ontology (for a related, but different use of this term, see Dopfer 2005). I argue that in order to fully understand the phenomenon of evolution, it is essential to consider two modes of existence; one is the matterenergy mode, the other is the mode of information, which I call the semiotic mode. In order to make this distinction clear right from the beginning, consider the example of a snowflake (compare Campbell 1974a). Snowflakes are physical phenomena of high complexity and high degrees of order (for a survey of the physical theory of snowflakes, see Libbrecht 2005). We can approach them in the matterenergy mode, comprehending the physical causality underlying their formation: That means, we identify the sequence of events that result in a certain shape of this snowflake. At the same time, every snowflake is a sign, which stores the entire information about the environmental conditions that prevailed on the trajectory from its formation to its fall to the ground. A snowflake is environmental information, in the sense of information theory (Floridi 2003): There is no sender and receiver, as in the theory of communication, but the information could be decoded by an observer. So far, we lack the theoretical tools to access this information, but it is there, like the rings of a tree. Further, a snowflake could also serve as storage of information if we assigned a certain function to it: For example, since every snowflake is unique, so we could use snowflakes as representing human individuals in a bijective mapping.

So, bimodality implies that we can approach the snowflake in these two modes, that is the matterenergy mode, which would appear to be the domain of efficient–causal explanations, and the semiotic mode, which is the domain of final and formal causal explanations. In the semiotic mode, we can approach the snowflake in terms of the information stored in its structure. This information relates with certain physical processes which are thermodynamic in nature. The physical explanation of the shape and size of snowflakes is still very incomplete and faces formidable mathematical challenges, in particular when all dimensions are considered (again, see Libbrecht 2005). This even holds for crucial qualitative aspects, although the principles are well known, such as the diffusion mechanism, the phase transitions or the processes that lead to energetic equilibria. One fundamental fact is the very tight interaction between temperature and pattern formation, which seems to be related to a boundary phenomenon, that is the complex processes of surface melting that leverage the effects of emerging surface structures. This implies that there is a direct interaction between structure formation and the attachment dynamics, especially in the sense of achieving efficiency in energy throughput, and in the sense of positive feedback loops, especially with dendritic growth. The entire process can be disturbed, speeded up and blocked by the smallest changes in environmental determinants and mechanism. Thus, in the recent theoretical treatments the concept of a 'structure–dependent attachment kinetics' was proposed. This term immediately reveals the interaction between information and physical processes: For example, in dendritic growth the states that have been realized favour new states energetically, hence functionally stabilizing their growth trajectory. That means, the realized structure obtains the role of a directional determinant of the efficient–causal processes.

In other words, if we ask the question why the snowflake obtains its shape, we point towards two different kinds of explanation: one is the efficient–causal sequence of individual events, the other is the identification of the most probable state of the snowflake in terms of its entire structure, which is an 'anisotropic' explanation in the previously established sense, hence it involves reference to formal and final causes. The linkage between the different causal modes is reflected in the hypothesis of 'structure–dependent attachment kinetics'.

This example of the snowflake illustrates a general problem in purely efficient–causal explanations of molecular structure in chemistry, which cannot be fully reduced to quantum interactions, even though in theory this is possible. The very notion of a molecular structure varies with the experimental interaction between the observer and the chemical process, as an extension of the quantum mechanical constellation, which can be interpreted as the transfer of information via structures as signs (Del Re 1998; Zeidler 2000). The conceptual constructs of 'molecular structure' and the notion of a 'chemical bond' underlie the representation of molecules in the chemical formalism, hence a sign in the down-to-earth sense. However, the notion of a bond cannot be given any exact meaning in terms of the wave equations for the molecule, because the energy of the molecule is not additive with regard to pairs of atoms, which means the electrons are delocalized (Vemulapalli 2006); practically, this means that quantum theoretic reductions are only feasible if certain molecular configurations are put in 'by hand' (Hendry 2006). Thus, even though the molecule is clearly a result of quantum mechanical processes, the empirical description on the part of the observer depends on a concept, that is the 'chemical bond', which implies references to energetically favoured states of the entire molecule. In very practical terms, this is reflected in the peculiar formalism of chemistry which is a sign language depicting those structural properties. Similar problems of reduction emerge when the concept of 'molecular shape' is scrutinized (van Brakel 2000: chapter 5). At the same time, these constructs are sufficiently powerful to explain specifically chemical causal powers. Again, we can make sense of these intricacies in referring to structure as final and formal causes, and the quantum level determinants as efficient causes.

In this analysis, we meet a particular constellation between the observer and the object. From the viewpoint of a purely efficient–causal explanation, the role of 'structures' and other higher–level phenomena may be simply seen as conceptual constructions on part of the observer that reflect her limited knowledge about the phenomena in question. This is also one interpretation of anisotropic explanations in general: Thermodynamics is seen as referring to macrostates because our information about the microstates is limited; therefore we need to argue on probabilistic terms. However, there is another view which assigns an autonomous ontological status to those concepts, as the previous examples also suggest. Indeed, Peirce even argued that mechanical laws themselves evolve from a state of randomness and are not fixed properties of the world; this represents evolving information in the current sense.

This view has been elaborated in terms of a physical theory in much detail recently by B. Roy Frieden (2004). The basic idea is that all physical laws emerge from information generating interactions between observers and objects. It is important to notice that this concept of information differs from the concept that was introduced by Shannon and which relates with processes of communication, so being just a quantity of information, defined relative to a space of possible states. To the contrary, physical information is 'information about' in the sense of Kåhre (2002) (who therefore even coined a new term, inf(*B*@*A*), the information that *B* gives about *A*). Frieden adds the idea that this 'about' is information, in turn. Consider our knowledge about the physical world: We generate this knowledge by causally interacting with this world; we receive causal feedback, which constitutes information about the unknown state of the world. Then, think of the total amount of potential information that would be necessary to describe and explain the object, J. J is the information source which embodies 'bound information'. By means of interacting with this source, we gain information I. This information does not simply refer to the object, but to the regularities involved in the causal interaction between observer and object. Then, we can think of observation as a process that evolves towards the minimization of the difference between I and J, following an extremum principle: $K = I - J =$ *extrem*. Frieden tries to show in numerous applications that this 'Extreme Physical Information' EPI Principle generates the physical laws which govern the object domain.

Figure 1.1 Physical information

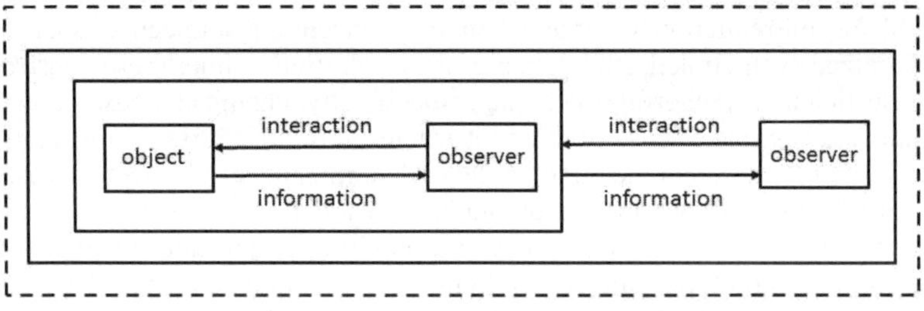

Note: Frieden's (2004) Principle of Extreme Physical Information states that all physical interactions result in the generation of information, hence can be seen as observations. These observations are physical objects in turn which generate information by further interactions. This information is a physical object, in turn, and so forth.

I come back to Frieden's approach later. At this point, I emphasize that Frieden follows Peirce in arguing that the regularities that make up our knowledge about the world are emergent properties of these causal interactions, and that this also implies that the EPI Principle is not dependent on the existence of human observers. To the contrary, one can argue that all physical processes imply the generation of information via causal interactions. This is what we have seen in the example of the snowflake: The interactions between crystal formation and environment result in structures which accumulate information that impacts on the further development of structure. This implies that 'observation' is a physical process, in turn, which is ontologically independent from human observers. Against the background of philosophical naturalism, this is only surprising on first sight, because after all every human act of observation is ultimately based on physical interactions, and there can be nothing non-physical involved. Human observation is of the same physical nature as the snowflake's observation of its environment.

How is this possible? This is because the original information–generating process is causally linked with another process of observation that builds on this information (figure 1.1). That means, we can interpret a physical process as an 'observation' because it results in information that can be observed, in turn. This is the dynamical aspect of bimodality which rests upon the simple fact that all signs are physical phenomena, too, and do not constitute an ontologically separate kind of substance.

1.1.6. Externalism and naturalism in economics

So, the most fundamental principle of naturalism is that in the physical world, there is a recurrent emergence of causal mechanisms that transform information into new information. The principle of causal closure therefore means, bimodally, that the universe is a system of accumulating information; in recent physical theorizing, this has been stated viewing the universe as a computational system (for example Zeilinger 1996, 1999; Wolfram 2002; Lloyd 1999, 2001, 2006). This is the modern transformation of Peirce's vision to see all reality ultimately as a 'mental' phenomenon, or to assign the status of reality to concepts, thus eschewing nominalism in ontology. All these philosophical quandaries of centuries can be resolved by the recognition of the ontological status of information as physical.

This has far-reaching consequences for economics. The concept of knowledge in economics is mostly equated with states of knowledge of human individuals (Samuelson 2004). If the naturalistic turn in economics sails with the naturalistic view on information, however, the consequence would be to treat knowledge as a physical phenomenon in economics, too. Indeed, this is a core idea of this book: Knowledge is physical (thus modifying Landauer's 1961 clarion call in the computer sciences, 'information is physical!'). I approach the economy as a system of knowledge that is embodied in physical structures, and interpret economic evolution as the growth of knowledge, understood in this way. The common economic approach to knowledge refers to human states of knowledge exclusively, even if those were interpreted in physical terms, such as states of the brain. But at a second sight, this would be seriously misleading if we just think about the knowledge stored in the entire biosphere of Planet Earth:

Bacteria, oaks and eels are physical stores of knowledge that human beings struggle to reconstruct by means of their theories and data collections, but certainly have to count as accumulated information generated by evolutionary processes. In the context of the human economy, all this knowledge is active in generating economic processes, such as in agriculture. However, according to the aforementioned generalizations over the concept of physical information we have to recognize that 'knowledge' is a universal aspect of the physical world, and hence the role of knowledge in the economy is just a special case of this universal physical knowledge.

I use the terms 'information' and 'knowledge' in a somewhat sloppy way, often appearing as close substitutes. Both terms refer to the same physical bases, with 'knowledge' seen as a stock, and 'information' as a flow adding to this stock (for related views in economics, see Wesseling 1991: 27; however, most of these approaches refer to human epistemic subjects exclusively). Further, knowledge is a set of regularities that emerge from actions that result in information and act upon information; regularities evolve via flows of information: So, in many contexts information would appear to be the 'data' and knowledge is the regularities that can be retrieved from the data. So, the distinction between knowledge and information is certainly meaningful, even though the term 'knowledge' has the disadvantage of suggesting close reference to human knowledge and mentalist interpretations.

What does this naturalistic approach imply for the analysis of human knowledge? The naturalistic approach to knowledge is strictly externalist, in the sense that knowledge is seen as a disposition to act successfully in relation to any kind of criterion of success, and that this disposition can be described as a causal mechanism connecting external causes and internal processes (Schantz 2004, MacDonald and Papineau 2006). Externalism in the analysis of human mind compares with internalism, which would assume that there are irreducible internal mental phenomena that are not caused by any external determinant (for example, assuming 'free will' is an internalist proposition). Both Hegel and Peirce proposed an externalist theory of mind. For example, Peirce formulated an externalist approach to mental content in stating that there is no content beyond the actions generated in response to some environmental impact (for an overview on modern statements of externalism with regard to mental content, see for example the overview by Lau and Deutsch 2012). In modern Philosophy of Mind, externalism refers to all theories about mental phenomena which claim that physical causal closure holds for the emergence of mental content, such that there is no separate domain of 'mental causation' (Kim 2009). However, considering this position against the background of the previous discussion of Peirce, we can surmise that what appears to be the specifically 'mental' in human action relates with specific conjunctions of the different Aristotelian causal modes. So we are back with the Principle of Bimodality. This is what I will explore in the next section.

It has to be noted that externalism is well-known to economics, although many parts of economics are strictly internalist and mentalist with regard to knowledge. A mentalist approach to knowledge describes knowledge as states of mind, and in particular assumes that the epistemic subject knows what it knows. The externalist declares this so-called 'KK principle' to be unnecessary because 'knowing how' does not necessarily presuppose 'knowing that' (Ryle 1949; see Schantz 2004). This viewpoint clearly prevails in certain fields of economics, which are close to evolutionary approaches, such as in the concepts of 'embodied knowledge' or 'routines as tacit knowledge' (for a survey, see Foray 2004). Yet, even the most generic uses of the term in the notion of 'stock of knowledge' remain actually silent on where this knowledge is actually embodied, and treats 'ideas' as a sort of capital, thus mixing up a mentalist term with the implicit externalist operationalization (for example Jones 2002; compare the critical discussion by Metcalfe 2001, 2002). All these uses of the term 'knowledge' in economics point towards a naturalistic interpretation; that is, they treat knowledge as regularities that are embodied in physical phenomena and enable certain actions, given certain causal impacts that qualify as 'information' relative to this 'embodied knowledge'.

To summarize, in my view the naturalistic turn in economics needs to be systematically completed in terms of developing a naturalistic theory of knowledge as a physical phenomenon. This approach needs to be built on principles that apply universally and thus go far beyond economics proper. This is meant by elaborating on the 'foundations' of economic evolution in this book. As we have already seen, one of the core issues in this field is the concept of mind.

1.2. TOWARDS A PRINCIPLED THEORY OF ECONOMICS: IMPOSSIBILITY THEOREMS ON MIND

1.2.1. Impossibility theorems and theory construction

Albert Einstein once distinguished between two kinds of theories, principled and constructive (for pertinent statements of modern physicists, see Smolin 2006: 11, or Bub 2006). Constructive theories build our picture of the world by assuming certain fundamental elements and then constructing mechanisms that explain observed phenomena based on interactions between those elements. They follow the principle of 'corpuscularism' that has driven Western science over many centuries (Wilson 2004: 96ff, 130ff). In contrast, principled theories start out from fundamental principles, which are impossibility theorems. Theories are built in a way to obey to these impossibility theorems in order to explain observed facts. Thus, for example, Einstein's theory of special relativity was built on the assumption of the impossibility of superluminal velocities. Principled theories can be subject to the most rigorous of all tests, namely falsification by one single event, which is regarded to be impossible. One physical theory that will form a crucial reference of my arguments to come, Thermodynamics, is entirely built on impossibility theorems, namely the First and Second Laws, and hence the principled exclusion of the possibility of a *perpetuum mobile* of both the first and the second kind (Atkins 2007).

In scientific practice, both approaches find widespread application; the special role of impossibility theorems is often neglected in favour of the generation of positive hypotheses about certain phenomena. However, this disguises the fact that positive hypotheses also express propositions about what is not possible. If they do not, instances of refutations may not exert a strong impact on the further evolution of the theory, because they might still be regarded as possible. This is of particular importance for all theories that deal with complex phenomena (Hayek 1972): Complex phenomena allow for a vast range of possible events in an open state space of the world, such that there can be many competing hypotheses about those possible events. These possibilities might be tested by statistical procedures, as is regular practice in economics today. So, following Hayek, the seemingly surprising conclusion follows that what appears to be an extremely strict criterion of validating theories, that is presenting impossibility theorems, is the most appropriate approach (for a pertinent discussion with reference to a particular example of cross–disciplinary research, see West 2006: 16ff). This is a very important insight, as impossibility theorems allow for a much wider variance in the detail and scope of positive hypotheses. This is aptly illustrated by Hayek's (1972) discussion of the Darwinian theory of evolution: This theory vastly differs from physical theories with regard to its capacity to generate positive predictions about the future, but nevertheless submits propositions about impossible events; the latter establishes its status as a scientific theory (which was disputed by Popper for a long time).

Further, impossibility theorems have the important advantage that they hold cross-disciplinary. One of the hallmarks of a principled approach to theories is that no particular scientific discipline is allowed to embark on the construction of theories which violates impossibility theorems stated in other disciplines (for an earlier statement of this, see Herrmann-Pillath 2008). Impossibility is a truly universal ontological concept. Therefore, the unity of science can be built on impossibility theorems. Positive hypotheses mostly carry much more conceptual load of the different disciplinary methodologies, such that unification becomes more tedious and can be even blocked via the limits to conceptual integration.

In the past, economics was designed as a constructive theory. To this, economists added a peculiar stance towards the impossible: Following instrumentalism, they regarded the assumption of the impossible just as an innocuous approach to an 'idealization' of their theories. A standard argument is to assume 'friction' away and to formulate hypotheses with reference to a 'frictionless' world. So, for example, assuming zero transport costs in international trade would certainly assume the impossible, even in the sense of the impossibility of superluminal velocities (zero transport costs imply instantaneous physical transfers), but that was just regarded to be a helpful simplification that was not seen as jeopardizing the theory. So, the basic elements of the theory were established by referring to impossible states of the world, and the further development worked via the stepwise relaxation of these constraints. However, in this process there is a large conceptual and empirical distance between the basic assumptions (which include many other simplifications, such as referring to a limited number of countries and commodities) and the econometric tests of more realistic hypotheses (for an immanent critical evaluation, see Leamer 1992, Leamer and Levinsohn 1995).

From the viewpoint of principled theories, impossibilities can never be assumed away. Compared with the methodological premise formulated by Hayek, economics failed to adopt the approach that is most appropriate in dealing with complex systems, that is starting out from the recognition of constraints on the possible states of the world. Instead, economics mainly relies on statistical arguments in order to test hypotheses that are otherwise seen as an idealization, hence positively state impossibility. Certainly, idealization and stating the impossible can interact in a complex relationship. An example is the assumption of an ideal gas in physics: The crucial question is whether one can identify an empirically meaningful way to approximate the ideal state as far as possible, and in particular, beyond some reasonable standard of measurement and operationability. But this is different from stating the impossible: For example, in thermodynamics there is no way of building a theory that would assume the existence of a *perpetuum mobile* in terms of an 'ideal' state to which empirical operations can converge, and then deduce statistically testable hypotheses based on this 'idealization'. With regard to our example from economics, the question is under which category the assumption of zero transport costs actually falls. For example, one could argue that this assumption is only one aspect of trade costs in general (as in Anderson and van Wincoop 2004). Then, the neglect of trade costs means that the activity of trading conducted by international traders is not included in the theory at all (which is explicitly stated in a major advanced textbook on international trade, Feenstra 2004: 371, who only introduces trading in the context of the theory of the international firm; other leading advanced textbooks such as Bhagwati et al. 1998 only include transportation costs in very few and limited applications, neglecting general trade costs completely). We can certainly submit that trade without trading is impossible, hence we are not dealing with a simple idealization (for a full discussion of this, see Herrmann-Pillath 2001b, 2006). So, it comes as no surprise that one of the most important challenges to the theory of international trade results from the explicit recognition of geographical factors which determine trading activities (for an overview, see World Trade Report 2008: 81ff).

I adopt the principled approach to economics. In fact, there is already a rich set of impossibility theorems in economics, such as the impossibility of pricing and aggregating capital (Cambridge controversy), the Condorcet–Arrow theorem on the impossibility of aggregating individual preferences to one consistent collective preference function, or the Sonnenschein–Mantel–Debreu theorem on the impossibility to reduce aggregate demand functions to a unique set of well-behaved individual demand functions obeying to the weak axiom of revealed preference. However, in this chapter, I will concentrate on more general impossibility theorems in science and philosophy, which do not only hold for economics. This is because I aim at presenting a universal evolutionary approach, in which economics is part and parcel of a larger cross–disciplinary synthesis. One of the great challenges to the social sciences is the fragmentation into different disciplines which partly deal with the same phenomena; psychology deals with consumer behaviour, as well as economics, or sociology deals with the emergence of markets, as well as economics, and so forth.

1.2.2. The Hayek impossibility theorem on brain and mind

Against the background of the discussion in section 1.1, I concentrate on one impossibility theorem that has been proposed by an economist in his research into the human mind, Friedrich August v. Hayek. The 'Hayek impossibility theorem' states that the brain can never be able to fully explain and hence understand its own functioning (Hayek 1952: 189ff). As Hayek recognized later (Hayek 1967), this theorem is just one version of the universal Gödel impossibility theorems on the incompleteness of all formal systems, given that all propositions of these systems are to meet the simultaneous criteria of consistency, truth and provability (for a succinct survey, see Kennedy 2012; on Hayek, compare Steele 2002). In a nutshell, it says that the brain cannot internally construct a neuronal representation of its own structure, because that would require a higher level of complexity, which is unattainable by that structure. This theorem is only a single instance of a large class of paradoxa and impossibility propositions that result from the phenomenon of self–reference, with household names such as the 'Cretan liar' (Bolander 2012).

Penrose (1989: 138ff) offers a very condensed and simple version of the Gödel theorem, which I summarize (for more detail, the reader is referred to the original source). We refer to an arbitrary formal system of symbols which can be arranged into strings; we consider all possible strings, that is the expressions in these systems, and a lexicographic ordering of these strings, by which it is possible to assign one and only one natural number to every proposition (the so-called 'Gödel numbers' whose construction was one of the most challenging part of his original work). So, we get an ordered, numerated sequence of propositional functions about variables w, with the *n*th function being $P_n(w)$: Given the method of construction, this is an arithmetically correct statement about the natural numbers *n* and *w*.

In such a formal system, we also have a sequence of proofs of those propositions Π_n. Proofs can also be numbered in the same way. We can then think of the proposition

$$\neg\exists x[\Pi_x provesP_w(w)]$$

which states that there is no proof of the proposition which applies $P_w(\ )$ on itself. The point in this procedure is that because of the particular construction of the lexicographic ordering, these propositions are arithmetic statements about the natural numbers that identify propositions and proofs. As the previous expression is an arithmetically correct statement in our system, it will also have a number in the series of statements, so it is $P_k(w)$. Then we can construct a specific proposition in which $k=w$:

$$\neg\exists x[\Pi_x provesP_k(k)] = P_k(k)$$

This proposition, however, cannot be proven, because it states just the non-existence of such a proof, resulting in a contradiction. Yet, the proposition is an arithmetically correct one. But that would mean that the proposition is true. So we have a true, but improvable proposition in the system. The same holds true for the negation of $P_k(k)$, which completes the Gödel theorem. This seemingly negative result is actually a positive one, because it shows that there can be true propositions that cannot be proven to be true within the formal system.

The Gödel approach is based on Cantor's diagonal method, which is used to prove the uncountability of real numbers, among other propositions (for a survey of this and its many applications in different areas of mathematics, logics and computer sciences, see Chaitin 2005). Imagine an infinite list of infinite sequences of zeros and ones, hence $s_n=(s_{n,1}, s_{n,2},\ldots s_{n,n})$. Then one can build a sequence s_0 where the *n*ths element is always the opposite of the *n*th element of the *n*th list, that means, results from taking just the opposite of the diagonal in the s_n written top down. However, this new sequence cannot be contained in the list s_n, because otherwise $s_{0,n}=s_{n,n}$, which is not possible, given the rule of constructing s_n. So the set of all infinite sequences of zeros and ones cannot be listed completely, because it is possible to construct a sequence which is both within and without the set. The set is larger than the infinite set of natural numbers.

This phenomenon of formal self–reference also explodes the Gödel construction. Basically, the Gödel construction is similar to the paradox of the Cretan liar who asserts 'I am a liar', which is a statement which cannot be proven to be truthful or not (as when asking about the barber who shaves all the people who do not shave themselves, thus cannot shave himself). Russell's paradox also belongs to this family of paradoxes, with Gödel's theorem being the most elaborate and extensive one because it directly relates to arithmetics and hence the foundations of mathematics. Russell's paradox creates similar problems for simple set theory and just results from the two statements,

$$P = \{x | P(x = true) \ , \ P = x \notin x \ .$$

The Hayek impossibility theorem is a material illustration of all these sorts of paradoxes when referring to a neuronal system and submitting that all expressions in these neuronal system must be neuronal phenomena in turn, especially neuronal states that are supposed to describe or identify other neuronal states. That is, the impossibility theorem inheres in the naturalistic approach to human mind as sketched in the previous section. It is important to notice that Hayek's application on a physical system such as the human brain is fully vindicated by more recent contributions to the topic (such as Ben-Jacob 1998 on genomes). In particular, Wolpert (2001, 2008; see also Lloyd 2006: 51ff and Binder 2008) has shown that on a most general and abstract level, the physical universe could be subdivided into an observing and an observed part, which both together make up the universe. Then, it is impossible that the observing part predicts events in the observed parts before these happen. By implication, the universe as a computational system could only simulate its own operations simultaneously and in real time, because operating a model of itself 'from within' would lead to paradoxes of the Gödel kind (for a related analysis, see Wolfram 2002: Chapter 12). This analysis is formally similar to Hayek's point, because a brain that cannot explain itself cannot predict what it will do in the future, even if all external determinants were known. Like the universe, the brain can only run a synchronous simulation of its own activities, if at all.

1.2.3. The gap between brain and mind

The Hayek impossibility theorem is of central importance for this book because Hayek provides an evolutionary explanation for the category of the 'mental' (Hayek 1952: 191). The question is, if we assume that all phenomena are physical, and hence mind and brain are identical, why do we experience certain phenomena which we tend to identify as purely 'mental' ones which are lacking any physical interpretation? This includes essential phenomena such as the experience of consciousness or the role of 'qualia', that is subjective states such as feelings that seem to accompany neuronal states, or finally and most importantly, our feeling that 'we' are free to take choices about future actions, independent from the states of the neuronal system (for example, we can exert conscious efforts to control expressions of pain).

In Hayek's view, the 'mental' reflects the explanatory gap between the brain and itself (for a modern discussion of this gap, see Levine 1983, 2009). The 'mental' solves the dilemma of self–referential paradoxes in offering a new category that makes meaningful action possible. This view matches with a long tradition of interpreting the Gödel results in the context of analysing the human mind; it has produced the idea that the negative result of incompleteness actually points to the sources of human creativity and freedom (Lucas 1961; Penrose 1995; for a critical view, see Dennett 1995: Chapter 15). In other words, the category of the 'mental' itself can be explained by an evolutionary argument. Given the emergence of complexity in the brain along with the emergent capacity of self–reference, this capacity can only be transformed into a viable behavioural feature if it is accompanied by the idea of mind, which relates to notions of free will, intentionality and consciousness. In other words, the idea of the mind enables action in the context of the larger systems in which human beings need to live. Mind has a function relative to systems external to mind (van Gulick 2009; for a related argument on 'free will', see Sommers 2007).

This fits exactly with Peirce's notion of the 'mental'. The foundational principle of his pragmatism is the idea that there is nothing in mind than successful action in the environment (such as Peirce 1998: 331ff). This idea leads back to Hegel's approach to the expressive nature of mind, or spirit (Taylor 1985). Beyond Hayek's focus on single human brains, Hegel already pointed out that the mental (his 'spirit') can only emerge from interaction between human individuals. In fact, he grounded his entire metaphysics on another variant of impossibility theorem: Namely, that one cannot recognize oneself as a conscious being unless this is mediated via the recognition by another conscious being whose consciousness is recognized by oneself, in turn (the famous 'lord and bondsman' dialectic in the *Phenomenology of Spirit*; for an overview, see Redding 2008). Thus, we can draw a positive conclusion from Hayek's impossibility theorem: Mind emerges as an interactionist phenomenon which closes the self–explanatory gap in human brains by means of enabling externalized actions. This is the most fundamental reason why mind can only be properly conceived in externalist terms.

1.2.4. Peircian triadism

In order to fully clarify this point, it is necessary to introduce the Peircian view on 'triadism' (compare Millikan 2009 for a reception of Peirce in the modern Philosophy of Mind to which we referred so far). According to Peirce's famous distinction between 'Firstness', 'Secondness' and 'Thirdness', all phenomena are triadic in nature, if considered in their ontological entirety. This is not the place to indulge into the exegesis of Peirce. I simply adopt a 'Peircian' view that mainly follows Short's (2007) brilliant analysis that prepares the ground for a coherent naturalistic interpretation of Peirce's philosophy (for a seminal early view, see Emmeche and Hoffmeyer 1991). This approach focuses on the fundamental ontological role of signs; the relevant process is called 'semiosis'.

Peirce distinguished between the three fundamental ontological categories, 'Firstness', 'Secondness' and 'Thirdness', which he treated as a sort of universal conceptual structure that applies for many areas (Burch 2010). In the subsequently developed Peircian triad (figure 1.2; compare other visualizations such as in El-Hani et al. 2006), Firstness is the object, Secondness is the sign, and Thirdness is the observer, with Secondness, however, also applying for all single connections. If one tries to extract a common ground across all uses by Peirce (Bergman and Paavola 2003), Firstness applies on entities without any relation to others, Secondness refers to a connection with others, and Thirdness sets this relation relative to another entity. This corresponds to the distinction between 'object' as cause in our diagram, its effect and the way how this causal relation is interpreted in a functioning. Peirce referred to the observer as 'interpretant', which I treat as a purely terminological nuance here.

Regarding proper Peirce exegesis, there is a problem here because Peirce presented many arguments where 'Firstness' clearly refers to a phenomenon in the sense of a quality of perception, that is, becomes close to a mental phenomenon. This is also evident from his entire theory of signs, which focuses on the process of interpretation, which is also a mental phenomenon, in many of his statements. From this follow two tendencies. One tendency is to expand the scope of semiosis, which is the process of signification, beyond the human realm, which is turned into a programmatic approach in biosemiotics (for example Emmeche 2002; Vehkavaara 2002). This is because the ontological relations between the object, the sign, and the interpretant are universal, so that the interpretant can be any kind of entity (compare Ji's 2012: chapter 6 discussion of semiosis in chemistry). But given the Peircian definitions, this also can imply that the entire ontology is seen as mentalistic, as it is a common assumption in panpsychism (Seager and Allen-Hermanson 2012). That means, semiosis would entail the assumption that many more phenomena than the human mind actually have 'meaning', as for instance in Hoffmeyer (1999) and Brier (2008). Certainly this corresponds to Peirce's original ideas about 'agapism' and the spiritual unity of the world. As we have seen and will continue to explore, this implication falls apart if we properly consider the mental as an emergent property of physical systems, without being ontologically separate.

In Peircian ontology, the interaction between epistemic subject and object is always mediated via a sign (figure 1.2). The subject obtains the role of an 'interpretant' of the object, and this interpretation is mediated by the sign that represents the object. At this point, the more complex taxonomy of signs does not matter that Peirce developed through his lifetime. We can relate this triadic view to the aforementioned Frieden (2004) approach to information: There is an information source J, the object, and there is a transmission of data, the information I, that is the sign. The observer assumes certain states in which the difference between I and J obtains a function. In the case of the scientific observer, this is tantamount to the application of the EPI Principle, that is the application of extremum principles which results in a maximum of information transfer. This is the 'physical information' $K = I - J$. To take the human brain as an example again, researchers have developed models where the brain minimizes 'surprise' as measured by the so-called 'free energy' in the conjunctions of statistical variations of environment and brain states (Friston 2010).

Figure 1.2 The Peircian triad and Frieden's fundamental physical categories of information

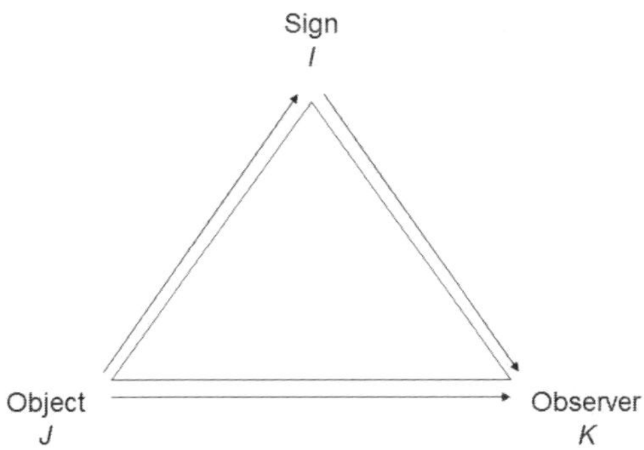

Note: Peircian triadism approaches the relationship between epistemic subject and object always as being mediated via signs. We treat the subject as an 'observer' which stands in a causal interaction with an object. The transmission of information J between the object and the observer is mediated via the sign, which corresponds to I. The observer retrieves physical information K following the EPI principle $K \equiv I - J = extrem$. It is essential to notice that there is always a part of the direct causal interaction which does not transfer information, so implying a loss of information J, unless we refer to quantum level regularities.

Now, Peirce's pragmatism implies that the observer, the interpretant, evaluates the information that is obtained via the semiotic process in terms of its effects on its actions. Faced with certain data as embodied in signs, the observer conducts a process of inference that approaches the true state of the object, given certain criteria which result from the goal of the observation. Therefore, we can say that the observer relates with a function. In science, the function of observation is to improve our knowledge about reality. There are other observational processes, such as in life, where functions relate to survival and reproduction. This corresponds to the approach of teleosemantics in the Philosophy of Mind, which dissolves the category of 'meaning' into the notion of 'proper functioning', see MacDonald and Papineau (2006) and Millikan (1989, 2009). So, biosemiotics understood in naturalistic way would explore how animals perceive the world, in relation to their evolved adaptive functions (for an example, see Neander 2006). Therefore, I propose to complement the Peircian triad by means of reference to a generalized notion of selection (compare Hull et al. 2001): Functions relate semiosis to a criterion of selection. In life, this is survival and reproduction, in science, methodological standards such as applying rigorous methods of empirical testing.

Figure 1.3 Semiosis and function

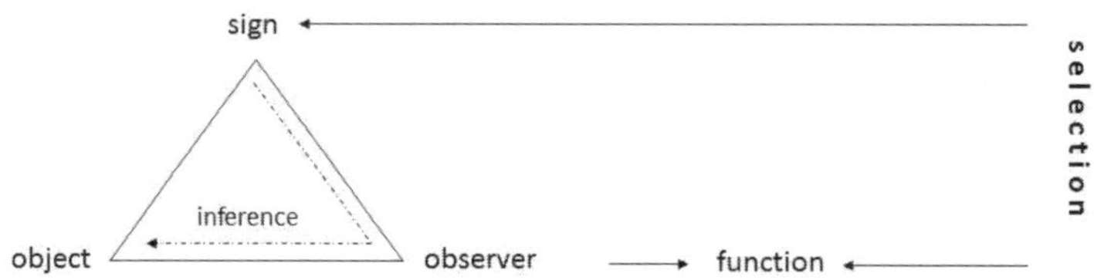

Note: The semiotic triad relates with functions that observations have and which determine the process of information extraction from signs, that is the inference. Functions relate with criteria of selection via forces springing from the environment. Selection enables the inference process on the population level.

Figure 1.3 establishes the close relationship between the Peircian approach and evolutionary approaches in epistemology, featuring under the heading of Evolutionary Epistemology, in both senses as being practised so far (for overviews, see Bradie and Harms 2012): The first is to apply evolutionary principles in the analysis of human knowledge (with seminal approaches such as Campbell 1960 or Popper 1972), and the second is to put human knowledge into the context of the biological theory of evolution (beginning with Konrad Lorenz 1973, and with recent extensions of the Darwinian paradigm such as Dennett 1995).

1.2.5. Minds are signs

We can apply the basic semiotic model on the relationship between the observer and the brain. Following Hayek's argument, we would assume that there is a brain that observes itself; but the brain cannot directly access all its neuronal states, even in the case of modern neuroscience. Brains only perceive signs of neuronal states via proprioperception of the body. For example, we perceive 'feelings' that represent neuronal states (Damasio 2010: 108ff). So, we can state that what is conventionally designated as 'mind' corresponds to sets of signs that relate with brains. This fits to Peirce's view that all mental phenomena are semiotic in nature.

In Peirce's view, the mind is a system of signs, and viewed as a process, is semiosis. Hence, even though substance monism is adopted, this does not simply end up in the mind–brain identity hypothesis (for a related modern view that comes close, see Dretske's 1995 representational theory of the mind which relates representations with informational functions; compare Adams 2003). The mind is a sign of the brain: So, the mind is not the brain, in the same way as smoke is not fire, though both are physical facts. Signs are by no means co-extensive with the set of neuronal phenomena that they relate with, even though they are embodied in neuronal states: My feelings of neuronal states are neuronal states, in turn. Yet, there is a fundamental ontological difference because if the mind is a set of signs, the meaning of these signs is defined by the function that the resulting actions of the observer have relative to the environment. These actions, however, cannot be described in terms of neuronal states, as they are other physical states, such as the posture of my body, a movement with my arm to fetch an object and so forth. Therefore, the mind is the conjunction between signs and the expressions resulting from semiosis. This is the externalist approach to the gap between brain and mind.

The mind is the set of products of neuronal phenomena and thus extends far beyond the neuronal matter and includes all creations of the human brain. This directly corresponds to the Hegelian notion of 'objective spirit'. Then, we can also refer to Hegel's version of the impossibility theorem on mind and state that brains cannot observe themselves, but only other brains. This observational relationship between brains is constituted via the externalized actions of brains, which are the signs of brain states.

Figure 1.4 Brains and minds

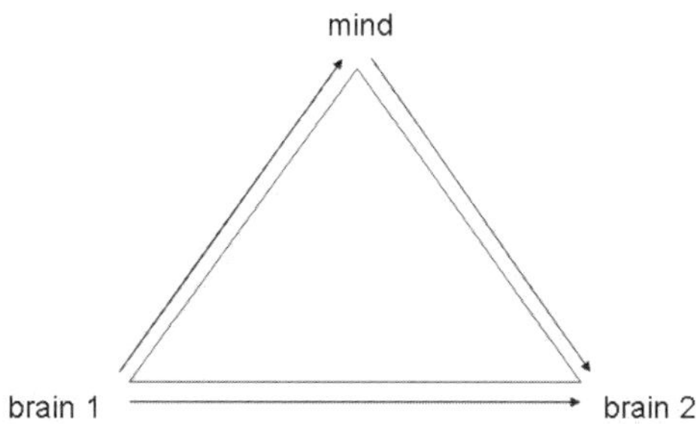

Note: In the Peircian view, which corresponds to Hegel's dialectical analysis of 'spirit', the mind is the set of signs that mediates between different brains, thus enabling brains to observe other brains. Signs are expressions of brain states, and minds enable inferences about brain states of Alter. This relationship differs from the direct causal interaction between brains with bodies. Semiosis relates these interactions with functions relative to the environment.

So, we can say that in the reconstruction of the brain/mind relationship, we cannot assume that the observer is the brain itself: The observer is one member of the society of brains that interact via the mediation of signs. Hence, following Hegel, mind as 'spirit' is a collective phenomenon, not an individual one. This view does not imply any sort of revived substance dualism or the hypostasis of collectives, which is a frequent misunderstanding of Hegel's viewpoint. In the simplest way, we can rewrite figure 1.2 as a relationship between two brains that is mediated via mind as an externalized set of signs (figure 1.4). Interestingly, this idea has also been discussed in the brain sciences, in particular by Edelman (1987: 308ff) who argued that the increasing complexity of information processing by neuronal systems is only possible if there is intra–species communication across those systems as embodied in different individuals, or, in the most general sense, a language (see also Sacks 1995). Again, this implies that there are two aspects of what can be the same physical process. Consider somebody touching another person: As brains are incomplete without bodies (Damasio 2010), this can be regarded as a causal interaction between brains, ultimately. But the 'meaning' of this physical interaction is only accessible by analysing the accompanying semiosis; this would refer to the function of the touching behaviour (such as expressing care, which might relate to biological functions such as parenting, and so forth).

1.2.6. Naturalizing Wittgenstein's 'Private Language' argument

The mind is the mediator by which brains observe and understand other brains. I will explore this idea in detail in Chapter Four. At this point, it is essential to conclude that mind is therefore a population–level phenomenon, and not an individual–level one. Minds as individuals result from self–reference of brains as a special case. Self–reference is one expression of consciousness; consciousness means that brains refer to themselves via the mind: this is why infants only develop consciousness of themselves through interaction with others, and are not born with a fully-fledged consciousness available on the first day of individual existence (Carpendale and Lewis 2004). Infants learn to rely on externalized products of the brain in order to refer to themselves. These products are not limited to own products, for sure. As we shall see in Chapter Four, the coordination of expressions of brains in interactions between individuals is essential for developing even the distinction between own and others' products.

With regard to the Hayek impossibility theorem, this opens up a fresh perspective: Brains cannot explain themselves, but minds can, because they are higher–level systems of signs, relative to the level of neuronal structure. For these, the Gödel theorems also apply with full force, of course, but at the same time the related systems of brains and minds can manifest certain logical properties that result in local solutions to the Gödel dilemma, such as the formation of hierarchies of conceptual systems. That is, the isolated brain cannot refer to itself without falling into the trap of paradoxes, but other brains can refer to brains via a system with an autonomous structure, that is the mind as a semiotic structure, which is even ontologically different from sets of neuronal states (on the role of nested hierarchies in resolving Gödel–type paradoxes, see Kennedy 2012).

This argument relates with another famous impossibility theorem in philosophy, namely Wittgenstein's (1958) argument on the impossibility of a 'private language' (survey in Candlish and Wrisley 2012). Wittgenstein's philosophy of 'ordinary' language, which departed from his early philosophy of ideal language, has been mainly received by philosophers (such as Richard Rorty) who aimed at establishing a pragmatist theory of meaning which claims the irreducibility of meanings. In the current context, a naturalization of Wittgenstein's views offers itself, just because those maintain the originally Peircian idea that all meaning lies in the regularities of action which relates with the use of signs. I will use Wittgenstein's private language argument as one of the central impossibility theorems in this book, as it shows the impossibility of a language of 'mentalese' in the sense of a sign system that would be unique to individual brains. Even internal uses of signs need to be population–level phenomena in the sense that the proper use of signs can only be fixed by referring to population–level regularities of use. Wittgenstein's original point was that a truly private language is impossible because the individual would not be able to establish stable criteria of meaning, given the fact that reference to past uses would also be mediated via those meanings. In other words, there can be no fixation of meanings without an external anchor, which is the use of signs in communities of users. As we shall see in later chapters, this view is essential for establishing an evolutionary approach to the mind which tightly relates the analysis of meaning and language back to the general theory of evolution (Aunger 2002: 261ff; Millikan 2005).

1.2.7. The externalist approach to brain and mind

Naturalism implies externalism of the theory of mind. Externalism applies for both Hegel and Peirce in their fundamental stance that the mind is what the mind produces. This is not the place to delve deeper into the intricacies of the Philosophy of Mind. Every statement is open to dispute, and there is a very substantial literature, even on single concepts. I will not refer to this vast domain in detail but just present my own approach here; it is outlined in figure 1.5.

Externalism means that brains operate on the basis of signs. Both brains and signs are physical phenomena, albeit of different kinds. That means, following Hegel, I adopt substance monism but reject brain–mind monism. This is a radical alternative to most approaches in the modern philosophy of mind, which mostly interprets substance monism in terms of a brain/mind identity; this results in very intricate discussions about the supervenience of mental properties on neuronal properties, sometimes leading to complicated constructions such as 'anomalous monism' (Davidson 1970/2006: Chapter 5; for an overview, see Yoo 2009). Signs are external to the brain, but there are also signs in the neuronal system, such as neurotransmitters, once we approach the brain in a deconstructed way (as I will do in Chapter Four). Thus, the mental rests upon causal interactions between internal and external signs, such as the causal impact of the sound waves of a word in human language on the brain. However, according to the Hayek impossibility theorem the mental is also a construction of the brain that enables actions in closing the self–explanatory gap, and which relies on the emergent properties of brain–brain interactions.

Figure 1.5 The Hayekian view on brain and mind

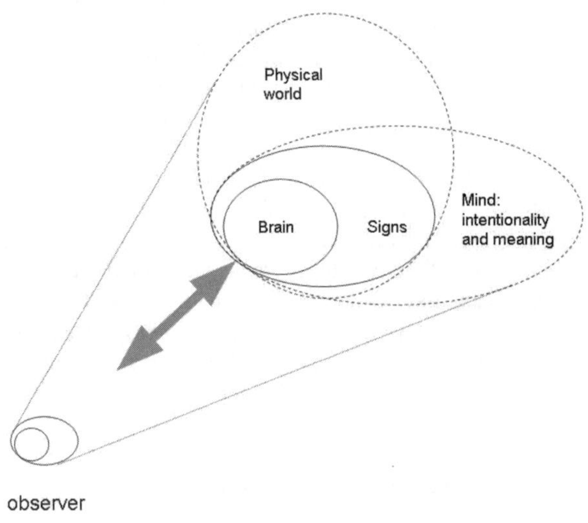

Note: From the viewpoint of a human observer, the brain is a state of the physical world. Brains are accessible via signs, which include states of brains (neuronal states are signs relative to other neuronal states) and all external physical expressions of brains (such as linguistic expressions, bodily movements etc.). However, if the observer's brain observes itself, it cannot do this without mediation via those signs, that is the mind. Mental categories such as intentionality close the gap between brain and mind. From the observer's perspective, these categories appear to be distinct from physical phenomena. Hence, as indicated by the broken lines, the two domains of the physical and the mental emerge from the self–reference of observing brains. They do not constitute different substances in the Cartesian sense, but aspects relative to the observer.

In figure 1.5, this is indicated by duplicating the system in terms of a self–referential observation. The mental transcends the physical world in the peculiar sense that it cannot be fully reduced to physical phenomena by any human being. As a result, there are two circles, one the physical world, the other the mind with its peculiar phenomena, in particular intentionality and meaning. Note that this picture represents an aspectual dualism, but not substance dualism. It is of utmost importance to realize that this argument does not refer to mind/brain supervenience which would presuppose brain/mind identity or congruence. Following Hayek, I propose that the mental is an external physical construction of brains in interaction with other brains that enables action and self–expression. Minds supervene on signs as population–level phenomena, but not on brains, and the 'mental' is an emergent property of self–referential brains interacting with signs.

1.2.8. The two worlds

Thus, the Hayek impossibility theorem actually reinstates the division between the *Geisteswissenschaften* and the *Naturwissenschaften*. This is reflected in the Peircian view that highlights the role of creativity. Human action is creative in a fundamental sense, that is, it generates novelty via the interaction between paradoxical self–reference and reference to others. This creativity is the natural object of the *Geisteswissenschaften*.

That being said, however, there is a unity that resides in the fully fledged triadic framework. Then, it is straightforward to see that the opposition between the two approaches was just resulting from a biased and one-sided emphasis on either of the two sides of the triad (figure 1.6).

- The positivistic stance focuses on the physical causality that results in the generation of signs and the effects that signs exert on observers: For example, this is the idea prevailing in recent neuroeconomics where neuronal activity is seen as generating certain actions such as the expression of social preferences. In the positivistic stance, all mental phenomena would be seen as being reducible to neuronal mechanisms (programmatically stated in neuroeconomics by Glimcher 2011).
- The hermeneutic stance focuses only on the interpretation of signs, such as when exploring the cultural meaning of social interaction. Against the background of our initial section, this also includes the interpretive approach to the formalism of economics. Then, subjective preferences would be seen as interpretations of the observer, and 'rationality', in the Weberian sense, would be a construct to 'understand' human action irrespective of the underlying physical causalities. According to this view, neuroeconomics is completely irrelevant to economics (Rubinstein 2008).

A comprehensive naturalistic approach would have to take both aspects into consideration, with no methodological predilection. In brain research this shows up in the need to combine a bottom-up and a top-down approach in explaining the complex experimental observations (such as in research on empathy, see Frith and Singer 2008). I have already indicated the conceptual means that enables us to achieve this. In particular, we relate the observer qua interpretant to the realization of a function: For the interpretant, the same principles apply as for the analysis of the signs, namely that interpretation cannot refer to an 'inner' mental state of the interpretant but to the action that is triggered by the sign, and results into the realization of a function, such as maintaining meaningful social interaction (again, this corresponds to 'teleosemantics', see MacDonald and Papineau 2006; Neander 2012).

Figure 1.6 Triadic synthesis of the 'two worlds'

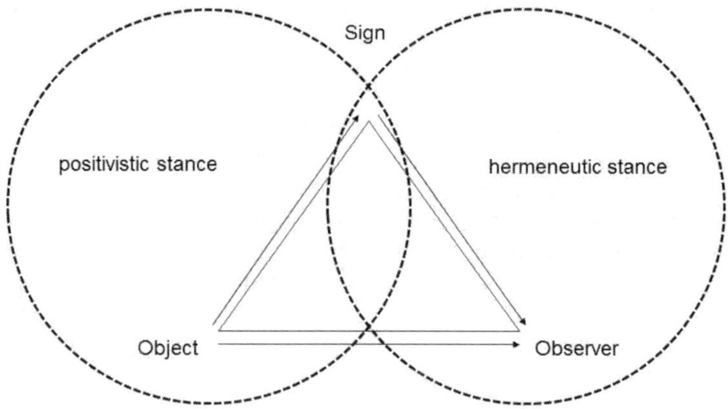

Note: The 'two worlds' of the sciences and the humanities are represented by the positivistic and the naturalistic stance. The positivistic stance concentrates on the sequences of efficient–causal processes that underlie the generation of signs and their effects on the observer. The hermeneutic stance focuses on the interpretive activities of the observer. However, in the triadic and externalist approach to mind, these interpretations are not internal mental states of the observer, but functions relative to the environment in which the observer acts. So, meanings are expressions triggered by signs.

In this view, the principled opposition between the two stances is misguided (compare Mantzavinos 2005). However, this does not mean that the hermeneutic stance is reduced to the positivistic stance, but that the two are sublated in a truly Hegelian fashion within the triadic framework. If we refer this back to the analysis of the Aristotelian distinctions between modes of causality, we can therefore assign the modes to the two stances. Then, the positivistic stance refers to all kinds of explanations that only refer to efficient causality, whereas the hermeneutic stance refers to the conjunction of formal and final causality that is involved in the emergence of functions. In this view, signs have a separate ontological role because they are constitutive in assigning objects to classes of objects represented by the signs (so, 'smoke' identifies the class of objects which is 'fire'), hence formal causality; and they trigger actions by observers which realize a function, which means fulfil a purpose, hence final causality.

1.2.9. Signs and existence

The ontological role of signs as being constitutive for minds can be further clarified if we pay brief attention to the notions of causality and existence (which we will explore in more detail in Chapter 2). The principle of physical closure posits that everything that exists must cause an effect, or must be an effect of a cause (Bunge 1977: 160, 271 refers to this as *the panta rhei* principle; cf Papineau 2009). In other words, effects prove existence; we cannot state the existence of something that does not cause any effect. This idea underlies another important impossibility theorem, namely that the existence of a mental substance different from matterenergy substance is impossible (Dennett 1991: 33ff); in Ryle's (1949) famous terms, there is no 'ghost in the machine'. If mental substance existed, it would need to have physical effects. Today, the claim of mental causation is made only in a very careful way, mostly in terms of the epiphenomenal view – which treats mental phenomena as supervening on material phenomena but without ontologically autonomous causal powers (for an overview, see Robb and Heil 2009; for a critical position, Kim 2009). Otherwise, the effects of mental causes must be of the same matterenergy quality than the mental causes. A mental substance could only have mental effects, in order to avoid causal over-determination; in other words, the assumption of an ontologically distinct mind could not explain human action in the physical world.

The important consequence of this impossibility theorem is that naturalism assigns 'existence' to signs because they cause effects (which is a modified version of Bhaskar's 1989 argument on the causal nature of social entities). Based on this, all creations of human brains exist as a part of the physical world (thus rejecting Popper's 1972 hypothesis of the 'Three Worlds', with one 'world' separately containing the creations of mind). Although Ockham's razor is certainly a wise strategy, the question is what defines the bottom line of necessity. In the naturalistic view, the creations of the human mind are just another kind of physical entity. But this entity is not reducible to lower–level physical facts, as they stand alone as causes. In this view, one cannot even argue that these phenomena supervene on other physical phenomena: Signs are just that, signs. Thus, for example, a religious belief that causes a terrorist to explode a bomb exists, in terms of physical facts such as books, artefacts and standardized bodily movements. Clearly, this causal pattern cannot be simply reduced to a mechanical or electromagnetic physical cause. There is a special class of causes that emerge at the interpretant part of the triad. In order to understand this cause, we need appropriate theories which have been explored in the *Geisteswissenschaften*. Of those, the social sciences can be seen as part and parcel insofar as they necessarily need to cope with the phenomenon of meaning. The fundamental idea of the naturalistic approach to mind is to explain this category of meaning in terms of the notion of function, in the pragmatist tradition.

This view results in a peculiar ontological position which also characterizes Hegel: Hegel adopts 'conceptual realism', that is introduces the notion of the existence of concepts, which is also accepted by Peirce in his rejection of nominalism (for Hegel, see Stern 2008; on Peirce, see Houser in Peirce 1998: XXIVff). However, as we have seen, this does not mean that concepts are a separate 'ideational' domain of the world, in the sense of Platonic ideas. Concepts are a special kind of physical phenomena, such as classes of actions of human individuals. Hence, Hegel speaks of 'objective spirit' which is embodied in external structures of society.

Now, we can relate this naturalistic approach to semiosis with the analysis of knowledge. Most simply, knowledge is signs; hence, the naturalistic concept of knowledge is based on the conjunction of causal modes in the Peircian triad.

1.3. OBSERVER RELATIVITY AND THE SEMIOTIC TRIAD: KNOWLEDGE AS A PHYSICAL STRUCTURE

1.3.1. Observer independent and observer relative facts

The naturalistic ontology of mind developed so far can be made more operational by relying on the distinction between observer independent and observer relative facts that has been introduced by Searle (1995) in order to analyse human institutions. Different from Searle's (2010) recent writings on these matters, I stick to the earlier notion of 'observer' because this term denotes a most general physical entity: As we have seen, I do not equate observers with human beings exclusively but with a generic function that can be realized in many different ways; for example, a sunflower is an observer relative to the sun. I equate observers with the Peircian interpretant and follow the argument developed by Short (2007: 156ff) who presented the definition of the interpretant in terms of a response R to the sign: That is, strictly following Peirce's pragmatism, the content of the interpretation is the action caused by the sign. Observers relate with other physical entities in that they extract and accumulate information in order to realize other causal processes, thus constituting a function relative to their environment. I will extend on these ideas in much detail in Chapter Two.

The concept of the observer is of fundamental ontological significance. This is also evident from modern physics, where observers play a distinct role for the analysis of quantum level phenomena: According to one of the most widely accepted interpretations of Quantum Theory, the Copenhagen view, it is only the causal intervention of observers that causes the transition from the quantum to the classical world of causal interactions (Faye 2008). As we shall see in the next chapter, observers also play a crucial role in Thermodynamics. This corresponds to the general information–theoretic framework established by Frieden (2004). Then, we can distinguish between the different modes of information *J* as the information bound to the physical object independent from an observer and the information *I* that is generated by means of an observation, hence constituting observer relative facts. The physical information *K* reflects how far the latter approaches the former, thus establishing the convergence between observer relative conceptions of the world and the underlying 'Kantian' reality of the '*Ding an sich*'. Interestingly, in Frieden's analysis, the equality of *I* and *J* applies for the quantum level entanglements between observer and object which result into the collapse of the wave equations, thus constituting the 'reality' of the classical physical world (Frieden 2004: 86f, 119ff).

An observer relative fact is a real entity which only exists if it can cause an effect on the observer. Clearly, this definition has differentiating power if we just focus on human observers and imply reference to intentionality. In this case, observer relative facts are facts which only exist relative to human action, which is driven by intentions. Hence, a rock is an observer independent fact, but a holy rock is an observer relative fact. If the rock falls on my head for some physical reason, and my skull is broken, this is an observer independent fact that does not relate to my intentions relative to the rock. But if I regard the rock as holy, and therefore smash it on my head, this physical interaction between rock and skull has to be explained by explicit reference to my states as an observer, even though the effect may be physically identical, that is a fissure in my skull.

Yet, in closer detail, the designation of a rock (being different from 'pebbles' or 'wooden pieces' of similar size) is also an observer relative fact, because all facts of language are observer relative. Insofar as physical reality is only accessible via concepts and theories that are maintained by observers, all reality consists of observer relative facts, which, however, refer to other sets of facts that are assumed to be observer independent, in the sense of Frieden's duality of *I* and *J*. Realism implies observer independence of the world (Searle 1995 has an extended discussion of realism, for that reason). So, we end up with a Kantian picture, namely assuming an observer independent reality which we can only approach as observer relative facts.

This classical philosophical dilemma can be resolved if we extend the notion of the observer in the sense already indicated above, namely referring to any kind of information generating process. Observers, in this sense, include all living systems, such as populations of bacteria, plants or human beings. Further, evidently we cannot simply relate the notion of 'observation' to single entities, as the accumulation of information in living systems is only possible on the level of evolving populations of entities. In this sense, observers are lineages of evolving living systems. If we continue this line of thinking to the ultimate consequence, we can say that the entire 'tree of life' is analytically identical with one single 'observer'. In Frieden's approach, this view would extend to the sequences of observational processes, which are physical processes for which the distinction between 'living' and other systems is irrelevant (in the sense of figure 1.1). However, this means that we consider complex sequences of physical measurements by which the relationship between two physical processes constituted by efficient–causal interactions results into regularities which imply the categorization of those events.

1.3.2. The emergence of information

This abstract point is best illustrated by means of an example taken from physics (Penrose 2004: 820 who also discusses the information–theoretic aspects). Consider the following experiment. Imagine a photo lamp that emits photons. The photons hit a mirror tilted with 45°, a so-called beam splitter. In the straight direction there is a receptor. The photon will be split by the mirror in two super–imposed states, one arriving at the receptor and one hitting the surrounding wall. When the photon hits the receptor, the wave function collapses, and the measurement takes place with a probability of 1/2. Thus, we can predict the state of the photon with probability 1/2. Now, consider the inverse: Which probability holds for the originating state of the lamp emitting the photon, given that we observe a photon at the receptor? In this case, we would distinguish between two possible origins of the photon, the lamp or that the photon just jumps out of the wall. Penrose's point is that applying the Schrödinger wave equations on the two different processes, which is prediction and retrodiction, is formally the same, so assigning 1/2 to both respective scenarios. Yet, evidently, the quantum state reduction by the measurement at the receptor renders the process time–asymmetric, because we do not conclude from the measurement that there is a probability of 1/2 that the photon was emitted by the lamp and of 1/2 that it just jumped out of the wall. Given the experimental setting, we know with certainty that the photon was emitted by the lamp. But this is actually what we do not get from calculating the Schrödinger equations.

This example is fundamental because it shows that causality and information flows work in opposite directions (Dretske 1981: 26ff; actually, if one pursues the same direction, the standard conception of information breaks down and needs to be substituted by a new one, see Brukner and Zeilinger 2005, 2006). That means, in the analysis of knowledge and causality we have to distinguish between knowledge about the causes and knowledge about the effects, and the information about the causes that we can get from knowledge concerning the effects. In the example of the beam splitter, we do not know exactly whether the photon will hit the receptor, only with a probability of 1/2. There is no way to reduce this uncertainty. Yet, the very fact of the photon hitting the receptor gives rise to certain information: This is that the photon was emitted by the lamp, and did not jump out of the wall.

Now, think of the receptor being connected with the intricate mechanism designed in the famous thought experiment of 'Schrödinger's Cat': the receptor connects with a lever that kills a cat in a container that is not accessible for any external observer (for a detailed discussion of this extension, see Penrose 1989: 375ff). As long as we do not open the container, we only know with a probability of 1/2 whether the cat is dead or alive. According to certain interpretations of Quantum Theory, this means that until observation takes place, the cat is indeed both dead and alive, for example, in two different worlds as posited by the 'many worlds' interpretation by Everett. Therefore, if we open the container and see the dead cat, this reflects the fact that the arrival of the photon at the receptor resulted in a state of information which connects with this fact, both as observer independent facts of reality. Or, consider two observers, one sitting in the container together with the cat and the other outside: At no point of time, the observer inside the container will be uncertain of the state of the cat; yet, for the outside observer the cat lingers in a quantum state of linear superposition of the two states 'dead' and 'alive'.

The essential point of this example is that the sequence of events of the experiment is itself independent from the observer who only comes into play as the designer of the experimental setting. But then every kind of configuration of physical settings which manifests causal chains of the same kind would also imply the generation of information, in the sense of 'environmental' information. In other words, the transition from the quantum level to the classical world is tantamount to the generation of information (Zeilinger 1996, 1999).

If we approach these reflections from the triadic perspective, we can say that the observer relates to objects via the mediation of signs. Signs, such as environmental information, can be seen as propensities of the world to generate information: This means, the sign is a potential cause of an effect that happens with observers relating to the sign (Peirce himself adopted this propensity view only in the later stages of his thinking, see Short 2007: 54ff). In Frieden's terms, I is a sign of J that generates physical information K by means of the actions of the observer, that is the measurement. Coming back to the snowflake, the snowflake is a propensity of information to be generated by an observer via interpreting it in a particular way. What kind of information is this? Thinking in Peircian terms, the information accumulating in the observer is itself an action, namely contingent on a particular function that the observer actualizes relative to a particular environment. This leads to the conclusion that this action itself is potentially information relative to another observer which realizes a function, hence obtains the status of a sign, too. This concatenation of signs is infinite, in principle, and can be called 'infinite semiosis', which establishes a potential informational unity of the world, hence seen as one stock of knowledge (Peirce actually vacillated over this idea, see Atkin 2010; Short 2007: 56ff).

Now, in the light of the previous exemplary experiment, we can say that this sequence of information generating events implies that the accumulating knowledge structure simply is the world: In Frieden's approach, this means that *I* and *J* converge to the same value. The world is just a stock of accumulated information, with no distinction between observer independent and observer relative facts; reality is what observers see: viewed from the perspective of information flow, the receptor clearly indicates that the received photon is a sign that reflects with certainty the fact that the photon was emitted by the lamp. In turn, once the receptor received the photon, and we know this, it is also certain that the cat is dead. On the other hand, given the construction of the experiment, if we observe that the cat is dead, we can regard this as a sign that allows us to infer that the photon was emitted by the lamp. This inference, though being observer relative, corresponds to an observer independent causal chain in the world.

1.3.3. Fisher information and dynamic epistemics

Peirce's philosophy is evolutionary in a most fundamental sense. However, he employed a rather artificial terminology, adopting the principles of tychism, synechism and evolution. 'Tychism' refers to the assumption that the world is random in a fundamental sense, which means it is constituted by propensities as real possibilities. Synechism refers to the universal and gradualist connectedness of all phenomena, and evolution to the possibility of emergence. In the current context, this amounts to the idea that the evolution of the world is ontologically both the emergence of regularities and the evolution of knowledge about it. This is the meaning of Peirce's idea that the mental is the primordial ontological category, which can be easily misconceived as panpsychism if associated with common notions of 'mind'. Signs are not psychic phenomena but 'mental' ones, seen as a special kind of physical facts, namely observer relative ones.

Peirce's tychism can be formally interpreted in terms of Frieden's approach, again, which, as we shall see later (Chapter 3) can be closely integrated with evolutionary theory. Frieden shows that the relationship between *J* and *I* can be formally specified as 'Fisher information' in foundational theories of statistics. Consider a certain state of the world. We think that these states reflect certain regularities, which are not known to us. Then, we enact a series of measurements. These measurements relate with the source of the information *J* in a probabilistic way, which means there is a range of random fluctuations in the data around the supposed 'true' determinants of the measurements. Fisher information measures the amount of information that we can retrieve from the measurement about the parameters of the probability distribution. So, with the variables X and a parameter θ of the probability distribution that governs the occurrence of the X, Fisher information is the expectation value of θ, given certain measurements:

$$I(\theta) = E\left[\left(\frac{\delta}{\delta\theta}\log f(X;\theta)\right)^2 \middle| \theta\right]$$

The Cramer–Rao inequality holds for Fisher information as defined in that way, stating a reciprocal relationship between Fisher information and the mean square error:

$$e^2 I \geq 1$$

This shows that increases of Fisher information correspond to increases of the estimation quality, thus substantiating formally Peirce's notion of inference resulting from semiosis. Fisher information can be also interpreted as a measure of order (Frieden 2004: 41ff), thus capturing the common notion that 'high order' implies high information content.

Now, Frieden shows that laws of physics can be deduced as Fisher information resulting from applying the extremum principle $K = I - J = extrem$. This means, that the process of measurement is analysed into three different constituents. One is the probabilistic fluctuations in the object, the other is the probabilistic fluctuation in the measurement; the third is the regularities governing the measurement process (such as the physical effects underlying the workings of lenses in optical measurement). Frieden shows, in a Peircian fashion, that physical laws can be deduced as the regularities that govern the causal interaction between the inputs and the outputs of measurement, hence result from a process of maximizing the Fisher information in the measurement. This results from the fact that all measurements also perturb the object, such that these effects themselves become the origin of knowledge about physical regularities.

This idea applies on any sort of measurement. For example, consider the actions of economic actors on markets; they aim at gaining information about the true state of the market, such as the true level of scarcity of a certain resource. This is a probabilistic phenomenon of its own, as the market is a complex system subject to recurrent shocks. The economic actor probes the market by conducting certain actions, such as buying a certain amount of the resource. This action is a measurement. If we consider a series of measurements, these are probabilistic phenomena in turn. Then, Frieden's approach means that sequences of these measurements result in the maximization of Fisher information about the original object probability distribution, if the aforementioned extremum principle is applied. This application results into the identification of regularities that determine the market process. Thus, as we shall elaborate in detail in Chapter Eight, the 'market price' is a regularity in recurrent sequences of economic actions on the marketplace.

One can regard this approach as a formal operationalization of the Peircian dynamic epistemology which distinguishes between different kinds of objects and interpretants, namely the dynamical object and the immediate object on the one hand, and the immediate, dynamic and final interpretant on the other hand (surveyed by Short 2007: 187ff). The immediate interpretant is the immanent reference of a sign without being actually interpreted by any observer, hence the propensity of a sign to generate information, which is realized by dynamical interpretants as the sequence of real observations. The final interpretant would refer to a state where all possible interpretants converge on the same interpretation: this would constitute 'reality' in terms of what would ultimately be observer independent, because there is no longer any difference between different acts of observation. Correspondingly, the immediate object is the object as given by a particular act of observation, and the dynamical object is the object in terms of the convergence of different sequences of observation.

1.3.4. The fundamental semiotic triad in knowledge generation

The interpretation of the dynamic epistemic process as an extremum principle can only be fully understood as a real world phenomenon in turn if we follow Peirce in recognizing the full range of different notions of causality (Peirce 1998: 120ff; for a succinct analysis, see Short 2007: Chapters 4 and 5). In particular, a Peircian view recognizes the role of final and formal causality beyond the role of efficient causality. Final causality refers to the directional effect of any kind of selective process taking place in nature; in the general case of the measurement, this is the function of the measurement relative to the context of the observer. The fundamental question is whether this function has a universal physical property of its own. Peirce was fully aware of a connection that I will explore in the next chapter, namely the relationship between evolution and thermodynamics, with the latter providing the ultimate physical foundations for finality as directionality. In the current context, we can state that final causality refers to the selection of observers relative to a criterion of selection that is co-evolving with the semiotic process.

Let us consider a simple example, referring back to the diagram of the triad (figure 1.7; see figure 1.2). In this example, we apply the previous considerations on a biosemiotic context, that is animal cognition. So, in Frieden's terms, we refer to two probabilistic processes. One is the flow of events in the environment of an animal, such as the appearance of snakes of different shapes and kinds at different places. The other is the flow of reactions and types of reactions of a certain animal species that evolves through time, that is the sequence of generations in a population of animals, such as the evolution of rabbits in their interaction with evolving species of snakes. The question is how true knowledge about snakes emerges, that is knowledge about what objects are regularly snakes and what objects are other kinds of objects (for a related teleosemantic analysis, see Neander 2006).

Figure 1.7 Semiosis and evolved function

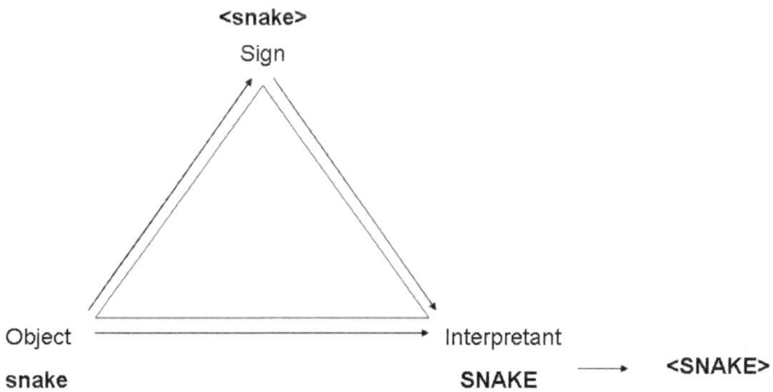

Note: In the biosemiotic application of the Peircian triad, we distinguish between real world objects, such as **snakes**, the signs of those objects **<snakes>** and the reactions of animals to those objects **SNAKES**. These reactions can become signs in turn, that is **<SNAKES>** for other observing animals. The reaction of animals to **snakes** is mediated semiotically via **<snakes>**.

So, I consider a **snake** and an animal that could suffer from its poisonous bite. The animal depends on the proper recognition of **snakes** in order to ensure survival. This recognition relies on the quick and timely processing of information in an uncertain environment. The identification of **snakes** is mediated via signs of **snakes** **<snakes>**, which might include all sorts of physical characteristics of snakes and their impact on the environment (such as traces). For example, a sign of a **snake** can be a certain pattern of movement. The animal does not need to process all the possible information about a single **snake**, such as recognizing all the facets of a **snake**'s skin. The only criterion for the selection of particular signs by the animal qua interpretant is that the resulting action, that is its response, will ensure survival. This is in turn established on the population level, hence resulting from variation, selection and retention of information generated in earlier generations of animals meeting snakes recurrently. So, the sign of the **snake** relates with functions, which can be in turn analysed in more or less detail, reaching from the assurance of fast withdrawal to the most general functions of survival and reproduction. It is essential to notice that the meaning of **<snake>** does not refer to any kind of internal state of the interpretant, but only to the action directed towards the environment, which therefore defines a **SNAKE** in pragmatist terms.

In this analysis, we can identify the special role of final and formal causality beyond the role of efficient causality in triggering certain actions of the animal (for example, photons arriving at the eyes of the animal which trigger neuronal chains that end up with certain motor actions). The evolutionary process establishes final causality in terms of the functions for which the animals as interpretants are selected. The relationship between sign and action is in turn a formal–causal one. This is evident if we consider the possibility of failure: A snake can be misidentified in the sense of the two fundamental statistical failures, that is mistaking a worm for a **snake**, or mistaking a **snake** for a worm. Thus, the sign classifies certain mechanisms that ensure proper responses. Precisely because this sort of error can happen, we can say that the sign is an observer relative fact, as it has causal powers which are independent from the **snake**. It can cause **SNAKE** even if there is no **snake**.

So, formal causality involves the process of cognitive categorization of **snakes** in a way such that true knowledge about snakes is realized in terms of proper responses to the appearance of **snakes** in the environment. These categorizations are the **<snakes>**, and the proper responses are the knowledge about **snakes**, that is **SNAKES**. If this knowledge is true knowledge, **SNAKES** are **snakes**. As we refer this process of knowledge generation to a population level process, we can directly apply Frieden's framework here and argue that the true knowledge reflects an extremum principle which underlies the selection process. This extremum principle conjoins two processes that fluctuate probabilistically, namely the sequences of events that involve **snakes** and **snake**–like objects, and the sequences of actions of rabbits towards these events. The emerging information is the proper identification of **snakes** by means of adaptive actions taken by rabbits.

I generalize over this example in figure 1.8. Here, I dissect the semiotic triad into more detail, building on the analysis by Robinson and Southgate (2010; firstly presented in Herrmann-Pillath and Salthe 2011). This diagram plays a central analytical role in this book, therefore I emphasize that it does not represent particular causal processes directly, but represents the conceptual framework of evolutionary analysis in relating the different causal modes to each other, and referring them to a general principle of selection. Therefore, at the same time it states an ontological structure, and a principle for the conceptual organization of particular phenomena in terms of the different kinds of causal processes that are conjoined in evolution. So, the diagram is to be understood as representing ontology, and is therefore independent from particular interpretations in different empirical domains. So, I will apply the diagram across the different levels of analysis that I will subsequently unfold.

Figure 1.8 The complete model of the Peircian triad

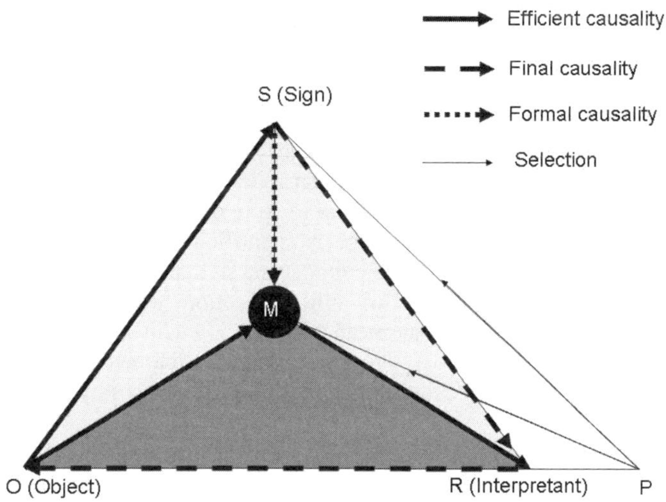

Note: In the fully-fledged version of the Peircian triad, we distinguish between two channels of efficient causation of the response of the interpretant, the observer, to an object: the causal linkages between the object and the response *OMR* (such as physical impacts on sensory organs connecting with motor responses via neuronal reaction chains), and the semiotic channel *OSR* which supervenes on efficient causal mechanisms (such as physical differences between inputs indicating different shapes of objects). Both channels converge in generating the response, resulting from evolutionary forces of selection relating with a general purpose *P* for which behaviour is selected, such as survival. These forces establish the final causality of semiosis. They result in categorizations of mechanisms *OMR* which embody knowledge about the object, and hence represent the formal–causal mode. The diagram represents ontology, and can be projected onto different empirical domains, as in the case of the different levels of analysis in this book.

I distinguish between two channels of efficient causation (for a related approach in biosemiotics, see Emmeche 2002). The channel *OMR* is the efficient–causal physical mechanism that connects an object *O* with the interpretant, the response *R*. A **snake** connects with the animal via many physical phenomena of light, sounds or smells impacting on the different sensory organs. However, these impacts do not suffice to explain *why* the animal withdraws from the **snake**, as there is no direct physical impact such as a mechanical push driving the animal away. Rather, the physical impact runs via the semiotic channel, namely *OSR*, which operates efficient–causally, too, if considered in isolation. This channel does not introduce a separate kind of entities; thus we can say that semiotic causality supervenes on physical causality, but without having mere epiphenomenal status: The movement of the **snake** is a **<snake>**, but it has independent causal powers in being observer relative; at the same time, we cannot simply say that the **<snake>** is 'within' the interpretant (corresponding to the idea of the **snake** in mentalist terms), because it is an external cause of effects with the latter. The *OSR* chain stands in a formal–causal relation with the *OMR* chain in classifying certain behavioural mechanisms as being responses to **<snakes>**. The realization of those mechanisms can fail in the sense that either the real object did generate a sign of the **snake** in spite of not being a **snake**, such as a worm, or that the sign was properly identified but did not generate the correct reaction, that is **SNAKE**. One central hypothesis of evolutionary theory is that in the course of time, selection will tend towards the minimization of failures. That means, as is shown in figure 1.8, selection works on both channels of causation, namely the evolved relationship between objects and signs, and the elicitation of responses by the occurrence of signs.

Both the sign and the response are evolved physical phenomena which refer to physical properties of objects (in this discussion, for convenience of the argument we omit reference to different Peircian kinds of signs, such as icons, indices etc. which differ in terms of the causal connectivity between signs and objects, thus including, for example, also purely conventional causal associations between a sign and an object relative to a population of sign users). Through time, selection relates those phenomena to ultimate final causes, which I designate as 'purposes' *P*, following Short (2007: 108ff). Purposes are generic criteria of selection, such as selecting for survival. Because the sign means a **snake**, and because insufficient withdrawal reduces the chances for survival, the response *R* emerges as a regularity in the behaviour of the animal. This regularity is particular knowledge about **snakes**. So, the sign classifies sets of mechanism into adaptive ones, that is, those reactions to certain snake–like aspects of reality which help to avoid real snakes, and therefore help to realize the general purpose of animals, that is survival. It is essential to re-emphasize that the physical reality of snakes does not matter directly here, because final causality only focuses on properties of snakes that impact on the animals' functionings. Therefore, a sign of the **snake** is not a **snake**, even though it is a physical part of the snake.

All this leads to the radical conclusion that ultimately, **snakes** are what is manifest in the responses. Indeed, another animal observing withdrawal may treat this as a sign of a snake, hence **<SNAKE>** in figure 1.7, thus making the meaning of the behaviour explicit. Therefore the complete triadic framework includes 'systems of interpretance' (figure 1.9), in which different kinds of interpretants relate with each other (this term was coined by Salthe 2009). So, an ecological community of animals is a network of interpretants, in which the chain of functionings connects different animal species, reflecting certain categorizations: For example, for predators certain kinds of prey are categorized according to certain generic properties they have, such that particular properties of individuals do not matter. That means, the physical functions in ecosystems such as the flows of nutrients and energy resources are mediated via semiotic structures in which the different species–level categorizations connect with each other: **Snakes** perceive **rabbits** as **<rabbits>**, **rabbits** perceive **snakes** as **<snakes>**, and the real world functions of the ecosystem are realized via the interaction between **SNAKES** and **RABBITS**. Then, in this systemic view, and following Short (2007) again, we can distinguish between the chains of responses *R, R'*, *R''*,... and the final purpose *P* that defines the most general function under which the responses *R* are selected. This most universal purpose unifies all the different processes of selection that result in the chains of responses; for all animals connected causally in the ecosystem, the general purpose of ensuring survival applies.

Figure 1.9 System of interpretance

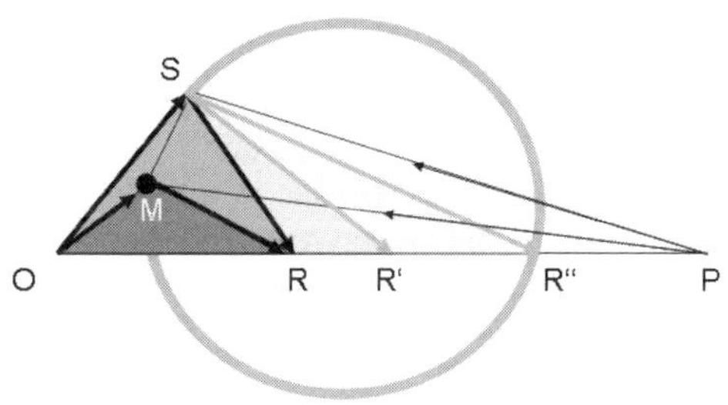

Note: Semiotic triads manifest the causal connectivity between causally connected responses under the impact of a most universal principle of selection, purpose *P*. So, the different species in an ecosystem are causally connected, which is manifest in physical flows of nutrients, energy etc. However, these flows can only be explained with reference to the semiotically mediated responses of the different species towards responses of other species. These are types of responses, hence regularities which embody the information generated by the evolution of the ecosystem. The ecosystem is a system of interpretance.

1.3.5. Semiotic realism and the semioverse

We can now draw a fundamental conclusion about the status of signs in general ontology which goes beyond the refutation of the Cartesian dualism of signs which would locate the signs in the meaning assigned to them by means of a purely 'mental' process. This would correspond to a nominalist ontology which would not treat signs as existing as physical objects in terms of their status as categories under which other physical phenomena are subsumed. This view would treat signs as 'names' that are arbitrarily assigned to physical objects. However, this is not what results from the analysis of the semiotic triad, because the signs are physical phenomena that relate with physical effects, that is the responses on part of the interpretant. On the one hand, the sign is efficient–causally produced by the object; on the other hand, its 'meaning' is embodied in the response as a physical process.

Both Hegel and Peirce converge on what might best be designated as 'conceptual realism' (Stern 2008) All signs are concepts in the sense of involving a type/token distinction, with the generic regularities of the type defining the sign as a concept; all reality is only accessible via concept formation, because knowledge about reality can only consist of recognizing regularities (true predictions which are merely chance events cannot be knowledge, see Dretske 1981: chapter 4). As we have seen, this results from formal causality. The sign of the **snake <snake>** is a concept of the **snake** in the sense of the regularities that guide the proper use of the sign by the interpretant, that is the **SNAKE**. As such, the concept does not reside in the interpretant, but only relative to it. Thus, concepts are a part of reality. They are the triadic conjunction of objects, signs and responses, and as such reflect the conjunction of the three causal modes in the real world. In other words, the realism vs. nominalism controversy can only occur if one only considers efficient causality as a constituent part of reality. If one pays due respect to the other causal modes, the Peircian view is validated that concepts are a constitutive part of reality. This approach also makes sense in the physical approach to information as championed by Frieden. Here, concepts are the emergent physical regularities that result from the accumulation of Fisher information in causal processes of observation. For example, 'mass' is a concept that relates with certain physical laws and has to be seen as being distinct from the single events that make up the probability distributions in a fundamentally random world. Yet, 'mass' has a physical reality in terms of its relationship with the physical laws that inhere in the probabilistic flow of events.

We can extend the Peircian ontology to the notion of the 'semioverse' (figure 1.10) which can be deduced from an argument presented by Deutsch (1997: 187ff). The term builds on Lotman's 2005 notion of the 'semiosphere' and also relates with Peirce's 1998: 362 idea of the 'phaneron', cf Short 2007: 66ff, but in the naturalistic interpretation (apparently, it first popped up in Heibach 2000 in the entirely different context of media studies). Peircian 'tychism' clearly resonates with modern conceptions of quantum mechanics which assume a multiplicity of universes that exist parallel to each other, representing different propensities of fundamentally random quantum events (the so-called Everett interpretation of quantum mechanics, for an overview see Penrose 2004: 782ff). For example, in the previous discussion of 'Schrödinger's cat', the two states of the cat, 'dead' and 'alive', would be seen as states of two different parallel universes which both exist. The entirety of the set of parallel 'worlds' is called the 'multiverse' (a term which, interestingly, stems from Peirce's contemporary William James). Then, the question arises whether there is a physical connection which unifies these different parallel universes.

Figure 1.10 The semioverse

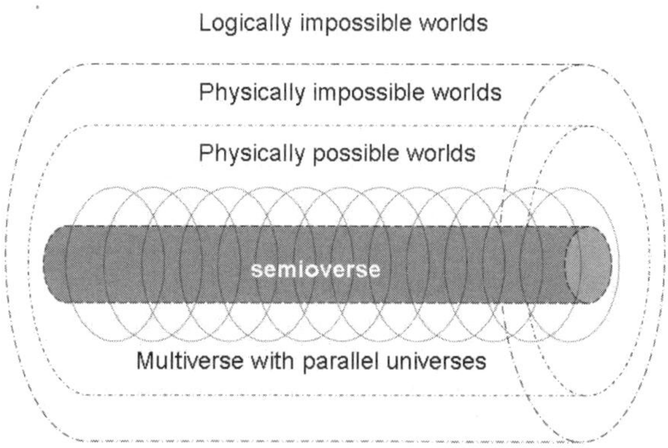

Note: In modern physics, one of the authoritative interpretations of quantum mechanics sees quantum probabilities as representing different states of the multiverse in terms of 'many worlds' that represent different causal flows of events triggered by probabilistic collapses of the Schrödinger wave function. The physicist David Deutsch (1997) argues that evolution imposes constraints on these chains of events which embody knowledge that converges across the multiverse. I call this the 'semioverse'. So, we distinguish between five different sets of states, the logically and the physically impossible states in contrast to the physically possible states which realize via quantum mechanisms into parallel universes, and the semioverse as the convergent set of states of physically embodied knowledge.

Now, Deutsch argues that these parallel universes are unified via the phenomenon of information that results from evolution, or, the stock of physically embodied knowledge. This is because evolution introduces the element of necessity into a random world: Depending on currently prevailing selective forces, present physical structures are constrained by past selection and the information embodied by it, and these constraints converge across the multiverse. Thus, for example, DNA in different parallel universes will converge, as a result of past selection across all possible worlds, whereas pebbles at the seaside manifest less constrained diversity, as there are no equivalent convergent forces of selection operating on pebbles as compared to DNA. Accumulation of information is basically the growth of constraints on possible states of the world as multiverse, seen as the set of parallel universes. So, Deutsch argues that across the parallel universes, physical phenomena that are subject to evolution will converge in spite of the fundamentally probabilistic nature of the physical processes. This idea matches with Frieden's view of the universe as a structure of information, which argues that physical regularities are the result of the generation of Fisher information via causal interactions.

In my parlance, that means that the signs are the unifying strand that holds the multiverse together. Deutsch's hypothesis can be regarded to be another version of the much-debated 'anthropic principle' in physics, hence may be re-labelled as 'semiotic principle' (for a controversial discussion of the anthropic principle, see Smolin 1997, 2007; Penrose 2004: 1030; Susskind 2006: 170ff). The anthropic principle states that the physical world evolved in a way that the emergent natural laws, especially the unique physical constants (dubbed the 'fine-tuning' of the laws), take a form that makes life and human observers possible. The 'semiotic principle' would follow Deutsch and state that the multiverse evolves in a way that knowledge about it is possible as an emergent and unifying physical property. This evolutionary process unfolds in a state space that is made up by physically possible worlds, a notion that I will further explore in Chapter Two.

1.3.6. Physical information generation

This perspective allows for generalizing the semiotic triad to a universal information generating structure resulting from the interplay between three causalities, efficient, formal and material (figure 1.11). Information is a difference that makes a difference (thus, this idea builds on Bateson 1979). That means, random variation turns into an information if it generates regularity in the world, which takes a difference as a starting point, which is manifest in this regularity: In terms of Peircian categories, the random event is Firstness, the difference it makes relative to an environment, Secondness, and the regularity Thirdness.

This generalization requires the extension of evolutionary principles. This is possible in referring to Frieden's Extreme Physical Information Principle, again, which introduces a general notion of 'measurement' that inheres to all causal processes that involve regularity. For example, if two bodies interact causally as a result of random events, and if this interaction is governed by the masses that the bodies have, we can say that one body 'measures' the other body in the sense that for the resulting effects a large number of other properties of the body do not make a difference, but differences in mass. Frieden argues that therefore the physical regularities relative to which a difference matters emerge by means of the causal conjunction between two different probability distributions, namely the probability distribution that governs the events and the probability distributions in the measurements, which we can equate with the effects in a Peircian fashion. Then, the principle of Extreme Physical Information obtains an ontological status, and is not merely an epistemological principle: It governs the emergence of physical regularities as real-world phenomena, and not just as states of subjective knowledge on part of observers with minds. This captures Deutsch's notion of treating knowledge as a physical feature of the world.

Figure 1.11 Generation of information

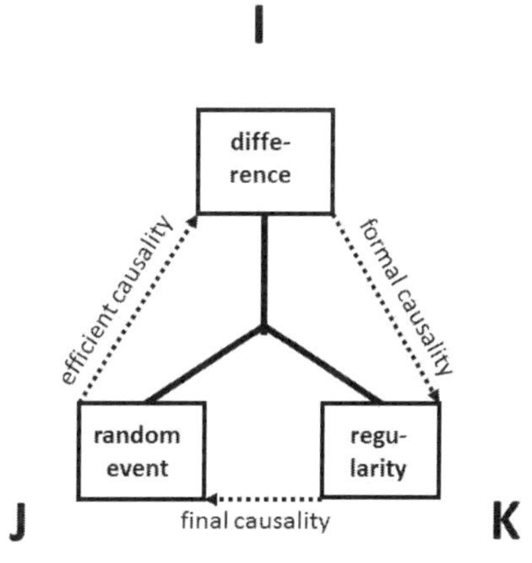

Note: This diagram conjoins Bateson's definition of information as a 'difference that makes a difference' with Frieden's Principle of Extreme Physical Information and the Peircian conjunction of causal modes. In a random world, certain events constitute differences with other events, which obtain a separate causal power on other events. This implies the transition to a higher logical level, that is differences that cause differences. This can be captured formally by Frieden's extremum principle that governs the relationship between information source *J* and information output via measurement *I*. The resulting regularities ('concepts' in terms of higher–level logical types) are physical information *K*.

Therefore, we can generalize the notion of the 'observer' into the concept of a 'physical inference device' PID (the term is Wolpert's 2008). A physical inference device is a mechanism that is subject to selection of any kind and thus enables the accumulation of physical information; it can be analysed in terms of the triadic conceptual structure. In other words, on the ontological level, the semiotic triad represents the generic structure of PIDs. I call this process of information generation 'physiosemiosis', in order to highlight the fact information is strictly seen as a physical phenomenon, thus avoiding any potential intrusion of 'mentalist' accounts of information which often tend to dominate semiotics (for instance Brier 2008). Again, it is important to recognize that PIDs are coupled with other PIDs. Thus, a regularity that emerges in a primordial stage can in turn serve as an information–generating sign for another regularity. The most basic feature of information processing in the world is therefore the emergence of *n*–th order regularities (figure 1.12). We conceive the growth of the physical world as a process of physical accumulation of knowledge via information flows that are generated by PIDs, which themselves result from evolution. A snowflake is a PID that accumulates information about environmental conditions prevailing during its fall. A sunflower is a PID that stores the information which flowed via past selection of sunflowers; it is also a sign that causes information flows, such as pointing towards the position of the sun. All ecological systems can ultimately be interpreted as *n*–th order physical systems of knowledge. Therefore, as pointed out before, regularities observed by observers are themselves physical embodiments of knowledge.

Figure 1.12 Knowledge as embedded regularities

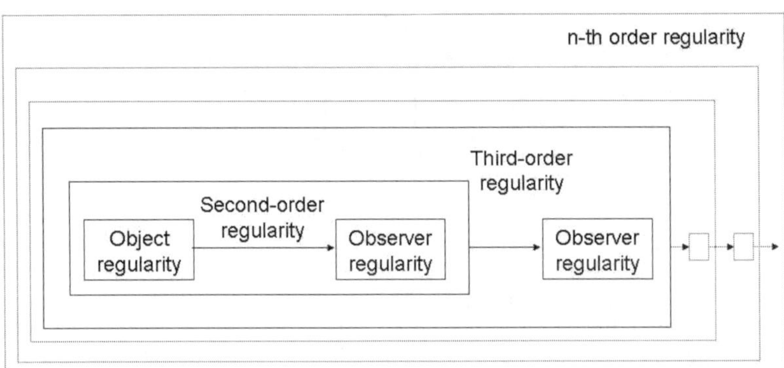

Note: This diagram extends on figure 1.1 and shows how physical knowledge is embodied in embedded regularities. There are object regularities which correspond with observer regularities. The causal connections between these two are second–order regularities. These can become the object of another process of observation, thus resulting into third–order regularities, and so forth.

The central idea in this book is to approach the economy as a complex physical system of evolving knowledge. This goes beyond regarding the economy as a mere information processing system; it includes a view on both knowledge stocks and information flows and directly identifies physical functions that drive the evolution of knowledge. Further, economic knowledge is seen as being physically embodied, such as in neuronal states, technological artefacts or physical changes in ecosystems. The essential aspect of knowledge is the causal conjunction of those states as embedded responses to certain general purposes of selection.

1.4. CONSILIENCE AND ECONOMIC ANALYSIS

1.4.1. Four approaches to reality

A simple classification of general ontology can now be posited, which follows from the principle of bimodality in combination with the distinction between the two different kinds of facts (for related, though different ideas, see Kull 2007). We distinguish, on the one hand, between observer independence and observer relativity, and on the other between the matterenergy mode and the semiotic mode (table 1.1). All physical objects can be approached as observer independent facts and in the matterenergy mode, such as water or the human heart. Then there are physical objects that we can approach in the matterenergy mode but which are observer relative facts. A class of examples are technological artefacts. An engine produces physical effects that are observer independent, but the reason why these effects occur at all can only be understood if we refer to the purpose of the engine, namely its function. This is a case in point for the Aristotelian distinction between modes of causality, as the technological artefact necessarily requires reference to a particular instance of final causality, that is human design. But as the discussion of the previous section has shown, if we generalize over the notion of observation in terms of evolutionary theory, the observer relative mode also applies, for example, on biological functions, such as the heart.

Table 1.1 Bimodality in basic ontology

	Observer independent	**Observer relative**
Matterenergy mode	physical objects	artefacts
Semiotic mode	numbers	institutions

Next, we have phenomena that are observer independent but which are in the semiotic mode. This categorization corresponds to the position of conceptual realism and as such is in no way uncontroversial. One of the phenomena that might claim widespread acceptance in this context is mathematics and the concept of numbers. According to many philosophers and scientists, the world manifests a mathematical structure which is observer independent, which means that it can be discovered by scientists, but has causal powers that are independent from those observers (Penrose 2004: Chapter 1). Numbers are signs in the strict sense. So, we can say that even though signs are observer relative in an essential way, we can consider signs, as we have already done previously, as physical propensities to generate information, which do not relate to human observers in the real world. In this sense, mathematical entities are propensities which can be realized by mathematical discovery. For example, if physical mechanisms reflect the quantitative regularities of physical laws, these mathematical properties are real and go back, as we have seen, to a physical process of information generation by means of measurements. So, the numbers are an integral ontological component of Frieden's information source J, and they result in quantitative information I.

Finally, we consider phenomena in the semiotic mode which are observer relative. The classical case for this is human institutions, as analysed by Searle. Looking at institutions in this way makes it clear why there is an ambiguity between treating institutions as observable regularities of behaviour and as rules that govern behaviour. For example, we might explain the institution of the 'holy cow' in terms of agro-ecological functions, so that it would actually be seen as a 'technology', hence belong to the upper right box (this is the position of Harris 1979), or we would regard the 'holy cow' as a socially constituted behaviour which only results from the assignment of meaning by the believers who accept and follow this rule (which was the position of Sahlins 1976 in the famous dispute with Harris).

It is important to emphasize that in the bimodal approach to ontology these four approaches to real phenomena are not mutually exclusive. All cows are physical objects and hence observer independent facts. Yet, if we want to explain the cows, we might need to refer to artificial breeding by human actors, such that they appear to be artefacts (cf Perlman 2009). At the same time, cows obtain a holy status in Indian culture. If we want to explain certain physical processes involving cows, such as the behaviour of cars with human drivers relative to cows, we need to refer to this dimension of ontology. So, which aspect is emphasized depends on the question directed to the respective state of the world. Therefore, I think that many controversies in the sciences and especially between the sciences and the social sciences actually result from the neglect of this conjunction of aspects; so, behaving like the four blind men who touch different parts of the elephant and quarrel about its proper description, even claiming that they actually refer to four different animals.

Table 1.2 Kinds of knowledge

	Observer independent	**Observer relative**
Matterenergy mode	Physical processes/ regularities of the object–system	Functionings/ physical processes of the observer system
Semiotic mode	Theories/ 'objective knowledge'	Functional representations/ 'subjective knowledge'

We can also use this classification to distinguish between different kinds of phenomena which ultimately relate to different kinds of knowledge that emerge in the relationship between object and observer (table 1.2). In the upper left box we find physical processes which exist, which are realizations in the multiverse and not just possibilities. This corresponds to the regularities of the information source *J* in Frieden's view. In the upper right box we find functions, which we can see as dispositions to produce certain causal effects, relative to an environment which determines the function of these effects. In the case of functions, we distinguish between proper functions and malfunctions, as we have seen in the discussion of the semiotic triad. But this means that what counts as knowledge is the proper realization of function, and not whether this is a truthful representation of the object. So, whether a frog really understands the physical properties of flies does not matter for its survival. Yet, if this knowledge contradicted physical knowledge about the object, this error could certainly be a major reason for malfunctioning. If we consider the particular function of scientific research, that is the aim of generating truthful knowledge about the world, this corresponds to Frieden's *I*, namely the results of the physical measurement processes. *I* is thus observer relative in the physical sense, as different measurement processes will result in different data sets causally related with the information source *J*.

That compares with the lower left box, where we find the results of the applications of the Principle of Extreme Physical Information, hence *K*. There are sets of objective knowledge, that is theories approaching a truthful picture of objects in the upper left box, and which refer to sets of data that have been generated by measurements. In the lower right box, we find subjective knowledge that we need to access via interpretive methods. In physics, this subjective knowledge refers to principled approaches to interpret reality, such as the different interpretations of quantum probabilities as real propensities or Bayesian subjective probabilities, thus reflecting states of ignorance on part of the observer. I claim that all four perspectives are indispensable in order to achieve a complete picture of reality, especially if we deal with economics, or, more general, human action, and understand the role of knowledge in this reality.

1.4.2. Implications for economics as a science

The last statement can be illustrated by looking at the role of economics in understanding the economy. Many economists would claim that economics is located in the lower left box, hence constituting 'objective knowledge'. However, that would presuppose that 'the economy' is an object in the physical world, in the sense of a system that exists and is characterized by specific causal powers. However, 'the economy' might be a system of functions and thus possibly constitute a technology, which would raise the question for the relevant observer or designer of that function. Modern economics provides only broad and quite vague answers to this question under the heading of 'consumer sovereignty': in this view, the economy serves the function of satisfying consumer needs. It is important to notice that this introduces an important possible break between different research questions in economics. For example, the phenomenon of economic growth would be approached in purely mechanistic terms in the first view, such as investigating into causal mechanisms between investment and growth. In the second view, researchers would ask firstly about the functions of growth in relating 'the economy' with its environment, and then explain realized growth by means of these functions. This is one perspective taken in this book.

However, non-materialistic factors such as a religious belief may also satisfy consumer needs in general, which therefore might not be satisfied by 'the economy'; there can be many other functions which an economy could serve, such as maintaining ecological equilibrium. On the other hand, we can also ponder whether 'the economy' actually belongs to the lower right box; it would then be conceived as a reflection of interpretive activities of human beings, similar to a religion. In this case, 'the economy' would only assume existence in being a system of rules that are followed by human beings, and would assume causal powers only as a result of this. For example, these distinctions stand behind fundamental cross-disciplinary controversies in the social sciences over the meaning of 'capitalism': One might see capitalism as a necessary outcome of technological change (as in Marxian materialism), and the other as a cultural construct (as in Max Weber's analysis of 'rationalization'). Correspondingly, causal analyses of historical processes such as China's failure to industrialize will differ in fundamental terms. In the first view, 'the economy' determined China's cultural evolution, in the second view, China's culture determined her economic evolution.

The question arises whether we define economics in terms of specific theoretical hypotheses or in terms of a specific object of research. I cannot give a full response to this question at this point because some conceptual tools have not yet been introduced (see Chapter 8, section 1). However, I posit that given the need for multidisciplinary approaches, the latter approach seems to be the preferable. At the moment, this can be based on the argument that economics as a science is a set of knowledge, with all the implications of this notion that have already been discussed. We can therefore start with the statement that economic knowledge must be part and parcel of the physical world. Then, we ask for the causal powers of economics. These causal powers are observer relative, that is, they relate with the human actors that use economic knowledge. In Peircian terms, we would therefore define economics by what economics does (in variation of the adage that economics is what economists do). One idea to be developed in this book is that economics is one of the determining forces of the emergence of economic systems, or of markets. Economics actually co-creates the economy, and only in this sense can it be regarded as a kind of knowledge. This would imply that economics would belong to the lower right box in table 1.2, considering that 'subjective' knowledge does not necessarily refer to individual knowledge but mainly to knowledge distributed among collectives of actors.

We then need to identify a certain set of physical phenomena that are the objects of the knowledge that we call 'economics'. Recently, economics as a set of theories has been substantially expanded, even into the realm of biology (such as Noë et al. 2001). Thus, we could ask whether animals or food webs are an object of economics. I am not in favour of these extensions because they do not lead to a sustainable arrangement between the different scientific disciplines. Extensions of economics into other realms are of the same quality as extensions of physics into economics: There are certain conceptual and analytical tools that can be of cross–disciplinary use, but this does not imply that these extensions have an ontological status of their own – unless they assume the role of interpretive activities and thus constitute causal powers in turn. Financial traders are not particles of an ideal gas, even though we might find statistical mechanics useful to describe the aggregate phenomena on financial markets (Baaquie 2004). The same applies for extensions of economics into other disciplinary domains: A fish is not an economic agent, even though some tools of utility theory may be useful in analysing foraging activities. However, there is a fundamental difference between physics as applied on human actors and economics as applied on animals: physics as economics can result in interpretive activities that have causal powers because they impact on human action (who use physics in taking decisions on financial markets), whereas such an impact is not possible for animal action. However, for example fishes can become objects of economics and therefore transform their status as an object in the physical world insofar as the human activity of fishing is concerned, see Holm and Nielsen 2007).

The next question is what kind of object offers the defining reference for economics as a science. I will argue that this is a special kind of evolved artefact, namely markets. Markets are complex systems of social interaction in human societies which involve the use of particular objects, such as goods, prices and money. The use of the term 'object' is meant in a literal sense here: for example, a price is a thing, such as a price tag, and money is a coin. Evidently, we are talking about signs in the Peircian sense; money is a sign, and as such it is a physical object. Economics would then be defined as the study of this particular class of signs, including the role of economics in the creation of these signs. As we shall see later, this approach conjoins economics as a science and all other kinds of interpretive activity that result in the constitution of 'the economy', that is also non-scientific beliefs about 'the economy' (Callon 2007; Çaliskan and Callon 2009). This also means that economics as a science is rooted in such beliefs, which are for instance visible in the role of political value propositions in driving certain directions and results of economic inquiry.

This view also includes the conception of markets as distributed knowledge, an idea familiar to economists especially in the Hayekian tradition. Hayek and many others saw this idea in mentalist terms: Markets would coordinate inner mental states of knowledge of agents. In the naturalistic approach, we directly view markets as physical phenomena displaying certain regularities; these constitute knowledge that can be partly embodied in human agents, in the sense of their brains, but also and foremost in other physical structures, most generally signs, and specifically, signs that are peculiar to economic transactions, as defined by the knowledge that we designate as 'economics' (compare Swedberg 2008).

Table 1.3 The ontology of markets

	Observer independent	**Observer relative**
Matterenergy mode	Markets and ecology	Markets and technology
Semiotic mode	Markets and structures	Markets and institutions

Taking this as a provisional point of departure, we can ask how to locate markets in the classification of different kinds of knowledge (table 1.3). First, it is possible to conceive of a market as a physical structure through which matterenergy flows are channelled. This is done, for example, in the context of industrial ecology (Ayres and Ayres 2002). There would be no reference to prices but, for example, explicit tracking of certain chemicals which have a certain impact on the environment. Second, we can analyse markets as technologies, including institutions as control structures of technological artefacts. In this case, we ask for the functions that technology has relative to the environment of the market. This view has long been neglected in economics: Marxian thinking about substructure/superstructure is one of the most influential views in this context, but institutionalist contributions which built on Veblen's (1921) dualism of engineering efficiency and markets are also notable.

Thirdly, we can analyse markets as abstract mathematical structures. This has been the dominant approach in the twentieth century. It certainly does not mean that the relevant theories directly describe reality in terms of the underlying physical processes, but would assume that they manifest mathematical properties qua signs that can be analysed by economics. For example, this is the meaning of the revealed preference approach to utility (Gul and Pesendorfer 2008). It implies that economics would in fact not deal with actions by 'real' human individuals, but with systems of actions which constitute an object on their own (cf Ross 2005). So, considering a sequence of individual actions, these manifest certain mathematical properties which can be described by means of utility functions, but whether these functions describe individuals as physical objects is irrelevant for economics understood in this sense. 'Individuals' only have these properties in the sense of abstract entities in markets which are analysed as mathematical structures in turn.

Fourthly, economic systems can be interpreted as sets of institutions that provide meaning to individuals' actions manifesting these institutions, and that result from their interpretive activities. One major consequence of this view is that markets would not be seen as universal categories applying on abstract systems which could be projected on any sort of pattern of interactions, including, for example, animals, but as being fundamentally contingent on human interpretive activities. Markets are thus historically and culturally specific phenomena, as in much of the institutionalist literature (with classics such as Karl Polanyi).

I claim that a naturalistic approach to markets has to recognize all these four dimensions. For example, it would be wrong to confront the right lower and the left lower box, namely general equilibrium vs. institutionalist approaches. Instead, the question has to be asked when and why markets might display certain mathematical structures which could be stated in terms of equilibrium theory. The explanation cannot rely on these theories exclusively, as they do not explain certain fundamentals, such as prices as observer relative facts: Equilibrium theory does not explain why prices come into existence in the real world. In this view, prices are already seen as part and parcel of the economic ontology. Therefore, in order to understand real world prices, one would need to move to the lower right hand box, which would relate prices to institutions that determine price related behaviour, but also to the upper right box, where the function of pricing technologies would be scrutinized, as in recent materialist approaches to economic sociology.

1.4.3. Consilience

The fundamental ontological scheme developed in the previous sections serves as an organizing structure for enabling coherent cross–disciplinary research. The naturalistic approach to economics thus aims at consilience, a term coined by Edward O. Wilson (1998). As a basic methodological guideline, consilience requires to heed respect to all scientific disciplines in order to understand phenomena in one single discipline. This means, first, that all impossibility theorems are respected cross–disciplinary, and second, that disciplinary propositions should not fundamentally contradict results from other disciplines unless the reasons are also presented in the methods and language of this original discipline. In other words, economists claiming to explain a phenomenon so far treated by psychologists would have to posit their arguments in terms of the disciplinary concepts of psychology (for an intriguing discussion of the Becker's economic theory of addiction from the cross–disciplinary perspective, see West 2006).

Figure 1.13 Consilience

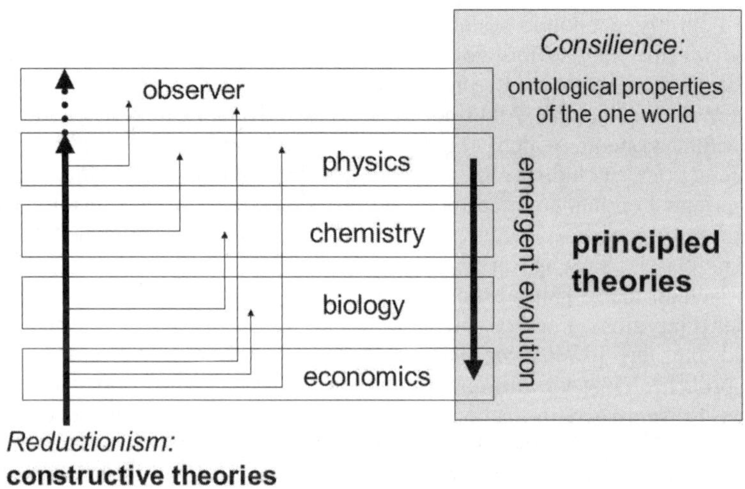

Note: There are two possible ways to achieve consilience. Reductionism would aim at explaining all higher–level phenomena in terms of lower–level theories and causalities. Ultimately, however, it would need to explain the observer, which ends up with limits to knowledge identified by the Hayek impossibility theorem. Consilience in principled theories is enabled by the universal validity of impossibility theorems and recognizes the emergence of ontological novelties on different levels.

This approach to consilience differs partly from Wilson's as Wilson tends to favour reductionist approaches to explanations, which relates consilience with constructive theories exclusively (Wilson 1998: 57ff). In figure 1.13 I once again compare the two approaches to theory building. Constructive theories aim at reductionism, with different reach according to the complexity of different levels of reality. For example the behaviour of financial traders is explained by referring to particular hormones in the human body (for example Coates et al. 2010); this reduces economics to biology and even chemistry. Reduction can also work via abstraction. As mentioned previously, statistical mechanics can be applied to financial markets; this does not mean that they are seen as gases, but simply that there are physical processes of an abstract kind which have different manifestations on different levels in complex systems (for example Roehner 2002). Ultimately, however, all reductionist approaches would end up with making the role of the observer explicit, if only in the realm of quantum phenomena, such as suggested by the Copenhagen interpretation. Therefore, reductionism always contains the seed of its own paradoxical 'sublation' in Hegelian terms in it: This directly follows from the Hayek impossibility theorem.

Reductionism could only be complete if it also fully explained the role of the human observer in any kind of science, in particular on the quantum level. Only this would account for all scientific theories in reductionist terms: That is, we would need to explain why the human brain constructs a certain kind of theory, given certain inputs to this brain. However, apart from the sheer complexity of this task, there is another impossibility theorem involved, that I dub the 'Popper impossibility theorem' (Popper 1982: 11ff, 49ff): As we know, all science only leads to fallible propositions, and our knowledge grows continuously. Now, if we want to reduce a particular theory held to be approximately true today, we would also need to explain why this theory fails to be true in the future. But this would require that we know the true theory already, because only based on this theory we would be able to identify the errors of the current theory in terms of the exact identification of why this wrong theory departs from reality. Therefore, we can never arrive at a full reduction of the role of the human observer in the growth of knowledge: We would need to be able to explain why the human observer errs, and to which degree; but this would require being able to assume a position that is independent from any human observer including ourselves. This conclusion also follows from Hayek's impossibility theorem, but can be further specified. In particular, it follows from Popper's impossibility theorem of the impossibility to predict the measurement requirements of any future theory that might possibly improve on the currently held theory (this relationship ultimately roots in Gödelian limits to fallibilism as a coherent and consistent epistemic strategy, see Post 1987): We are not able to predict, based on the current theory, in which way we could improve it, without knowing already the new theory.

This discussion is directly relevant for economics. Economics is apparently able to show that the human observer often errs, which results into a list of so-called 'anomalies' in applying rational choice theory. In this case, we compare a theory with pre-scientific ways of reasoning. Then, we can even calculate the distance between the errors and the truthful state of the world, for example when comparing subjectively estimated probabilities and true probabilities. However, even in this case we face the problem that the economic theory of rationality is in turn falsified by these very facts as a theory of human behaviour. Therefore, we cannot yet answer the question why human choice does not match with the predictions of the theory. A comprehensive theory would have to explain the reasons for the failures. However, this theory would be closer to the true state of the world, and hence would substitute for the economic theory of rationality as a theory of human behaviour, which would also affect our assessment of the measured human errors. Therefore, as long as we do not know this new theory, we cannot adequately evaluate the observed human errors. There is the possibility that the new theory might discover that these errors serve another purpose, and therefore would turn out to be 'optimal' relative to this.

The evolutionary approach to consilience does not aim at reductionism; quite to the opposite, it tries to explain the emergence of irreducible novelty, such as the emergence of life from chemical processes. It treats the role of the observer as fundamental, as emergence is seen as essentially related to information generation and accumulation. Therefore, reduction can be helpful to understand the connection between different levels of reality that are reflected in different disciplines; but what is more fundamental is to show how novelty emerges, and why. This question imposes the discipline of consilience on theorizing: Even if a phenomenon is seen as emergent ex post, it is not possible to explain its emergence on the basis of regularities specific to this emergent level. In other words, for example, if we accept the economic model of rationality, and ask the question why it holds, we cannot explain this presumed fact by referring to economics, but to some other theory, such as biology (as in Robson 2001). Or, if we want to explain the origin of life, we would need to draw on principles of physics and chemistry, and would not implicate already any sort of phenomenon which is specifically biological. Notwithstanding, once life has come into existence, we need to recognize that there are phenomena which are specific to life and cannot be reduced to physics and chemistry.

Therefore, in Husserl's (1913/1985: 112ff) words, consilience does not preclude the formulation of 'regional ontologies' as a foundation for the different sciences. Regional ontologies are reflected in particular irreducible concepts (for one of the many modern formulations of a related thought, see for example Fodor 1974). The question is then how we can identify certain theoretical notions that are specific to an academic discipline, in the sense of denoting emergent properties of the Husserlian regional ontology. Here, I propose to follow the approach of the 'New Structuralism' in philosophy of science, which has not been widely received but was recognized as a valuable frame of reference in the philosophy of economics by Hausman (1992). This position starts out from the observation that in all specific scientific domains, there are theoretical concepts which can only be measured if the relevant theory is already presupposed. So, the Newtonian physical magnitudes of force, acceleration, mass etc. form a theoretical system in which those magnitudes are only defined within that system and presuppose the Newtonian laws in measurements.

In Stegmüller's (1973, 1986) comprehensive development of the new-structuralist approach, terms such as 'mass' are called 't-theoretical terms,' indicating that they are theoretical with reference to the theory itself (for an overview of the entire approach, see figure 1.14, Stegmüller 1986: 48ff). Then, two levels can be distinguished, theory dependent sets and non-theory dependent sets (t-theoretical, non-t-theoretical). This is familiar from economics: Since the neoclassical revolution, 'value' has been related with 'price'; this means that prices have been turned into t-theoretical magnitudes because they always need to be related to the competitive model of the market. Tons of grain, in contrast, is non-t-theoretical. The relationship between the levels is established via theoretical terms. The terms are parts of fundamental laws, which define the general framework of a theory (such as marginalism in neoclassical economics): applications require the addition of special laws in order to render the theory applicable empirically (such as a specific form of the production function in economics, see in detail Herrmann-Pillath 2001a: 205ff, 2002). Thus, a theory appears to be a complex pattern of different sets of models, in which essential parts of the measurement language are relative to the theory in question. So, there is a theory which is defined by a set of fundamental laws and circumscribes a set of potential models of the theory, which are transformed into models by adding certain special laws, as well as certain constraints (such as the physical constants). These models can be related to empirical applications in terms of partial potential models. Thus, for example, a real world market can be a partial–potential model of a neoclassical theory of markets, which implies that the empirical prices are interpreted in terms of the t-theoretical prices of that theory (compare Balzer 1982).

Now, with regard to consilience it is essential to recognize that the non-t-theoretical terms are not a theory-free observational language in the sense of positivism. They are only non-t-theoretical with reference to this theory (call it T1), but are t-theoretical with reference to another theory, or theories (henceforth called T2). But this implies that the empirical validity of T1 rests upon the existence of T2 which is independent from T1, and which establish sets of entities, magnitudes etc. which can serve as a non-t-theoretical reference for T1.

Figure 1.14 Structuralist approach to theories

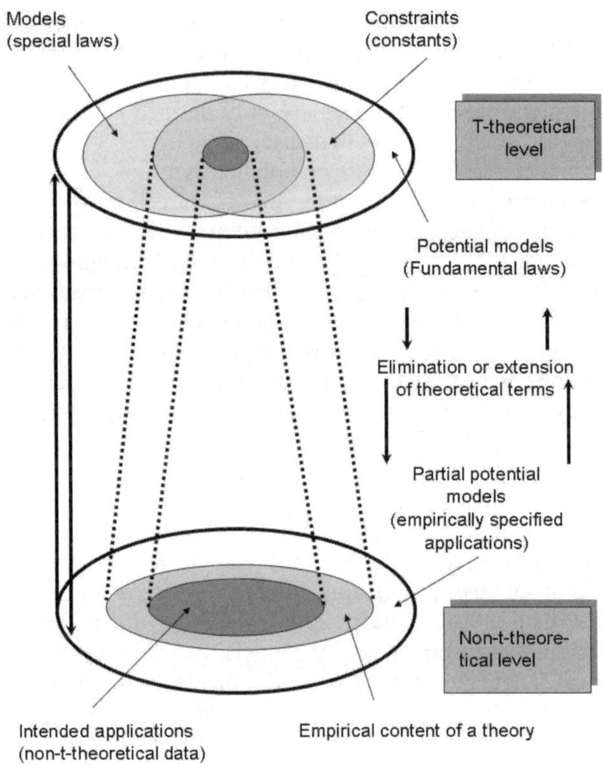

Note: Stegmüller's 'New Structuralism' in the Philosophy of Science analyses theories into different sets of models which involve theoretical terms of a theory and non-theoretical terms, both taken relative to one particular theory T. On the t-theoretical level, there is a set of constraints and special laws which results into sets of potential models of a theory, that is theoretically enriched descriptions of reality. These models refer to intended applications which are defined by means of non-t-theoretical data. These applications are subsets of the set of partial potential models of the theory, which is projected by means of t-theoretical terms into the set of potential models of the theory.

We can conclude that the ultimate reduction to a 'theory of everything' must necessarily fail because this theory would lack non-t-theoretical magnitudes. Consilience would correspond to a structuralist view of theories as networked and heterarchic structures; our view of 'reality' emerges precisely at the interfaces between theories and therefore necessarily relies on the absence of full reductionism (for a survey on related views, see Cat 2010). In other words, it is only in a non-reductionist network of theories that we expect 'scientific facts' to emerge. For example, we would not try to reduce economics to biology, but focus on the relationship between the two theories at interfaces which are empirically relevant, such as consumer choice. An empirical fact such as addiction would then need to be explained by both theories independently, but also establish a mutual reference, such that economic theory would analyse addiction in t-theoretical terms that correspond to distinct psychological phenomena which are non-t-theoretical with reference to economics, but t-theoretical with reference to psychology.

It is possible to elaborate a conceptual framework for consilience which undergirds the construction of complex cross-disciplinary conceptual structures. This conceptual structure is not arbitrary, or driven by criteria such as simplicity or elegance. It is grounded in fundamental ontological notions that can be created in doing Natural Philosophy. As we have seen in this chapter, these fundamental notions include a rich conception of causality, which builds on the Aristotelian distinction between efficient, formal and final causality. This distinction emerges from the Principle of Bimodality, which distinguishes interactions in the real world into the matterenergy mode and the semiotic mode. We can specify this in the ontological framework of the Peircian triad. We have seen that the Peircian triad corresponds to a physical inference device, which is a mechanism that explains the emergence of physical information. In this view, the world is knowledge about the world, that is the world is accumulated physical information. We will explore in the next two chapters how this accumulation can be further analysed. The accumulation of physical information is evolution.

2. Causation

It may well be a consequence of the uniqueness of the world that the attempt to describe it in terms of universal theories leads to an infinite sequence of approximations, not unlike the attempt to describe an irrational number in terms of ratios of natural numbers. Our attempt to describe the world in terms of universal theories may be an attempt to rationalize the unique, the irrational, in terms of our self-made universal laws (Karl R. Popper 1982: 46).

2.1. THERMODYNAMICS AND KNOWLEDGE

2.1.1. The conceptual framework of Thermodynamics

In this chapter I will further explore the idea of a physics of knowledge as the foundation of the theory of economic evolution. For this it is necessary to explore the notion of causation in more detail, in two senses; one is the question of the directionality of causal changes, the other is the role of regularities in causation. This requires elucidating the relationship between energy and knowledge. The relationship between energy and knowledge is straightforward from the perspective of Natural Philosophy: Ontologically, 'energy' can be defined as a potential for change entities have relative to a reference frame (Bunge 1977: 240); knowledge refers to the set of regularities that are manifest in these changes.

The core theoretical concept linking both notions is 'entropy'. This is because entropy has two formally homologous interpretations, one in Phenomenological Thermodynamics and one in Information Theory, with Statistical Mechanics bridging the two via the famous Boltzmann formula. There is a deep physical and hence ontological relationship between energy, entropy and information, that is knowledge. In this chapter, I will explore this relationship based on the ontological concepts developed in Chapter One. Although this is still a highly abstract argument, I will end up with a framework that directly connects with economics in terms of the physical processes that underlie economic production in an ecological context; this view on the economy was seminally developed by Nicholas Georgescu-Roegen (1971; for a survey of his life and work, see Gowdy and Mesner

1998). One of my aims is to show how we can conceive the Earth System in an abstract way as a system of accumulating knowledge, driven by energetic throughputs. In this view, the fundamental component of the Earth System is physical inference devices PID that enable physiosemiosis. Physiosemiosis requires energetic throughputs. This analysis of the Earth System is fundamental for understanding the role of the human economy in the larger process of physical knowledge evolution.

In order to understand such a system, we need to develop principled approaches to causation that relate energy and information, and which then can be applied on empirical systems. For these approaches, the notion of 'entropy' is fundamental. Entropy was introduced into economics by Georgescu-Roegen with an explicit emphasis on Phenomenological Thermodynamics (1971, 1976). His ideas have attracted a lot of criticism, especially by one of the leading theorists of entropy as a measure of information, the physicist E.T. Jaynes (for instance 1982; compare Kåberger and Månsson 2001), but also by economists (for example Khalil 1990), if for different reasons. However, as I will show in this chapter, the ideas developed by Jaynes are very productive in re-instating the case for entropy in economics, because we can elucidate the relationship between energy and knowledge (for a seminal related view, see Raine et al. 2006). So, in spite of the fact that my argument remains mainly ontological, there are direct implications for economics, parallel to the earlier efforts by Georgescu-Roegen.

To begin with, it is certainly necessary to review some of the fundamental concepts of Thermodynamics, as far as they are needed for my argument. Thermodynamics divides into the two branches of Classical, namely Phenomenological Thermodynamics, and Statistical Thermodynamics. The two branches approach states of physical systems in two different ways; the 'state of a system' refers to a particular state space which has certain dimensions in which it is possible to identify the system (for example, in Mechanics we can identify a system in a phase space which has the dimensions of position and momentum of particles, such that a particular state of a mechanical system is one point in a state space that has the enormous dimensions of the position and momentum of all the single particles which make up the system at a certain point of time). Phenomenological Thermodynamics analyses the relationships between certain properties of macrostates of physical systems, in particular energy, temperature and entropy, conjoined with special properties in different kinds of systems, such as gases with volume and pressure; further, it analyses the interactions between those systems and the environment in terms of flows, in particular heat and work. Statistical Thermodynamics explains these phenomena in terms of microstates, ultimately connecting with the quantum level. The central point of connection is the energetic states of atoms or molecules, which are probabilistic phenomena. There is a limited number of energetic states that can be occupied, and which rank in terms of levels of energy. The macrostate property of temperature is a measure of the probability of a population of molecules to stay at those different levels: Low temperature means that most molecules stay at lower levels, high temperature means that the distribution approaches equality across all levels. This fact establishes the connection with probability and information: At states of high temperature, we can tell with much less certainty at which energetic state a particular molecule is located, whereas at low temperatures we know with much higher certainty that these are low energetic states.

Classical Thermodynamics is defined via three or four laws, often numbered beginning with the Zeroth Law (as in Atkins 2007), so that sometimes the 'Fourth Law' is the 'Third Law', which results in confusion when some authors claim to have added a new 'Fourth Law' (for example, Georgescu-Roegen raised this claim). The Zeroth Law is a statement about the transitivity of thermodynamic states of causally connected physical systems in equilibrium, such as in case of the measurement of temperature (if A is in thermal equilibrium with B, and C is in equilibrium with B, this also holds for A and C). The First Law states the conservation of energy, defined as the internal energy of a system. Then, for an isolated system the First Law posits that the internal energy U is constant, or, what is more important in our context, that:

$$dU = dQ - dW$$

where Q is the energy added to the system via the external environment, such as a flow of heat, and W is the energy that flows out of the system, hence exerts an impact on the external environment as physical work. Now, a fundamental idea of Classical Thermodynamics, stemming from the earliest investigations into steam engines, is that in these interactions between environment and system, there is a distinction between two kinds of interactions. One is 'work', such as using a steam engine to move a weight, and the other is dissipating 'heat' which cannot be used for work. This leads to a distinction between two kinds or qualities of energy, energy that can be used for work, and energy that dissipates. The former is called 'free energy'. Then, the free energy is defined as the potential of work A generated from the system:

$A = U - TS$; so that in combination with the previous formula

$$dW = -dA$$

which means that the amount of work that can be produced by a system relative to its environment corresponds to the change of free energy. Here, the quantity S appears: the 'entropy' of the system. Entropy is a measure of the quality of energy and is defined in the Second Law of Thermodynamics which simply states for systems in equilibrium:

$\frac{dS}{dt} \geq 0$, with entropy defined classically as $dS = \frac{dQ}{T}$.

This implies that the generation of work is impossible without increasing the entropy of the ensemble of system *and* environment. In other words, if work flows into a system and therefore causes a reduction of entropy of the system, this is always accompanied by at least an equal increase of entropy in the environment of the system. That means, as stated in the Third Law, that it is impossible to achieve the point of zero absolute temperature because the work needed to implement this state would always generate entropy, and therefore the state of zero entropy at zero temperature cannot be ultimately achieved, only approximately.

The latter observation reinstates the relationship between entropy and information which also evident from the formal equivalence between the Boltzmann definition of entropy:

$$S = -k\sum P_i \ln P_i$$

and the Shannon information–theoretic definition of entropy:

$$H = -\sum_{i=1}^{N} P_i \log_2 P_i \ .$$

This formal equivalence results from the fact that the Boltzmann approach defines entropy as a probability distribution over a number of microstates which have certain energetic values; this corresponds to the state space in Shannon information. The distinction between the two only seem to lie in the use of different constants and bases for the logarithm, yet there is no direct Shannon equivalent to the relationship between microstates and macrostates in thermodynamics. Then, the relationship between entropy and probability is established in Boltzmann's formula as:

$$P = e^{S/k}$$

showing that the probability of a state increases exponentially with the entropy. This relationship establishes the connection between phenomenological and the statistical definitions of entropy and lies at the root of the two additional uses of the term, namely firstly, as a measure of order of a system, as evaluated in terms of the distance from the equiprobability of its states, and a measure of ignorance of observers, such that those probabilities actually reflect the limitations of observers in identifying the microstates, given certain information about macrostates.

If systems are open and manifest matterenergy flows between environment and system, their total change of entropy results as the sum of internal changes and the entropy imported or exported by the system via the matterenergy flows:

$$dS = d_iS + d_eS$$

Open systems with volume *V* can be characterized by the specific dissipation function σ:

$$\frac{d_iS}{dt} = \int \sigma dV \geq 0$$

which allows characterizing the dynamics of the systems. Open systems can obtain stationary states in which:

$$\frac{d\sigma}{dt} < 0 \text{ , approaching } \frac{d\sigma}{dt} = 0$$

However, for the subsequent argument it is important that this only holds for states close to equilibrium, and not for systems that maintain states far from equilibrium by means of growing matterenergy flows. The most important case of this is living systems on all scales, that is individual organisms or ecosystems.

2.1.2. Entropy and generation of information

The significance of Thermodynamics for the foundations of economics results from two considerations. One stayed at the centre of Georgescu-Roegen's attention, namely that Thermodynamics consists of a set of impossibility theorems that must hold also for economics, in particular because all economic processes of production are energetic transformations (Bünstorf 2004; Ruth 2005). The other consideration has not yet been explored in economics, namely that the concept of entropy can be used as a conceptual bridge between the analysis of those energetic transformations and the generation of knowledge in the economy.

This linkage can be uncovered if we go back to the physical notion of information developed in Chapter One. Then, it is straightforward to realize that any kind of observation is a causal interaction that involves energetic transformations (compare Collier 1996). Then, the impossibility theorems of thermodynamics must also apply for this fundamental process. This has been elucidated in recent theories about quantum decoherence which argue that the superpositions of quantum states decohere in interactions between quantum systems and environment (of which 'observation' is one of the most important cases), such that the order of phases is lost via entanglements with quantum states of the environment (for surveys, see Zeh 2005; Bacciagaluppi 2012). Then, although universal superposition holds for the systems of object, measurement device, observer and environment, locally one single state becomes observable. This is what explains the observations in Penrose's experiment sketched in Chapter One: Now we can add that this emergence of information comes at a cost, namely the loss of information and order in terms of quantum decoherence (for a related view, see Brukner and Zeilinger 2006). For example, there are experiments in which this loss is avoided, such as when observing the two superimposed quantum states of a photon in the double–slit experiment; but in the vast majority of measurements, these result in a 'classical' situation, which means we cannot observe all superimposed states, but only one; this one is our 'reality', and we are perfectly certain about this. However, in fact we can say that the Second Law holds for the emergence of physical processes on the quantum level of observational processes, and that our certainty actually reflects our ignorance about all other quantum states. In other words, the growth of certainty comes at the cost of the loss of information about all other possible states.

Figure 2.1 Generation of work (modified after Chaisson 2001: 21)

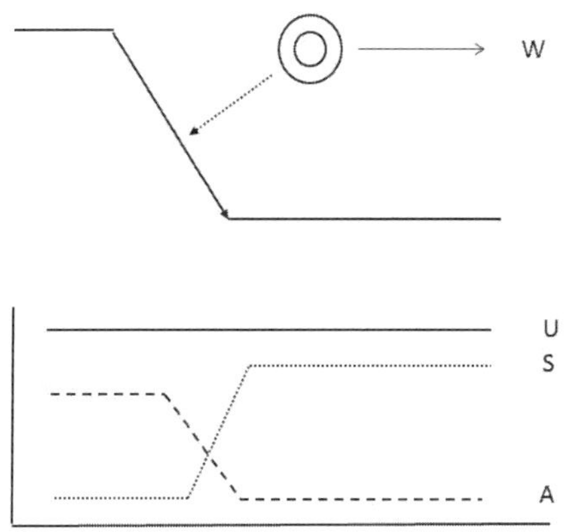

Note: We consider a waterfall. The bottom diagram visualizes the changes of thermodynamic state variables. When the water flows downwards, the internal energy *U* remains constant; however, its quality changes with the gradual dissipation of free energy *A*, so that entropy *S* increases. *A* could be converted into work *W* by inserting a wheel into the flow. Then, we can also say that the wheel measures the free energy potential of the waterfall in terms of the work produced. For this, we also need to know the degree of dissipation by the wheel, that is its thermodynamic efficiency in generating work. So, the outcome of the measurement depends on the measurement device, and our knowledge about it.

On the macro–level, we can interpret the relationship between entropy, energy and information in terms of the concept of 'work'. Consider the following simple example (figure 2.1, cf Chaisson 2001: 21): In a waterfall, free energy of water dissipates into the environment, thus increasing the entropy of its state until equilibrium is reached at the bottom state where the free energy (the gravitational potential) can no longer be used for generating work. We can add a mechanism, such as a wheel, to transform this energy into work. This is possible within the limits of the Second Law: The mechanism interacts with the water flow and dissipates energy in turn, for example through friction. This is why we cannot build a *perpetuum mobile*, using the wheel to drive a pump that would restore the original state of the water, thus creating a cyclical process. The free energy needed to maintain the process would always be larger than the work generated.

Now, we can say that this mechanism is also a measurement, as the amount of work generated can be seen as measurement of the free energy of the system, given the structure of the measurement device. In other words, any process that generates work also generates information. This information inheres in the macro–state that is created via the work generated by the wheel (compare Kauffman 2000: 96ff). Further, we can conclude that all measurements also entail a loss of information, which is the increase of entropy resulting from the causal interactions of the process of measurement. This increase of entropy happens in the conjunction of object, observer, device and environment, as in the case of quantum decoherence. In this sense, the Second Law is indeed one of the most fundamental physical laws.

Now, considering this necessary interaction between observer and object, and the resulting necessary co-occurrence of the emergence and the loss of information, there is the question what this implies for the possibility to gain full knowledge about objects. On the one hand, we can say that the Second Law therefore also means that the generation of information always faces a limit. On the other hand, in defining this limit, we also have a criterion to define the maximum possible information that we can get. This has been elucidated in Frieden's approach (sketched in Chapter One) in stating that in the relationship between information source J, information I and physical information K, the Principle of Extremum Physical Information implies that in most circumstances, there is a loss of information such that:

$$I = \kappa J$$

This is based on Brillouin's 'equivalence' principle which states that in any process of measurement, there is always a relationship between Shannon information gained H and information lost in terms of thermodynamic entropy S such that:

$$\Delta S \geq \Delta H$$

This relationship directly reflects the Second Law as applied on information generating processes, so that the Second Law can also be reinstated as a 'Law of Diminishing Information' I:

$$\frac{dI(t)}{dt} \leq 0 \text{ (Frieden 2004: 43)}$$

This law holds for sequences of information generating processes in ensembles of objects, devices observers and environments, such that, as in the case of thermodynamics, the increase of local information is entirely possible, while the change of information in the total ensemble is always equal to or less than zero (the term 'Law of Diminishing Information' was coined by Kåhre 2002 in a different, though closely related context without considering the physical dimension).

2.1.3. Entropy and observation

Frieden's use of Fisher information to explain the generation of physical laws from measurements that involve probabilistic interactions between information sources and observers is closely related with the method of Maximum Entropy (Frieden 2004: 10f). The difference between the two approaches lies in the mathematical formalism which specifies the former as a local and the latter as a global solution to what is basically the same problem (as we shall see later in Chapter Three in applications on evolution). In this chapter, I will mainly refer to the Maximum Entropy notion, because this establishes the more direct conceptual connection with Phenomenological Thermodynamics (further, the Maximum Entropy approach is formally more mature than Frieden's approach which needs to be overhauled in many details of the formal implementation, see Lavis and Streater 2002).

As I have noticed previously, the concept of entropy has been interpreted in numerous different ways; one is that the statistical interpretation of entropy directly relates to the interaction between observer and object and hence describes states of ignorance of the observer. This approach has been developed by E.T. Jaynes. His MaxEnt approach is also well known in another context of economics, namely econometrics (Golan 2002). This is because Jaynes introduced the Maximum Entropy estimation method, which exploits the fundamental ambiguity of the term, namely the thermodynamic versus the information theoretic meaning, and which is based on Jaynes's theory of probability (Jaynes 2003). Basically, this concept builds on the Shannon definition of entropy, as stated previously.

Jaynes proposed the Maximum Entropy approach to testing theories which states that given a number of constraints on realizable macrostates of a system, and facing our ignorance about the possible microstates it can assume, the most effective estimation technique is to assume that the microstates will maximize entropy, which means will achieve the equiprobability distribution under the constraints. This corresponds to the thermodynamic notion of entropy: For example, the state space of a gas is described physically as the phase space of its molecules in terms of the distribution across energetic levels and positions; this microstate corresponds to a certain macrostate as measured by means of magnitudes such as pressure and temperature. Observers can identify the macrostates, but cannot access all information about the generating microstates. The thermodynamic laws tell us that the gas will arrive at a state in which the most probable distribution of microstates will be achieved, tending towards equidistribution of molecules in a container, for example. This state also defines the macrostate variables, which therefore are only meaningful in equilibrium (we can only determine the temperature of a body if the ensemble of measurement device and body stays in equilibrium). This physical process can also be interpreted in the MaxEnt way, such that the observer predicts the macrostate based on the assumption of equidistribution. This is because the MaxEnt assumption would imply that the observer has exploited all necessary information to determine the causal impact of the constraints on the observed system, so that the equiprobability assumption does not entail any loss of information necessary to predict the behaviour of the system.

Figure 2.2 The MaxEnt Principle

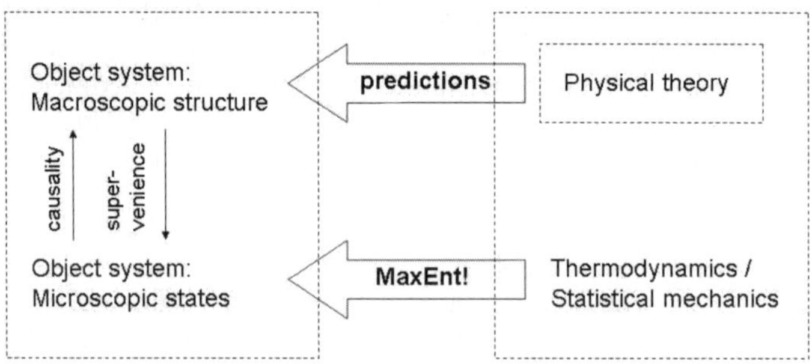

Note: Dewar's treatment of the MaxEnt approach as a methodological principle means that physical theories attempt at making predictions about macrostates, facing fundamental limitations to knowledge about all the underlying microstates that cause the macrostates. Then, the principles of Statistical Thermodynamics suggest that those macrostates will realize in which the unknown microstates obtain the maximum entropy distribution. If this cannot be shown, this indicates that certain constraints on the system have not been properly identified, thus resulting into modifications of the theory. Ontologically, this implies that the macrostates supervene on the microstates, as there is multiple realizability of the former via the latter.

Therefore, Dewar (2009) argues that the MaxEnt principle is a methodology to test any kind of physical theory (see figure 2.2), such that observed violations of MaxEnt would reveal at least the information that the assumptions of the theory leave some constraints with causal impact out of sight. The role of this principle could be explained by computational efficiency, because stating MaxEnt is the most economical assumption in terms of computational costs. This argument is essential for the extension to evolutionary theory that I will unfold in this chapter: If we conceive evolution as a knowledge generating process, MaxEnt would capture one of its essential statistical properties, because evolution selects for efficient mechanisms of information extraction and accumulation (compare Frank 2009a).

It is important to notice that the relationship between the microstates and the macrostates is a complex one. One the one hand, MaxEnt seems to be a purely observer relative notion relating with the degree of ignorance of the observer. On the other hand, one would assume firstly, that the microstates cause the system to adopt certain macrostates, and second, that the macrostates supervene on the microstates (Sklar 2009). For example, in Thermodynamics temperature is a macrostate, which supervenes on the microstates, which cannot have this property (single particles do not have a temperature); yet, the movements of the particles together cause the system to have a certain temperature (Bunge 1977: 97f; Laughlin 2005: 15ff). Further, systems with very different qualitative microstates can manifest the same macrostate (such as solids and liquids of different substances having the same temperature).

Figure 2.3 Two kinds of entropy

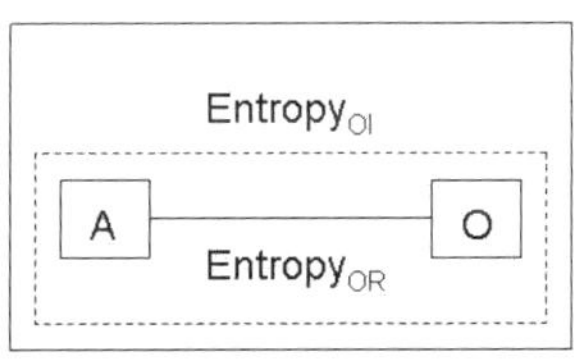

Note: According to Jaynes, observers measuring entropy define a particular setting of measurement, such as describing a system in terms of volume and pressure, or in terms of temperature and electrical polarization. This relationship renders entropy into an observer relative magnitude Entropy$_{OR}$; the results of measurements differ across different experimental settings. At the same time, we can define the entropy of the ensemble of observer and object, which is observer independent Entropy$_{OI}$. However, as we can only access this entropy by means of another measurement, this would be rendered as Entropy$_{OR}$ in turn.

Jaynes's approach reveals one fundamental property of the concept of entropy, which is that it refers both to an observer independent and an observer relative fact. This is because the measurement of entropy depends on the definition of the relevant physical ensemble, which is relative to the observer and the way how she defines the relevant parameters (Jaynes 1965: 397ff; Zeh 2005: 68ff). In other words, we can distinguish between the entropy of an object, which is the object of a measurement that intends to measure this entropy as an observer independent physical magnitude, and the entropy of the ensemble of observer and object (figure 2.3). Once we consider the observer, we have to recognize that the measurement of observer independent entropy depends on the experimental setting and the fixation of relevant parameters by the observer: Thus, entropy turns out to be an observer relative magnitude. On the other hand, considering the ensemble of observer and object, the entropy of this ensemble is observer independent.

So, we need to distinguish between two conceptual variants of entropy, the observer relative entropy and the observer independent entropy (Salthe 1993: chapter 3, distinguishes between internalist and externalist notions of entropy). Entropy_{OR} refers to entropy in the sense of the MaxEnt principle; Entropy_{OI} would refer to the physical entropy which includes the observer. Evidently, the measurement of the latter would always imply that there is another observer observing the original ensemble: This intricate logical structure of the concept of entropy introduces Gödelian limitations to its complete theoretical treatment, because we face an infinite regress of observational relations that would be necessary to render entropy into a purely observer independent magnitude. These limitations ultimately go back to the conceptual difficulties that relate to the notion of randomness that is intimately connected with the concept of entropy.

2.2. RANDOMNESS

2.2.1. Entropy: The view from Natural Philosophy

The crucial idea on which this chapter builds is to continue with our analysis of observation in Chapter One. Then, we can extend the notion of entropy to the analysis of physical inference devices PIDs. PIDs have been analysed in terms of the semiotic triad as being related with the realization of a function relative to the environment. As we have seen in the analysis of the waterfall example, we can view this realization of a function as 'work' (for a related idea, see Zurek 1989a, b). All functions are realizations of work. This reinstates the close relationship between the two notions of 'work' and 'information' (Collier 1996). Consider the wheel and the waterfall, again. The wheel is a physical structure that embodies knowledge of the human designer; this structure interacts with the flow of the waterfall to transform free energy into work. Now, we can think of two scenarios. One is just to let the wheel spin and dissipate energy, in turn. The other is to connect the wheel with another mechanism to generate another type of work. In the latter case we say that the wheel has a function. This extends to the waterfall: Because there are the mechanisms in place, we can say that the waterfall obtains a function. Viewed from the perspective of a measurement process, this function is reflected in the generation of information by means of the wheel; in terms of generating work, the wheel generates information about the waterfall, namely the amount of free energy available in it. This amount fixes the amount of work that can be activated by the function, such as the weight that could by lifted by a mechanism connected with the wheel.

Thus, I claim that the generalization of the notion of entropy directly leads us to a further elaboration on the Peircian framework of causality. This approach is a case in point for my understanding of natural philosophy, and in this sense follows up to Georgescu-Roegen's approach (Herrmann-Pillath 2011). This philosophical perspective is meaningful in the context of exploring the notion of entropy, because there are still a number of foundational ambiguities in physics related with that term (for an overview, see Uffink 2001). The most important ones are firstly, that entropy is only defined for equilibrium states, but at the same time any kind of change of these states presupposes an interaction with an environment, which would violate the condition of closed systems which is fundamental for Classical Thermodynamics; this relates to the additional problem that the theory always implies a relationship with an environment, which would in turn already have a thermodynamic state, thus would need to be a closed system on its own (which corresponds to our discussion of figure 2.3). Secondly, the information theoretic interpretation of entropy raises difficult questions about the conceptual status of the notion of probability, which is essential for the definition.

The conceptual connection between entropy and knowledge runs via the notion of randomness. As we have seen, randomness is a fundamental assumption in Peirce's thinking, dubbed with the neologism 'tychism'. The assumption that the world is fundamentally random induces a seemingly paradoxical idea about how to explain the other phenomenon Peirce was concerned about, namely directedness of change: This is that the world evolves into the most probable state (Short 2007: chapter 5). For grasping the essence of the ideas presented in this chapter it is absolutely necessary to recognize this fundamental shift of perspective: For example, if we as human observers regard the emergence of life as an extremely unlikely phenomenon, that perception would fail to see the fact that under the given physical constraints of planet Earth at a certain point of time, the emergence of life would have been a most probable event (Whitfield 2005, 2007). Such a view clearly refers to an observer independent notion of entropy in assuming that there are physical forces that drive systems into their most probable states: This is the core connection between the analysis of micro–level and macro–level phenomena in Thermodynamics, otherwise understood as referring merely to states of ignorance of observers (Volkenstein 2009: 105ff): Entropy results to be an observer independent measure of the impossibility of knowledge under certain given local conditions, which translates into the subjective impossibility to access the necessary information. However, as the argument has shown, this limitation to knowledge has a dual side; this is that once we arrive at the limit, that is the MaxEnt configuration, we also know what we can know for certain.

2.2.2. Randomness: Observer relative or observer independent?

To clarify these complicated questions, it is necessary to consider the relationship between randomness and causation. Randomness stands in a direct contradiction with the conventional idea of causality, in a double sense. If we understand causality in the traditional sense as expressing efficient causality, then randomness means that an event, a 'token', happens without a cause that can be described by reference to a 'type' of causation: All singular causal propositions at least implicitly refer to a regularity to state causality (Stegmüller 1983: 512ff; Woodward 2003: chapter 6 refers to 'invariances'). That means, causality cannot be stated only as a sequence of singular events, but always needs reference to a regularity that would render the sequence necessary; this fact had resulted into many sceptical attitudes towards the notion of causality in general, beginning with Hume and radically expressed by Bertrand Russell who argued that the entire idea of causality is pre-scientific (Dowe 2008; Ladyman et al. 2007: 258ff).

For example, the decay of an individual radioactive atom cannot be explained by means of a cause, so it is a truly random event, which can only be assigned to a probability measure that applies for the total population of atoms. Clearly, our perception of a causeless event depends on our need to refer causes to causal laws; in the case of the decay, we can only state population–level statistical regularities, which are not statements about causality themselves: The probability of decay is not a causal force. The other tension with our notion of causality results if we adopt the framework developed in the first chapter, as randomness would stand in opposite to 'order' resulting from functions. Then, we say that a phenomenon is not random if it manifests a function, that is a purpose. These two interpretations converge on an abstract level and simply relate with the notion of regularity: A phenomenon is truly random, if it does not follow a particular regularity.

So, we need to clarify the concept of 'regularity'. Obviously, we can relate this to both the observer independent and the observer relative mode. In the first case, we would state that the regularity is an aspect of the physical world. In the second case, we would assume that the regularity relates with the observer and its knowledge. Then, in my approach it is also straightforward to approach this regularity on part of the observer as an observer independent fact in turn, because the state of the observer is itself a physical fact. For example, if I have a physical law 'in mind', this is a state of my brain coupled with external artefacts, and this conjunction is a physical fact that is observer independent. Yet, if a higher order observer wants to explain this fact, it has to identify the function of the state corresponding to the physical law. This view is implied by Frieden's approach to physical laws as regularities that emerge from the interaction between observer and object: The two possible interpretations of regularity collapse into one, because the regularity is only possible to be defined and to be identified via the physical interactions of measurements.

The ambiguity in the term 'regularity' is reflected in two fundamentally different approaches to randomness as well. One approach states that randomness is an observer independent fact, thus is a property of the world. The other would treat randomness as observer relative. In this case, randomness would be seen as describing the state of knowledge of an observer. This distinction is of fundamental ontological significance, and we cannot present sufficient evidence for either of the two, as this relates with a perennial problem of science: Do we believe that all phenomena in the world are governed by laws, hence are reflecting universal regularities, or do we reject this view? In the former case, we would assume that in principle, we can hope that one day science will be able to state all regularities that are needed to explain everything. The implication is that randomness, as seen today, is merely 'subjective' or, in my parlance, observer relative. In a nutshell, randomness would be ignorance.

This distinction between two notions of randomness is reflected in different notions of probabilities as analytical descriptors of randomness. There are objective and subjective notions of probability (for an overview, see Hájek 2012). This difference is of central significance for my argument, as entropy in the information theoretic sense directly refers to probability, and this information theoretic approach mirrors the Statistical Mechanics view of entropy that was introduced by Boltzmann and Gibbs. Jaynes (2003) opted for the interpretation of probabilities as subjective probabilities, but at the same time showed how this interpretation also matches with the thermodynamic uses of the term 'entropy'. The trouble with the economic use of entropy by Georgescu-Roegen results from the fact that Georgescu-Roegen rejected the Statistical Mechanics interpretation of entropy (and until today, almost all economic discussions of entropy refer to Phenomenological Thermodynamics, see Gillett 2006 vs. Lozada 2006). I intend to offer another view which might reconcile the two opposing ideas.

Turning back to Peirce here, we notice that Peirce treated randomness as an ontological category which does not primarily relate with states of knowledge of the observer. This thinking is shared by Popper (1982) in his later works, and ends up with the denotation of probability as a 'propensity'. Jaynes was a staunch critique of the propensity notion (Jaynes 2003: 43f, 60f, pointing to the 'mind projection fallacy') and exclusively relied on subjective, which means Bayesian interpretations of probability, because he ultimately maintained the idea that science needs to rely on deterministic causal laws. I do not follow Jaynes here, although I receive many of his insights. The reason lies in the point previously mentioned, namely that I regard the observer itself to be a physical phenomenon. Then, all 'subjective probabilities' are themselves physical states of an observer, hence part and parcel of the one world: There are no exogenous observers.

2.2.3. Lessons taught by Maxwell's demon

The *locus classicus* for this discussion is the story of 'Maxwell's demon,' which continues to produce a substantial literature until today (overview in Maroney 2009). Maxwell's demon is a core analytical metaphor in my argument because all constructions of the demon in the physics literature until today refer to the fundamental issue whether an information processing system can produce work while violating the laws of Phenomenological Thermodynamics: In other words, whether information follows physical laws, as we know them. The metaphor refers to the question whether we can imagine an information processing mechanism by which a gas in a container can be separated into two segments with different velocities without increasing entropy, thus violating the Second Law. The demon would just observe the atoms of the gas and move a separator accordingly (in later expositions, the demon was substituted by a physical mechanism, without essentially affecting the arguments). On this scenario, the point about the relevant ensemble directly applies (in short, Volkenstein 2009: 154ff). The demon would need to expend energy for two purposes: Firstly, it would need to realize observations as physical interactions with the gas atoms, which would involve quantum level processes, as observation is a physical process; secondly, it would need to store the information about the locations of the atoms, and erase its memory (if it is not infinite, which is physically impossible) to track the changing locations. In spite of the fact that the demon is mythical figure anyway, the realistic assumption of a limited memory capacity would imply that the demon would have to incur energetic costs for erasing information in its memory. As a consequence, we can state that the demon will always need to incur energetic costs to implement its function, so that it would contribute to entropy production in the entire ensemble of demon, container and environment. Then, it is impossible to sort the gas into two segments without net entropy production in the ensemble. In other words, information processing is always a thermodynamic process.

Consequently, we can submit a simple hypothesis that sets the scene for this chapter: If the demon aims at maximizing the amount and the speed of information processing in order to sort the gas, it will also consume maximal energetic outlays, and thus produce a maximum in ensemble entropy. So, even if the entropy in the gas is reduced by sorting its molecules, the entire ensemble will continue to evolve towards maximum states of entropy, just because the demon is accumulating information, hence building stocks of knowledge, and reorganizing them via erasures. In this case, we might surmise that if a mathematically sophisticated demon applies Maximum Entropy methods to sort the molecules, these methods would also reflect the physical production of entropy in the ensemble. In other words, the ensemble would represent the Law of Diminishing Information as stated above, but this also implies that if the demon needs to expend work in order to accumulate information; the most efficient state of information will be defined by the MaxEnt assumption, as we have seen previously. In this sense, the maximization of entropy is also a process of optimizing information processing, given the Second Law. Think of a thermometer: In equilibrium, it will attain a certain macrostate that carries information about its object; this macrostate supervenes on a number of microstates which are themselves randomizing, thus tending towards maximum entropy, given the constraints of the measurement process. As for the observer of the thermometer, the proper interpretation of the measured value presupposes the assumption that equilibrium has been reached, which means microscopic information has become irrelevant and information about the constraints and the measured temperature is sufficient. I will make this argument step by step, but want to keep it as a beacon from now on.

The connection between information and energy has been well established by computer scientists fifty years ago and is called 'Landauer's principle' (Landauer 1961). Meanwhile, Landauer's principle can be treated like a natural law (cf. Bérut et al. 2012), stating that every bit of information at least equates:

$$E \geq kT \ln 2$$

which are the energetic costs of erasure (with k the Boltzmann constant) (for physical deductions of this inequality, see for example Bub 2002; Volkenstein 2009: 157f). Only observers with infinite memory capacity could avoid these costs (Bennett 2003). This is what we experience with our personal computers: They consume energy and heat up the environment. The processing and accumulation of information and energy use are two sides of one coin.

There is a most simple way to express this fundamental physical fact (Ayres 1994: 37ff): The essence of the concept of 'information' lies in the notion of 'distinguishability': that means, a state carries information if it is distinguishable from its environment (if not, it is equiprobable in the ensemble context). But this statement corresponds to the notion in Phenomenological Thermodynamics that a system can only generate work if there is a temperature difference with the environment, which reflects its thermodynamic potential A, the measure of available useful work (without a cold sink, work cannot be generated, see Atkins 2007: 49ff). Then, the Shannon information H stored in a system relative to the environment with temperature T_0 is simply:

$$H = \frac{A}{T_0}$$

So, turning back to the notion of probability, we can say that there are physical reasons why we cannot treat probabilities as merely subjective phenomena, even if we refer them to observers as observer relative facts: This is because the observers assume physical states themselves that process probabilistic information. This corresponds to the observer independent nature of entropy as outlined previously: Observers and objects constitute ensembles, and subjective ignorance is an objective property of the interactions between the two.

2.2.4. Propensities and probabilities

I propose to classify the existing approaches to probabilities in terms of the fundamental ontological modes identified in Chapter One as follows (cf Hájek 2012):

- The upper left box is the propensity of the world to manifest certain phenomena at certain points in spacetime, hence a physical phenomenon. These propensities root in quantum level phenomena: On the one hand, the totality of entangled quantum states defines one singular state of the universe; on the other hand, as we have seen, the physical interaction between observer and object results into singular realizations of particular states. This is a propensity which also applies for singular events, hence, for example, the outbreak of war or my marriage. In all these cases, the realization of the particular physical state is a causeless event in the sense that we cannot determine a regularity which explains with necessity that this state materializes, and not another one.

Table 2.1 The ontology of probability

	Observer independent	**Observer relative**
Matterenergy mode	Propensity (single events)	Propensity (sequences of events)
Semiotic mode	Frequentist probability	Subjectivist probability

- The upper right box is the propensity in the sense of Popper (1982), which refers to certain recurrent constellations of events, which can also be artificially constructed, such as in an experiment. The design of this experiment is observer relative, which would imply that propensities are contextual magnitudes, not just properties of single things or spacetime locations. This also applies for 'natural experiments,' hence in particular, all sorts of evolutionary processes that involve selection by the environment. In this case, observer relativity inheres in the necessary demarcation of the relevant properties of the context of the event to which a propensity is assigned. In fact, this is catching a major part of Jaynes' original approach to probability in the context of entropy, which emphasizes the relativity of measurements of entropy relative to the experimental setting and its focus of different aspects of physical macrostates (Jaynes 1957a, 1965). This view of propensity is also implied by the Frieden approach to information, because if refers to regularities that emerge from recurrent interactions between observers and objects. We can interpret the relationship between the two propensities in terms of figure 1.11, that is randomness as a property of the world and probabilistic regularity that emerges from causal interactions.

- The lower boxes contain the two classical approaches to probability as a mathematical measure, which is why it is assigned to the semiotic mode: Probabilities are numbers. One is the frequentist approach, which is observer independent in the sense that the frequencies are seen as properties of the world. However, the frequencies depend on the definition of the state space, which is an observer relative construct in turn; the choice of state space or measure space happens when the basic population of events is fixed by the observer. So, the frequentist approach requires reference to a state space which is itself observer independent: For example, the phase space of mechanics is assumed to be observer independent, that is position and momentum as dimensions of the phase space. Then, the pertinent state probabilities, such as in movements of gas molecules to other states, are seen as observer independent.
- Finally, the Bayesian subjectivist interpretation of this measure is observer relative, which means, in the original sense of Jaynes, that probabilities reflect states of knowledge of observers. This we can also refer to observer relative definitions of state space, which marks the essential difference between the statistical approach to entropy in Statistical Mechanics and the Shannon information–theoretic one. Shannon entropy is entirely contingent on the definition of the state space (compare Kåhre 2002: 182ff). So, for example, we can approach this page of the book in terms of the English language and the distribution of letters in the text, or in terms of the distribution of ink molecules on the paper. This observer relative nature of the state space is also implied by the notion of 'coarse graining' introduced by Gibbs into Thermodynamics: We can redefine the phase space in terms of averages over particles in larger components of the mechanical space. This coarse graining reflects ignorance of the observer.

The ontological dimension of this classification is most evident when considering quantum phenomena. The Schrödinger wave equation allows calculating exactly the probabilities of the outcome of a measurement, but these are not probabilities of the standard kind (Penrose 2004: 519; Bub 2006). The so-called 'measurement parodox' links the wave function, which is actually the description of universally entangled quantum states, to the fixation into one state of the classical world view, the 'measurement', which is an interference with a classical causal process in the world. The different solutions to this paradox (overviewed in Penrose 2004: 782ff; compare the discussion in Brukner and Zeilinger 2006) also vacillate between the boxes of the table 2.1. For example, the radical subjectivist follow-up to the Copenhagen view would fit into the lower-right box, hence understanding the wave equation as a description of states of ignorance on part of the observer (such as Fuchs 2002; which, however, does not seem to match with Bohr's original ideas, see Faye 2008), whereas the many–worlds interpretation (underlying my use of the term 'multiverse' in Chapter One) would directly refer to the upper-left box. In this case, the propensity would no longer be a property of single events, but of different multiverses as a whole.

From this discussion I conclude that 'probability' is not the primordial concept, but 'propensity'. This follows Bunge's (1977) systematic ontology. Bunge distinguishes between two kinds of propensities, the causal propensity and the chance propensity (Bunge 1977: 179ff, 194ff). A causal disposition refers to contextual causality, that is, relates a state of the world with other states of the world which condition a change of the former. The causal propensity is the susceptibility of the thing to undergo this change, given certain circumstances, that is the context. Chance propensity is context–free. This distinction is ontologically fundamental, because it refers to two different ways how energy, as defined previously, manifests its potential for change.

- Causal propensities always find expression via a causal intervention of any kind (which also defines the transition from the quantum world to the classical world), where these interventions produce effects against the background of certain invariants (Woodward 2003). So, causal propensities would correspond to the upper right box notion of propensity in table 2.1; in this view, determinacy and indeterminacy is not a criterion of distinguishing non-random from random events. This corresponds to our intuition: The final state of a die that we throw is indeterminate, but still be can explain it by a causal process, referring to the configuration of actions that produce this result. Notice that these actions operate on macrostates, whereas indeterminacy results from the microstate processes.
- Chance propensities, if they are not conjoined with a mechanism that manifests causal propensities in turn (such as a Geiger tube that would

connect radioactive decay with another causal mechanism such as ringing a bell, or as the just mentioned configuration of throwing a dice), dissipate energy with no other effect than producing 'physical heat': Mathematically, this is caught in the concept of 'Brownian motion,' which is an abstract approach to describe the resulting random processes. This is a microstate phenomenon.

Then, based on the latter observation, we can relate the duality of propensities to the previously made conjunction of work and information. A causal propensity refers to a particular regularity, such that the corresponding dissipation of energy takes the form of 'physical work': so, the wheel is driven by the waterfall, and there is a certain propensity of the corresponding energetic transformations. At the same time, some energy is transformed into heat, which reflects random variations in the physical transformation of free energy into heat. In other words, the information that inheres in work is actualized via the constraints under which the dissipation of energy occurs such that part of the dissipation results into the directed change of macrostates, such as lifting a weight by means of the waterfall and the wheel.

2.2.5. 'Individuals' as a fundamental ontological category

Peirce's tychism is a theory of propensities, meaning it assumes that randomness is a fundamental ontological property of the world. What is the relationship between randomness and regularity? I have already stated in Chapter One that the Peircian view, which corresponds to Frieden's physical approach to information, adopts a radical perspective even on natural laws, seeing all regularities as emergent properties of the world, thus ultimately equating knowledge with the world, insofar as all knowledge is at the same time a particular regularity in and of the world. This seemingly radical conclusion actually flows out from the philosophical reflection about the core idea behind regularity, namely the notion of causality. Since Hume we know that causality can only be stated with reference to a regularity which is observer relative, namely a law that is stated by an observer. This makes directly clear why our understanding of randomness is itself subject to certain limitations which go back to fundamental impossibility theorems in science and mathematics.

Let us consider the Bayesian interpretation of randomness as a state of subjective knowledge. Given a certain state of knowledge, can we actually decide whether a phenomenon is random? The first answer is 'no', because we can only state that our knowledge is limited, so we do not know. But there is a more complicated issue involved here. This is Borel's paradox (Chaitin 2005: 123ff). It is impossible to prove that a phenomenon is random, because proving means to subsume the phenomenon under a particular regularity; but that would exactly imply that the phenomenon is non-random. This is basically a Gödelian statement, because we might be able to state truthfully that a phenomenon is random, but we can never prove this, in principle (Volkenstein 2009: 185f). The only possibility that we have is to refute the assumption of randomness, if we can show that we can subsume the phenomenon under a particular regularity. There is a fundamental logical asymmetry here.

The most common way today to express this difficulty is the notion of algorithmic incompressibility that is applied on a sequence of phenomena, such as a sequence of numbers (Küppers 1986). Then, we state that a phenomenon is truly random if we cannot identify a single algorithm that can generate this sequence by means of an algorithm that has less information content than the sequence itself; that means, a generating sequence would be just a copy of that sequence. Obviously, there are different kinds of randomness, depending on whether such an algorithm exists. For example, the number π is a random sequence, but we can identify the regularity how to produce it, namely to calculate the ratio between the circumference of a circle and its diameter. The number of bits to describe this prescription is certainly far lower than the number of bits to describe the sequence of digits of π, which is actually infinite. So, a truly random phenomenon would be one where no such algorithm can be identified. This identification problem leads into non-computable problems, which relate with Turing's halting problem and therefore, ultimately with Gödelian impossibility results (such as computing the probability to pick a halting program from the set of all possible programs, see Chaitin 1995, 2005).

It is important to recognize that this approach allows for a specific interpretation of the interaction between observer and object that has been scrutinized by Zurek (1989a, b) (compare Ladyman et al. 2007: 213ff). Zurek approaches Maxwell's demon in distinguishing between the subjective states of knowledge and the objective states of the demon, and defines physical ensemble entropy as the sum of both. That means, on the one hand the demon might be highly intelligent and applies complex procedures to approach a solution to its problem by powerful statistical means, which reduces its state of subjective ignorance. On the other hand, the demon needs to build structures that store information and track its experience in solving the problems, which are random in the sense formally defined above, namely the structures are algorithmically incompressible. Therefore, even if the first aspect would result in entropy decreases, the rise of algorithmic complexity would reflect entropy increases. From this follows, as we have already seen previously, that there is a direct relationship between information processing and thermodynamics, in the sense that an information processing entity that extracts energy to produce work faces fundamental thermodynamic limitations that result from the algorithmic complexity of its memory, and the energetic costs of resetting the memory. So, physical entropy is always internal in the sense of including the observer. Then, the relationship between physical entropy and Shannon entropy in the ensemble of observer and object would be:

$$S = H + K$$

namely the sum of Shannon entropy and algorithmic randomness K. Referring to figure 2.3, S is $\text{Entropy}_{\text{OI}}$, whereas H is $\text{Entropy}_{\text{OR}}$. The gap between the two is defined by the algorithmically irreducible aspects of states of the observer. From the Second Law as scrutinized above, it follows for all information processing systems:

$$\langle \Delta H \rangle \leq \langle \Delta K \rangle$$

which means that gains of Shannon information will always be accompanied by at least the same increase in algorithmic irreducibility, that is randomness of states of the observer. This is a corresponding statement to Brillouin's principle, showing how the generation of information is always associated with costs, and hence the 'Law of Diminishing Information'. From this we can conclude that any consideration of physical entropy in evolution needs to consider the fact that if we conceive of evolution as an information processing mechanism, the physical states that store information have to be seen as being part and parcel of the thermodynamic process. So, we can establish a direct thermodynamic interpretation of the duality of information and knowledge, because we can identify the irreducibly complex structures that store the information as 'knowledge'. Then, considering the emergence of life, it is straightforward to realize that 'order' is not simply the regularity that is mapped into those irreducibly complex structures, but those structures as physical embodiments. This is paradoxical, but only on surface: In terms of its functions, knowledge is a set of regularities, but in terms of its physical embodiment, it is random in being irreducibly complex.

Borel's paradox makes a point clear that Peirce already expressed: Because our knowledge is always expressed in stating regularities, we cannot easily recognize that the world is fundamentally random. In this sense, we can never know, but only state the fact, without any hope to justify it in terms of a proof (cf Volkenstein 2009: 185f). This allows for another interpretation of this observation, which goes back to a notion of medieval ontology. This is that formally, randomness is the same as 'individuality' in the strict sense. A phenomenon is individual if we cannot describe it in terms of conceptual classes: This is the '*individuum est ineffabile*' thesis of scholastics (Pieper 1974). It relates with the fundamental limits to predication: All predication is an assignment of certain objects to conceptual classes. All classes are defined by the regularities that make of their definition or in modern parlance, their use. As such, classes can be shared by any number of individuals. So, what makes an individual truly singular, cannot be a property that relates with a class. But as we cannot speak unless by assigning predicates to entities, *individuum est ineffabile.*

This analysis shows why we need a specific theoretical framework to deal with the emergence of knowledge in a random world. This is the theory of evolution. The theory of evolution as developed by Darwin establishes a new relationship between individuals and regularities in taking individuals as the 'substance' of the reality of evolving biological information. Every biological individual is unique, and at the same time represents a set of regularities that evolves on the level of the population of individuals.

2.3. EMERGENT INFORMATION AND THE SECOND LAW

2.3.1. Regularities as kinds of constraints on change

Genuine randomness is genuine individuality: This insight is of prime importance. We can submit the fundamental ontological proposition that only individuals exist; this also implies that the world in its entirety is an individual, hence reflecting its fundamentally random nature (Bunge 1977: 30, 157) (physically, this individuality of the world is salient in the role of physical constants). The idea that 'existence' is a special ontological property of individuals can be justified, among other reasons, by the problematic and even self–contradictory status of the predicate 'to exist' (overview in Nelson 2012). As we have already seen in Chapter One, this is a contentious proposition in general ontology, because both Hegel and Peirce are conceptual realists. This problem can be traced back to medieval philosophy and the controversy between realism and nominalism. Nominalists subscribe to the statement that only individuals exist, whereas realists assume that concepts exist, such as Platonic ideas. Peirce clearly rejected the nominalist position, but we can now offer a solution to the tensions between the different positions: This is that concepts are higher order individuals, which directly follows from treating knowledge as a physical phenomenon. Since every concept is also a physical state of an information processing system, those states are individuals in the ontological sense.

We can make this point more precise if we distinguish between different kinds of regularities in an evolving state space of the world. The notion of the state space is itself a tricky one, because it depends on the way how we classify events (Bunge 1977: 123ff). For example, a state space in physical mechanics, the phase space, such as used when describing a gas, has $6N$ dimensions (three for position, three for momentum, for every of N particles). The state space of biological evolution might be described, for example, by the possible combinations of the DNA which relate with 'traits' that refer to biological functions under selection (Grafen 2002). Even if we take this for unrealistic, it suffices to show why there is a fundamental difference between the mechanical and the evolutionary view. This is because the state space of evolution evolves, as new combinations of atoms and molecules emerge which can in turn combine with existing combinations, and which result into new 'traits'.

Against this background, we can define a particular regularity just as a constraint on a state space which manifests itself recurrently. Physical laws have universal validity, thus every physical object in the universe manifests their constraint: Physical laws are universal impossibility theorems in the sense that they hold universally, namely allow for no exception. This is different from properties that chemical substances have. A chemical substance manifests certain properties (such as the phase transitions of water and the corresponding temperatures) which are universal, but only relate with this substance. Again, it is impossible that water does not manifest these properties, but this is not a physical law in the conventional sense. Finally, there are regularities that only apply for individuals: For example, I cannot run as fast as Usain Bolt. This certainly does not qualify as a natural law, but still is a strict impossibility statement. It is important to emphasize that one cannot simply say that my incapacity to run as fast as Bolt does not relate with natural laws, because, after all, Bolt can run faster than me. The impossibility results from the individual constitution of my body.

Figure 2.4 Kinds of regularities in the state space

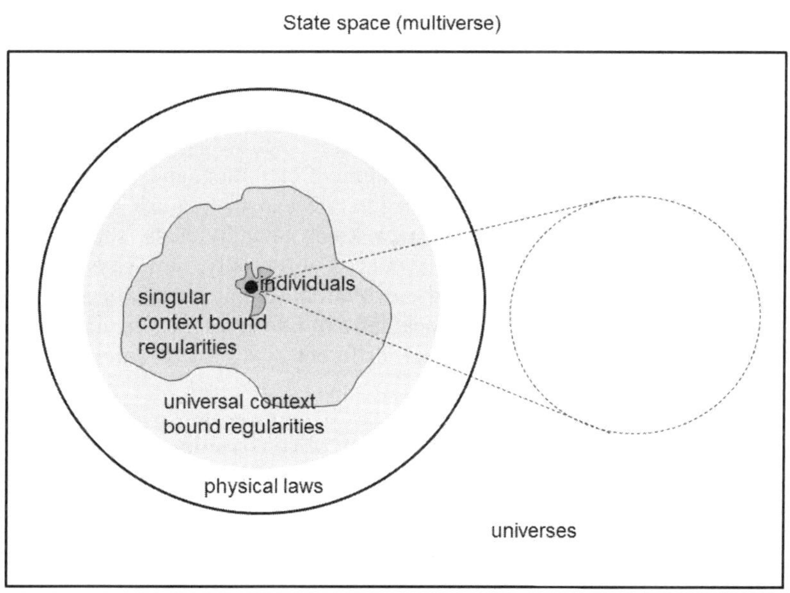

Note: There are three different kinds of regularities in the multiverse; regularities are constraints on possible states of its state space, hence define impossibilities. Singular context bound regularities are constraints that only hold for single individuals. Universal context bound regularities hold for kinds of individuals, such as chemical substances. Physical laws hold universally. Some theories of the multiverse suppose that single universes are individuals in terms of the particular physical constants that appear in physical laws. In this sense, physical laws are singular context bound regularities relative to the multiverse, as they define universes as individuals.

I summarize these distinctions in figure 2.4, where I denote the three cases as 'physical laws', 'universal context bound regularities' and 'singular context bound regularities'. Contextualization restricts the range of the resulting impossibility statements, but still we have a regularity which can be checked for example by falsification (Popper's situational logic, see Caldwell 1991). As we see in figure 2.4, this distinction ultimately holds for the multiverse as the different constituent parts, the single universes, are themselves individuals. Even the physical laws, with regard to the constants, can be individual context bound regularities from this point of view (Susskind 2006). The essential point is that we can conceive of all regularities as being evolved constraints on the possible states of the state space: In being constraints that result into impossibilities, the distinction between laws and more restricted regularities becomes less significant. At the same time, we can posit that as knowledge is a physical state itself, it turns into a constraint on possible states of the world (which corresponds to the Deutsch hypothesis underlying my concept of the semioverse). Stated as such, we can also say that regularities are constraints on the evolution of states, that is restrictions on possible states. Then, we can distinguish between two different kinds of change: One is change within a given state space, and another is change within a changing state space; a changing state space means that there are new kinds of states emerging.

According to the common understanding of evolution, and with reference to our previous discussion of knowledge, we can distinguish between the emergence of new individuals and new kinds of individuals, such as new chemical substances. As physical laws hold universally, new physical laws can only emerge on the level of the evolution of universes, which implies that relative to the multiverse, physical laws of universes are singular context bound regularities (as envisaged in different ways by Smolin 1997 or Susskind 2006).

2.3.2. Evolution of knowledge as evolution of constraints

These thoughts can be put in more general terms if we introduce the concept of 'accessibility' (Stadler et al. 2001; Fontana 2007). Considering the state space, the point is that regularities restrict accessibility of possible states. Then, it is evident that evolution implies the decreasing accessibility of the evolving state space, because new entities on the one hand increase the potential for new possible states, but at the same time the realized states impose constraints reflecting the regularities specific to them. In other words, the essence of evolution lies in the fact that evolution increases the number of possible states of the world, but at the same time accumulates restrictions to accessibility of possible states, relative to the expanding state space. This conclusion can be further sharpened if we consider one particularly powerful determinant of the emergence of new possible states of the world, which is recombination. Recombination means that existing states are combined into new states which have properties that did not exist previously.

The implications of this can best be illustrated by considering molecular evolution. The chemical properties of macromolecules are determined by the molecular shape which is a property of the ensemble of atoms, and not just a property of the atoms (Ramsey 2000). So, if a new kind of macromolecule happens to form by means of a recombination of pre-existing atoms and molecules, this increases the number of possible states of the world, because this molecule can in turn become the object of recombination. However, given the energetic constraints on the realization of shapes, this state of the macromolecule cannot be achieved from any starting configuration, and it cannot move to any arbitrary other shape via incremental change of configurations. So, the shape is a constraint for the emergence of other possible shapes out of the macromolecule. At the same time, there is the possibility that there are changes of configurations that are neutral with reference to this shape, which is therefore realizable in multiple ways. These neutral changes can open the way for the sudden emergence of new shapes, if at a certain neutral configuration, one single additional change would suffice to realize the transition (Fontana and Buss 1996; compare Kauffman 1993).

Thus, there are complex determinants of the accessibility of states. One important consequence of this is that changes of the molecular state space are path–dependent, because transition probabilities are asymmetric for the vast majority of cases. That means, if there is a change from one to another state with different shapes, the probability of a reversal is different. This implies that the shapes qua evolving constraints create a particular path of molecular evolution, which at the same time manifests the property of an increasing number of possible states, but decreasing accessibility, in relative terms. It is essential to realize that this asymmetry also holds because of the Second Law: Since the direction of change is always determined by increasing the probability of states, physical systems will move to ever larger segments of the state space, such that the movement back to particular states with lower probability becomes close to impossible (Penrose 1989: 400ff).

This example of molecular evolution just illustrates a general principle which we can formulate in this way: The evolution of the state space of the world manifests an increasing role of context bound regularities in constraining accessibility, while maintaining and increasing the potential for the emergence of new possible states. Consider the transition from physical to biological and cultural evolution: There is an increasing significance of context bound regularities, which means, that physical laws as such are becoming less and less important as constraints on newly emerging possible states. So, the different capacities of different animal species are determined by their species specific constraints, but not by the physical laws directly: There is no physical law that would constrain the possible evolution of wings that would allow humans to fly. Similarly, the human potential for innovation is not constrained by our biological features, but by the cultural context. In other words, the further the state space evolves, the more salient become individual context bound regularities. In terms of Zurek's duality of constituents of entropy, that means that the algorithmically incompressible complex aspects of the world become more and more salient, reflecting growth of knowledge as a physical structure. But this also implies that the potential for new possible states of the world grows continuously. We can state this as the most fundamental principle of the evolution of the semioverse, as defined in Chapter One.

2.3.3. Growth of knowledge as expression of the Second Law

Now, considering the information–theoretic notion of entropy, according to which the entropy of a realized state depends on its distribution across a state space:

$$S = -k\sum_{i=1}^{M} P_i \ln P_i \ ,$$

the relationship between entropy and evolution requires considering the change of entropy that happens if the number of possible states M is also evolving. Then, evolutionary transitions to new actual states have to be considered in two different contexts, namely relative to the initial state space, and relative to the new state space, with the two being connected via the increased number of possible states by means of recombination.

Now, Layzer (1988) and Frautschi (1988) introduced the following essential idea (figure 2.5) (for a related approach, see for example Landsberg 1984). In an expanding universe, even when only considering the static state space of physics with reference to the possible $6N$ dimensions, the number of possible states (though of the same quality) is increasing continuously with the expansion. Since at the same time the law of the conservation of energy and matter holds, this means that the realized states project into this increasing state space such that even if the realized states follow the Second Law in terms of increasing disorder, the order in terms of decreasing entropy relative to the expanding state space increases. That means, in an expanding universe the Second Law holds for both the growth of potential and realized entropy, but the gap between the two grows continuously, too. From this follows that there is increasing information content in the realized states which become less probable; physically, this information content is the dual of the free energy that is embodied in the states manifesting the increasing entropy gap. However, we need to recognize that this information content can reflect all the different kinds of regularities that we identified previously. We have already noticed that empirically, the relevance of context–bound regularities increases, which is a plausible assumption because the transition to state spaces with new possible states is itself a random process. We can refer this to Frieden's categories of information in the following way; if we define Frieden's J as the maximum information capacity of states of the universe, then actual information represents the gap to its full realization, which we denoted as $\kappa J = I$. Then, adapting the notation in Layzer (1988: 26), we have:

$$S_{act} + \kappa J = S_{\max} = J$$

Figure 2.5 Growth of information I *in the universe (after Frautschi 1988: 18 and Chaisson 2001: 130)*

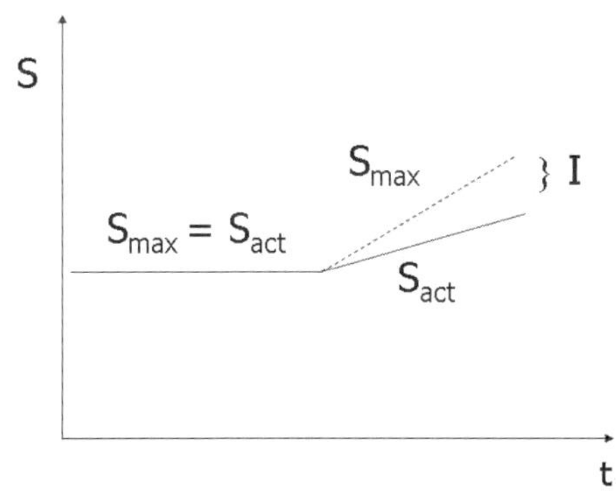

Note: In an expanding universe, the Second Law holds for the evolution of realized states with entropy S_{act}. However, after a certain initial period (presumably extremely short) S_{act} grows slower than the number of possible states of the universe. Hence, the realized states, while manifesting increasing entropy, nevertheless embody increasing amounts of Shannon information, relative to S_{max}. This corresponds to Frieden information I, whereas Frieden's J would corresponds to the maximum information capacity in terms of S_{max}.

One simple mathematical approach to this relationship between actualized states and possible states in evolution has been proposed by Weitzman (1998) in his notion of 'recombinant growth'. We can directly transfer his results about biological evolution to a state space which evolves via the recombination of existing states into new possible kinds of states. Weitzman considers plant cultivation, with different cultivated varieties C. If one starts out from analysing binary pairings from N objects, there is a function:

$$C_2(N) = (N \cdot (N-1))/2$$

such that we can define a binary recombinant expansion process which is the solution to a second-order differential equation:

$$N(t+1) - N(t) = \alpha[C_2(N(t)) - C_2(N(t-1))]$$

where α is a positive constant which gives the proportion of hybrids that yield a new variety. There is a minimum threshold for the process, which is that the number of next-generation varieties should not fall below the previous generation number, otherwise the process will collapse. If this is fulfilled, Weitzman can prove that, with a and b any positive constants, there is a positive integer T such that, for all $t \geq T$:

$$N(t) > a(1+b)^t$$

Hence, the binary recombinant expansion process will always grow stronger that an exponential process. This generalizes over all expansion processes of class m which are generated by a difference equation of the form:

$$M(t+1) - M(t) = \alpha[C_m(M(t)) - C_2(M(t-1))]$$

Where α is a positive constant and $C_m(M)$ is the number of different ways how the M objects can be combined:

$$C_m(M) = M!/[(M-m)!m!]$$

The expansion process of class ∞ means that:

$$C_\infty \equiv 2^M$$

For this generalization, every higher–class expansion process dominates the lower class expansion process. From this analysis follows that the growth of space of possible states, which evolves via recombination of states, will always be stronger than the growth of actualized states. Then, we can say that relative to the set of possible states the information content of the realized states increases continuously; this corresponds to the approach of Frautschi and Layzer that posits that in an expanding universe, free energy and information can increase continuously while the Second Law continues to apply for the entire evolutionary trajectory.

2.3.4. Irreversibility and causation

Following Zurek's previously considered argument, we can surmise that this interaction between actual and potential entropy is directly manifested in the algorithmic complexity of the accumulating physical structures of information storage. One way to measure this complexity is the notion of 'thermodynamic depth' proposed by Lloyd and Pagel (1988) (for a related, though alternative approach to 'logical depth' see Ladyman et al. 2007: 210ff). Thermodynamic depth measures the information content of the causal chain that is needed to produce a current state. For example, in purely entropic terms a random collection of letters and a poem have the same information content in the aggregate, which results from the observer relativity of entropy measures (for a pertinent discussion, see Kåhre 2002:

181ff). Yet, non-random states manifest a peculiar causal history which is non-random; that means, they are only accessible via a particular number of steps, which cannot be changed arbitrarily. So, all random combinations of letters relative to a certain set of letters are equally improbable. Some of them may contain meaningful sentences. We can distinguish between the two in terms of thermodynamic depth, so that random combinations just result from mixing, whereas non-random combinations require a complex causal chain that involves human grammar, semantics and so forth.

As Crutchfield and Shalizi (1998, 1999) demonstrate, however, this measure still fails to give an unequivocal account of complexity, because the depth depends on the choice of the macrostates relative to which the information content of realized states is measured. Crutchfield and Shalizi propose to identify the macrostates as 'causal states'. That is, a macrostate is a causal state. States are delimited by the criterion whether a state distinction makes any differences for the probability distribution over the future states. That means, possible trajectories of past states are regarded as being the same, if there is the same uncertainty over the future. Further, the states are chosen as to minimize thermodynamic depth. Thus, the causal states are the ones that identify the historical information in the system: These are exactly the constraints that differentiate possible and actual entropy, or, demarcate the states that are accessible.

So, this idea reflects the point made above, namely that the growing information content of the evolving state space is actualized in terms of decreasing accessibility with increasing potential for new combinations. That means, the growing gap I is also manifest in increasing thermodynamic depth of actualized states of the world. So, for example, in order to explain why I am sitting at this desk and type this manuscript, it is not sufficient to relate to physical laws and just point out that this is a highly improbable state of the universe. The complexity of my state results from the complexity of the causal chain that leads to my current activity, and which cannot be grasped by mere reference to physical laws. Referring back to figure 2.5, this approach means that the physical growth of knowledge has to be analysed in terms of two aspects of the same process. One aspect is S_{act}, which is the degree of algorithmic incompressibility of the realized states; this has to be evaluated in terms of thermodynamic depth, which means to refer to the sequence of causal macrostates that have led to this state. This sequence reflects the regularities under which the process operates, and which determine constraints on accessibility of states, hence the information in terms of the gap between S_{max} and S_{act}.

The concept of thermodynamic depth actually means that the evolution of the states shows an increasing property of historicity, that is, it is non-ergodic. Non-ergodicity means that the probability that a state returns to the original state goes arbitrarily close to zero, even if the time span considered approaches infinity. In Statistical Mechanics, this has been stated as the 'fluctuation theorem' according to which the probability of a system to return to the same state A is:

$$\frac{\Pr\left(\overline{\Sigma}_t = A\right)}{\Pr\left(\overline{\Sigma}_t = -A\right)} = e^{At}$$

There are intricate conceptual problems with the related notion of 'irreversibility', since the crucial thermodynamic state variables, in particular, entropy, are not defined out of equilibrium, and equilibrium states are necessarily reversible states; on the other hand, irreversibility is often seen as the most important implication of the Second Law (the 'Arrow of Time'). However, there are different interpretations of 'reversibility' which refer to whether the reversed process also goes all the intermediating steps backwards (as in mechanical reversibility); 'irrecoverability' would not require this (Uffink 2001). In our context, this second interpretation is the relevant one: It refers to the loss of information during a process so that it is impossible to recover the initial state by means of a causal process that is non-random. This corresponds to the fluctuation theorem in stating that there is an arbitrarily small probability that the process can be recovered by a random event.

This allows making clear the sense in which the Second Law implies 'irreversibility as irrecoverability.' Figure 2.6 is reproduced from Dewar (2005) and visualizes the classical deduction of the Second Law by Jaynes (1965; 1998; see also Gull 1989), which considers the transition from macrostate A to a macrostate B, where the information about the corresponding microstate is uncertain. According to Liouville's theorem, for a reproducible adiabatic process moving from one thermal equilibrium to another one, the phase volume of the unknown microstates W_A and $W'_{A'}$ is the same, such that the entropy in the sense of the probability distribution over this ensemble is constant. However, as the system moves into another state B, this is embedded into a new region of the state space (W_B) which cannot be smaller than the original one, because otherwise it would not be a reproducible process. This implies that the mechanical causation of the microstates is reversible, but is (almost) impossible to reproduce the original macrostate A by exerting causal powers on macrostate B. This means that information is lost in an irrecoverable way, even though the underlying process would follow mechanical causation which is reversible. This information loss reflects the Second Law. It is important to emphasize that ontologically, the random nature of the world is adequately reflected in the fact that the Second Law also needs to be stated as a probabilistic proposition: That means, although the Second Law is an impossibility theorem, it has to be stated in a probabilistic form, which is the fluctuation theorem.

Figure 2.6 The Second Law, the state space and irrecoverability (Dewar 2005: 46)

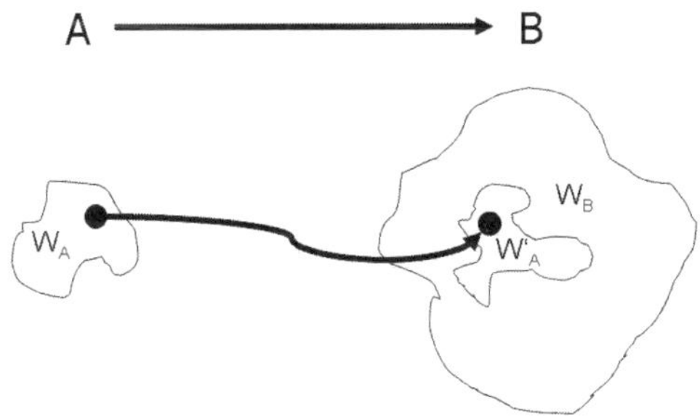

$$S_A = k\log W_A = k\log W'_A \leq k\log W_B = S_B$$

Note: Thermodynamic irrecoverability is compatible with mechanical reversibility if one considers a system changing from macrostate A to macrostate B, such that Liouville's theorem holds, that is the phase volume of the microstates W_A and W'_A remains constant. However, as this microstate is embedded into a new state W_B with at least the same phase volume, it is impossible to recover the original microstate by exerting causal powers on the macrostate B such that the microstate W'_A would be fixed that would lead back to W_A. So, for example, even though the expansion of a gas with a given number of molecules is a reversible process in mechanical terms, we cannot recover the initial microstate of the gas by changing macrostate properties after expansion, such as volume or temperature. This corresponds to irrecoverable loss of information, and manifests the Second Law.

2.3.5. The Second Law and finality

This previous analysis allows presenting a concise definition of what we mean when we call a process 'historical'. History means that we can identify a clear-cut causal chain of events leading towards a certain present state. Yet, at the same time this sequence appears to be contingent in a fundamental way, which means that we cannot identify the relevant causal microstates unequivocally, and we are unable to figure out any current action by which the original state could be recovered exactly. There are many possible worlds which could have led to another result, and also many possible worlds which could have led to the same result. By implication, the thermodynamic depth of the description in terms of causal states is high, because many alternative causal paths need to be excluded.

The notion of causality is itself dependent on the identification of causal states. This is evident from the problematic status of causality in the sciences (overview in Dowe 2008). On the one hand, there is a simple notion of causality which would relate a physical cause with an effect. However, this identification itself always depends on the statement of regularities by an observer, which in turn needs to refer to counterfactuals, namely the set of possible worlds that is excluded by the realized causal chain. For example, if I cause a forest fire by throwing away a cigarette, this causation depends on many contextual factors, dividing into sets of necessary and sufficient conditions. The clear identification of the main cause may be very difficult and requires reference to counterfactuals which exclude certain sets of events from actualization. So, stating that I caused the fire requires reference to a complex causal theory. This is what emerges from the discussion of thermodynamic depth: Complexity increases if the set of possible causal states increases. These states, however, differ from the realized states in the sense that there is a range of alternative constellations over those states which might be neutral.

We can refer this back to our discussion of knowledge in Chapter One: Causal states can only be defined relative to a regularity that is stated by an observer. Since we treat all observers as endogenous, this means that the regularities themselves are states of knowledge. This is the ontological foundation of conceptual realism: There is no causality without involving classes of phenomena; classes of phenomena can only be defined relative to an observer which is a physical process.

This reference to observers implies the transition from the simple concept of efficient causality to the Peircian triadic model of causality. In this view, evolution leads towards the emergence of information carrying states in the sense that via final causality formal causal mechanisms emerge in which certain causal macrostates manifest themselves as higher level regularities; these macrostates can be conceived as signs relative to the generating microstates. So, for example, if an ice block falls on the table and causes damage, this causal effect does not only depend on the molecular properties of water, but on the realized phase, that is being an ice block, and not steam. The adoption of this state is itself determined by thermodynamic processes, which result in a division of possible states of water into different phases which can be described as having certain properties. The causal powers of ice as opposed to liquid water do not only depend on the molecular properties, but on the ensemble properties of the crystal. The classification of these properties relates with final causality, insofar as the phase transitions are driven by thermodynamic regularities.

The universal physical source of final causal powers is the Second Law: For example, in the early stages of the universe gravitational energy was dissipated according to the Second Law in the formation of physical structures which were confined to certain areas of spacetime. These structures generated new causal powers (such as the possibility of collision), which combined with the workings of the Second Law. These new causal powers result from the changes of the state space that are driven by the

Second Law, yet result in states with new kinds of properties; properties are defined as causes that produce effects that did not exist previously. For example, in an initial state of the universe with radiation only, 'shadow' does not exist as a possible state of the world. Once the Second Law resulted into the formation of solid bodies, shadow became possible. Shadow implies the possibility of temperature differences between different parts of solid bodies, which determines further thermodynamic processes. Thus, the Second Law drives the direction of changes of the state space, without, however, determining the specific result of the changes. The emergence of 'shadow' as a property of the state space is not determined by a pre-existing goal of its evolution.

So, we are able to build a triadic conception of causality on a simple physical definition of efficient causality, thus achieving a physical interpretation of the triadic causal modes (compare Tuisku et al. 2009). We can define a most simple notion of physical efficient causation that builds on the concept of energy and energy transfers (Bunge 1977: 240, 326; Fair 1979; this is a more specific formulation of the conservable quantities approaches to causation, see Dowe 2008). If we conceive of energy in a most general sense as a potential for change, causation means a transfer of energy across two states. As we have seen previously, this needs to be further differentiated into dissipation, which means to refer to causeless causes, that is random phenomena which result in changes of microstates, and causality in the sense of regularities that tie up different macrostates, and to which we refer as 'physical work'. Then, the notion of physical work is essentially related to the notion of regularity and hence, a state of information (compare Kauffman 2000: 96ff; Collier 1996). For example, a body sliding down an incline is exerting physical work in terms of the changes of its macrostates, that is the physical location. At the same time, friction occurs, which involves random changes of its microstates. Both changes can be conceived in terms of efficient causality, namely energy transfers and transformations. But only the macroscopic changes involve a direction of change. This direction is implied by the particular configurations of the context of the changes, such as the slope of the incline. If we want to explain the particular pattern of changes, we would also need to explain how this configuration came into place. One possibility is that we would need to refer to a human designer who created an experimental setting in which the change happens. Thus, the regularities that are manifest in the generation of work relate with the interaction between observer and object. Alternatively, the configuration can be seen as a result of physical evolution, such as the geological formations.

Therefore, we can distinguish between work and dissipation also in information theoretic terms. This simply follows from the observation that work implies uniform movements of particles in the environment in which the process takes place, whereas dissipation as heat implies random movements (Gillett 2006; Atkins 2007: 32f). At the same time, we can say that work also means to turn states into ordered states which are random otherwise. This leads to the distinction between 'information' and 'information capacity'. States with high entropy represent states with high information capacity because they could be transformed into states with high information content via energetic inputs. Therefore, the distinction between work and dissipation is not a physical one in the narrow meaning of the term, but an information theoretic one (compare Salthe 2007). This becomes only evident if we reflect upon the physical notion of work in terms of the relationship between observer and object, and also recognize that observation is a physical process that involves work, that is the transformation of macrostates of observers. This implies that work itself can be interpreted as a dual to the process of observation: The environmental configuration of the body sliding down the slope observes this body, and the resultant macrostate embodies information about the initial macrostate, such as its location, free energy etc.

In this context, important cases are the dissipative states far from equilibrium that result in patterns, such as the much-cited case of Benard cells. These seem to suggest that the underlying energetic transformations could be conceived as work, in spite of being just dissipative. However, according to the current analysis we could only refer to this as 'work' if the resulting states have causal powers as independent macrostates, thus would connect causally with other macrostates. Otherwise, the 'patterns' are only relevant in terms of the relationship with the human observer. However, if we consider states in which the emergent macrostates feedback causally to the original microstates, then we might qualify this interaction as work. This is the perspective on synergetics which marks the transition to triadic causal analysis as the macrostates operate as constraints on the microstates in terms of 'order parameters' (Haken 1983).

Work that produces causal effects in terms of macrostates transforms information and stores information (Collier 1996). So, we can refer this to the triadic analysis in stating that the identification of macrostates occurs via formal causality which relates macrostates as causes with macrostates as effects. This is the only way how work can be distinguished from heat, as both are efficient causal processes. The emergence of those macrostates needs to be explained via final causation, that is, by identifying the causal chain that leads towards the emergence of mechanisms that result in those macrostates. Final causation is not meant to refer to a goal of the process, but to the directionality that reflects the Second Law. Therefore, if we adopt the ontological framework of triadic causality, the common opposition between the Second Law and teleological processes with growth of complexity becomes redundant (as in Faber and Proops 1998). So, in the previous example, if the dissipation of gravitational energy leads towards the emergence of celestial bodies, this in turn leads towards the emergence of new kinds of macrostates, such as shadowing certain parts of those bodies.

These effects create temperature differences which in turn drive energy dissipation.

Therefore, we can now restate the Peircian triad of causal modes in the following summary way:

- Efficient causality refers to the energetic transfers and transformations of the microstates of systems.
- Formal causality refers to the transformation of macrostates of systems and defines the distinction between physical work and dissipation, that is heat; formal causality reveals the transformations of information that is embodied in the physical structures;
- Final causality refers to the directionality of transformations that results from the Second Law, and relates with the emergence of new forms of formal–causal phenomena.

2.3.6. Triadic causal modes, generation of information and irreversibility

This approach offers another solution to the conundrum of reversibility versus irreversibility in thermodynamics. From the mechanical point of view, all efficient causal processes are reversible. In the debates of the late nineteenth century, this was seen as a contradiction to the phenomenological laws of Thermodynamics which refer to macrostates (Cohen 1996). However, we can say that irreversibility occurs on the macrostate level because of the involvement of formal and final causality, and is reflected in irrecoverability of initial states by macroscopic processes. I now expand the proposed Peircian interpretation of thermodynamics which applies triadic analysis on this problem (building on Herrmann-Pillath and Salthe 2011). I present the conceptual framework first, and then proceed with more detailed analyses in the next section. This philosophical interpretation is radically different from the established approach in physics, because it considers the full Aristotelian scope of causalities. I claim that this is legitimate, because we meet with a peculiar relationship between physics and information theory, and semiotics offers an ontological framework for the latter.

Then, we approach the notion of the 'macrostates' as being 'signs' of the microstates (figure 2.7). This corresponds to the Gibbsian notion of 'coarse graining' in Thermodynamics: A macrostate represents a set of microstates to the observer, who cannot access all the information of the microstates. The observer is equated with the environment which selects certain thermodynamic states (in the most simple way, the distinction between the system and the environment is a temperature difference, and the effects of this difference can be conceived as a 'measurement'). Then, we can approach physiosemiosis as a process in which one macrostate results into another macrostate, relative to the observer, that is the environment. In this view, the notion of work directly connects with a physical inference device in terms of the ensemble of object, process and environment.

Figure 2.7 Physical inference devices, physiosemiosis and generation of information

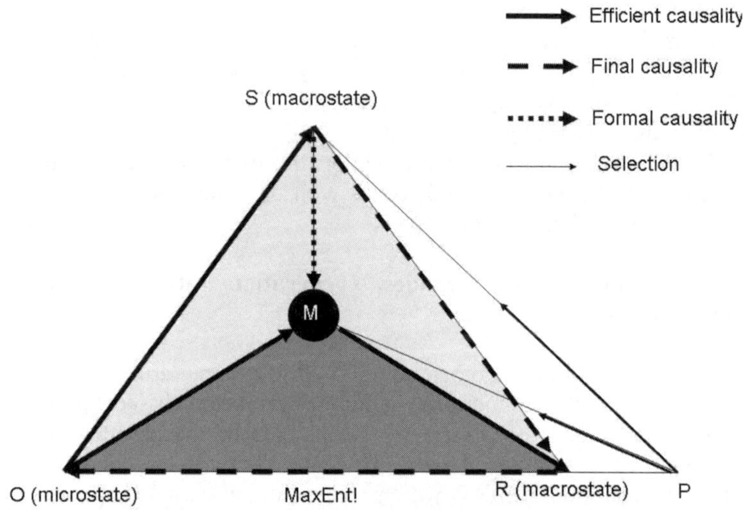

Note: The emergence of physical information can be analysed in terms of the triadic analysis of physical inference devices. Efficient causality relates microstates of objects with microstates of observers, thus establishing entanglements of both (*OMR*). Observers relate with the environment via the function of observation *P*, which implies that they only refer to macrostates of objects, with a corresponding loss of information ('coarse graining'); this is the formal–causal mode via *OSR*. These macrostates are signs of objects in an observational interaction. The MaxEnt hypothesis means that populations of observers will attain macrostates relative to the functions of the observation that tend to maximize entropy in the entangled system of observer and object. These are states in which the relationship between sign and object implies that the microstates tend towards the maximum entropy state under the given constraints. This is the state in which information relative to the selection by *P* emerges. Therefore, the inference process of PIDs supervenes on thermodynamic processes.

Consider the Penrose experiment again (Chapter One, section 1.3.2.). If the photon arrives at the detector, this is a macrostate in two senses, namely there is a state of the receptor, and this state can relate with the human observer. This macrostate is a sign of the lamp that emitted the photon. On the quantum level, there is randomness of microstates because the photon can also attain another state at the beam splitter. However, relative to the environmental configuration, if the macrostate at the receptor materializes, information about the initial macrostate can be inferred with certainty. In this experiment, selection operates via the experimental design of the physicist. On the quantum level, the generation of entropy occurs via decoherence of the entangled states of observer and object, as discussed previously.

Against this background, it is straightforward to apply the MaxEnt concept as envisaged by Jaynes, because we can posit that the resulting macrostate is one in which entropy tends to become maximal, with reference to the mapping of microstates into the macrostate, and relative to the constraints. So, if the temperature is equalized between system and environment, this is a 'measurement' which results into maximum entropy of the ensemble, that is thermodynamic equilibrium between object and thermometer. In the Penrose experiment, we would refer to the underlying quantum decoherence which results into the macrostate of the receptor, but involves the increase of entropy in terms of the dissociation of phases of the quantum states. These processes materialize under the given constraints of the process setting, such as the experimental configuration of lamp, beam splitter and receptor.

Alternatively, though not differing in principle, we can approach this in terms of Frieden's concept of Extreme Physical Information. Then, the entanglement between observer and object implies the maximum possible minimization of the difference between information source and information generated. This corresponds to the maximum entropy solution because the latter implies that the entire potential for generating information is realized, as the maximum entropy state means that there is no further information to be gained, given the information available via the accessible macrostates and the constraints. In other words, the MaxEnt state is the state at which Frieden's κ is minimal.

Now, in terms of the triadic notion of causality we can say that firstly, the partitioning of the state space into macro–states equates with formal causality, and the realization of the most probable state in the relationship between observer and object corresponds to final causality. That means, firstly, that we can give a clear-cut physical notion of final causality which avoids any reference to teleology, because the directionality only results from the fact that the systems tends towards its most probable state. Secondly, formal causality represents a property of the state space in terms of its observer relative nature. However, observer relativity is a strictly physical notion here, as this refers to the effects of selection by the environment, which is itself a physical phenomenon.

We can analyse this conceptual framework in more detail as depicted in figure 2.8 which simplifies the triad in omitting explicit reference to M, to avoid cluttering. We start with noting that the macrostates are efficiently caused by the microstates, as stated previously. However, if we compare two microstates through time, they connect via two different macrostates which are related to each other via final causality. Finality means that macrostate *B* is the more probable one, which is achieved via the microstates obtaining the maximum entropy state, relative to that macrostate. Macrostates stay in a formal–causal relationship with microstates, which reflects the fact that they are observer relative, in the specific sense that they relate with an environment that selects those states. The entire process is driven by energy dissipation, which is the direct physical manifestation of efficient causality. For this dissipation of energy, the Second Law holds.

Figure 2.8 Triadic causal modes and the Second Law

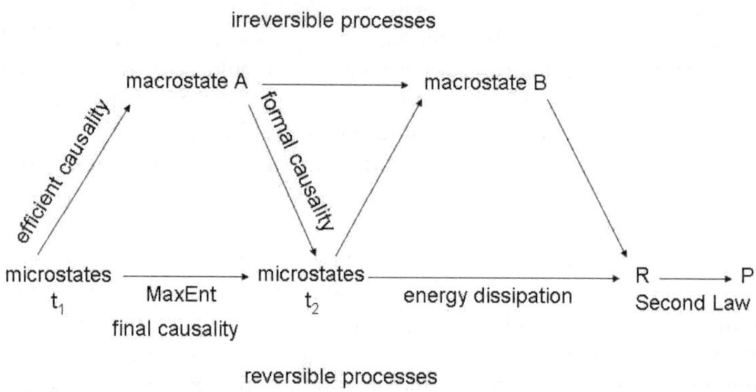

Note: In the triadic analysis, macrostates stay in a formal–causal relationship with evolving microstates. The evolution of microstates manifests the Second Law and results into dissipation of energy, which establishes final causality. However, microstates also cause macrostates relative to observers such that entropy tends to be maximal in the entangled observer–object relation. This relation evolves on the macro–level, where macrostates emerge into constraints on further evolving macrostates. Thus, irreversibility is established on the macro–level in terms of the irrecoverability of initial microstates by means of causal interventions on the macro–level. The resulting loss of information about microstates corresponds to the energetic dissipation in terms of a continuous loss of information, while evolving macrostates embody growing information (as stated in figure 2.5).

Consider the example of the snowflake again that I introduced in Chapter One. The formation of shapes of snowflakes is a process in which macrostates assume a formal–causal role via the specific structure–dependent attachment dynamics, which is efficient–causally connecting the corresponding macrostates. Then, the snowflake is a more probable macrostate in which the atmospheric conditions during its formation are reflected, and where the emergent structure constrains the further processes of crystallization. The snowflake accumulates information about its environment, which is structurally embodied, and this is accompanied by the achievement of thermodynamic equilibria under the evolving structural constraints which imply the manifestation of the Second Law. So, we can say that the snowflake emerges as an observer of the efficient–causal entanglements between its surroundings (the 'object') and itself, evolving under selection of the changing environments during its fall.

Then, we can distinguish between two aspects of finality. One is the finality involved in the attainment of more probable states, the other is the efficient–causal mechanism M that results into the respective macrostates (see figure 2.7). This mechanism manifests a causal energetics which is also determined by the macrostates in the sense that the macrostates determine the specific way by which the dissipation of energy is realized. This refers to the relationship of the resultant macrostate with the environment and its selective forces (so, the structure of the emerging snowflake selects further crystallization together with the environment). Then, we can achieve a conceptual distinction between work and heat, in the sense of dissipation, in considering the interdependence between mechanism and selection. Therefore, the special combination of reversibility and irrecoverability in the Second Law results from the interaction between the different causal modes. Final causality determines the transition between macrostates, and efficient causality determines the mechanisms that result in the realization of the most probable states. This realization is therefore reversible in terms of the micro–mechanics, but irrecoverable in terms of the loss of information about the causal dependency of the macrostates on the microstates through time.

We have already stated in Chapter One that in a modern conceptualization of Peirce's triadic modes we can say that the 'interpretant' is a response to selection by the environment; the response can be technically termed a 'function'. Therefore, we can say that PIDs establish the special causal category of 'function', comparing with efficient causes. Functions represent the essence of the conjunction of the three causal modes considered so far. I summarize the entire argument so far in figure 2.9, which also serves as a beacon for its further deployment in this chapter.

We consider processes through time, and the relationship between the Second Law and evolution. Evolution is seen as change of the space of possible states of the world, and as formation of knowledge. Knowledge is the dual to ignorance, in the sense that the storage of knowledge, memory, requires the availability of information capacity. Information capacity emerges from dissipation processes; it inheres in the random nature of the world. Information emerges from the formation of constraints on possible states of the world. These constraints operate on the macro–level, such that ignorance is defined as a lack of information on the corresponding micro–states. The Second Law operates physically on the micro–level, as far as efficient causation is concerned, namely dissipation and randomization. Evolution operates on the macro–level, and builds on the full triadic causal modes, converging into the emergence of functions. Functions establish the distinction between work and heat via the emergence of physical information, that is knowledge. The upshot is that evolution and the Second Law do not stay in contradiction with each other, as in Schrödinger's famous view, but to the contrary, the Second Law is the physical force that drives evolution. Evolution is the physical process of increasing the rates of dissipation via the formation of structure, namely constraints that accumulate physical information.

Figure 2.9 Evolution and the Second Law

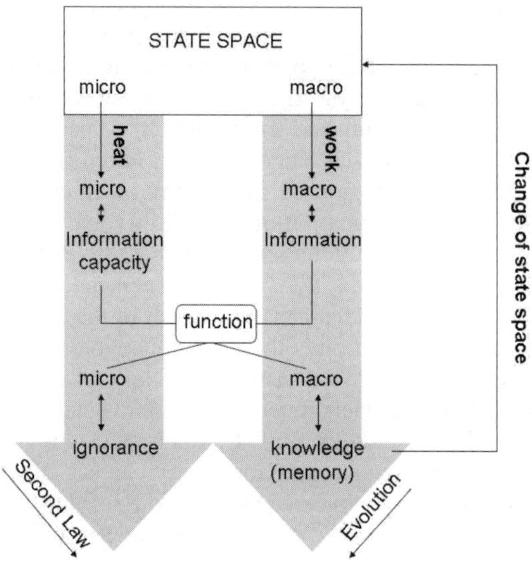

Note: This diagram summarizes the argument so far. We conceive of evolution as change of the state space of the world, in terms of accessibility of expanding possible states. The state space is defined relative to endogenous observers, that is PIDs, and therefore manifests the distinction between microstates and macrostates. Evolving macrostates represent causal regularities that relate physical work with information; information accumulates via the evolving constraints on possible states, hence resulting into knowledge ('memory' in the Maxwell's demon metaphor). PIDs realize functions and operate in the triadic causal modes, such that macrostates and microstates relate via the Maximum Entropy Principle. Relative to macrostates, microstates maximize entropy, which implies that the evolution of macrostates follows the Second Law on the macro–level. On the micro–level, we observe mere dissipation of energy, whereas on the macro–level we observe pattern formation. The two phenomena are two sides of the same coin, as accumulating information represents knowledge, whereas entropy production creates information capacity. This relationship is captured in the fundamental hypothesis that growth of information occurs because of the growing gap between potential and actual entropy in the expanding state space.

2.4. FUNCTIONS AND MAXIMUM ENTROPY PRODUCTION

2.4.1. Fundamental forms of functions

We can now proceed to distinguish two fundamental cases. One case is that a certain system changes its macrostates by releasing its free potential energy, like a waterfall running downwards. The other is the case of a system that is driven by continuous energy throughputs. In the latter case, we can further distinguish between systems where this throughput is not determined by the system mechanics, and systems which realize a system dynamics that feeds back on that energy throughput. All systems that rely on continuous energy throughputs can maintain states far from thermodynamic equilibrium. The central point of this distinction is that according to the previous analysis, a continuous process of knowledge generation via information flows is only possible if the increase of entropy that occurs because of the energetic transformations in the observer–object interaction is made up by energetic inflows that reduce entropy again. In other words, the capacity of systems to generate information (which is their 'evolvability', different from information capacity in terms of storage capacity) depends on energetic throughputs. Computers can only run with being connected to power. As we shall see, this includes the special case of those PIDs which manifest causal feedback loops such that energetic throughputs are also directly instrumental for generating this capacity. These PIDs are living systems. In this view, processes of information generation and accumulation are necessarily processes far from thermodynamic equilibrium: Thermodynamic equilibrium means that no further information can be generated, beyond the information stored in the structures that constrain the equilibrium. The Second Law implies that those structures will also erode through time, unless they are sustained by energetic throughputs.

In the triadic analysis of PIDs we have seen that the macrostate representing knowledge results from the relationship between the observation and its function relative to the environment. I will now explore the notion of function in more detail. As a most general definition, functions can be defined as follows (Wright 1973):

The function of *X* is *Z* means:

(a) *X* is there because it does *Z*, and

(b) *Z* is a consequence (or result) of *X*'s being there.

So, in figure 2.10a we see that there are two parts of the causal mechanism that makes up a function (building on Herrmann-Pillath 2010). First, a cause *X* produces an effect *Z*, and second that *Z* is a reason why *X* exists. This loop is embedded into a higher level function *Z'* of *Z*. So, the efficient causal part of the function inheres (b), whereas (a) reflects the final causal part. It is important to notice that in the recent philosophical discussion about functions (overview in Perlman 2009) even naturalistic and reductionist approaches converge on a notion of 'teleofunctions', which results into the need to distinguish between proper functionings and malfunctioning even if no external goal is assumed; this in turn raises the question of how the criteria for proper functioning are established. This problem leads back to the role of the observer in identifying functional causality (for example, Searle 1995: 120ff posits that all functions are observer relative even in the strong sense as referring to human observers, compare Searle 2010: 58f). In my approach, this conceptual problem can be resolved in arguing that all forms of functional causality root in evolutionary processes which result in certain configurations of efficient causal processes that manifest functions relative to the environment which selected those configurations. This relationship with the environment counts as observer relativity.

Figure 2.10 Functions

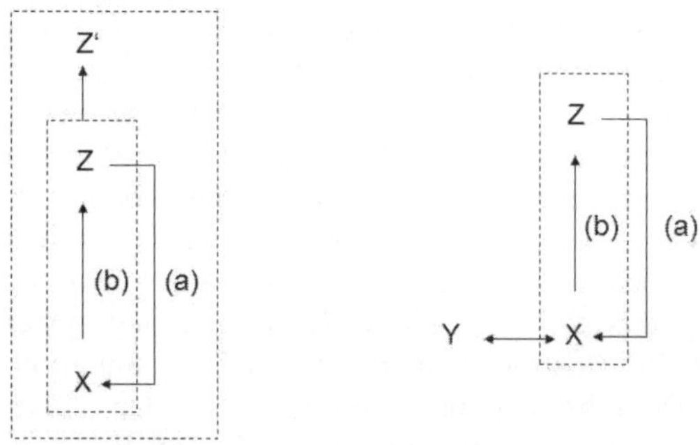

2-10a **2-10b**

Note: We can distinguish between two fundamental kinds of functions, which differ by the nature of feedback cycles. Generally (2.10a), a function consists of an efficient causal relation between *X* and *Z*, such that there is a final–causal feedback which turns *Z* into a reason for the existence of *X*; this relationship is embedded into a higher–level function *Z'*. The heart exists because it pumps blood, and this function is the reason why hearts were selected for in evolution, which establishes a relation with higher level functions, such as ultimately survival. In comparison, autocatalytic circuits are functions in which the product of an interaction between *Y* and *X*, *Z* becomes a reason for the existence of the interaction; in chemical autocatalytic cycles, the product of the reaction catalyses the reaction.

There is an important variant of functions which are called 'autocatalytic' in chemistry, and which will play an important role in the subsequent chapters (fig. 2.10b). This means that the function *Z* results into a feedback loop to an original causal interaction such that this is reinforced. For example, a chemical reaction between *Y* and *X* is catalysed by its product *Z*. Then, product *Z* obtains the function to catalyse its own production. Autocatalytic functions are central to evolutionary theory. In autocatalytic functions it is most evident that all functions build on efficient causality, because (a) is straightforwardly identifiable as such. Reductionist approaches to functions simply claim that in the case of 2.10a the causal chain connecting *Z'* and *X* is only more indirect and complicated, but remains efficient–causal. In the triadic view, this is only correct in the sense that final functional causality supervenes on efficient causality: If we ask the question why *Z* exists, the answer cannot simply point to the efficient–causation by *X*, but needs to point to the selective process by which the function of *Z* emerged.

2.4.2. Autocatalytic functions and hypercycles

The importance of autocatalytic functions in chemistry results from the fact that they lower the energetic threshold of efficient causal interactions. This makes clear that functions depend on energetic throughputs if they manifest themselves recurrently. In a solution with different chemical components autocatalytic functions will be favoured energetically, such that they come to dominate the result of the reaction processes. This is a process of selection which occurs on the population level, that is cannot be just identified in considering a single realization of the reaction. So, we realize that functions, though physically manifest in tokens of processes, actually refer to types of processes that emerge in sequences of many processes co-occurring in larger ensembles of processes and environment.

Figure 2.11 Elementary autocatalytic cycle

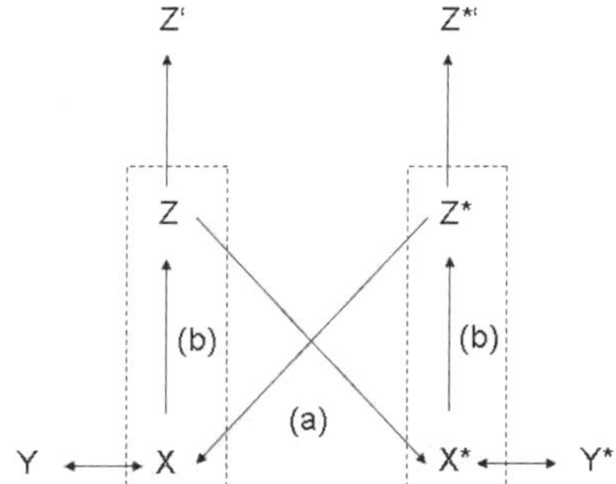

Note: In the elementary autocatalytic cycle, two functions *Z* and *Z** which relate with higher level functions *Z'* and *Z*'* are cyclically connected because the output of the first function *Z* also catalyses the realization of the other function *Z**; the output of this function also catalyses the former function *Z*, while being embedded into another higher level function. Functions of this kind are general functions that can be realized in many different physical forms. The elementary physical cause is cyclically connected chemical reactions; but for example ecosystems can also be conceived as autocatalytic cycles. For instance, flowers contribute to the reproduction of bees, while reproducing themselves, and bees do the same in turn. The autocatalytic function only emerges on the conjunction of the processes, that is on a higher hierarchical level of categorizing the functions.

In the context of evolution, the most important sort of a function results from the formation of autocatalytic cycles. In an autocatalytic cycle, functions get interconnected via the catalytic effects that a functional output exerts on other functions, and vice versa. This is shown for the simplest case of two functions in figure 2.11 (for a more general formal framework, see, for example, Hordijk et al. 2010). The functions mutually catalyse their realization, while being embedded into specific higher–level functions of their own; as a result, the autocatalytic function is only emerging on the higher hierarchical level of the conjunction of the functions. In living systems, autocatalytic cycles involve self–replicating functions, which we consider in Chapter Three in more detail; in this case, they are called 'hypercycles' in which the self–replicating functions generate catalysts for other functions which connect over longer chains into a cycle (figure 2.12).

Figure 2.12 Hypercycle

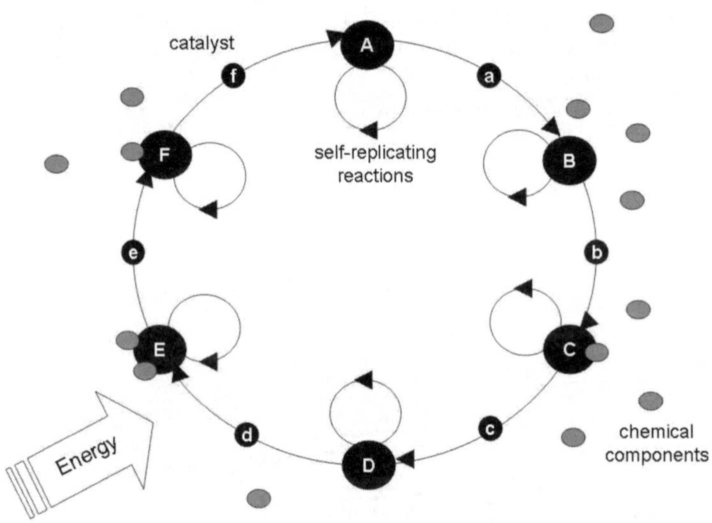

Note: Hypercycles are constituted by causal circuits in which different self–reproducing processes get interconnected such that single processes catalyse other processes, ultimately establishing a causally closed circuit. They feed on energy throughputs and are energetically favoured compared to other processes because of the catalytic functions. Therefore, hypercycles are emergent chemical structures that attract components in their environment, thus resulting into new sets of possible chemical states. The model was originally developed by Manfred Eigen to explain the first emergence of living systems as embodied in the primordial chemical substrates. In this view, chemical reaction systems such as the DNA–RNA circuits in living cells are based on primordial hypercycles. Again, as in the general case of autocatalytic cycles, the generic model can be applied in many different domains, such as neuronal systems or ecosystems.

The importance of autocatalytic cycles results from the fact that they undergird the emergence of hierarchies in functional systems and hence the emergence of higher–level entities in evolution, thus changing the state space qualitatively (Maynard Smith and Szathmáry 1995: 51ff; compare Brooks and Wiley 1988: 75ff). This effect is independent from the physical basis in the sense that autocatalytic interactions are also possible in causal cycles which are not chemical in nature, such as between economic processes (Padgett 1997, Padgett et al. 2003) or institutions (Teubner 1990). As we shall see in later chapters, the autocatalytic circuitry is then termed an 'externality'.

Ulanowicz (1997) presents an analysis of autocatalytic cycles that also applies the triadic analysis of causality (in figure 2.13 the bottom level concepts refer to his analysis, which uses different terms, following Salthe's 1985 approach to hierarchies). He identifies the following properties of autocatalytic cycles. Firstly, autocatalytic cycles support the emergence of a partly autonomous structure that exerts 'internal selection' on the component processes; in the Peircian triad, this is formal causality. This is because component processes can be substituted by variant processes as long as these processes maintain the cross–catalytic effects and the higher–level pattern of interactions. At the same time, different kinds of cycles are subject to external selection, thus establishing final causality: Imagine a population with different cycles that co-exist in a chemical solution. The different cycles will consume the available components competitively, and the cycle with the strongest effects on the reaction kinetics, that is the energetic throughputs, will tend to dominate the population, which means determine the composition of the final solution. So, two forces of selection, internal and external selection, or, formal and final causality, work together in determining the direction of change.

This results into a second property of autocatalytic cycles, namely centripetality. Centripetality means that selection of cycles will converge on certain structural patterns that are autonomous to a certain degree, relative to the constituent processes and their components. The third feature relates with this phenomenon, that is growth. Autocatalytic cycles lower the reaction thresholds and therefore increase reaction rates, with lower energetic throughputs for the single reactions, but increasing throughputs in terms of the reaction rates for the entire population of cycles, namely relating to throughput per unit of time. Hence, they manifest the property of growth with directional change. It is important to notice that all these properties go back on efficient causality operating on the level of the single processes.

Figure 2.13 Triadic analysis of autocatalysis

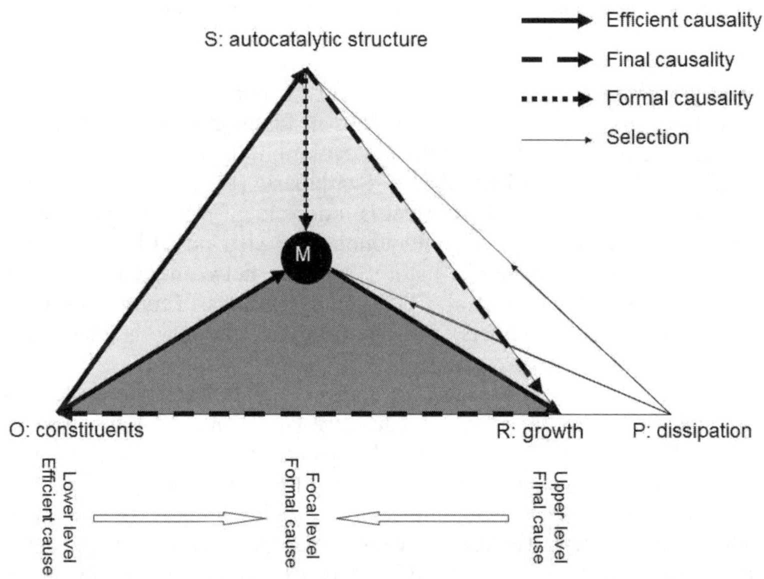

Note: Autocatalytic cycles can be analysed in terms of the triadic causal modes. In the bottom part of the diagram, I refer this analysis to the corresponding analysis of Ulanowicz (1997). The function of the autocatalytic structure is determined by the final causality of the Second Law, namely maximizing energetic throughputs and therefore dissipation ultimately; growth, driven by the lowering of energetic reaction thresholds, is the function that achieves this ultimate result. The emerging autocatalytic structure selects different combinations of components, thus obtains a formal–causal force on the range of possible processes in a population of components. Therefore, extending on Ulanowicz, we can say that the autocatalytic structure is a sign, that is an emerging macrostate of the original object domain that formal–causally selects efficient–causal mechanisms that result into increasing rates of energetic dissipation, ultimately.

In the triadic analysis, we can see that autocatalytic cycles establish a function that can be related to the Second Law in the sense of the tendency to maximize energetic throughputs by increasing reaction rates of the processes involved (compare the application of triadic analysis in Ji 2012). This refers to final causality, whereas the autonomous structure assumes the role of formal causality that imposes a pattern on the underlying constituent processes. The function is realized by efficient causal mechanisms.

2.4.3. Lotka's Maximum Power Principle

Based on this analysis, we can now state a fundamental theorem in evolution, which is Lotka's Maximum Power Principle MPP (Lotka 1922a, b). The MPP states that all functions, as defined previously, evolve to maximize power generation via the throughput of free energy. Thus, for example, the emergence of autocatalytic cycles is favoured by selection, and once those have emerged, they leverage this selection effect in becoming part of the selective environment of other functions. Considering populations of functions, selection implies the MPP. The MPP is of foundational relevance because it states a regularity in the sense of a propensity which is based on an important physical regularity, namely that for a certain class of physical phenomena, the state with maximum power does not correspond to the state of maximum efficiency, defined in terms of minimizing the inputs relative to the outputs (similar to electric circuits which manifest Jacobi's Law, where maximum power generation is not achieved at the point of maximum efficiency, unless the electrical resistance at the source approaches zero, see Cartwright 2008; cf. Odum 2007: 32ff). Thus, if we observe a stable state which would manifest MPP, this has to result from evolutionary processes that favour maximum power. For example, an animal that needs to avoid predators will not realize capacities to realize maximum efficiency but to manifest maximum power, because only maximum power would result in competitive speed ranges or prowess in fighting. However, this implies that MPP is a propensity (such as a bodily disposition or capacity), but does not manifest itself necessarily under any condition, in the sense of a universal physical law; any kind of evolutionary process will manifest the tendency to maximize power, but will not necessarily always reflect a state of MPP. In other words, the MPP principle is not an equilibrium principle, so cannot be a permanent or stable feature of certain states. This means, MPP cannot be simply falsified by identifying states that fail to actualize maximum power production. The animal that has the capacity to generate maximum power output, such as highest speed, might meet efficiency criteria during regular activities, though under the given structural constraints of the evolved capacity to maximize power output.

Thus, the MPP consists of two related hypotheses: Firstly, evolution tends towards recurrent states in which energetic throughputs generating power outputs tend towards maxima, given the constraints of the generating system, and secondly, the structural features of the generating system evolve towards manifesting this property in terms of a propensity, which realizes depending on environmental parameters. I may own a Ferrari, but under regular circumstances I drive the car in an energy–efficient way, namely at lower speeds. Yet, the design of the car aims at generating maximum power, which also constrains the achievable absolute levels of efficiency in the efficient states.

So, it is important to notice that MPP holds for systems far from equilibrium, but will give way to the minimum dissipation principle that was stated by Prigogine for systems near to equilibrium (see the survey by Sciubba 2011). That means, the actualization of MPP depends on the evolutionary context: Only as long as evolutionary forces reign, MPP will tend to manifest in empirical observations. This observation highlights the essential point that MPP only holds for the case of functions, and therefore always relates with the functions that are realized by energy throughputs. That means, the energy throughput should only be seen as a proximate, but not an ultimate mechanism. It is not the purpose of a function to maximize power, but functions that are subject to selection will tend to favour configurations by which maximum power is selected for in relationship to the realization of functions, relative to the environment. That means, MPP does not state a particular regularity over single functions, but about evolutionary processes that take place with populations of functions.

Figure 2.14 Functions and selection

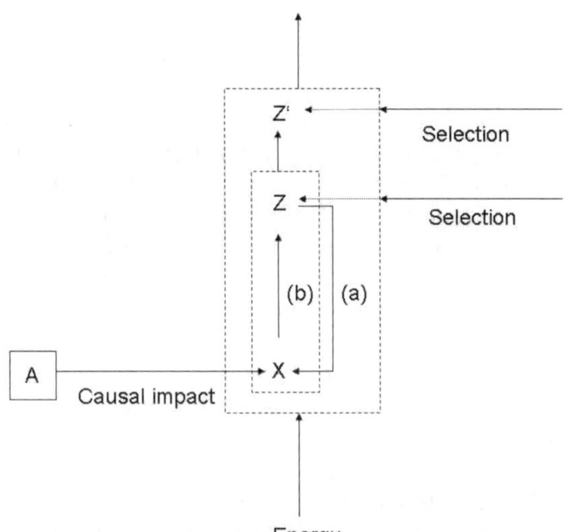

Note: The complete model of functions, building on figure 2.10a, includes the role of selective forces that operate on the different levels of embedded functions; for example, the function of the heart evolves via specific selective forces working on that level, and there are other, though related selective forces that work on the level of the organism of which the heart is a part. Functions are triggered by efficient–causal impacts that go hand in hand with external energy throughput necessary to maintain the functioning, both in terms of the flow output and the structure enabling the function.

So we arrive at a more complete picture of functions, only considering a most elementary single function here (figure 2.14). This picture shows that functions are subject to selection; hence the phenomena discussed so far refer to a population level analysis exclusively. Functions emerge from selection, thus accumulating information about the environment from which selective forces generate (Lord 2010 presents a related approach to functions that avoids this reference, however, because the empirical reconstruction of selective trajectories may be difficult). Functions are always embedded into hierarchies of functions, in the sense that MPP refers to a function relative to the environment, which in turn consists of systems that realize functions. Therefore, the analysis of functions always needs to establish the contexts of systems of interpretance (see figure 1.9). As all functions build on causal mechanisms that are energy transformations, maintenance of functions presupposes continuous energy throughputs.

With reference to biological evolution, the MPP is an alternative way to conceptualize the biological notion of 'fitness' that I will scrutinize in more detail in Chapter Three. There is a long tradition to refer fitness to optimization, hence efficiency (overview in Leigh 2001). However, as Grafen (2008) has shown formally (yet without drawing the final consequences), there is a paradox of evolution if one adheres to the interpretation of fitness as optimality: Firstly, if every individual optimizes, then there is no selection, and vice versa, secondly, if there is no selection, every individual optimizes. This is the necessary result from the fact that optimality always implies reference to an equilibrium state, but selection can only work on non-equilibrium states. Evolution is a non-equilibrium phenomenon; therefore, the notion of optimality needs to be substituted by the MPP which states, firstly, that evolution tends to favour expressions of MPP, and secondly, that these expressions drive evolution, thus maintaining the non-equilibrium states that make up evolutionary sequences. This connection between 'fitness' and MPP results from the more general relationship between proper functioning and the actualization of work directed towards the environment that exerts selective forces on functions. For example, 'fitness' as reflected in higher speeds of escaping predators does not reflect optimality principles, but MPP in the sense of the capacity to mobilize higher energetic throughputs to realize this function. This interpretation matches with the general approaches in Evolutionary Ecology that relate fitness the sense of differential reproduction with the generic 'currency' of energy harvested in foraging activities (for a classical approach, see Stephens and Krebs 1987; for an overview, see Kramer 2001). So, if energy is considered as generic currency for fitness, it seems appropriate to see MPP as the correlated physical non–equilibrium phenomenon.

2.4.4. Maximum Power and Maximum Entropy Production

Considering the specific example of living systems, physical manifestations of MPP depend on the boundary of the system in question and therefore the specific interfaces at which the evolutionary forces impact on the system. All living systems are complex configurations of many functions that work together. This does not only refer to the functions that connect within an organism, but also on the species level and even the level of the ecological system. Therefore, the actualization of MPP can occur via a manifold of mechanisms that result in the manifestation of physical power in the context of ecology and selection (Vermeij 2004 builds his 'economy of nature' picture on this idea). For example, MPP can be expressed in size increases of organisms, speeds and ranges of movements, numbers of descendants and so forth. Ultimately, all expressions of MPP must converge on the ecosystem level, because selection operates on the integrated systems, too, and not only on the level of single organisms. For this level, it can be shown that all different possible generic ecological goal functions converge on the MPP, including minimum dissipation theorems (for an extensive comparison and evaluation, see Fath et al. 2001; compare Lozada 2006 on the relationship between 'minimum energy' and 'maximum entropy').

The MPP has been presented by Lotka as another law–like statement in Thermodynamics that applies for life and evolution, thus elucidating the relationship between evolution and the Second Law, in particular (however, Bünstorf 2000 argues that Lotka's Principles can hold without direct reference to fundamental thermodynamic laws, only building on the analysis of evolutionary processes). There are a large number of attempts to extend the laws of Phenomenological Thermodynamics to reconcile thermodynamics with the fact of evolution. Although these attempts often present themselves as alternatives, it seems that they converge on the MPP. Then, the relationship between the MPP and the concept of entropy is straightforward to establish as the maximization of energy throughput ultimately results into the production of entropy; this conclusion needs to refer both to the flow of energy throughputs and the ultimate decay of the structures that generate the flows (compare Salthe's 1993 emphasis on the senescence of living systems). Then, we can say that the MPP principle entails the Maximum Entropy Production Principle, the MEPP; of course, this means that the MPP is grounded in the MEPP ontologically. The MEPP relates with the MaxEnt Principle in stating that the application of the MaxEnt Principle on certain ensembles of observers and observed systems, thus manifesting a distinction between macro– and micro–level aspects of the state space, will identify states which also physically maximize entropy production, relative to the environment in which they exist. Again, two points are essential to emphasize (compare Niven 2010): Firstly, the MEPP is itself a statement of a most universal propensity of evolutionary processes, so that it does not manifest itself with reference to equilibrium states, but as a tendency of systems far from equilibrium; secondly, the empirical validation of MEPP depends on the proper identification of systems boundaries, both in space and time (compare Vallino 2010; Virgo 2010).

Dewar (2010) gives the example of plant optimization. Plants are systems that optimize over many parameters, such as leaf production, root allocation etc. Standard ecological models aim at specifying the different maximands and solve the underlying optimization problem directly. The MEPP approach does not need to do that but just has to identify the constraints that operate on plant development and calculate the MEPP state, following MaxEnt methods. The relevant physical process is plant respiration. This refers to different levels, that is partial processes in the plant such as photosynthesis, whole plants and ecosystems with plants. In the latter case, MEPP applies to both plant and soil respiration. Respiration is equivalent with maximization of photosynthesis, and can therefore be interpreted as maximization of power production in Lotka's sense, such that MEPP only fully applies for the entire ecosystem which also includes the debris resulting from the death of the plant. In other words, ecological systems connect a multitude of MPP processes with the finality resulting from MEPP on the highest systemic level on which evolutionary forces operate. This implies that subsystems can manifest deviations from MEPP, because what only counts is the most encompassing system boundary, both spatially and temporally (compare the discussion in Volk and Pauluis 2010).

I summarize the relationship between MaxEnt, MPP and MEP established so far in figure 2.15. The fundamental idea is that the conjunction of these three principles is the physical expression of the Second Law in non–equilibrium systems that manifest causal structures of functions. In these systems, the realization of functions is physical work that relates macrostates of populations of observing systems with observed systems (such as the population of plants of a particular species relating with their ecological niche). This relationship is based on information transfers, with both systems distinguishing macro and microstates (such as species level traits of plants as distinguished from individual varieties). Observing systems relate functions with macrostates of observed systems, such that proper functioning is possible (such as plant growth and reproduction responding to species specific, hence observer relative properties of the natural environment, the niche). Proper functioning results from states of information processing in which MaxEnt states are realized, which correspond to energy dissipation as heat in physical terms (such as the exuberant growth of individual plant varieties in the population of a plant species, where the varieties do not accumulate information unless they are selected for as new types of functions on the population level). Functions tend towards MPP as a response to the impact of selection (such as the exponential growth of a plant population in its ecological niche). Ultimately, the dissipation of work in the actualization of functions results into MEP (such as the total amount of plant respiration and debris over several life cycles of a plant population). In other words, viewed over the entire chain of causation, information flows, generation of work relative to functions and entropy production are deeply physically related (Karnani et al. 2009).

Figure 2.15 Relationship between the principles of MaxEnt, MPP and MEP

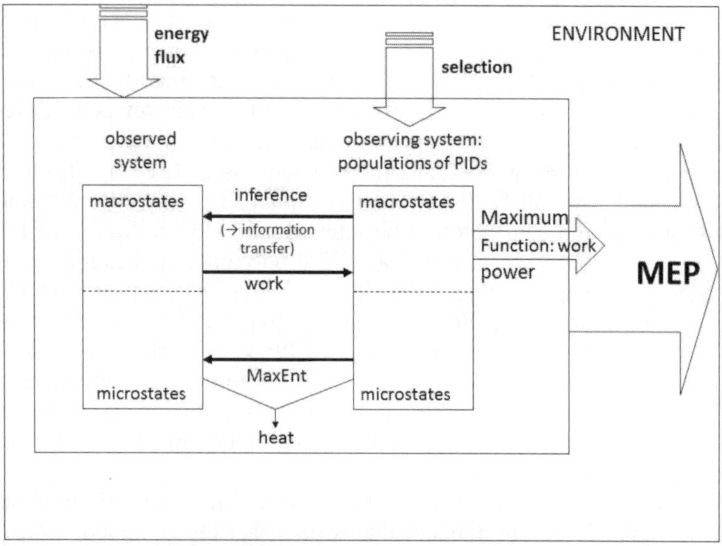

Note: This diagram details the process patterns outlined in figure 2.9, elucidating the interaction between three thermodynamic principles for open systems far from equilibrium. We analyse the causal interaction between an observed system, the object, and an observing system, which is a population of PIDs under selection by the environment. PIDs interact with the object macroscopically and microscopically, with macrostates supervening on microstates: Microstate interactions manifest efficient causality, macrostate interactions manifest the conjunction of triadic causal modes. Relative to the selective forces, macrostates of PIDs realize functions which generate physical work. These functions are Peircian interpretants relative to the object macro–states which they identify semiotically; hence generate information via semiotically intermediated inferences. This means that on the micro–level, the populations of PIDs tend towards MaxEnt states, thus mapping constraints of objects into macrostates of PIDs, such that the underlying variants of PIDs, their microstates, approach maximum entropy. The causal interactions between objects and PIDs differentiate into work and heat physically, which means that some interactions are intermediated macro-scopically, such that the interaction between objects and PIDs is driven by the generation of work that supports the realization of PID functions; this transforms the energetic input into work relative to the environment. Given forces of selection, the functions manifest the propensity to generate maximum power, hence obey to the MPP principle. Ultimately, the MPP principle results into MEP, considering both the energetic flows and the ultimate decay of the physical structures that maintain the functions.

2.4.5. Maximum Entropy Production and the Constructal Law

There is one alternative proposal of an additional law of Thermodynamics for non–equilibrium systems which covers all the aspects discussed so far, too, the Constructal Law (even though the author himself denies any relationship with the MEPP; for overviews see Bejan and Lorente 2006, 2010). The Constructal Law helps to clarify one important point: Following Schrödinger's (1944) famous exposition, the emergence of life and the Second Law have mostly been seen as staying in tension with each other, because life is a phenomenon of increasing order and complexity (see for example Faber and Proops 1998: 85ff). However, this idea confuses levels of analysis, as the Second Law can only hold for the encompassing systems in which living systems interact, as we have seen. Therefore, the question is not whether the systems themselves manifest higher levels of order, but whether the systems contribute to the manifestation of the Second Law, especially in the sense that they increase the rate of entropy production relative to the state without these systems. In this regard, it has to be noticed that physical laws constrain entropy production in a manifold of ways: For example, it is physically impossible that the Earth suddenly explodes into one big bang of dissipation. More complex living systems can therefore increase the rate of entropy production by more simple physical mechanisms (for example, earthworms increase the gradients of water flows and hence energy dissipation in soils, see Zehe et al. 2010; generally, see Mäkela and Annila 2010). In other words, increasing structural complexity of functions is a manifestation of the Second Law with reference to the ensembles of functions and environment.

This can be stated more concisely in the Constructal Law, which posits that flow systems will always attain states in which the gradients of the dissipation of the flows will be maximal. For example, river systems attain branching shapes which maximize the water flows. The Constructal Law relates the concept of work and heat in the context of non–equilibrium systems. In a non–equilibrium state, the rate of work is the relevant magnitude, that is 'power'. Then, as depicted in figure 2.16, the Constructal Law states that in a structured flow system, the energy inflow will be processed by the system in such a way that power output is maximal, with minimum dissipation as heat, conditioned on the MPP (that is, minimization is a tendency, but not a state characteristics in the sense of efficiency). So, in this view, the river system has the purpose to channel water to a state which is ultimately described as the equilibrium state. Evidently, this also means that the structure itself does not approach an equilibrium state, because it is maintained in the process: These are the macrostates of the branching pattern, supervening on the micro–level dissipation by water transport. The structure can be destroyed in the course of time by the dissipation of energy that necessarily accompanies power production, for example, by soil erosion and sedimentation in river beds. Thus, maintenance of structure is also an important aspect of work in non-equilibrium systems, which requires energy throughputs, in turn. This is the hallmark of living systems.

Figure 2.16 The Constructal Law (after Bejan and Lorente 2010: 1341)

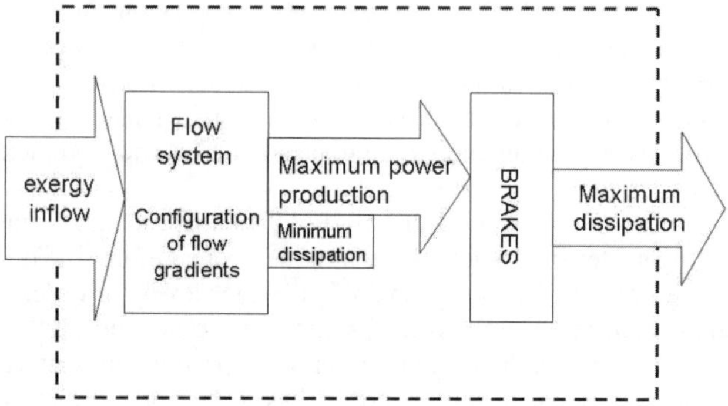

Note: The Constructal Law states that all flow systems evolve towards structural states (establishing flow gradients) in which throughputs of flows are maximal. Flows are useful energy, often termed exergy; the distinction between exergy and energy is established relative to the structures of the flow system (recall figure 2.1). In order to maximize power output, a tendency of minimum dissipation occurs. However, ultimately the entire power output dissipates via all kinds of processes that are called 'brakes' here, such as senescence. Thus, ultimately MPP implies maximum dissipation. The Constructal Law can be empirically validated for all sorts of flow systems, physical (such as river systems), and biological (such as respiration systems) or technological (such as heating systems). Take, for example, the evolving population of engines for cars. There is an evolutionary trend towards maximizing power output by cars while achieving high efficiency, established by the forces of selection (in this case, the uses of cars in different contexts). Maximum dissipation does not only happen via the forces that bring engines to stop, but also via the ultimate waste produced by engines getting out of use.

The central insight gained by the Constructal Law is that the entire process ultimately follows the Second Law, because MPP ultimately will also lead towards states of maximum entropy, in the sense of a complete dissipation of the energy throughput. In figure 2.16, this is indicated by the generalized notion of a 'brake'. Water does not flow eternally, but arrives in a standstill state. Living systems can be regarded as a flow system which maximize power generation, but ultimately will cease to operate and decay, thus increasing entropy production further (Salthe 1993). The same is true for the on-going power production and the resulting actions, such as running and stopping, with the latter ultimately dissipating energy. So, the Constructal Law offers the conceptual way to unify the two notions of evolution, in the sense of evolving structural complexity, and the Second Law, in the sense of increasing entropy: The Constructal Law states that evolving structural complexity is a means to dissipate energy at a maximum rate.

Figure 2.17 Relationship between fundamental thermodynamic principles in the analysis of the evolution of physical information aka knowledge

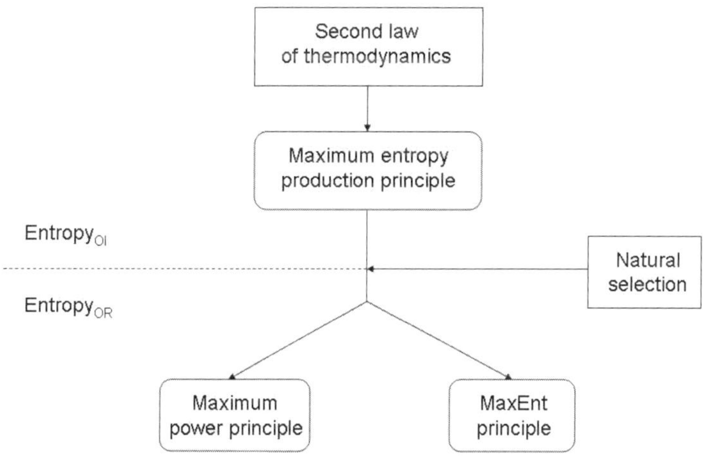

Note: The conceptual relationship between the different principles that relate thermodynamics with evolution and the growth of knowledge is shaped by the distinction between observer independent and observer relative processes and the corresponding notions of entropy. The Second Law establishes an observer independent reference for the analysis of thermodynamic processes, which relates with a specific hypothesis about systems far from equilibrium, the MEPP. Considering the relationship between entropy and information, these systems manifest the property of accumulating physical information via triadic causal processes. These need to be analysed by means of observer relative concepts. The MaxEnt principle applies for the dynamics of the information generating processes, the MPP relates to the functions that are realized by means of the information that accumulates.

To conclude this section, in figure 2.17 I overview the relationship between the different fundamental thermodynamic principles. All principles are expressions of the Second Law. The MEPP is a specification of the Second Law for systems far from equilibrium which have the propensity to assume steady states with continuous energy throughputs (Martyushev and Seleznev 2006). Then, considering the case of natural selection, we specify the MEPP for ensembles of observing and observed systems which manifest physical information generation and processing. This entails the distinction between Entropy_{OI} and Entropy_{OR}. The former is related with MEPP conceptually, the latter with MPP and MaxEnt. MaxEnt reflects the statistical properties of information processing, whereas MPP refers to the functions that are realized by means of this. Both principles underlie observer relative physical phenomena, interpreted as endogenous evolution of knowledge, namely accumulating physical information.

2.5. PHYSIOSEMIOSIS AND GAIA

2.5.1. Kauffman's 'Fourth Law' restated in triadic terms

Stuart Kauffman has proposed an alternative extension of Thermodynamics which states, in vernacular, that "the biosphere maximizes the average secular construction of the diversity of autonomous agents and the ways how these agents make a living and propagate further" (Kauffman 2000: 4f; his argument ignores many related approaches, such as Collier and Hooker 1999). I argue that this principle reflects the information processing dual of the aforementioned principles, that is MPP and MEPP, as stated in the Peircian approach to semiosis so far. In this section, I relate Kauffman's approach to the biosphere with the general analysis of the Earth System as the physical entity that embodies the physical information that accumulates via physiosemiosis, with biological evolution as the central mechanism that maintains states of the Earth System far from equilibrium. I begin with showing the equivalence between Kauffman's approach and the Peircian approach developed so far. So, the brief review of Kauffman's theory also serves as a rehearsal of what we have elaborated on so far.

Kauffman needs a set of other hypotheses and principles to generate this hypothesis. The first is the concept of an 'autonomous agent'. An autonomous agent is defined as a reproducing system that carries out at least one thermodynamic work cycle. So, the notion of agency is directly related with the notion of thermodynamic disequilibrium: An agent manifests agency because it is able to generate work: Hence, this notion corresponds to the generic concept of 'function' that I have established in the previous section. A further criterion is that the processes are cyclic, in the sense of a simple thermodynamic engine, such that the state of disequilibrium is reproduced concomitant to the throughput of energy.

The full definition involves all the concepts that I have developed so far. The first is that of an 'autocatalytic cycle', as defined in the previous section. All autonomous agents build on autocatalytic cycles. The second concept is 'work', again in the general sense developed previously. Kauffman argues that the physical concept of work is underspecified because the structure of constraints is only posited implicitly which determines the distinction between energy dissipation, that is heat, and work. For example, a mechanical construction that generates work such as moving a weight is actually designed by an experimenter in a way such that a certain amount of energy is released under the constraints. However, the same is true of any sort of work, which operates under naturally emerged physical constraints (Salthe 2007). From this follows that 'work' is a physical magnitude that cannot be defined independently from context, that is, the physical structure that receives the energy throughput, which is not a universal regularity in nature, but a singular combination of physical properties specific to particular spacetime coordinates. This is particularly true if work relates with a function: Functions arrange causal mechanisms which relate causal macro–states with purposes and goals which emerge in knowledge generating processes. So, for example, a stream in a river might transport objects downstream randomly, but the stream can also be exploited by fishes for actualizing evolved purposeful activities. This holds in general: Evolution consists of the emergence of systems that transform energy into work related to their reproduction.

Now, a special case of work is work directed at constructing the constraints under which work is generated. This is a defining feature of autonomous agents: Autonomous agents work on their environment in a way that some of the causal effects feedback on the constraints under which they operate, including the structural features of their autocatalytic processes. These feedback circuits are driven by the actions of autonomous agents. The most general feature of these actions is an input–output linkage which connects a measurement with work. Measurement inheres in the processes which lead autonomous agents to open up sources of energy that feed their autocatalytic processes. Work output includes actions that are directed at those sources. Thus, for example a bacterium detects nutrient gradients in the environment and moves accordingly (on a related analysis of this example, compare Ben Jacob et al. 2006).

Now, thinking about populations of autonomous agents that compete over a set of possible sources of energy, we can say that a given spatiotemporal distribution of agents and their structural properties reflects the history of the interaction between agents and the environment. This history is non–ergodic, as the space of possible states increases with the number of possible combinations and partitions of the state space. This argument that I have already elucidated in the previous sections, is the most fundamental ontological basis of the 'Fourth Law' as claimed by Kauffman. He introduces the notion of the 'adjacent possible': when referring to the set of realized chemical entities in the universe, the adjacent possible is the next reaction step that can result from their interactions and its product. This reaction step can lead towards the creation of a new chemical entity which manifests properties that did not exist previously. In this sense, the evolution of the chemical universe manifests growth in the dimensions of its state space. It is essential to notice that this process is driven by the fundamental thermodynamic forces, because chemical reactions are driven by energy dissipation. Further, it is also evident that the possibility of autocatalysis and cycles is a mover of the emergence of new structural features. Stable autocatalytic cycles can in turn interact with other chemical entities, thus possibly connecting to other higher–level entities and so forth.

Figure 2.18 Physiosemiosis and Maximum Entropy

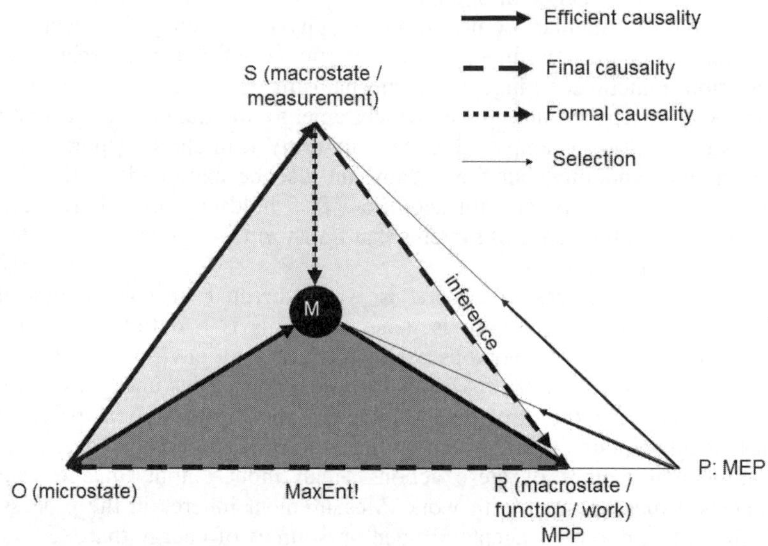

Note: This triadic diagram of a physical inference device (extending on figure 2.7) puts together Kauffman's notion of the 'autonomous agent' with the principles of physiosemiosis established so far. Kauffman posits that autonomous agents conduct measurements in order to generate physical work that maintains their existence. Measurements are signs as macrostates that enable inferences about objects. These inferences enable functions, for which the MPP principle holds. The inferences result into MaxEnt states, which corresponds to the Kauffman notion that evolution maximizes the 'adjacent possible', namely maximizes evolvability. Ultimately, this corresponds to the MEP principle which states that energetic dissipation occurs by the conjunction of the flows enabled by functions that generate work (MPP) and by the production of maximum non–functional variety in the population of autonomous agents, which is necessary to ensure evolvability into a growing 'adjacent possible' state space.

Kauffman's categories directly correspond to the categories in the semiotic triad, so that 'measurement' refers to the relationship between signs and objects such that certain classes of mechanisms are identified which entail certain functional responses. The latter relate with ultimate purposes. This relationship is based on the physical category of 'work', which refers to the realization of functions. Then, it is straightforward to further specify

Kauffman's version of the 'Fourth Law' by actually rendering it obsolete, because it is only a superficial description of the more fundamental principles that we have identified in the previous section. This is summarized in figure 2.18, which combines the previous analysis with the results of section 2.4.

Then we see that the notion of 'measurement' and the corresponding process of inference refers to the conjunction of two macrostates such that the relationship between the functional state and the object realizes the MaxEnt principle: So, the MaxEnt principle corresponds to the principle of the maximization of the variety of functional manifestations of PIDs, which relates with Kauffman's notion of the 'adjacent possible'. That means, we can provide an explanation for one of the essential characteristics of evolution, that is the tendency of generating an exuberance of individual variants within the set of functional classes in a population, such as the variety of individuals of the members of a biological species (or, more figuratively, the 'waste' of myriads of individually unique descendants that perish before reproduction). In other words, the distinct process pattern of evolution highlighted by Darwin for the first time, which is the exuberance of individual variants together with the emergence of population level shared patterns, can be seen as directly reflecting the Second Law.

The generation of variety follows the MaxEnt principle because it is driven by the fundamental thermodynamic forces, that is MPP and MEP. MPP refers to the effect of selection on the realization of functions via the generation of physical work. As we have seen, this ultimately results in entropy production, with the tendency to maximize. So, MaxEnt and MEP relate in this view via the conjunction of causalities in physiosemiosis. MEP drives the growth of the exuberance of individualized functions in terms of MPP, because the functions are ultimately mechanisms to enhance MEP. At the same time, this state reflects 'fitness' of functions in the sense that the conjunction of measurement with functions results into classes of responses, relative to which the varieties are non-functional, hence randomize without direct causal relevance for the functional performance. Yet, the evolutionary process of inference implies that under certain circumstances, variants can prove to become functional if they make new states of the state space accessible, hence realizing new or improved ways of functioning.

2.5.2. PIDs as self–referential heat engines

One aspect of the original Kauffman approach deserves further scrutiny, which is the idea that autonomous agents apply work on themselves in order to enhance the capacity to realize work via increased energy throughputs. I further specify autonomous agent as being self–referential thermodynamic engines along the lines proposed by Garrett (2011a, b) (with 'self–referential' my own terminological addition).

Figure 2.19 Self–referential heat engines (Garrett 2011a)

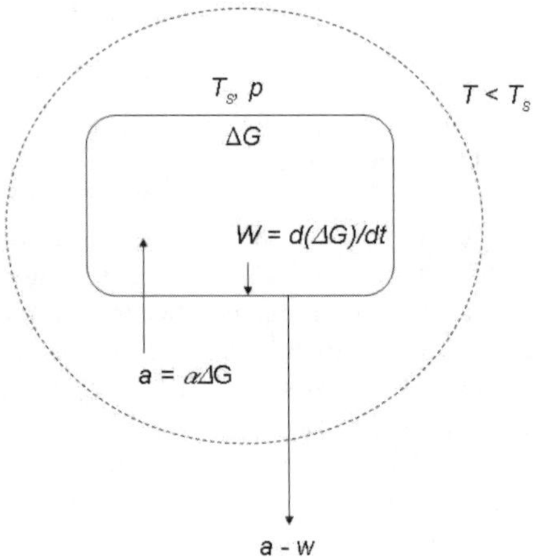

Note: Self–referential heat engines exert work W on expanding their energetic interface ΔG that determines throughputs a, while dissipating heat $a - w$ into the surroundings, into which the system environment is embedded as a source of throughputs, with a temperature differential (hence, a thermodynamic sink).

Garrett distinguishes between an entity and its environment, with the line of separation drawn by a permeable boundary such as a membrane (see figure 2.19) (this relates with the role of membranes in biosemiotics, thus connects the informational and the thermodynamic view, see Hoffmeyer 2000). The system consisting of the entity and its environment is embedded into surroundings with lower temperature $T < T_s$ such that heat can be exported. The interface between the entity x and its environment constitutes an energy potential ΔG. The available potential energy in the environment is transformed into unavailable forms by means of transfer of matter across the boundary, which can be measured at the rate $a = \alpha\Delta G$, where α is a system-specific coefficient which reflects the intrinsic physical characteristics of the system that influence the availability of energy throughputs (such as access to flows, or conductivity etc.). The energy made available to the entity is transformed by its operations into either work output w or into heat dissipation $a - w$.

The notion of a self–referential heat engine means that the work output is directed at creating, maintaining and expanding the energy potential ΔG, such that $a = \alpha\Delta G$ and $\mathrm{d}\Delta G/\mathrm{d}t = w$. The efficiency of the heat engine is defined as $\varepsilon = w/a$. Garrett concludes that a system of this kind manifests a growth process, where a rate of return η can be defined as (Garrett 2011b eq. 2):

$$\frac{da}{dt} = \alpha \frac{d(\Delta G)}{dt} = \alpha \cdot w = \alpha \cdot \varepsilon \cdot a \equiv \eta \cdot a$$

Thus, a self–referential heat engine manifests continuous growth of energy throughputs, depending on the efficiency of the engine.

The model of self–referential heat engines demonstrates, in a most simple way, how the information processing dimension of physiosemiosis relates with the thermodynamic dimension. This is because the enhancement of the access to energy throughputs is only possible via the accumulation of information in the heat engine. So, all PIDs are self–referential heat engines. This is the essence of physiosemiosis, which is hence conceivable as a phenomenon that unifies the different expressions of the Second Law in the expansion of the multiverse. As we have already seen from the discussion of Layzer (1988), this expansion is the ultimate physical cause why the growth of information and knowledge is possible and corresponds with the combinatorial growth of the state space of the world. In principle, this reflects the fundamental physical relationship that we have already identified in section 2.1, namely between information capacity and the temperature difference between a system and its environment. This argument has been applied on a cosmological level by Chaisson (2001).

2.5.3. A measure for evolving information in physiosemiosis

Chaisson (2001: 127f) proposes a physical measure that catches the corresponding energetics of evolution. The only way that growth is possible is firstly, in an open system with an external source of energy, and secondly, if there is an increasing gap between the possible entropy and the realized entropy, namely the space of possible states and the realized states. The former possibility is practically the most important, as, for example, the Earth is an open system with the sun as an external source of energy. The latter is ontologically more fundamental, because it relates to the structure of the universe as the total system into which all other open systems are embedded. We can refer this to the change of the state space in the following way, which is a natural result of the expansion of the universe. If the number of states is Ω_a before and Ω_p after the change, the resulting change in entropy is:

$$\Delta S = S_a - S_p = k_B \ln(\Omega_p / \Omega_a)$$

Chaisson argues that if a reduction of possible states takes place between an initial state space Ω_i and a final state Ω_f, then the change of information I is:

$$\partial I = I_f - I_i = K \log(\Omega_i / \Omega_f)$$

This equation and the previous one can be combined, with substituting S_i / k_B and S_f / k_B for ln B_i and ln B_f, respectively, and absorbing the 2.3 difference between natural and decimal logarithms in the new constant K / k_B. This results in:

$$\Delta I = K k_B^{-1}\left(S_a - S_p\right)$$

This can be related to the fundamental thermodynamic definition of entropy, which conjoins heat with temperature. Now consider that maximum entropy is obtained by the minimum of T. If this is defined by the average temperature of matter T_m, this is always smaller than the temperature of radiation T_r, so that the evolution of the potential information in the world is macroscopically:

$$I = K k_B^{-1}\left(T_m^{-1} - T_r^{-1}\right)$$

This is the total possible gain of information that can result from the temperature gradient in the universe. Thus, the expanding universe is the ultimate source of a growth of information as long as the temperature gradient is maintained; the growth of information does not contradict the Second Law, but is its physical expression.

Based on this theoretical consideration, Chaisson proposes a measure of energy throughput which takes into account the physical mass of the functional unit. This is the 'free energy rate intensity'. Free energy rate intensity Φ_m (measured in erg/s/g) is an intensive measure of complexity which includes the efficiency of a system in processing energy flows. Empirically, we can hypothesize about a general law of increasing Φ_m during the evolution of the multiverse, which also applies to systems and subsystems. For example, protocells have a lower Φ_m than plants, or the human brain has much higher energy rate intensity than the human body (figure 2.20, from Chaisson 2001: 192). Again, this tendency is a stochastic phenomenon, such that especially within lineages, deviations from the general trend are possible. Yet, there is a clear-cut regularity that matches the growth on information as embodied in physical entities with the rate of energy throughputs. Thus, we can regard this measure as an expression of the MPP.

Consequently, we can interpret human evolution as a part of the overarching 'big history' of the universe (overview in Aunger 2007). This refers the unification of evolution as the trajectory of different domains of information and energy processing across different stages, with certain regularities that express the Second Law, such as the intensification of free energy rate intensity, but also the increasing speed of changes, with a continuous shortening of the periods that demarcate major qualitative changes, such as the time elapsed between the emergence of simple cells and of complex multicellular units, or by comparison, the time elapsed between the domestication of fire and the emergence of agriculture. Those transitions are 'non-equilibrium steady state transitions' which demarcate certain universal structural patterns of physiosemiosis, in my parlance. So, the multicellular units and hence, the organism, are distinct patterns of PIDs as compared to simple cells, or the industrial society built on fossil resources is a distinct pattern as compared to societies built on direct photosynthesis, such as agricultural societies. The different patterns relate with distinct processes that nevertheless basically follow the general functional logic of self–referential heat engines, namely the 'work cycle' in the sense of Kauffman's. That means, the systems exploit energy throughputs in order to maintain and expand basically similar structures that enable this functioning.

Figure 2.20 Growth of free energy rate intensity (after Chaisson 2001: 192)

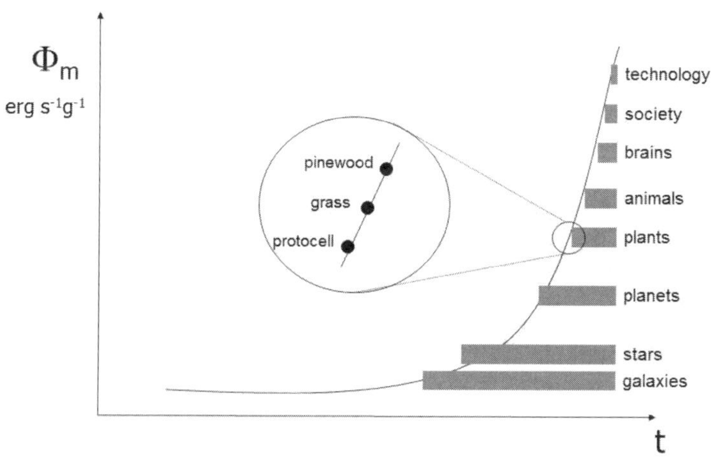

Note: Chaisson presents this qualitative diagram on the evolution of free energy rate intensity Φ_m which measures the energy throughputs per units of mass and time. This measure reflects the complexity of different physical entities, and hence directly expresses the embodied physical information. So, for example, brains have higher free energy rate intensities than simple organisms, or microchips higher than simple machines. Chaisson argues that a unifying trend in evolution across different domains (physical, chemical, biological, technological) is increasing free energy rate intensity, taking stochastic fluctuations and structural constraints in particular lineages of evolution into consideration.

Following Aunger, one way to distinguish 'eras' in 'big history' is to differentiate between cosmological and terrestrial evolution, with the 'material' era representing cosmology until the onset of biological evolution on Earth (we do not know for sure whether a similar transition happened elsewhere in the multiverse, but there is a very high probability, given the universality of MPP and MEPP). The Biological Era is followed by the Cultural Era and the Technological Era. The eras manifest distinct basic patterns of functions which remain central to the subsequent eras, but are combined with qualitatively new functions. Thus, the biological era differs from the material era in the emergence of the function of 'replication' that I will scrutinize in the next chapter. The Cultural Era introduces a multiplicity of mechanisms of information processing and storage that builds on 'minds' as physical structures that combine external artefacts and neuronal structures (as we shall see in Chapter Four). The Technological Era features the autonomous evolution of artefacts, which even harness entirely new physical mechanisms, thus changing the patterns of functions in the Material Era as well (as scrutinized in Chapter Seven).

2.5.4. Emergent hierarchies in physiosemiosis and 'Gaia'

The unifying principle in this unfolding of terrestrial evolution as embedded into cosmological physiosemiosis is that of 'hierarchy' (compare Annila and Kuismanen 2009). Hierarchies evolve in all self–referential heat engines when the energetic throughputs that enable information processing in turn control other energetic throughputs, such that the former can be of much smaller scale than the latter. This function directly relates with the semiotic causation in the Peircian triad, that is emerging from the energetic requirements to maintain the special function of sign processing. So, an essential aspect of physiosemiosis is the emergence of 'control information' (in the sense of Corning 2005: 361ff; for a related approach, see Lahav et al. 2001, Elitzur 2005).

Control information changes the rates of entropy production in the entire Earth System. In order to understand this role of emergent control information, it is useful to distinguish between two kinds of hierarchy, subsumptive and compositional (following Salthe 1986, 2002). We will explore this distinction in the next chapter; just suffice to present the definition here: Subsumptive hierarchies refer to the relations of descendence between different kinds of functional systems, hence the diachronic dimension of unfolding physiosemiosis, whereas the compositional hierarchy refers to the construction of complexity by means of evolution. For example, 'compositional hierarchy' refers to ecosystems and their functioning at present time, whereas 'subsumptive hierarchy' reflects the relations of descendence between ecosystem components which result from the emergence of control information through time.

Then, as depicted in figure 2.21, we can analyse complex composite self–referential heat engines such as ecosystems in terms of their energetic flows top-down and bottom up: For example, in an ecosystem complex food chains result into maintaining the composition of its functionings across different biological organisms, thus resulting in energy flows that maintain this structure, hence the constitutive functions. At the same time, certain functionings are coordinative, hence represent energy flows of control information, such as the role of large predators in maintaining certain levels of productivity in the entire ecosystem (compare Vermeij 2004: 111ff, 286).

Figure 2.21 Hierarchies of self–referential heat engines

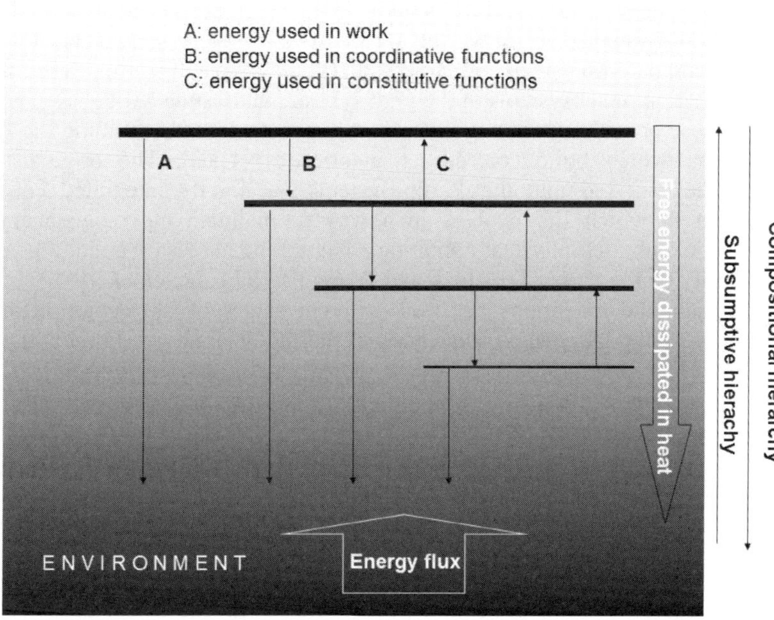

Note: Complex hierarchical systems of PIDs qua self–referential heat engines create ordered systems of gradients of energy dissipation while mobilizing growing energy throughputs. These systems can be analysed in dual terms. Synchronically, the compositional hierarchy reflects the subordination of systems components under higher structures of control information. For example, large predators are sustained by ecosystems, but at the same time regulate and enhance the energetic productivity of the entire ecosystem. Extinction of large predators typically reduces ecosystem productivity. Diachronically, the subsumptive hierarchy reflects the generative sequences that resulted into the constitution of the higher level systems, such as the phylogenetic history of the different species that make up an ecosystem. Entirely new species suddenly invading an existing ecosystem can radically destroy its control information and trigger ecosystem decline, as it happened with many island ecosystems in the past. In both cases, extinction of predators and sudden introduction of new species, the total potential of energy dissipation declines in spite of entropic ecosystem degradation.

Considering the entire hierarchical structure, both spatially and through time, ultimately it results into dissipation of free energy, enabled by the composite structures that operate by means of emergent control information. As proposed by Corning, this role of control information could be captured by the ratio between energy used in processing control information and systemic energy throughput that are activated by it. It is important to re-emphasize that in the context of hierarchical systems, MEP does not necessarily apply for single subsystems, but only, yet always to the system *in toto* and through time (compare Meysman and Bruers 2010). Of course, this implies to ask for the function of subsystems in the total system manifesting MEP.

These considerations suggest a new approach to understanding the Earth System, which builds on earlier theories of 'Gaia'. The original Gaia hypothesis stated that the Earth System is a tightly integrated complex system in which life evolves in a way to maintain the biogeochemical, climatic and other physical conditions that are the necessary conditions of its viability (for example Lovelock and Margulis 1974, Lovelock 1990). In this approach, the transitions between different stages of the evolution of the Earth System are seen as sequences of thermodynamic equilibria (Margulis 1999). The new approach (I follow the exposition by Kleidon 2009, 2010, 2011) defines the Earth System as a non–equilibrium system; the evolution of this system drives the emergence of new states which are even farther away from equilibrium. This reflects the working of the Second Law via its expressions of MPP and MEPP. So, in this new view Gaia is a self–reinforcing non-equilibrium system. Life – and I add human technology, as we shall see later – is the basic mechanism of physiosemiosis that drives these sequence of non–equilibrium steady states.

There are certain levels and subsystems of the Earth system in which thermodynamic disequilibrium is generated and maintained by energy throughputs that are exogenous to this level and subsystem. These states of disequilibrium are a potential for work generated by the release, dissipation and transformation of free energy. The physical mechanism generating work is contingent to other levels and subsystems on which thermodynamic forces operate, given their structural features. The result of this causal impact is to drive those other subsystems further away from thermodynamic equilibrium, thus creating a further potential for work. So, the entire process appears to be like a fountain with different levels, in which an initial thermodynamic disequilibrium propagates through a manifold of levels which are connected via energy flows that reflect the causal impact of work outputs which are generated by the receiving levels in the flow of energy.

In other words, if viewed dynamically in the time dimension, the thermodynamic machinery of the Earth System is conceived as a hierarchical system of power flows. In this system, two sources of energy loom especially large. One is solar radiation; the other is photosynthesis, which depends on the former. The latter is central to the entire system, because without photosynthesis, the low thermodynamic efficiency of all other physical processes would only maintain relatively small deviations from thermodynamic equilibrium. This is the most fundamental example for the pattern that I have already emphasized when discussing the Constructal Law: The emergence of photosynthesis enabled physical mechanisms of increased dissipation rates that are impossible to achieve without it, given the constraints of physical laws.

It is important to emphasize that this view focuses on average entropy production per unit of time (a distinction that is also important in the generic thermodynamics of information, see Maroney 2009). The First and the Second Law of thermodynamics imply that there is an upper bound of the energy budget of the entire process, hence also for the potential of entropy production. The MEPP, as applied on the hierarchical Earth System, claims that the emergence of hierarchy firstly, increases the speed by which energy is dissipated (cf Vallino 2010), and secondly, increases the variety of mechanisms how this can happen (cf Niven 2010), given the constraints of physical laws, and given the basic requirement of maintaining the structural viability of the hierarchy. So, the Earth System appears to be a physically viable local hot spot of entropy production.

2.5.5. Maximum Entropy Production in the Earth System

Empirically, this approach requires establishing causal chains in which transformations across different forms of energy take place. So, the differentiated analysis of material fluxes that are concomitant to the fundamental thermodynamic processes is the core of Kleidon's previously cited approach. The basic form is the free energy that is generated from heat gradients, both caused by solar radiation and by the heating in inner Earth. The other forms are mechanical energy, geopotential energy, kinetic energy and chemical energy. Releasing these forms of energy results into processes that work towards thermodynamic equilibrium, but never reach it, because of the continuous throughput of solar radiation, and which hence maximize entropy. So, the fundamental heat gradient generates the process of diffusion, mechanical and kinetic energy result in mass transport and friction, or chemical energy results into chemical reactions. All of these processes, taken in isolation, would simply result into the dissipation of free energy. However, in a causally connected Earth System the processes impact on each other, especially in the form of chains, networks and, most importantly, cycles. In order to analyse these processes, the physical notion of 'work' is central.

In this view, the change of entropy of the entire system can be expressed as (Kleidon 2011, eq. 14):

$$dS_{tot} = \frac{dU + dW}{T} \equiv dS_{heat} + dS_{diseq}$$

which results from the combination of the First Law with the standard definition of entropy. In this formulation, dS_{diseq} corresponds to the work done or exerted upon a system. From this follows, when considering changes through time, that the change of free energy is directly proportional to the degree how far disequilibrium is diminishing in a process (Kleidon 2011, eq. 16):

$$\frac{dA}{dt} = \frac{dU}{dt} - T \cdot \frac{dS_{tot}}{dt} = -T \cdot \frac{dS_{diseq}}{dt}$$

Based on this, one can define the net amount of work that is exerted on a thermodynamic variable as resulting from the interaction between two forces, one is the inflow of power, the other is the dissipation rate of free energy. It is important to realize that for this interaction, time scales matter essentially, that is, the processes resulting in equilibrium depend on the rates of power inputs and the dissipation rates, which in turn are determined by certain structural properties of the processes (such as soil erosion as compared to a taifun).

In this framework, Kleidon defines the notion of 'entropic force', which results from the interaction between different subsystems of the Earth System. The entropic force strictly obeys the Second Law in the sense that the resulting dynamics follows the gradient of energy dissipation and hence entropy generation over a certain distance *dx* (Kleidon 2011, eq. 23):

$$dW = \vec{F} \cdot d\vec{x} = TdS$$

and for the rate *D* of the dissipation of free energy (Kleidon 2011, eq. 24):

$$D = T \cdot \frac{dS_{diseq}}{dt} = \vec{F} \cdot \vec{v}$$

Now, for positing the MEP hypothesis, it is essential to establish the correspondence between entropy production and power production, that is work generated per unit of time. Power extraction can be measured by Carnot efficiency, however, one has to consider the role of heat generation and competing processes in a system. In this case, the MEPP directly connects to the MPP. The MEPP framework is completed in considering the causal interaction between subsystems which results from the impact of power fluxes across subsystems with different modes of energy, such as the impact of heat transport on water flows. For every subsystem, one can formulate a basic descriptor of thermodynamic fluxes which result from the impact of power on the subsystem. The power input drives the system away from equilibrium, which generates another source of power fluxes. Since the adaptive forces driving the subsystem back to equilibrium do not operate instantaneously, the subsystem maintains a state of disequilibrium, depending on the continuous power flux, and therefore can in turn become a continuous source of power inputs for other subsystems. As has been emphasized previously, the time structure of the processes matters much (relative speeds and scales).

Figure 2.22 Gaia and physiosemiosis

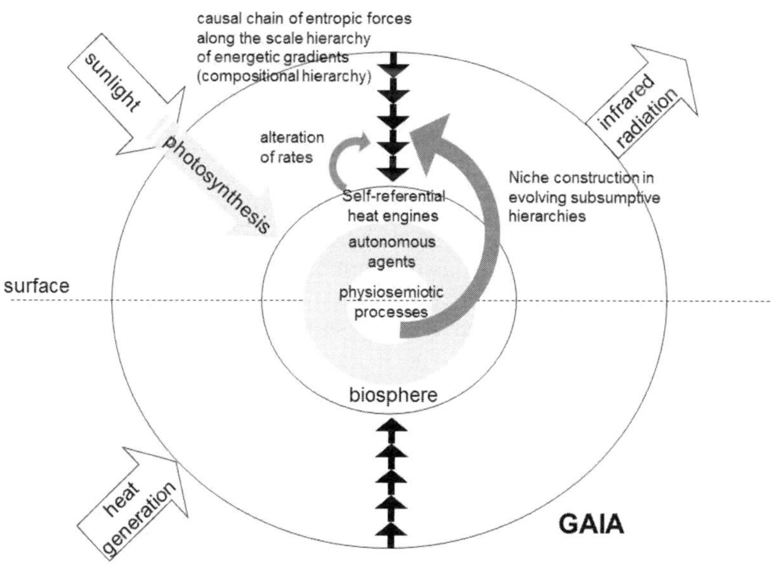

Note: The Earth System Gaia is conceived as a system that is continuously driven farther away from thermodynamic equilibrium by means of physiosemiosis; physiosemiosis is physically enabled by continuous energy throughputs from solar radiation (I neglect heat generation from inner Earth for simplicity). Physiosemiosis results into niche construction via evolution, which relates the accumulation of information with the emerging functions of Maximum Power Production (subsumptive hierarchies). Physically, this results into hierarchically ordered gradients of energy dissipation; rates of dissipation are endogenous to the on-going process of physiosemiosis. In this picture, physiosemiosis is the most general notion that includes all forms of accumulating physical information (such as snowflakes); autonomous agents à la Kauffman are PIDs that have the special property of self–referential heat engines in which work generated positively feeds back on the capacity to harness energy. Therefore, only the biosphere can maintain a state far from equilibrium, which makes accumulation of physical information possible. This view is very different from the conventional view of Gaia, where the biosphere is seen as an equilibrating system. However, this view cannot be reconciled with the fact that evolution accumulates new information, as this is only possible far from thermodynamic equilibrium.

The Kleidon approach results into the picture of diagram 2.22 which builds on a diagram in Kleidon 2011, but simplifies this, while adding the analytical categories developed in this chapter.

The Gaia system is driven by the energetic flows generated exogenously, namely solar radiation and Earth's inner heat (subsequently, we leave the latter out of the discussion and the diagram, in order to avoid cluttering). The biosphere is a phenomenon close to the surface of the Earth, but extending beyond in both directions. It stands out as a second source of energetic flow resulting from phototrophic life. The diagram does not present the details about the levels of gradients across which the entropic forces generate work which connects into chains and loops (compare the original, more detailed Kleidon 2011 diagram). This is the efficient–causal process that underlies the physiosemiotic process, thus providing the ultimate justification for extending the notion of semiosis into physiosemiosis.

We distinguish between three analytical layers in analysing the biosphere. One is provided by the most general notion of a self–referential heat engine, which catches the Kauffman conception of work as energy dissipated under constraints, and impacting on those constraints. As we have seen, this notion of a self–referential heat engine is essential to explain the evolutionary directedness of the biospheres' changes through time, in the sense of driving Gaia further and further away from thermodynamic equilibrium (Kleidon's definition). Thus, the entire biosphere is a self–referential heat engine. Further, we distinguish between this generic case, which applies for all kinds of ecosystems, and the more specific analytical layer of autonomous agents. In the sense of the bi-directionality of hierarchies, compositional and subsumptive, autonomous agents build the biosphere, and the biosphere constitutes the physical system in which they evolve, increasingly internalizing the Earth System as a whole.

In this context, it is essential to highlight two points. The first is that the biosphere influences the chain of energetic flows (and hence, entropy production) by changing their rates. This is a physical effect that is emergent on the entire biosphere, even though triggered by the single events and action patterns on the constituent individual level of the biosphere (that is the organisms, i.e. the autonomous agents). For example, even climate change triggered by human action cannot simply be reduced to the latter alone, but on the entire network of feedback effects in the biosphere. Second, the distinction between autonomous agents and self–referential heat engines refers to the fact that the interaction of autonomous agents triggers emergent phenomena on the ecosystem level which do not imply agency. This distinction is necessary to avoid teleological interpretations of the Gaia hypothesis, but reflects the triadic causality of physiosemiosis. These emergent properties, in the current context, centre around the features of self–referential heat engines, in the sense of intermediating causal chains that redirect work on the constraints under which the biosphere evolves.

Autonomous agents have the properties outlined in the previous sections. Especially, they build on autocatalytic cycles, which are the physical foundation for the emergence of supervening triadic causal mechanism in Gaia. Thus, we argue that a fully-fledged analysis of Gaia needs to move beyond the analysis of efficient–causal chains of entropic forces in order to explain the directedness of changes and the continuous tendency to move away from thermodynamic equilibrium. In the context of autonomous agents, this interplay of causal forces stays at the core of physiosemiosis, which opens the view on the dual of the entropic flows, namely the emergence and evolution of information that is embodied in the structure of the biosphere. Now, physiosemiosis also establishes the second major feedback mechanism in the evolution of Gaia, which is the process of niche construction (see Chapter Three in more detail). Niches define environments in terms of semiotically mediated processes of energetic dissipation. This results in the twofold hierarchical structure of compositional and subsumptive hierarchies, which changes the nature of the efficient–causal entropic forces fundamentally, as they become embedded into the structure of niches. The concept of niche reflects the principle that has been highlighted by Kauffman, namely that the physical conception of work, as applied in empirical contexts, is fundamentally dependent on the structure of constraints that channel the dissipation of free energy. Therefore, evolving niches continuously transform the physical expression of work.

In sum, analysing Gaia solely in terms of the causal chains of entropic forces remains a purely descriptive statement. The more fundamental causal hypothesis of Maximum Entropy Production requires a more powerful explanatory approach. The ultimate explanation is the physiosemiotic one, which shows that the MaxEnt principle and the MEP principle are inherent features of evolution as a process of accumulation of information via the emergence of novelty.

In this chapter I have tried to elucidate basic physical and ontological characteristics of evolution as growth of information and knowledge. The essence lies in the idea that the growth of knowledge is an expression of the Second Law, because the ultimate purpose of information is to harness energy sources in order to produce work, which in turn increases the gradients of energy dissipation, and hence the rate of entropy production. To understand this basic ontological pattern of causation, it is necessary to adopt the view of Peircian triadism, and to acknowledge the fundamental role of randomness in the fabric of the world. In the next chapter, I will turn to the analysis of more specific functional mechanisms that drive evolution in living systems, of which I regard human economic systems to be part and parcel. Evolution is defined via the emergence of novelties. This includes the emergence of novelties of evolutionary mechanisms, that is mechanisms of information processing and knowledge generation. Evolution evolves. Evolving evolution provides the setting in which the human economy has to be located ontologically. Evolution evolves via the emergence of new forms of physical information, namely kinds of physical inference devices. Thus, the concept of PIDs serves as a unifying conceptual framework for analysing different forms of evolution, in particular, biological and cultural. As we have seen, in analysing PIDs Peirce's philosophical approach provides a powerful conceptual framework which allows integrating different scientific disciplines, in particular, Thermodynamics, Information Theory and Evolutionary Theory, into one single and unified ontology of evolution.

3. Evolution

> Thus, and in summary, for the unifocal and noninteractive Darwinian models of exclusively organismal selection, causal flow from an environmental outside to an organismal inside, and a microevolutionary locus for mechanisms of change that smoothly extrapolate all scales, we substitute a hierarchical selectionist theory of numerous interacting levels, a balanced and bidirectional flow of causality between external selection and internal constraint (interaction of functionalist and structuralist perspectives), and causal interaction among tiers of time (Stephen Jay Gould 2002: 32).

3.1. EVOLUTION, ENTROPY AND INFORMATION

3.1.1. The meanings of 'evolution'

The previous chapter established the general principles of evolution, which are based on the thermodynamics of information. This chapter aims at exploring specific aspects of evolutionary causation, which apply for living systems in particular. This corresponds to one general tendency in many scientific domains, especially in economics, to interpret the term 'evolution' in the sense of biology. Yet, this still allows for many different approaches, such as claiming ontological continuity between economic and biological evolution, while rejecting certain theoretical concepts more specific to the latter (for example Witt 2003), or elaborating on a 'generalized Darwinism' (Hodgson and Knudsen 2006b; Aldrich et al. 2008).

Even when adopting an integrationist approach to biological and economic evolution, the problem with the biological use of the term is that there are many competing evolutionary theories even within biology, especially in the recent three decades, after many second thoughts came up regarding the so-called Neo-Darwinian 'synthesis' of classical Darwinism and population genetics (Hodgson 1997). These discussions are of crucial relevance for my argument because they gyrate over a special assumption about causal structure in evolution, namely the genetic theory of evolution and the distinction between genotype and phenotype in the analysis of information flows across generations. These assumptions have also exerted a strong impact on debates in economics (Knudsen 2002; Vromen 2006).

The central question here is whether and how specific evolutionary causation can be further dissected into two different kinds of functions: The replicator function and the interactor function, two terms which are conceptual generalizations over the distinction between genotype and phenotype. The debate over the validity of this distinction covers many other important points of dissent, especially the question of the levels of selection, which includes the role of group selection; this is because it entails the conceptual distinction between units of selection, units of inheritance and units of evolution, which ultimately boils down to the question of where biological information is stored and transmitted. So, regarding the group selection question, the issue at stake is whether groups are merely phenotypical phenomena, such that certain selectively relevant properties are generated on this level, but the information that underlies this generation is exclusively genotypical.

The core idea of the Neodarwinian synthesis is that all information accumulating in evolution is transmitted via the genotype, and that all selection effects are mediated via the phenotype which is the ontogenetic expression of the genotype. Therefore, no phenotypic information (acquired traits) can be transmitted in evolution (refutation of 'Lamarckism', see the corresponding debate in economics, Nelson 2006 vs. Hodgson and Knudsen 2006a, 2007). Today, we know that this theory was partly wrong, as there are many non-genetic channels by which information is stored and accumulates even in biological evolution (for surveys, see Jablonka and Lamb 2006 or Danchin et al. 2011). This is of particular importance for studying human systems, because this implies the possibility of a unified evolutionary theory that combines biological and cultural evolution. In this chapter, I outline the fundamentals of such an approach, which will offer the overarching paradigm for the analysis focusing on the human economy in the subsequent chapters. My main objective is to identify generic principles of evolution that can be applied across different ontological domains, without necessarily implying that the material mechanisms of evolution are the same (this corresponds to Witt's 2003, 2008 notion of 'ontological continuity').

With regard to the question of where biological information is located, one central task of this chapter is to show that the idea was misguided to assume that biological information is stored in atom–like units of information, the genes and the related structures (for related radical critiques, see for instance Oyama 2000, 2001). Based on the analysis of Chapter Two, we can develop an alternative approach that equates accumulating information with constraints on possible states of the world. In living systems, constraints emerge on different levels via the process of development, that is ontogeny, in particular environmental contexts. Information transmission through evolutionary time occurs via the correlation and stability of constraints in recurrent ontogenetic processes which are triggered by genetically embodied information; this genetic information, however, is being interpreted by the emergent complex living systems, such that we cannot say that its 'meaning' qua function is stored in the genes. Development and evolution are closely entwined sides of one trajectory of the growth of knowledge (compare Salthe 1993). I will argue that the Thermodynamics of knowledge as outlined in Chapter Two offers a framework to analyse this duality. As we shall see, this approach matches with recent developments in evolutionary theory that approach evolution as a statistical phenomenon, building on early, but neglected contributions by George Price. So, my claim is that these statistical approaches are the other side of the coin of the physical processes that drive and result from evolution, and which essentially are structured processes of energetic dissipation.

3.1.2. Dissipation of energy and origins of life

I begin with elaborating on the general question how evolution and entropy relate with each other in the context of energetic dissipation by living systems. In the previous chapter, we have established that evolution manifests the conjunction of three principles, the MEP principle, the MPP principle and the MaxEnt principle, which are all expressions of the Second Law. Evolutionary systems evolve into most probable states, which corresponds to states which tend towards maxima of power throughput and hence entropy production (Whitfield 2007). I re-emphasize that this is a proposition about propensities, not about necessary deterministic properties of states of systems. In this view, the Schrödinger (1944) conjecture is misguided to argue that life is a phenomenon reflecting states with low probability because it manifests high complexity: What counts is the conjunction of ensembles of living systems and their environments, and in these conjunctions more complex structures actually increase the entropic rates, such that the Second Law continues to hold for the ensemble. Living systems are systems of functions that are ultimately directed towards the most universal purpose in nature, the dissipation of energy (Annila and Salthe 2010). From this it follows that evolution is a telenomic process, that is it manifests directionality of change. Directionality and increases of complexity are expressions of the Second Law, and do not contradict it. As we shall see in the course of this chapter, in the context of the biological theory of evolution this means to define 'adaptation' in terms of a state which is the most probable one, given constraints. In fact, this is a simple, almost common-sense idea: If certain processes converge to certain states, they are the most likely ones by definition. The fact that living systems are complex simply mirrors their irreducible individuality, as elucidated in the previous chapters in ontological terms.

We have already seen that this view is the dual of the information theoretic view. Living systems are physical inference devices, PIDs.

Populations of living systems manifest a distinct pattern of functionings. They maximize entropy in the sense of producing the highest possible number of individual variants, given the constraints on the growth of the population. The random distribution of these variants therefore does not store information in the Shannon sense, but would actually reflect the loss of information that goes hand in hand with the dissipation of energy. However, the PIDs are subject to selective impacts from the environment; these impacts are reflected in the stable structural features of the functions that populations of PIDs share through time, and which drive power throughputs that evolve according to the MPP principle. Information is stored in those structures, and we can say that this information, in most general senses, is information about how to harness, use and dissipate energy.

This picture is most explicit in recent theories about the origin of life. Lahav et al. (2001) offer an overview of different theories and summarize the common aspects in thermodynamic perspective (see also Elitzur 2005; Michaelean 2011). The conceptual basis for this approach is the analysis of autocatalytic cycles as presented in the previous chapter. All theories of the emergence of life build on the idea that a certain class of chemical reactions turns into self–sustaining and self–replicating chemical structures with ring–like connectivity, by which control information (in the sense of Corning's 2005) emerges that results into increased thermodynamic rates of energetic dissipation via those reactions. That means, information inheres in the difference between the energetic flows in the two states, without and with control information. Then, as explicitly stated in approaches as proposed by Michaelean (2011), we need to recognize that this emergent information ultimately serves to increase the rates of energy dissipation in the entire Earth System. For example, Michaelean argues that the emergent RNA/DNA circuits were especially efficacious in transforming high–energy ultraviolet light into heat, with the resulting temperature differences and turbulences during the day/night cycle operating as heat machines that could trigger further dissipative processes, thus coupling emergent biotic and abiotic processes of entropy production.

In our context, the detailed assumptions of different chemical theories about the origin of life do not matter. Once this kind of 'accidental' chemical information emerged, it turned into the starting point for the further evolution of life, leading back to this chemical LUCA (Last Universal Common Ancestor) in an unbroken line, the 'tree of life'. In the previous chapter, I called this process 'physiosemiosis': evolving chemical structures drive the emergence of structural features that involve representation and information transmission that is ontologically autonomous from the actual chemical processes that reproduce these structures (Elitzur 2005 calls these structures 'forms'; for a related view, see Ben Jacob, Shapira and Tauber 2006). According to Lahav et al. (2001: 110), these structures manifest the fundamental characteristics of life, as we know it, and which identify a more special class of PIDs, manifesting the properties of:

- Metabolism, that is processing matterenergy throughputs in exchange with the environment;
- Autonomy, that is operating as a self–referential heat engine that maintains its boundaries to the environment;
- Teleonomy, that is the conjunction of feedback mechanisms, reproduction and development of structural features in interaction with the environment;
- Learning, that is development of structure involves the growth of control information.

Thus, with all life on Earth going back to the primordial LUCA, all living systems reflect the same fundamental principles of chemical evolution throughout the unfolding of its forms. Therefore, origins of life theories are of universal relevance for the theory of evolution (Küppers 1986). They are fundamental facts that support the general theory developed so far, and they impose certain constraints on evolutionary theories that also explain later stages of evolution.

3.1.3. Entropy and evolution: Fundamentals

We can analyse the most general patterns of evolution in terms of the conceptual model developed by Layzer (1988) that we have already explored in Chapter Two (following the seminal work by Brooks and Wiley 1988). Then, our results so far can be summarized in figure 3.1. This is a purely qualitative diagram that visualizes the central claims of the general thermodynamic theory of evolution. Firstly, evolution is reflected in a temporal sequence of functions, which determine processes of energy dissipation. These processes have two sides. One is that they maximize entropy in the sense of creating a maximum of information capacity (which is the random distribution of variants of PIDs). The other is that they maximize energy throughput and hence entropy production, as specified in the Constructal Law. The additional clarification provided by diagram 3.1 is that we can relate these two processes, sides of the same coin, namely the functions, to the two different notions of entropy, observer relative and observer independent entropy.

MaxEnt processes constitute $\text{Entropy}_{\text{OR}}$, in the sense of the fact that the evolution of functions towards states of MaxEnt reflects the constraints that impact on that evolution. In other words, randomness is relative to the constraints that hold. On the other hand, insofar as the physically embodied functions incorporate information about those constraints, they enable the dissipation of energy. This is a physical process that relates to $\text{Entropy}_{\text{OI}}$, since energy is an observer independent magnitude for which a conservation law holds, the First Law.

Figure 3.1 Evolution and entropy

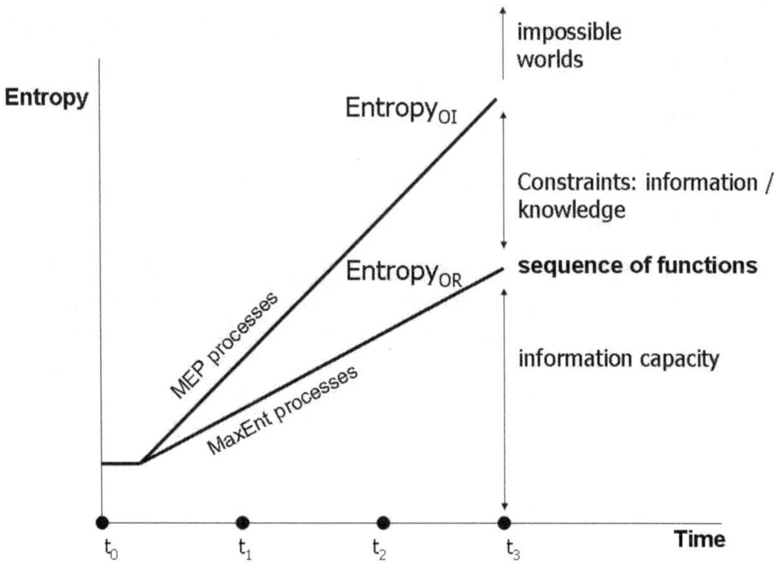

Note: This diagram presents a qualitative view on the trajectory of physiosemiosis in evolution, based on the conceptual framework developed in Chapter Two. Extending and modifying seminal contributions by Layzer (1988) and Brooks and Wiley (1988), we distinguish between potential entropy and actualized entropy, with the gap (measuring information) being determined by evolving constraints on possible states of the world. Evolving constraints are functions of PIDs that reflect forces of selection. Realized states of populations of PIDs manifest the tendency to maximise variety, hence reflect MaxEnt processes, resulting into accumulating information capacity, measured as algorithmic incompressibility of the individual states. This is Entropy$_{OR}$, relative to the functions of PIDs. Functions are embodied in these individual states, but information inheres in the resulting constraints on possible states. Entropy$_{OI}$ corresponds to the sum of information and information capacity.

The diagram also reflects one important point that has already transpired in our analysis of the semioverse: Namely, that the sequence of functions also establishes constraints on the further evolution of functions, thus limiting the accessibility of possible states in the state space of evolution. Functions reflect constraints, and they are constraints. These constraints add to the operation of physical constraints on possible worlds. Again, the latter are observer independent, but the former are observer relative, namely, relative to the established patterns of functions. The latter separates physically possible states of the world from evolutionarily accessible states. The evolution of constraints is the accumulation of information, the growth of randomness under constraints is the growth of information capacity (I should mention that this interpretation differs from Brooks and Wiley 1988: 41ff, who treat potential entropy as information capacity, whereas I treat realized entropy as information capacity, because selection can only operate on realized states, not potential states).

Finally, we realize that the distinction between the two kinds of entropy, relative to the functions, corresponds to Zurek's (1989a, b) definition of physical entropy in terms of the sum of the Shannon information measure and the algorithmic complexity of the function relative to which Shannon information is measured. The former reflects the information that is represented in the functions and the embodied constraints, relative to the state of maximum randomness. The latter reflects the individuality of evolved constraints, in the sense of thermodynamic depth, that is the causal sequence that has resulted from the contingent selection impacts through time (for a related analysis, see Collier and Hooker 1998 who introduce a set of new terms to capture the different notions of information and entropy, such as defining 'enformation' as the information embodied in structural constraints that enable dissipation in the form of work, that is realization of functions).

So we can modify figure 3.1 into figure 3.2. The additional insight gained from this diagram is that our picture of evolution also fits into the most fundamental ontological structures outlined in Chapters One and Two. Firstly, the random distribution of functions is the set of individuals, for which the ontological criterion of existence holds, in the strong sense of being observer independent objects. Thus, the theory of evolution takes ontological individuals as the core, that is posits ontological individualism. At the same time, all functions represent signs: This refers to the shared classes of functionings (the 'forms' of Elitzur, or 'concepts' in the Peircian and Hegelian approach to conceptual realism). The signs are essential for defining the process of information accumulation, or knowledge. So, for example, the fins of sharks come in myriads of individual variants, with the individual sharks anchoring the ontology of evolution. But the information stored in these fins relates with a type of fin which reflects certain physical causalities in determining speed and agility of swimming movements. As long as individual variants do not affect these generic functionings, they do not matter, and evolution will maximize diversity of its shapes. So, for example, human intelligence can distil the information stored in these structures and re-build fins as technological artefacts that manifest similar functions. The relationship between functions, functionings and populations of embodied functions underlies the special field of biology dealing with morphology. From this viewpoint, morphology studies the semiotic aspect of evolving biological information (for a related view, see Riedl 1983).

Figure 3.2 Evolution and the semioverse

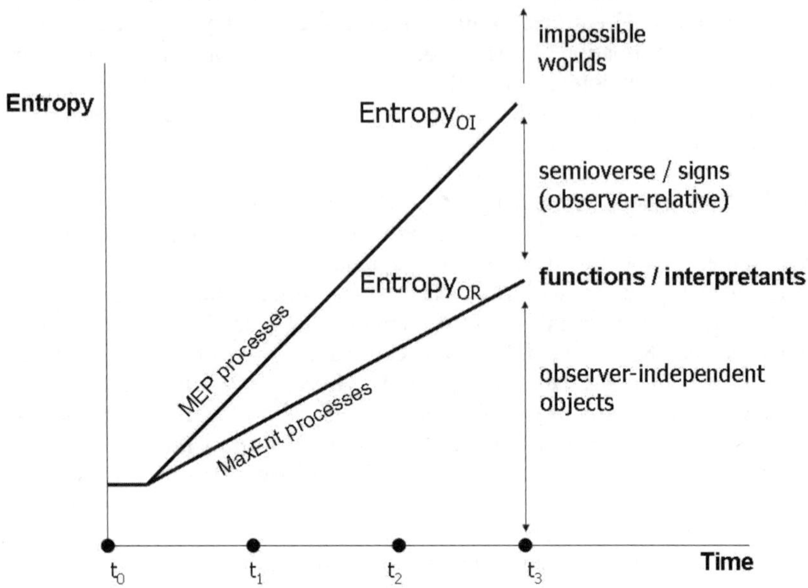

Note: This diagram translates figure 3.1 into ontological categories, relating with the analysis of the semioverse (figure 1.10). Functions are embodied in populations of individuals; individuals exist, therefore constitute observer independent objects. Functions emerge from physiosemiosis and hence relate to the set of signs as observer relative objects making up the semioverse. This view corresponds to the fundamental philosophical positions of Hegel and Peirce, that is conceptual realism, and matches with Deutsch's approach to evolution in the context of a many–worlds interpretation of quantum mechanics. That means, the world is seen as being constituted by two types of facts, observer independent and observer relative, with individuals constituting the former, and signs the latter. Signs relate with embodied functions in the triadic analysis of PIDs. They are the physical embodiments of accumulation information aka knowledge in the multiverse.

How can we arrive at more specific propositions about this evolutionary process? The central insight is that evolution builds on random processes. As we have seen, along the lines of Peircian tychism, the world is fundamentally random. Evolution in turn operates via random processes, which means is based on ontological individuality. So, the fundamental property of evolution is that two random processes are conjoined such that information emerges. This is most obvious in the case of physical laws: So, the shark's fin embodies information about the physical constraints on swimming, beyond the mere random impacts. This information has been accumulating via a random process generating myriads of individual variants subject to selection. Things become much more complex in the case of other regularities. The fin may also be determined by the functionings resulting from interaction between prey and predators. In this case, we are not referring to physical laws, but to evolved regularities by which living systems mutually impose constraints. Then, evolution conjoins two different sequences of functions which emerge from randomized causal interactions in the first place. This analysis corresponds to the nested embeddedness of observer–object interactions as analysed in Chapter One (figures 1.1, 1.12).

3.1.4. Evolution maximizes Fisher information

This abstract reasoning can be put into a more concise framework for analysing the dynamics of evolution by means of the concept of Fisher information that has been introduced recently by Steven Frank into evolutionary theory (2009a, 2011b; Frank and Smith 2010, 2011), building on Frieden's (2004) general theory of the emergence of physical information that I introduced also in the previous chapters. So, we can directly relate Frank's approach to the ontological categories that underlie the analysis of physical information and the growth of knowledge. The general idea is that evolution extracts and maximizes Fisher information in entangling two different processes which are driven by random events, namely environmental changes and the generation of variants in populations embodying biological functions. The evolving populations interact with the environment and jointly construct regularities.

So, statistically, evolution can be conceived as a process which tends towards maximizing Fisher information about the environment. As we have seen in Chapter One, Fisher information is a measure in statistics which refers to the information that the observation of a random variable reveals about certain statistical parameters of the distribution that governs the occurrence of the information generated by the single observation. Hence, we conceive of the evolutionary process as a process of statistical estimation: Because the world manifests fundamental randomness, information accumulation will always occur in terms of improvements of expectations which would correspond to improved statistical estimates. Again, we generalize over this in extending the notion of the 'observer' to population based processes: That is, following the argument in Chapter One, we do not think of a human observer who applies some statistical tools to identify the distribution, but to a process of selection of PIDs that evolve into stable causal feedback circles which are described by the 'expectations'; as we shall see in detail, these expectations can be grasped by a statistical approach to the notion of 'fitness'. In other words, we classify populations of PIDs, conceived as random evolutionary processes, more specifically as being mechanisms of statistical inference. Then, it is straightforward to argue that the evolution of PIDs maximizes Fisher information; with the endogenization of the observer, we also realize that embodied Fisher information itself is an emergent pattern of regularities in the ensembles of observers and objects.

Seen from another angle, if we observe certain rates of evolutionary change in a population of PIDs, hence directed changes of functions and their speed of change, we can interpret this as Fisher information. This has been demonstrated by Frank (2009a) in a most basic way, which I summarize in the remaining part of this section, relating to the considerations of the previous chapters. We consider a probability distribution function $p(y|\theta)$ of a random variable y and a parameter θ, simplifying into p_y in the notation; p' denotes $p(y|\theta + d\theta)$. Against the background of the discussion of the concept of probability in Chapter Two, it is important to notice that these pdf's reflect propensities, hence properties of the world, and cannot be just reduced to statistical mappings of the observer's ignorance.

We now introduce a central term in the biological theory of evolution, 'fitness'. In Chapter Two, I already related 'fitness' to a particular generic function, that is maximization of power. In the statistical approach to evolution, this physical interpretation is not used directly, as we only refer to relative frequencies of certain phenomena. Then, we define 'fitness' as the determinant of the changes of the probability distribution function through time; if we consider discretionary change (such as generational change), one step of change is:

$$p'_y = p_y\left(\frac{w_y}{\overline{w}}\right)$$

with w_y the fitness of the y trait, and

$$\overline{w} = \sum p_y w_y$$

the average fitness. Frank then adopts a specific definition of fitness: p'_y does not refer to the frequency of a trait in the descendant population, but to the fraction of the descendant population that derives from the parent population, given the parameters of the statistical distribution at t_0. That corresponds to the general idea in biology that fitness is expressed in the numbers of progeny of individual organisms. So, if we consider a population of total size N, statistically the number of individuals with trait y is determined as $N_y = Np_y$. The same holds for the proportions in the descendant population. Then, average fitness is $\overline{w} = N'/N$ and trait specific fitness is $w_y = N'_y/N_y$.

Now, equipped with these definitions we can also consider rates of change, that is population growth rates m. Evolutionary change is the rate of change (indicated by dots) of the frequencies of traits:

$$\frac{\dot{p}_y}{p_y} = \dot{\log}(p_y)$$

Since the frequency is just N_y / N and therefore the change of the frequency the difference between the logs of N, this can be transformed into:

$$\frac{\dot{N}_y}{N_y} - \frac{\dot{N}}{N} = m_y - \overline{m} = a_y$$

which is the average excess of fitness of type y, expressed in terms of the rates of growth of the numbers of individuals with trait y.

Now, we consider the definition of Fisher information. In one technical interpretation, Fisher information measures the distance between two frequency distributions if a change in a parameter θ happens, with the frequency distribution $p(y|\theta)$ of the random variable y. Adopting the simplified notation for the pdf as used previously, Fisher information is defined as:

$$F = \sum_y p_y \left(\frac{d \log(p_y)}{d\theta} \right)^2$$

Frank proposes a notational variant as follows, where the overdots mean differentiation with respect to θ:

$$F = \sum_y p_y \left(\frac{\dot{p}_y}{p_y} \right)^2$$

Then, we can relate this to the analysis of fitness by simply substituting the previous result in the definition of Fisher information, ending up with:

$$P = \sum_y p_y \left(\frac{\dot{p}_y}{p_y} \right)^2 = \sum_y p_y a_y^2$$

where P denotes the Fisher information in the frequency distribution of trait y about the parameter θ that determines the occurrence of the observations. This directly shows that evolutionary change, as measured in population frequencies and growth rates of populations with certain traits, corresponds to the accumulation of Fisher information, in the sense that the random distribution of variants reflects the impact of parameters, that is constraints, on the occurrence of the single events.

More intuitively, Fisher information is a measure of the acceleration of change that occurs with the frequencies of trait, such that this acceleration reflects the increase of information. That is:

$$\mathrm{d}p_y = p'_y - p_y = p_y a_y \mathrm{d}\theta$$

so that a_y actually measures the frequency distribution over impacts of the parameter θ. Most generally, the excess fitness reflects the mismatch of the given distribution of traits with the environment as measured with reference to θ.

It is important to notice that this notion directly establishes a connection between Fisher information and Shannon information, because the above quoted definition of Fisher information can be shown to be formally homologous to the measure of the acceleration of increases of Shannon information (Frank 2009a: 242). With Shannon information being defined as:

$$H = -\sum_y p_y \log(p_y)$$

Fisher information is:

$$\ddot{H} = F = \sum_y p_y \left(\frac{\dot{p}_y}{p_y} \right)^2$$

which means that the acceleration of Shannon information is measured as squared distance between the two frequency distributions over the scale of the parameter θ. In other words, acceleration of information reflects the strength of the selective forces that inhere in the environment, as measured at the scale of the parameter.

By this brief formal reasoning developed by Frank (2009a) we can directly show how the entropic principles relate with the accumulation of information through evolution, which relates to the other side of the coin, the growth of information capacity. It is useful to refer to Ayres's (1994: 46) distinction between 'D–information' and 'SR–information' here. The growth of Shannon information is the growth of 'distinguishability information' which is made possible via the growth of individual variants of PIDs. Shannon information, in terms of the framework established in figure 3.1, can only be measured relative to the set of possible states of the state space of evolution, hence is observer relative. This growth of Shannon information corresponds to the growth of Fisher information, which is 'survival–relevant information' in the sense of accumulating information about the statistical distributions that govern the causal feedbacks between the environment and the population of PIDs. Fisher information is embodied in the frequency distributions over traits of populations of individuals that embody those traits, and which are observer independent entities.

If we ask for the fundamental semantics of this information, we can state in most general terms that it expresses the 'fitness' of the evolving PIDs: 'Fitness' means that information is accumulating that reflects the environment in a way such that the structures of PIDs, namely the evolving functions, become sustainable through time, as reflected in their differential reproduction, which translates in changing statistical distributions over variants and kinds of PIDs. In this particular sense, evolving knowledge is observer relative by necessity: This means, it does not refer to the 'truth' criterion, in the sense of reflecting 'true' states of the world, but to the 'fitness' criterion (Küppers 1986). This is a precise restatement of Peirce's pragmatist approach to knowledge in evolutionary terms: Evolving biological information improves actions of living systems in the world, and this is reflected in 'fitness' as increasing Fisher information. It is meaningless, then, to refer evolving knowledge to any standard of 'truth'. So, the analysis of the role of Fisher information in evolution resolves one fundamental issue in traditional epistemology, along the lines of Evolutionary Epistemology. The core phenomenon driving this result is selection. So I turn to the more detailed analysis of this fundamental process of evolution.

3.2. THE THEORY OF SELECTION

3.2.1. Price's equation and heredity

Selection is a fundamental notion in the general theory of evolution. Yet, it did not receive a sufficient analytical treatment for a long time, because it was mixed up with many empirical aspects of selection in biology, which were then partly transferred to other scientific domains, often causing ill-conceived concerns for example about 'Social Darwinism'. The general theory of selection was only developed in the past three decades, after the work of George Price in the early 1970s was lifted out of obscurity, although he also played a pivotal role in the development of evolutionary game theory. Again, Steven Frank (1995b, 2012a) contributed central insights. The 'Price's equation' is a most general proposition about the logic of selection in probabilistic terms, stating that observed evolutionary changes of traits (which corresponds to the 'functions' in our context) result statistically from two determinants, firstly, the covariance between the trait and population shares of individuals embodying the trait, and secondly, an expectation term which captures forces of change which are independent from selection.

Frank (2009a) is also able to show that this most general theoretical approach to selection and evolution can be directly inferred from Fisher information. For achieving this, we introduce the distinction between types of individuals y with traits z, so that z_y is the average value of z for the individuals of type y. If overdots designate changes with respect of a variable over the scale θ, Frank shows that the expression:

$$\dot{\bar{z}} = \frac{\sum p'_y z'_y - \sum p_y z_y}{\mathrm{d}\theta}$$

is equivalent to:

$$\operatorname{cov}(m, z) + E(\dot{z}) + \operatorname{cov}(m, \mathrm{d}z)$$

and hence, because d*z* → 0, we arrive at one possible formulation of the Price's equation:

$$\dot{\bar{z}} = \operatorname{cov}(m, z) + \mathrm{E}(\dot{z})$$

which states that the rate of the change of the average value of a trait *z* in a population is the sum of the covariance between the trait and the growth rate of the share of individuals with the trait in the population and the expectation over autonomous changes of the trait.

There is also an incipient reception of the Price approach in economics (for example Andersen 2004; Knudsen 2004) which takes the central importance of replicator dynamics in evolutionary modelling as a point of departure (for example Metcalfe 1998, 2001; overview in Safarzyńska and van den Berg 2010). The significance of the Price's equation results from the fact that it describes general statistical properties of any kind of process of selection, and does not make any specific assumptions about the underlying causality (Price 1973/1995). This is of utmost significance for establishing an evolutionary theory that encompasses different levels of evolution, such as biological and cultural (Kerr and Godfrey-Smith 2008, Helanterä and Uller 2010). The central point is that one of the core notions of evolutionary theory, heredity, is defined independently from the underlying causal mechanisms. That means, heredity is only conceived as a statistical correlation between parent and descendant populations, such that the distribution of certain properties in the descendant population is partly determined by the properties of the parent population, beyond the impact of autonomous changes resulting from other factors. Basically, this approach matches with the definition of heredity in Population Genetics (for an overview, see Downes 2010). Then, most generally,

$$H^2 = \frac{V_g}{V_z}$$

That means, the heredity of a type is measured by the relationship between the variance of the traits *z* and the variance of the determinants *g*, which are the breeding values in population genetics, and correspond to fitness as a trait (we will discuss later, in section 3.5, that this raises intricate issues in treating fitness as a predictor in a probabilistic setting). In the context of biology, heredity compares phenotypic and genotypic variance, if the latter is seen as the only causal determinant of the properties of the descendant population. More specifically, one can distinguish between broad and narrow heredity. This separates the additive genetic variation between individuals from the genotypic variance in general. The latter is implicated by epistatic interactions among genes and dominance, for example. There is also the possibility that genes and the environment interact in the statistical sense, for example, when genes for body height interact with a tendency of individuals to move to nutrient-rich environments. Thus, a complete formula for heredity would be:

$$\frac{V_A + V_D + V_i + V_E + V_{G\times E} + Cov(G,E)}{V_A + V_D + V_I}$$

with V_A the additive genetic variance, V_D the dominance variance, V_I the epistatically caused variance, V_E the environmental variance, V_{GE} the variance resulting from interactions between genes and the environment, and *Cov(G,E)* the covariance of genes and the environment. Heredity is exclusively determined by the statistical properties of the determinants and the characteristics, and not by the single determinants. Thus, heredity is a population level phenomenon. Therefore heredity has nothing to do with any specific idea about the causal mechanisms of heredity. The concept is purely phenomenological, that is statistical. Still, the minimum requirement for a measure of heredity is the identification of a set of relevant characteristics and a set of determinants.

3.2.2. Fisher's 'Fundamental Theorem' as an impossibility theorem

Against this background, we will now consider Price's equation in some more detail, following the exposition by Frank again (1995a; for a more recent overview, see Frank 2012a). We define a population as a set of types with index *i*. Each type has a trait z_i, which defines its dissimilarity with others, which means it is a distinctive feature. We can then define the relative frequency q_i by which the type occurs in the population. Then, we follow the previous definitions and denote as q_i' the fraction of types *i* in a population that is derived from the type *i* in the ancestral population. Then we can state:

$$\bar{z}' = \sum q_i' z_i'$$

as the population average of the trait of the descendants of type *i*. Heredity is about the relationship between two sets of populations, the ancestral one and a descendant one. We can define the change in the average trait z_i:

$$\Delta\bar{z} = \sum_i q_i' z_i' - \sum_i q_i z_i$$

We introduce the contribution w_i of type *i* of the ancestral population to the descendant population, such that:

$$q_i' = q_i w_i / \overline{w}$$

where w is the average contribution of types i. The contribution w_i is called the 'fitness' of type i. This is a purely descriptive term denoting a statistical relation, without any implications about causality.

If the average trait value z_i' is weighted by the share in total fitness, we obtain the expression:

$$\Delta\bar{z} = \sum_i q_i(w_i/\bar{w})(z_i + \Delta z_i) - \sum_i q_i z_i = \sum_i q_i(w_i/\bar{w} - 1)z_i + \sum_i q_i(w_i/\bar{w})\Delta z_i$$

The right-hand expression, following the standard definitions of covariance *Cov* and expectation *E*, can be reformulated as Price's equation in the proper sense:

$$\bar{w}\Delta\bar{z} = Cov(w, z) + E(w\Delta z)$$

which can be specified with indices i.

The Price's equation states that the average change of a character trait in a population can be explained as the sum between the covariance of the fitness and the trait and the expectation value of the change of the trait:

- The covariance measures the so-called 'selection effect'. This is the phenomenological expression of all factors determining the fitness of a character, relative to the environment. The covariance of a character and its fitness is just the observed statistical correlation between the two features.
- The expectation term grasps the pure effect of the transmission of a trait. This term captures all autonomous determinants of heredity, such as innovations, imitation or learning among individuals.

Now, one can introduce a crucial theoretical twist if one realizes that traits can refer to any property of the individual, thus not only including phenotypical characteristics in the standard sense, but also all factors that determine reproduction, such as the genes carried by the individual, or fitness itself, understood as the reproduction coefficients of different types. In the latter case, the Price's equation can be written as:

$$w\Delta w = Cov(w_i, w_i) = Var(w_i)$$

if we also ignore the impact of autonomous changes, which is often justified in population genetics by assuming that in large randomly interbreeding populations, these effects cancel out, thus resulting into an expectation value of zero. This special interpretation of the Price's equation is of fundamental, though complex significance. In treating fitness as a trait, we conflate observed fitness and predicted fitness, with the latter actually implicit to this step. As we shall see in section 3.5, this needs full consideration. Currently, the important point is that what we get is Fisher's 'fundamental theorem' which plays a crucial role in the theory of natural selection. It states that the speed of change of the average traits of a population depends on the variance of that characteristic. Thus, Fisher's Fundamental Theorem follows from the general framework of Price's equation, but only if we apply the notion of fitness in a self–referential way, which means treating fitness as a trait. As we shall see, this indicates a substantial limitation of the theorem in analysing evolution.

The Fundamental Theorem underlies a specification that is also widely used in economics (for example Metcalfe 1998), the replicator dynamics:

$$\dot{q}_i = q_i\left[w_i(q) - \sum_{i=1}^{n} q_i w_i(q)\right]$$

where q is the vector of the relative frequencies of elements $q_1,\ldots q_n$. The replicator dynamics grasps the forces underlying Fisher's theorem, namely that the change of the population shares q_i depends positively on the 'distance from the mean', that is the distance between individual fitness and average fitness. Again, the problem is that two interpretations of fitness are conflated; therefore, in certain specifications of the replicator dynamics one would substitute fitness by the determinants of fitness. However, this would actually presuppose to have a powerful theory with empirical basis that allows identifying those determinants.

It is important to notice that Fisher himself pointed out that the Fundamental Theorem can be compared with the Second Law (Gould 2002: 511f). Indeed, the Fundamental Theorem states a comparable equilibrium notion about evolution: Fitness increases over time will reduce the variety of fitness, such that ultimately a state will be reached in which all potential for change has been exhausted. In a sense, variety is the free energy of evolution; once it has dissipated, no further change is possible.

Fisher's theorem describes a fundamental property of selection without considering any other autonomous force of change. As is shown in Frank (1995b: 382), Fisher partitioned the evolutionary change of fitness into the following components:

$$\Delta\overline{w} = \left(\overline{w}'|E - \overline{w}|E\right) + \left(\overline{w}'|E' - \overline{w}'|E\right)$$

The first term measures the change in fitness within a stable, given environment, the latter measures the pure effect on current fitness that results from the change in the environment. Only the first effect would be called 'natural selection'. In Fisher's approach, this was analytically necessary because only if the reference frame is a stable one can neatly identify the effects of the environment on the genetic changes that proceed through time, given an initial environmental status. If the environment changes, there is the possibility that a positively selected change of gene frequencies can fail to be adaptive, such that the observed evolution does not manifest a direct correspondence between changes of gene frequencies and adaptation.

This means, Fisher's fundamental theorem does not refer to evolutionary change in general. This is of utmost importance, as therefore we can deduce two fundamental statements about natural selection. The first is that natural selection consumes its own fuel, in the sense that selection will fade out over time because variance will be continuously reduced. This would correspond to a state of equilibrium. In other words, evolution would no longer occur if only forces of natural selection prevail. Therefore, Fisher's fundamental theorem is fundamental with reference to natural selection, but not with reference to evolution.

The second statement is even more foundational, because it establishes a conservation principle for evolution (Frank 2012b). In the original statement of the theorem, Fisher argued that natural selection tends to result in fitness increases, but at the same time these changes imply a deterioration of the environment. Thus, Fisher actually assumed that evolution is always frequency dependent, while isolating natural selection as a frequency–independent process theoretically: Just consider a population approaching the carrying capacity of an environment, when population growth directly affects fitness changes of its members. However, this implies that mean fitness of a population cannot increase over time, but tends to remain constant. A simple justification based on Malthusian parameters would be a sort of knife edge theorem about growth as reflecting fitness. That means, if a population grew continuously stronger than other populations, it would grow infinitively, if it grew continuously less than the average, it would become extinct. Therefore, the mean fitness of a population is constant. This is the fundamental conservation law of evolution, which is also an impossibility theorem: Fitness cannot increase but in temporary states of disequilibrium, and considered partially.

3.2.3. Fitness and maximum entropy

It is therefore essential to realize that a clear cut conceptual distinction needs to be made between two core notions of evolutionary theory, fitness and adaptation. Fitness exclusively refers to the statistical correlations of heredity and their mapping into relative growth rates of types with certain traits. Adaptation refers to the causal mechanisms that determine the capacity to grow, such as the specific behaviours in foraging, reproductive activities and so forth.

From this observation follows another distinction, namely, between the observed fitness and the determinants of heredity. In the statistical view, those determinants carry the information that accumulates via evolution. That means, the determinants can be predictors of the observed fitness. This relates with an important methodological issue, namely whether 'fitness' is a purely descriptive magnitude, and thus tautologically true, or whether any assumption about fitness can be falsified (again, I will pursue this in more detail in section 3.5). In population genetics, this predictor is the breeding value, which refers to predictors, the genes, which are seen as being contained in different types of individuals making up a population. Then, each type y contains x_{yj} copies of a particular predictor, the hereditary particle j. In terms of growth rates, the average excess fitness m_y of a type y is (Frank 2009a: 237).

$$a_y = m_y - \overline{m} = \sum_j \alpha_j x_{yj} + \varepsilon_y$$

where we consider predictors of fitness indexed with j, and the α's denote the pertinent regression coefficients of fitness. In standard population genetics, the sum term on the right-hand side is called the 'breeding value' g_y, so that we can simply write:

$$a_y = g_y + \varepsilon_y$$

which states that the observed average fitness values are the sum of the predicted fitness values and the deviations, that is the unexplained stochastic disturbances. One can then argue that the accumulation of Fisher information by means of evolution is tantamount to a process in which the disturbance term is minimized through time.

Most simply, with Frank (2009a) we can say that the variance E in a trait distribution that is caused by the environment is:

$$E = P - G$$

where P denotes the total variance and G denotes the variance which is explained by the predictors of fitness. So, P is the total amount of Fisher information, of which only a part is stored in the predictors G, and another part, E, is lost by environmental disturbances. This distinction directly corresponds to our dual view on the evolution of functions in relation to entropy: The predictors accumulate structural information, whereas the environmental disturbances relate to all other random aspects of the states of the functions.

From this a very important conclusion follows: There is no material presumption about the nature of those predictors. In population genetics, the standard assumption is that the predictors are the genes and the genotypes. But these should be conceived as purely theoretical entities, which can, but need not exclusively refer to 'genes' in the biochemical sense. In contrast, we can simply say that the stability and the performance of the predictors determine which material entities operate as such. In other words, evolution determines endogenously which entities carry information. There is no ontological *a priori* about the material nature of the predictors. This is especially important when considering different time scales in changes, such as rapidly changing environments, whose disturbances might even destabilize information that already accumulated via the predictors. So, the stability of the predictions determines the nature of the predictors, precisely because they are subject to selection.

Based on the most general conceptualization of Fisher information in the context of Price's equation, we can interpret evolution as a process which follows the principle of Extremum Physical Information as proposed by Frieden (2004). In this approach, we think of the environment as a source of information J with which a process interacts that generates information I via measurements. Then, evolution implies an extremum principle for the difference $I - J$. This is expressed formally as the accumulation of Fisher information. It is essential that in this view the two processes are entangled in the sense that the regularities which embody the information in J are only accessible and therefore come into existence via the interaction with the observational process. This corresponds to the ontological approach to the physics of information outlined in Chapter Two. So, the question is how the approach to evolution outlined so far connects with the more fundamental entropic framework.

In biology, one way to illustrate this is to consider the species abundance distribution, SAD (Pueyo et al. 2007; McGill 2010; Frank 2011a). The SAD is the distribution of species in a sample of species taken from a certain geographical area. Against the backdrop of the previous analysis, we can see species as sets of traits which manifest certain frequency distributions, and which represent processes of information extraction relative to the environment. These distributions show certain properties empirically, such as log-normal distributions, power laws, and, on a most general level, gamma distributions. Considering the most general properties of the interaction between environment and differential population growth, such as certain constraints regarding the average number of entities relative to carrying capacity, and of the mechanism of growth, it is possible to show that these distributions can be reduced to a MaxEnt formalism, with the aforementioned prior information. In other words, the empirical statistical patterns can be interpreted as the result of a statistical process by which the information that is retrievable from the environment is embodied in a state of the populations which maximizes entropy in terms of the distribution of species and variants. In addition, Frank (2011a) argues that the generality of the gamma distribution, which combines logarithmic scaling with small magnitudes and linear scaling with large magnitudes, reflects the nature of the growth process in ecological settings: Then, we can interpret the standard logistic growth pattern as one where with low population densities, relative to carrying capacity, there is much more scope for stochastic variations that induce growth of information (hence the logarithmic scale typical for power law dynamics), whereas when abundance approaches carrying capacity, information growth scales linearly, manifesting the approximation to a state where the information extraction is complete, unless new perturbations of the environment happen.

So, we can argue that for living systems, it is essential to take into consideration the function of idiosyncratic variation on the different levels (individuals of species, species in an ecosystem) for firstly, the generation of information, and secondly, for achieving stability in terms of the average trait distribution across species, which in turn reflects the gain of information that results from the diffusion of species, in the sense of the observed frequency distributions (Pueyo et al. 2007). Therefore, we can give a physical meaning to the fact that those statistical distributions that we observe in nature can be deduced from the MaxEnt framework, considering certain most general constraints on the underlying random processes (for the formal argument, see Frank and Smith 2010, 2011; Frank 2009b; compare Grönholm and Annila 2007).

Figure 3.3 Triadic view on evolution and information

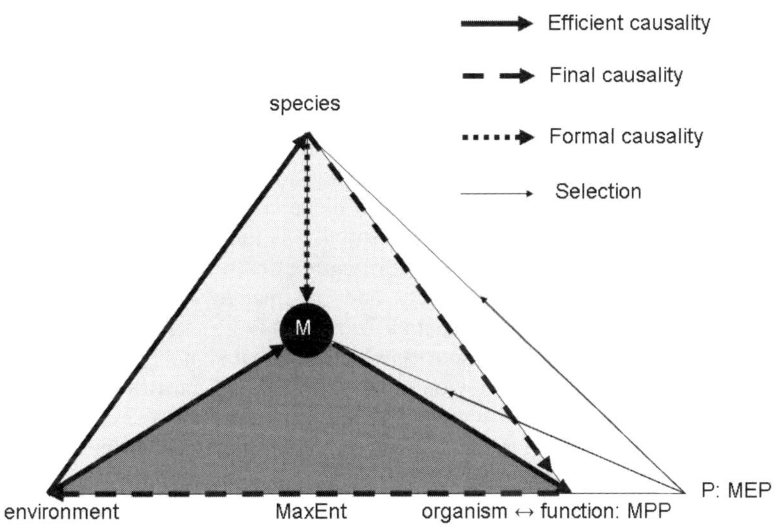

Note: In the triadic framework, the concept of 'species' relates with the semiotic dimension of functions which emerge via forces of selection that operate on evolving populations of living systems qua PIDs. Populations accumulate information that is embodied in their functions which most generically manifest the Maximum Power Principle. Functions involve the formal–causal categorizations of efficient–causal mechanisms on which the signs supervene; in biology, signs correspond to the morphology of organisms that embody the functions. Evolution ultimately manifests the MEP principle via two entangled processes. One is the realization of MPP via the functions, the other is the MaxEnt principle that is manifest in the maximum variety and number of individuals in evolving populations (literally, the 'waste' of evolution). Thus, evolution accumulates information while expanding information capacity.

We can put the previous analysis into the generic triadic framework (figure 3.3). Here, we give a special interpretation to the notion of the 'average' in the statistical approach. The average is the 'species' in biology, which corresponds to a sign in the semiotic analysis. The interpretant is the organism, which embodies the biological function in populations of individuals. This actualization of the biological function is mediated via a set of efficient–causal mechanisms *M*. This analysis provides an important insight about the status of the species concept, which has been the object of substantial controversies over two centuries (Mayr 1982; Gould 2002; Ereshevsky 2010). On the one hand, species are considered as mere conceptual categories in the taxonomy of biological individuals, hence literally a mere 'sign' in biological conventions of taxonomy. This is a nominalist approach to species and underlies the population approach that was inaugurated by Darwin who criticized the essentialist species concept of previous taxonomists. However, until today the idea is also proposed that species 'exist', in the sense of higher level individuals (for example Ghiselin 1997). This corresponds to realism with regard to species.

We can resolve this controversy in clarifying that species are signs in the triadic causal framework, and hence exist as observer relative facts. Species characteristics mediate information about the environment in the sense of a set of traits that represent regularities relative to a species specific niche. In this sense, the two notions of species and niche are conjoined: The organism cannot process all the information potentially available in the environment, so that it filters out a set of relevant information that represents regularities in the mediation between environment and organismic functions (the *OMR* chain of efficient causality) (Kull et al. 2009 speak of a 'semiotic niche'). For example, a mouse might react to certain patterns that signal the presence of a snake in species–specific behavioural patterns. So, regularities in behaviour, that is the responses, relate with regularities in perceiving the environment, which constitutes the sign/niche relation. The signs qua species–specific regularities formally–cause the internal selection of behavioural mechanisms *M*; thus, they overlay the individual responses with a classification system. This opens up the possibility of misrepresentation, as well as of behavioural novelty. For example, there might be a new sort of snake migrating into the environment of a certain rodent species. Some individuals misrepresent the snake as a lizard, and do not flee. Others properly classify the snake. However, both behaviours are actually failures in applying the past behaviour inductively, because even in the second case the new snake was taken as a 'familiar' snake, which is also not true. Yet, surviving individuals will realize their functions more successfully, which enables reproduction, and thus the incremental inclusion of the new behaviour into the species level set of regularities. This is the process of evolutionary inference, which builds on the final causality resulting from the forces of selection.

Then, we can properly assign the role of the different entropic principles. Relative to the species, the individual organisms in the population are PIDs which manifest MaxEnt states in tending towards a maximum variety of *OMR* mechanisms across different PIDs in the population that connect with certain functionings. This variety forms the basis of selection, which results into MPP, which means that the organismic functions relative to the environment tend towards the maximization of power throughput. This is in turn causes the manifestation of the more fundamental principle of MEP. In terms of the Extreme Physical Information concept it can be shown, for example (Frieden and Gatenby 2011), that the evolutionary transition from prokaryotes to eukaryotes distinguishes states with low energetic throughputs and low information from states with accumulating information, high energetic throughputs and corresponding rates of entropy generation in the environment. So, we can analyse biological evolution in terms of physiosemiosis, such that a core concept of Darwinian Theory, the species in terms of population thinking, can be interpreted in terms of the triadic model. This conjunction of causal modes is also necessary for understanding evolution in time.

3.3. Hierarchies and the many dimensions of evolution

3.3.1. Synchrony and diachrony in evolution

Charles Darwin's central concern was to explain the tree of life and to understand the bewildering diversity of life on Earth. These two perspectives reflect two different notions of hierarchy in evolutionary theory (figure 3.4). One is the diachronic hierarchy, which is manifest in the tree of life, namely the unbroken succession of parent and descendant populations, ultimately leading back to the LUCA. The other is the synchronic hierarchy, namely the functional networks in ecosystems, which also displays hierarchical structures as already analysed in Chapter Two, that is structures of control information, such as embodied in large predators. The synchronic hierarchy is mainly analysed in terms of the distribution of species and individuals in space, whereas the diachronic hierarchy focuses on the temporal dimension. In the classical theory of speciation, both dimensions interact: This is one solution to the problem of gradualism versus qualitative change in evolution: How can genuine novelties emerge from mere gradual change of what exists already? The diachronic hierarchy represents gradual change, so that it is difficult to explain how strong separations between species can emerge and the junctures of the tree of life. One way is spatial isolation, which introduces the possibility of gradually accumulating divergences of traits, ending up in reproductive isolation even in the case of a subsequent spatial merger.

In the synchronic hierarchy of embedded functions, individual characteristics do not matter in essence, as the variations cancel out in the synchronic snapshot. What remains, are the species level regularities in the interaction between different organisms. Individual differences cannot be seen in the light of their evolutionary potential, which only realizes through time (on this fundamental point, see Dennett 1995: 282ff). However, we cannot understand the role of the species level regularities unless we can give an evolutionary explanation, which would imply the reconstruction of the diachronic hierarchy (which was the essential step taken by Darwin). This is important to understand that current functioning is not necessarily optimal in any sense. In fact, if the environment undergoes rapid changes, current functioning may even fail, which implies that one cannot interpret synchronic observations by referring to present adaptation, but only to past sequences of adaptations. This difference cannot be simply reduced to differences in speeds, because the emergence of novelties is involved. We need to think in terms of two hierarchies of evolution beyond the dimension of time.

Figure 3.4 Hierarchies in evolution

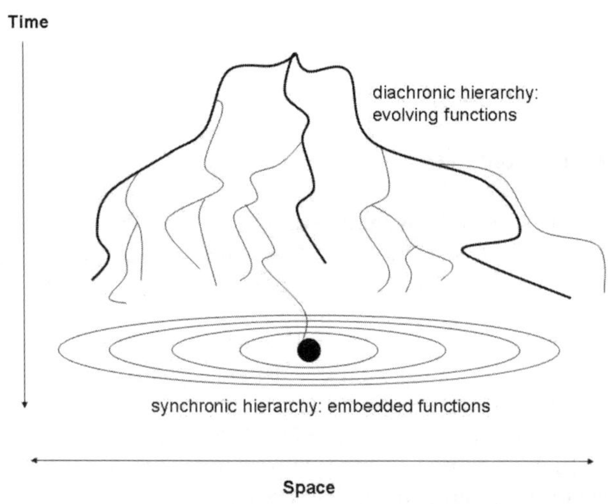

Note: We consider two hierarchies in evolution. In the synchronic hierarchy, we analyse functional interdependencies of organisms at a certain point of time; this is the approach of ecology. These interdependencies typically manifest spatial patterns, such as the distribution of species in a particular habitat. So, for example, we would consider the function of a large predator in an ecosystem; the predator realizes certain functions in terms of adaptation, but also is a part of the ecosystem function in embodying higher–level control information, which results into increased ecosystem productivity. In the diachronic hierarchy, we look at the relations of descendence between evolving function through time. So, we would explain current functions of the predator by referring to past sequences of selection events that shaped these functions, and relate this back to causally connected ancestral states.

Hence, we see that the two notions of hierarchy actually reflect two different kinds of conceptual hierarchies, the subsumptive and the compositional hierarchy which we have already introduced in Chapter Two section 2.5 (following Salthe 1985). Therefore, the interaction between the two hierarchies can be analysed in the triadic framework (figure 3.5). In the compositional hierarchy, we focus on the mutual interaction between functions in terms of the efficient causality driving the MPP and the MEP. So, for example, we analyse food chains in ecosystems which determine their total biomass production and energy dissipation. However, these mechanisms are seen in the light of the regularities which are displayed between individuals. Thus, the compositional hierarchy is one of classes of mechanisms, such as predator–prey interactions on the species level. Since we cannot reasonably measure all individual interactions in an ecosystem, we construct the compositional hierarchy on the basis of behavioural and performance averages over the individuals of different species. This is reflected in the possibility to reduce SAD patterns to the Maximum Entropy distributions, as we have seen previously: The species distribution reflects all functional interactions across an ecosystem that result in its aggregate patterns of energetic distribution, with individual variance obtaining the maximum, thus reflecting the fundamental fact that the delineation of functions via species boundaries captures all the information embodied in the functions.

This approach is warranted because the functionings themselves are guided by the emergent regularities on the species level. This connects the compositional hierarchy with the subsumptive hierarchy. In the subsumptive hierarchy, we focus on the relationships between different levels of signs representing regularities of mechanisms. For example, there are shared properties of vertebrates, and all vertebrates are subsumed under these regularities. Thus, the subsumptive hierarchy reflects the phylogenetic relationships between individuals. It is essential to realize that this implies that individual variance happens on different levels here, namely variance between individuals and higher level groups of individuals, such as genera and taxa. As a consequence, the two hierarchies actually differ in a more fundamental way (compare Ereshefsky 2010): In the compositional hierarchy, two species with convergent functionings can play a similar role in the causal connectivity of ecosystem flows, without being genealogically related: The relationship between the different regularities is one between a member and a class in a sequence of embedded sets. In the subsumptive hierarchy, we deal with a part and whole relationship, because the members of a genealogically connected species are defined via their interaction with other members of the species, which therefore makes up the interactive whole, the lineage. Lineages find synchronic expressions in specific behaviours, such as related to reproduction, which results into constraints on interbreeding.

Figure 3.5 Subsumptive and compositional hierarchies

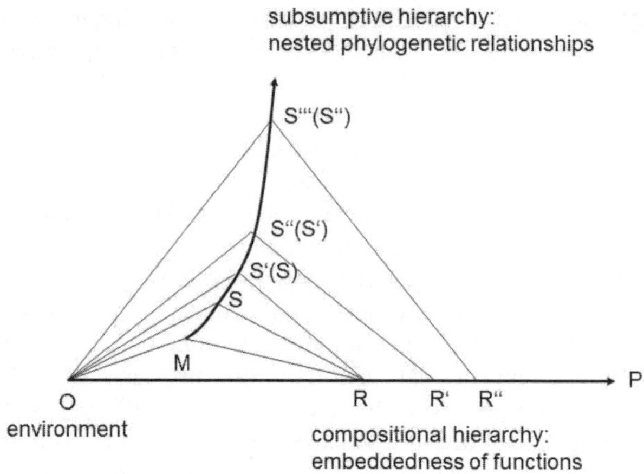

Note: Diachronic and synchronic hierarchy reflect the triadic distinction between compositional and subsumptive hierarchy. The compositional hierarchy refers to the embeddedness of functions, hence regularities relative to a purpose, that is forces of selection. The subsumptive hierarchy refers to the emergence of signs related to particular functions in the compositional hierarchy. The relationship between the two hierarchies reflects the role of signs in inferring the information that is physically embodied in the functions. Thus, the compositional hierarchy embodies the regularities of embedded functions in living systems (organisms, ecosystems etc.), and the subsumptive hierarchy reflects their phylogenetic relatedness.

3.3.2. The different ways of biology

In this analysis, one cannot simply state that current populations are adapted to the current environment, and therefore, that they were adapted to any of the earlier environments, having been the then current environments at that time. The deeper reason for this does not lie primarily in the possibility of misrepresentation and therefore maladaptation because of asynchrony, but in the fact that the environment is just the totality of all species specific niches. The niches of single species include all other species, so that we can speak of species–niche coevolution. An example for a biological theory which covers this argument is the approach on 'niche–constructing phenotypes' put forward by Odling-Smee (1988) and Odling-Smee et al. (2003).

Odling-Smee argues that there are two channels of evolution, one the genetic and one working via the 'bequeath' of better environments for anticipated genes. This means that organisms adapt the environment to their needs, and not the other way round, and that selection actually operates on these niche–constructing strategies which compete against each other, continuously transforming the environment. Following a proposal by Lewontin, this means that the fundamental evolutionary processes are coupled:

$$\frac{dO}{dt} = f(O, E)$$

$$\frac{dE}{dt} = g(O, E)$$

with O denoting the organism and E the environment. Clearly, the change in the environment does not follow the mechanisms of genetic evolution. Odling-Smee (1988) calls the corresponding co-evolutionary unit 'environ'. Therefore, he proposes to expand the equations in the way that the g–function refers to the environment E_i that is specific to an organism O_i, and adds a h-function that describes the structural features of the relationship:

$$\frac{d(O_i E_i)}{dt} = h(O_i, E)$$

From this analysis, we reach the fundamental conclusion that we cannot separate the two hierarchies which are actually conjoined into one triadic ontology. Then, the tension between the phylogenetic notion of species and the adaptationist notion evaporates because we relate the species/niche distinction to different positions of observers. We can analyse this in terms of the bimodal approach to ontology as in table 3.1. Here, we see that different areas of biology actually refer to different aspects of the same unified evolutionary process. Ecology is the study of networks and flows of matterenergy in populations of living systems, thus adopts the matterenergy mode with observer independent measurement criteria, such as biomass. In contrast, functional biology analyses the interaction between different organismic functions, which requires identifying observer relative relationships, in the sense of the goal structure of the functions; to re-emphasize, with 'observers' referring to evolutionary processes, and 'observers' in terms of the scientists, for example, as aiming at reconstructions of these processes, hence searching for functional explanations, such as explanations in terms of adaptation. Clearly, we can ask the same for the ecosystem, if we enquire for the mutual interdependence of selection processes that result in a certain pattern such as of mutualism.

Table 3.1 Bimodality of evolution

	Observer independent	**Observer relative**
Matterenergy mode	Energy dispersal (ecology)	Coordinative functions (functional biology)
Semiotic mode	Constitutive processes (population genetics)	Interpretants/functions (taxonomy/phylogeny)

In the semiotic mode, we focus on the information process that is aspectually embodied in the matterenergy flows. One important example is population genetics which investigates evolving frequencies of genes and genotypes, relative to traits. These are constitutive processes in the context of ontogeny, and therefore relate to observer independent aspects, such as the efficient causality between a certain genotype and the phenotype. Although population genetics can serve to identify genealogical relationships between different individuals and populations, there is one fundamental problem which relates to the demarcation of a population. Demarcations can only be identified in an observer relative way, either via criteria of the external observer, or via the criteria of the participant observers, such as members of the population interacting with others in reproductive activities. Therefore, taxonomy in terms of delineating species and taxa is only possible in terms of identifying observer relative facts (compare Riedl 1983).

Against the background of this analysis, it is misleading to oppose these different approaches to living systems. This is most evident from considering fundamental paradoxes that emerge from a single–aspectual approach. So, for example, considering heredity, the only reliable criterion of identifying heredity is to refer to non–functional items for which one cannot assume that there are other forces that lead towards the adoption of this trait. However, this would imply that the establishment of evolutionary lineages would not relate with the continuity of the information transmission path, that is the core feature of evolution, but only with the random part, in the sense of genuine individuality. A similar paradox applies for the demarcation of populations, which are strictly defined as randomly interbreeding sets of individuals in standard Population Genetics. This definition is tautological, unless an external criterion of demarcation is introduced. So, we realize that one essential aspect of evolution is the emergence of observer relative mechanisms that identify boundaries between populations. Therefore, as we have seen, the species concept appears to be problematic as long as it is only considered in the single–aspectual mode.

3.3.3. Levels of selection, group selection and semiosis

The triadic approach resolves one of the most complicated conceptual issues in biology of the past decades, namely the issue of group selection, which I approach as a problem of levels of selection, involving the emergence of semiotic processes. This is because I can approach the group selection issue as one expression of the more fundamental distinction between integration and isolation in evolution, or, the question of the relationship between units and levels of evolution (Bonner 1988). This issue relates with the general problem in evolutionary theory how to define the distinctions between the levels at which the different processes of variation, selection, adaptation and evolution proceed. One of the major innovations in evolutionary theory of the past decades was the widespread acceptance of kin selection theory which introduced the distinction between the unit of selection, the individual, and the unit of adaptation, which follows inclusive fitness maximization of genetically related individuals (Gardner and Grafen 2008). This literature directly relates with the question of how composite individuals emerge in evolution (Maynard Smith and Szathmáry 1995).

In this view, there is no fundamental distinction between groups and organisms, and between intra–organismic information processing and population–level information processing. In the original version of this debate, it centred on the question whether individual behaviour can be altruistic with reference to the species as a group (for example Trivers 1985). This discussion results from the one-sided emphasis of on different modes of the evolutionary process. Once we consider the independent ontological role of signs, and realize that all causal interactions are also mediated semiotically, we can understand the role of the species vs. population distinction. The species distinction can only be analysed in terms of observer relativity, whereas the population distinction (as commonly established in Population Genetics) is only based on direct reproductive interactions, which follow efficient causality (for instance the standard definition of randomly interbreeding populations, see Hartl 2000), and hence seem to relate with observer independent facts (such as realized copulations). However, at a closer look those observer independent facts can only come into existence as semiotically intermediated facts.

This is evident when considering the establishment of population boundaries, which is a specific expression of a group boundary. All population boundaries are ultimately established semiotically, in the sense that signs indicate the existence of con-specifics, potential reproductive partners or predators on that species, for example. There are efficient–causal mechanisms that make reproduction between different species impossible, but mostly behavioural and other forms of signalling suffice to establish group markers and the respective group boundaries. Therefore, the evolution of group markers is ontologically autonomous from the evolution of mechanisms in a principled way, although it cannot decouple entirely from those mechanisms, because selection only operates on the triadic conjunction of the causal modes. Taken together, this means that the population and the species perspective are just two parts of the triadic conjunction of different causal modes in determining group boundaries. Efficient–causal interactions such as copulations are essentially related with formal–causal categorizations of those mechanisms, which are observable in signalling behaviour, for example. This leads to the important conclusion that the species concept as a semiotic concept can relate to two different kinds of observers, namely the members of a population or the scientific observer who extracts the species categorization from observations about events in the population.

Viewed in the synchronic perspective, group markers establish correlated behaviour; viewed in the diachronic perspective, correlated behaviour establishes group markers. In evolutionary game theory, correlated behaviour is a concept that is essential to explain the emergence of cooperative behaviour (for example Bergstrom 2002; Skyrms 2004). There is a class of behaviours which manifests the principled problem of cooperation. Firstly, there is a cooperative solution which contributes to the interests of all actors, and could therefore be sustainable even if actors do not act altruistically, but that secondly, can be undermined by self-interested actions because there are action options in which the short-term benefit for singular actors is even larger. The emergence of correlated behaviour ultimately means that the range of strategies becomes more constrained or that the pay–off structure is changed, such that the incentives for deviation become less strong (for example, the prisoners' dilemma would be transformed into a stag hunt game, as discussed by Skyrms 2004; there is also the general case of coordination problems, see Robson and Samuelson 2010).

The classical example for this situation is the prisoners' dilemma, which can be used to describe commons problems. The tragedy of the commons especially in a multi–generation setting, results from the fact that short-term gains are only outweighed by group level advantages in the longer run. Whereas in the prisoners' dilemma this conflict is mirrored in the impossibility to reach a rational agreement about the cooperative solution that is maintained endogenously by the actions of the self–interested actors, in the evolutionary context the time dimension is essential: That means, the self–interested actions lead to short-term gains in the reproduction of behaviours, which therefore spreads in population, but is counterproductive in the longer run, even from the perspective of self–interest. This difference of time horizons translates into differences across populations that would adopt different behavioural patterns: In this case, the collective rationality of the PD Nash equilibrium converges with the individually optimal solution because what counts is the diffusion of behaviour across different populations, such that the individually embodied collectively rational solution would lead to higher fitness of individuals belonging to that population. This result is well-known from cellular automata PD models of randomly interacting neighbourhoods of individuals, in which cooperation can diffuse beyond cooperating neighbourhoods (Hegselmann 1996). In this case, a particular spatial pattern of repeated interaction can suffice to maintain cooperative equilibria.

Now, the interesting point is how spatial patterns interact with signalling. All signalling creates the additional problem of how to distinguish between cooperators and non–cooperators, or cheaters and non–cheaters, if the signals themselves can be open to cheating. This is a problem in the semiotic domain: The question is how the different types of actors can be distinguished in a population. Cooperative equilibria can be sustainable if actors can reliably distinguish between cooperators and non–cooperators, which presupposes signalling devices which are cooperative in turn (for a classical analysis, see Frank 1988). However, these signals are themselves potentially open to cheating. Consider a population that has evolved a reliable signalling mechanism, then it is always possible that a new variant invades this population that is able to fake cooperators' signals.

From this it follows that for cooperation to be maintained, it is essential that two factors play together: firstly, there is a system of signs that correlate behaviour, and secondly, this must be supported by some physical impediments to invasion. In other words, cooperative signalling can emerge from spatially structured interactions, which in turn create the condition for cooperation in the original strategic situation. The most universal phenomenon in this regard is the spatial ordering of groups which simultaneously share signals of group identity. Both mechanisms alone may not lead towards stable cooperation, but if they mutually reinforce each other, cooperation becomes possible. This is warranted if we assume that signalling itself has a spatial structure: So, we actually consider a two–level game, on one level the signals emerge, supported by spatially structured interaction patterns, and on the other level credible signalling supports the cooperative solution. In this argument, there is no need to assume any sort of genetic connectivity between the different individuals, because only the fact of correlated behaviour counts, if it results in group level advantages. For example, there might be species–level advantages of correlated behaviour, or forms of mutualism and symbiotic relationships between different species. Independent from the biological nature of the relationships, the semiotic emergence of behavioural correlation is crucial.

It is important to emphasize that in this argument there is no assumption of altruism, that is, the correlated behaviour is advantageous to all individual actors, once it diffuses on the population level. We have already met with the most universal structure of this kind, the autocatalytic cycle, which can be analysed in terms of positive externalities across different actors in the evolutionary process. These positive externalities constitute a 'commons'. Consider, for example, a population of bacteria with different strains, that is groups, in an environment rich of nutrients (Ben Jacob et al. 2006). There are two forces that determine reproductive success of such a group of individual bacteria. One is that there is competition within the group in which individual bacteria can achieve larger reproductive success than other members of the population. But populations of bacteria also rely on certain positive externalities within the group, the most important of which is the coordination of behaviour via signals that indicate nutrient gradients in the environment. As a result, there is another factor that determines reproductive success, namely information processing on the group level, which is reflected in the quantity of descendants that the group can fission off; on this level, the different strains of bacteria compete against each other.

We can generalize this observation into one fundamental impossibility theorem in the theory of evolution: It is impossible to define a criterion for individual advantage in evolution that is exclusively related to one level of evolution, because at least the most general criterion of individual advantage, which means evolvability in response to environmental changes, is a population–level property (compare Gould 2002: 656ff, 1282ff). In simple terms, if we consider individual advantage from the perspective of a single gene, the 'selfish' perspective of that gene would need to include the dimension of being capable to change, if selective forces change. Yet, this capability is not a property on that level, but on the population level. Viewed from the perspective of the lower level, the higher level property is a 'commons', to which the lower level contributes. One of the most hotly debated issues in biology with regard to this problem is the evolution of sex, which implies high individual costs to females, which lose one half of their genetic representation in the descendant population. One explanation is the gain in evolvability on the population level, for example, in the interaction with parasites that have a much faster reproduction cycle, hence pattern of evolvability. Sex is even more complicated, because females who produce females contribute to a public good, as the production of males would increase their competitive advantage relative to other females (males can fertilize many females within in a given period). Yet, the total number of offspring is limited by the number of females, such that, again, evolvability requires a sex ratio that resolves this commons problem with regard to the group of females (Frank 2009c). Interestingly, the most productive approach in terms of population growth in commercial livestock breeding is to limit the number of males, which implies the suppression of competitive behaviour by the females.

3.3.4. Price's equation approach to group selection

From the previous impossibility theorem we can conclude that the fundamental analytical distinction in the theory of group selection is not between individual selection and group selection, but between within–group selection and between–group selection. The notion of 'group' is a most general and abstract term which relates to the distinction between two arbitrarily defined, though related levels of evolution, or, the trade–off between integration and isolation, demarcated by a boundary.

This approach can be covered by the recursive structure of the Price's equation (Frank 1995a).

$$\overline{w}\Delta\overline{z} = Cov(w_i, z_i) + E_i\{Cov_j(w_{j \cdot i}, z_{j \cdot i}) + E_j(w_{j \cdot i}\Delta z_{j \cdot i})\}$$

Here, w stands for fitness as defined in section 3.2.1, and z refers to traits that determine fitness. This is the so-called 'expansion' of Price's equation. It builds on the fact that in the original equation, the expectation term is structurally similar to the left-hand term, which means that we can recursively insert Price's equation into itself. In the expanded equation the subscripts $j \cdot i$ refer to sub-partitions of type i into subtypes j. There are no constraints on the partitions, so that there are two possibilities. Firstly, we could imagine pushing the expansion until the expectation term approaches zero. That is, by a proper definition of partitions of types we could explain evolution entirely by means of the selection effect. Secondly, and more important, the partition amounts to the analysis of hierarchical selection. In the equation this means that the w_i and z_i are averages of the type i groups, and the $w_{j.i}$ and $z_{j.i}$ are the averages of the subgroups. Another way to express the expanded equation makes this recursive structure even more visible:

$$\overline{w}\Delta\overline{z} = Cov(w_i, z_i) + E\{Cov(w_{j \cdot i}, z_{j \cdot i})\} + E\{E(w_{j \cdot i}\Delta z_{j \cdot i})\}$$

Then, following the Fisher theorem, we can assume that there is no innovation effect, so that the evolution of the population average characteristics would only depend on the balance of the between–group and the within–group selection effect. Clearly, the dominance of group characteristics over sub-group characteristics will depend on the relative strength of the different selection forces. In particular, if:

$$Cov(w_i, z_i) > -E\{Cov(w_{j \cdot i}, z_{j \cdot i})\}$$

the group characteristics will outweigh the within–group characteristics. This relation is of particular importance to analysing group selection.

It is important to realize the implications of this step: Considering two levels of selection, there are evolutionary processes that take place between groups, and follow the logic of natural selection, and there are evolutionary processes within groups. In this view, group selection is more fundamental, in the sense that within–group selection firstly appears to result in a pure transmission effect. Only in the next step we decompose this level of evolution into processes that follow natural selection. Therefore, we overturn the standard perspective on group selection, which firstly looks at the sub-group level selection and then asks whether there are positive contributions on the group level. The central significance of this view is evident if we consider that individual organisms can also be interpreted as groups of cells which potentially compete against each other. In other words, the group notion is the more general and fundamental one than the notion of the individual organism (ontologically, of course, groups are to be regarded as individuals themselves).

This conclusion is based on the simple statistics of the so-called 'averaging fallacy' or 'Simpson paradox' that is put into the centre of the analysis of Price's equation in Sober and Wilson (1998: 23ff) (for a survey on the Simpson paradox, see Malinas and Bigelow, 2012). The Simpson paradox refers to the difference between averages of sub-groups and averages of groups: If there is a group–level effect of individual behaviour these averages can move into the opposite direction. For example, if for the case of an isolated population a particular behaviour would lead to an individual disadvantage in within–group competition, the positive effect on the group level would not matter. But if the group competes with other groups in a larger group, thus would be a sub-group, such that there would be a distinction between the sub-group and the group–level average for this behaviour, there is the possibility that a decreasing sub-group level average will correspond to an increasing group–level average, because the sub-group will grow stronger relative to other sub-groups. However, the crucial condition for this to occur is that no random mixing of sub-groups is possible.

Frank (2009c, 2011b: 228ff) offers a simplified formalization of this core point of the theory of evolution, which I summarize here (for the detailed argument, refer to Frank 2011b). Corresponding to the Fisher duality between natural selection and environmental forces, one can most generally distinguish between evolutionary change caused by changes of forces of selection and by forces of transmission, which work against each other. Then, Price's equation boils down to:

$$\overline{w}\Delta\overline{z} = \Delta S + \Delta\tau$$

with ΔS referring to fitness changes caused by selection and $\Delta\tau$ changes caused autonomous forces of transmission. In equilibrium (that is total change amounting to zero) $\Delta S = -\Delta\tau$ holds. Generally, following Fisher's fundamental theorem, one can analyse the forces of selection in terms of the selective intensity of a character z, s_z, and its variance V_z (selective intensity is the absolute amount of the regression coefficient of w on z, hence the breeding value):

$$\Delta S = s_z V_z$$

Then, considering the partition of Price's equation, we can rewrite the balance between transmission and selection in the following way, if we distinguish between selection among groups S_b and selection within groups S_w, which substitutes for τ:

$$s_b V_b = -s_w V_w$$

As total variance V_t of the group is the sum of both between– and within–group variance, we can write:

$$s_b V_b = -s_w (V_t - V_a)$$

We can then define the correlation coefficient $r = V_a / V_t$, divide by V_t and end up with:

$$s_b r = -s_w (1 - r)$$

The advantage of this formulation, compared to the full decomposition of the Price's equation, is the identification of the crucial relationship r, which shows the relative weightings of within–group and between–group selection. We can relate this with a simple analysis of the relationship between competitive behaviour and group performance. We consider the trait z as describing the intensity of competitive behaviour of an individual towards other members of the group, which results into a certain appropriation of group–level performance. So, this relative share would reflect the relationship between individual competitiveness and average competitiveness in the group $z/\bar{z}_g$, which determines the fitness w. Now, if group performance is negatively affected by the level of individual competitiveness, we can simply assume that this is $1 - \bar{z}_g$. Then, we can write fitness as:

$$w = \frac{z}{z_g}(1 - z_g)$$

Now, these reasonable assumptions about the relationship between individual competitiveness, group performance and fitness imply that selective intensity s_b is -1, and selective intensity s_w is $(1 - z_g) / z_g$. Then, we can write the equation for the balance between within–group and between–group selection as:

$$-r = -\frac{1 - z_g}{z_g}(1 - r)$$

which allows to calculate the ESS z^* which ends up with the simple expression:

$$z^* = 1 - r$$

Therefore, we realize that the balance between competitive and cooperative behaviour is directly determined by the co-variances between the different levels. If this co-variance is low, individual competitiveness will achieve a higher equilibrium value, if it is high, group orientation will prevail.

It is of the utmost importance to see that this correlation can have two different reasons. One reason has been emphasized in the earlier literature on group selection, namely shared interests between members of sub-groups and groups. In biology, shared interests were defined as interests of genes, such that cooperation would only be explained in terms of kin selection: In fact, agency in terms of behaviour would be determined by the structure of gene clusters dispersed across different individuals, which determine the level of relatedness. However, as we have seen, the same effect can be explained in terms of behavioural correlation within a group. In the most simple terms, behavioural correlation would mean strategic convergence in competitiveness, such that within–group selective intensity decreases. This would result in cooperative behaviour.

For this reason, in considering the relationship between individuals and groups in evolution, we always have to distinguish neatly between two different causes of co-variances between the levels. One is causation that starts out from the mechanisms that relate individual behavioural variation with certain functions relative to an environment. The other is the semiotic channel which classifies individual behavioural variations into certain classes of behaviour which manifest different degrees of similarity between members of a group. This reflects the essential role of externalities between individual behaviour in interactions with other individuals. As it was emphasized previously, these externalities do not necessarily relate with particular mechanisms of establishing relatedness. Yet, we can also say that the semiotic channel presupposes some mechanisms that enable the individuals to display this kind of behaviour (for a related analysis of human 'groupishness', see Van Veelen and Hopfensitz 2007). If these mechanisms are genetically grounded, this implies that ultimately the consequences of the behaviour need to converge with the inclusive fitness of these genes, because they would otherwise erode via random drift. From this follows an argument that I will explore in more detail in the next section, namely that shared interests operate as a constraint on the unfolding of all other possible mechanisms, but do not necessarily directly determine group–level phenomena.

3.3.5. Triadic analysis of groups

In the triadic view (figure 3.6) we can approach these issues in the way that we treat the relationship between individual and environment as being mediated via the group. Functions that establish the niche relate with populations of individuals which manifest large variety of individual traits. These connect via mechanisms with the functions. However, there are many functions which involve interdependencies between the individuals of a population. These functions are mediated via group level semiosis, especially in terms of establishing boundaries between populations.

In this view, it becomes clear that the group relative to the individual is central to the process of inference in evolution. Group–level correlation of behaviour is tantamount to the evolution of constraints, hence physical embodiments of information. Then, evidently it does not make sense to search for a physical embodiment of this information on the genetic level: The genetic level reflects this information, as it co-evolves with the constraints, but only in the sense that it is subject to the same evolutionary forces, including those ones that emerge on the group–level as constraints on behaviour. This specific pattern of causation is the Baldwin effect that I scrutinize in more detail in the final section: In other words, genetic relatedness is the result of group selection, but not its ultimate cause.

Figure 3.6 Groups and individuals in the triadic view

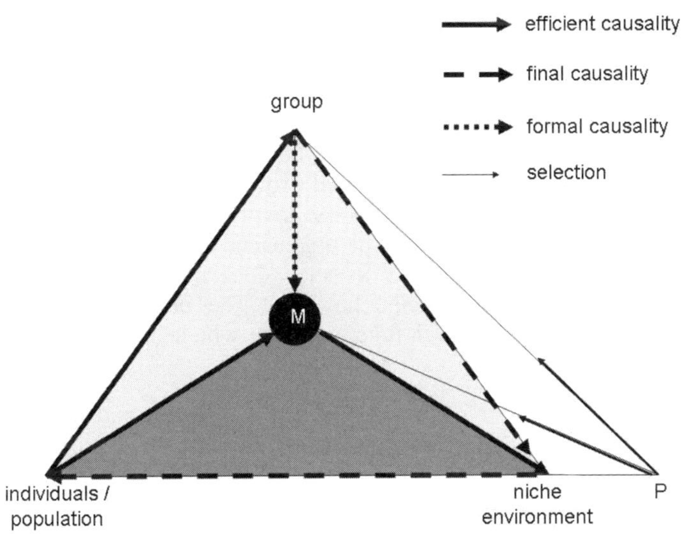

Note: In the triadic view, the group is a semiotic structure that mediates between individuals as members of a population and their niche as embodiment of functions relative to the environment. This structure categorizes certain mechanisms that result in adaptation by determining population boundaries via the generation of correlated behaviour. As all individuals of a population also form a part of the environment of all other individuals, there is a feedback mechanism between the formation of the niche by correlated behaviours and physical embodiments of information on the individual level. Thus, genetic relatedness can emerge from semiotically mediated population boundaries.

Group selection is a notion that directly reflects the role of constraints in the accumulation of information, with the constraints themselves forming complex hierarchies as analysed in terms of the distinction between subsumptive and compositional hierarchies. Then, it follows that the distinction between 'individuals' and 'groups' is meaningless. Indeed, there is the possibility of the evolutionary transition from groups to individuals in the case that the semiotic mechanisms of group–level correlated behaviour obtain a central role in group–level information processing such that the original individual actors evolve into physical structures which become complementary to each other in functional terms, including complex hierarchical control information. These transformations are major transitions in evolution, such as the transition from the single–cellular to the multi–cellular organism. In other words, all higher–level individuals can be analysed in terms of lower–level groups which maintain strongly cooperative strategies. So, for example, a human organism is a group of lower–level functional units, most basically a group of functionally specialized cells.

This is a basic insight that we will pursue further in Chapter Four: Individuals are composite entities which can be analysed in group terms. The suppression on competitive behaviour on the level of the individual constituents of these group–individuals can collapse: This is cancer (Gould 2002: 695ff). 'Cancer' is the covering name for a large number of organismic dysfunctions on the level of cells where the suppressed competitive behaviour is set free; hence unregulated growth of tissue happens. Frieden and Gatenby (2011) show how cancer involves the rapid decay of the information which is embodied in the organismic structures. One cannot say that the genome of cancer cells as such does not 'store' more or less information than the other cells, however. The decay results from the destruction of the group–level functions into which different cells of the organism are integrated.

3.4. THE CAUSAL STRUCTURE OF EVOLUTION

3.4.1. The standard model of evolutionary causation

In the previous analysis, important aspects of the causal mechanisms of evolution have not yet been sufficiently detailed. This causal structure has been most generally analysed in the paradigm of 'Darwinism'. There is a very complex and substantial debate over the meaning of Darwinism in modern biology, in which questions such as the role of group selection have played an important role. The following elements of Darwin's theory can be regarded to be essential, in my view:

- *The VSR principle*, that is variation, selection and retention: It states that evolutionary processes are dissected phenomenologically into three theoretical stages, namely variation (however generated), selection of variations relative to an environment which is the cause of those selective forces, and retention, that is mechanisms that maintain certain results of selection against forces of entropic degradation. We have already scrutinized the notion of selection in the previous section. I add the important observation that variation is 'blind' in the sense that variation is mostly independent from its future consequences. So, for example, intentional action under fundamental ignorance about future consequences is as 'blind' as random genetic mutation (compare Campbell 1960). This means, at a closer look, that what counts as 'variation' are varieties without function: Thinking of an evolving state space through time, 'variation' means that the emergence of a new state is not functionally connected with successor states, and that therefore the new state is algorithmically incompressible as it cannot be reduced to a functional regularity.

- *Population thinking*: Darwin himself was sceptical about the species notion, so that existence is only ascribed to populations of individuals, and the existence of higher–level groups is denied (that is refutation of species essentialism). However, insofar as groups obtain properties of individuals, those higher–level individuals exist. These are structural properties of groups such as evolvability or group boundaries established via semiosis. Hence, population thinking combines with the notion of levels of selection, as we have detailed in the previous sections.
- *Heredity*: Evolution results in the establishment of lineages of descent, with heredity being expressed in certain shared regularities and similarities between parent and descendent populations across time. This principle has also been already established in the previous sections.
- *Growth*: Growth is the essential idea that Darwin adopted from Malthus, which implies that forces of selection are necessarily generated endogenously, because exponential growth always drives populations towards the limits of the carrying capacities of their niches. This principle needs to be combined with the Weitzman notion of combinatorial growth that we applied on the state space of evolution in the previous chapter. The most important consequence of growth is the fact that evolution is frequency–dependent in a fundamental way, which I will explore in the next section.
- *Fitness*: The outcomes of selection are described as differential reproductive success in the process of population growth, which is termed 'fitness'. Fitness in this sense is a Malthusian parameter, that is differential growth of different lineages of variants in populations and ecosystems. Thus, fitness captures the statistical aspects of evolution as scrutinized by means of the Price's equation and related theorems. We have already seen that a fundamental conservation principle applies for fitness in this sense, the consequences of which will be explored in the next section. In modern biology, 'fitness' is defined as 'inclusive fitness', which refers to groups which are defined by relatedness resulting from heredity (Leigh Jr. 2009).

- *Adaptation*: Adaptation describes the outcomes of selection in terms of the causal mechanisms that determine fitness. These causal mechanisms include all aspects of behaviour, thus also encompassing extra–somatic phenomena (artefacts, patterns of interactions etc.). If the terms are kept separately, as it should be done (they are often conflated), adaptation is a predictor of fitness. This is one condition which needs to hold in order to render evolutionary theory falsifiable. In a most general sense developed already in Chapter Two, the state of 'adaptation' means that the likeliest state is achieved, given the constraints resulting from selection. This is the basis for evolutionary convergence. Fitness and adaptation relate via the notion that evolution leads towards the optimization of design (Grafen 2007).

It is crucial to see that one of the core elements of modern evolutionary theory, namely genetics, does not show up in this list. Viewed from the history of biology, this is only natural because Darwin had no understanding about genetics. Therefore, it is appropriate to turn back to the roots and re-write the role of genetics in a universal theory of evolution.

The major conceptual progress in this regard was the introduction of the replicator/interactor distinction by Dawkins (1989) and Hull (1988). This distinction relates with the distinction between ontogeny and phylogeny. In most general terms, and on first sight, this is the distinction between information and function: The replicator is the mechanism by which information is maintained and transferred across the different generations, and the interactor is the set of functions that is enacted by this information; clearly, transmission of information is a function in turn, which allows for the self–referential application of the Price's equation, as we have seen previously (such that, for example, genes are also properties of phenotypes).

Hence, replicators are a particular class of functions that relate a source of information with its copy. To count as a replicator, the following conditions must be fulfilled (Aunger 2002: 73; compare Hull and Wilkins 2008):

- The source of the information is causally involved in the production of the copy. Thus, for example, a document that is copied by fax is not a replicator, because the document does not control the fax machine in any way. In contrast, a gene is directly involved in the reproduction of itself.
- The copy must be similar to the source, including the information that is necessary to make the copy similar to the source. So, in copying genes the resultant phenotype is similar to the source and includes the mechanisms that generate this similarity, that is the genes. This is the necessary condition for the emergence of lineages of descent. So, a fake product might be as close to the original as possible, but it does not contain the information of how to achieve this. This condition also implies that replication is not controlled by any source of information

outside the process, as in the case of fake products, where external engineering information is involved.

- The copying process results into at least two copies, including the original. This is the necessary condition for growth and the emergence of evolutionary lineages.

In Dawkin's original approach, replicators are the only entities that count for the analysis of evolutionary change. Replicators are carried by interactors, the vehicles, but they do not unequivocally relate with them: That means, similar replicators may be dispersed across many interactors. Further, replicators create interactors, and selection of replicators operates via the mediation of interactors, namely the functions towards the environment.

Figure 3.7 Standard model of the causal structure of evolution (after Lewontin 2011)

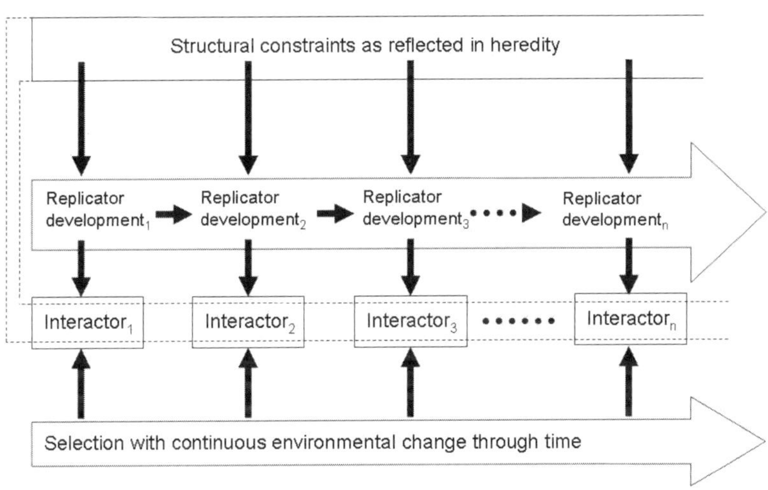

Note: The standard model of the causal structure of evolution conjoins two processes, evolution and development, which are subject to selective forces of the environment, which is changing through time. Evolution proceeds through the succession of states of replicators which cause development. Development results into sets of interactors which manifest the functions that emerge from selection. Replicators are connected causally through time, interactors are causally disconnected. However, even in the standard model there is the possibility that interactors manifest structural constraints on the accessibility of new replicator states. Then, these structural constraints would also operate as a channel of heredity. As interactors are always defined as interfaces to particular environments (the 'niches'), this also implies that environments can be part of evolutionary heredity. Then, the Weismann doctrine would no longer hold that states that information only flows through the replicator line.

We can analyse the resulting formal structure as in figure 3.7 (after Lewontin 2011). In the established Neodarwinian synthesis of Darwinism with population genetics, the so-called 'Weismann doctrine' holds. This means, that there is a neat distinction between the functions that receive the impact of selection and the mechanisms by which information is transmitted. The replicator is the control information of the process of ontogeny by which the interactor is developed, in a succession of interactors. In the original biological context, the interactor is the phenotype. Forces of selection only impact on the interactor, resulting into differential reproduction on the population level. This happens via the transmission of replicators which are carried by the interactors. Therefore, the changing composition of replicators results into changing variance on the interactor level. Interactors never transmit information across generations of replicators (no transmission of acquired traits, which means rejection of 'Lamarckism').

Figure 3.8 The causal interdependence of replicator and interactor

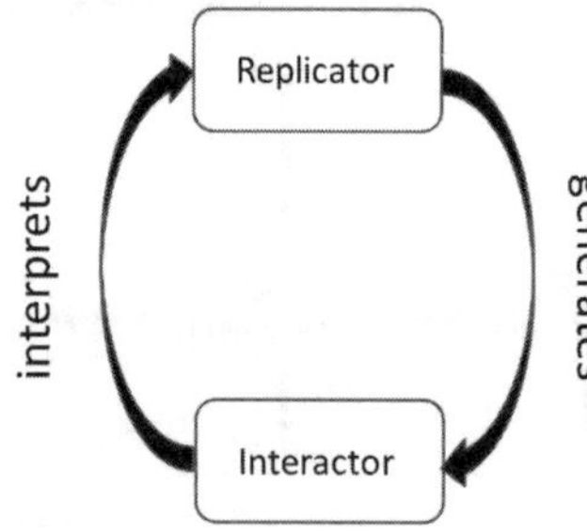

Note: Replicator and interactor are causally enmeshed in a principled way. Replicators generate descendant interactors, but this generation depends on the interpretation of replicators by the current generation interactors. Hence, the information transmitted to the descendant population has to be referred to this complete interpretive process, and not only to the replicator and its material structure.

However, in this standard model there is one central ambiguity which is easily accessible in figure 3.8. Replicators cannot create interactors 'out of thin air': that means, with the possible exception of the origin of life scenario that we touched upon in section 3.1.2, all replicators rely on the interactor of the previous generation in order to create the next-generation interactor: Mothers carry the fertilized egg. Then, we can say that replicators generate interactors, but interactors interpret replicators: In other words, the generative process depends partly on the role of the interactor. This raises the question where biological information is ultimately located.

3.4.2. Triadic analysis of biological information and the replicator

The central problem in the standard account is the use of the term 'information' (Maynard Smith 2000). There is the idea that information is carried over as being embodied in the replicators. This analysis adopts the sender/receiver dualism in Shannon information: The replicator 'sends' information to the next generation where it is decoded in ontogeny. Clearly, this way of thinking seems to suggest that information is independent from its material embodiment, in the sense that the replicator is a map of that information, as stated in the term 'genetic code'. At a closer look, this is ontologically wrong, as we cannot identify the information independent from the process (Oyama 2000). This is evident in the Peircian view, because information only inheres into the triadic semiosis, such that the interpretant, that is the function, embodies the information (compare the discussion in El-Hani et al. 2006). That means, as the interactor carries the entire chemical machinery that is necessary to interpret the replicator (cells interpret genotypes, and so forth), we cannot say that information is only embodied in the replicator. Furthermore, in this analysis the so-called parity thesis applies, which in information theory states the equivalence between channel and source, that is the message (Griffiths 2001). Then, the channel is the environment, such that one can always also argue that the environment transmits the information. This is evident from the fact that the interpreting interactor is also the interface to the environment, and hence defines the 'niche' as the selectively relevant part of it. Thus, the ontological troubles with assigning the exclusive role of information transmission to the replicator is straightforwardly depicted, but also resolved, in the semiotic analysis (figure 3.9).

This diagram picks up the line of thinking that we have begun with the analysis of levels of selection. The argument involves a shift in perspective: Previously, we approached evolution as a process by which information is accumulating about the environment; now, we consider the replicator, in the course of evolution, as the object about which information accumulates via the selection by the environment. In the triadic view, the environment in the most general sense is the interpretant, establishing the functions by means of selection that relate replicators with the niche via the generated mechanisms *M*. It is important to recognize that the 'environment' includes all levels of selection, viewed from the perspective that is established by the identification of the replicator. Thus, for example, if one equates the replicator with the genotype, the cell is part of the environment of the replicator, such that we ask for the function of the replicator in the cell (for an alternative semiotic view, see El-Hani et al. 2006). However, one can argue that the genotype cannot fully reproduce itself without being embedded into the cell which operates the reproduction mechanisms. Then, the cell might be seen as the replicator and the organ as the first–level environment. This duality of perspectives can be grasped by the notion of the 'system of interpretance':

As indicated in the lower diagram, the 'environment' needs to be dissected into levels of selection which constitute functions in turn.

Figure 3.9 Triadic analysis of replicator and interactor: Basic unit and system of interpretance

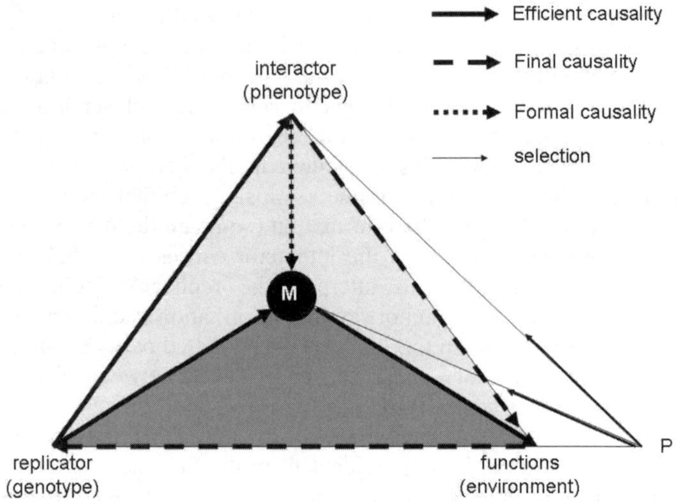

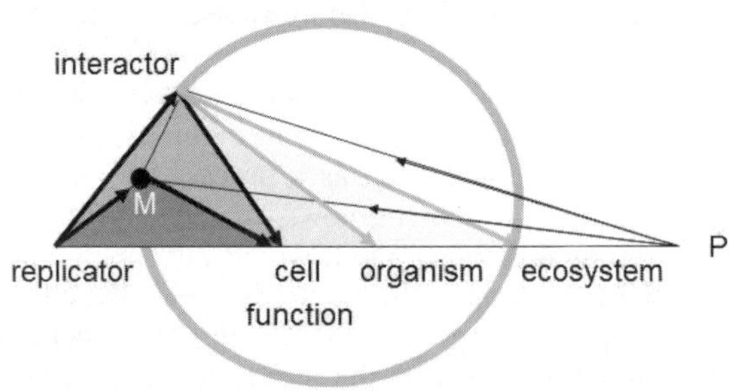

Note: In the triadic analysis of the relationship between the replicator and the interactor, replicators connect efficient–causally with the realization of functions, which are defined relative to the selective forces of the environment. As shown in the lower diagram, the environment is constitutive for a system of interpretance: The replicator is embedded into a hierarchy of interpretants qua functions, such as the cell which enables reproduction, and which is in turn part of an organism, and so forth. On the one hand, replicators connect with different mechanisms of genetic control of developmental processes or organismic reactions to external stimuli, for example. However, in the developmental process, replicators can only obtain this role in being interpreted by the interactors which carry them, and which establish the relationship with the different levels in the system of interpretance. Therefore, replicators obtain the position of the 'object' in biosemiosis, which means that their functions are always mediated via interactors as signs. This general semiotic structure explains why the relationship between replicators and functions is much more complex than originally thought, with many different and interacting roles of genes in the process of gene expression, and why there are numerous direct feedbacks of the environment on gene expression. Further, it explains why it is so difficult to assign a function to all genetic differences in a replicator (reflected in the notion of 'genetic junk').

Another essential point relates with the time dimension in which we analyse the mechanisms. In the context of the general theory of evolution, this is referring to 'development': Development is the efficient–causal process by which replicators produce certain functions relative to the environment. As indicated in figure 3.7, development and evolution are conjoined in the role of the replicator. Therefore, in the triadic analysis we can resolve a difficult issue in biology, namely how functions, which actualize adaptation, and development under constraints relate, because development always occurs under constraints (Amundson 2001; for a biosemiotic view, see Andrade 2007): Constraints cannot be simply seen as adaptations in turn, because they also constrain the evolution of theoretical improvements of functions. Constraints are structural principles which may not only relate to the species level, but also to higher taxonomic levels, often designated as 'Bauplan'. So, if we do not only consider the realization of functions at a point of time (such as the capability to flee a predator with a certain speed), we need to consider the developmental process by which the capacity to actualize this function is generated. Then, the relationship between function and ultimate purposes in the triadic analysis needs to be analysed in terms of entire life–cycles of organisms. Only in these life cycles the entire system of interpretance unfolds.

Replicators come in a large number of variants which include variants in mechanisms generating functions. Evolution results into regularities that define the borderline between functional causal mechanisms (macrostates) and non–functional random variation (microstates). The emergence of these regularities is mediated by the interactor. Comparing with previous figures, we can therefore realize the close connection between the interactor notion and notions such as the species. This is because the interactor defines regularities which result in functions, including, for example, functions such as group boundaries. Hence, the interactor plays a central role in determining response patterns, relative to ultimate purposes. In this view, it is very misleading to focus only on the efficient–causal relationship between replicator and function, in the sense of the attempt at reducing functions to replicators, such as reducing behaviour to genetics. This is because the replicator is a set of microstates (such as the chemical composition of the genome), whereas the function is a macrostate that is intermediated by another macrostate, that is the interactor. For example, humans have a set of affectual mechanisms that are genetically rooted, such as fear, but there is no direct mechanism that links fear with environmental stimuli (which do exist, for example, if humans eat poisonous stuff). The generation of fear is determined by functions that emerge from developmental processes. In the triadic view, the efficient–causal mechanisms rooted in the chemical microstates of the replicator are interpreted by these macrostates. This leaves much space for random expressions of fear, such as individual variations in expressions of fear.

Based on this analysis, it is obvious that we cannot assign information to the replicator exclusively, if at all. Information inheres in the entire triadic structure, and in particular the relationship between interactor and environment. The semiotic analysis shows that the common notion that replicators carry information actually means that replicators are objects which are being interpreted by interpretants, which I conceive as functions relative to the environment. This approach allows for making sense of two central insights of recent research into genotype/phenotype relations. Firstly, genotypes are complex structures which do not relate in a simple and unidirectional way with particular organismic functions. This is not the place to review this research, but what emerges as essential is the distinction between coding and non–coding genes, as well as of complex feedback structures between genes and genotypes and genes and phenotypes (Jablonka and Lamb 2006). That means, gene expressions are determined by interactions with other genes, and these interactions can be in turn influenced by phenotypic properties (methylation etc.). Secondly, even if we pay respect to this complexity, there remains the additional fact that all relations seem to be multivalued, that is, the mapping is many–to–many (Lewontin 2011). One important aspect of this is that the increase of phenotypical complexity is not reflected in any straightforward way in the genotype, which seems not to differ much between different species to account for all the phenotypic differences.

3.4.3. Species, functions, groups

In the semiotic view, this complex and multi–valued relationship between function and replicator is one of macrostate and microstate. Replicators efficiently–cause functions via mechanisms, which relates to development or ontogeny. However, this does not imply that all microscopic properties of replicators unequivocally match with macro–level functional properties. The semiotic causation works in the opposite direction: Emergent functions interpret replicator distinctions. This is the 'bookkeeping' role of genes, as compared to the supposed information carrying role (Gould 2002: 632ff). Of course, the 'accounts' reflect information, but this information is not 'internal' to the replicators. It emerges from the interactions (Oyama 2000). In other words, genotypes do not carry information that directly controls phenotypes, but phenotype/environment interactions interpret genotypes in terms of enabled functions (for a related view, see Sterelny 2005). This insight is also important for the analysis of group selection in the discussion of the previous section: The ambiguity of the term 'group' (see for example Sober and Wilson 1998 vs. West et al. 2006; cf. Leigh Jr 2009) results from the fact that group–level adaptations relate with genes as 'bookkeepers' that are not necessarily located in one individual, but are dispersed across many individuals: Hence, we can also interpret the 'inclusive fitness' approach in terms of the 'bookkeeping' functions of genes qua replicators. Inclusive fitness does not mean that the pertinent biological information is located in the genotype.

This view is further vindicated by considering the interactor. In the original replicator/interactor dichotomy, interactors and functions are merged into one concept. This would always imply optimal adaptation and would not allow for misrepresentation. In my view, replicators generate interactors as macro–level properties that correspond to species level properties. Those species level properties relate with certain aspects of the environment, that is the niche. Therefore, this relationship between 'species' and 'interactor' is tantamount to the distinction between a type and a token of a semiotically mediated function, with functions being causal regularities in the interaction between organism and environment. The type/token distinction emerges from formal causality, as the species notion relates with the categorization of mechanisms generating functions: For example, species–specific courtship behaviour is manifest with token of functions, that is individual interactors, but operates as a categorization of individuals into species, which means as a type. Thus, formal causality comes into play in different respects. Courtship behaviour is individual, but reflects species–level regularities. These regularities are observer relative in a double sense: Firstly, they result in regularities in the interaction between con-specifics, of which the recognition of a con-specific is one of the most fundamental acts of classification, hence a semiotic process; secondly, these regularities also underpin the species classification by the external observers. In the case of artificial breeding, these external observers can even become a part of evolution. These regularities define the interactor, whereas the individual behaviour relates with the organism and its functions, as emerging from the developmental process.

From this follows, that varieties relative to the species level interactor properties, which are efficiently caused by the replicator without carrying information in the first place, can give rise to emergent information, if they are positively selected for. This shows that replicator micro–level variance comes first, and is then interpreted and enriched via the evolutionary process. This idea has been always implicit to the notion of 'mutation' of course, but obtains a different meaning now, since any sort of idiosyncratic property of the replicator is part of its information capacity, resulting from any kind of process. In particular, this can also refer to properties that do not change at all, if they are put into another singular selective context. So, information is only emergent on triadic conjunctions of causal modes, and one cannot assign a primordial role to the replicator in the sense of the replicator efficiently–causing information generation and transmission.

This approach allows taking another fresh look at the relationship between groups and individuals, with reference to genetics. In the selfish gene hypothesis, the assumption is made that only genes carry information, and therefore all interactors are mere vehicles to transfer this information. By implication, only genes are ontologically relevant, which would imply that individuals as higher–level entities do not actually exist in the sense of determining evolutionary causation. As a result, cooperation can only be explained by gene clusters that cross individuals, that is cooperation between same or similar replicators. As we have seen previously, this view neglects the essential role of signs in establishing correlated behaviour and group boundaries. Therefore, the relationship between genes and groups is a much more complex one which directly reflects the role of the two hierarchies, compositional and subsumptive.

So, in figure 3.10 I overview the relationship between genes and species with reference to the two hierarchies (for a related analysis of the relationship between gene flow and species, see Barker and Wilson 2010). In the subsumptive dimension, genes relate with gene clusters that result in kin groups and populations. In the compositional dimension, genes connect with individuals and groups in which functional interdependencies are established. Therefore, if we conceive of the two hierarchies meeting in the concept of the 'species', then we recognize that the term is bimodal in a fundamental sense, because species level behaviour and performance has to be explained in both dimensions. Thus, for example, it is not possible to reduce cooperative behaviour solely on the genetic cluster perspective, because, as we have seen, the relative role of within–group competitiveness of behaviour is not only determined genetically, but also by the degree of behavioural correlation which can also be established via semiosis.

This duality of hierarchies is also important to understand the relationship between development and evolution. In figure 3.7, replicators have a double function in guiding development synchronically and information transmission diachronically. However, development is a process that establishes a direct connection between genetic and non–genetic channels of information transmission, such that the genetic effects themselves become endogenous to the evolutionary process. Take, for example, maternal effects through which certain chemical features of the maternal environment during ontogeny influence gene expression, such that there is a two-fold channel of information transmission: So, for example, certain environmental factors might trigger maternal behaviour that influences gene expression epigenetically; in turn, those gene expressions trigger that maternal behaviour in the next generation, such that environment, maternal behaviour and gene expressions co-evolve. This causal circuitry is not determined by the genes directly, this counts as non-genetic information transmission.

Figure 3.10 Genes and species in two hierarchies

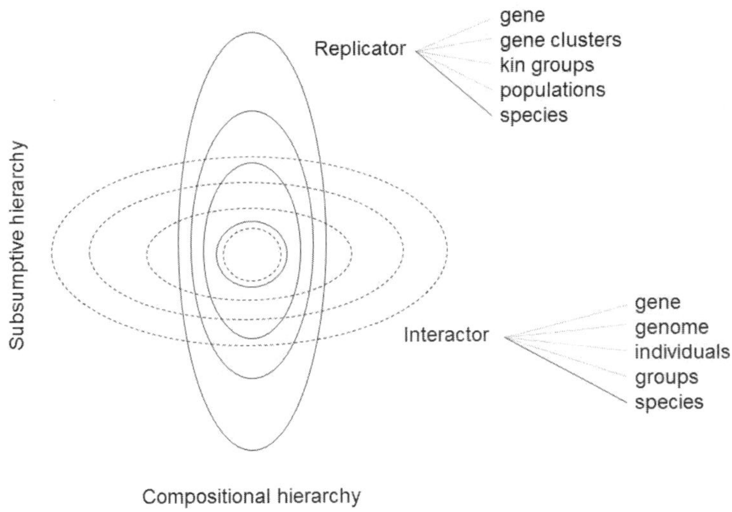

Note: The relationship between genes and species is embedded into the two hierarchies, subsumptive and compositional. The subsumptive hierarchy refers to the genealogical connectivity between genes and populations in which individuals share genes, resulting into gene clusters that relate individuals, especially in terms of kin groups. These relationships underlie the theoretical notion of 'inclusive fitness' in the common understanding. In the triadic analysis, genetic information is only created via the functions qua interpretants. Functions are embedded into compositional hierarchies in which species relate to connected functionings, such as populations in the context of ecosystems. This relationship is foremost reflected in the role of signs in determining population boundaries. Therefore, the possibility of group selection emerges in both dimensions of hierarchy, genetic relatedness and semiosis, that is correlated behaviour.

We can now understand the central role of structural constraints in the evolving replicator/interactor relationships. Structural constraints operate in two directions. Firstly, there are structural constraints on development: This means, the variance of interactors versus replicators is determined by the structural constraints that inhere in the developmental process. This need to be distinguished from the traditional emphasis on direct genotype–phenotype interactions: In my view, the genetic replicator is a set of boundary conditions for variety, but does not determine micro–level variety directly. The second directions are structural constraints on phylogeny, which directly connects with the first point. In other words, it we say that biological information inheres into an evolving structure of nested constraints, we can reinstate the conceptual unity of the theory of evolution in arguing that the genotype is one level of constraints among many others.

3.4.4. Co-evolution of constraints and multi–level evolution

One important example for this role of genetic replicators as constraints is the role of cultural transmission of information. Cultural transmission clearly differs fundamentally from genetic transmission because it operates also horizontally, that is information transfer happens with co-existing generations and also within generations, and also involves individuals which are not connected genetically (for a classical analysis, see Boyd and Richerson 1985). Therefore, one cannot reduce cultural information transmission to genetic factors. However, on the other hand we need to distinguish between cultural transmission and the capacity for culture (Rindos 1985, 1986; Ingold 1986: 364). The capacity for culture must be rooted in genetic factors, because otherwise it would succumb to random drift factors, given continuing selection operating on the genetic level. So, if cultural evolution became completely autonomous from genetic evolution, the capacity for culture would erode in the long run. Therefore, the genetic replicator operates as a constraint on cultural evolution. This argument matches with my previous argument on group selection: Mechanisms that establish certain correlations of behaviour need not be directly determined by genetic replicators, but the capacity to generate those mechanisms need to be, the maintenance of which therefore requires that they meet with this constraint.

We can argue in a similar way for all other sorts of non–genetic evolution, especially when considering the possibility that there is a feedback between all kinds of phenotypical evolution and the forces of natural selection operating on the genetic level. This is the Baldwin effect, which catches the causal interaction between niche creation and selection that I have scrutinized previously, and specifies another feedback mechanism between interactor and replicator. The Baldwin effect establishes a causal circuit between genetic evolution, environment and behaviour in the sense that behavioural changes result in the creation of niches through which the capacity to generate this behaviour is positively selected for, ultimately ending up in genetic adaptations that incorporate this information in the genetic transmission mechanism. So, we can conclude that both extreme positions are misplaced, rigorous genetic reductionism on the one hand, and denying biological influences on non–genetic information transmission at all. Evolution always proceeds in different dimensions, and for certain phenomena the different dimensions may weigh differently, but do not reduce to complete irrelevance. Constraints remain constraints.

We can grasp all these effects with the distinction between levels of selection, that is between within–group and between–group, corresponding to the Price's equation formalism. This is because we can refer to groups either as constituting environments for individuals which induce certain effects of information transmission on the lower level, or as arrangements of traits that can be transmitted via any sort of mechanism, that is the population boundaries (Helanterä and Uller 2010: 9). Then, the notion of the 'group' refers to classes of interactors which determine the direction of evolution via development. If we designate these patterns most generally as 'forms' (signs, in the semiotic framework), thus referring to the biological field of morphology, we can state that forms emerge from evolution, but at the same time operate as selective forces on development; development of forms feeds back to evolution. Developmental constraints operate as internal selection relative to the external selection exerted by the environment (compare Wuketits 1987). So, the organism can be considered as a group, and new variants (mutations) are internally selected, whereas the entire organism faces external selection between other organisms. On the other hand, viewed from the relationship between species and individual, phylogenetic constraints relate to within group internal selection of organisms, thus of species level properties, and between group selection to the environment as external selection.

We can relate this reasoning back to the general entropic framework (figure 3.11). Then, we see that internal selection via developmental constraints corresponds to the evolution of functions as observer relative states through which information accumulates. For example, variations of wings in birds will be subject to internal selection because there are many interactions between wings and other body parts which would cause deleterious effects on the entire performance of the organism, and which would be expressed during development. On the other hand, constraints, which reflect species–level forms, allow for a large variety of combinations which are subject to external selection *in toto*, especially if we consider entire life–cycles. This developmental variety constitutes individuality in the population context, and therefore the material substrate for information capacity. Thus, we see that the concept of forms as constraints in classifying species represents the interface between the two processes of development and evolution: Forms emerge by evolution, and they operate as constraints on development. One expression of this relationship is the temporary occurrence of earlier phylogenetic forms in individual ontogeny. Another is the fact that many Hox genes, that is gene clusters that regulate positions of organism parts, are often very old in phylogenetic terms (compare the extensive discussion in Gould 2002: 1147ff).

Figure 3.11 Phylogeny, ontogeny and entropy

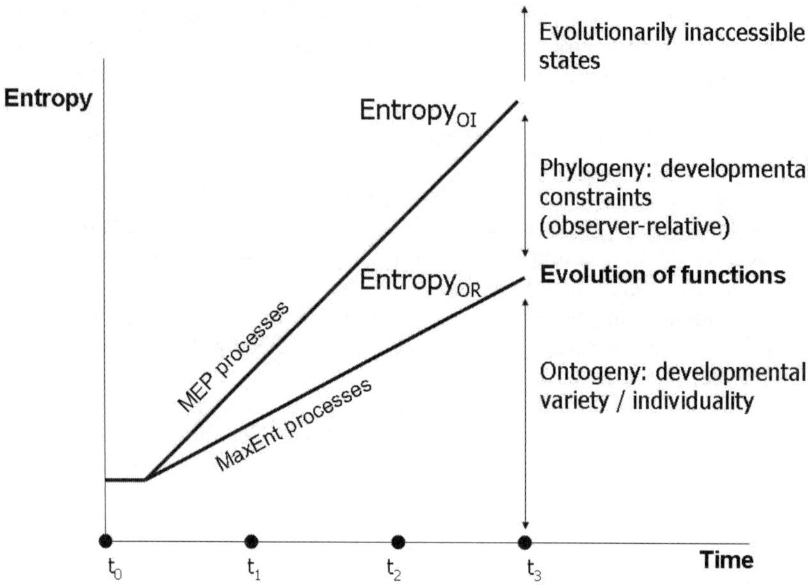

Note: The relationship between evolution and development or phylogeny and ontogeny can be understood against the background of entropic analysis that highlights the general role of constraints in the accumulation of information. Ontogeny is the process that generates variety in terms of irreducible individuality of members of a population. This corresponds to the MaxEnt principle, considering the relationship between variety and species–level types of traits. These types evolve during phylogeny, resulting into constraints that are a dual of functions (for example, a wing of a bird species comes in a large number of varieties, but develops in order to realize a type of function, such that the constraints channel development towards this goal). Thus, phylogeny is a set of observer relative facts, which embody the ultimate physical functions of living systems, that is dissipation of energy (the wing enables energy uses to maintain the life cycles of the population of birds). As we have seen previously, this function is embodied in the nested hierarchies of ecosystems that are made up from species interactions.

3.4.5. Inclusive inheritance

We can now systematize the previous considerations in the following way, turning back to the analysis of heredity as a statistical phenomenon. In the new notion of 'inclusive inheritance' the idea is no longer maintained that the replicator is only embodied in the genetic substrate (Danchin et al. 2011). In the original Price approach, this statement boils down to the simple fact that the transmission term receives more direct attention and is no longer regarded as the source of noise in analysing natural selection as operating via the germ line. Then, we can distinguish between different modes of transmission in terms of the direction. The genetic mode is almost exclusively vertical, although we know today that there are instances of horizontal gene transmission, too. On the other extreme, there is cultural transmission, which operates both vertically and horizontally. Cultural transmission can be regarded as one expression of group–level transmission in the sense of distinguishing between levels of selection (compare Richerson et al. 2010). Therefore, one essential question in evolutionary analysis is whether evolution on these higher levels of selection can be also analysed in terms of the replicator/interactor duality. This has been proposed by the theory of 'memetics', on which I will come back in the next chapter (for a survey, see Aunger 2000). Memetics posits that cultural evolution operates on the basis of specific replicators and thus follows the same Darwinian logic as characterized in the beginning of this chapter.

Cultural evolution is one special expression of the more general phenomenon of ecological transmission. Ecological transmission refers to the mainly vertical and partly horizontal transfer of information via the niches of species. As we have seen, this can include interaction with other mechanisms, such as genetic ones. A much quoted human example for this interaction is lactose tolerance of human populations that evolved as a response to the emergence and sustainable cultural pattern of pastoralism and dairy farming: Large parts of the global human population show decreasing production of lactase after weaning off.

There are two further channels of information transmission which are vertical exclusively, namely epigenetic inheritance and parental effects, as briefly sketched above. Helanterä and Uller (2010) propose to arrange these different mechanisms into three larger classes, namely vertical transmission, induction and acquisition. 'Induction' refers to all effects that result from environmental channelling, and 'acquisition' to all effects that involve current generations and partly active learning (but also includes horizontal gene transfers). One can then discuss the different effects in terms of their impact on the expectation term in the original Price's equation, namely distinguishing between natural selection and transmission in general. Then, there are three possibilities:

- Random impact of transmission: This means that the transmission weakens the directionality of genetic vertical transmission similar to the effects of mutation.
- Directional impact of transmission: This includes materially as different cases such as environmentally induced mutation rates or biased cultural transmission; generally, these effects occur if trait adoption is frequency dependent.
- Fitness increasing impact: Transmission works in the same direction as genetic change, such as in the Baldwin effect.

Figure 3.12 The general model of heredity (Danchin et al. 2011)

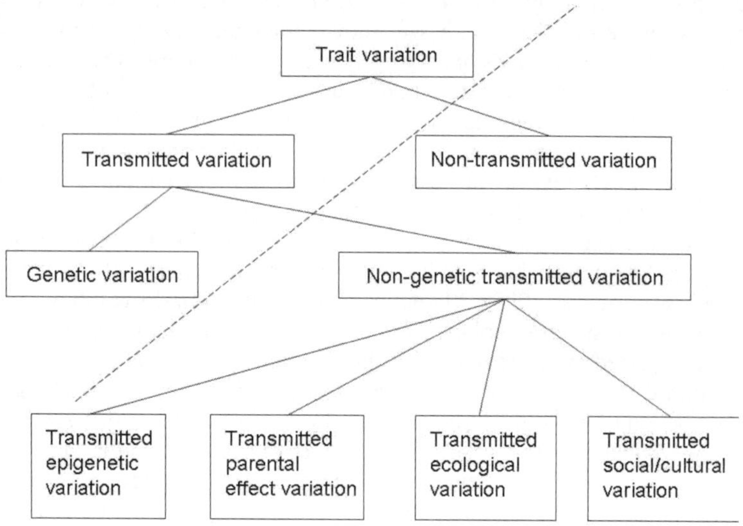

Note: The new evolutionary paradigm of inclusive inheritance posits that evolution proceeds via different channels of information transmission. The broken line indicates the distinction with regard to the conventional view which only allows for transmission of genetic variation. The new approach distinguishes between four other channels of non–genetic transmission, which can be systematized in the systems of interpretance view. That means, the channels operate on different levels of evolution. For example, the epigenetic channel operates on the level of the cell and the chemical mechanisms determining gene expressions such as methylation patterns, or the ecological channel operates via the ecosystem niches in which organisms exist, and which are jointly constructed by organisms and selective forces.

If we keep with the original phenomenological distinction between the different channels, which is useful if we want to concentrate on human systems in particular, where cultural and environmental transmission play an important role, we can adopt the systematic scheme proposed by Danchin et al. (2011), on which the general model of heredity can be applied (figure 3.12). In this model, trait variation and correlations between trait variations are essential. The standard model is indicated by the broken line: It excludes the possibility of non–transmitted genetic variation in evolution. The new more universal theory of evolution includes the latter, which is differentiated into the four different channels of transmission.

This picture already emerged in earlier theories of gene/culture co-evolution (for example Lumsden and Wilson 1981; Boyd and Richerson 1985; Richerson and Boyd 2005), on which I will come back in the next chapter. So, the main advantage of the new approaches is to clearly state the formal unity of the general theory of evolution. This has been made possible by the theory of selection that has been introduced by George Price.

3.5. FREQUENCY DEPENDENCY, COMPLEXITY OF ADAPTATION AND MEP

3.5.1. Analytical primacy of frequency dependency in evolutionary theory

One of the essential ideas of Darwinism is that adaptation increases fitness. As I have already mentioned, the two terms are often conflated, as the 'fittest' is also the 'best adapted'. Burian (1983) gives a full account of these problems and relates them to different notions of adaptation. These are: absolute, relative and selected engineering fitness on the one hand, and realized and expected Darwinian fitness on the other hand. The first three closely relate fitness with the notion of adaptation as functioning; the first two among them just consider engineering aspects (such as shape of fins viewed hydrodynamically), whereas the third one explicitly refers to forces of selection. In comparison, Darwinian fitness does not relate to adaptation, but only focuses on differential reproductive success, which translates into a statistical conceptualization as outlined in the previous sections. Then, we can distinguish between realized differential reproductive success and a theoretical magnitude that corresponds to the predictors of reproductive success in the statistical models of evolution.

Of these, realized fitness can be regarded as tautological (an observation that led the early Popper to discount Darwinism as 'unscientific'). Yet, Burian argues that even in the case of Darwinian realized fitness, the danger of tautology can be avoided if one distinguishes between fitness in terms of probabilities and fitness in terms of the single observations (that means, as realized fitness is a statistical value, as in the Price's equation, single organisms can still fail to reproduce). Rosenberg and Bouchard (2010) elaborate on this problem and show that the probabilistic interpretation of fitness faces all the problems that emerge from the foundations of statistics and probabilities, such as in this case the frequentist interpretation. For example, and most simply, the probability to leave a number of offspring does not directly determine the actual number of offspring over time, which is also strongly influenced by the variance across time and location. Rosenberg and Bouchard conclude that Darwinian fitness cannot be fully independent from 'ecological fitness' (which is basically Burian's engineering fitness) in order to make full sense, that is, if it is interpreted strictly as a term that can be used in predictions and therefore would be falsifiable. That means, however, that fitness would relate with adaptation, and certain hypotheses about adaptation on the individual and population level would be used to generate predictions about differential reproductive success.

In our context, these debates can be resolved in arguing that fitness should not be interpreted as 'fitness with reference to a given environment' (which corresponds to Burian's engineering fitness), but only as 'fitness relative to other individuals, given an evolving and endogenous state space'. So, the two notions of fitness and adaptation would be kept strictly separate. From this follows the important point that fitness is always frequency–dependent: Absolute fitness values are meaningless, because differential reproductive success is the expression of an ordinal rank order over individuals in a population, and rank is defined by relative positions, not by absolute individual properties. In the context of Fisher's fundamental theorem, this apparent conceptual problem can be simply resolved in considering the fact that from the viewpoint of a single individual, all other individuals are a part of the environment. However, this implies that one cannot refer 'fitness' to only natural selection in the original sense of Fisher's, because individual actions and individual reproduction always change the state space in which selection happens. The environment is not independent from individual change. This observation already inheres in Darwin's distinction between 'natural selection' and 'sexual selection', where the latter can be conceived as a special case of selection between conspecifics (competition between mates and over mates). Sexual selection is always frequency–dependent because it involves interactions between the reproduction of individuals in a population (for example, the previously discussed common pool problem of shares of females in a population relative to males is frequency–dependent).

Biologists have doubted for long that fitness maximization necessarily entails optimization in terms of adaptation. Grafen (2002, 2008) has shown that if one approaches this issue in the Price's equation framework, it is possible to show mathematically that fitness maximization entails optimization. However, this is both a positive and a negative result. It follows from the purely logical fact that in a population that manifests no change of trait, frequencies would no longer be subject to selection, which implies that all individuals have achieved optimal states; vice versa, if all individuals have achieved optimal states, selection would no longer occur, so that no changes of trait frequencies are observable. As such, Grafen's approach is about equilibrium, but builds on the dynamics that is reflected in Price's equation. That is, out of equilibrium change will happen into the direction that is implied by optimization. But in equilibrium, the two notions cannot apply together: Optimized states manifest no selection, and selection can only operate on non–optimal states.

There is one observation that directly supports both Grafen's claims and its deflationist interpretation: This is the much-neglected fact that change is not the most remarkable fact about evolution, but stasis (Gould 2002: 874ff).

Stasis refers to the long-run stability of trait features of organisms, often even in the very long run evolutionary time horizon, and even applying for simple organisms. Stasis can be seen as the most direct manifestation of selection, and not change; this is because change would be the default case anyway, in the form of evolutionary drift, that is random changes (which directly express the Second Law) (compare Brandon 2010). In this context, the notion of 'punctuated equilibrium' looms large, which can be interpreted as the observation that given stasis as reflecting certain optimal states of evolution (local or global), change will only happen under special circumstances and if so, then with relatively increased speed. However, those differences in speed do not imply that there are substantially different evolutionary mechanisms at work (Dennett 1995: 282ff). One can say that selection does not only drive continuous gradual change, but works as a retention mechanism that is reflected in stasis of achieved states.

One can certainly argue that the more complex the optimization process, the more probable stasis of achieved states becomes. This is because the more complex an organism becomes, the probability of negative changes in adaptation is much higher than the probability of improvements. In complex organisms, optimization requires the solution of many trade-offs, which are increasingly discussed in terms of economic models in biology (for example Noë et al. 2001). This is particularly true when considering the interaction between evolution and development, as economic trade-offs stay in the centre of the analysis of life-cycle phenomena, such as the evolution of different patterns of fecundity and size of offspring, gametes etc. (for a survey see Roff, 2001). As many of these trade-offs are related to sexual selection, they are embedded into a frequency–dependent selective context and can therefore manifest very complex causal interdependencies. Thus, there might be a trade-off between fecundity and size both with reference to the parent and the offspring generation. In the parent generation, size and maturity are normally negatively related, because size requires the investment of energy and body-mass, which needs time, so that maturity is delayed. However, larger size might help survival and hence increases the probability of successful reproduction. Similarly, the smaller the size of the off-spring becomes, the higher the fecundity in single litters, but possibly also the lower the probability of survival of the offspring. These are already relatively complex trade-offs in stable environments, however, they become much more complex once the intra– and inter–species competition is taken into consideration. Then, we can conceive of Grafen's argument in terms of equilibria as stasis of solutions of complex trade-offs, and selection as the force that operates on random departures from equilibrium, predominantly weeding out negative changes, thus finding foremost expression in the absence of change (for related discussion on the relationship between selection and 'rationality' of animal behaviour, see Houston et al. 2007).

This argument about interdependencies is related to Stuart Kauffman's (1993) *NK* models of biological evolution, which describe so-called 'rugged fitness landscapes'. These models refer to genomes, but can be also transferred to networks among organisms in ecosystems. If we just assume that trade-offs in adaptation are embodied in interactions among genes (even if only in the 'bookkeeping' sense), Kauffman's analysis directly applies on the previous discussion. In case of genomes, the model ascribes a fitness value to single locations in the genotype which can mutate, that is the alleles. If there are only two alleles, the total number of genotypes is $2N$, with N the number of genes. With two alleles, every gene locus can obtain the value of 0 or 1. For each gene, the number of K other genes can be identified which affects its fitness. If a complete list of those interactions can be made, for each gene its fitness is determined by its own allele and the allele at the other K loci, so that the list has $2K+1$ entries. The fitness of the entire genotype is determined as the average of the fitness of the N loci with K epistatic interactions. Depending on those interactions, a mutation can drive the genotype to different local optima or suboptimal states, even if the isolated fitness effect would be positive. In the NK model, with $K=0$ every mutation will either increase or decrease the total fitness, which implies that selection will drive the changes monotonically to the global optimum. That would correspond to the theoretical case of frequency independent selection. With $K=N-1$, every possible epistatic interaction is actual, resulting in what Kauffman calls 'fully random fitness landscapes'. This circumstance results into a large number of local optima; the latter fact implies in turn that there is a very low probability that a global optimum can be reached. Kauffman shows that with increasing N the local optima fall toward the mean fitness of the space of possible genotypes. This is the state of maximum entropy with equiprobability of all microstates, namely loss of structuration in the sense of accumulation of information. Kauffman calls this a 'complexity catastrophe'.

As Kauffman (2000: 194ff) therefore states, evolution proceeds as the co-evolution of fitness landscapes and organisms, or organisms and environment. Stasis reflects optima in terms of constraints on possible changes, thus reducing the accessibility of possible states, thus avoiding the erosion of achieved complex adaptation by randomizing changes. This corresponds to the tenets of niche–construction theory (Odling-Smee et al. 2003): Evolution is the co-evolution of organisms and niches. Again, we have a statement about levels of selection, because the niche can be regarded as a commons relative to the other organisms. The fundamental issue is, again, evolvability. There are a large number of fitness landscapes which would jeopardize evolvability in the sense of resulting into complexity catastrophes. Therefore, the question is whether organisms evolve into states where the environments that they mutually constitute for each other are ones by which the evolvability of the different organisms or species is maintained or even maximized. The latter requirement results from the fact that optimization in the real world operates under uncertainty, so that the capacity for adaptation is itself subject to an optimization process. From this follows, that it is not possible simply to argue that adaptation happens relative to 'the environment' (for an early statement, see Dobzhansky 1974). The co-evolution of environments and organisms in constrained interactions is the core process in general evolution.

3.5.2. Exaptation

In order to understand these interactions in more detail, it is important to go back to our most general analysis of the state space and accessibility. If there are many possible interactions between different loci of information transmission, there is the possibility that incremental changes of loci may result in major restructurings of the state space, if new combinatorial possibilities for interactions are created. The emergence of autocatalytic cycles is a most generic case in point. Once an autocatalytic cycle comes into existence, this changes the fitness landscape, that is the state space, for all other processes in an ensemble, such that the direction of evolutionary change is altered fundamentally. Therefore, it is misleading to assume that natural selection proceeds in a given state space, namely an environment that is fixed.

In order to grasp this interdependence, we need to modify the term adaptation. I propose to put the term 'exaptation' at the centre of evolutionary analysis, following Gould (2002: 1229ff). Exaptation refers to the functional transformation of traits which evolved either randomly or with reference to other functions. Whereas 'adaptation' emphasises the efficient match between environment and trait, exaptation covers the creative dimension of evolution in the sense of the interaction between environment and organism. This is because exaptation does not focus on realized functions, but explains the emergence of functions via effects that emerge via environment–organism interactions. Thus, the concept is a powerful means to overcome the difficulties in explaining the gradual evolution of adaptive traits which are non–functional during the period of their formation. The classical example is feathers of birds, which served and serve different functions in the course of evolution, such as heat regulation, competitive displays and flying. As we shall see in the next chapter, many hominid innovations can also be interpreted as exaptations, such as when changes in the locomotion patterns enabled the use of hands for other activities, or when certain existing mechanisms of vocalization where merged with primordial functions of gesturing in the emergence of human language.

There are different classes of exaptations (extending on Gould 2002: 1233).

- A trait that was already selected for meets with changing environmental conditions and assumes new adaptive functions, which includes functional shifts within similar or related functional domains.
- Existing traits can adopt new functions while keeping the original functions, thus evolving multi–functionality.

- A trait that was emerging randomly is producing adaptive effects relative to changing environments, which includes non–adaptive functions that turn into adaptive functions.
- Further, exaptations include the case of positive feedback cycles between changes of the environment caused by one organism, resulting into changes with other organisms that in turn trigger adaptations on part of the original organism; in this case, we have an autocatalytic dynamics, which cannot be simply reduced to adaptation towards a stable environment, because the original change could not possibly anticipate the resulting changes.

Especially the last case shows that exaptation relates with the levels of selection, because traits might be generated that prove to be advantageous on another level of selection, such that the processes on different systemic levels generate novelty on other levels. This becomes evident if we consider the fact that all changes are interdependent with changes that they cause to happen, such that the unanticipated causal feedbacks lead to the emergence of exaptations. In other words, exaptation results into adaptation under the conditions of frequency–dependent selection and uncertainty, that is the impossibility to anticipate the consequences of trait changes.

Exaptation is also different from adaptation because the criteria for adaptation are contingent to the level of selection, which is to be understood as an emergent systemic functionality, such as in a newly emergent ecosystem with autocatalytic properties. The classical example that we met already is the role of predators in ecosystems, which also leverage general ecosystem productivity, thus generating an externality that also feeds back to them. A property generated on the individual level might prove to be adaptive on the species level. This is to be distinguished from the mere multi–functionality of traits that might evolve through time, that is an adaptive feature might prove to be also functional in another context, as in the case of a simultaneous use of a trait as a solution to an engineering problem and to a signalling problem. Although such phenomena also count as exaptation, if the other function is a newly emerging one, what is more important are cross–level functional phenomena, because they give rise to novelty which cannot occur within one level, thus widening the scope for the growing state space considerably. It is crucial to understand that these effects can be even seen as operating with the gene as the fundamental unit of control, in the sense that processes on different levels of evolution activate particular genetic structures which are superfluous or even detrimental on other levels.

3.5.3. The Red Queen Principle

We can put together the previous considerations in one fundamental theorem of evolution, the Red Queen Principle (for a survey, see Robson 2005).

Empirically, the Red Queen Principle relates to the observation that certain biological phenomena manifest convergence, such as convergence of extinction rates across taxa or the phenomenon of stasis, in general, which manifests convergence of individual traits to a generic species pattern shared by all individuals. The Red Queen Principle describes the arms race of evolution: All changes of traits induce changes in the environments of other organisms and thus trigger changes which in turn feedback on the original organism. The metaphor of arms races refers to the observation that in arms races, the competitors always tend to converge on ever increasing levels of armament, while keeping relative positions stable, or converging to a balance of powers; in the balance of powers, relative levels of armaments do not differ, though absolute levels are continuously increasing. The Red Queen Principle applies this thought on the notions of fitness and adaptation.

In this view, fitness is only conceivable as a relative magnitude, in the original sense of differential reproductive success, which is reflected in relative trait frequencies. In this view, 'maximization' is no force of nature, but simply reflecting the statistical arithmetic that results if, for whatever reason, one organism differentially reproduces more than another organism. However, because of the frequency–dependent relationship between the interacting organisms, fitness is a concept of relative status, which means if one organism improves fitness, another organism will lose. 'Maximizing fitness' is a meaningless concept, then, because it is impossible to maximize independent from the behaviours prevailing in all other parts of reference populations. This idea is very familiar to economists: In a competitive economy, all companies strive to maximize profits, but in the aggregate they cannot do that, ending up in a zero–profit state in which a 'balance of armaments' is achieved. That means, it is meaningless to refer the notion of maximization to the population level, even if it can apply on the individual level. Individual level maximization leads to minimization on the population level. This simple, though basic argument casts doubt on the relevance of the notion of 'average fitness' which is used in the context of statistical analysis of selection, as outlined in the previous sections.

Considering the meaning of 'average fitness', we meet a most simple argument in favour of the distinction between individual and group selection: If fitness is a relative concept, the average fitness of a group of individuals can only be meaningfully defined as being the relative fitness of the group as compared to other groups. If only one group were considered, averages of relative fitness are meaningless, like the average score of two basketball teams in a tournament. As we have seen previously in the discussion of the Price's equation, relative fitness in the context of replicator dynamics is always defined as difference between individual fitness and average fitness. However, this simple formalism is flawed in one fundamental sense: For differential reproductive success, only the individual relative differences count, in a sequence through time. That means, one always needs to consider the expanded Price's equation which compares relative fitness across groups and sub-groups. Then, the Simpson paradox applies, as discussed in section 3.3.4. Here, average fitness would always relate to differential reproduction across groups, and does not relate with differential reproduction within groups. This holds for all applications of the replicator dynamics reasoning: Consider firms in an industry as a population and different industries as groups; then, for the success of individual firms within the industry absolute levels of profits do not count but relative profits, reflected in a rank order of firms. For this rank order, averages of absolute profits are meaningless. However, if we ask for the relative expansion of industries as groups, which also determines individual firm's success, the differences between average absolute profits count, yielding a rank order of industries; however, on the inter–industry level, we are back with the irrelevance of the inter–industry averages.

From this it follows that fitness cannot be treated as an absolute value that increases through time. It is meaningless to ask whether bacteria, horses or humans are 'fitter' than other organisms. If we did so, bacteria would certainly appear to be the 'fittest' organisms on the world, for sheer numbers. In Fisher's Fundamental Theorem, this idea was introduced only by means of excluding frequency dependency. This was done to identify the fundamental driving force of the dynamics: Out of equilibrium, fitness will increase, depending on the existing variety of traits. However, frequency dependency implies the conservation principle in the sense of Frank's (2012b), which we can now relate to the nature of fitness as relative status. In evolution, fitness is a constant, relative to a reference frame, and amounts to zero.

Now, based on Grafen's theorems about the relationship between optimization and fitness, we can state the following. Fitness is a conserved quantity in evolution, whereas adaptation is measurable in a multi–dimensional state space, which allows defining measures in which 'optimization' can be made operational in terms of relative improvements or deteriorations (Burian's 'engineering fitness'). One of the most general measures, for example, is energy harvested in foraging activities (Kramer 2001). Theoretically, one can therefore define a scale in which adaptation is measured. Empirically, the multidimensionality of adaptation prevents aggregation in any meaningful sense, because it is impossible to evaluate all complex trade-offs in terms of energetics, for example. Then, increases in adaptation are driven by the Red Queen principle that applies for fitness: In the arms race metaphor, adaptation refers to the absolute levels of armament, fitness to the relative status. All improvements of traits are reflected in changes of relative fitness of single individuals out of equilibrium. This implies that partially, organisms can realize fitness improvements, but on the aggregate population level, the conservation principle applies, that is, fitness cannot increase but for limited out–of–equilibrium states.

Figure 3.13 Adaptation, exaptation and fitness

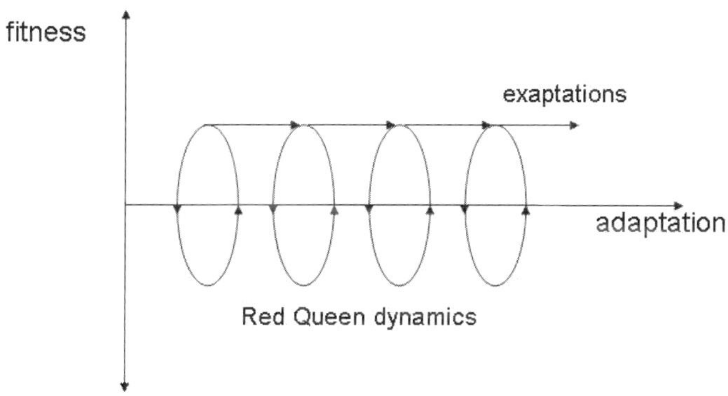

Note: This diagram establishes the basic relationship between the three concepts of fitness, adaptation and exaptation, which is mediated by the Red Queen Principle. Fitness is a relative term in the sense of the differential contribution of individuals to successor generations. Therefore, fitness is constant in the aggregate, approaching zero, and individual increases of fitness are only possible in disequilibrium states (this dynamics is indicated by the circles). For fitness, the Red Queen Principle applies, that is in frequency–dependent selection an arms race takes place in which positive changes of adaptive functions will never lead to sustainable fitness advantages. However, Red Queen competition can result into exaptations, that is, to functional novelties of traits that emerge in these arm's races. These novelties drive absolute improvements of adaptations, relative to selective forces of the environment. Thus, exaptation covers the creative aspect of evolution.

The interaction between fitness and adaptation can be conceptualized by the notion of exaptation. Exaptations drive the qualitative changes in the ensembles of organisms and niches, and therefore change the patterns of adaptation. This interaction between the three forces of evolution is shown in figure 3.13. So, we see that evolution proceeds via sequences of disequilibria in fitness maximization, such that in the long run, fitness is a conserved quantity. For adaptation, we can state propositions about positive change. The Red Queen dynamics of fitness maximization drives the emergence of exaptations that result in adaptations in the course of time. It is important to notice that exaptation also works in the context of the multidimensionality of adaptation, and probably this is even the most general case. For example, a trait that is selected for in sexual competition might prove to be adaptive in another dimension (such as prowess in intra–specific combats that is helpful in interactions with predators). Of course, this also implies that traits developed in one dimension can be detrimental in another dimension. This is what turns the relationship between adaptation and fitness multivalued.

The Red Queen Principle is essential for maintaining evolvability, because adaptation, if considered in isolation, would certainly tend to get stuck in local optima, given the complexity of the state space (compare the Kauffman argument presented previously). Frequency–dependent selection creates forces that continuously break up those equilibria, which includes changes of the state space itself, which can render realized equilibria obsolete, and trigger exaptations in other respects (compare Brown 2001; Hutteger 2010 shows that frequency–dependent interactions break up the link between evolutionary equilibria as modelled by evolutionary game theory and adaptation). Thus, absolute advances in adaptation require continuous generation of exaptations which drive functional transformations. This force is more fundamental than environmental changes in the narrow meaning of natural selection, because these changes cannot directly explain how functional transformations become possible. So, the Red Queen Principle drives the evolution of what Gould (2002: 1270ff) calls the 'exaptive pool' and what we have previously identified as 'information capacity' in the generic evolutionary framework. This insight enables us to establish the conceptual bridge between fitness, adaptation and the thermodynamics of evolution.

3.5.4. Size, complexity and Maximum Entropy in evolution

We can now ask the question how adaptation relates with the general evolutionary principles of MPP and MEPP. It is important to notice that the analysis in figure 3.14 does not imply that evolution follows a teleological track. There is no intelligent design behind the interaction between adaptation and environment as actualized in exaptations. On the other hand, we can follow Lotka's conjecture and argue that the most fundamental measure of adaptation is power, in the sense of the capacity to harness useful energy for the realizations of functions which maintain and enhance the capacity for harnessing energy. As I have already mentioned, this idea corresponds to general approaches in evolutionary ecology which treat energy harvested as a universal 'currency' that relates with differential reproductive success ('optimal foraging theory'). The MPP principle, however, does not simply apply on the level of single organisms, but needs to take the interaction in ecosystems into consideration. This matches with the fundamental approach in Thermodynamics to always consider ensembles of systems and environments. In this view, we can posit that the directedness of evolution only emerges on the level of these general principles, but not in the sense of anagenesis, namely directed improvements of adaptation according to some external standard. In this view, human beings are not 'better adapted' than bacteria, though being more complex. But human beings harness larger energy throughputs per unit of mass and time (which means manifest higher values of free energy rate intensity as outlined in Chapter Two) and have expanded the scope and reach of their ecosystem interactions continuously. Therefore, we can say that ultimately, adaptation corresponds to the principles of MPP and MEPP. As I have already pointed out, the MEPP also matches with the MaxEnt perspective, as we can surmise that adaptation means that organisms adopt traits which are the most probable states, given the constraints. Hence, it is entirely misleading to view the growth of complexity in evolution as the transition to less probable states. In fact, adaptation to constraints means that organisms adopt the likeliest state; the likeliest state by definition is the one towards which evolution converges, if interpreted as optimization.

These general ideas can be scrutinized in some more detail when considering the role of size in evolution, following the seminal analysis of 'nature's economy' by Vermeij (2004). Again, size can be approached both in absolute and relative terms. One of the most general aspects of adaptation is the relationship between absolute size and diversity, both internal and external. Absolute size is an important aspect in evolution, for different reasons. One is that size effects truncate the statistical distribution of variants (Gould 2002: 899ff). Given a certain pattern of organismic functioning, there is a minimum size below which proper functioning collapses. As a result, a purely stochastic effect will induce growth of size. Size increases therefore tend towards the realization of tendencies towards power maximization, as size, considered over the life cycle, and including the final production of debris, correlates positively with power generation. It is important to notice that this does not necessarily mean that the driving force is adaptation in the sense of functional improvements. The truncated probability distribution simply shows that highest levels of complexity are simply very rare events, and lower levels of complexity by far dominate the relative abundance of species. Yet, this interpretation fits into the entropic view on evolution, if we broaden the view to include levels of selection. Then, we consider the entire distribution of sizes across the range of species and organisms, and would conclude that the observed distribution is the likeliest one, given constraints on growth of size and complexity.

In this case, we need to consider additional ratchet effects that result from exaptation. That means, if certain novelties in organismic structure result in increases of minimum sizes for certain kinds of organisms, the aforementioned stochastic principle applies on different levels. Therefore, we can state that a major aspect of evolution is the transition between levels, the levels defined as different forms of integration among individuals. For example, the transition from monocellular to multicellular organisms implies different minimum size thresholds. We have already seen that these transitions generally follow the logic of autocatalytic cycles (Maynard Smith and Szathmáry 1995). Thus, it is important to keep the formal equivalence of the 'level' and the 'group' notion in mind: All higher levels emerge from group–level positive externalities. These externalities create ratchet effects in the growth of minimum sizes of composite organisms. Thus, the application of the MPP and the MEP principles on autocatalytic cycles in general transfers to the current context (see Chapter Two).

Figure 3.14 The size–complexity link in evolution (simplified after Bonner 1988: 226)

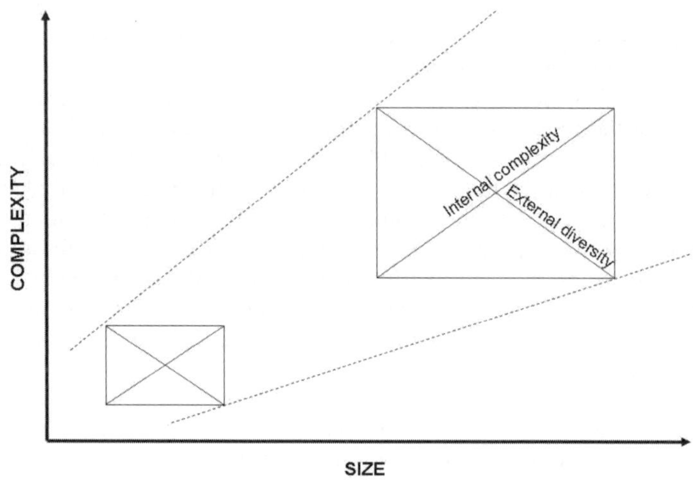

Note: A general pattern in evolution is the interdependence of size and complexity. Firstly, there is a general trend to increase size of living systems which can be interpreted as an expression of the Maximum Power Principle, as size increases require growing energy throughputs, and result in larger dissipation, considering current flows and ultimate decay. Secondly, size increases enable increasing internal complexity, which creates ratchet effects, as certain levels of achieved complexity can only be maintained beyond certain minimum size levels. Thirdly, increasing size, relative to the niche of living systems, correlates with decreasing external diversity of the species distribution, resulting from the competitive pressures of size increases.

In this view, internal and external diversity of organisms refer to the same fundamental notion of variety, with the difference resulting from the intervening levels of selection which define the boundary between internal and external structures. So, external cell–type diversity for monocellular organisms transforms into internal complexity in terms of cell types for multi–cellular organisms. Internal complexity relates with size, because the functional viability of internal complexity depends on minimum sizes. In diagram 3.14, I summarize the relevant generalizations made by Bonner (1988). Generally, we can state that evolution has resulted into continuous increases of size and complexity. Complexity is simply measured by the number of different types of internal constituents of an organism. Size, in my view, and following Vermeij (2004: 136ff), reflects the MPP, and needs to be considered not only in terms of the size of the body, but also the reach of bodily actions, among other aspects. For example, a bird may be small, but the reach of its movements can be thousands of kilometres. Then, we can state that there is a trade-off between internal complexity and external diversity. For one, internal complexity increases with size, because size simply enables the inclusion of more different sub-components. On the other hand, relative to a certain niche and ecological environment, size increases correlate with decreasing diversity of variants and species, thus reflecting the adaptive advantage of size, and the endogenous selective pressure on other organisms.

Then, we can surmise the hypothesis that with decreasing external diversity, on which external selection operates, evolvability declines. Therefore, evolution proceeds in leaps by which the trade-off between size and diversity is moved to a higher level (compare Ingold 1986: 17ff). This is enabled via integration, that is the transformation of groups into individuals, which does not necessarily imply full-scale organismic integration, but for example includes integration by means of communication (so, for example, bacteria form colonies with shared chemical information systems). Once a higher level is achieved, the trade-off between internal complexity and external diversity applies again. Evidently, this view matches with the general entropic framework developed in the first section of this chapter. Internal complexity, in the most general sense, relates with the individuality of the organism and hence the stored information; external diversity relates with the information capacity on the population level.

3.5.5. The Handicap Principle, size and metabolism

Now, if size, groups and levels are also constituted by communication, we can introduce the final general principle of evolution, the Handicap Principle (Zahavi and Zahavi 1997; compare Dawkins 1989: 313ff). The Handicap Principle is the companion principle to the Red Queen Principle in the sense that it focuses on the role of signals in interactions: Signals are an essential aspect in behavioural coordination, because they transmit information across individuals, so that the Red Queen Principle also applies for signalling: signals play a pivotal role in intra– and inter–species behavioural coordination, and thus can determine the outcome of frequency–dependent selection (for example, signals in sexual competition often manifest Red Queen effects, such as exaggeration of traits).

The Handicap Principle goes back to one fundamental problem in information processing, which results from the generation of information externalities. In the physical approach to information, all information processing is costly in energetic terms. Viewed from the single organism, therefore competition over resources would imply that organisms minimize this cost. One way to achieve this is to use information that is processed by other organisms, similar to a parasite. For example, in searching for food, individuals may just follow the tracks of others, in order to save search costs. By implication, individuals that process information that is somehow accessible to others by cheaper means, such as simple observation, create a positive externality for others. Therefore, information processing is always governed by the Red Queen Principle because individuals may get an advantage if they can exploit information processed by others, and these individuals may protect their advantage if they keep the information 'private', or even have the capability to drive a wedge between private information and accessible information, including active cheating of others (however, cheating is costly in turn, for example, if it requires to maintain complicated combinations of different behaviours directed at different observers). It is important to notice that 'cheating' does not necessarily presuppose intentional action, but can evolve by VSR processes, such as in the case of mimicry.

However, in communication and information processing there are many constellations where group–level interactions also favour the sharing of information, in the sense of making truthful information of one individual accessible to others. One is the case of information sharing cycles, which is basically reciprocity in the flow of information externalities: Animal rituals in front of audiences of con-specifics are a case in point, which results in a general containment of lethal violence in those populations. As in the previous analysis of group selection, we can surmise that these effects can occur both via shared interests (as in genetically integrated social insects) or via correlated behaviour (as in cultural interaction among humans). Another constellation is the case of conflict, where under certain conditions it is advantageous to both sides of the signalling relationship to reveal true information about comparative strength and prowess, as in mate competition or predator–prey relations. For example, a prey that is able to signal reliably its capacity to flee, would save energy costs to the predator which would try in vain to get hold of it, and, of course, would ensure its own survival.

Zahavi and Zahavi (1997) call this form of selection 'signal selection'. I posit that the duality of signal selection and natural selection directly reflects the bimodality of evolution. Natural selection operates on mechanisms; signal selection operates on signs, hence in the semiotic mode. The generation of signs is a mechanism in turn, so that the two processes are fundamentally entangled. Yet, the essential difference lies in the coordination of signalling mechanisms between different individuals, such that the effect of the signal does not rest upon its physical impact, but on the interpretation, that is the function in behavioural coordination. For example, if a predator catches a prey and devours it, this is a mechanism directly generated by the predator and impacting on the prey. If the prey sends a signal to the predator, and both achieve behavioural coordination, the impact of the signal on the predator essentially depends on the way how it interprets the signal.

Signal selection is a generalization of the biological notion of sexual selection, and therefore a fundamental form of frequency–dependent selection. In sexual selection, signalling plays a very important role to attract mating partners. These signals may run against criteria of optimality in natural selection, as has been modelled early in Fisher's concept of 'runaway selection'. Runaway selection happens if the genes determining a certain characteristic and the genes determining the preferences of the mating partner for that characteristic co-evolve and cause the exaggeration of characteristics. However, this analysis overlooks the fact that signalling is semantically complex because the fact that a trait violates adaptive optimality in one dimension may actually signal optimality in another dimension, or, even more so, in the aggregate. For example, if deer develops huge antlers that impede movements, this violates certain criteria of optimality, but signals strengths for that very reason: The deer is so strong to be able to afford this signal.

This is the meaning of the term 'Handicap Principle': the costs of traits obtain the status of a signal that reveals information about the true qualities of other traits. These costs play a double role, because it is also essential that the costs prevent the possibility of fakes. Grafen (1990) distinguishes between different kinds of handicaps, of which the so-called 'strategic choice' handicap is the central one. It is based on the assumption that one side has private information and has to decide about the proper way to signal that information reliably. For the receiver, it is important to detect cheaters. The evolutionary stable strategy implies that signals have to be costly in fitness terms, and that signals are more costly for those senders with higher quality, which implies, however, that the opportunity costs for them are lower than for senders with less quality. This is the reason why the signals are truthful and cannot be faked by low quality senders. This constellation has the result that the sender–receiver system will rapidly expand the signalling system, if the lower threshold of quality is small. The reason is that signals are sent by senders on every level of quality, such that, the more levels there are, the more effort will be invested into distinguishing the levels. That means, signalling on the lowest level actually drives up all signalling costs on the higher levels: If individuals with very low quality start to differentiate themselves from the worst individual, this requires the next–higher individuals to start to invest into signalling, and so forth; then, aggregate levels of signalling are driven by the minimum level at which signalling starts to operate (see Grafen 1990: 524).

There is a close connection to the game–theoretic debate over 'cheap talk' (Skyrms 2004: chapter 5). It has been shown that under certain conditions 'cheap talk' can also improve coordination if it triggers correlated equilibria. This happens via the destabilization of less efficient equilibria, such as PD equilibria, because cooperators can invade those populations if they base their cooperation on cheap pre-play communication, which is innovative in the sense of exploiting an unused signal, which is therefore not yet devalued by cheating ('secret handshake'). The point is that in the equilibrium, the information in the signals is back to zero, so there is also no use for fakes, however. The effect only results from the partitioning of the population, which makes equilibria accessible which were inaccessible without the signal, but do not depend on the signal to persist. This formalizes the previous analysis of group selection with reference to signalling, population boundaries and spatial structure: Signalling can lead to spatial structuration, and one spatial structuration persists, cooperation becomes possible without signalling, even if it persists.

The Handicap Principle can be interpreted in a most general way with reference to size: Size is a signal of its own, which implies that size may achieve magnitudes that go beyond optimal sizes in terms of efficiency; for example, animals might create super–large territories, relative to the foraging goals and cost–benefit considerations of locomotion expenses relative to energy harvested, because this is a signal in sexual competition, or in predator–prey interactions. In other words, large size can become a handicap, and precisely for that reason signals high quality of the larger individual (so, to be fat might not be healthy, but to be able to maintain the fat status signals that all other organismic systems are in good shape, being able to cope with fatness). Therefore, the Handicap Principle, together with the Red Queen Principle, plays an essential role in analysing the evolutionary causal dynamics that leads towards the MPP, especially in comparison to hypothetical states of efficiency. Both principles favour the maximization of power throughput. In other words, size increases in evolution can be interpreted as directly reflecting the MPP. We can argue that the causal mechanisms that are analysed with the Red Queen Principle are the forces that drive the actualization of the MPP, in the strict sense of Lotka's Principle.

Therefore, the relationship between power maximization and size allows considering one final aspect of evolution which also relates with the size/complexity trade-off: Size and internal complexity relate with particular physical mechanisms of how matterenergy flows are processed in systems, thus an aspect of living systems that I have neglected so far, metabolism. The most general way to approach this is to consider the networks through which energy flows are processed. This perspective applies for both the internal organization of organisms and the external systemic interactions in ecosystems. Therefore, we consider the issue of size in relation with the Constructal Law as exposed in Chapter Two. The Constructal Law posits another principle of 'optimality' and hence adaptation which states that living systems will obtain structural states by which they maximize power throughputs, once all possibilities of structural adaptation have been exploited. In the context of evolution, however, this implies that one essential expression of the Constructal Law is also that systems that keep the capacity for structural adaptation will be favoured in selection, if they can achieve states in which flows are further enhanced. In other words, structural adaptation happens in the context of a trade-off between optimality and evolvability: Flow–maximizing structures need to maintain evolvability

(Bejan and Lorente 2006: 21ff). Evolvability may require the maintenance of structural states which are theoretically suboptimal in a hypothetical environment that is stable.

Most generally, according to the Constructal Law living systems are seen as flow architectures, both internally (metabolism) as externally (ecosystems). The evolution of these systems happens in a state space that can be most generally characterized in terms of the following properties:

- External size of the system, that is relative to other living systems;
- Internal size, which is internal complexity in terms of flow mechanisms (that is ducts of matterenergy flows);
- Performance relative to the selective forces operating on the system;
- Configuration of metabolism;
- Evolvability.

Systems evolve in solving trade-offs in those dimensions. This results in certain regularities in nature, the allometric scaling laws (West, Brown and Enquist 1997; West and Brown 2005). In biology, allometry is the general study of quantitative relationships between parts and shapes of organisms, such as the body proportions or the relationship between muscles and bones. The importance of this field results from the fact that during development, and also during larger scale evolutionary changes, growth of size would normally have to meet certain constraints of geometry, such as the changes of volume versus changes of surface. Real world organisms do not directly reflect these constrains, as there are systematic changes of proportions with size changes, which are called 'allometric'.

An allometric scaling law has the general form of a power law, thus reflects the underlying principles of maximum entropy in generating certain distributions in nature (Grönholm and Annila 2007; Frank 2009b). This power law has the general form:

$$Y = Y_0 M_b^{\,b}$$

where Y designates a certain biological quantity, such as lifespan or growth rate and M_b is the mass of the organism. One of the most famous scaling laws is Kleiber's law which states that the basic metabolic rate of organisms scales with mass by an exponent of ¾. This law applies across vastly different orders of size, such as single cells and cell components such as mitochondria, or mammals. One possible explanation is that metabolism requires the transport of energy to all parts of the organism, which implies certain structural principles which have a universal mathematical validity. These principles go back on one particular aspect of the Constructal Law, which states that internal dissipation by flows tends towards minimization, thus resulting into maximization of power throughputs and outputs, considering both the matterenergy of the flow architecture and its output, which includes, in the life cycle perspective, decay and entropic dissolution. Thus, allometric scaling laws reflect the efficiency of adaptation in most general terms, relating to the underlying thermodynamic principles.

Allometric scaling laws are one of the immediate expressions of the interaction between physical constraints on energetic dissipation and the evolutionary dynamics of accumulating information. Summarizing these interactions as elucidated in this chapter, we may emphasize one central insight: Biological information grows via the evolution of complex constraints on living systems that manifest the phenomenon of heredity, thus result in lineages and nested hierarchies of diachronic connectedness. This picture differs in two fundamental senses from the synthesis between Darwinism and population genetics that was dominant in the second half of the twentieth century, and matches with recent theorizing about 'inclusive inheritance':

- Firstly, it eschews the idea that biological information is stored and transmitted by certain hereditary particles, the genes: Genes are just one set of constraints in those complex evolving hierarchies, though an essential one. Biological information emerges from interactions between replicators and interactors, and interactors are systems which conjoin organisms and their niches. Therefore, biological information is transmitted via multiple channels of heredity; this is a crucial result for reconciling biology with the study of human culture and economy.
- The second fundamental difference lies in the radicalization of the statistical analysis of heredity, generalizing over Price's equation. Heredity is not defined via the transmission of hereditary particles, but via statistical correlations across levels of evolution; here, the notion of the 'group' plays a central role. Individuals are groups, groups are individuals: Accordingly, selection happens on different levels, intra–group and inter–group, and major evolutionary novelties occur via the integration of groups of individuals into higher level individuals. In these processes, correlated behaviours play a driving force, ultimately embodied in the genetic material as 'bookkeeping device' of biological evolution. Yet, in the statistical view on evolution this 'bookkeeping' function is endogenous and can be realized also by alternative physical entities.

Evolution has two sides. One is the accumulation of information aka knowledge, embodied in constraints on further evolution. The other is the evolution of evolvability, or the growth of information capacity. These two sides reflect the fundamental physics of knowledge as elucidated in the previous chapters. This relationship was clearly recognized by Ronald Fisher who established the statistical view on evolution, when he compared his Fundamental Theorem with the Second Law: The role of variety as a driver of evolution in the Fundamental Theorem just states the necessary relationship between information capacity and information accumulation in the general model of evolving physical information. The evolving constraints of living systems are part and parcel of the Earth system, hence are a special kind of PIDs that ultimately increase the rates of energy dissipation; therefore, evolution is an expression of the Second Law, and does not work against it.

One of the most intriguing insights by Charles Darwin was to recognize the interaction of growth, variety and complexity in evolution (beautifully summarized in the image of the 'entangled bank' that he paints in the concluding paragraph of his 'Origin of Species'). Living systems are the most complex physical entities on Earth, and they are sustainable in the process of variation, selection and retention; at the same time, they manifest a bewildering diversity on every level of evolution, beginning with the diversity of individuals in a population. Finally, life is growth: Growth of numbers, growth of size, growth of systems, growth of energy throughputs and biomass production. These three fundamental aspects of evolution are direct expressions of the principles of the Thermodynamics of knowledge, the Second Law, the Maximum Power Principle and the Maximum Entropy Production Principle.

4. Individuals

The minds that individuals have are already the minds of individuals in groups (Robert A. Wilson 2004: 307).

4.1. THE METHODOLOGICAL STATUS OF INDIVIDUALISM AND RATIONALITY IN THE EVOLUTIONARY APPROACH TO ECONOMICS

4.1.1. Individualism, 'methodological' and evolutionary

The notion of the individual is of fundamental significance for economics as it stands. Economics adopts the beacon of methodological individualism, which means that all social phenomena are explained with reference to individual agency, additionally cast into a set of axiomatic assumptions that define individual rationality, seen as conceptually neatly separate from collective rationality (Elster 1989a: 13ff). Even in this framework, we can distinguish between fundamentally different paradigms depending on how far the role of uncertainty and ignorance is acknowledged. This is because under ignorance, the notion of unintended consequences looms large. This line separates strands of thought such as neoclassical equilibrium economics from others such as Austrian economics. Yet, all these different strands converge to the stance of individualism (Heath 2011).

In this chapter, I will explore the evolutionary theory of the individual; I emphasize that this does not mean developing an *economic* theory of the individual (akin to Dopfer 2004; Gintis 2006; or Hodgson 2010; for a general discussion in the context of Evolutionary Economics, see Vromen 2001). The difference will become clear in the course of the subsequent chapters. Suffice to state at the current point that the economic theory of the individual must be a theory of economic agents in complex systems called 'markets' (as stated in Ross 2005, 2007a). The evolutionary theory of the individual is a theory of the special kind of living systems that emerged from biological evolution, and which is supposed to be the empirical reference of the economic theory of the individual (compare Robson 2002). The 'naturalistic turn' in economics that I discussed in Chapter One implies that the latter may put substantial constraints on the theoretical conceptualization of the former; yet, the two notions need to be kept distinct. One essential conclusion of this chapter is that this separation follows from the evolutionary approach to the individual: Human individuals can be shown to be 'systemic' phenomena on evolutionary grounds, and therefore the economic approach to this systemic nature is just a special case. This view is Hegelian in essence: Hegel's individualism is about individuals as constituted by the systems in which they live, that is institutions, social norms and social interactions. This philosophical perspective is the bedrock on which the connection between the evolutionary and the economic view of the individual can be built.

I do not introduce the individual as a given, but venture to explain in evolutionary terms what individuals are and why they manifest certain structural features that are reflected in individual actions. This approach is based on the fundamental position of ontological individualism that I have outlined in Chapter One. Ontological individualism posits that only individuals exist, and that this definition of individualism relies on the criteria of irreducibility to regularities, following formal notions such as algorithmic incompressibility. Therefore, ontological individualism does not make any specifications regarding the material nature of individuals. If economics claims that only human individuals are to be recognized in analysing economic systems, this is a proposition that needs justification on evolutionary terms. After all, in certain applications of economic theory it is regarded as quite natural to treat 'firms' as individuals. Ontologically, this is fully legitimate, if we approach the population of firms as a set of irreducible individuals, which, however, seems to conflict with methodological individualism, strictly spoken. Methodological individualism differs from ontological individualism in submitting the explicit claim that only certain kinds of individuals count for the analysis of human systems, namely individuals as being implicitly defined by human organisms. A major task of this chapter is to show that a naturalistic approach to the individual results into a systemic view. This is externalist in a fundamental sense: Individuals are constituted by organism–environment causal interactions, and there is no primordial causal and logical role for individuals as being demarcated by the boundaries of the body.

4.1.2. The tension between externalism and internalism in the economic theory of the individual

My position points towards deep issues with the immanent consistency of the economic approach. This is because it mixes up two contradictory foundational approaches to the Philosophy of Mind, externalism and internalism (cf. Wilson 2005: chapter 4). Normatively as well as intuitively, methodological individualism in economics is internalist, thus tracing all causes that drive economic processes back to internal states of individuals, treated as 'subjective preferences' and 'utility functions'. However, it is important to acknowledge that, in fact, the formal use of methodological individualism in economics does not make claims about the material substrate of economic systems, even though most economists would intuitively equate 'individuals' with human individuals as defined by the boundaries of the body. With the deployment of equilibrium analysis in the twentieth century, 'individuals' in economic theory are purely abstract entities which are defined relative to these theoretical systems (Ross 2007b). Economics does not claim that any real human individual behaves like these abstract entities. The background of this approach is twofold.

One is Friedman's (1953) instrumentalism. That means, economics uses highly abstract and therefore certainly empirically vacuous assumptions in order to economize on formulating predictions. So, the proof of the pudding lies in the successful explanation and prediction of observed facts about human behaviour (the ideal–typical approach is Becker 1976). If that works out, there is no need to revise the theoretical assumptions, even if it is plainly obvious that they do not describe reality. The other reason for adopting methodological individualism is that the set of axioms about human agents in fact does not describe real world actors but 'agents' in economic systems. That means, economic systems manifest certain properties in which agents appear to act in a way that can be described by means of these axiomatic assumptions. So, the empirical reference of the theory is the system, not the individual. Then, methodological individualism is a program of theoretical reductionism: it means that systems–level phenomena can be reduced to individual–level phenomena, which are theoretical entities, not real–world entities in the first place. There are different ways to relate this argument with the real world, such as arguing that economic competition is a force that will only allow for the manifestation of certain kinds of behaviour (this is the classical Alchian 1977 argument; a more general version is the 'money pump' argument, see Cubitt and Sugden 2001). In other words, people are not rational, but they are selected to be(come) rational by acting in the context of economic systems. By implication, theoretical rational agents appear to be powerful analytical means to analyse those systems (such as 'representative agents').

From the philosophical perspective, the second interpretation of methodological individualism is of considerable interest, because it factually adopts an externalist approach to rationality. The externalist approach is empirically validated by many results of experimental economics, especially experimental markets (Smith 2003; yet, the empirical record in the field is mixed, see Fehr and Tyran 2005). This research has shown that agents behave 'as if' they act as rational optimizers if markets are designed in certain ways. In the most extreme case, even zero–intelligence agents can behave in a way that on the aggregate, the equilibrium result based on perfect rationality can materialize. From this follows, that the economic assumption of rationality is an externalist one, which states that rationality is a systems property (that is of institutions), but not a property of individuals (for a most elaborate statement of this insight, see Ross 2005). This is also true for the theory of revealed preferences. Obviously, the methodological dilemma of the standard theory results from the fact that the term 'subjectivity' with relation to preferences clearly suggests an internalist interpretation, which therefore stands in tension with the externalism of the formal theory of rationality. This is even more pronounced if one considers the recent attempts at developing a neuroscience reduction of the notion of subjective utility, resulting into neuroeconomic internalism (Knutson et al. 2009; Glimcher 2011; cf. Herrmann-Pillath 2012a, Ross 2012).

Apparently, the externalist interpretation of rationality raises the important question of how far the economic assumptions can be extended beyond the realm of economic systems and markets in particular. This was a central tenet of economics in the past decades and often labelled 'economic imperialism' (Radnitzky and Bernholz 1987). Indeed, economics has even intruded biology (Hammerstein 2001). However, in this particular case we meet an explicit methodological correspondence to the externalist view on rationality: Economic applications in biology do not assume that living systems are rational actors, but that evolution results into certain systemic states which can be analysed 'as if' agents act as rational optimizers. To the contrary, the extensions of economics into broader domains of the human sciences assume that the material assumption of individual rationality is essential. It should be mentioned that this view also relates with other philosophical value statements because the assumption of rationality comes along with the emphasis on human choice, and hence the idea of human autonomy, consciousness and self-determination. This establishes the broader basis for methodological individualism in ethics and politics, as epitomized in classical writings such as Popper (1945).

As I adopt the externalist approach to mind and knowledge, I accept the economic reasoning, if understood in the externalist way. However, I conclude that this means that rationality is certainly specific to certain domains of interactions, and dependent on the prevailing regularities, that is social norms, institutions etc. This is basically the position of Max Weber, who may be duly regarded as the intellectual father of the notion of methodological individualism in the social sciences in general (Weber 1922: 2, 6). Max Weber used the idea of (individual) rationality in two senses. The first approximates Friedman's instrumentalism in stating that rationality is indispensable to arrive at scientific explanations, because all other factors seem to be random 'disturbances'. The other is that rationality as 'rationalism' is an emergent phenomenon of certain societies, in particular modern capitalism (cf. Schluchter 1979). Naturally, the externalist notion of rationality therefore lends itself to sociological interpretations. This is an important insight, because we realize that existing disciplinary barriers break down in the evolutionary perspective: In fact, economic instrumentalism is a disguised form of sociological reasoning, because it factually adopts an externalist approach to rationality, inappropriately cast into internalist language.

In this context, one important result of Chapter Three looms large: This is that groups are the primordial analytical category in evolutionary analysis, because all individuals can be understood in terms of highly integrated groups of phylogenetically older and simpler individuals. If one takes as one distinctive feature of economics relative to sociology the question whether individuals or groups are primordial, it is evident that the idea that individuals are composite entities immediately renders this disciplinary demarcation line obsolete. The question is how we can make empirical sense of the idea that individuals are groups, referring both to the internal structure of individuals and their embeddedness into external relations. This is one important task of this chapter: The idea that individuals are groups can be interpreted in terms of recent theories in the brain sciences that approach the brain as a complex system of modules, and eschew the idea of a centralized decision making structure.

4.1.3. Brains, minds and individuals

In establishing this argument, we consider the relationship between brains and mind again, building on the results of Chapter One. An important (though also disputed) result of the modern brain sciences is that the brain evolved as a modularized system. This view underlies recent developments in entirely new branches of the human sciences, in particular Evolutionary Psychology (Tooby and Cosmides 2005), and looks back on radically new perspectives developed in as different disciplines as Artificial Intelligence (for example Minsky's 1986 famous notion of the 'society of mind') or economics (for example Elster's 1986 edited volume on 'multiple selves'). On an even more basic level, the brain is seen as an evolutionary system of its own that evolved into complex structures with many interacting components of different evolutionary age. This observation provides the empirical basis for the idea that individuals are to be seen as composites (though this would not imply, rhetoric aside, that these composites are 'selves,' see Damasio 2010). This contradicts the view that there is a central decision agency in the brain (dubbed the 'homunculus' by Dennett 1991), and therefore would lead to question the economic notion of a 'general purpose rationality' governing all human decision making.

However, this apparent contradiction only applies if economics is interpreted in the internalist way. The externalist interpretation of the traditional economic view means that the individuals are actually functions in an evolving economic system: For example, the function of a trader is to make profit, because if she does not make profit, she will be selected negatively. Externalism implies that certain economic behaviours are determined by the environment, and hence proximately can be seen as functions that maintain the larger system in which the agents operate. Then, in terms of the biological notions of selection and adaptation, individual behaviour would be seen as an integral part of adaptive functions realized on the group level, with selective forces also impinging on this level, beyond the individual level. In other words, traders make profits in order to be sustainable agents in a market environment, and they contribute to the collective making of markets by this kind of behaviour. This argument can even be lifted to a higher level of complexity in supposing that the belief that actors are rational and consistent decision makers may have a function in maintaining the larger systems (for a related argument on 'free will', see Sommers 2007).

Therefore, I approach 'rationality' in terms of a function, and not as an intrinsic property actors have: This also means that 'agency' is a system level phenomenon, and not related to individuals as defined by bodily boundaries (for a related view on economics, see Wilson 2004: 116). The question is how the brain takes part in realizing this function. In this regard, the rise of Behavioural Economics, Experimental Economics and Neuroeconomics in the recent decades has been perceived by many as shaking the foundations of economic analysis. I will come back on the results of this research in due course of the argument; suffice to state at this point that there is a plethora of empirical results that demonstrate convincingly that the brain does not operate in terms of 'rationality' as defined by economic theory (for a comprehensive textbook exposition, see Wilkinson and Klaes 2012). This result can be most generally explained in terms of the modularity of the brain: For example, we are able to learn to calculate probabilities correctly with certain parts of the brain, but if we are not primed to do so, our reactions to situations that involve probabilities are influenced by processes in other parts of the brain, that end up into violations of mathematical probability calculations. This results into the contextualization of our capability to calculate probabilities (for example, when faced with the task to detect cheating, our performance is much better than in answering questions cast into numerical terms, see Gigerenzer 1996, 1997).

Now, relying on an important insight of Chapter One, I do not claim that these observations directly question the economic approach, because it confuses the origination of actions with the emergence of functions. The central question is how we deal with the category of 'mind' in economics. One root of the current methodological troubles is the fact that standard economics is mentalist, whereas the new approaches are naturalistic. Surely, mentalism in economics is also a misplaced reflection of the aforementioned methodological status of rationality as a systemic principle, but mostly inheres in the applications of the concept, for example, in the purely inferential use of rationality in Game Theory. Rationality is a property of mind, and the problem with recent empirical results is perceived to be that they seem to suggest that brains do not operate as such, as brains and minds are seen as co-extensive.

Figure 4.1 Brain, mind and individual

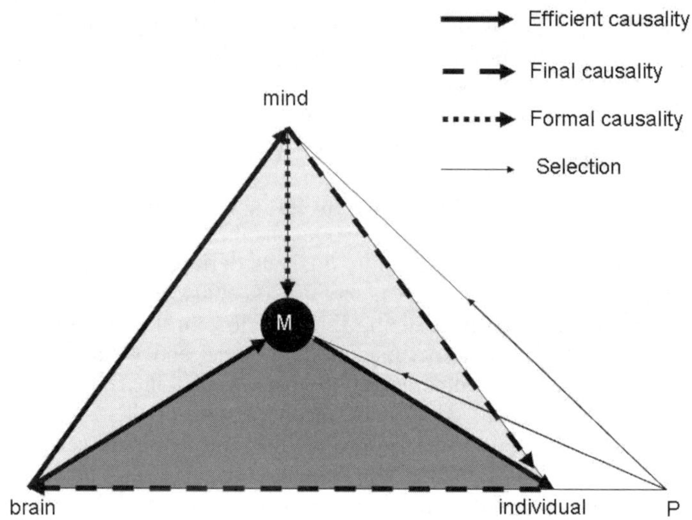

Note: The triadic approach to individuals states that individuals are functions in systems into which they are embedded as agents, and from which selective forces originate that shape the evolution of those functions. Functions are human actions which are efficiently–caused by brain mechanisms. The information embodied in the functions emerges from semiosis, which constitutes the mind. Hence, the mind is a set of signs that refer formal–causally to efficient–causal brain mechanisms that generate actions. Thus, functions as actions relate essentially with meanings of signs; signs are population level entities that efficient–causally relate with brains, but assume meaning because they enable communication between brains (compare Chapter One, fig. 1.4). Thus, brains of individuals are confined to the boundaries of the body, but minds of individuals transcend these boundaries as population–level phenomena.

Now, we can resolve this problem in adopting the triadic Peircian view in the following way (figure 4.1). As I have stated in Chapter One, in the externalist view mind is a semiotic phenomenon, which means is a set of signs that mediates causally between different brains. This is also the Hegelian view, meaning that mind emerges from externalized actions that are efficiently caused by brains. Therefore, mind is a population–level phenomenon, in evolutionary jargon. This drives a deep conceptual wedge between all reductionist approaches that aim at explaining mind via the brain. In the triadic view, this boils down to the simple assertion that individual behaviour roots in efficient–causal mechanisms that involve the brain, but this should not be confused with a full scale causal explanation, because the function of behaviour is determined on the population level, via the evolution of signs that make up the mind. 'Mental' processes can be interpreted in terms of formal causality, that is as categorization of efficient causal mechanisms, and functions evolve through the working of final causality by which the basic brain mechanisms are imbued with meaning as function. This analysis makes clear why all attempts in the past failed to analyse human behaviour in terms of simple stimulus–response models, which had already been eschewed in Hayek's analysis of categorization in the human brain.

This observation helps us to make sense of the current methodological frictions in economics. If we conceive of rationality as a function, then we cannot possibly reduce this function to the brain. Vice versa, it is meaningless to use observations about the brain (psychological, neuroscientific etc.) to refute propositions about rationality (which vindicates certain strong reactions against Neuroeconomics expressed in current economic thinking, for example Harrison 2008; Gul and Pesendorfer 2008; Rubinstein 2008). Rationality as function emerges from the semiotic conjunction of causalities that is mediated via mind. Minds as population level phenomena constitute sign systems that channel brain actions in such a way that rational action in terms of function is made possible. This seemingly abstract argument is easy to understand empirically.

Take, for example, a financial trader. If she acts rationally on a financial market, this depends on mental processes. A mental process is not a brain process, although it involves brain processes in an essential way. Yet, many brain processes deviate from rationality. So, observing a real world individual may result in the identification of mechanisms M that cause even dysfunctional behaviour. So, researchers may identify hormone mechanisms that determine the behaviour of financial traders (for surveys, see Coates et al. 2010; Wargo et al. 2010). Yet, this is not sufficient to understand the behaviour of traders, as it is emerging from thick descriptions of the field data (for example Zaloom 2003, 2004; Beunza and Stark 2008). The standard argument in economics is that one can approach the aggregate behaviour of traders with the notion of rationality because this applies for the average behaviour, with all irrationalities cancelling out. Thus, the rational agent can be even approached as the 'representative agent', where the population is substituted by one single actor. In the triadic view, this is misplaced because it unnecessarily leaves the role of mind unexplained. Mind is an emergent property of the semiotic systems in which traders operate.

For example, traders receive a certain education, they follow certain social norms of the trading communities, and they mostly obey to certain institutions. Rationality emerges from the complex confluence of brain processes and these manifestations of Hegelian 'objective spirit'. This operates via the conjunction of causal modes: For example, social norms classify certain mechanisms (such as the emotion of loss aversion) and may transform them in a way that they do no longer stay in tension with realizing the function of rationality (Smith and Dickhaut 2005 show that emotional responses to auction institutions vary with the design of the institutions).

This manifests formal causality. Then, rationality is an evolving property of financial markets which results from historically contingent selective forces, reflecting final causality. So, in this picture the efficient causal analysis of brain mechanisms that generate certain behaviours is by far insufficient to understand the functioning of real world actors on real world financial markets (for a related view, see MacKenzie 2006: 266ff). However, this enlarged perspective implies that economics needs to heed attention to the disciplinary perspectives of sociology, anthropology and other social sciences, precisely in order to vindicate its original stance towards rationality.

4.1.4. Minds as systems of interpretance

We can grasp this fundamental point in figure 4.2, which shows how the analysis in this Chapter relates with the subsequent ones (compare Chapter One, figure 1.9).

Figure 4.2 The human system of interpretance

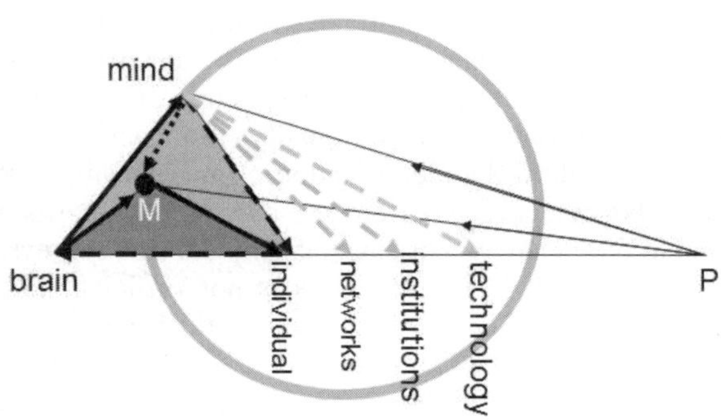

Note: In the triadic view, individuals are functions in hierarchies of embedded functions, that is systems of interpretance. This view matches with recent approaches to the 'extended mind' in cognitive sciences. 'Mental' phenomena refer to functions in different contexts, with the most basic being networks between brains. Networks manifest the emergent property of institutions, and they include artefacts, that is technology. Hence, minds are made up of these three main ingredients, networks, institutions, and technology, which interact in creating human individuals qua agents realizing functions.

This is a most simple visualization of structures of 'objective spirit' which lie behind the economic assumption of rationality. This is still a simplified analysis because I do not yet make the hierarchical structure of mind explicit, which emerges from the fully-fledged evolutionary approach as deployed in Chapter Three. What is important to fix now is that the triadic conjunction of brain, mind and individual happens in complex systems of interpretance of human systems. These systems manifest different levels, which I classify into three most general ones. The first is the notion already referred to in Chapter One, namely the connectivity of human actors, that is brains, via minds, which is the level of networks (for a seminal approach in cognitive sciences, see Hutchins 1995; compare Sterelny 2004). The notion of network is the most straightforward specification of the generic term of 'group' in Evolutionary Theory. This corresponds to the most abstract view of markets as networks of interactions; however, real world markets today show the strong impact of the other levels, too. The next level is the level of institutions, which emerges from regularities of network interactions. Mind obtains institutional characteristics on this level, quite in the original Hegelian sense. Finally, I scrutinize technology as an element of mind, a perspective which is much emphasized in recent thought about the 'extended mind' (Clark 2011). Both institutions and technology can be seen as artefacts created by collective human action, feeding back on the fundamentals of this action.

So, coming back to the example of financial markets, rationality of traders emerges firstly, from the level of interactions in networks, such as information transmission, emergent social norms, copying etc. Next, rationality is further enhanced by the emergence of institutions, such as regulatory institutions, accounting standards etc. And finally, rationality is further shaped by the diffusion of technologies that support or even partly substitute human decision making, such as computerized trades. Once these systems of interpretance are made explicit, it may appear to be reasonable and justifiable to approach the resulting economic system of financial markets in terms of models that focus on the systemic level, and simplify human 'actors' into rational 'agents'. This would imply, as stated at the beginning of this section, that the evolutionary theory of the individual ultimately supports a particular kind of economic theory of the individual (for more on that, see Chapter Eight).

Yet, the same approach does not automatically justify the standard notion of rationality in other contexts, such as consumer behaviour (for a related abstract conceptualization of markets, see Sugden 2004). In this regard, the insights of Behavioural Economics may apply with full rigour (aptly overviewed by Kahneman 2003). In this chapter, I concentrate on individuals, and I postpone the analysis of the larger systems of interpretance to the following chapters. Therefore, I make full use of this rich recent research in order to construct a naturalistic approach to the human individual. I begin with understanding the human brain in evolutionary terms, thus following the methodological standard that I introduced at the beginning of this chapter: Which properties of brains can we ground in theories and empirical evidence about the evolution of the human brain?

4.2. COOPERATION, ENERGY AND THE EVOLUTION OF THE BRAIN

4.2.1. Brains as exaptatively emergent adaptations

Brains are structures of neuronal mechanisms that allow for specific kinds of problem solving and information transmission. As such, brain structure reflects human phylogeny, as has been stated classically in MacLean's theory of the triune brain, distinguishing between the 'reptile', the 'limbic' and the 'neocortex' brain structures which constitute partly autonomous units connected via specific neuronal pathways (for a critical assessment of MacLean's approach in the context of modern brain sciences, see LeDoux 1997: 92ff, 2000; Konner 2002: 135ff). Typically, the 'reptile brain' contains systems of homeostatic regulation and fixed response patterns, the 'limbic system' encompasses basic emotions and survival related valuation systems, and the 'neocortex' includes all the higher level functions. Those three systems evolved gradually, a process which continued also in latest stages of human phylogeny, in which the growth of the prefrontal cortex was the crucial phenomenon, which is home to most higher–level cognitive operations typical for the human species. Although this triune theory is certainly over-simplifying to a large degree, the basic perspective is still useful to make the fundamental point about the modularity of the brain and its relationship with human phylogeny. For example, in Damasio's (2010) approach to consciousness and the self these phenomena are seen as emergent features of a complex interaction between brain modules of different phylogenetic age, such as the brain stem and the posteromedial cortices. For the argument presented in this chapter, the specific patterns of functional localisation do not matter.

One of the most important functions of brains is to enable vicarious selection processes based on internal models of the environment (Dennett 1995: 374ff), recently dubbed 'Bayesian brains' (Friston 2010). Organisms with brains can virtually explore environments and predict future events, and they can design corresponding problem solutions, without trying those solutions in the real world, fully succumbing to trial–and–error selection. Hence, vicarious selection is a powerful means of enhancing survival chances. Therefore, brains also enable and enhance phenotypic plasticity, resulting from the flexibility of internal models of vicarious selection, which is ultimately reflected in behavioural outputs.

At the same time, brains enable communication of information between con-specifics, in particular. Therefore, brains and communication systems on the population level need to be seen as necessary complements (Edelman 1987: 313ff): On the one hand, brains enable communication, on the other hand, as we shall see, their internal operations essentially depend on sign systems that emerge from communication. The evolutionary rationale behind this linkage is that communicating brains enable population level learning, thus further containing the costs of individual–level trial–and–error selection (Boyd and Richerson 1985 is a classic on this).

We can surmise that there are a number of adaptive advantages of brains which can explain why brains emerged and grew, just because brains are extremely expensive to maintain (on the following, see Smil 1999: 80f): Brains consume more than 20 per cent of all metabolic throughput of humans (that is the Basic Metabolic Rate), only surpassed by the liver; presumably, the evolution of human cognitive capacities went hand in hand with continuous energetic intensification of brain metabolism (Khaitovich et al. 2008). During ontogeny, and especially in the early stages, the development of the brain consumes more than 40 per cent. If one compares the cumulative energetic costs of developing brains between chimpanzees and humans, the difference is staggering: To achieve the brain weight of about 400 grams, the chimpanzee value is about 0,7 GJ, whereas the human brain needs more than 2 GJ to build a 1300 gram brain. So it is obvious that we need to explain two facts at the same time, namely the benefits that accrue to individuals with larger brains, and the means by which these benefits could be made energetically sustainable. This point is essential: All propositions about human brains must be based on arguments that refer to adaptive functions of brains under tight energetic constraints. So, the evolutionary theory of the individual can be systematically grounded in the general analysis of evolution outlined in Chapter Two.

However, in this context we also need to make full use of the insights gained in Chapter Three. The evolution of the brain can be seen as a case in point for the conjunction of the Red Queen Principle and the Handicap Principle as exposed there: Brains are essential devices for information processing, and hence played an important role in the evolutionary arms race over the exploitation of information and signalling for enhancing survival chances and reproduction opportunities. This also suggests that the brain is an exaptation, at least with reference to functions that it adopted in later stages of its evolution. In other words, we should avoid any kind of shortcut explanation which interprets the evolution of brains in terms of their functions today, but have to take into consideration that these functions are exaptations which result from other evolutionary forces and resulting functions in the phylogenetic past: For example, whereas human intelligence was once mainly seen as being expressed in tool use, hence technology, today researchers believe that social intelligence is more fundamental and evolved earlier, such that the former may be seen as an exaptation of the latter (for example Goody 1995b). This is also important to recognize the possible tension between certain brain functions and emergent functions as exaptations: Since the brain is a complex modular structure, exaptations emerging for some modules need not stay in harmony with adaptations in other modules. To the contrary, we even need to take into consideration that exaptations today may be even jeopardizing other adaptive functions. For example, brains may be especially exapted to cultural transmission of information, but this might stay in tension with biological adaptation even in the most general sense, that is differential reproduction (Richerson and Boyd 2005: chapter 5) (for example, in many societies individuals with an especially strong cultural role forsake reproduction opportunities, for example in the context of religion). However, this possibility does not contradict the general evolutionary theory sketched in Chapter Three.

One of the simplest forms of applying these general evolutionary principles is to regard brains as handicaps, precisely because they are energetically expensive (Dutton 2003). Then, brains and the corresponding shapes of the skull would be conceived as signals in intra–specific competition that transfer information about strength and health of individuals. This includes the possibility of runaway selection, which might be even empirically vindicated, given the very rapid growth of the forebrain in an evolutionary timescale. However, there are more sophisticated versions of applying those principles on brain evolution. These relate with general arguments on why the evolution of brains was adaptive.

These arguments concentrate on the human capacity to cooperate in groups and to organize complex group activities (Goody 1995a; Tomasello 2008). This statement should not be interpreted in value terms, such as viewing cooperation as intrinsically good. There is no fundamental contradiction with 'Machiavellian' approaches to the social origins of human cognitive skills (Byrne 1995), since many 'Machiavellian' strategies also require cooperation. This also affects many theories about the possible role of warfare in human evolution (for classical statements, see Alexander 1979 or Corning 2003: 232ff), as warfare also requires cooperation.

Cooperation in human groups presupposes three capabilities:

- Firstly, the capability to adopt a detached stance from one's own position to understand the perspectives of others;
- Secondly, the capability to planning in advance, especially for situations in which individuals are absent and not directly controllable via behavioural signals;
- Thirdly, the capability to credibly communicate the pertinent intentions and plans.

It seems elusive to construct 'just so stories' about the adaptiveness of group action here, because the basic point seems more than obvious, for example, with regard to hunting large game or game capable of fast movements. What is more important is that the evolved capacities would have produced far-reaching implications for the further evolution of brains. This is because all of these capacities enhance the capacity for cheating, too. This is where the Red Queen Principle applies with a vengeance: The evolution of brains was driven by an arms race in signalling.

4.2.2. Signalling and brain evolution

The generic situation has been modelled by Skyrms (2004) as the Stag Hunt Game. This generic structure is closely connected with the Prisoners' Dilemma, another classic pattern of social cooperation and its fallacies. In the original Rousseau version, the story is about a group of hunters who need to cooperate to hunt a deer. Deer is a very valuable prey, so everyone wants to get it, and there are ways to share without conflict. However, the group has to disperse, with some members rushing and baiting the prey, and some possibly lucky to kill it. While doing this, hares may pass by. Nobody knows in advance whether the group will make the big kill. So there are strong incentives to leave the team and just to catch the hare, so that the cooperative venture will fail. Then we have a situation which is similar to the PD: As the members of the group are dispersed, they cannot communicate. Yet, there is a fundamental difference between the Stag Hunt and the PD structure, namely that the former has two Nash equilibria, cooperation and defection, the latter only one, defection (see table 4.1). This analysis implies, especially, that all PD structures transform into a Stag Hunt structure if they involve repeated play and the possibility of punishment (indicated by -2 in the brackets of the PD pay-offs in table 4.1), which would reduce the defectors' payoff sufficiently in order to establish the pay–off structure of a Stag Hunt game. Therefore, the Stag Hunt structure is indeed the more universal one. This implies further, as has been shown extensively by Skyrms, that mechanisms of aligning social behaviour obtain a central role in social evolution, as the Stag Hunt at its core is a coordination problem, and less a social dilemma.

Table 4.1 Stag Hunt Game

	Prisoners' dilemma		Stag hunt	
	cooperate	defect	cooperate	defect
cooperate	2 / 2	0 / 3(-2)	2 / 2	0 / 1
defect	3(-2) / 0	1 / 1	1 / 0	1 / 1

Now, it is important to reflect upon the methodological role of these game–theoretic structures in the evolutionary context. The standard approach is offered by Evolutionary Game Theory, which would identify evolutionary stable strategies that are defined as states of interactions which cannot be invaded by any mutant with other strategies. However, this view is too narrow. The more fundamental evolutionary analysis would proceed to ask the question: If there are potential losses to every actor, how would their evolution change the actors themselves in a way such that the problems would no longer occur?

In this context, it is essential to draw a line between standard economic analysis and evolutionary analysis. As it is easy to see from the Stag Hunt structure, the emergence of cooperative strategies cannot be counted as group–oriented or even altruistic behaviour here, because there is a clear individual benefit in the cooperative solutions, even relative to the cheater strategies. Therefore, in principle the emergence of corresponding behaviour can be rationalized in terms of the inclusive fitness concept. Yet, this even applies, and more importantly, for the PD structure, which manifests relative disadvantages of the cheater strategy in the Nash equilibrium. Thus, adopting cooperative strategies is fitness maximizing in the biological sense, though individually irrational in the economic sense (for a pertinent discussion, see West et al. 2006; on the resulting empirical complexities, see Gurven 2004). This applies for both the level of the individual and the level of the group (Bowles at al. 2003). This reflects the dissociation between the Pareto optimum and the Nash equilibrium in those game theoretic structures: Hence, solutions to those dilemmata are always possible in an evolutionary setting (as modelled for example by means of cellular automata and genetic algorithms, see the overview in Miller and Page 2008: chapter 10).

The key notion in this context is reciprocity, because unless a particular behaviour is genuinely altruistic in the sense of creating negative fitness effects on the actor, but positive ones for others, mechanisms are always possible that stabilize the reciprocal exchange of benefits, even if a short term cost is involved (Binmore 2005: Chapter 5). Reciprocity is a problem because it is sequential, that is, if one individual concedes a benefit first to another individual, a free–rider constellation is created, allowing the other to exploit the former. Therefore, in classical problems of social coordination backward induction typically leads towards the unravelling of patterns of coordination which would certainly benefit all interaction partners, that is, would not contradict the criterion of individual benefit in the final stage, which, however, cannot be attained by individual optimization (Hollis 1998). This problem cannot be solved by inferential rationality commonly assumed in economics, because endogenous signalling via observed actions does not create the common knowledge necessary to assess the types of agents correctly (Knudsen 1993; Binmore 1997). Therefore, from the economic point of view the attainment of cooperative solutions can only be based on weak altruism as defined by Field (2001). This kind of behaviour is also found in real world experimental applications of the centipede game, for example (Camerer 2003: 94f, 218ff). That means, individuals have to invest into an 'advance' of cooperation which faces the risk of cheating on the other side. However, from the biological point of view, which takes the long run perspective of evolution, a population that attains this solution can maximize individual benefits *both* individually and in the aggregate. So, the emergence of capacities to generate these solutions should be favoured by natural selection operating on multiple levels, as analysed in Chapter Three.

Against the background of this analysis, the more significant issue in evolutionary terms is the role of cheating in terms of players' identities, because cooperative solutions can always be sustainable if players can credibly communicate that they will cooperate. The standard economic dilemmata result from the fact that this communication is not possible, given the assumptions about individual rationality. The possibility of cheating triggers the Red Queen dynamics in the sense that one can argue that cooperation was a driving evolutionary force in both senses, namely, enabling cooperation, and coping with the problems for cooperation that result from precisely those factors that enable cooperation. The central role is played by language here. This is because language also creates the capability to communicate lies, that is, to create fictitious scenarios for action that mislead others (on deception in signalling systems in general, see Skyrms 2010: 73ff). Most generally, this means that language can also serve for cheating about the identity of players.

Ross (2005: 291ff) has a game–theoretic argument that helps to clarify this point. Following Binmore (1994), he distinguishes between two levels of games, one, *G''*, encompassing the biological aspect of interaction, and the other, *G*, the specific strategic context of actual interactions among actors. Biological reductionism would claim that the results of this game are ultimately determined by natural selection, as in sociobiology. Ross argues that this picture leaves another level out of sight, which is the series of recurrent and interrelated games *G'* in which the agents mutually coordinate their identities as players. From this, a dependency of the results of the games of type *G* emerges on the results of the games *G'* in which it is determined which identity the players in *G* games will assume. This argument is closely related to the analysis of Skyrms (2004: Chapter 5) which shows how signalling makes pre-coordination in games *G* possible by sorting populations of players into subsets of a similar kind, hence similar identity, thus changing the games *G* into games with correlated equilibria. Skyrms also shows that these 'identities' lose informational significance after the equilibria have been established, because, for example, they just stabilize the path leading to the selection of a particular equilibrium in a multiple equilibrium setting. That is, in equilibrium, the level of *G'* seems to be causally irrelevant. This corresponds to the everyday perception that language is just a medium for expressing given preferences. In fact, however, it is the medium in which identities emerge, and without which the equilibria could never be attained which ex post are seen to be based on neutral stabilizing incentive patterns (for a different, though related analysis introducing lexicographic preferences for honesty, which might reflect shared identities, see Demichelis and Weibull 2008).

There are two aspects that are essential for the processes that result in certain patterns of *G'* games. One is the process of signalling, the other is the capacities of actors to adopt identities that they share with others. Beginning with the second aspect first, Sugden (2000) argued that for analysing human agency, team preferences are more general and fundamental than individual preferences; the latter are actually special cases of the former. This idea can be related to Tuomela's (2007) detailed analysis of the two modes in which human individuals can operate, the 'I–mode' and the 'we–mode': Most simply, the 'we–mode' is a cognitive and behavioural stance or mode of reasoning, in which individuals perceive and act as members of groups, whereas the 'I–mode' is the purely individualistic stance. Tuomela argues on evolutionary grounds that humans evolved the capacity to switch between different modes of action, which are based on respective cognitive attitudes (I present related arguments and evidence in the subsequent sections). Correspondingly, even for the case of cooperation there are different modes, such as, for example, purely I–mode based cooperation as compared to strongly We–mode based cooperation: For example, the prisoners in the PD game might adopt the I–mode, in which the classical dilemmata of cooperation emerge, yet could be overcome by certain mechanisms, such as Tit-for-Tat; or, they adopt a We–mode, which directly enables them to go for the cooperative solution because they know for certain that the other will adopt the same in the We–mode.

The adaptiveness of the We-mode results from the fact that cooperative functions can be realized more efficiently. One most general reason for this difference is that the We–mode does not fall into the trap of circularity which is possible in all I–mode approaches to cooperation which are typically analysed in game theory, such as the tit-for-tat strategies and related topics. Circularity always pops up if the I-mode action depends on others' actions, whereas the We–mode action directly presupposes that everybody acts on the basis of shared intentionality. As in Sugden's analysis, this means that the typical strategic pay–off structures of game theory collapse into single–valued joint strategies of the group. This argument, however, does not establish group–level entities, as the We–mode is strictly a property of individuals (compare Tuomela 1995: 369ff). Yet, individuals share collective attitudes and collective intentionality in terms of the 'we'.

Although this approach may seem to do away fundamental problems of social philosophy with a sleight of hand, Tuomela's strong point is that the We–mode is not just a cognitive mode that can be adopted in an arbitrary way but is a permanent, genetically fixed feature of human action that nonetheless needs to be activated by certain signals. That means, on the one hand humans do not cooperate in the We–mode necessarily, but they have the natural capacity to do so. So, the thrust of this philosophical analysis is that human brains are 'social' in their basic structure, meaning that sociality is independent from any kind of 'rational' decision-making process that proceeds by higher–level cognitive functions.

In this peculiar sense, the We–mode might reflect 'irrational' aspects of human decisions and behaviour. This leads us back to the initial observations about brain structure: In the triune picture of the brain, 'rational' behaviour is associated with the neocortex, especially the forebrain, and 'irrational' behaviour with the phylogenetically older brain structures. Then, the question seems appropriate whether at least some aspects of the capacity to switch between modes and in particular, to adopt the We–mode, relate with particular patterns of brain structure; in this context, specifically with those structures that relate higher–level cognitive processes with the processing of emotions and even visceral processes in general. This is the most straightforward way to demonstrate that the adoption of the We–mode is not a question of arbitrary choices by higher–level cognitive processes, and thus cannot succumb to the dilemmata of rationality as analysed by standard strategic Game Theory.

4.2.3. Enabling brains for living in groups

One important argument refers to the co-evolution between brain size and group size. In a recent survey, Dunbar and Shultz (2007) show that there was a feedback between the performance of the 'social brain' and the adaptive effects related to group–level performance. The evolution of the neocortex took place under energetic constraints, as I have emphasized already. Therefore, it could only happen if the resulting effects were functional in terms of the energetic return on investment. This implies that if the neocortex indeed improved interactions in groups, these interactions also contributed to an increased energy throughput on the individual level. This differs from a purely individual optimization, as, in economic parlance, gains from cooperation on the group–level in the sense of collective goods would have loomed large. The core issue results whether the growth of the neocortex preceded the increasing complexity of social interactions, thus enabling the latter, or whether social complexity was a driver of neocortex growth. So, energetic or ecological constraints operated on two different levels, one is the level of brain size as such, and the other is the level of group size. On the latter, cognitive constraints operate, too, which are determined by brain size.

If the human brain co-evolved with human groups, the question results what is the most universal brain mechanism undergirding this co-evolution. I posit that this is imitation. Imitation plays a central role in co-evolutionary theories of biology and culture, such as Boyd and Richerson (1985), Richerson and Boyd (2005). Imitation is a uniquely human capacity (Tomasello 2008: 23ff, 102ff). It is important to emphasize, that in spite of its cognitive complexity, imitation is not based on conscious forms of intentionality. It is the basic form of human learning during ontogeny and separates human infants from apes (for example, apes learn most of their species–specific gestures by ontogenetic ritualization, but not from imitating others, which would enable much larger phenotypic plasticity, as in humans). Human infants develop the capacity to imitate others' actions in a context–free way, that is, they become able to separate goals of actions from individual perspectives, and they can replicate intentions in their own actions. This is important to emphasize because one great advantage of the concept of imitation is its simplicity in terms of modelling. Imitation can be simply conceived as copying, which allows us to apply all sorts of network models of group interaction, the core topic of the next chapter (Bentley and Shennan 2003, Bentley et al. 2007; Rendell et al. 2010).

The analysis of imitation is related to the recently burgeoning literature on empathy (overview in Kirman and Teschl 2010). Empathy is a fundamental human feature that has been entirely neglected in economics, although a related concept played a foundational role in Adam Smith's theory (the 'Theory of Moral Sentiments,' Smith 1759). Empathy has also been identified as a foundational category in Game Theory by Ken Binmore (1994). Again, strategic coordination requires the capability to understand the position and interests of others, and only then the emergence of 'common knowledge' is possible: For example, one often used tacit assumption in Game Theory is that the players know that they perceive themselves as playing the same game, which enables them to cognitively reconstruct the position of the other; this would include the capability to empathize with other's valuations of outcomes.

It is important to emphasize that even on the level of brain mechanisms empathy is a complex phenomenon which has to be differentiated into cognitive and emotional empathy (surveys in Hein and Singer 2008; Molnar-Szakacs 2011). Emotional empathy means that Ego feels similar emotions as another person, just by observing the other. For example, Alter hits her knee at the desk, and Ego feels the pain. This mechanism goes back on the neuronal mirror systems that I will overview in the next section. Emotional empathy depends on cognitive categorizations, especially on perceived identities. The degree of empathy depends on how close individuals feel to each other, such as in married couples. This implies that different perceptions can change empathy. This is covered by the notion of cognitive empathy, which is conscious to a large degree, and is also related to intentional imitation. Cognitive empathy is neuronally independent from emotional empathy, as has been demonstrated in several experimental and brain lesion studies. It means that Ego reconstructs the position of Alter without feeling the same (which is, by the way, close to Smith's notion of 'sympathy', see the detailed discussion by Sugden 2002). However, when doing the same this will result in similar feelings. For example, I hear somebody singing a beautiful song, and I start to imitate this, because I have an idea about the inner feelings related to the singing. When singing, I begin to feel similarly. To summarize, human empathy reflects a complex interaction between bottom-up processes (epigenetically caused emotional mechanisms) and top-down processes (higher level cognitive categorizations) (Singer and Lamm 2009).

In economics, empathy can be regarded to be the underlying brain mechanism of 'social preferences' (Fehr 2009). There is strong empirical support for the assumption that human individuals have social preferences in two senses, namely as other–regarding preferences and as contextual preferences, in the sense of comparative assessments on one's own situation (such as fairness norms, for a survey see Bowles 2003: 109ff). The important insight derived from recent neuroscience research is that these preferences have a proximate physical representation in the brain, because the respective behaviour is directly manifest in the generalized reward structures of the human brain, that is the dopaminergic circuits. For example, if individuals apply social punishments on others, this activates reward mechanisms in the brain (cf. Hopfensitz and Reuben 2009). From this perspective, one cannot analyse these mechanisms along the lines of an argument that would treat other–regarding behaviour as 'altruistic' in any sense, because this behaviour triggers the same rewards as individual consumption. However, from the evolutionary perspective this fact simply demonstrates that the behaviour is adaptive, and therefore undergirded by appropriate internal mechanisms that elicit this behaviour (Field 2001). This establishes the connection across the different levels of group selection as analysed in Chapter Three: Especially, the capacity to manifest social preferences via appropriate internal reward mechanisms needs to be coupled with signalling mechanisms that establish the relevant group boundaries (which renders all simplistic theoretical reductions meaningless, see Gurven 2004). Empirically, the mere fact of communication can enhance the tendency to cooperation considerably (Andreoni and Rao 2011). Hence, as in the case of empathy, we observe a conjunction of bottom-up and top-down mechanisms. These mechanisms are generic, hence genetically encoded, but they do not fix certain behavioural patterns in particular contexts of interaction. This is exactly what is needed to establish the capacity to switch between I–mode and We–mode, and which enables correlated behaviour as scrutinized in Chapter 3 as essential element of group selection (Frank 2009c).

So, the discussion so far has identified essential mechanisms how correlated behaviour can emerge through natural selection that operates on brain structures. If humans act in the We–mode, this results into suppression of competitive behaviour for the simple reason that the strategy space is curtailed. This is independent from the shared interest explanation of cooperation that dominates game theory so far. Therefore, it does not directly presuppose inclusive fitness effects. However, the argument applies again that was already presented in Chapter Three: If inclusive fitness were violated persistently, the capacity for adopting the We–mode would erode. Therefore, we can assume that there is much space for various We–modes independent from the biological substrate, however, the scope of variation is ultimately constrained by the inclusive fitness principle.

An interesting case in point is the empirical study of the diffusion of innovation by Spolaore and Wacziarg (2009): The authors argue that genetic distance between human populations is a differential barrier to the diffusion of technological knowledge, because genetic distance covers the differential effects of the entire intergenerational transmission of any traits that make human populations different, that is, in the sense of inclusive inheritance. This is because non-genetic differences also feed back onto genetic difference in constraining random inter–breeding, basically similar to all other forms of exchange, such as knowledge transmission. In other words, genetic differences do not determine group boundaries, but reflect group boundaries, thus reversing cause and effect. This is exactly what we know as the 'bookkeeping' function of genes in Chapter Three. Therefore, the empirical result can make sense that the diffusion of technological knowledge directly reflects genetic distance between human populations, even though technology is not determined genetically: Both technology diffusion and inter–breeding are influenced by group boundaries which are established and maintained by non-genetic transmission channels in the inclusive inheritance framework as established in Chapter Three.

So, to summarize the results derived so far, we can say that the evolutionary theory of the individual establishes a number of principled reasons why human brains may have adopted certain structural characteristics which prepare them to solve problems of cooperation in a way that group identities are established. I will scrutinize this insight further in the next sections. Before doing this, we need to conclude the argument in this section by showing explicitly how brain evolution may have been driven by the need to cope with energetic constraints, while reflecting the basic forces of maximizing energetic throughputs. The human brain, as we have noticed, is a highly energy intensive structure: But what is even more important is how the control information processed by this structure may have contributed to expanding energetic throughputs in the course of human evolution. Then, the question is how far we can relate brain evolution with specific mechanisms that firstly, result in increased energetic throughputs of the human organism, and secondly, that are directly caused by group level interactions. The ideal-typical story about hunting presented so far is only touching this issue superficially. I argue that the central phenomenon is the harnessing of external energy sources for food processing, resulting into the enhancement of the supply with energy and nutrient inputs.

4.2.4. Brain evolution, groups and energy

One outstanding feature of human behaviour is the prevalence of cooking. Cooking emerged from the discovery of one of the fundamental technologies of the human species, namely the controlled use of fire. Although there is a dispute over the emergence of cooking, most observers agree that it is sufficiently old to be evolutionarily significant, that is, about at least 250.000 years (for an overview, see Bowman et al. 2009). My analysis follows Wrangham et al. (1999) and Wrangham and Conklin-Brittain (2003). There is considerable leeway in determining the time of the emergence of cooking which relates with the problem of how to identify the first use of fire.

Further, cooking in general can be independent from the controlled use of fire, if early humans just exploited opportunities of naturally occurring fires. Thus, one can adopt the extreme position proposed by Wrangham that locates the first use of cooking to the first traces of fire in the context of human activities: This is the emergence of Homo erectus, 1.9 million years ago. The time line for proven controlled use of fire is very different, about 400.000 years ago maximum. Thus, the entire argument about cooking can also refer to a different scenario in which cooking emerged about 250.000 years ago. Those uncertainties set apart, even for the shorter periods the argument on the evolutionary impact of cooking applies, especially with regard to the evolution of brain size. Even for Homo sapiens, the period is still long enough to make genetic adaptations possible, especially runaway selection.

The direct relevance of cooking for human evolution arises from the fact that cooking changes the chemical structure of raw food and therefore vastly enlarges the human capability to harness the energy potential of food resources in the local environment. This includes both the scope and intensity of resource use. For example, many plants were made accessible via cooking which were inedible otherwise. One important aspect of cooking is the change of the time constraints governing the trade-off between foraging and eating activities. The eating of raw food needs considerably more time to be devoted to the activities of chewing and dissecting the food. That is particularly true for raw meat, which would easily require many hours a day to meet the caloric needs of humans. Only cooking changes the structure of meat in a way to enable the eater to digest larger relevant quantities in order to cover caloric needs in a way to leave sufficient time for foraging. Taken together, therefore cooking was not only crucial in shifting time constraints related to foraging, but also to other human activities, especially regarding social exchange and sociality, and also generic creative activities.

The more and the longer the human species relied on cooking, the more the digestive system could adapt to this technology even on the physiological and anatomical level. Therefore, cooking is an excellent example for the biological concept of the extended phenotype (Dawkins 1982) and niche construction (Odling-Smee et al. 2003). The human species has enhanced the digestive system by means of an external technology which in turn fed back on the further evolution of the digestive system. Beyond that immediate effect on the availability of nutrients, cooking plays a central role in relieving the human immune system from a large number of possible sources of infections etc. To take meat as an example, as I have mentioned, cooking enabled humans to digest a much larger quantity of meat in a much shorter time because of the greatly enhanced tenderness, thus reducing the need for chewing. At the same time, cooking is a disinfection device, which almost certainly contributed to reduced infant mortality with humans as compared to other primates. The interdependence between technology and body is evident from a number of adaptations that resulted from the use of cooking. In particular, there has been a reduction of the size of teeth and the jaw and presumably also a change of the muscular apparatus needed to process food with the required strength. Another substantial change was the reduction of gut size.

One central evolutionary problem in body organization is the investment into different kind of tissues, hence organs. The human brain is an extremely expensive organ, both in terms of the investment and time to grow. Therefore, cooking could have been a central invention in triggering the expansion of the neocortex in particular. This is for two reasons. Firstly, as we have seen, cooking vastly enhanced the productivity of foraging in terms of final energy consumption. Secondly, cooking enabled disinvestment into gut size. Of course it is difficult to estimate the bioengineering requirements resulting from the specifically human life form, but it seems to be reasonable to assume that this kind of disinvestment could not as easily happen with other parts of the human body, such as the heart or the lungs. In a sense, gut size could be easily dispensed with, once cooking enabled external processing of food. This released resources for the formation of larger brains. But clearly, precisely this growth of brains also enabled human beings to develop more complex social relations and skills that pushed forward the further evolution of the technology.

Finally, cooking relies on the use of fire. The use of fire requires a particular social organization, as fire is a contrived good, similar to large game (Ofek 2001). That means, fire, once under control, can be individually appropriated in the sense of excludability. But at the same time, lending fire from an existing fire does not reduce its utility, so that there is no rivalry of consumption. The same holds true for large game, which, once killed, will decay in a short time. With no preservation technologies, the hunter can exclude others from participating, but at the same time he can afford giving away, because he is not able to devour all the meat. So, fire is a good that can be freely shared, but only after it has been created at all. An essential part of the fire technology are therefore social regulations of access and positioning in a community, as in the case of larger game, with social regulations about differential access to different parts of the game etc. Fire as a physical phenomenon is directly related to the emergence of social institutions, and without social structuration the causal mechanisms might unravel that bring fire into place. After all, fire is also a highly destructive technology that needs control and attention.

What we have described so far is a hypercyclic evolutionary transition. It can be summarized in figure 4.3. There are two sources of energy driving the hypercycle. One is the energy released from food intake, which is secured by foraging and, in later stages, food production. The second is the technological release of energy stored in physical structures especially of plants, such as wood. This is fire. The availability of the additional source of energy allowed for another technological innovation, that is cooking. Cooking triggered far-reaching changes in bodily structure, especially in terms of the brain/gut trade off, that is to say, reduced gut size enabled larger brain size. Thus, increased energy availability allowed for an increase in brain size, which in turn enabled the emergence of more complex forms of social organization (for an economic model specifying this interdependence, see Robson and Kaplan 2003). These forms allowed for the emergence of more efficacious ways of organizing foraging and hunting, as well as the emergence of a broader social framework for food consumption. For the sake of simplicity, the picture does not show the self–replicative part. For example, fire is self–replicative as long as sufficient resources are available, which precisely causes a control problem. Brain size is self–replicative, given the underlying structure of Neural Darwinism. Cooking is self–replicative via the imitative mechanisms of human cultural transmission of information, and so forth.

Figure 4.3 Energy, brains and groups: The primordial human hypercycle

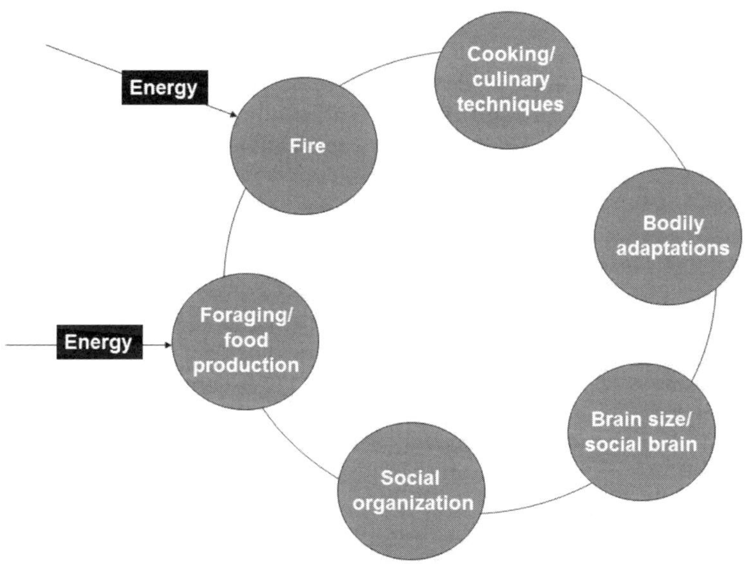

Note: The primordial hypercycle in the emergence of the recent brain structures of homo sapiens works via the externalities linking up changes in brain size, social organization and food production and processing. The domestication of fire enabled cooking, which enhanced the availability of energy per unit of time and the energetic return on investment on foraging and food processing. This allowed for the contraction of gut size, thus further leveraging the availability of energy for maintaining larger brains. Larger brains enable more complex social organization, which allows for innovations in foraging activities and other forms of cooperation in harnessing energy sources, such as controlling fire.

To conclude, we can show that there is a strong autocatalytic feedback mechanism that links the evolution of the human brain with the impact of two of its major capacities on the potential for processing energy, namely the capacity to cooperate in groups and the capacity to discover means of technological control of the environment (for related aspects of the co-evolution of fire and cognition, see, for example, Brown et al. 2009). In this chapter, I will not pursue the topic of technology further. This is because the handling of technology, even in the simple case of the controlled use of fire, requires cooperation. So, the human capacity to act in groups is the primordial capacity. I will now turn to the more detailed analysis of brain mechanisms that underlie this capacity.

4.3. BRAIN SEMIOSIS, EXTERNALISM AND THE EMERGENCE OF GROUP MINDEDNESS

4.3.1. Connectionism

The brain is the most complex structure of the universe as we know it. This is not the place to delve into the details of brain anatomy and process. I concentrate on certain essentials that are important to further detail the evolutionary theory of the individual in terms of identifying the mechanisms that result into interaction between individual and group level that I have studied so far. In doing this, I follow certain views the brain sciences, and ignore others, which implies that my account is biased, as these positions might be under dispute. I leave these open questions to the disciplinary debates, as my major concern is how to fit existing results in a coherent evolutionary theory; so, my broader theoretical stance biases the reception of the brain sciences. In addition, I complement these insights with additional concepts that are necessary to establish the cross–disciplinary bridges, especially with regard to the general theory of evolution, and with regard to the causal interdependence between brain processes and signs, that is Peircian semiosis.

The basic perspective in analysing brain/sign systems is connectionism. Connectionism was first defined as a paradigm of the brain sciences by Donald Hebb, who proposed a theory of neuronal connectivity which is very similar to Hayek's, on which we drew in Chapter Two. This approach is more general than the connectionist paradigm that emerged later and which posed a fundamental challenge to established views about the brain as a computer which processes symbols according to a certain syntax (for a survey, see Garson 2012). Connectionism directly builds on the formal theory of neural networks, in which all information is deposited in differential weights of neuronal connections and the resulting network patterns. This implies, for example, that there is no inner 'language of thought' in which external symbols would be reflected by similar, yet neuronal entities, but that the correspondence of an external symbol is a pattern, a 'Gestalt' of neuronal connectivity which might, in the extreme, encompass the entire brain as an intermittent state in its rapid flow of configurations of neuronal activity. As connectionism builds on the formal theory of neural networks, it is not delimited to physical neuronal structures. The formal theory features the term 'neuronal', but can be used to analyse any kind of connected elementary entities. Thus, one can also analyse semantic spaces in terms of neural networks; then, the application of the same method to describe evolving patterns of connectivity implies the possibility of a mapping between two different kinds of structures, semantic and neuronal (for a seminal study, see Strauss and Quinn 1997). The formal homology between internal network structures and external network structures provides the physical foundation for the externalist view on mind. Or, we can argue that connectionism unifies internal brain networks, external sign networks, and neuron–sign causal networks into one single methodological framework (for an exemplary related computational approach, see Ryder 2004, 2006).

So, connectionism claims that human thinking and acting takes place in complex and evolving architectures of neural connections, which relate with external causes. These neural connections constitute statistical correlations between subsets of neuronal connections that are active in different areas of the brain. Through these statistical correlations internal mappings emerge between different areas in the brain that ultimately establish causal circuits between sensory inputs and behaviour, namely motor outputs in the most general sense (Friston et al. 2010). As these mappings manifest a manifold of internal relations, they constitute the ground on which conceptual systems emerge endogenously (Gallese and Lakoff 2005).

There are many different modelling approaches to understand this structure: Suffice to mention only the recent efforts by Karl Friston to conceive the brain as a Bayesian machine (Friston 2010, Friston and Stephan 2006; compare Ryder 2004). This approach is especially interesting in our context, because it introduces formal methods that are closely connected with the MaxEnt formalism. Friston puts the minimization of 'free energy' into the centre of his brain theory, which is a statistical notion related to the degree of 'surprise' of new sensory inputs (via the statistical mechanics formalism this notion of free energy corresponds to recent adoptions of the free energy concept in Maximum Entropy modelling of Thermodynamics, see Niven 2010). This grasps the fact that in the optimal state of adaptation, the brain achieves high degrees of order, in the sense of convergent patterns of the distribution of priors and the distribution of new sensory inputs; in these states, 'surprises' appear to be formally similar to 'free energy' generating information, and resulting into a final state with minimum 'free energy', which is lowest possible surprises, thus reflecting optimal information processing by the brain in its interactions with the environment.

However, the brain has two levers to achieve this adaptation, along the lines of the evolutionary analysis of Chapter Three: One is the correction of the priors, the other is accommodation via motor action towards the environment, which corresponds to niche construction (for an early related argument about cognitive homeostasis in those two aspects, see Piaget 1975). This approach comes close to a MaxEnt analysis, because it focuses on the maximization of prediction success, thus adopting a selectionist framework, while still leaving out of sight the dynamics of evolution in the sense that a static minimization of surprise by fixing the corresponding structures would stop further accumulation of new information. In other words, only the MaxEnt framework would account for both the maximization of information and the maximization of information capacity.

Figure 4.4 Basic feedback mechanism of the Bayesian brain (after Friston et al. 2010)

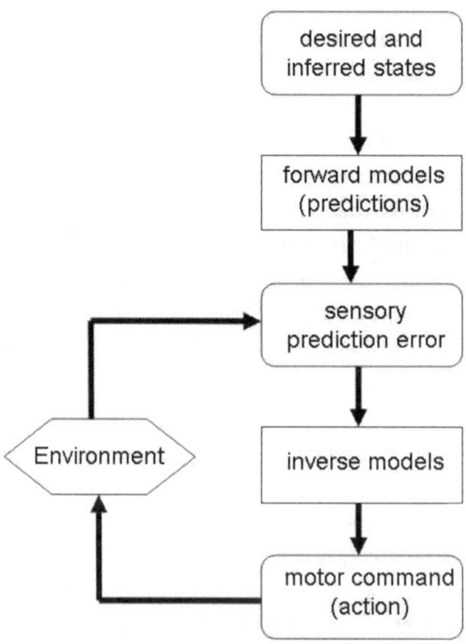

Note: The central component of the Bayesian brain is the use of inverse models to link action results with predictions. The brain operates on the basis of an internal state space that maps desired and inferred states of the environment, which is only accessible via neuronal representations. These internal maps generate predictions, which cannot refer directly to environmental states, but only to sensory maps of perceived results of motor actions in this environment. Prediction errors are fed into inverse models that relate motor outputs with sensory maps.

Connectionist processes are evolutionary in the strict sense of variation, selection and retention. So it is also the basic perspective underlying the theory of Neural Darwinism that was proposed by Edelman and which I adopt as a further elaboration of the Hayekian view (Edelman 1987, Edelman and Tononi 1995, Herrmann-Pillath 1992, Sacks 1995; Fernando et al. 2012). This theory starts out from the idea that the connectivity of neuronal structures evolves according to the VSR–mechanism, with fundamental constraints being the energetic and chemical resources necessary for the activation of neurons. Then, a neuronal net is seen as an evolving hierarchical system which is always in flux, hence also dependent on the recurrent inputs from the external world which stabilize certain patterns in spite of the forces of randomization that result from the on-going spontaneous firings of neurons. Thus, for example, aggregate 'mental' or psychological phenomena such as human learning can be explained in terms of the VSR dynamics (Hull et al. 2001).

There are proximate and ultimate causes of stabilizing certain neuronal patterns. The proximate causes work via neurobiological mechanisms and constraints, such as the distribution of energy potentials in the brain, qualitative differences between neurons and chemical substances etc. The ultimate causes of the first level (we will detail the other levels on a later stage of the argument) are successful actions in the environment, as being valued by intermediate indicators which are related to biological needs of the organism. It is important to emphasize with Friston and Stephan (2006), that the brain has no way to directly access the true states of the environment (compare the notion of the brain as an autopoietic system, see Roth 1992, following Varela and others, which also corresponds to the early Hayek view). All sensory data are already brain states, and all motor actions are brain states which are reflected in proprioperceptive states. Therefore, the causal mechanism that underlies information accumulation in the brain internalizes the environment via motor action, which results into sensory data that are evaluated in terms of prediction errors (see figure 4.4).

4.3.2. Neuromemes and somatic markers

Following Aunger (2002) I propose to designate the basic theoretical element in this evolutionary brain structure as a 'neuromeme'. By this term, I designate a replicator in evolving neuronal structures. Similar views have been presented earlier by other 'memeticists' (for example Delius 1989) and are closely related to other selectionist theories of the brain, such as Calvin's (1996, 1998), and are vindicated by statistical approaches to the brain as proposed by Friston (2010). All these theories share the idea that in the neuronal dynamics, certain patterns stabilize via recurrent reproduction, and can be part of emerging hierarchies which end up in the formation of concepts, as these are reflected in external signs. Based on these different conceptual approaches, Fernando et al. (2008, 2010) have recently proposed neuronal network mechanisms which enable copying and replication of neuronal structures without directly mapping the connectivity itself. This is one of the first formalizations of a purely topological replication in the sense of Aunger's (2002). As Fernando et al. (2012) have demonstrated recently, this approach allows modelling neuronal evolution strictly according to the Darwinian model, whereas the original Edelman theory was more general because it did not include a specific mechanism of copying information across different neuronal entities. However, all these models match with the general framework of evolution that I have sketched in Chapter Three and which takes the Price's equation as a core approach. In other words, there are good reasons to assume that brain processes are evolutionary in a principled sense (for example, as argued by Dennett 1995), and the open questions refer to the precise mechanisms by which this evolution materializes. I argue that the concept of 'neuromeme' might play a pivotal role in the conceptual framework.

Richard Dawkins (1989: chapter 11) proposed the theory of 'memes' in order to analyse cultural information transmission in an analogous way to biological information transmission. Memes were seen as a new set of replicators which also relate to the individual organism as interactor or vehicle: In Dawkin's view, memes hijack brains as their material resource, which implies in an even more radical fashion that 'mind' would be a population level phenomenon, exclusively confined to the set of evolving memes. A meme is a cultural unit (a song, an artistic pattern, a concept) that produces copies of itself, with the notion of a copy related to the endogenous boundaries of copying fidelity, namely a notion of stability through evolutionary processes. However, this theory has met with devastating criticism, both in theoretical and empirical terms (for a concise treatment, see Richerson and Boyd 2005: 80ff). The problem is that the cited empirical cases of 'memes' simply do not have the defining properties of replicators (such as copying fidelity) and even lack clear and consistent physical descriptions.

These difficulties can be avoided in the theory that has been proposed by Aunger (for a short summary, see Aunger 2002: 329). Aunger clearly distinguishes between 'meanings' and neuromemes (Aunger 2002: 221ff), that is, a neuromeme as such does not have a meaning, which resides in the functionings that are triggered by the neuromeme. This excludes many uses of the term which have been familiar since Dawkin's inception of the term 'meme', such as ideas, melodies etc. In Aunger's approach, neuromemes are physical structures like genes (which also do not have a 'meaning'). A neuromeme builds on a specific kind of causality in which physical constraints are reproduced in a causal chain (Aunger 2002: 149ff). The neuromeme itself is defined as 'a configuration in one node of a neuronal network that is able to induce the replication of its state in other nodes'. Thus, a neuromeme is simply neuronal activity, but a special sort of, involving the VSR mechanism. As the brain is connected to the outside world via sensory inputs, there is the possibility that certain inputs are related with particular neuromemes, which, though being based on dynamic neuronal actions, attain stability through the on-going process of replication. A neuromeme is not directly based on fixed neuronal connections, such as genetically wired ones.

I argue that this approach might also encompass the theory of somatic markers proposed by Damasio (1995), thus allowing to link the micro–level phenomenon of a neuromeme with higher–level neuronal regularities that can be more directly related with macro–level (that is individual organism level) functions (for a concise overview, see Bechara and Damasio 2005, for an evaluation in the context of economics see Reimann and Bechara 2010). A somatic marker is a stable and recurrent neuronal pattern in which certain inputs are connected with certain emotional states, with an emotional state being a certain mapping between pertinent brain areas, and which creates the disposition to take a particular sort of action. So, the somatic marker theory can be regarded as a 'meso' level neurological theory about brain operations that focuses on certain feedback loops between larger structures, such as the amygdala and the prefrontal cortex, which enable human action based on valuations that emerged from earlier experiences. Somatic markers can be induced by 'primary' inputs, namely sensory inputs from the environment, and 'secondary' inputs, which are other states of the brain and the body. So, the theory also includes feedback loops internal to the brain as well as brain–body feedback loops. Therefore it encompasses a number of other theories which have been recently introduced into economics, too, such as Loewenstein's (1996) theory of visceral determinants of decision making. Especially, the theory also encompasses the more 'micro level' theories about neuronal processes underlying human decisions, in particular, the analysis of dopaminergic circuits (Schultz 2009). All these different elements can be integrated into a generic approach to neuromemetics.

4.3.3. Basic semiotic patterns of causation in the brain

The somatic marker as such can be seen as being rooted in fundamental neuromemetic structures through which the regularities in the input/output connection are caused. This appears to be a conceptual requirement as somatic markers would always be activated by a range of similar inputs; this presupposes the operation of certain 'Gestalt' mechanisms. Such mechanisms are straightforward to model in terms of neuromemetic replication patterns in neighbourhoods of neuronal networks. Further, somatic markers always refer to causal conjunctions of inputs and neuronal mechanisms, which requires the reference to basic conceptual frames. This suggests a semiotic interpretation. I posit that signs are the mediators between inputs and outputs of neuronal activity. This is important to understand the interaction between sensory inputs and motor outputs. I sketch the basic causal structure underlying brain evolution and processes in figure 4.5 that was proposed by Hurley (2008) and is basically a model of layered cybernetic circles.

Figure 4.5 Basic causal structure of brain operations (modified after Hurley 2008)

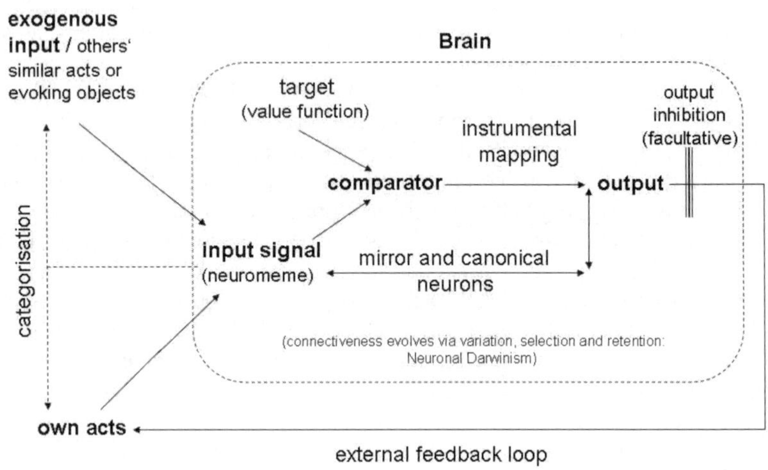

Note: The causal structure of the brain relates exogenous inputs with outputs and their results, mapped into inputs in turn (see figure 4.4). Outputs can be inhibited, which allows for vicarious modelling of actions in internal brain models. Input signals are recurrent neuromemetic structures which provide a stable map of the external environment which relate with value functions that result from individual, social and biological information accumulated in the past. Valuations map into instrumental functions. The relationship between outputs and inputs is embedded into specific types of neuronal connectivity which enable proprioperception and the comparison between others' and own actions. Via those sensorimotor feedback loops, external inputs are categorized into concepts. This central role of categorization had been already emphasized by Hayek and stays at the centre of modern theories of 'grounded cognition'.

The essential elements of the elementary neuronal unit of causality in brain/environment interactions are:

- Input signals which are neuronal structures on its own (which means should not be confused with the original environmental causes). These signals are neuromemes in terms of functioning as replicators that undergird the recurrent recognition of certain external phenomena. For example, a neuromeme is the stable pattern that leads to the recognition of a snake by the brain. Thus, neuromemes underlie the common

'Gestalt' effects in pattern recognition, when cues suffice to generate full perceptions of external phenomena.

- Input signals always relate with another class of neuronal structures, that is comparators, which establish a connection between those signals and certain fundamental value functions. Thus, a pattern caused by an external impact is compared with pre-existing patterns of 'snakes' which relate with past valuations, which can be both hard and soft wired, that is value functions can also be genetically fixed (in this case, snake–like patterns may be perceived as threats to survival). The conjunction of inputs and valuations result in neuronal patterns that I refer to as 'somatic markers'. They are physically embodied in more specific reward mechanisms of the brain, such as the dopaminergic circuits.
- Input signals trigger responses which are functional with reference to the valuation, which results into motor outputs. Outputs can be inhibited. In the latter case, inhibited motor outputs constitute the elements of internal representations of the world. This reflects the internalization of the environment as discussed previously. For example, the input of 'snake' can trigger the motor response to jump away, but can also trigger an internal representation of this response.
- Sensory inputs and motor outputs connect causally in feedback circles via mirror and canonical neurons. Mirror neurons connect an action with the perception of the action, both own and others. Canonical neurons reflect the affordances of objects to which actions relate. So, mirror neurons establish a direct feedback between Ego's attitude towards snakes and the observation of other's actions towards snakes, and canonical neurons prepare actions towards snakes based on any kind of visual or other representation of snakes.
- Motor outputs feed back to the brain via the proprioperception of these outputs. This is the basis for the emergence of categorizations. Thus, if a twig was misrepresented as snake, this is a failure of categorization which is then further processed by the previously sketched feedback mechanism. As a result of this closed chain of brain processes, all sensory inputs are categorized, thus reflecting a conceptual structure that is determined by the brain processes; these categorizations are directly related with valuations.

Now, the upshot of this analysis is that we can provide a neuroscientific foundation for the role of signs in brain operations. The interaction between sensory inputs and motor outputs means that the latter are signs that feed back to the brain as sensory inputs. In this most fundamental sense, the brain actualizes semiosis. From this follows the Hegelian approach to mind (in the sense of Taylor's 1985): Brain operations are impossible without externalization, because the stability of the neuronal patterns, namely the sustainability of the evolutionary dynamics, depends on the feedback between motor outputs and sensory inputs. This view has been systematically developed in recent theories about 'grounded cognition' (for example Garbarini and Adenzato 2004; Gallese and Lakoff 2005; Pecher and Zwaan 2005). These theories claim that all higher–level cognitive functions, which rely on concept formation, root in sensorimotor system structures, both materially, but possibly even in semantic terms, as has been especially emphasized by Lakoff (2008). This implies that the earlier separation between cognition and perception/action is another most recent expression of Cartesian dualism: To the contrary, all cognition is just an advanced state of neuronal processing of sensorimotor feedback loops, as sketched in figure 4.5. These advanced states result from internal mappings and circuits, which can be seen as 'signs' in the semiotic sense (for instance, Barsalou 1999 uses the term 'perceptual symbol systems'). This allows modifying the established approaches to grounded cognition in a specifically semiotic sense: Then, we relate sensorimotor processes directly with the handling of signs, and, vice versa, all sensorimotor processes result in the emergence of signs. For example, if canonical neurons trigger internal neuronal simulations of 'grasping an apple' by perceiving the apple, the apple is a sign via the affordances that connect causally with it (inducing the grasping), and the neuronal representations of 'grasping' are signs relative to other neuronal processes (cf. Fogassi 2011). Therefore, internal and external semiosis are inextricably enmeshed with each other (in grounded cognition theories, these is implicit to the central role assigned to 'simulation,' see Barsalou 2008).

So, the basic semiotic structure of brain functioning can be analysed as in figure 4.6. The fundamental unit of neuronal structure is the neuromeme, a material replicator that does not carry any meaning. This replicator is causally connected with motor outputs as externalized actions. This corresponds to the interactor function in general evolutionary analysis. The motor output is a sign that is being interpreted by the brain which is seen in its duality as a mind. As we have already analysed in Chapter One, this relationship between brain and mind, however, is not one of physical co-extension between one brain and one mind, but essentially depends on the interaction between brains, which is a function. This function is the mind. So, along the lines of Hegel's thinking, the mind is an external phenomenon that is mediated via motor outputs as signs. From this follows that the neuronal structure only acquires meaning via this externalized feedback loop. Isolated brains cannot think. We can further formalize this structure along the lines of Friston's approach, as referred to earlier, in detailing the interaction between the statistical distributions of sensory inputs and motor actions, related to results which translate into other sensory inputs. In this interaction, the motor outputs assume the role as the driver of the emergence of concepts, because they result in classes of responses, that is functionings (this also matches with the analyses of teleosemantics, for example Matthen 2006, Neander 2006 or Millikan 2009).

Figure 4.6 Brain semiosis

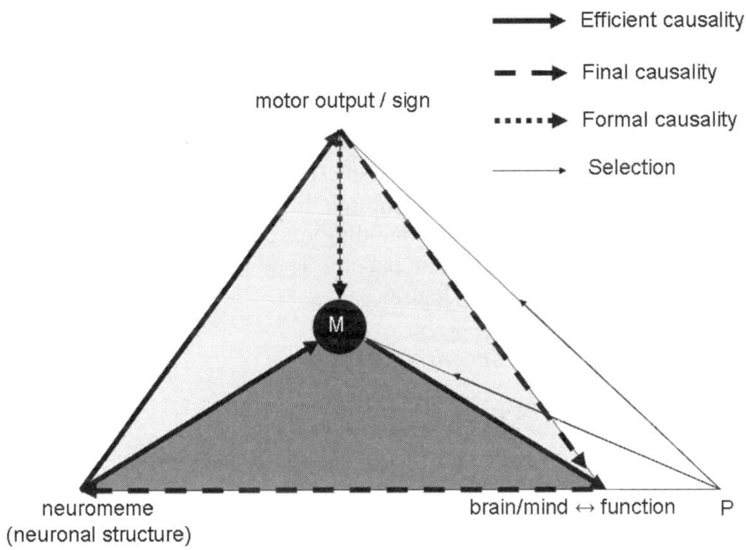

Note: The triadic view of causation in the brain posits that mind is a function relative to the environment in terms of actions taken, that is motor output. The functions interpret stable neuromemetic patterns in neuronal structure. Thus, neuronal patterns are seen as efficient–causally generating certain functions (for instance, a certain action directed at consuming an apple), but their meaning is only established via the evolved categorization by types of motor outputs (for example, 'consuming an apple' is a type learned via past sequences of actions, referring to both others' and own actions). This formal–causal role of motor outputs is reflected in the affordances of objects (such as the apple generating the sensorimotor pattern of grasping the apple). So, the semiotic analysis differs fundamentally from a simple stimulus–response model.

We can put the different parts of the analysis together in terms of figure 4.7. Here, we make the interaction between brains explicit. We identify three feedback circles (broken lines). Considering a single brain, one is the feedback circle between motor outputs as sensory inputs that maintain sustainable neuronal structures, which root in replicator processes, that is neuromemes. Consider an infant that learns to walk: she continuously observes her own actions which are fed back into the on-going process of building neuronal structures that enable walking. However, the motor output is also a sign to others, such as the parents. The infant and the parents continuously observe each other. Then, similar motor events, that is walking, are signs that are mutually recognized (for detailed discussion of these 'shared neural networks', see Singer 2009). By this, the fundamental process of imitation is triggered, that is brains can compare motor outputs of different brains (for example, smokers internally reproduce neuronal states of smoking activity when viewing others smoking, see Wagner et al. 2011). It is essential to see that in this process, especially in early stages of ontogeny, the difference between Ego and Alter does not exist, in the sense of being directly reflected in neuronal maps (of course, it exists as an objective physical difference between the different organisms, which also generates individual variations in sensorimotor circuits). This is because in the phenomenon of the sign, both are conflated: The sign is 'walking', no matter who is walking. Therefore, primordial minds are collective minds in a fundamental physical sense, namely building on conjunctions of signs with converging neuromemetic causation patterns (but not identical structures) distributed across different individuals.

Figure 4.7 Mind emerging from brain semiosis

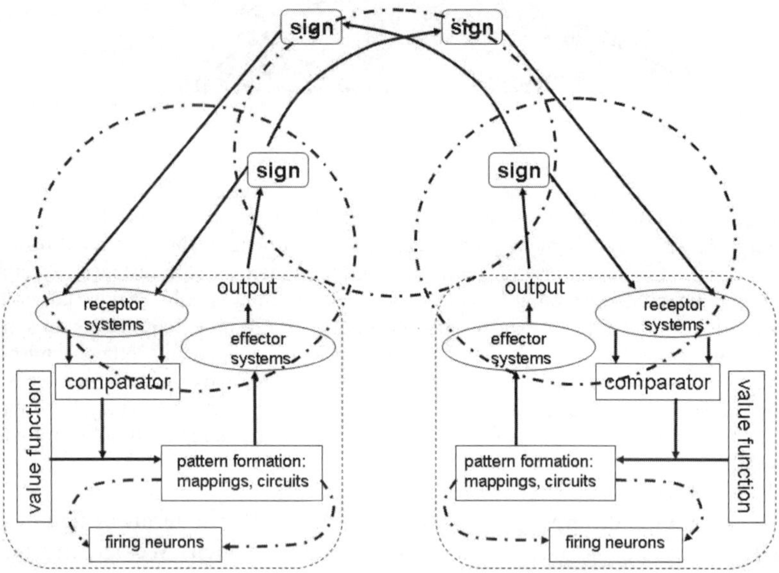

Note: The complete picture of the brain/mind interaction centres on the role of signs in both proprioperceptive feedback loops and in imitating others. Thus, motor outputs are signs for other brains as well as signs relative to the originating brain. So, signs intermediate functions between brains, such as when coordinating actions. At the same time, signs stabilize internal neuronal patterns of variation, selection and retention in enabling the emergence of concepts as categorizations (see figure 4.5 in more detail).

4.3.4. The naturalistic view on language

We can therefore conclude that semiosis is the foundation for the fusion of groups and individuals in human neuronal processes, in the sense of a synthesis of Ego and Alter in fundamental sensorimotor structures of the brain. This role of the Other in enabling Ego's cognition has been recently elaborated on in approaches to 'social cognition' (Lewis and Carpendale 2002). This research revives the ideas of Vygotsky, a Russian scholar of the early twentieth century who extended Marxian, and in that context, Hegelian ideas into psychology (Carpendale and Lewis 2004, Moll and Tomasello 2007). The Vygotskyian view explains human cognitive capabilities via the internalization of patterns of interaction between human individuals during child development. Vygotsky himself proposed, for example, that language and thought are connected in an externalist way, such that the development of speech in communication between infants and adults leads to a gradual internalization of those external patterns, resulting in 'inner speech' as the medium of thought. In modern approaches to social cognition, it is argued that the functional needs of human cooperation in groups require complex coordination, and that growing up in those contexts results into the formation of the required cognitive capacities. These capacities do not simply 'represent' aspects of the external environment, but internalize action patterns, which essentially connect object–related activities with communication. Even fundamental ontological beliefs develop out of interactions between adults and infants, which focus on objects, and are hence social in a most general sense (for example, via actions such as pointing, showing etc.).

The most elaborate human sign system is language. The semiotic approach to the human brain allows integrating recent developments in naturalizing the theory of language, too. This can be based on Wittgenstein's (1958) early approach to natural languages. Wittgenstein's view differs fundamentally from the approach to language that was developed in theories which follow a computational paradigm that neatly distinguishes between syntax and semantics (such as Chomsky's generative grammar) (overview in Lycan 1999), with the former being governed by 'grammars'. In the actual use of language, it is impossible to separate purely grammatical rules from semantic rules in establishing the correct formal structure of sentences (Pinker 2007: chapter 2, has many examples, such as verbs like 'march', when we can say both 'soldiers march home' and 'I march soldiers home' but we cannot say 'I come soldiers home', while saying 'soldiers come home'). The reason for this fusion of syntax and semantics is that language refers to actions in the physical world, with words reflecting the underlying ontology of action, such as a peculiar conception of causality. The recognition of this fact was the major insight of speech act theory that emerged from the criticism of the ideal formal language philosophy that dominated thinking about language in the mid of the twentieth century.

Today we might even radicalize this view further: Language is not simply a way of doing things, but language is deeply enmeshed with our doing. This view is a Wittgensteinian one, as Wittgenstein argued that meaning is not referential but inheres in the regularities of uses of words in certain communities of language users which share a certain life form. This view leads us to see language as inextricably enmeshed with action, and language being a particular kind of action.

Evolutionary approaches to language such as Millikan's (1989, 2005) can be seen as naturalizations of this Wittgensteinian thinking (there are related ideas in economics, such as in Rubinstein 2000: 25ff, Demichelis and Weibull 2008). Here, the VSR logic is directly applied on the emergence of regularities in language. This perspective also matches with Aunger's (2002) view on communication and memes. Language use is seen as a dynamical system in constant flux where users mutually correct their individual uses in pragmatic contexts. Language is an evolutionary system which follows no other rules than those emerging from the on-going flow of language involving actions. As such, the system shows both stasis and continuous innovation, which can be straightforwardly explained by evolutionary theory in general. Millikan emphasizes that in this perspective speaker intentions do not count at all, but only functions on part of the user, which of course feed back onto functions on part of the speaker. So, semantics is no more based on mental facts such as intentions, but the purpose of language use at least within minimum dyads of users. The receiver of a language message 'makes sense' of it in the context of her action pattern, and this feeds back on the action patterns of the sender.

The evolutionary view on language relates language with biological processes in a most general sense (Locke and Bogin 2006). So, language uses are foremost primordial ones in the context, for example, of courtship behaviour, cooperation in groups, or status competition. The role of language as a system that processes information about the environment is only subordinate to these original functions which means represents an exaptation. For example, parents who send truthful information to their children will gain a reproductive advantage relative to parents who do not. This also explains the central role of language in establishing identities in social interaction (Sterelny 2006). However, this very process is already an expression of the fact that language as an external phenomenon assumes a partly autonomous and endogenous evolutionary dynamics.

Language is one of the symbolic systems that human brains can manage, and therefore we can also refer back to the co-evolutionary approaches discussed in the previous section which rely on the Red Queen Principle to explain brain evolution: That is, language might have emerged as an exaptation of certain brain capacities (such as gesturing, in Tomasello's 2008 view), but once language came into existence, it triggered further evolution of the pertinent capacities (for a related view on extended minds in general, emphasizing the mutual leveraging of capacities, see Sterelny 2004). For example, a theory of the coevolution of the brain and of symbolic systems has been proposed by Blackmore (2000) in her account of gene/meme coevolution. She argues that memes need large brains as a resource for their replication. If people with a high-performance brain adopt the role of 'meme fountains' in their social environment, and if this exalted role correlates with the exploitation of more opportunities for physical reproduction, meme selection will be coupled with the selection of genes producing larger brains. This fits with empirical observations on the precedence of brain size (as reflected in bone structures) to the emergence of artefacts which presuppose the use of symbolic systems (see Finlay et al. 2001).

There is one radical consequence of these observations which finally settles the case in favour of the externalist approach to mind and hence, rationality in the economic sense. This is that consciousness is also the result of internalization, which applies both in the developmental view and the analysis of human action (for an early argument, see Dennett 1991). This relates to the fundamental human capacity to 'mentalize'. There are different approaches in the brain sciences that substantiate these claims, such as the 'mirror neuron hypothesis' which I have discussed previously. Mirror neurons are regarded to be the foundation for imitative learning and the capability to imagine the other (see for example Wicker et al. 2003; Gazzola et al. 2006; Fogassi 2011). A somewhat broader approach to mentalizing is to investigate into larger areas of the brain or particular patterns of modular activation (see Frith and Frith 2003). In all of these approaches, mentalizing can be seen as an essential precondition for being able to coordinate actions with others, because, for example, the joint manipulation of objects requires everybody to be able to imagine how particular movements appear from the perspective of others. Camerer et al. (2005: 47) emphasize that the formation of Ego's beliefs about Alter's beliefs seems to rely on a projection of Ego's beliefs onto the other, which presupposes an implicit assumption of similarity.

Now, we can posit that consciousness is actually the reflexivity of mentalizing: Humans learn to imagine themselves based on the capacity to imagine others as having a mind. In other words, the adaptation of becoming able to recognize the intentions of others is an exaptation that enables consciousness of the Self. This view seems to match with the aforementioned social cognition approaches to child development, which imply that the child's consciousness of itself is a result of social interaction, and not its precondition. One of the most conclusive evidences for this approach is the recent research on action generation, which highlights the fact that even in the case of intentional actions, the brain mechanisms that effectively cause the action precede the conscious decisions to take the action: This results into a most radical questioning of the notion of 'free will' as related to consciousness (Davies 2007). This observation also questions standard distinctions in analysing brain processes, which are based on dualisms such as 'conscious action' and 'automatic actions' (for example Camerer et al.

2005). One of the most important expressions of this fact is the phenomenon of coaction: Human individuals imitate the behaviour of others via many channels, without being aware of it, thus coordinating their behaviour (Wegner and Sparrow 2007; Oullier et al. 2008; Oullier and Kelso 2009). Another important evidence for the reflexivity of consciousness via the relatedness of different brains is the human capacity of self–deception, which includes even strong cases where the individual is not aware of self–deception (for related literature, see Mijovic-Prelec and Prelec 2010, von Hippel and Trivers 2011). Self–deception basically works via the perception of one's self as mediated via the perceptions of others. One related result is also the intransparency of one's self to oneself, which is also significant in order to be able to assume credible interaction patterns that are enabled by fundamental uncertainty of the types of agents (compare Humphrey 2007).

To summarize, and to simplify, the analysis of basic causal patterns of brain activity strongly suggests that human thinking and decision making is externalized in an essential way via the causal conjunction of neuronal processes and population level evolution of signs. Individual consciousness and intentionality is a result of this structure, but not its essence. From this follows that human behaviour manifests strong features of behavioural coordination in groups, therefore a tendency of correlation that favours the emergence of group oriented behaviour. This we can dub the 'group mindedness' of human individuals. I will now show how group mindedness can be included in more application–oriented conceptualizations of human choice, and therefore can be used in the context of economic analysis.

4.4. DUAL SELVES, WANTS AND NEEDS

4.4.1. 'Dual selves' approaches in the neurosciences and economics

I am going to present a most general theoretical approach to the human individual that builds on the previous analysis, and that aims at providing the basis for empirically valid approaches to the analysis of human choice. So, the aim is to present an evolutionary alternative to the standard economic model of subjective preferences and individual optimization. This is the dual selves approach.

Following empirical and theoretical research in different disciplines (neurosciences, sociology and economics) I propose to distinguish between two generic parts (qua modes, that is, without a primary spatial assignment) of the brain, the 'Object Self' and the 'Acting Self'. This is a purely theoretical distinction at the same level as the standard economic model (hence, it is a 'molar' as opposed to a 'molecular' approach in the sense of Ross 2008, 2012, and thus operates on the same conceptual level as the standard model, see Neumärker 2007). There is no claim whatsoever that this distinction corresponds to any particular process in the human brain (though there are already many empirical hints at how and where to locate those functions). However, the distinction follows from the triadic framework as it starts from the basic idea that all brain processes involve mappings and hence internal semiotic processes that are causally connected with external signs. This implies that all brain processes can be seen as duals that are integrated via a third, the interpretant qua function.

If we want to analyse human agency, the most straightforward approach is to assume that there is a fundamental distinction between the agent that evaluates and the agent that acts. In economics, this structure corresponds to a generic principal–agent model, in which the brain is split into an agency that guides and implements actions (the agent) and an entity for which this action is taken (the principal); between both entities information asymmetries limit complete coordination, and both follow partly autonomous goal functions (Brocas and Carrillo 2008). In neuroeconomic research, the microfoundations for this dual selves model have been provided with the analysis of the dopamine circuits in the brain, which undergird human choice, but are partly independent from the mechanisms that determine goal fulfilment and the corresponding valuations. The neurotransmitter dopamine circuits are related with goal oriented behaviour and learning, with dopamine signalling a closing distance between goal achievement and performance ('reward prediction error', for surveys, see Knutson and Wimmer 2007; Knutson and Greer 2008; Schultz 2009; Glimcher 2011). That is, increased dopamine levels reinforce a behavioural pattern that leads to improvements, thus providing the basis for reinforcement learning. This effect is generic, that is, independent from the valuation of the goal itself, which occurs in other neuronal structures, yet, dopamine levels are also related with general states of satisfaction.

This provides the foundation of the distinction between 'wanting' and 'liking' systems, which is also recognised by researchers who otherwise emphasize the 'unified currency' approach (Landreth and Bickle 2008; compare Glimcher 2009). The 'wanting' system would equate with the dopamine circuits, the 'liking system' with domain specific neuronal mechanisms that signal proper functioning (for a reception in economics, see Camerer 2006). An excellent example is eating behaviour, where the disjunction between the two systems is established knowledge (see surveys by Berridge 2009, Finlayson 2010). So, perceiving the sight and smell of a delicious food releases dopamine, if somebody is hungry, as goal attainment is close. However, this is different from the signalling of goal achievement qua proper functioning by the relevant homeostatic mechanisms that establish goal fulfilment, such as achieving the necessary supply of nutrients. Both processes interact, as dopamine levels also affect the capacity of the organism to process the corresponding inputs; for example, viewing a delicious food may increase the capacity of the digestive system to process food. This also explains why behaviour can even be dysfunctional, if the dopamine effects are stronger than the other signals: systematic overeating becomes possible, even leading towards individual states of dissatisfaction, or phenomena such as bulimia. Another well-researched example for this dissociation between the 'wanting' and the 'liking' system is gambling and addiction to gambling, where the joy of gambling may be related to the fact that addicted players constantly feel to be close to the goal, which increases dopamine levels, even though in the final result of their action they are accumulating losses (Ross et al. 2008; Clark 2010).

However, this is not the only way to conceive of dual selves in neuroscience terms. Another important strand of research relates with intertemporal optimization, where anomalies of rationality have been discovered early in the context of exponential vs. hyperbolic time preferences (Ainslie 1992). This problem has led to economic models of dual selves (such as Laibson 1997), which were later connected with brain research, thus showing a dichotomy between brain modules that evaluate immediate satisfaction and other modules that calculate costs and benefits in the future (McClure et al. 2007). One can generalize this into multiple selves approaches to individual life history, that is, on different points of time, where each current decision-maker is seen as an agent that acts on behalf of the principals of future selves, but falls prey to the structure of hyperbolic time–preferences in the present (Jamison and Wegener 2010). This leads to models of individual choice that differ from the standard economic model, but may possibly reinstate the individual decision maker beyond modularity, because she can rely on different commitment devices through time (Ainslie 2007). This comes close to economic approaches to these issues which show a similar tension between approaches that basically maintain a dual selves structure (see for example Bénabou and Tirole 2002, 2004; Fudenberg and Levine 2006) and others that maintain the integrated decision calculus (Gul and Pesendorfer 2001; Benhabib and Bisin 2005). The dual selves perspective is also supported by the psychological distinction between decision and experience utility, which induces systematic distortions, for instance, between current experiences and later memories which would underlie choices (Kahnemann et al. 1997).

My approach to distinguish between 'Object Self' and 'Acting Self' follows an entirely separate, and to my knowledge isolated strand of thought, which, however, easily connects with this rich literature: It is based on a proposal by the sociologist James Coleman (1990: 503ff). Coleman corresponds with the aforementioned literature because he argues that only a disjunction between two selves can explain systematic deviations from any kind of optimization behaviour, such as addictions (compare the more complex, but related view of modern addiction research in Redish et al. 2008, as evaluated by Herrmann-Pillath 2012a). However, he also emphasises an aspect that only recently is discussed by economists, too, namely that the dual selves approach can further generalize the principal–agent paradigm in economics, thus unifying the conceptual framework for analysing individuals and organizations (Brocas and Carrillo 2008). This argument is especially important in the context of my approach, which also generalizes over the concept of the individual. Thus, Coleman proposed to distinguish a principal, the Object Self, from the agent, the Acting Self. From this follows that intra–individual information asymmetries also play a central role in explaining observed individual behaviour.

The possibility of intra–individual information asymmetries follows from the fact that the brain is modularized: Firstly, different brain modules pursue different functions and hence process information differently, and secondly, information transmission within the brain is necessarily prone to entropic degradation of information. These information asymmetries even create the possibility that different modules 'cheat' other modules: This is most evident from the aforementioned phenomenon of self–deception (von Hippel and Trivers 2011). According to different adaptationist explanations of self–deception, this peculiar pattern of information processing enables individuals to commit themselves to strategies which would fail to be sustainable otherwise (for example, deceiving oneself about one's true physical strength might actually create the conditions for audacity that helps to win a struggle).

4.4.2. The semiotics of Acting Self and Object Self

We can analyse the semiosis of Acting and Object Self as in figure 4.8. The central idea is that we distinguish between the organism and the Object Self in the sense that, based on the physical structure of the brain/body, the Object Self evolves in terms of changing information about the realizations of organismic functionings. This growth of information is mediated via the Acting Self and the corresponding semiotic processes (for a related approach in economics, see Laibson's 2002 'cue–theory of consumption').

This implies that we cannot simply state that the Acting Self fulfils certain organismic functionings, even in the ultimate sense. This hypothesis is typically entailed by genetic–reductionist approaches to human agency. The triadic framework suggests that there is a fundamental knowledge problem in the identification of organismic functions, relative to the environment, and that therefore the generation of knowledge necessarily requires the duality of Acting Self and Object Self, as constituents of the semiotic process. This distinction can be justified also by means of a generic evolutionary argument, because the distinction between the two functions can be seen as a precondition for the very high degree of phenotypic plasticity of humans, enabling the capacity to learn in new and unknown environments. But then one cannot say that the Acting Self can be reduced to organismic functions, even though it is efficient–causally generated by the organism. As we shall see, the reason for this lies in the fact that the Acting Self is a semiotic phenomenon and hence is constituted by sign systems that are external to the organism. These sign systems include the own actions taken by the individual as one most essential element, as we have seen in the previous section.

Figure 4.8 Acting Self and Object Self

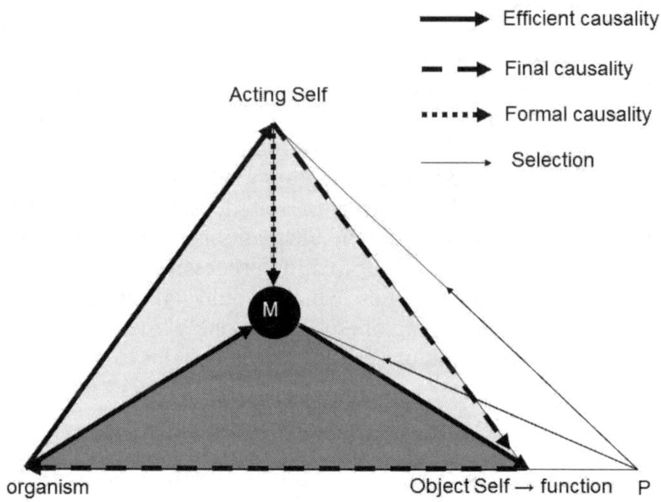

Note: The dual selves model of the individual posits that there is a fundamental gap of information between the decision making systems and the organism as far as the optimal choices are concerned (principal–agent problem). The Object Self represents the functions of the organism relative to the environment, namely embodies the valuations of outcomes of actions. These functions are semiotically mediated via the Acting Self. For example, the Object Self is constituted by the complex homeostatic mechanisms of eating and satiation, the Acting Self takes the decisions about eating based on external signs such as colours and shapes of food items. Thus eating behaviour does not directly causally connect organismic states with states of satisfaction, but mediated via semiosis. For example, eating behaviour is strongly shaped by cultural determinants.

There is one important insight that can be immediately reaped for the economic theory of consumption. This is that we cannot simply say that the Object Self represents an internal evaluation standard, because it is always also related with external functions, mediated via semiosis. A related approach has been recently developed by Dan Ariely and colleagues in two respects.

- Firstly, individuals seem to be often ignorant about their preferences and valuations and build current valuations on previous choices, which can be in turn caused by even arbitrary factors (Ariely et al. 2006; Ariely and Norton 2007). This is called 'coherent arbitrariness', which means that fundamental valuations are arbitrary, but individuals aim at consistency of value rankings afterwards. Hence, individuals actually form current preferences by means of imitating past selves in a basically same way as they copy others (so called 'self–herding'). This has the radical consequence that their current valuations can also be influenced by past prices which are seen as value indicators, such that the equilibrium states in the economic context are no longer independent from the preferences. In my parlance, this shows that the Object Self is externalized in an essential way, insofar as the functions are always mediated via the Acting Self, though remaining independent.

- Secondly, all human consumption acts can be interpreted in a dual sense, namely consisting of the material impact and of the related cognitive process; this is called 'conceptual consumption' (Ariely and Norton 2009; compare Witt 2010). For example, even simple tastes of drinks are directly influenced by prior conceptual framing which implies that individuals do not have 'independent' tastes in the sense of the underlying neurophysiological mechanisms. The two dimensions can be even separated in many consumption decisions, involving trade-offs and vicarious activities (see Wilcox et al. 2009). In my approach, this matches with the Object Self/Acting Self distinction, directly showing that the Acting Self operates on the basis of signs ('concepts'), that is chooses signs (and thereby becoming a sign itself, in terms of the proprioperception of consumption acts), whereas the Object Self processes information about fulfilment and satisfaction. All consumption is bimodal, that is consumption in the matterenergy mode (such as the physiological impact of a drink via the efficient–causal mechanisms *M*) and in the semiotic mode, that is consumption of signs (which can be reflected empirically, for example, in the strong impact of brand perceptions on taste evaluations, see the classical experiment by McClure et al. 2004 and related research as summarized by Plassmann et al. 2007 or Hubert and Kenning 2008).

4.4.3. Human choice and levels of evolution

Now, I put the analysis so far into the broader context of evolutionary theory which is outlined in figure 4.9 (for a seminal related analysis, see Elworthy 1993; also see Hodgson 2010). The basic idea is that considering the analysis of the brain/mind relationship so far, we can state that different levels of evolution are concerned (which leads back to another Hayekian idea, namely on the 'three sources of human values', see Hayek 1979: 153ff). For example, some fundamental value functions in brain mechanisms might be genetically encoded, whereas other value functions are exclusively mediated via culture. In the interactions of the Acting Self with the Object Self, these different levels are integrated, as in the example of cultural determinants of eating behaviour. Therefore, a complete evolutionary analysis needs to disentangle these different levels.

Figure 4.9 Individuals and levels of evolution

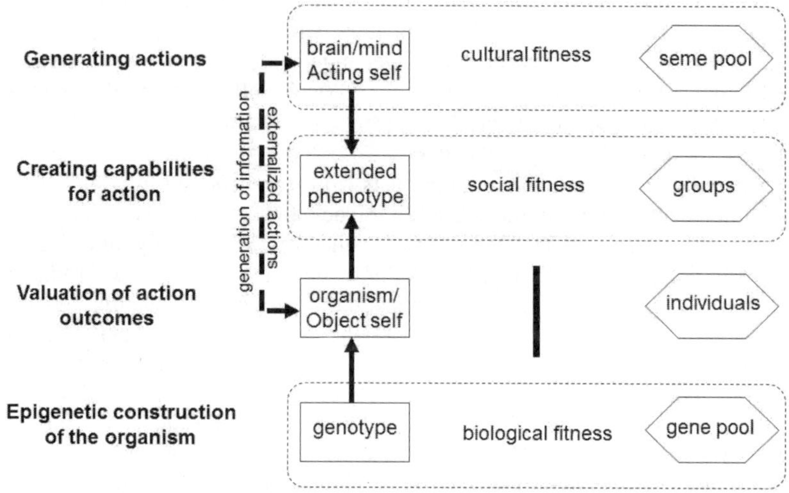

Note: The integrated model of the individual distinguishes between different levels of evolution, genetic, social and cultural, with corresponding fitness criteria. The levels connect via brain structure as analysed previously. Thus, certain basic valuations are embodied on the genetic level, hence relate to biological fitness. The Object Self is embodied in the organism, where a principled physical barrier to other organisms exists. The organism connects with other organisms, however, in groups via semiotic intermediation on the level of the Acting Self. The Acting Self is embodied externally, that is via neuromeme–sign patterns, with the signs being population level phenomena which manifest an independent evolutionary dynamics, namely cultural evolution in the seme pool (with semes defined as minimal carriers of meanings).

The theory of human choice has to take into consideration different levels of processes which are interconnected. The fundamental process is the epigenetic construction of the organism. This is the level of development, which therefore puts ontogeny at the centre. On this level, we already need to heed attention to the entire sequence of levels, which is made explicit in theories of social cognition: Human beings can only unfold their whole biological individuality if they grow up in social interaction. At the same time, we can approach this level separately. Then, a most basic mechanism is genetic reproduction, which focuses on biological fitness. This also implies that the individual organism is connected via shared genes with other organisms, which defines biological fitness as inclusive fitness. So, the relevant analytical framework is the gene pool, and the individual would just be perceived as a sample of genes within the boundaries of the body. However, this is a purely analytical separation, considering the inclusive inheritance paradigm explored in Chapter Three. Corresponding to this paradigm, we need to include all other levels in analysing human choices (thus eschewing sociobiological reductionism).

The next level is the level of the individual organisms, where we also locate the Object Self in material terms, that is as the physical location of somatic markers, neuromemes etc. This is also the level of proximate valuations, as compared to the ultimate valuations on the biological level. On this level, individuals are strictly separate from other individuals, because of the physical boundaries between organisms. This has the important implication that individuals rarely connect via direct physical impacts, such as during sexual intercourse or physical struggle. Yet, even in these cases internal states of other individuals can only be accessed via signs.

Now, considering the semiotic analysis of the brain/mind, the next level is the level of groups. Social cognition means that human individuals are always part of groups in a most fundamental sense. Biologically, one can refer to this as the extended phenotype of human individuals, in the sense that group connectivity is essential for realizing all cognitive functions that result in actions. In the group context, as I will analyse in more detail below, biological fitness does not directly matter, but social fitness. Social fitness is relative status in groups of interacting individuals (this will be scrutinized in detail in the subsequent chapter). It is important to recognize that we can relate this level with the generation of capabilities for action, which is almost the defining feature of 'social fitness' in the sense of defining those capabilities relative to the capabilities of other individuals.

Finally, the actions that are taken by an individual are determined on the level of the Acting Self, which is fundamentally based on semiosis. Semiosis connects the individual with the population level, however, not simply with other individuals, but with the signs that are used on the population level. I call this set of signs the 'seme pool', with the seme as a minimum sign carrying meaning. Semes connect with neuromemes in reproducing cultural patterns. This defines cultural fitness, in the sense of the differential reproduction of these patterns. As indicated by the direction of the arrows in figure 4.9, the cultural and the social level are closely enmeshed, as human capabilities for action include the capability to handle signs in coordinating actions with others. Further, there is a fundamental feedback loop that links the level of the Object Self and the Acting Self, because actions taken also generate information about basic valuations underlying choices through time.

Thus, individual action connects the three levels of the Object Self, the group and the Acting Self and is therefore the central determinant of information. Information is generated and accumulated on the population level and is embodied on the individual level in terms of the externalized actions (for example, a food custom is a population level phenomenon but materializes in individual eating behaviour). Hence, we can approach preferences in the same way as we have approached genes in Chapter Three: Individual preferences are the bookkeeping entities relative to the population level processes in which information evolves. The causal connection between the levels is established by the different brain mechanisms that we have identified so far. The individualization of preferences is a consequence of the complex interactions between the levels, but is not the ultimate driver of those processes (for a related approach to 'embodied economics', see Oullier and Basso 2010).

4.4.4. Wants and needs

We can proceed on this basis to develop some elementary notions for the analysis of human consumption, understood as a central category in economics (the 'demand side' of the economic process, see Nelson and Consoli 2010). I propose to relate the distinction between Acting Self and Object Self to the distinction between 'want' and 'need', which mirrors the neuroscience distinction between 'wanting' and 'liking' that I discussed previously. This is the evolutionary substitute of the notion of preferences in the dual selves approach (inspired by contributions such as Sartorius 2003 and Witt 2000). A 'want' is the category that defines the motivation for action on part of the Acting Self; a 'need' is the function that the resulting action fulfils. Again, this function is a complex phenomenon in terms of the duality of somatic markers and external functioning. On the one hand, we can relate the need with biological functions, such as the need for nutrients. But the need for nutrients is never directly determining satisfaction, as the need is always related to semiotically mediated external functions (bimodality). This is why even for the case of the elementary need of food we do not directly know what we need in terms of organismic function but rely on externalized standards such as eating habits and a whole set of environmental cues (Sobal and Wansink 2007).

Table 4.2 Bimodality of wants and needs

	Observer independent	**Observer relative**
Matterenergy mode	body states	need (function)
Semiotic mode	brain states	want

One can make this clear in terms of bimodal analysis in table 4.2. In the upper left box, we refer to body states in the sense of systems of matterenergy flows, that is metabolism. For example, we can analyse the processing of sugar in the body by purely chemical means. If we consider functions of metabolism, we move to the upper right box. Functions are observer relative in a way that differs from Searle's view on that matter (see Chapter Two, section 2.4.1.), because, as we have seen, in the triadic analysis needs, referring to the Object Self, establish a linkage between internal and external states, with the latter also determining internal valuations of body states. For example, the need to consume sugar is not simply determined by internal functions of metabolism, but also by the role sugar plays in the context of particular societies. Therefore, the consumption of sugar is a need that is partially culturally shaped (on sugar, see Ruprecht 2005; de Vries 2008: 151ff). This applies even for seemingly simple biological indicators, such as body height (Steckel 2008): Although height is a direct indicator of nutrition status, the appreciation of height is partly normative.

In the semiotic mode we analyse brain states which are based on physical neuronal mechanisms (such as somatic markers); so, they constitute observer independent semiotic processes. However, these processes only obtain meaning in the observer relative mode, which establishes 'wants'. A want is not necessarily a conscious phenomenon, but refers to the generation of individual intentions. As these are mediated via signs, the intentions cannot be simply reduced to internal subjective states, as in the economic analysis. Wants are individual states, but evolve on the population level.

We can also conduct this analysis in terms of the triadic structure (figure 4.10). This analysis helps to make sense of one fundamental tension in the economic analysis of preferences. On the one hand, for practical matters such as evaluating levels of development, we rely on external standards of life satisfaction to assess individual states, and we also recognize that these are partly contingent on levels of development, as in the basic needs approach. On the other hand, we recognize individual freedom in determining choices, and emphasize the subjectivity of all preferences. In the triadic view, this is straightforward to accommodate.

On the one hand, needs root in organismic states via mechanisms, such as the effects of nutrition on body height. At the same time, needs evolve relative to functions that are external to the organism, and may relate certain nutrition habits with roles in society, for example. These effects are mediated via signs, that is the Acting Self and its wants. Wants rely on population levels signals that select certain mechanisms formal–causally. As a result, even though we can identify certain mechanisms that relate food intake with the realization of body functions, we cannot straightforwardly draw conclusions on the realization of needs. For example, a status of relative malnutrition may result from the exertion of certain wants that evolve with cultural determinants of role perceptions (for example relative malnutrition of girls in India), thus realizing needs without necessarily affecting subjective perceptions of satisfactions negatively (such that even objective states of malnourishment, as in the early Industrial Revolution, partly result from preferences for food that fulfil signalling purposes with regard to status, see De Vries 2008: 116ff).

Figure 4.10 Triadic view on wants and needs

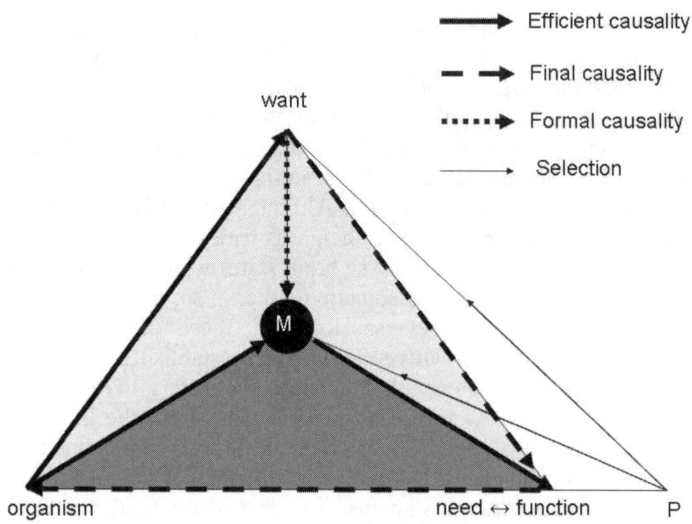

Note: The fulfilment of needs is always efficiently–caused by organismic states, but as needs are also functions relative to the environment, they are semiotically mediated by wants. For example, nutritional status can be measured in terms of physiological states of organisms, but individual choice of food intake is mediated via social and cultural determinants; this can even result into objective states of relative malnutrition, when alternative choices could be possible. Yet, individual satisfaction is determined by the fulfilment of functions.

Still, we can relate the analysis of wants and needs back to biological categories. This idea has been vigorously pursued by Corning over two decades (see Corning, 1983; 2005: Chapter 11; compare Cordes 2005). The starting point is to relate needs to adaptation; Corning himself refers to 'fitness', but this use seems to confuse the two notions, as elucidated in Chapter Three. That implies (Corning 2005: 301), in the end, a notion of individual adaptation defined as 'the capacity to function effectively in relation to the activities that are instrumental to survival, reproduction, and the nurturance of offspring in a given environment; it involves the ability to carry on normal functioning and to engage in productive activity'. This definition allows to establish a relationship with other attempts in economics to define objective conceptions of welfare, in particular Sen's (1984) approach, in which capabilities to function play a central role (I come back on this in the next chapter). Sen's functionings are mainly conceived as social functionings, without any biological foundation. But as Corning demonstrates, there is no basic contradiction involved, which is vindicated in my triadic view.

In Corning's elaboration, adaptive basic needs are: 1. thermoregulation; 2. waste elimination; 3. nutrition; 4. water; 5. mobility; 6. sleep; 7. respiration; 8. physical safety; 9. physical health; 10. mental health; 11. communication (information); 12. social relationships; 13. reproduction; 14. nurturance of offspring. On these basic needs, instrumental needs and wants build, in the sense that human action is geared towards gaining access to means of fulfilling those basic needs (compare Witt 2000, who speaks about 'consumer knowledge'). Thus, the actual means in different environments may display a wide variety. As the list shows, all human activities can be assigned to at least one category, with some of them being intrinsically related with the cultural level of evolution, in particular, the categories 10-12. In the literature on human preferences, sometimes it is emphasized that human beings somehow became culturally autonomous from their basic needs. This kind of sublimation is also implied in the highly influential hierarchy of wants that was proposed by Maslow in the 1950s, with material affluence fostering the higher spiritual needs. That may be the case, with affluence certainly being a relative concept, as the early cave paintings of our past ancestors demonstrate, who expressed their spiritual needs with clear meanings. But in fact the majority of consumption activities even in the most advanced industrial societies seems to be related to topics such as crime, sex, and fun, which perfectly match with an adaptationist basic needs approach (for an extensive discussion of the biological foundations of modern consumer behaviour, see Saad 2007). Further, as any visit to the museum will demonstrate, we have a very good understanding of the consumption items of even very remote civilizations, which also gyrate around the same fundamental categories.

We can analyse these interdependencies between cultural evolution and functions in terms of the two-dimensional hierarchy of semiosis as deployed in Chapter Three (figure 4.11). The complexity of human needs relative to the social and cultural context can be analysed in terms of the interaction between the subsumptive and the compositional hierarchy (in economics, this can be referred to regularities such as the Engel's Law; for a new approach emphasizing the relationship between biological functions and socio-economic development, see Chai and Moneta 2012, and for a seminal earlier approach, see Pasinetti 1981: 68ff.). In the compositional hierarchy, human needs are analysed similar to functions in ecosystems. That means, my individual need is always related with the realization of functions in social context. This reflects the compositional structure of society. This structure evolves, such as in the unfolding of the division of labour. On the other hand, this evolution interacts with the evolution of Acting Selves. In this hierarchy, we consider the evolution of the conceptual dimension of human wants, similar to the historical etymology of words in language. In actual consumption decisions, wants and needs interact. That means, on the one hand we can concentrate on the semiotic dimension of consumption, which would make the individual meaning of consumption acts explicit, as embedded into sign systems on the level of the population, that is the society (cf. Mick 1986; Mick et al. 2004). On the other hand, we would explore the function of consumption in maintaining individual roles in society, which includes, in particular, those functions in which the sustainability of individual states contributes to the sustainability of the larger structures.

Figure 4.11 Evolution of wants and needs

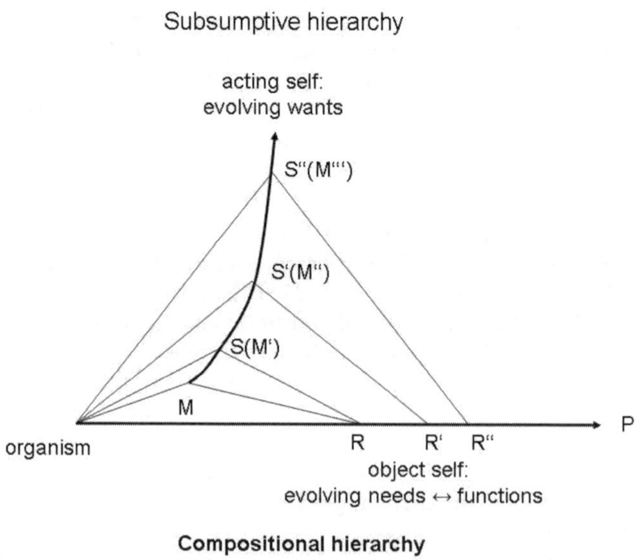

Note: The analysis of human choice has to consider the two-dimensional unfolding of the duality of wants and needs. Needs relate to the evolution of functions in human societies; for example, in a particular society, a certain pattern of consumption (such as gift–giving to children) might be necessary in order to properly fulfil the function of a mother. These patterns change alongside with social change. At the same time, these patterns are semiotically mediated via a system of cultural symbols, which can be traced back to cultural change in the past. So, symbols of motherhood correlate with functions of motherhood. Observed consumption patterns always need to be explained in terms of cultural history and current functions. For example, there is a distinct cultural history of sugar consumption in Western societies, which is distinct from the current functions of sugar in modern diets.

There are classical examples illustrating the validity of this dual approach, often manifesting clashes with apparently conflicting interpretations, which can be sublated in my approach. One famous case in point was the different interpretation of American beef consumption, which was interpreted by Sahlins (1976) as a purely cultural activity, related to fundamental meanings in the 'American way of life', whereas Harris (1979) offered a 'materialist' interpretation based on agro–ecological functions in the context of the North American continent. Both views play together in the emergence of needs from the semiotic intermediation of organismic states through the evolution of wants. In both cases, the argument also relies on the historical dimension, thus reconstructing the unfolding of the two hierarchies in evolution.

To summarize the argument presented in this section in a nutshell, the evolutionary approach to individuals allows the construction of an alternative model of human decision making, the dual selves model. One essential consequence of this model is that the information underlying human decisions is externalized in an elementary way. This differs from the tacit internalism of the economic model of preferences, but matches with the 'revealed preference' approach, if only in the radical sense that observed choices are the preferences. This insight also offers a solution to the fundamental quandary in current economic thought, namely to reconcile the vast number of empirical results about apparent 'irrationalities' and 'inconsistencies' in human behaviour with the idea that human actors are integrated decision makers. For this, we need a final building block for the theory of the individual, the concept of 'identity'. This is because the theory presented so far cannot explain why human individuals, in spite of the modularization of their brains, perceive themselves as individuals, and not as composites (although one has to recognize that many people also have this sort of experience, which is, after all, also the topic in many literary, religious and philosophical works). I will argue that integrated decision makers emerge from social interactions, and cannot therefore be taken as a fundamental determinant of sociality. Yet, this implies that under certain circumstances, the evolutionary theory of the individual can vindicate the economic theory of the individual, given certain contexts of interactions.

4.5. IDENTITY

4.5.1. Personal and social identity

In this final section I explore the notion of identity. I claim that the fundamental distinction between Acting Self and Object Self is sublated in the notion of identity which establishes the single human actor, in the sense of 'the Self'. Especially, I argue that phenomena such as consciousness, intentionality, agency and free will relate with individual identity. Individual identity is a paradoxical phenomenon which underlies much of human creativity and dynamics. On the one hand, individual identity relies on group identity. On the other hand, individual identity is experienced as being different from any shared group characteristics. The paradox consists in the fact that the latter can only be cognitively grasped as a difference from group traits, but is difficult to give a 'neutral' meaning: Following the discussion of singularity and individuality in Chapter Two (section 2.2.5), we can apply the medieval–Aristotelian dictum again, 'individuum est ineffabile'. Even though individuals are unique and singular, we can only talk about them in terms of group properties, that is predicates that they share with others (or, for that purpose, do not share). The individual is the limit of an infinite approximation to itself.

The concept of identity is the most fundamental category in the analytical treatment of individuality in evolutionary terms (for a related idea, see Ingold 1986: 126f). It can be reduced on two dimensions. One is the possibility to discriminate an individual from all other individuals, and the other is to re-identify an individual through time. This analysis of identity in two dimensions follows the seminal analysis by Davis (2003). Firstly, there is no necessary reason why human beings should be treated as identical through time, given the fact that the human brain is a modular and fluid evolutionary system. Economic theory normally assumes stability of preferences through time, which is a bold assumption which cannot be supported by the biological facts. Indeed, human malleability even includes fundamental changes as the transition between different genders during certain individual life histories. Many people experience fundamental transitions in their conceptions of life, which cause major ruptures in their relation with the social environment, such as in religious conversions or divorce. There is also the regularity of development, that is the transition through stages of childhood, adolescence and adulthood, which cannot be straightforwardly interpreted as a simple continuation of identity. Otherwise, the preferences of an infant would continue to reign over the preferences of an adult, which is in almost all societies rejected in terms of the custody of parents and adults over a child. Individual life history shows the same tension between singularity and individuality as the relationship between individual and group.

Against this background, I treat identity through time as the phenomenon of the individual construction of life histories on the level of consciousness. This means, firstly, that individuals perceive their individual history as a sequence of causally connected events which end up with their present state, and that they perceive regularities through the causal chain which are constant, especially with regard to their present state. Thus, identity is a form of constructed consistency of action through time (so, the 'coherent arbitrariness' approach by Ariely et al. 2006 that I referred to in the previous section can be seen in this light). Identity emerges as a narrative (for a related view in the brain sciences, here referring to the notion of 'Self', see Damasio 2010: 203ff). This, however, suggests an externalist approach to identity which is based on language. Interestingly, we can refer back this idea to the general approach proposed by Ross to three levels of games (see section 4.2.2.). Similarly, Bednar and Page (2007) argue that individuals develop identities through recurrent interactions across multiple games, which they classify as 'culturally' embedded; Camera and Casari (2009) show that publicly discernible individual identities enable cooperation in infinite social dilemma games. In the current context, this notion of culture can be dissected into narratives and the symbolic repertoires they rely on (compare DiMaggio 1997: 274f.).

We should, however, avoid the fast conclusion that language is a kind of tool to maintain a given identity. Language is itself the source of the problem that identity solves. This is because the emergence of symbolic systems causes the endemic contingency of all behavioural patterns, such that the possibility of fakes, cheats, and just arbitrary movements becomes universal. From this, a fundamental dilemma emerges, as symbolic systems on the one hand allow for a much greater behavioural plasticity, but at the same time introduce fundamental uncertainty, as genetically and epigenetically systems of behavioural coordination are superseded. The emergence of identity as a narrative solves this dilemma.

Regarding the differentiation of an individual from other individuals, much insight can be reaped from the economic analysis of Akerlof and Kranton (2000; 2005), expanded in terms of Davis's (2006) critique. Akerlof and Kranton remain within the scope of traditional utility theory and introduce two additional ideas. Firstly, identity becomes a part of the individual utility function and is therefore treated just as any ordinary good. Secondly, there are externalities across individuals, because identity is defined in terms of group traits, such that an individual that behaves in a deviant fashion will also affect the identity of other individuals.

The Akerlof and Kranton utility function is:

$$U_j = U_j\,(\mathbf{a}_j, \mathbf{a}_{-j}, I_j)$$

where individual utility depends one agent j's own actions $\mathbf{a}_j$ and the actions of others $\mathbf{a}_{-j}$, and where identity I_j enters as an independent argument in the utility function. Identity is given as:

$$I_j = I_j(\mathbf{a}_j, \mathbf{a}_{-j;}\ \mathbf{c}_j, \boldsymbol{\varepsilon}_j, \mathbf{P})$$

where **P** refers to social prescriptions that define the categories and features which are the terms of reference that underlie, firstly, the social categorizations $\mathbf{c}_j$ which apply for a particular individual j and which provide the standard to assess the actual individual features $\boldsymbol{\varepsilon}_j$. **P** and **c** are exogenously given and can be regarded to be embedded in symbolic systems. Thus, the $\mathbf{a}_j$ and the $\mathbf{a}_{-j,}$ enter the utility function twice, namely directly and indirectly via the impact on identity. The latter effect causes externalities in the Akerlof and Kranton model, that is, the actions of others might affect j's identity, without necessarily directly impinging on her organism. For example, if all other men change their valuations of masculinity, this devalues j's position so far, even if the others' actions do not physically connect to him.

In his extensive discussion of this proposal, Davis (2006) shows that it is about social identity, and not about personal identity, as it is mainly reproducing the sociological analysis of group assignments. Against the background of my approach, however, this precisely grasps the fact that individuality needs to be defined relative to the group level, which are the social categorizations. So, the more fundamental question is where these categorizations come from. If identity is just one constituent of the utility function, the explanation is only moved back on the level of this function which, of course, is precisely defining the identity of the economic agent. This raises the issue of self–reference, namely the question whether the utility function is actually consisting of metapreferences and preferences. Choosing one's preferences raises intricate issues in logical consistency and empirical robustness (see for example Elster 1979).

Davis (2006) therefore proposes an extension of the Akerlof and Kranton utility function:

$$\boldsymbol{PI}_j = \boldsymbol{PI}_j\,[U_j\,(\mathbf{a}_j, \mathbf{a}_{-j}, I_j)]$$

where $\boldsymbol{PI}_j$ is personal identity, thus treating I_j as social identity. With this extension, identity becomes reflective in the sense that the agent assesses the utility generated from social identity in terms of the contribution to personal identity. Davis argues that this assessment can only be based on a pre-existing deontology, which seems to lead back to more fundamental dimensions of culture and language.

Kirman and Teschl (2006) (see also Luchini and Teschl 2004, Horst et al. 2006) have added further complexity to the discussion in distinguishing between the 'what', 'where' and 'who' identity. The 'what' identity refers to the properties that make up an agent, such as having preferences in economic models. The 'where' identity refers to the Akerlof and Kranton notion of social identity, that is is the location of an individual in a social space. The 'who' identity relates with Davis' conception of personal identity, but adds a dynamical aspect. The 'who' identity indicates the kind of person which an agent wants to be. So, identity becomes also a property of trajectories of individual change and need not be stable through time (compare Sen 2007). Further, identities co-evolve with the network patterns that structure the social space, thus allowing for the application of evolutionary concepts such as 'niche' and 'exaptation' (for an illuminating example, see Brown and Feldman 2009).

I summarize both dimensions of analysis in the 'cross of identity' (figure 4.12) (for a closely related analysis, see Davis 2010: 200ff.). The cross of identity refers the notion of individual identity to the combination of the synchronic and the diachronic aspects of identity, with the synchronic dimension defining the social identity and the diachronic dimension defining the personal identity. Only the conjunction of the two makes agency rooted in structures of the Self possible. Agency relies on capabilities which emerge in a social context, and those capabilities can only be activated in the context of an individual trajectory of change. We can relate this to the previous discussion of wants, because the diachronic perspective includes processes on different levels, including the genetic, the cultural and the life history level.

Figure 4.12 The cross of identity

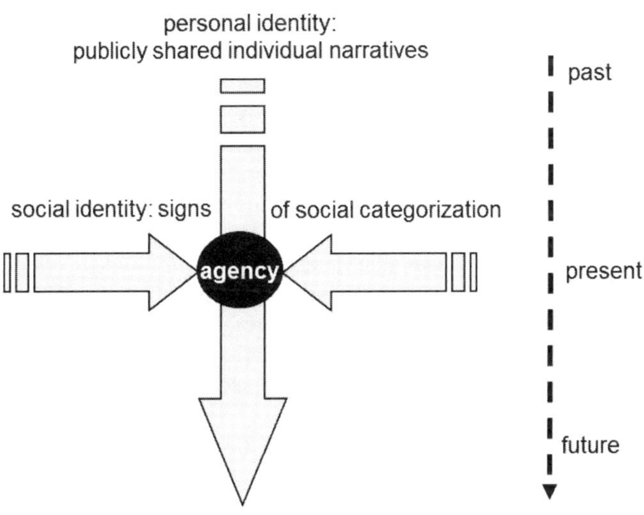

Note: Agency as rooted in stable structures of the Self goes back on the interaction of two processes involving personal identity and social identity, and the diachronic and synchronic dimension, respectively. Social identity reflects the social categorizations that apply for self–perception, as mediated by the perception through others. Personal identity results from the consistency of narratives about one's trajectory of life, including future projections of one self.

This implies that the emergence of identity corresponds to the proper functioning of the underlying biological systems. Even though the meaning of identity, that is, the content of the narrative, does not correspond to any functioning directly, it co-evolves with the more fundamental needs of behavioural coordination: Identities do not only have a function relative to the need to integrate individual behaviour and choice, but this also contributes to the creation and maintenance of social interactions (along the lines of the fundamental Ross model of three–level games). This mirrors the hierarchy of needs and wants that I have analysed in the previous section: Wants are integrated via the trajectory of individual identity, and they have functions in relation with human social interaction. So, we gain the insight that the evolutionary correspondence to the standard notion of the utility function is precisely the integration of wants in a notion of individual identity which is the reference for notions such as 'intentions' (for a related approach, see Foxall 2008). Especially, wants are embedded into a socially co-created individual identity, such that there is no independence of preferences from social interaction through time.

4.5.2. Identity and group markers

This allows drawing an important conclusion on the role of identity in the co-evolution of the different levels of evolution in the inclusive inheritance approach. There is a paradox involved in the relation between the levels, which comes to the fore in the many assertions that the most elaborate expressions of human symbolic systems seem to have no relation with biological functionings at all. More specifically, markers of group identity very often relate to behavioural phenomena and artefacts which have no direct functional significance apart from the fact that they define group boundaries. This raises the question how individual identity and group formation interact in evolutionary respects. We can refer this back to the analysis of group selection in Chapter Three: If the possibility of group selection emerges from the possibility of group–internal behavioural coordination, this would have to be seen as being manifest in individual identity. This is because the notion of identity implies a sort of absolute commitment that is necessary to fix behavioural convergence beyond the reach of individual opportunism.

Now, one can say that from the viewpoint of the logic of selection, no trait can directly serve as a reliable group boundary if it is adopted for functional reasons, because precisely if so, the trait would tend to diffuse across group boundaries, as long as the forces of selection and hence, adaptation, are converging. In other words, only functionless traits can serve the function of demarcating groups, because only they can withstand the convergent forces of selection. Thus, group boundaries are very often related to beliefs, ornaments and rituals. This, at the same time, is the very area where human creativity emerges, namely in the manipulation of symbols and meanings, and where individual identity seeks it primordial expression. Thus, the arts, music and performing skills have been defining characteristics of humanity since the early times (again, for a brain science viewpoint on this, see Damasio 2010: 288ff).

This hypothesis was first developed by anthropologist Rappaport (1979) and has been further developed into a fundamental evolutionary theorem by philosopher Munz (1993: 25f, 169ff; see also Herrmann-Pillath 1993). Rappaport had argued that the human capability to 'lie', that is to present a non–existing reality, underlies the phenomena of sanctity and other ritual creations of reality that ultimately are pillars of human social coordination, precisely because they cannot be questioned in the sense of being falsifiable, in that sense, are irrefutable 'lies.' Munz further accentuated a similar point by stating that only false beliefs can be sustainable indicators of group boundaries because only false beliefs offer a potentially infinite variety of possible demarcations, which are at the same time not susceptible to diffusion among populations for direct adaptive benefits (or, rational argument). This is an excellent example for the irreducibility of symbolic facts to genetic facts, while at the same time corresponding to proper (even biological) functionings.

This hypothesis can be tested empirically. For example, Rogers and Ehrlich (2008) report the analysis of traits of canoes in Polynesian societies (cf. Shennan 2008). Those traits can be distinguished into functional (for example shape) and symbolic (for example adornments). Functional traits are at least directly survival–relevant, whereas symbolic traits do not have a direct effect on the performance of canoes. For this reason, one can expect that functional traits evolve under strong selection, especially negative selection in the sense that traits that diverge from an established practice and do not work well, will be immediately abandoned again. So, functional traits can be expected to evolve only slowly. Symbolic traits can vary freely, and their main purpose, beyond pure expressiveness, is to signal group boundaries. Users of canoes can signal their identity also over distance. These differences are especially pronounced, if the populations are small, because the effects of drift are strong under this condition. The empirical patterns vindicate the hypothesis, namely that functional traits change much slower than symbolic traits. Symbolic traits evolve much more rapidly, resulting into a higher diversity of traits. This shows, on the one hand, that the symbolic traits are arbitrary in a fundamental sense, but at the same time they fulfil a generic function, namely to identify groups of users. This generic function is reflected in the on-going process of cultural creativity, also driven by the dynamics of group formation.

So, it is central to distinguish between the general type of response that drives the evolution of identities and the identity properly spoken. Precisely because the latter does not have a narrow function, it produces a general type of response that is in turn driven by natural selection. A most straightforward way to put this into the conceptual framework developed so far, is to see individual identity as the interface between semetic and genetic evolution, hence a phenomenon of co-evolution. In principle, both are de-coupled. But there is a criterion of setting mutual constraints which results from the long-run sustainability of the two processes. So, both processes need to fulfil certain most generic general types of responses which are endogenous to the respective processes. For semetic evolution, one essential criterion can be hypothesized to be the creation and maintenance of individual identity, which serves the general purpose of successful mutual coordination in groups, which is selectively relevant also in the genetic domain.

Now, we can relate this analysis with the previous analysis of the social brain. Identities play an essential role in determining solutions of strategic dilemmata in social interaction. Shared identities trigger correlated behaviour and therefore establish groups in terms of group selection (for a related view, see Wichardt 2008). Against this background, we still need to clarify why identities are relatively safe against fakes. If there is a reliable system to distinguish between cooperators and cheaters, the fitness–maximizing solutions in terms of reciprocity can be attained. Therefore, there are strong reasons to believe that the human brain evolved mechanisms to pre-coordinate behaviour in terms of similarities across groups of individuals.

The clearest expression of this is the peculiar pattern of brain ontogeny which changes the degree of behavioural plasticity during development. For example, even slightest differences in language may serve as group markers that trigger within–group reciprocity which is individually beneficial after the fact. The capability of adopting such differences changes considerably during the transition to adulthood, such that most people do no longer have the capability to fully acquire a foreign language and dialect without the slightest markers of their mother tongue. As a result, group markers established during ontogeny and socialization become almost immutably fixed after puberty the latest. This fact of human development can be easily explained in evolutionary terms if the importance for group recognition in reciprocal cooperation is acknowledged.

4.5.3. Emotions

As we see, this argument leads toward a specific form of group selection which does not require any form of altruism. The necessary condition for attaining the optimal states both individually and collectively is the existence of group markers which cannot be faked. Thus, we can assume that only those patterns will prevail in evolution, which support the emergence of these kind of group markers. This implies that these markers cannot be the object of conscious manipulation. I propose that this is exactly the systematic role of emotions in human behaviour which is fundamentally different from rational calculation. Again, this is a possible case of exaptation in the evolution of the human brain, as emotions are based on affects. However, affects are the much more general phenomenon and, most importantly, are not directly accessible to consciousness. In a simple sense, emotions are precisely the interface between the neocortical and the limbic systems, and are therefore crucial for the emergence of solutions to problems of social coordination which might otherwise result from intentional behaviour designed by the neocortex. In economics, this view has been seminally developed by Frank (1988; for further developments, see Elster 1998 and Kirman et al. 2010). This view does not imply that all emotions only serve these functions; but it means that phylogenetically older and universal affects across species can obtain these functions via exaptations.

The primary function of affects is the valuation of patterns of causal linkages between behaviour and results, which also applies for emotions (Price 2006). An affect is a somatic marker that stores valuable knowledge in terms of automatic responses. Thus, the classical case is operant conditioning, where indirect environmental cues are linked up with certain valuable actions in terms of expectations of resulting events. Thus, a signal related to the provision of food might trigger physiological reactions leading to the immediate readiness to eat. Or, a sudden light may signal danger and triggers immediate arousal and the readiness to take flight. According to somatic marker theory, this role of affects is universal, that is, without affects even rational decision making is impossible because the valuations are missing (for a comprehensive discussion, see Pham 2007). However, this does not simply imply that the valuations are themselves ordered in the sense of rationality, that is in terms of utility theory, as this approach assumes the existence of a unified decision calculus, thus conflicts with the modularity of the brain. On the other hand, integration can happen via the emergence of identities. This is translated across the levels of evolution into the contextuality of needs and wants, as we have seen. Thus, we can interpret reciprocity as being embedded into a hierarchy of needs and wants that are related to human social interaction and its objects. An excellent example is one of the most influential theories about individual behaviour in recent behavioural economics, 'prospect theory' which states that risk attitudes are asymmetric across losses and gains, leading towards the specific emotion of 'loss aversion' (for a survey including the neuroscience perspective, see Trepel et al. 2005; Knutson et al. 2008; Fox and Poldrack 2009). It is possible to reconstruct an evolutionary explanation of this shape of risk preferences based on animal foraging behaviour in general, such that risk taking is beneficial to survival and differential reproduction under conditions of environmental distress (McDermott et al. 2008; Netzer 2009; compare Santos and Chen 2009); yet, in certain contexts of human groups these basic affectual mechanisms can be framed in a way such that loss aversion is constrained (such as professional trading on financial markets, see Zaloom 2003, 2004).

Affects are causally related with external triggers. In the context of a social species, those external triggers include the behaviour of others. Therefore, I posit that emotions are the crucial mechanisms by which successful social coordination is made possible, by means of the internal coordination across different modules and mechanisms in the brain (Tooby and Cosmides 2005: 52ff; Livet 2010 approaches emotions as 'mixed' states involving different affectual components). In other words, I see emotions not as inner states of organisms, but in an essential way as the bridges across individuals: emotions are based on the neuromeme/sign conjunction that I elucidated previously. This is vindicated in recent psychological research which emphasizes the role of 'ecological rationality', that is relating emotions to successful and sustainable social interactions and conflict resolution (Pham 2007; Mercer 2010): An important aspect of the rationality of emotions is that they greatly enhance the coordination of valuations and behavioural expectations across different individuals, thus also providing the bedrock for 'social preferences' (Fehr 2009; Zak 2011).

An emotion can be defined as a socially embedded affectual circuit in the human brain which is partially reflected in consciousness ('feelings', see Phelps 2009; Damasio 2010). This implies that emotions are both universal and context–specific. The universality of emotions is based on the universality of certain affectual circuits in the human brain, mainly resulting from a common phylogenetic past (for a survey of human universals in the emotional domain, see Konner 2002). Thus, for instance, human beings are normally able to identify emotional states such as fear, anger or joy cross–culturally. At the same time, however, the triggers of these affects and the ways how they are reflected in consciousness are constructed during development, which leads towards a framing of the expressions of affects. Thus, emotions are framed affects (compare Cohen 2005; Matsumoto and Hwang 2011). This definition is important in two respects. The first is that emotions are a part of human phenotypical plasticity. For example, love can find different expressions in different societies, and there has been an evolution of forms of love during the centuries. However, the underlying affectual circuits are not as malleable as the framed emotions. This makes them particularly susceptible to evolve into reliable group markers. Thus, humans tend to perceive group distinctions mainly in affectual differences regarding the emotional responses in social interaction. As these differences are established during the transition to adulthood, and are typically reinforced in many social rites and customs, which are almost impossible to fake.

Thus, I reach the conclusion that the peculiar structure of the human brain is fundamentally shaped by group selection for group–internal cooperative behaviour. This is true independent from the specific object of the underlying needs. For example, a particular eating habit is directed at the need for nourishment, but at the same time can serve as a group marker. In a similar vein, many acquired wants of human beings are permeated by this mechanism of group identification. This is another expression of the multidimensionality of evolution in the sense that the role of emotions as group markers is, of course, only one of the functions of emotions. That is, emotions are multi–functional, and a whole account of the individual has to take their mutual relation into consideration. It is in this fundamental sense that we can state that individual identity is embedded into human groups. Phylogenetically, the human species is geared towards enabling human beings to benefit from cooperation within groups. Ontogenetically, human individuals develop an identity that activates this ability in a particular context. By this argument, I can provide a naturalistic foundation of the economic approach to identity.

4.5.4. Consumption, status and happiness

A radical consequence of the evolutionary theory of the individual is that the conventional economic theory of preferences can only make sense as a theory of agency in groups, which is a stark contradiction to methodological individualism. For instance, the stability of preferences cannot be treated as an axiom, but just the other way round, stability has to be explained. As we have seen, the straightforward explanation of stability lies in the identity of an individual, which is embedded into the group. In this fundamental sense, collective intentionality in consumption acts is the condition for individual intentionality. 'We consume' is the precondition of 'I consume'. This is sometimes treated in economics under the heading of 'habits' (for example Hodgson 2004), but this seems to treat the phenomenon as ephemeral. In the evolutionary approach, stability of consumption reaffirms individual identity in terms of conscious decision making through time. This necessarily relates individual consumption with collective phenomena.

This approach has important implications for the theory of consumption, because it implies that major aspects of individual consumption have to be interpreted as collective phenomena in the sense of manifesting a constant interaction between singular features of individuality and the evolution of shared features in a group (compare Reinstaller and Sanditov 2005). One should note, however, that this statement includes a paradox. Many so-called 'anomalies of rationality' manifest the underlying structures of the human brain. But at the same time, precisely the emergent properties of collective intentionality might even mitigate those anomalies. For example, in the case of hyperbolic time preferences which entail the possibility of 'irrational' preference reversals, group intentionality might actually commit individuals to stable time preferences following some established knowledge about optimal solutions. That is, group–bounded individual identities overcome internal conflicts over choice via workable commitment mechanisms (compare Ainslie 2007); for example, via the internalization of institutions (see Chapter Six on 'institutionally guided behavioural patterns) mechanisms can be activated that establish particular interactions between institutions and emotions (Smith and Dickhaut 2005). Thus, what appears to be individually rational might actually be the result of collective intentionality, thus at the same time contradicting the standard assumption of methodological individualism in economics. In other words, individuals might behave 'irrationally', but groups of individuals might behave 'individually rational'. However, the latter observation does by no means justify reinstating the standard economic modelling approach. We might even end up in a paradox: Problems of individual rationality in the context of collective decision making can be the result of group–level determinants of individual rationality. So, for example, a celebrated result in Experimental Economics is the cultural framing of behaviour in the standard ultimatum game, which shows, on the one hand, that 'irrational' cooperation is culturally determined, but also, of course, that the standard results of the economic model of rationality also emerge only in certain cultural contexts (Henrich et al. 2005).

Beyond this, consumption is a collective phenomenon as many forms of consumption directly express group affiliation in the sense of shared traits. For example, in human history eating habits and culinary customs always served as important group markers, a function which only weakened in modern societies with their multicultural cuisine. Yet, today eating habits may no longer be relevant as markers of ethnicity, but still may serve to delineate identities in terms of, for example, shared lifestyles in post-modern societies, such as being a vegetarian. Further, even the same attributes of goods very often signal group–internal status distinctions. Status goods are consumed to directly express status relations among individuals. These are both related to individual status differences and to status differences among groups. That means, consumption patterns that establish group identity can simultaneously signal status differences between groups, such that entire patterns (eating habits, clothing, sports etc.) arrange into an ensemble of consumption activities that marks one group off against another. This establishes group–specific consumption benchmarks, which also establish group–internal markers for status differences, as, for example, is most evident in the conspicuous consumption of luxury goods. Perceived status is also an important medium of second–order sanctions, as ostracism is a most powerful determinant of conformism (see next chapter).

The classic on status is Veblen (1899), of course. However, Adam Smith (1759) also assumed that the main driving force of economic activity is the yearning to win recognition by others, and that the beneficial effects on society only emerge when a competitive regime prevails. Status preferences have been systematically reintroduced into economics by Frank (1985) (for a recent survey, see Robson and Samuelson 2010). They are of tremendous significance because many conventional assumptions about rational choice and, in particular, strategic interaction, have to be changed or even discarded if it is assumed that people wish to maximize differences in consumption patterns and levels with respect to others, in particular, if these differences are measured on a linear scale (for a seminal analysis, see Taylor 1987; these considerations are essential in many theories about fairness, see for instance Bolton and Ockenfels 2000). A typical luxury good is defined both in terms of its idiosyncratic differences and in terms of its price, for example. In a Beckerian fashion one could argue that this kind of goods merely fulfils the special need of social recognition, however, its economic consequences are very different from ordinary goods. For example, there are externalities between different consumption activities: If I drive my car for prestige reasons, the new car of my neighbour might change its utility overnight. This example shows that the theory of status preferences is closely related to the theory of identity as it has been exposed by Akerlof and Kranton (2000), in which externalities in networks loom large. Via status preferences, all choices become interdependent across individuals because firstly, there needs to be a shared view (a 'we attitude' in the sense of Tuomela's 2007) about the criteria for status (I cannot define status exclusively for myself, because I need the recognition of others), and secondly, because all status oriented actions create externalities for others. Status preferences, among other properties, lead to an unending quest for satisfaction, that is, they offer a very simple reason for the insatiability of wants. This is because there is also a Red Queen effect at work, as even slightest differences can upturn a balance between different agents, reshuffling the status order (for a sociological classic on this role of the 'smallest difference', see Baudrillard 1970; on a detailed analysis of Red Queen effects, see Hopkins and Kornienko 2004).

In all human societies, status consumption is regulated by social norms (again, see Akerlof and Kranton 2000) which establish a connection between status, consumption and particular reference groups (for an evolutionary model, see Reinstaller and Sanditov 2005). With the growing multiplicity of social roles in modern societies, these norms have become less rigid but persist to exist (for example, an entrepreneur driving a Ferrari is accepted, whereas in the case of a politician many would think it as inappropriate). A major effect of those norms is to contain the harmful effects of status competition, with the result of stabilizing status orders, once established.

From the viewpoint of human biology, status certainly has an adaptive function, as it is directly related to reproductive success in animal and human societies, which also explains much of the seeming paradox of demographic transition. That is, in the average individuals with higher status in their reference groups also have more offspring, even in industrial societies, even if the average number across all individuals may have declined (for a classical discussion of the relation between status and reproductive success, see Betzig 1986). The second theoretical point follows from the observation that individuals have limited cognitive possibilities to ascertain the causal link between their actions and the results for their individual situation. Status is an information–processing signal which reveals whether one's actions indeed have improved the individual situation in the sense that given a particular environment and context, an individual has fared better than the others. This also explains why relatively successful individuals are copied in many ways, for example in terms of their consumption styles (Richerson and Boyd 2005: 124ff).

As status is a relational category, and status relations hence zero–sum, it follows that there is no possibility of satiation, because my status only depends on relative consumption. So, even if an apple becomes a status good, that would imply that I am never satiated with apples, if my neighbour still consumes more than me, or consumes more expensive kinds of apple. Because of this complexity of interactions, we can surmise that fundamental uncertainty reigns over the causal linkage between consumption decisions and individual satisfaction.

There is a fundamental issue here that is related to the Benthamite tradition in economics that posits that the aim of economic activity is to increase the level of individual pleasure or happiness. From the evolutionary viewpoint, this cannot be taken for granted, as happiness would only be an aim if it can be interpreted in terms of function. In the triadic view, happiness can only have an indicator function, unless it is shown that states of happiness have functions in the larger human systems. Happiness is not a need as such. But we can certainly state that people whose needs are not fulfilled are not happy. Thus, happiness or, better, unhappiness, seems to be an indicator that signals states of deficiency, but without specificity, thus triggering action which is not necessarily goal–oriented but may end up in results that reduce the state of deficiency.

This interpretation fits into the idea that human choice is driven by emotions, in which evaluations are based. That means, the economic idea of assigning particular utilities to particular items ('goods' and 'bads') seems to be fundamentally misleading, as those emotions are much more general in scope. Instead, there is a complex interaction between perceptions of individual states that are made up by combinations of external cues and signals that relate to the material determinants of that state. Most people identify states of happiness with streams of seamless doing, often without further reflection, and which is related to some meaningful activity, in the sense of pursuing a goal. Thus, playing is very often perceived as a flow, as it can be the working experience or following a religious rite. This kind of behaviour is embedded into what Veblen had called a 'scheme of life', which means it is related to one's identity. Thus, for example, jobless people will never be as happy as people with a job, because they cannot resume their feeling of flow that was related to their work. Retraining to another job might also fail to revive this experience of flow.

In the recent years, happiness research has become an important topic in economics (Frey and Stutzer, 2002). This followed Easterlin's classical result that increases in income are not reflected in increases of reported happiness. Even more astonishing is the fact that this result is also obtained if broader conceptions of determinants of well–being are added, such as improved health (Di Tella and McCulloch, 2006). That means, the entire economic progress of the advanced industrial societies is not directly and unequivocally reflected in greater happiness of individuals. There are several theoretical explanations for this observation that fit into the theory of the individual as outlined in this chapter. One of the most powerful is the assumption that people strive for relative status, so that their reference groups matter most. This directly implies that the effects of absolute increases do not cause greater happiness, if the reference group's standards also increase (Red Queen effect, see Hopkins and Kornienko 2004 with reference to happiness research; for a congenial overview of the empirical literature and theoretical approaches, see Clark et al. 2008). Happiness scores of people normally do show a response to higher incomes, but through time and across groups these always tend to flatten out and to show a 'ratchet effect'. Thus, for example, people might compare themselves with the average situation in their native country, such as when migrant workers maintain close communication with their native places. Even if they remain on the lower levels of the income ladder in their receiving countries, their improvement of income relative to their native region can be substantial. Accordingly, they experience great increases of status, resulting in high levels of happiness, even though they remain disadvantaged in their current situation, with reference to the host society. Once they integrate with the host society, this perception can change, as the reference group changes.

Happiness research has also shown that there is no unified internal measure and that it depends very much on the dynamics of changing from unpleasant states to better states (Kahnemann and Krueger 2006). There are strong drives to leave unpleasant states, as these are typically scoring high in individual perception. For example, past unpleasant states are mainly identified with the peak experience or the experience of the final stages, and not with the averages. Further, there is the fact of 'loss aversion', that is changes of satisfaction around a status quo weigh much stronger in the negative than in the positive (one seminal work is Thaler 1994, culminating into the 'prospect theory' approach championed by Kahneman and others). All this concurs with the hypothesis that individuals feel happy if there is a perception of growth and change to the positive, based on the stability of the status quo, which fits into the 'flow' argument previously developed. This also explains the second major reason for the Easterlin results that is normally given in the economic literature, namely that there is a habituation effect. Thus, people who win a lottery rarely score higher in sustained levels of happiness. Habituation is just the reflection of the more fundamental argument that happiness results from the perception of change, and not from the experience of states.

To summarize this section, the economic theory of consumption needs to eschew the traditional individualistic approach in terms of recognizing the social embeddedness of individual wants. Many forces converge here, such as learning from others by imitation or observing socially accepted standards of status. At the same time, we can also say that these forces flow together in the formation of individual identities. From the evolutionary view, human individuals have the capacity to form individual identities in groups, which are non-negotiable and therefore credible in interactions with others. In this way, human group–mindedness is even a precondition for forming individual rationality.

This picture seems to stay in stark contradiction with methodological individualism in economics. However, as I already clarified in the first section, we need to distinguish between the evolutionary and the economic theory of the individual. Human individuals co-evolve with the evolution of networks, institutions and technology. Therefore, in this chapter I only laid the foundation for this much more complex analysis. This approach to 'individualism' is Hegelian in essence: Precisely because we can show that human beings are group–minded in an essential way, we can also identify the conditions under which they constitute themselves as individuals in groups. Yet, Hegel's account of human social evolution is profoundly teleological, which stays in principled tension with Darwinian evolutionary theory. However, one core idea remains valid also in the evolutionary view: The individuals of economic theory are emergent phenomena in the evolution of systems that we call 'economic'.

A final point needs emphasis. Group–mindedness does not imply collectivism in attitudes and opinions. Ontological individuality means the uniqueness of the individual. All processes described in this chapter will always bear the mark of individual singularity, corresponding to the fundamental tenets of evolutionary theory. In this regard, the previous remarks raise awareness of the fact that the recognition of this irreducible singularity of the individual was an outcome of institutional and cultural developments in recent times (Taylor 1989).

5. Networks

> Our metaphorical river consists in stochastic flows of events. Ties and identities alike are bathed in uncertainty among crosscurrents from situations, on up through births and deaths. Switchings thus are endemic, across combinations of network and domain. Situations may be imbricated across multiple network-domains of identities. Signallings lead to utterances and thence stories that cluster for each network domain as a set, able to account for happenings with those ties. Participants, too, probe cohesion and connectivity and may come to perceive boundaries. Subsequently, identities and ties may string and profile under some circumstances into what you and I think of as persons (Harrison C. White (2008: xvii).

5.1. NETWORKS, INDIVIDUALS AND SIGNS

5.1.1. Networks, groups and distributed agency

In this chapter, I substantiate the abstract notion of the 'group' in general evolutionary theory in terms of the concept of networks. This concept matches with the paradigm of connectionism in the brain sciences, and it builds a bridge to general approaches in ecology, thus applying across vastly different levels of evolutionary analysis. In the first step, this reflects the generality of the mathematical notion of a 'network', which is just 'a collection of points joined together in pairs by lines' (Newman 2010: 1). One important task of this chapter is to relate this generic notion of a network with the specific biological characteristics of humans, in particular with reference to the theory of the individual. Human networks connect individuals, and so the question is what this implies for network analysis, both in theoretical and empirical terms. The pivotal point is the recognition that human brains fundamentally operate on the basis of semiotically embedded connectivity with other brains.

Networks and individuals connect in two respects. The first is that networks enable distributed cognition; the second is that networks establish distributed agency. Both aspects define the relationship between networks and groups. In this sense, in this chapter we go beyond the previous chapter which still treated We–modes as states of individuals. We–modes undergird the human capacity to form networks among individuals. In contrast, the notion of distributed cognition or 'extended mind' emphasizes the fact that networks enable cognitive capacities that are not accessible to isolated individuals. Hegel already established this in a most fundamental way in asserting that even advanced forms of knowing oneself can only be possible via the recognition by the Other, an idea that also applies on the collective level, such as stating that the culture of an community can only be recognized if reflected in the demarcation towards the culture of another community (Baecker 2000).

However, modern theories of distributed cognition, beginning with seminal studies such as Hutchins (1995), also refer to more specific cognitive capacities which are enabled by networks of individuals. For economics, this idea should not be strange, as we can regard markets as computational systems which make the valuation of scarcity possible in a large system of interacting individuals, which is not possible with other means, especially those ones in which the apparently necessary information would be concentrated in a central decision maker. This classical result of the 'socialist calculation debate' (see Hayek 1945) is generalized in the modern notion of markets as computational systems (Mirowski and Somefun 1998). Therefore, markets enable cognitive functions which are not accessible for individuals trying their best to collect all the information available in the market. This most general result applies on all different levels of networks, such as on the level of small groups or teams (Charness and Sutter 2012). This does not necessarily imply that the results of information processing are always more powerful (Lorenz et al. 2011). However, it is possible to show that, given certain conditions, networks of interacting individuals can achieve higher cognitive performances than single best decision makers. Page (2007) has established a set of pertinent theorems showing that these properties are truly emergent on the network level, because a major determinant is the diversity of actors: Under certain conditions a set of diverse actors can achieve better problem solutions than a more uniform set of individually best performers. So, cognitive performance on the network level is determined by network properties, and not only by the properties of the individual actors. This insight has been highly influential in contemporary thought about the role of diversity in human societies and business (for example Thomas 1991). These results are certainly limited to particular contexts, but they show how networks can obtain cognitive functions that go beyond the capacities of individual actors.

As we shall see, modern theories of distributed cognition go beyond the idea that networked individuals enable new cognitive capacities insofar as they explicitly include artefacts (Clark and Chalmers 1998). This is an aspect that is normally excluded from 'social network analysis'. However, there is the approach by 'actor–network' theory (surveyed by one of its founders,

Latour 2005) which argues that this is necessary. This is an important idea, especially in the context of economics, as it makes clear that markets as networks cannot simply be approached as networks among individuals, but have a material infrastructure, sometimes dubbed 'market devices' (Callon et al. 2007). Actor–network theory has extended this view into the analysis of agency (Callon 2008): 'Agencement' is distributed agency that includes networks between individuals as well as artefacts. So, for example, a financial trader is an actor whose cognitive capacities are partly distributed in network configurations with other actors (Beunza and Stark 2008 analyse the spatial configurations of actors in an investment bank office enabling complex perceptions of risk) and in the computers that she utilizes, embodying certain mathematical tools (MacKenzie 2006), and at the same time intermediating social networks among traders (Knorr Cetina and Brugger 2002). We will not scrutinize the role of technology explicitly in this chapter, which is left for Chapter Seven, but include this fundamental perspective here, in the sense of approaching networks bimodally, that is as configurations of individuals and signs, with signs seen as material entities.

The notion of distributed agency goes beyond the notion of distributed cognition and the notion of the 'We–mode' as I argue that in the context of human groups, group–level agents can emerge, in the sense of the corresponding function. As we have seen in the previous chapter, in the triadic analysis 'individuals' are constituted by functions (section 4.1.3.); so, there is no ontological necessity that agency is only located in the material body of individuals. There are evolutionary mechanisms that lead towards the emergence of more complex forms of agency in networks, such that under particular circumstances, groups act, enhanced by technological artefacts (Callon 2008 discusses the example of a pilot in a modern aircraft, who is just one part in a complex structure of *agencement*). This transition can be compared to phase transitions in physics: So, for example, a collection of individuals might transform into an angry mob that collectively moves to destroy a house of a collectively despised person. This collective state is enabled by certain emotional mechanisms that create We–attitudes and We–modes' enhanced by networked interactions, such that individual agency is at least partly moved to the collective level. There are many examples for such phase transitions, such as the emergence of 'group think' in teams that leads towards decisions that would not result from a mere aggregation of individual opinions (and which is a countervailing force to group effects related to diversity that I mentioned previously).

So, the concept of networks is the fundamental notion to analyse human groups. It is the most general way that within one unified paradigm we can both treat individuals *as* groups and individuals *in* groups: Approaching the brain in terms of connectionism means to apply a network model, and networks naturally emerge in the interaction among individuals. In this most basic sense, we can also think of disaggregating network analysis in the way of relating parts of individuals with parts of other individuals. One case in point are certain forms of self–deception (von Hippel and Trivers 2011): For example, an individual that self–aggrandizes himself and even deceives himself about this, may be supported in this behaviour by the recognition of others, which actually confirms the self–deceiving image; as this self–deception can be analysed in a dualistic way, that is, one brain module blocking and manipulating information towards another brain module, we can say that this self–aggrandizement is a network phenomenon, perhaps reflected in leadership behaviour and positioning in a social role, that focuses on parts of the brain, but not the entire brain of the individual, as internal information flows are channelled in a certain way.

5.1.2. Bimodality of networks

Modern network analysis currently comes in two versions. One is sociological Social Network Analysis; another is the application of physical models on social phenomena, including economics. There is still a disjunction here, because Social Network Analysis tends to focus on smaller (though not necessarily small) groups, whereas physical network analysis concentrates on very large groups. Indeed, physical network analysis has been driven by the emergence of the Worldwide Web, in particular (see for example Barabási 2002). Although this has led towards a certain lack of communication between the two approaches (Scott 2011), in fact they constitute one body of theory, if we just observe this distinction related to group size (see Newman 2010 as an attempt at a unified approach).

My own approach in the context of the Natural Philosophy of economics will build on these theories, but adds some new concepts. The first is that I adopt the bimodal framework of basic ontology. This leads to two modifications. One is that I regard all networks as networks between individuals *and* signs. A sign is a physical object. As I have already mentioned, this perspective has recently been developed in Actor–network Theory (though without the semiotic twist), which is the only approach that makes the role of artefacts explicit in human networks, as far as the social sciences are concerned (technological network analysis in engineering naturally includes both human decision makers and technological devices, see Batten et al. 1995). The emergence of the web 2.0 is a case in point: artefacts change the way how individuals interact in a fundamental way (such as Twittering). I generalize over this inclusion of artefacts in terms of the concept of the 'sign'. By doing this, I can provide the microfoundations for network dynamics in terms of the neuromeme/sign connectivity that I have elaborated on in the previous chapter. For example, if a group manifests high degrees of solidarity, this is based on certain signs that connect the individuals in the group, which activate certain emotional mechanisms in a recurrent fashion, such that the group–level pattern of solidarity emerges.

The second concept that I add is that I can explicitly conjoin the approaches focusing on network connectivity with other approaches that emphasize the role of meaning in networks. Classical Social Network Analysis emphasizes data that are accessible to external observers and therefore neglects interpretive activities (for an overview, see for example Knoke and Song 2008; for a typical disciplinary criticism, see the anthropologist Schweitzer 1996: 255ff; in general Hollstein 2011). This leads to an underestimation of the role of individual agency and creativity, for example, in the context of the fundamental network phenomenon in creating boundaries between networks. These complex questions have been dealt with in highly idiosyncratic network theories such as White (2008), and have been recently discussed more explicitly in the special approach of 'relational sociology' (Emirbayer 1997) emerging from these theories, but there are still many open questions (Mische 2011). One central idea in these views has been ventilated by White (2008: 17 for a summary) which is to relate the concept of identity with the concept of networks.

I argue that the semiotic approach offers some simple frameworks to deal with those issues, and we have already built the conceptual bridge in the previous chapter (figure 4.12): That is, in the network context identities fundamentally relate with the notion of mutual coordination and control of actions, such that individual identity, as stated previously, emerges from the history of network interactions, reflected in narratives, and the positioning in networks, reflected in categorizations. In both respects, signs play a central role. To a considerable extent, this view is already emerging in applications of Social Network Analysis on culture, where researchers investigate into mappings between configurations of actors and configurations of cultural items, such as linguistic expressions (DiMaggio 2011; Mohr and Rawlings 2012).

Table 5.1 Bimodality of networks

	Observer independent	**Observer relative**
Matterenergy mode	Network connectivity	Network structure/ function
Semiotic mode	Network signs	Network sign systems/ meaning

I can systematically present this unification of views in table 5.1 and in figure 5.1. Many approaches in network analysis, especially the physical ones, only concentrate on the upper left box. In this view, a network is a pattern of realized connections between individuals, such as the links in the WWW. In figure 5.1, this is the view on the left-hand side. Networks are constituted by configurations of individuals, the nodes, and their linkages, the edges. Viewed from this perspective, it is straightforward to apply mathematical methods from graph analysis to understand the more complex aspects of networks.

Figure 5.1 Two views of networks

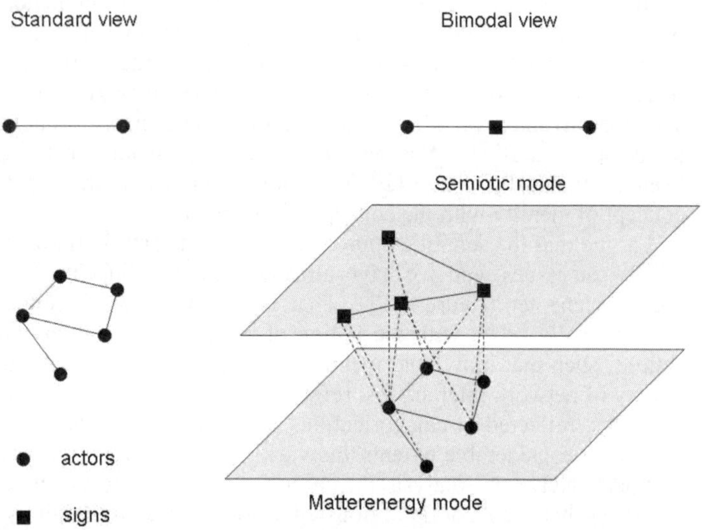

Note: The traditional approach to network analysis builds on simple graph–theoretic structures in which actors as elements are connected via certain kinds of interactions (for example, gift–giving, meetings etc.). The bimodal approach introduced in this chapter posits that all network connections are mediated via signs as physical entities. Signs manifest network connections on their own. For example, members of different ethnic groups meet, and during these interactions certain signs of ethnicity are active which stand in a multivalued relationship with the actors. The signs manifest an autonomous network pattern (such as the patterns of the semantic space in which they assume their cultural meaning). Based on this distinction, I argue that network analysis always needs to proceed bimodally, that is in the matterenergy mode and the semiotic mode.

The problem with these approaches is that they cannot make the role of actors' knowledge explicit in the analysis of networks. A simple case in point is that I may be connected even with all individuals of the world in some indirect way, but of course I do not know all individuals. Sometimes people meet and discover some connection, exclaiming 'It's a small world, indeed!' However, if they do not know, connectivity does not affect their actions, unless there is an additional mechanism that transfers the necessary information, or intermediates some causal effects: So, for example, I may be connected with farmers in South Africa by buying red wine, but their actions impact on me via signs, such as prices, and I am not aware of the connectivity on the level of the individuals. Further, if we want to understand certain actions, we also need to know how actors interpret certain network connections. Simple connectivity is, for example, realized if actors stay together in an elevator. However, from some other perspective this is meaningless, because they do not talk. Therefore, the question is which kind of interaction is of interest in defining connectivity. But this also depends on the meaning which actors give to those interactions. For that reason, it is important to approach networks in terms of observer relativity.

Here, we distinguish between the two modes. In the matterenergy mode, the distinction between types of connectivity concentrates on the function that networks have. This means to analyse network structure (upper right box in table 5.1). For example, we might ask which network structures result in the most rapid diffusion of information. Clearly this requires determining the pertinent function, because speed of diffusion might not necessarily be an aspect of proper functioning. For instance, this also applies for the speed of the transmission of an infectious disease, which might be counted as a dysfunction. Illness can be defined as a phenomenon in matterenergy terms, because it can be observed in terms of biochemical phenomena, but the analysis of the network dynamics depends on the identification of this particular function. So, in the upper right box we relate connectivity with function, which results into the identification of network structure.

Turning to the semiotic mode, we introduce the view on networks which is visualized in figure 5.1 on the right side, in terms of two levels in which we can approach networks. One is the level of the actors; the other is the level of the signs. Signs can be treated as observer independent objects in the sense of being physical entities. For example, if actors divide according to the colour of the skin, 'black' and 'white' can be defined as physical properties of actors, or, if there is a telephone line between two actors, we can define this in terms of the matterenergy characteristics of this artefact which turns human language into electric signals. The distinction of the two levels means that we have to recognize that if we separate the levels, connectivity can differ respectively. For example, we might consider the connectivity between actors of a population, which manifests complex patterns, but on the sign level we just see the connectivity patterns between black and white, thus resulting in a highly aggregate distinction between two groups of actors. So, the point is that we can define a mapping between actors and signs, and then consider connectivity on the two levels, and the mappings between these configurations. As we shall see, this distinction is especially important to understand perception and communication in networks. It is essential to recognize that all interactions in networks are mediated via signs, because all external action can operate as a sign, as we have seen in the previous chapter.

So, the bimodal view on networks directly refers back to the analysis of the brain/mind that I have presented there. For example, if I give money to somebody, this is a sign, both in the sense of using money as a sign, but also in terms of the action. However, as this example easily shows, it is impossible to identify the nature of the interaction just by relying on the observer independent dimension (namely the sign in terms of the physical properties of the coin). We need to make the actor's intentions explicit, which relates to the lower right box in table 5.1. This refers network analysis to meanings. For example, the transfer of money may be seen as a gift or as a commercial transaction. In the case of corruption, this may be difficult to establish. So, understanding the meaning of signs requires hermeneutic approaches in network analysis.

Figure 5.2 Triadic view on networks

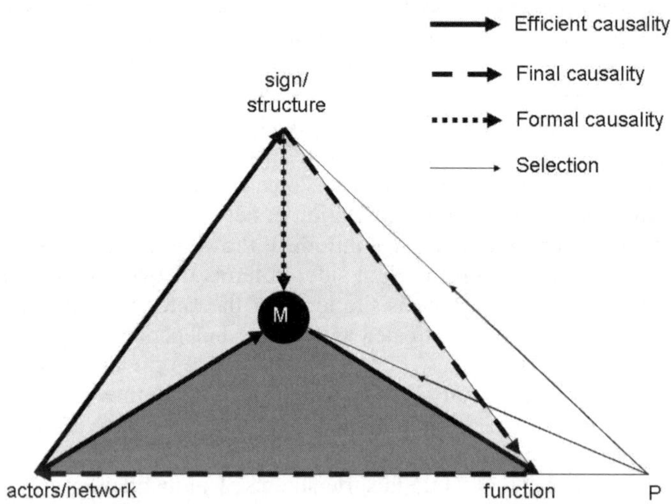

Note: In the triadic view on networks, groups of actors have functions relative to an environment. These functions are efficiently–caused by the actions of actors. However, they are semiotically intermediated via the categorizations of network structure and the corresponding classifications of types of actions. For example, producers and consumers relate via networks of markets, but the particular pattern of interactions also depends on categorizations (types of producers, types of products etc.).

We can therefore reformulate table 5.1 by means of the general triadic framework (figure 5.2). Then, we approach networks as realized patterns of connectivity among actors. These networks, such as a market, have certain functions, which are selected for by the environment to which networks relate. Thus, markets may have the function to connect producers and consumers in a society. Functions and network configurations relate via efficient–causal mechanisms. However, we cannot explain these mechanisms without referring to the level of signs. More specifically, signs are essential to mediate structure relative to function. For example, signs determine which kinds of actors actually realize certain functions of markets, and in which way, such as identifying a certain kind of professional traders. Producers and consumers might not get in touch directly, but via intermediation. Signs result in a classification of mechanisms that relate with the realization of functions, thus defining a network structure (distinguishing between producers, intermediaries and consumers, connected via certain classes of configurations). So, ultimately final causality determines the conjunction of mechanism and network evolution: The efficient realization of the function of distributing consumer goods may rely on the identification of particular kinds of intermediaries which are identified via sets of signs. For example, certain trades might be dominated by ethnic traders in a certain society.

From this follows that it is impossible to understand network phenomena only in terms of connectivity patterns in the matterenergy mode, which proves to be a major limitation of standard network analysis. On the other hand, connectivity patterns play an important causal role. In the ontological view, this causal role establishes the existence of network structure. So, network analysis gives a very simple justification for the distinction between what are traditionally individualistic approaches to actor agency and sociological approaches. For example, if a certain actor occupies a certain position in a network structure, this might give it an especially central position in connecting other actors, such as a gatekeeper. This position is not an intrinsic property of the actor, however, it can give the actor considerable power, depending on the nature of the interaction. This power is not an intrinsic property of the actors, yet, whether and how it is used depends on the actor, his social skills, his intelligence etc.

5.1.3. Causation and network structure: Methodological implications

Therefore, if we want to explain the actions of the actor, network structure plays an independent causal role, and hence exists in the ontological sense. This has the important methodological consequence that mathematical network measures such as measures of centrality (overview in Knoke and Song 2008: 62ff; Hannemann and Riddle 2005) describe empirical facts: We can distinguish between observer independent and observer relative aspects of these facts, as the original centrality measures refer to observer independent facts (so, they can be used for human systems as well as for technological networks or protein networks, cf. Newman 2010: 78ff), yet the resulting network processes involving human actors depend essentially on how this is reflected in internal knowledge states, both individually and collectively. As a result, the naturalistic notion of causality in networks includes both individual agency and network structure (compare Bhaskar 1989).

I introduce the conceptual distinction between configuration and structure, which relates with the micro/macro distinction in many social sciences, including economics (terminologically, this goes back to Elias's 1969a, b conception of a 'configurational sociology'). Configurations refer to the realized patterns of connectivity between particular actors. Structures are shared properties of configurations across different networks (a notion which is reflected in so-called 'blockmodel analysis' in standard SNA approaches, see Knoke and Yang 2008: 85ff). For example, if we consider a military hierarchy, this results in shared properties of all platoons in an army, thus defining a structure. However, the specific configurations between platoon leaders and soldiers might vary across the platoons. Identifying most general structures is an important aspect of hypothesis building in network analysis, such as identifying gatekeeper structures, which have general implications for the power position of an actor. Yet, the particular network configuration may differ. For example, a gatekeeper might be very open to any kind of inflowing interaction, or highly selective.

Another important methodological consequence of the network approach comes to the fore in comparing the notion of the 'group' with the notion of the 'class'. If I conceive of groups as 'networks', I define the 'group' as a category of individuals who interact directly or indirectly, with indirect interactions sorted along certain criteria of categorization which impose boundaries of interactions. So, for example, the Chinese farmer who grows apples that are sold in a UK supermarket is indirectly connected with a British customer, even with relatively few intermittent interactions. Still, we would not count the two as belonging to the same group, of any size. The criterion has been already identified by Max Weber: It is essential that actors are aware of the connectivity, and also of the mutual interdependence of actions. Yet, even this criterion is difficult to substantiate, if, for example, we assume that the Chinese farmer receives some feedback about British tastes via the trading company, and thus tries to imagine their responses to some new sorts of apples (though one needs to distinguish carefully between the awareness of a class of customers and of individual customers). Yet, the basic principle applies.

In comparison, a class of individuals is based on a shared property and the corresponding assignment to a category, without necessarily assuming that the individuals interact. For example, all fans of Madonna are a class of people, but they only form a group if they form an internet community via which the members of the community exchange opinions and information. This difference is of fundamental methodological significance. For example, if a theory is proposed which explains a revolution in terms of certain social structures, very often the error is committed to view structure as a shared property of individuals, and therefore draw some causal consequences. Thus, the industrial workers may appear to be in a shared structural position, and therefore are assumed to share certain interests and resulting action potential. However, the mere assignment to a class is of no causal relevance, unless it can be shown that this class characteristic is directly linked with network connectivity and actions. Workers need to form a group in order to become causally relevant for network processes. So, for example, they might become aware of the fact that they share a common structural position, and therefore start to interact, thus building action potential.

This example shows that the interaction between classes and groups can be approached on bimodal terms, if we can show that the signs that map the classes turn into causal determinants of actions. So, we can imagine a situation in which all members of a class take similar actions without actually interacting with each other, because they respond to the same sign that maps their assignment to that class. Further, perception of signals that indicate similar structural positions can cause actions that result in the formation of groups in terms of network connectivity. So, for example, workers may start to perceive their similarities in terms of structural position and start to network across local groups in order to build a workers' social movement.

The distinction between groups and classes is also reflected in certain cognitive and emotional mechanisms of human individuals, as far as the transition between the I–mode and the We–mode is concerned. There are distinct cultural differences in establishing group orientation (so-called 'collectivism' in cross-cultural research), with some cultures focusing on the relational nature of groups, and others on categorization (Nisbett 2003; Shavitt et al. 2011). These different attitudes are apparently based on cognitive mechanisms that result into different degrees of so-called 'field dependency' of cognition (Ji et al. 2000, 2004; compare Yamagishi 2012). So, for example, individuals who emphasize interactions in groups more than categories of people, will also sort words in linguistic sorting tasks mainly according to relationships between entities (such as 'monkey eat banana') than conceptual categories (such as 'monkey and horses are animals'). This has implications for the ways in which the individuals establish identities in groups: Cultures with less field–dependence manifest stronger inclination to identify with abstract groups like 'the company,' whereas more field–dependent individuals focus on actual relationships.

The distinction between groups and classes is of crucial methodological relevance for the selection of empirical methods in network analysis, resulting into a principled difference from most established methods in economics. Economics, in particular econometrics, builds causal hypotheses by identifying classes of individuals in order to show how certain class properties correlate in samples of individuals. For example, in estimating network effects in international trade, economists would test for the causal impact of ethnic classes on trade patterns, or shared languages etc. in the context of the gravity equation approach (such as Rauch 2001). From the viewpoint of network analysis, these methods are flawed as they are not based on relational data, that is samples of realized interactions between pairs of individuals. The explanatory variables are classes, and the dependent variables are dyadic trade transactions: What is missing here is how the class assignments can actually cause the creation of the pertinent interactions. Even the assignment to the same class of language or dialect does not imply that people really talk to each other. Therefore, network analysis builds on different sets of data, namely relational data that directly cover interactions, and not just classes of individuals (on this issue, see Knoke and Yang 2008: 15ff).

5.2. GROWTH OF INFORMATION IN EVOLVING NETWORKS

5.2.1. Information, entropy and non-integral networks

Regarding the relationship between economics and network analysis, there is one fundamental observation: All markets are networks. In economics, we meet the assumption that the most efficient way of organizing markets is to establish universal connectivity. This is because in this case information is accessible to every actor, and the range of possible choices of actions is at the maximum. So, the market in terms of perfect competition is the universally connected network. Then, all deviations from this structure are seen as imperfections, such as imperfect competition.

From the viewpoint of the theory of knowledge and information established so far, this is fundamentally wrong, as networks can only accumulate information if structure differs from the hypothetical state of perfect connectivity (following the arguments in Potts 2000, 2001, and Loasby 2001). This is because perfect connectivity would realize the maximum state of entropy of the social interactions: All connections tend to become equally probable. The argument applies also for less connected networks, if these are random networks, in which the equiprobability of network connectivity of single nodes applies.

We can make this point clear if we project the standard framework of entropy and evolution on networks. Consider an evolving system of interactions which unfolds via the growth of possible connections, such as via population growth, migration and the increasing scope of interactions caused by the extension of communication and transport. This means that the number of possible connections increases according to the simple principles of combinatorial arithmetic. This is the state of maximum possible entropy, in the sense of a random network with full connectivity. In this case, however, the network structure would not carry any information independent from the information that is carried by the nodes: This corresponds to the notion in economics that in a perfect market, all information is dispersed and already contained in the prices, such that observed price movements follow a random walk, so do not carry any information. Information accumulates in the structure if connectivity is less that complete. So, networks accumulate information via the formation of structure.

We can state this as the principle of non-integral network configurations in evolution (Potts 2000). This has far-reaching implications for economics, because it means that information processing in markets presupposes deviations from the standard model of perfect competition. Markets only accumulate information if they are 'imperfect' in this conceptual framework (a most general case in point is the structure of monopolistic competition which can be seen as revealing information about varieties in consumer preferences, which would not be processed under perfect competition as the incentives for diversification do not exist). Evidently, the notion of 'imperfectness' is somewhat misleading here, since the imperfectness is necessary for establishing the function. For example, firms represent imperfections of markets, but this means that they are indispensable for making information accumulation possible in markets. As I will argue in Chapter Eight, information accumulation in markets only proceeds via the co-evolution of firms and markets.

This analysis does not imply that certain results of standard analysis of competition lose force. For example, a monopolist assumes positions of power, which has certain effects on competition, and one cannot simply say that the monopolist is a necessary state in terms of information processing in networks. The specific analysis depends on the identification of functions relative to which information is operative. However, as we shall see in the final section of this chapter, this example also makes clear that network structure always has implications for relative power positions, and that the true meaning of the perfect connectivity paradigm is to define a state of homogenous power distribution across actors.

We can further substantiate this analysis in figure 5.3. Then, we recognize that networks, first of all, manifest a large number of complex interactions. However, only a certain number of these interactions are functional, which is determined by network structure. In adopting this view, we can also immediately apply the other principles of entropic analysis. Thus, we can state that network evolution will follow the MaxEnt principle in the specific way that together with the emergence of structure, network configurations will manifest a tendency to diversify as much as possible in a given set of populations of actors. For example, in the consumer goods market there will be certain general structural homogeneity of types of transactions, but at the same time there will be many variants deviating from this. This variety establishes the information capacity of market evolution, in the sense of the potential for the emergence of new structures. So, we can state that information accumulation in networks happens via the formation of network structures. Realized configurations manifest a large diversity of variations of these structures, which builds the capacity for further accumulation of information via the selection of newly emerging structures.

The growth of networks in terms of size (that is number of individuals) results into the growth of possible connectivity, of which only a subset is realized through time. The growing gap between possible connectivity and realized connectivity defines the amount of information that is accumulating in the network structures.

Figure 5.3 Entropy and networks

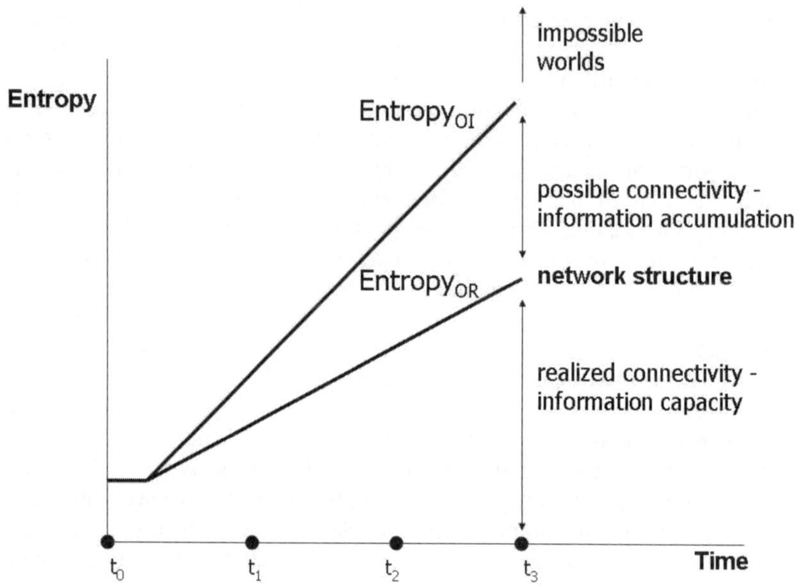

Note: Network evolution can be analysed in terms of the standard entropic model of Chapter Two. Information accumulates via the formation of network structure which is a constraint on possibly connectivity. This presupposes growth of networks, such that the gap between realized and possible connectivity increases. Realized connectivity manifests variety under constraints and hence constitutes information capacity for further network evolution. So, total entropy in terms of Entropy$_{OI}$ results from the conjunction of network diversity under constraints and the information embodied in network structure.

So, the entropic framework is fruitful to open the eyes for many foundational aspects of human network evolution, because it explains why structure and information relate as two sides of one coin. There is one general conclusion already resulting from the picture provided in figure 5.3: Consider phenomena such as globalization. Most observers emphasize the increasing global connectivity, but as a matter of fact, realized connectivity grows slower than potential connectivity (for some penetrating observations on that see the recent academic debates over popular slogans such as 'The World Is

Flat', see Leamer 2007). This means that the information carried in realized connectivity grows, in a similar way as in the original Layzer model of the expansion of the universe. In other words, in the conventional view on globalization we only see the growth of realized connectivity, but we do not see the growing gap to potential connectivity. In this view, the expansion of what has been called the 'human web' in the past 5000 years (McNeill and McNeill 2003) is indeed the major force of the growth of information in human systems, but that needs to be analysed in terms of the relationship between structure and potential connectivity.

We can relate this with the general evolutionary approaches that I sketched in Chapter Three, especially Kauffman's (1993) analysis of epistatic interactions in genomes and the notion of the 'complexity catastrophe'. In this context, the trade-off between complexity and incompleteness has also been cast into the hypothesis that 'order emerges at the edge of chaos' (compare Miller and Page 2007: 129ff). This refers to the basic distinction between three possible global regimes of complex systems, the ordered one, the chaotic one and the interface regime between the two (Wolfram's 2002: 235ff 'class 4 systems'). The chaotic one does not show any sustainable structures through time, and the ordered one features absence of evolution. The interface regime can be a steady state through time, though also showing continuous evolutionary change. The intuitive rationale behind the hypothesis is that at the 'edge of chaos', the trade-off between the need for novelty and the need for structure and memory is balanced.

One way to model this result is the analysis of networks as 'Boolean networks' (Kauffman 2000: Chapter 8). In general, all these approaches apply generic mathematical models to generic networks, which can be interpreted as different real world networks. In this case, network transactions are described by means of logical relations which grasp particular combinatorial properties of networks. For example, a consequential transaction can be caused by either a conjunction or a disjunction of two other transactions. The advantage of this approach is that network causality can be described by 'logical propositions' of unlimited complexity (like language), in the sense of describing outputs as true or false consequences, and describing the input combinations by means of Boolean structures. Now, one important phenomenon that emerges in Boolean structures is that limitations to complexity occur. The argument builds on the mechanisms that operate in networks of ecological systems, but easily extend to all other kinds of networks. In an ecological system, a predator species might survive if at least one of a number of alternative preys is available (disjunction), but may have to rely on one essential food ingredient (conjunction) or on the absence of certain lethal factors (conjunction with a negative). This corresponds to a Boolean system in the following way.

There is a set of 'clauses' containing disjunctions of variables which are true or false, such that the clause is true or false, correspondingly. Clauses are put together as conjunctions to form expressions. Conjunctions are only true if all constituent clauses are also true. Then, a simple theorem can be proven that states that there is a phase transition from a regime in which many resulting expressions are feasible to a regime where few expressions are feasible. The idea behind that theorem is intuitive. Consider a Boolean system where the number of variables is kept stable but the number of possible clauses increases. Then, if the ratio between clauses and variables goes up, it becomes more and more improbable that the resulting expressions will be true. It has been shown by means of simulation, that this transition does not happen gradually, but at a critical point, that is, it is a phase transition. On the other hand, if the number of variables increases, this phase transition is postponed. From this follows, that there are limits to complexity as long as the diversity of components does not increase. In network terms, types and scope of network configurations, which can be seen as clauses and expressions in Boolean systems, are limited in number and scope, as long as the number of types of actors involved is limited. On the other hand, even if the diversity of actors increases, there are limitations to the complexity of their combinations, in order to hold the network viable.

Evidently, this theorem provides a specific rationale for the entropic dynamics depicted in figure 5.3, that is, with increasing degrees of diversity network connectivity increases, but at the same time less than potential connectivity, if the evolutionary trajectory is sustainable, such that it does not succumb to a complexity catastrophe. Related results have also be obtained in economics, considering the computational viability of standard general equilibrium models, which would be perfectly connected integral networks: There are proofs that these are actually non-computable, such that only decentralized exchange processes with local reach may lead to feasible results that approach the efficiency frontier (for example Axtell 2005; for seminal approaches, see Albin 1998; for a general evaluation of this literature, see Markose 2005).

5.2.2. Ascendency and growth

Kauffman's model offers a micro–level analysis that directly links the individual patterns of connectivity with the emergence of structures. An alternative way to grasp the fundamental insight that non-integral structures carry information is to use the framework in ecology that has been developed by Ulanowicz (1997: 71ff; compare Ulanowicz et al. 2009). This framework is most appropriate for my analysis, because it relates network structure with throughputs, which are in the ecological context energetic throughputs. Thus, we can directly relate network analysis with the physical dimension of information growth. However, we will not explore this particular aspect in this chapter, as this requires including technology, which is the topic of Chapter Seven. So, I use the term 'throughput' in the most general bimodal sense, which means also referring to information flows.

In ecological science, attempts have been made to measure the interaction between the throughput that is governed by the network relations and the information content of the network structure (called 'system' here). This measure is the so-called 'ascendency', which is calculated as the product of the Total Network Throughput times the Average Mutual Information in the network, namely referring to the two aspects of networks, the physical flows and the network configurations. In principle, the TNT can be measured in terms of any physical flow (such as energy, carbon etc.), whereas the AMI measures the degree of constraint in the direction of flows though different network connections (which in the case of equality of connections would measure zero). We can then submit a general hypothesis that reflects the entropic principles in the context of network analysis, especially the Constructal Law and Lotka's Maximum Power Principle. This hypothesis states that through time, ascendency will increase such that Total Network Throughput will tend to grow; this means, in terms of the Constructal Law, that power throughput tends towards a maximum by means of a corresponding change of network structure, which is measured in terms of the mutual information. As in the statement of the Constructal Law, one has to distinguish neatly between the harnessing of throughputs at a given information structure and the evolvability of that structure by means of which access to new sources of throughputs is achieved.

The dynamic that underlies this evolutionary trend is depicted in figure 5.4. There, 'ascendency' would be seen as a measure of the interface between realized and possible connectivity, with the latter referring to a state of disorganized diversity, which means diversity that is not related with the realization of a network function. In ecology, this is called the 'system overhead'. Then, a system consisting of physical flows and a networked information structure has a certain developmental capacity that is the composite of ascendency and overhead, that is the structure of constraints on realized connectivity and the disorganized flows that are open to the emergence of further organization. Increasing ascendency only relates with a trend toward growing throughputs if through time system overhead is transformed into structure. This corresponds to the relationship between power maximization and efficiency in the Constructal Law: Without changing accessibility of throughputs, increases in ascendency will manifest as relative declines of throughputs, that is increasing efficiency.

It is essential to realize that the growth of TNT, which reflects the Maximum Power Principle, requires a balance between ascendency and overhead, that is realized and potential connectivity. This is because the overhead represents the potential from which ascendency is generated through time. In a simplified qualitative diagram, we can relate the two as in figure 5.4. The exact relation between overhead and ascendency depends on empirical determinants and does not matter for the general argument. It will differ for different kinds of network systems and even across individual systems. I describe a stylized developmental trajectory for a network, thus linking the two notions of development and evolution, as discussed in Chapter Three.

Figure 5.4 Ascendency and Maximum Power (modified after Ulanowicz 1997: 126)

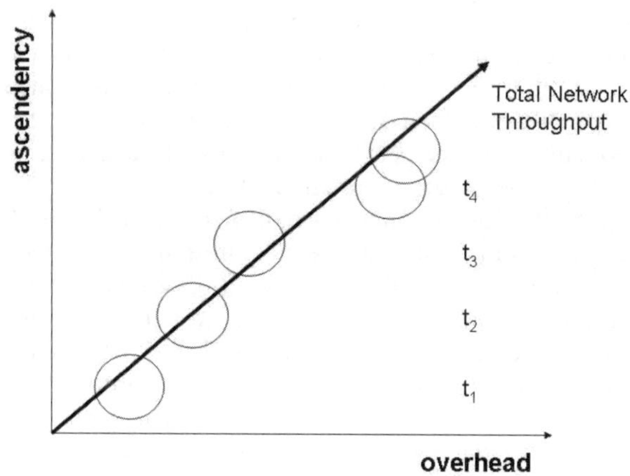

Note: In a generalization of related approaches in ecological science, Total Network Throughput (conceived bimodally as flows of energy and information) is seen as increasing through time (Lotka's MPP), conditional on a balance between ascendency and system overhead. Ascendency (defined as product of TNT and Average Mutual Information in a network) is a measure of organized complexity, overhead is a measure of disorganized complexity. The former corresponds to the evolution of network structure and its embodied information in figure 5.3, the latter corresponds to network diversity unrelated to the realization of network functions.

Development is driven by the Maximum Power Principle, which translates into a trajectory along which the TNT continuously grows. This does not necessarily imply that a maximizing state will be achieved, as there are continuous disturbances of the system, but it means that ceteris paribus, the trajectory is a growth trajectory. This is directly driven by the developmental cycle (going back on ideas firstly elaborated on in Salthe 1993). In the early stages, overhead is much larger than ascendency, which reflects the openness and redundancy of network connectivity, and the strong weight of potential connectivity that is available in on-going transactions. As the system matures, ascendency increases, which means that redundancy is reduced and the realized connectivity becomes more constrained relative to the possible connectivity. Finally, the system enters into the state of senescence, which means that the overhead shrinks below a level which is necessary to maintain the possibility of novelty, hence evolvability. The system 'dies', which means that a new network configuration emerges from the old system via a radical reshuffling of components. This allows for further growth, though on a higher level of TNT.

Hence, a crucial magnitude is the overhead, which results from diverse sources, of which the following are of particular interest (Ulanowicz 1997: 82ff).

- First, the size of input flows determines overheads as long as the resulting outputs are not themselves recycled into the system, that is as long as the inputs are not themselves governed by the network. To take an example from the original application in ecology, soil is an input that contributes to overhead as long as it is not integrated into the agricultural system, such that it becomes a part of ascendency (for example transition from slash and burn agriculture to sedentary farming turns soil from overhead into element of ascendency). So, internalization of inputs is one mechanism how overhead is transformed into ascendency. At the same time, however, maintaining a sufficient throughput of external inputs is a major precondition for maintaining evolvability of a system. This is tantamount to stating that achieving the highest levels of efficiency violates the conditions of evolvability, if this means that input flows are entirely internalized into the control configurations of a network. This idea can be generalized in terms of network analysis, stating that the sustainability of network evolution presupposes the coexistence of loosely connected different network domains (for example, innovation dynamics of markets might depend on the existence of non-market domains in science and the arts). On a most fundamental level, this can also be interpreted with reference to the relationship between individuals and networks: 'Oversocialized' views of networks would imply that individual diversity would no longer work as a source of overhead that contributes to evolvability; thus, individual autonomy is a precondition for network evolution (interestingly, this corresponds to views such as in Luhmann's 1984 theory of social systems that individual minds are 'disturbances' of systems processes).
- Second, overhead is reflected in the dissipative processes, which I have already elucidated in the analysis of Chapter Two. On the one hand, overhead directly reflects the working of the Second Law, but at the same time dissipation also reflects the fact that because of the Second Law, the generation of dissipation is a necessary condition to create and maintain systems at all. This is familiar from the notion of production in economics: No production without incurring costs, in particular the wear and tear of equipment which is reflected in depreciation. From that viewpoint, increasing costs, in particular depreciation, while maintaining the drive towards minimizing the costs, reflect higher productivity in terms of throughputs. Thus, increasing dissipation in networks is

necessarily concomitant to the rise of ascendency, thus rebalancing the relation with the overhead, while increasing TNT. Again, we can generalize over this ecological argument in terms of network analysis in different respects. One is that we can conceive of information flows bimodally as TNT, such that dissipation would be equated to the generation of useless information. This is easy to observe in the economy, for example, where the 'blockbuster' phenomenon relates to the observation that in industries such as pharmaceuticals and the creative industries the 'winner takes all effects' result in a voluminous production of outputs which fail to succeed on the marketplace, or parallel investments are 'wasted' in patent races.

- Third, and related to the first point on internalization, system exports can contribute to the continuous re-balancing between overheads and ascendency if they do not directly contribute to imports, as in internalization, but if they contribute to higher–level feedback cycles, of which the archetypical example is the hypercycle. That means, exports differ from dissipation in that they represent useful work for another system, independent from the functions of the generating system. If that system is connected back with the exporting system via positive externalities, the exports contribute to the growth of the latter. It is important to emphasize that the functionality of exports is not determined by the exporting system, which establishes the difference to the first case with internalization. In this sense, exports are always uncertain, in the evolutionary context. This is why they constitute overhead. A system may export more, but if that fails to be integrated in higher–level systems, the exports only contribute to further dissipation, thus ultimately driving system decline, compared to other systems that establish positive feedbacks via exports. Transferring these arguments into general network analysis and economics, this can be related to classical arguments in favour of international trade, but also to more general phenomena such as the cross–fertilization of networks in different domains, such as between the domain of the sciences and the domain of markets, or even between the domain of human networks and biological networks. To take an extreme example: Global warming can be both dissipation and exports, because in the latter case we can identify biological systems, such as in Siberia, which might actually transform these externalities of human economic activity into useful work in creating and maintaining new variants of ecological systems. This might open up new growth potential for the human economy, in spite of the detrimental effects of global warming in other regards.
- Fourth, internal redundancy is an important part of overhead, even though from the perspective of ascendency it is a loss, as stated in the first case. That means, redundancy contributes to overhead and re-balances with ascendency if it is continuously re-created, though step wisely being eliminated in the developmental trajectory. In other words, ascendency

results from the reduction of redundancy, whereas evolution introduces a ratchet effect that drives redundancies upwards that contribute to evolutionary potential, hence overhead. A typical example in human networks and economics is the product and industry life cycle, which initially manifests a large variety of product versions and firms, which then undergoes a shake-out process, resulting into a considerable reduction of diversity and numbers, typically associated with lower level of costs (for instance by economies of scale of mass production of standardized variants) and higher levels of efficiency. This is tantamount to the reduction of redundancy. However, this process also leads towards a loss of developmental flexibility and evolutionary potential, thus eventually leading towards industrial decline, unless the entrepreneurial process and hence the redundancies is reinvigorated. So, standard conceptualizations of the industry life cycle directly correspond to the dynamics of ascendency as outlined in figure 5.4.

These four determinants of overhead imply for network analysis that network evolution drives TNT and hence manifests the Maximum Power Principle because it leads to increasing degrees of ascendency, while driving overhead up, thus recurrently creating the need for re-balancing. Re-balancing drives TNT, eventually. As we have seen, industries and market relationships may be considered as a network that manifests ascendency in continuously moving towards greater efficiency, which means, ascendency. But efficiency needs to be counterbalanced with the creation of a potential for evolvability, which means, overhead. Overhead is created via 'slack' in industrial organization, such as, for example, redundant buyer–seller relations, or the maintenance of higher levels of labour input than necessary. These interdependencies can be summarized in terms of the Constructal Law as stated in Chapter Two, that is, networks evolve in terms of maximizing accessibility to flows of any kind; interestingly, also in the original formulations of this law, Bejan and Lorente (2006) emphasize that imperfectness of flow configurations is an essential precondition for evolvability.

Ulanowicz's approach allows highlighting one particular aspect of network evolution in human contexts, which is the typical pattern of growth and decline, such as the growth and decline of empires, or the growth and decline of leading industries and companies. In all these life cycle phenomena, a deeper commonality seems to be the tension between the rising ascendency in terms of greater information processing efficiency and the need to maintain evolvability in terms of overhead, which necessarily implies 'inefficiencies' with reference to established network functionings. Further, it makes abundantly clear why and how human networks always involve the physical dimension, linking up ecology and economy. As we shall see in Chapter Seven, the most important expression of this fact is urbanization (McNeill and McNeill 2003: 279ff). Human networks evolve together with the physical infrastructures that maintain them, such as transport, communication and settlement structures. Via these structures, matterenergy flows and semiosis work together, in bimodal terms. There are clear indications how the evolution of certain large–scale network structures relates with the evolutionary potential of networks in terms of information processing. So, urban networks are typically the most creative and dynamic segments in human networks and drive economic growth (Florida 2002). The driving force of the emergence of urban networks is spatially circumscribed hypercyclic connectivity, which has been already identified by Alfred Marshall in the context of the analysis of industrial agglomerations (for a modern restatement, see Krugman 1991): In the parlance of economics, this refers to the positive information externalities that emerge in those structures, and that mutually connect the different actors (for a related analysis in the context of industrial clusters building on complexity theory, see Lane 2002). This is one of the topics that I will explore in the next sections.

5.3. DIMENSIONS OF EVOLVING NETWORK STRUCTURE

5.3.1. Transaction, communication, perception

So far, I have analysed generic principles of bimodal network connectivity. However, in analysing human networks we need to distinguish between different dimensions of connectivity. I distinguish between transaction, perception and communication:

- Transaction is the efficient-causal interaction between two actors which results into changes of the states of these actors (for example, a market transaction changes the composition of goods owned by actors and enables them to certain consumption activities).
- Perception is the unidirectional transfer of information between actors (for example, an investor observes stock market transactions of other actors on the computer screen).
- Communication is the bidirectional transfer of information (for example, a company issues a report that is read and interpreted by investors).

This is a functional differentiation. For example, communication always involves a transaction, because there is the physical transfer of a sign between the actors, and the states of actors change. However, this transaction can be analysed separately from the information transfer.

Standard network analysis concentrates on transactions in the sense that classes of interactions are scrutinized, such as people meeting at certain places, gift giving as transfers of objects or the exchange of messages (Knoke and Yang 2008: 12). The advantage of this approach is that transactions, in principle, can be accessed from the position of an external scientific observer. However, it does not allow discerning the meaning of these interactions, and how the interactions relate with the knowledge dimension on interactions, as we have seen previously. It is important to notice that different disciplinary approaches to networks differ in this respect. The modelling of network processes in the Complex Adaptive Systems approach typically also adopts a multi–dimensional distinction between modes of interaction, mostly in line with my distinction (see for example the seminal contributions by Epstein and Axtell 1996 or Holland 1995 and the survey by Miller and Page 2007: Chapter 7, who refer to the multidimensionality issue as the 'Eightfold Way' to model systems).

Perception refers to all phenomena that can be analysed as observations. For example, people observe others doing something. Observations result in information transmission. However, it is essential to recognize that this does not mean that knowledge of other actors is transferred. For example, if *A* observes *B* buying an apple at a market stall, this does not transfer the knowledge of *B* to *A* directly. Strictly speaking, the only information that is transferred is that *B* buys an apple. All other information are inferences of *A*, such as that this might imply that the quality of apples is high (actually, *B* does not know the quality, but is a friend of the stall owner). So, information flows and transactions differ in a fundamental way, as far as perception is concerned.

There are other reasons for this divergence. First, information flows are constrained by impediments to observation. Thus, actors' internal states are not accessible to other actors, which is a fundamental phenomenon. As we have seen, this is a complex issue, as there is also the possibility that this information is not accessible to the subject itself, in terms of the Acting Self. So, for example, an observer may actually be able to observe the true internal state ('Are you really feeling well?'), and the subject has not yet realized this. As mentioned earlier, there is the important phenomenon of self–deception, which systematically implies that certain states of an agent may not be accessible to this actor, but possibly to others.

Other impediments to observation result from the mere physical limits to observation. I cannot observe all other actors with which I am connected indirectly all the time. I grasp this fact with the notion of the 'perceptual field'. Perceptual fields are structured by physical constraints on observation. These are determined by the technologies of observation. For example, I cannot observe my children on the playground, if I stay at home, but I could install a camera. Generally, the evolution of the media determines the scope of perception: I can watch television footage about a disaster in real time, hearing victims talk about their plight. When people refer to 'globalization' today, very often they refer to the technological determined expansion of perceptual fields.

This observation also applies for communication. Communication involves perception, because it presupposes the perception of the message.

However, the concept is even more complicated than perception. Firstly, I can perceive a message without perceiving the sender. For example, I can collect a bottle with a letter, and wonder who the sender is, yet understand the message. Further, perceiving a message does not necessarily imply that I know the internal state of the sender. The sender can send wrong information intentionally. This point makes one aspect of communication very clear that is not treated adequately in many theories about communication, with Grice's one being very influential (Lycan 1999: 102ff; for the critical assessment of Grice's approach in terms of evolutionary theory, see Aunger 2002: 259ff). These theories claim that communication involves transfer of information from sender to receiver based on the intention of the sender to send this information via a message and through a channel. Then, the meaning of the message is based on sender intentions. However, meaning and information are entirely distinct concepts (Dretske 1981: 41ff). For example, a message that is based on false information has a meaning, and this meaning is independent from the speaker's intentions in the sense that the intended misinformation is actually based on population level meanings of the message. So, if I tell my friend who wants to visit me 'It does not rain', but in fact it is raining, my friend does not receive any information, but believes to receive information that is based on the meaning of this sentence, which is independent from my intention to abuse the meaning in order to cheat my friend.

Therefore, we see that communication is based on two essential phenomena. Firstly, there is a set of population level signs which have a meaning that is used in the messages of the sender. Secondly, the information transfer only operates via the receiver, and is completely independent from the sender (compare Millikan 1989, 2005). Therefore, communication is similar to perception in this regard. This is most evident from the phenomenon of misunderstanding: Even is *A* tries hard to transfer information to *B*, *B* might still not be able to retrieve it, and misunderstands the message.

Communication is also shaped by available communication technologies. Communication technologies determine the directionality of information flows. For example, somebody might be able to communicate her ideas on television, but there is no direct response by the audience (yet, the communication depends on the information processing by the audience). We can generalize this into the distinction of audiences and actors in networks (the notion of 'audience' is borrowed from organizational ecology, see Hsu and Hannan 2005). Audiences are endogenous observers in networks. Audiences minimally perceive the actions of others, and based on this determine the transactions with the actors. For example, customers on the marketplace are the audience of sellers, and based on perceptions some members of the audience decide to buy. Sellers are aware of this, so they try to manipulate perceptions via communication. For example, they arrange vegetables in a particular way to hide the more rotten ones, and send corresponding signals. This is communication; we realize that communication is multimodal and relies on any kind of signs. Communication can turn into bilateral communication if a buyer approaches a booth and starts to haggle over the price in order to realize a transaction.

Figure 5.5 Dimensions of networks

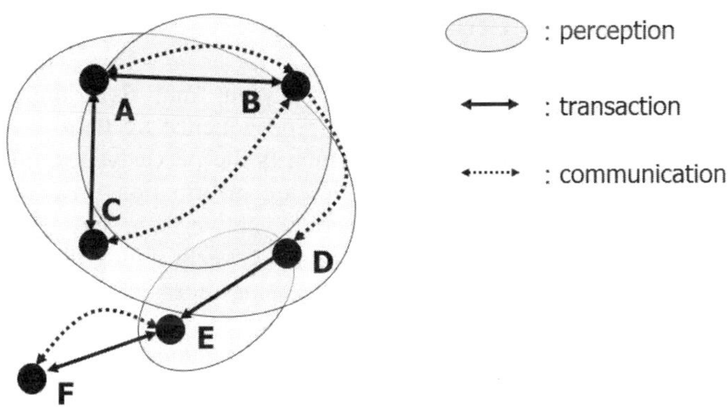

Note: Evolutionary network analysis considers three dimensions of networks, as it is also done in the context of Complex Adaptive Systems approaches. Actors entertain transactions with other actors, they conduct communication with them and they observe other actors in perceptual fields that they maintain behaviourally and technologically. In these three dimensions, peculiar structures of information flows emerge. For example, in the diagram *A* transacts with *B* and *C*, and *B* communicates with *C*. *C* is not included in *A*'s perceptual field, but in *B*'s. *B* communicates with *C*. This structure pictures *B* as a middleman who enables the transaction between *A* and *C* by making information about *C* accessible to *A*. *B* also transfers information to *D*, causing *D* to make a unilateral transaction with *E*, such as a donation. *E* is not in *B*'s perceptual field, but in *E*'s. This pictures *B* using *D* as an agent. The relationship between *E* and *F* pictures a type of exchange where both sides do not include each other in a perceptual field: Think of using a vending machine, where buyer and seller do not know each other in person, yet communicate and transact.

So, we end up with a view on networks which is much more complex than standard Social Network Analysis (figure 5.5 exemplifies this). This complexity results from the fact that the interactions in the three dimensions are not necessarily isomorphic and congruent. So, for example, if a company sets up a vending machine, this is a technological device that separates transactions and communication: I can buy a bottle of soda without communicating with the seller directly, and without perceiving him. Yet, even some communication can take place, such as advertisement or placing a complaint. But this also applies for selling the soda via a supermarket: I might communicate with sales personnel, but I do not communicate with the producer of the soda. From this possibility of dissociation, complex structures of information processing emerge (for a related approach in economics, see Casson 1997: 117ff). As we have already seen, perception and communication can be dissociated, as, for example, I can perceive the message but cannot perceive the sender, when reading a newspaper, and just read the name of the writer, without a faint idea who that is.

5.3.2. Information externalities

I will explore the implications of the previous analysis in the course of this chapter. But there is one fundamental consequence for network analysis that obtains a central theoretical role, which is the pervasiveness of information externalities. Information externalities are information flows which are not functional in relation to the original network process by which the information is generated. For example, eavesdropping is an information externality. Information externalities are ubiquitous in networks, because we can assume that perceptual fields are normally more encompassing than communication and transaction, such that the latter continuously create non-functional information on part of the observers (for an empirical example, see Cai et al. 2009). We can analyse the archetypical case in figure 5.6.

Consider the example of *B* buying an apple with *A*, again, and *C* observing this transaction. This original transaction might be based on complete mutual observation of *B* and *A* and on the communication between them. Now, if for some reason *C* interprets this perception in a way that she thinks that apples must be of excellent quality, she might approach *B* as well, and just buy one, with a minimum of communication apart from 'hello' and handing over the money.

This is an information externality which is created by the fact that information flows separately from structures of communication and transaction, only via perception. From the economic point of view, the externality results from the fact that *B* might have invested resources (at least, time) into collecting the information about the quality of apples, and *C* does not need to invest. I argue that externalities are the central force driving the evolution of networks and actions in networks, because selection always works towards the minimization of costs of information processing. The central phenomenon is imitation resulting from information externalities. *C* imitates *A*. Of course, externalities can be positive or negative. *C* might misinterpret the situation, and ends up with a bad apple. Even if the result is positive, she might still depend on wrong information.

Figure 5.6 Information externalities

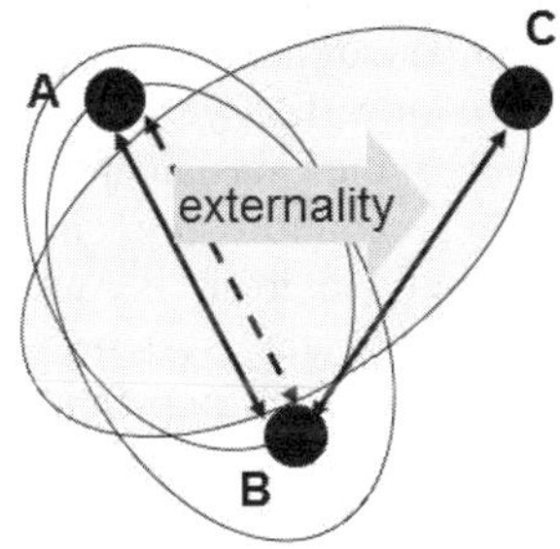

Note: This is a simple network structure involving an information externality. *A* and *B* transact, communicate and mutually perceive each other. This is observed by *C*. Based on the information gained by this observation, *C* transacts with *B* even without separate bilateral communication (such as by placing an order by letter). This information 'comes for free'; however, it does not necessarily reflect the information that is underlying the original transaction, that is knowledge of *A* and *B*. The information that *C* gains is what she observes about transactions and possibly communication, and what she interprets.

As information externalities are pervasive in networks, given the impossibility to make all three dimensions of networks fully congruent, we realize that the fundamental unit of network analysis is the triad, and not the dyad (this sociological use of the term should not be confused with the Peircian triad). This differs fundamentally from standard economic analysis which highlights the dyad, in the sense of the two sides of the market. The notion of the triad had been emphasized for the first time as fundamental unit in the analysis of society by the sociologist Georg Simmel (Nooteboom 2006 edits some fragments where Simmel makes a systematic distinction between dyads and triads in sociology). Third parties play a crucial role in transforming bilateral network relations, which is summarized in typical roles, such as the arbitrator, the intermediator, the observer etc., which go beyond the structure underlying the concept of information externality (compare Burt 1992). Actually, one might say that the triad is the basic unit of a 'society', whereas the dyad cannot yet be counted to be a 'society' (Hanneman and Riddle 2005: Chapter 8). Interestingly, we notice that Adam Smith (1759) already anticipated this view in emphasizing the role of observers in evaluating social interactions, which includes the possibility of the internalization of the observer (Smith's 'spectator').

Information externalities are the most important form of externalities in networks, but there are others, for example relating with the physical channels of transactions: If I build a bridge to connect with another village, because my lover dwells there, others can use it, if I do not keep them out, which creates an externality. So, the network theory concept of externality includes the economic notion of externality, which focuses on markets as types of networks exclusively. However, the economic concept of externality and its theoretical elaboration can be extended to the generic network theory concept. This raises the question how far we can also apply the related concept of transaction costs, which in the Coasian approach to externalities is seen as an essential element of explanations why internalization does not occur. This point is of considerable interest, because, as we have seen, externalities are an important part of the system overhead that creates evolvability of networks by means of non-functional exports. This relationship between network growth and externalities is also well known from economics in the context of New Growth Theory, where externalities that remain non-internalized are seen as one of the most important causes of sustainable growth (Helpman 2004: 36ff). Therefore, I propose to generalize over the notion of transaction costs.

5.3.3. Interaction costs and the emergence of hypercycles

All network interactions require the expense of 'interaction costs', of which information costs are of special significance. This term refers to all costs of inducing and implementing interactions, which directly accrue to the agents and therefore determine their actions and decisions. In economics, the notion is mainly related to contracting, but we can extend it to network processes in general. So, we distinguish between costs of transactions, perceptions and communications. There are costs of perception which are the costs of awareness or directing attention to a certain object, which basically relate to opportunity costs of time. Costs of communication relate to costs of time and effort to coordinate the interactions. Transaction costs include the costs of perceptions and communication, apart from physical expenses such as transport costs, because all activities that enable transactions also work in these dimensions. The economic notion of transaction costs often is restricted to the transactions in a particular systemic context, namely markets (as in the classical approach by Williamson 1985; for a survey see Wang 2003).

Interaction costs are a form of opportunity costs, because all activities that enable interactions imply that other activities are not selected. In the evolutionary approach, this means that the information about interaction costs also emerges from the process and cannot be simply regarded as an input to the decision process. This is a major difference to the economic use of the term, where in principle transaction costs can be the object of rational choice. But this assumption actually runs into a paradox, which reveals that interaction costs relate with an important impossibility theorem (Herrmann-Pillath 1990, 2000). This theorem results from the dilemma of an actor who would need to weigh between two options, namely choosing a certain interaction right now, with implications for the assessment of opportunity costs, or incurring further interaction costs in order to improve the information about alternatives. Evidently, this decision could never be based on the true information about opportunity costs, because this is not accessible without incurring further interaction costs (this argument generalizes over the famous Arrow proposition about the impossibility of assessing the value of new information in advance). However, as these costs are also opportunity costs, it is not possible to compare the two alternatives of choosing now or postponing, as the true interaction costs are also unknown. From this it follows that, in the context of pure economic theory, transaction costs could only be identified in the state of general equilibrium, but it is this state in which no transaction costs need to be incurred, as all necessary information has already been processed in the economy.

This argument builds on a general point about opportunity costs that has been made by Buchanan (1969) in a classic work. Although the entire New Institutional Economics builds on the notion of transaction costs (see for example North 1990, Richter and Furubotn 1996, or specifically North and Wallis 1994), the fundamental theoretical dilemma has been rarely recognized, and if so, mostly in the context of the Coasean theory of the firm, namely arguing that it is impossible to optimize over the firm vs. markets choice based on transaction costs (for variants of my more general argument, see for example Schneider 1986; Dunn 1992; Kiwit 1994; Hallwood 1997a, b). Streit and Wegner (1993) present the most general version, in the context of criticising the assumption that is often made in the theory of international trade, namely that transaction costs can be treated in a way homologous to transport costs, thus allowing for optimization of trading patterns.

So we realize that there is a fundamental tension between the forces driving network evolution and the capacities underlying agency in networks (for a practical application of this idea in the context of networks in economic regions, see Storper 1995). All interactions involve costs of interactions, but knowledge about these costs is always incomplete and fallible. Interaction costs are revealed via the actual comparison of realized interactions, which, however, has only limited relevance for future interactions, especially new ones in novel contexts. Again, this fact has two sides. One is the simple conclusion that all actions that relate with interactions costs are necessarily dysfunctional, compared to a hypothetical state of complete information. On the other hand, for this reason the evolutionary process also generates novelties in network patterns which reveal the information about those costs, among other aspects. This is one of the reasons why we posit that knowledge is stored in incomplete network configurations.

With reference to information externalities, we can therefore say that information externalities are a fundamental driver of network evolution, as they substantially impact on the general level of interaction costs, via aggregate effects and via the bias that cost saving efforts introduce on the level of individual actions. This ubiquity of information externalities implies that there is the possibility of the emergence of hypercycles in networks as defined in Chapter Two. This is because we can directly compare the concept of interaction costs with the energetic costs of chemical reactions: An information externality works as a catalyst on the realization of other network interactions by lowering their interaction cost threshold.

Hypercyclic structures relate to the emergence of boundaries in networks, as in the original reference to the role of compartmentalization in biology (Maynard Smith and Szathmáry 1995). Boundaries emerge from the particular conjunction of positive and negative externalities, akin to the operations of a neural network. That is, considering a single interaction, this interaction can exert a positive externality on another interaction, thereby lowering the interaction costs. At the same time, the interaction may exert a negative externality on another interaction, thus decreasing the probability of its occurrence. This can work via direct inhibition; or happens just because the realization of an interaction depletes the resources available to interactions in general. For example, if an interaction causes a positive information externality, this will pull the resources of another actor in, such as attention. Then, less attention is available for other interactions, which are therefore inhibited.

The step towards establishing the possibility of hypercycles is immediate: If positive externalities form cyclic chains, an initial interaction is also reinforced by some indirectly connected interaction, such that the entire chain achieves a lowering of the interaction cost thresholds relative to the environment. If this happens, the corresponding network configuration is stabilized. In real–world societies, we meet many examples of this sort of configuration, such as friendship relations, where friends of friends help friends of friends, so that everybody, ultimately, expects a return of some services, or the aforementioned clustering effects in urban industrial districts, where each firm expects a return flow of knowledge when offering access to its own knowledge.

The standard properties of hypercycles (see Chapter Two, section 2.4.2.) directly apply on networks. These are, especially, the properties of internal selection and centripetality. Thus, the hypercycle model allows us to explain the pervasiveness of the homophily principle (which I scrutinize below), because the emerging network boundary selects those members of a network which contribute to the positive externalities. We can hypothesize that similarities of any kind enable the occurrence of positive externalities, because they increase the potential for adoption. For example, similar ideas and cognitive structure make mutual understanding easier, so that learning processes are improved. If we consider that all network interactions also compete for resources, centripetality results. From the perspective of the network, the most central resource is actors themselves, even though actors can be members in multiple networks. But some interactions are mutually exclusive because of the effects of negative externalities. Therefore, some network configurations will grow faster than others, thus attracting actors, and will therefore put limits on the emergence of other network configurations. So, in the end, directionality of network evolution emerges: Networks typically manifest the dominance of certain types of structures over other types, and the emergence of interlocking convergent structures. This fact has been well recognized in economics: One much-cited example is the analysis of medieval Mediterranean trade by Greif (1993, 1994), where Arab and Italian traders developed distinct network structures that competed against the other, with the Arab traders relying on elaborate kinship networks and the Genoese traders relying on contractual relationships with formal enforcement powers. This divergent development happened against the background of a common selective context, which is the organization of long-distance maritime trade, and resulted into functionally equivalent patterns of network structures. In modern economies, we observe similar developments such as in the formation of different patterns of global supply chains with divergent structures of combining markets and firms in the global network structure of trade and production (Feenstra et al. 1999; Gibbon et al. 2008).

Further, there is a trade-off between sustainability and diversity in the evolution of hypercycles. The reason is straightforward to identify: A hypercycle that is growing rapidly might ultimately undermine its very survival in depleting the environment of resources necessary for its growth. This corresponds to the analysis of ascendency and system overhead in the previous section: the increasing loss of non-functional diversity because of the centripetality effect will ultimately dampen the evolutionary potential for novelty. Finally, there is a limit to growth resulting from the brittleness of configurations that include larger numbers of steps in the hypercyclic change with many components, because the probability increases that a single component in the chain might not be present in the environment any more, with the immediate effect of the collapse of the entire chain. Therefore, hypercycles cannot grow complexity without limits, but manifest certain trends towards simplicity of configurations and limitations to size and scope.

5.3.4. Triadic view on network structure

We finalize this section in relating the dimensions of network structure with triadic analysis (figure 5.7). Then, we make the conceptual relationship between groups and networks explicit. In the generic evolutionary approach developed in Chapter Three, groups are seen as units of correlated behaviour which generate certain group–level adaptive benefits that accrue to all group members. As we have seen, hypercycles of information externalities in networks are the primordial example of this general phenomenon, because they create a group–level adaptive benefit in lowering interaction cost thresholds for the entire group and for all its members, and because they manifest the property of centripetality, that is support convergent structures in networks. So, as a result of interactions, the actors that are related within a group change their states in a particular direction which is determined by the evolved functions.

Figure 5.7 Triadic view of groups and networks

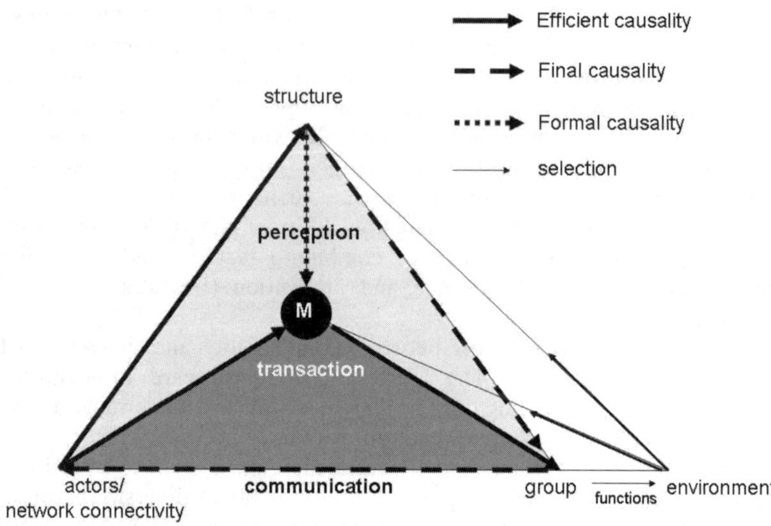

Note: The triadic approach allows clarifying the relationship between groups, networks and actors. Groups realize functions relative to an environment that are enabled by network structure. The three network dimensions of transaction, communication and perception correspond to distinct causal forces in the triadic analysis. Transactions are the efficient–causal driver of group level functions. Perceptions relate with the formal–causal categorization of network structures, such as the formation of particular roles of actors in evolving network configurations. The realization of functions goes hand in hand with communication processes by which information is transmitted and accumulated that further enhances network functions on the group level. For example, the emergence of professional traders in markets pushes the formation of particular structures of transactions, which improves information transmission by means of domain-specific communication.

Functions are relative to the group environment. So, for example, a group of hunter and gatherers needs to realize survival functions via foraging activities, which is based on transactions among them, such as hunting together and sharing the game. These transactions within the group are determined by network structure. Now, we can relate this with perception: the categorization of transactions within the group introduces a formal–causal force in network evolution. So, for example, transactions between females and males are determined by the categorization of their roles and hence, by the perception of those transactions. Group level functions fundamentally depend on this semiotic dimension of network connectivity.

Functions emerge from forces of selection impinging from the environment. Therefore, network structure is the precondition for the operation of group selection. It is important to note that the concept of information externality directly relates with the analysis of identity proposed by Akerlof and Kranton (2000) that we referred to in Chapter Four. Information externalities also involve information about oneself, that is work via the Acting Self in establishing functions of the Object Self. For example, once roles emerge in network structure, information externalities also affect the identities of actors that fulfil these roles. Therefore, roles stabilize in being rooted in individual identities.

Triadic analysis also details the group–level emergence of information, which results from patterns of communication in the relationship between the group and the network connectivity of actors. This means, configurations of connectivity carry information, and hence behaviour of actors communicates information. That means, given the interplay of the three dimensions, certain behaviours are always a communication as they are a signal against the background of semiosis. This also applies for divergent behaviour: If I behave differently from the categorization of transactions, this might be interpreted as a communication of information. Therefore, this view of communication is not dependent on sender intentions, but only emerges on the population level via receiver interpretations. For example, in the emergence of roles of females and males in the aforementioned group of hunter and gatherers, the convergence of behaviour communicates information about the effects of individual behaviour on group–level functions.

However, we can refer back at this point to the analysis of ascendency and complete the picture in making the role of the MaxEnt Principle explicit: If network evolution simultaneously enhances proper functioning and evolvability, the evolution of roles needs to reflect MaxEnt in allowing both for the formation of structure while growing the non-functional diversity of behaviour. This is exactly what the MaxEnt Principle predicts about the general features of any evolutionary process of information accumulation: Networks will evolve structural convergence in terms of constraints on behaviour (such as roles of actors), but they also maximize variety of realized behaviour (such as individual variants of role fulfilment or non-role related behaviour) which is the precondition for the emergence of new information in network evolution. Thus, the analysis of ascendency and Maximum Power in the previous section can be completed by highlighting the role of the MaxEnt Principle in the interaction between convergence and diversity in networks.

We have now established important aspects of information accumulation in networks. I will now turn to the question of whether we can further specify these observations by establishing a closer relationship with the insights of Chapter Four. Thus, we will be able to formulate more specific hypotheses about the structures of distributed cognition in human networks.

5.4. NETWORK STRUCTURE AND INFORMATION DIFFUSION IN NETWORKS

5.4.1. Biological constraints on network evolution and group size

As we have seen, one of the core determinants of network evolution is the costs of interaction. This cost is endogenous to network evolution, because networks generate externalities that determine these costs in turn. One important consequence of this fundamental fact is that basic biological constraints of human cognition impact on the evolution network structure.

I have already elaborated on the interdependence of group size and brain size in Chapter Four. The given structure of the brain imposes certain constraints on the processing of information in networks, which directly affect group size. However, at the same time brain capacities relate with the emergence of new cognitive functions, intermediated semiotically, that introduce new forms of interactions that change this relationship between group size and brain size. This means, there is a feedback circuit between structures of distributed cognition and evolving network structures: The latter may contribute in terms of exaptation to the enhancement of the former, which in turn creates the possibility of the emergence of new network structures. For example, the creation of the Worldwide Web enables new forms of knowledge processing, which in turn enables the emergence of new forms of the WWW.

The basic condition is given by the limitations to individual information processing in social relations (for a survey, see Dunbar 2011; for a reception of this idea in social network theory, see White 2008: 32, 344; in economics, see North et al. 2009: 14). Roughly speaking, human individuals are able to process individual information about 150 other individuals in their simultaneous interactions. In the sense of the fundamental ontological distinctions, this refers to individuality, as different from categorizations. In fact, the circle of individuals which we can truly appreciate in terms of their individuality is even smaller, about 50 individuals maximum. Beyond the scale of 150 individuals, we perceive other individuals mostly in terms of their social roles, that is in terms of their categorization. So, I may know the salespeople in the supermarket which I regularly visit for shopping, but I do not know their individual features beyond accidental information. This suffices to maintain the interaction. Now, considering the conjunction of the three network dimensions, especially with reference to transactions, there is plenty of evidence that this is also limited in scale, probably around a number of 1500. Beyond this scale, categorization applies with a vengeance, and information flows become much more asymmetric. The effect of technologies of interactions becomes especially strong.

Based on these empirical considerations, we can distinguish systematically between small groups and large groups. Interestingly, this is a distinction that has achieved a certain prominence in economics and social philosophy since Hume (cf. Kliemt 1985), and was emphasized by Hayek (1988), in particular. A small group, with the upper limit of 150 individuals, is a group in which humans can maintain individualized interactions in all three dimensions simultaneously. Large groups are defined beyond that size and manifest the essential role of categorizations in determining social interactions. Therefore, there is a distinct difference between the technologies of interaction, which increasingly concentrate on signal processing in few or even single dimensions. Within the small group, signal processing is multimodal and includes all five senses. The larger the group, the more constrained the channels of signal processing. This also opens up the possibility to enhance certain signal processing via technologies.

Consider a soccer stadium. Via communication technologies, one person can address the entire audience. This is limited to the auditory channel, even though signals of facial expressions can also be transmitted via a screen. The speaker cannot perceive the feedback of single individuals to his message, but some population–level signs, such as incipient movements of larger groups of people, chorus-like oral messages etc. Within the audience, similar interactions happen. A fan club may sit together and therefore realizes small group interactions with full scope. The members perceive the entire audience also based on aggregate signals that emerge on the population level. This is determined by the architecture of the stadium which allows almost complete mutual perception of the crowds.

So, the distinction between large and small groups essentially depends on the role of categorizations that result from the processing of signs: The individual in the stadium cannot interact with all other individuals, but perceives signals that relate with collective behaviour of the large group. This applies generally: Human management of large group interactions is based on categorizations. From this, the important psychological process of stereotyping results: in large groups, we classify other individuals according to certain categorizations and build our behavioural expectations correspondingly. Stereotyping is a central analytical category in network analysis because it directly relates with the notion of identity. As we have seen in Chapter Four, identity determines agency via the confluence of personal and social identity. Personal identity is rooted in the narratives agents tell and listen to, whereas social identity reflects the synchronic ascription of social categories. These are precisely the stereotyping processes. Stereotyping reflects the fundamental cognitive constraints in managing information about larger groups. At the same time, stereotyping establishes the in-group/out-group boundary and hence is the precondition of higher levels of cooperation within a group (see below; compare Charness et al. 2007 on salient indicators of group membership reinforcing in-group cooperation; or Van Veelen and Hopfensitz 2007 on human 'groupishness'). Therefore, we can identify two evolutionary causes of the emergence of stereotyping, information economy and group selection.

Once stereotyping produces social identities in networks, a new kind of externality becomes possible, because all individual actions that relate to a stereotype may affect the identities of others, even if there is no transaction in place (compare Chapter Four, section 4.5, following the Akerlof and Kranton 2000 model). This compares with an information externality, but a negative one in the sense that any kind of action that departs from a stereotype increases the uncertainty of other agents. If there are stereotypes about male behaviour in a society, and Ego departs from that, this increases uncertainty of the identities of Alter. As we shall see below, this results in specific problems of maintaining the categorizations by means of social sanctions in large groups, because in large groups there are also widespread free–rider issues of enforcement.

Such free–rider issues do not exist in small groups. The typical configuration of a small group is the primordial structure of human and primate societies. In small groups, individuals can interact with all other individuals, and there are few constraints on mutual perception and communication. We can assume that our cognitive and emotional brain structures are primarily adapted to this primordial group structure (Tooby and Cosmides 2005; Seabright 2004).

However, even for the primordial case we have to consider the fact that group boundaries do not preclude interaction between groups. This defines the next step in the evolution of group structures which has been identified by several researchers as a 'tribe' (compare Hill et al. 2011). Tribes are intermediate forms between small groups and large groups, because they build not only on categorizations, but also individualized connectivity among a limited number of individuals. This is the typical pattern in primordial human societies: Tribes are connected small groups within a certain territory, where connections can result from regular trading relationships, exchange of brides and other forms of interactions which also involve more complex dimensions of interactions, beyond simple categorizations such as the classification into different small groups. Most essentially, tribes relate with the emergence of shared categorizations, such as shared linguistic features, such that the smallest unit of language may be defined on this level.

So, to summarize, we can conclude that biological constraints on the capacity of human individuals to handle network interactions result in the distinction between small groups, tribes and large groups. Small groups allow for multimodal interactions, large groups mainly build on categorizations to enable interactions, which can be enhanced by technology, and tribes combine the two modes in relying on categorizations, but maintaining interactions via multimodal interactions by a limited number of individuals connecting small groups in tribes.

5.4.2. Group size and patterns of information diffusion

Now, the tribe structure is essential to define one of the most important phenomena of information flows in large groups, which is the 'small world effect'. In social network theory the notion of the 'small world' is quantified in terms of the two observations that in social networks the distance between nodes is normally small, and that furthermore the diameter of networks is also small (for an extensive analysis, see Watts 1999; for a summary and updated analysis, see Newman 2010: 552ff). The diameter is the shortest possible connection between arbitrary nodes. This relation is approximated by the statement that the diameter is only proportional to the number of nodes in log terms. This implies that even very large networks are in fact 'small' in terms of the possible reach of connections (for a vivid description, see Barabási 2002: 41f). In modelling approaches, 'small world models' have been developed out of networks with only limited reach of connections (so that, for example, the reach of connections in a one-dimensional lattice is only 3 nodes) in adding cross–linkages randomly. Already a very small number of such linkages lead to radical reduction of the diameter of the network (see Newman 2003 for a simple illustration).

Figure 5.8 Small worlds and tribes (after Watts 1999: 102ff)

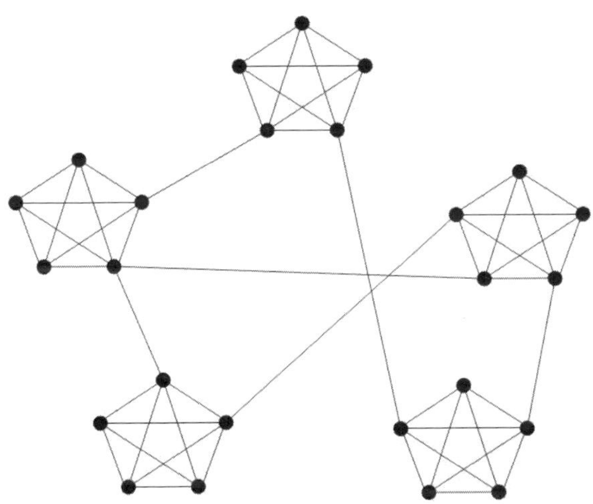

Note: Tribes consist of closely–knit small groups ('villages' in this example) that are connected via sparse relationships between few individuals. The 'small world effect' means that in spite of the low level of overall connectivity, the few connections suffice to reduce the mean geodesic distance of sequences of interactions considerably. This implies, for instance, that information flows fast in the entire network.

So, in figure 5.8, we imagine a set of five villages where most inhabitants closely interact with the other inhabitants, and only few people travel between the villages. In spite of the low density of the connections between the groups, information or diseases will flow rapidly between the groups. That means, in spite of the fact that the villages are relatively isolated from each other, and form closed communities, the network can be highly integrated in terms of information diffusion. A case in point is the rapid shrinkage of spoken languages in the world during the past centuries, which was triggered by the increased connectivity across local communities: High levels of local linguistic distinctness can only survive with very high degrees of local seclusion (see McNeill and McNeill 2003: 263, 271).

This phenomenon has also been scrutinized for larger networks and gave rise to popular topics such as the 'six degrees of separation' and even parlour games. However, one has to distinguish between the connectivity that is possible or can be mobilized by certain means, and the realized connectivity which is limited by the scope of the cross–connections. This is why there is still a distinction between tribes and large groups in general: Tribes manifest a convergence of certain behavioural patterns, such as the aforementioned linguistic convergence, which contribute higher connectivity than within the larger group context. The connectivity across tribes can support convergence in large groups.

The distinction between large groups, tribes and small groups is of fundamental importance for network analysis. In economic sociology, one pertinent conceptualization is the distinction between 'strong ties' and 'weak ties' (Granovetter 1985, 2005; Lin 2001). As we shall see below in more detail, one important difference between small group and large group settings is the fact that in small groups, interactions can be monitored by many more mechanisms than in large groups, especially with reference to the mobilization of emotions (compare Bowles and Gintis 2001a). Small groups mostly include:

- The close mutual observation of behaviour;
- The possibility of simultaneous signalling over different channels, such as vocal expressions, facial gestures etc.;
- Continuing interaction over longer time periods which allow for recurrent enforcement mechanisms which are also observable to the group;
- More intensive forms of We–attitudes and We–modes which make cooperation easier;
- Strong enforcement mechanisms based on ostracism with different degrees, including expulsion from the group.

These are some characteristics of strong ties. Therefore, one general hypothesis in network analysis is that small groups enable stronger and more diverse forms of cooperation (Coleman 1990). However, at the same time small group structures imply that there is also a high degree of informational integration within the group, given the ease of information externalities and the readiness to share information. Therefore, there is a low probability that new information will emerge within the structure (which has been pointed out in Granovetter's seminal 1985 study of labour markets). New information mostly is generated in the larger networks into which small groups are embedded, typically via the sparse connections. These are the weak ties. So, a major hypothesis in network analysis is that new information is mostly generated and spreading via weak ties. Although from the viewpoint of the larger network structure, the connecting ties might be of weak or strong nature, if only they are cross-cutting small groups, typically those ties are weak in the sense that they are not continuous and frequently recurring, and that they are lacking the multidimensionality of small group interactions.

Figure 5.9 Network configuration and information processing (Burt 2000)

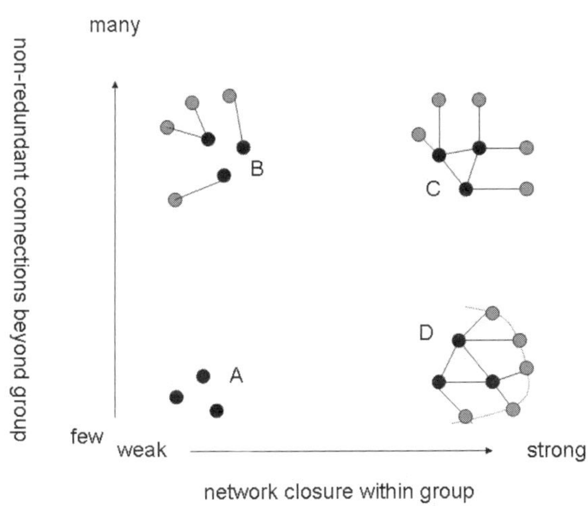

Note: Generic network patterns can be classified into four ideal types in the two dimensions of closure and diverse external connectivity. Closure determines internal cooperation, hence sharing of information, and diverse external connectivity determines accessibility of new information. So, network *D* with high degrees of closure and similarity of actors in terms of their external connections will manifest a high level of information sharing, but low intensity of novelties (think of a traditional village). Network *C* combines closure with diversity of external connectivity, which is the hallmark of highly innovative modern firms, for example.

Following Burt (2000), we can therefore distinguish between four different ideal-typical constellations of network structures, depending on the combination of strong and weak ties within or across groups (figure 5.9). We consider a local cluster of people, which might constitute a small group with different degrees of integration ('closure' in the case of high integration). Small groups can result from an exogenous combination of people, such as combining a new research team from scratch. Whether strong ties develop, is a question of the prevailing local conditions. Then, we have different possible combinations of strong and weak ties, which describe the degree of internal cohesion and the degree of variety in external connectivity. That means, for example, that a small group may manifest strong ties inside, but also diverse weak ties outside. Such a group will therefore rapidly accumulate new information, but also share this information inside. A group with diverse weak ties outside, but lacking strong ties inside, will accumulate new information, but that information is not shared easily within the group.

Thus, the interaction between small group and large group characteristics is crucial for the patterns of information diffusion in human systems. One important general mechanism that impacts on these patterns is the homophily principle (for a survey, see Lin 2001: 46ff). The homophily principle states that human individuals tend to create and strengthen connectivity with other individuals that they perceive to be similar. Homophily is self–reinforcing because increasing connectivity also strengthens similarities, for two simple reasons. Firstly, patterns of connectivity are criteria of similarity on their own terms, that is in the reflective sense. Secondly, more intensive connections disperse information and therefore support convergence to similar patterns of behaviour. Thus, small groups that are not enforced by outside intervention normally closely reflect homophily forces.

However, the homophily principle applies also for large groups because perceived similarities can be supported by any mechanism of categorization. There are celebrated results from social psychology that show how human individuals can respond to any kind of arbitrary classification of different groups in terms of homophily (this is Tajfel's social identity theory, for a survey see Smith and Bond 1993: 75ff). This reveals that there are strong, probably genetically fixed mechanisms of establishing in–group and out–group boundaries, which directly depend on the formation of respective We–modes, in terms of the 'us against them'. We can refer these mechanisms to the concept of identity that has been explored in Chapter Four. The most important cause of in–group/out–group boundaries is the role of shared identities in determining the members of the in–group.

5.4.3. The in–group/out–group distinction

In–group/out–group distinctions are pervasive in human networks and are being continuously created in any contexts, resulting from any kind of categorization pattern. There are several important behavioural universals which result from this distinction, and which relate to the causal attribution processes of social action and its results. For example, if a group is successful relative to others, they will causally attribute this to its own excellence, if it is not successful, it will attribute this to some external influences. Vice versa, the failure of the other group will be attributed to its own weakness, but not to external causes. This attribution pattern is the determinant of one important consequence of the in–group/out–group distinction, namely discrimination. All human societies manifest different forms and degrees of discrimination between different social groups, with different degrees of intensity, if only in a seemingly playful way, as discrimination between different fan communities in sports. However, all these forms go back to the same fundamental network mechanism, which relates homophily with the psychological capacity of stereotyping as elucidated previously.

The evolutionary cause of the emergence of the homophily principle is easy to establish, because it is the other side of the coin of the We–mode. Suffice to add that the principle also provides the basis for one of the most important forms of social punishment, which is ostracism, expelling a group member beyond the group boundary to the out–group status (Bowles and Gintis 2001b). Ostracism does not need to be implemented by direct physical means, but already happens via many forms of weak signalling and refusals of cooperation in any contexts (Binmore 2005: 4). Therefore, discrimination is also a powerful means to enforce cooperation. Without the in–group/out–group boundary, ostracism would not be a punishment mechanism. It is important to recognize that the possibility of ostracism also depends on physical characteristics of network structure, such as settlement patterns of groups, thus highlighting once again the actor–artefact configurations (Michalopoulos 2012 shows that the diversity of land quality and characteristics explains ethnolinguistic diversity across the world; for an illuminating case study of collective action, see Barnes 1995: 179ff.).

Hence, we can root the possibility of group selection in human societies to this capacity of discrimination. As we have seen, group selection becomes possible if there are mechanisms that result in the suppression of competitive behaviour, thus limiting the range of those behavioural variants. The homophily principle directly entails different mechanisms that lead towards this effect (Frank 2009c): Firstly, imitation effects support behavioural convergence and hence cooperation (for example Mengel 2009); secondly, the possibility of ostracism implies a policing mechanism. Again, it is important to state that this does not mean that social punishments are altruistic by necessity, as it is often assumed in the economics literature (Bowles 2004: 443ff). Ostracism often happens on the collective level, and thus is an individually low–cost behaviour, and in addition, the effects of group–level cooperation may vindicate the behaviour in terms of inclusive fitness, if there is a general tendency of convergence between genetic relatedness and group structure.

Based on the analysis of identity presented in Chapter Four, and in particular referring to the notion of externalities as proposed by Akerlof and

Kranton (2000), we can further develop this argument in considering the possibility of '*n*–th order punishments' (Bowles 2004: 387ff). This goes back to the triangular basic unit of network analysis that I developed in the context of information externalities. Second–order punishments are directed at individuals who are observed by others not to apply first–order punishments on other deviating individuals. As we have seen, behavioural deviations exert a negative externality on other actors, who supposedly share this identity. However, the same argument also applies on punishments, because these express identities. So, if an individual does not exert a punishment, this also exerts a negative externality on third parties. This mechanism explains the pervasiveness of discrimination in human societies: In a racist setting, a White who does not show despise towards Blacks might be ostracised by other Whites, even though she is not Black. Following the analysis of Akerlof and Kranton, we realize that these mechanisms are actually internalizing the externalities of individual action, thus balancing the costs of deviant action with the costs of punishments. In this sense, social structuration in terms of in–group/out–group boundaries is akin to the role of property rights in economic markets.

One consequence of the network patterns that I have described so far is that one fundamental divergence between large and small groups can result from assortative mixing based on the homophily principle (Kranton 1996). Assortative mixing leads to a distinct difference between the resulting pattern of small and large groups: There is the possibility that cooperation levels within small groups are high, and low within large groups, considering interactions across in–group/out–group boundaries (Hargreaves Heap and Zizzo 2009). Homophily implies that social preferences are stronger in small groups, thus favouring more efficient and cooperative coordination (see Chen and Li 2009; Chen and Chen 2011). This effect is further reinforced via the discrimination mechanism, in the more general sense that individuals who are more cooperative, given certain conditions of small group formation, will tend to interact more frequently and intensively, whereas in purely large group settings less cooperative individuals dominate the interactions (Bowles 1998). This is an important result in the context of the emergence of market interactions, which are often defined as interactions between strangers (Seabright 2004). If market interactions presuppose certain levels of cooperation to suppress cheating, there are only two ways to overcome the effects of assortative mixing. Either the small group context is activated in the context of market organization, or some alternative mechanism is created that offers other ways of sanctioning cheating in large group contexts. This is the conventional explanation of the emergence of institutions that we will explore in the next chapter.

There is an important other mechanism that results from assortative mixing, and which occurs in the large group context. Assortative mechanisms support the general mechanism of preferential attachment. Preferential attachment means that in any sort of sequences of interactions, individuals tend to choose that interaction which is similar to the previous ones, for example, in the sense of being the most frequent one in this class of interactions. For example, in the analysis of migration preferential attachment means that migrants will move to that place where many other migrants have already moved to. Or, scholars will tend to cite a paper that has already been cited frequently. The theoretical importance of this mechanism results from the fact that the emerging distributions of interactions will always follow the pattern of a Power Law (Newman 2006; Miller and Page 2007: 165ff). For example, a famous example that refers to the migration case is Zipf's Law of the distribution of cities. As we shall see in the next section, power laws are a driving force of the emergence and stabilization of status in human networks.

We can also surmise that preferential attachment is just another expression of the fundamental human behavioural tendency to imitate. We have already established the brain mechanisms in Chapter Four that underlie imitation (section 4.2.3). Imitation results into preferential attachment, in a most general way. However, we can distinguish between different structural forms of imitation, most generally random copying and all forms of non-random copying (Bentley et al. 2007; Richerson and Boyd 2005: 69).

5.4.4. Imitation and frequency dependency of network processes

In the case of random copying, the homophily principle is actually undermined by a random factor, even though the underlying behavioural pattern is imitation, hence the tendency to assimilate behaviour to the observed behaviour of others. However, the selection of the target of imitation is randomized. For example, somebody who is otherwise strongly attached to a certain group, walks along the street and just catches up the way of dressing of an arbitrarily chosen stranger. If she starts to copy it independently from the patterns prevailing in her small group, the homophily principle may erode, yet the mechanism is based on the same tendency, namely to behave similarly to other people. Random copying is a powerful explanation of many forms of human behaviour that relate to non-functional signs, such as fashion styles (if unrelated to identities) or children's names.

With regard to non-random copying, Boyd and Richerson distinguish between guided variation and biased transmission (for related analyses, see for example Feldman 2001; Rendell et al. 2010). Guided variation refers to learning processes. Biased transmission affects the imitation process, and can be further differentiated into content–based, frequency–based and model–based bias. Content–based bias relates to special cognitive effects that makes transmission of certain behaviours easier. Frequency–based bias is a subset of frequency dependency in general. Model–based bias is status based imitation, with status mostly defined as success in a certain social context. That means, model–based bias can also include effects that only relate to observed efficacy of actions. However, success also contributes to status. I come back on the special role of status in the next section.

The importance of imitation cannot be underestimated for the evolutionary theory of networks, as imitation leads to different forms of frequency–dependent selection of connectivity. We can distinguish between two different kinds of frequency dependency, global and local. These kinds relate with different modelling approaches in analysing diffusion patterns in networks, with far-reaching consequences for the differential performance of networks in terms of functions:

- Global frequency dependency refers to a pattern of imitation in which the individuals have access to information about the relative frequency of certain behaviours in a population, or in which a global constraint determines the adoption frequencies. The ideal-typical case of global frequency dependency is the logistic diffusion curve (the S–curve) which is used in many different contexts, reaching from ecology (with carrying capacity as the global constraint) to technology diffusion and market dynamics (with total demand or number of customers as the global constraint). The logistic curve is of fundamental interest because depending on the parameters, logistic growth processes can manifest all sorts of dynamics, including chaotic behaviour (Haken 1983: 305ff; Wolfram 2002: 149ff).
- Local frequency dependency relates the adoption of a certain behaviour with the frequency of that behaviour in a neighbourhood or, more specifically, with the direct interactions with neighbours. These models have been introduced into economics with Schelling's (1978) classical work on 'checkerboard' models of racial discrimination and urban settlement structures, and are today widely used in models of cellular automata (for a general approach, see Wolfram 2002). The importance of these models results from the fact that there can be a divergence between the goal structures of individual agents and the aggregate outcomes (such as in the original Schelling model, where racial segregation can emerge without any individual actual preferring it). This divergence also allows us to overcome certain dilemmata of social cooperation, because in local contexts, cooperation is possible, and can spread over a number of local groups via neighbourhood contamination (for the Prisoners' Dilemma, see for example Hegselmann 1996).

There is one question that deserves more scrutiny, namely whether the information that is processed in network structures that I have described so far is functional in the sense of maintaining proper systems functioning. Very often, this depends on whether the information is truthful, that it depicts real world facts accurately, relative to the functions. The homophily principle and the corresponding mechanism of imitation can result in information flows which systematically lead towards dysfunctional states. This happens because there is the fundamental split between private and public information in any kind of network interaction. We have already stated previously, that individuals do not have access to internal states of other individuals. Therefore, they do not know private information, unless this is revealed truthfully. Even in the case that private information is revealed, this might be cheating. Therefore, there is the possibility that cheap talk prevails, which means even though individuals reveal information, this is not trusted, so that it does not have an impact on the behaviour of others (Farrell and Rabin 1996). So, generally speaking, individuals will rely on the observed behaviour of others to choose their own behaviour. As we have seen, in this case there is no necessary connection between the private and the public information: I observe another individual buying an apple with a certain seller, but falsely assume that this signals high quality apples, yet the two were just friends.

Now, it is possible to show that in this case, information cascades are possible by which information diffusion becomes dysfunctional. The basic model of information cascades has been developed by Bikhchandani et al. (1992; 1998), which is a specific example of 'social learning models' and another manifestation of frequency dependency in networks (seminally, Gale 1996; exemplary Çelen and Kariv 2004). They distinguish between an observable action and an observable signal scenario. This is slightly different from my description because they assume that the signals automatically become a part of a pool of public information, that means of common knowledge. Thus, there is no modelling of the communication process in a network. Yet, the principles of information cascades are the same. Their point is that in an observable signal scenario, the public knowledge of the individuals will converge to a truthful state in a process that is Bayesian in nature, such that individual signals will only change the distribution of knowledge in a probabilistic way, but this does not jeopardize convergence. This is different in the observable actions scenario, where signals remain private to the individuals. This scenario emerges under plausible conditions about information transmission. If individual *B* observes the action of individual *A* and simultaneously perceives private information (a signal), she will be indifferent about the choice, if the two pieces of information contradict each other. If she then just tosses a coin, the information transmitted by her own action to individual *C* becomes zero, without, however, being recognizable by this individual. Thus, it is possible that *B* takes a wrong action, but *C* follows, if the two previous individuals also took this choice, even though individual *B* did receive contradictory information, as assumed. The same principle applies for subsequent individuals, so that in the end the information cascade only depends on imitative behaviour, and is no more affected by the private information that the individuals extract from reality. This is particularly pronounced if signals are very noisy. Imitative behaviour is supported by the fact that information flows in the cascade are positive externalities. Imitation does not add to the pool of public knowledge, only dissenting behaviour that is based on private information. This implies that following the crowd is rational, whereas acting on private information is altruistic.

The model of information cascades has met with criticism, because the underlying modelling of network interactions is somewhat simplistic; the specific results cannot be generalized, for example, into multi–agent models, see for example De Vany and Lee (2008). More general models of social learning in networks add much more structure to the underlying network configurations. For example, in applied research in the context of development economics (Bandiera and Rasul 2006), a case in point is knowledge diffusion in agricultural extension, where it can be shown that diffusion is strongly influenced by kinship structures and other group affiliations, such as shared religion. At the same time, this research also clearly reveals the relevance of externalities, because on the one hand, there are strong frequency–dependent effects, such that diffusion speeds up, the higher the share of adopters, but there are also countervailing forces, as externalities imply a free–rider problem in generating the knowledge in the first place. That is, third parties might simply wait for others to take the risk of adoption.

5.4.5. Human society

To conclude this section, information diffusion in networks is strongly influenced by network configurations and structure, and evolves endogenously, resulting in very complex dynamics of frequency dependency. Further, there is a direct impact of biological constraints of human information processing on the evolution of network structure. This further underscores the general point made already in the second section, that in network evolution, simplicity can be a virtue. High levels of connectivity and speed of diffusion may engender destabilizing dynamics which ultimately might jeopardize network functions. Therefore, the question arises of which kinds of structural stability in networks also contribute to sustainability of networks.

Based on the analysis of the previous section, we can summarize the structure of human societies in figure 5.10. This structure provides the bedrock for the emergence of institutions that we explore in the next chapter. So, we see that one of the major flaws of many approaches in the economics of institutions is actually to assume that institutions can operate on the level of 'society' or 'markets'. As we shall see in the next chapter, all institutions build on the diverse mechanisms that go back to the different levels of the complex hierarchy of groups in human societies. In particular, the standard view (such as North 1990) that distinguishes between market mechanisms that prevail in small group regimes (the 'bazaar') and those in large 'anonymous' societies is misleading in analysing economic interactions with any reach and scope. In order to understand societies, it is essential to identify the structures in which causal mechanisms on all levels are integrated in order to realize certain functions, which can in turn be realized on the different levels. For example, the realization of the functions of global financial markets can rely on small–group mechanisms mediated via technologies, or the stability of families may depend on policies and laws emerging from national political processes.

Figure 5.10 The network structure of society

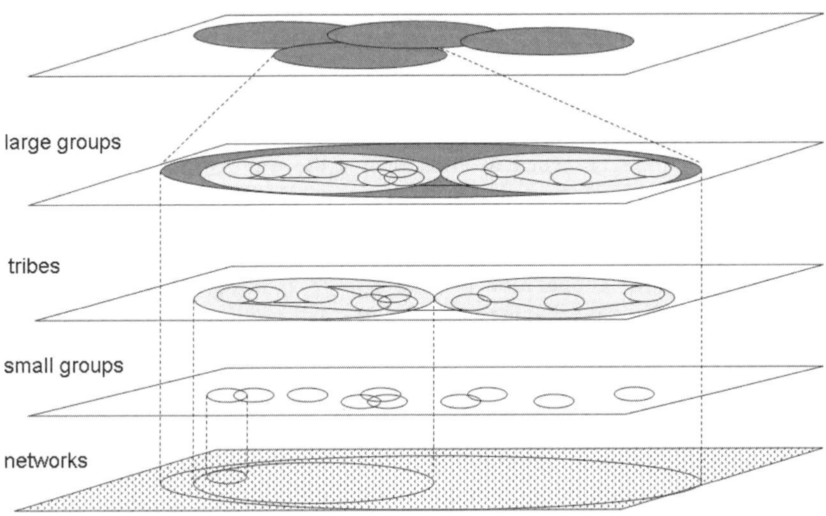

Note: Human societies manifest a peculiar hierarchy of network structures. The basic level is constituted by network interactions. Given biological constraints on information processing and the human proclivity to establish in–group/out–group boundaries, these networks organize into overlapping small–group structures. Small–group structures coalesce into tribes via the generic small–world effect in networks. In tribes, interactions are partly shaped by endogenously emergent categorizations. Categorizations based on stereotyping further decrease costs of group formation, so that large groups can emerge endogenously, especially with new communication technologies. Large groups overlap and intersect via different social identities of actors, mediated via categorizations.

The network structure of human society is highly complex. Given the complex dynamics of network evolution, the observed stability of human societies over long periods, though punctuated with episodes of rapid change, needs explanation. I propose that this explanation can be found in analysing the phenomenon of power. I argue that power is an emergent property of network structure, and that power is the single most important determinant of the emergence and stabilization of institutions.

5.5. TRUST, POWER AND STATUS

5.5.1. The trust dilemma in large groups

I will now analyse three phenomena that are specific to networks, yet play an essential role in the emergence and evolution of network properties related with institutions. These phenomena are trust, power and status.

There is a fundamental problem of trust in the transition from small groups to large groups, which directly connects with the economic analysis of rationality. Following the celebrated 'folk theorem' in game theory, and already established in the previous section, small groups would always offer contexts in which cooperative solutions are possible, because interaction in small groups is recurrent, thus opening the way for mechanisms of credible announcements of retaliation (Binmore 1994: 115ff). So, even though small groups manifest all emotional mechanisms of strong ties, it is almost paradoxical that precisely in this setting, cooperation is rational anyway. In other words, cooperation in small groups is always possible, even without deploying the mechanisms specific to small groups. So, the genuine problem of cooperation emerges in the large group setting (as emphasized by Seabright 2004).

In this context, we can generalize over a famous paradigm in the economic analysis of markets, the 'Lemons Problem' (Akerlof 1970). The Lemons Problem applies for large groups because of the central role of cognitive categorizations in the coordination of interactions. In economics, it results from the fact that the buyer builds probabilistic expectations about the average quality of a product on a market, if he cannot directly ascertain the quality of the single product. This implies, however, that a seller with higher quality has no way to signal this fact credibly. Thus, she will not be able to fetch an appropriate price, causing her to withdraw. If high–quality products are withdrawn from the market, the average quality declines. This will cause other sellers with higher quality to withdraw, as prices that buyers are willing to pay will further decline, thus triggering a downward spiral leading towards the collapse of the market.

From the viewpoint of network theory, this analysis presupposes that the market is entirely anonymous in the sense that the buyer can only infer one single property of the seller, which is to maximize profits opportunistically. The 'market' is conceived as a class of sellers who are not related to each other and who are only classified in the class of 'opportunistically egoistic individuals'. This, however, is a very specific network configuration. The Lemons Problem is a direct outcome of this peculiar network configuration, and it does not emerge in alternative configurations. Especially, in the configuration described so far, the sellers are perceived as a class of individuals with certain properties, and there are no group configurations. If buyer and seller, for example, were part of a local group, the problem of signalling quality would evaporate, because there are other mechanisms of sanctioning a cheating seller, and other mechanisms to collect information about trustworthiness (compare List 2006). This also applies for larger groups, even if there is a perfectly anonymous setting, provided that a proper technology of perception is available, such as in EBay auctions. The new auction technology allows for the processing of quality and reputation related information, such that the Lemon's Problem loses its bite.

The Lemon's Problem can be generalized for networks. Networks can unravel if there is uncertainty about the quality of other actors and related interactions, and if perceptions are limited to class characteristics on a high level of aggregation. This is sufficient to generate the destructive dynamics of changing population averages and the withdrawal of actors from transactions. The discussion also shows that this effect will not occur if networks manifest a certain structure that combines small group and large group configurations, and that involve certain perceptual patterns. The important effect of these structures is the creation of trusting behaviour, so that individuals are willing to invest into high–quality transactions, which contributes to the sustainability of the network in confirming expectations of others.

Empirically, as shown in large-scale surveys such as the World Value Survey, human societies show very different levels of trust, depending on the reference, such as society at large, neighbourhoods or kinship relations. In the economic context, trust into society at large is of special interest because this relates to the notion of anonymous markets (Tabellini 2008). In this view, trust is a major determinant of transaction costs: If trust unravels, individuals need to incur much more cost in drafting and enforcing contracts, collecting information about potential trading partners etc. Experimental research on so-called 'trust games' has shown that it is important to distinguish between 'trust' and 'trustworthiness' (for example Glaeser et al. 2000; Karlan 2005; Bohnet et al. 2010). An actor can manifest trusting behaviour, and the interacting actor may manifest trustworthiness. Trust as a network characteristic emerges from the interplay of the different forces that impact on these two different phenomena. Trustworthiness is a complex phenomenon, because it does not just depend on intrinsic characteristics of a person, which in large groups are not observable anyway, but mainly on network configurations which determine the perceived incentives to cheat. In a small group, trustworthiness can arise if actors know about the constraints and incentives that operate on other actors, such that they expect, as part of common knowledge, that everybody will avoid cheating. In the large group setting, this is not straightforward to establish and a major factor of the increased risk levels of transactions. In comparison, trusting behaviour is simpler, if we restrict the meaning of the term to the weakly altruistic act of transacting beyond the degree that is justified by rational risk assessments in a particular context.

Trust has become a major issue in social science and economics, because there is a clear relationship between the general level of trust in a society and economic, social and political development (Platteau 1994; Tabellini 2008). Nooteboom (2002) is an extensive treatment of trust as an analytical category. There is a paradox inhering all rational choice explanations of trust (such as in Coleman 1990), which is, if trust can be explained as a rational behaviour, it loses its essential characteristics, and even more pronounced, opens the way for mistrust. This is because rational choice is opportunistic in a fundamental sense, meaning if Ego trusts Alter because she can reconstruct Alter's behaviour as being rational, she can also anticipate that the behaviour will change if the external conditions change. In other words, if trust could be justified rationally, it is no longer necessary. Trust always transcends rational calculation.

This is precisely the argument propounded by Field (2001) who argues that trust is a weakly altruistic act, in the sense of a tit–for–tat strategy: The trusting individual advances a potentially costly interaction, which is rewarded if the partner is trustworthy. If this kind of trust is supported by further transactions, it is stabilized, but still cannot be completely reduced to rational choice in the initial stage, though rationalized in the sense of Skyrms (2004): Given the recurrence of the interactions, trusting behaviour is rational. Whether such equilibria are open to cheating invaders depends on the reliability of the signalling mechanisms, as discussed previously. In this framework, trust is not altruistic ex post, which implies that the evolution of the capacity to act in a weakly altruistic way ex ante matches with the inclusive fitness criterion (in the sense of West et al. 2006, see Chapter Three, section 3.3.3; compare Binmore 2005, Chapters 7 and 8). From that follows, that we can assume that human individuals have the capacity to trusting behaviour, but this needs to be triggered by contextual factors, in particular those ones determining the perception of trustworthiness, which is in turn determined by network structures (for a comparison between Arab and Western countries, see Bohnet et al. 2010). Further, trusting behaviour can manifest self–deception in the sense of von Hippel and Trivers (2011), such that individuals self–deceive themselves about true levels of trustworthiness, including own trustworthiness, therefore generating a higher incidence of trusting behaviour, which, however, creates the conditions for the emergence of stable cooperation patterns ex post. Therefore, one way to trigger these 'advance payments' of trust is to create shared 'We–modes (along the lines of Hollis' 1998 argument).

5.5.2. Capabilities and functions in network evolution

Trust relates with the general category of the capacity to transact. A most general form of trust is the actor's confidence that she has the capacity to transact. All trust relationships are based on this self–referential form of trust: For example, if I trust my friend and cooperate with her, I trust my capacity to enact this network interaction. Primordial and weakly altruistic trust enables the initiation of interactions and builds on trusting into one's own capacity to interact successfully.

I call this the 'capabilities' of an actor in the network context, thus importing a conceptual distinction introduced by Sen (1984; for an overview see Clark 2005). In Sen's framework, capabilities are relative to 'functionings', which connects easily with the notion of function in the triadic approach of this book. Interactions have functions that go beyond the mere intentions of an actor, as has been made clear in the triadic analysis of networks. For example, the function of my work may go beyond even what I know about it, so that my intentions only focus on a partial aspect of the functions. However, the linkage between functions and intentions is established via the feedback mechanisms that signal proper functioning to the actor, which, most generally, refer to selection in a population context. For example, the entrepreneur may not be fully aware of her functions in a complex market economy, and even the selection effect of competition may not fully reflect the reasons why success or failure happens. But competition results into reinforcing or containing certain action patterns. Then, the question is how capabilities of actors relate with their functions, both in the sense of the intentional and the non-intentional functions (the worker might believe that she does her work very well, but on the societal level the job is becoming obsolete because of technological progress, thus eroding the functional relevance of her capabilities).

We can say that proper functioning is an essential condition for the resilience and sustainability of networks. Functional failures lead to failures in transactions and can ultimately trigger the Lemons effects in unravelling the network, especially those ones building on large groups. So, the match between capabilities and functions is crucial in network evolution, insofar as this is reflected in the mutual stabilization of expectations. This allows relating the notion of trust with a very general notion of 'equilibrium' that matches economic views with sociological ones such as Luhmann's (1984): 'Equilibrium' refers to the recurrent matching of mutual behavioural expectations in network interactions, such that those interactions are sustainable through time.

Now, capabilities in general share important characteristics with trustworthiness: To re-emphasize, trustworthiness is not just an intrinsic property of actors, but is a contextual property that emerges from network configurations. In the distributed cognition and distributed agency perspective, all capabilities of actors are network phenomena to a large extent. For example, my capability to drive a car relies on the proper functioning of the car manufacturer in producing reliable quality or the qualification of service providers, thus going far beyond my skills of a driver (see F1 competitions, where, in spite of the fame of the drivers, actually teams win). At this point, we do not need to go into the details of this argument, but concentrate on the general aspect, which is that capabilities are emergent network properties, which are, however, assigned to individuals in the particular sense of the locus of confidence into capabilities which gives rise to trusting behaviour. So, for example, if I drive a car I express my confidence into my capability to do so, which in fact reflects my trust in the networked *agencements* which enable this action. Here, trusting is already a part of the expression of confidence. Beyond that, capabilities imply that if an actor is confident about her capabilities, this means that she will trust in the success of transactions. By further implication, this means that capabilities and trustworthiness are deeply connected. My capabilities include all network properties that increase the trustworthiness of the other actors. For example, if I know that a business partner is a friend of a friend of mines, this implies that in a case of cheating I might also ask for support from my friend. So, this particular network pattern is part of my capabilities to transact, leading towards a match between emergent trustworthiness of my partners and my trusting behaviour.

Figure 5.11 Power, capabilities and functionings

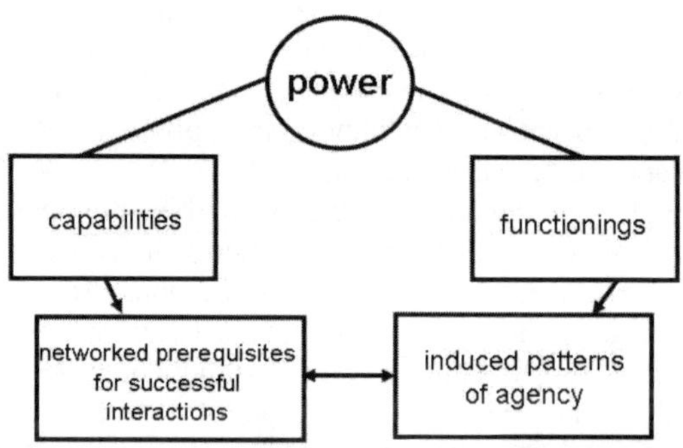

Note: The theoretical concept of 'power' relates to patterns of causation in network evolution and is a property of network configurations of actors that is only assigned to (but not ontologically manifest in) actors because it is reflected in successful interactions of actors. One the one hand, power relates with capabilities of actors that are emergent in network configurations. For example, an actor might control essential gateways in information flows, and possesses the capacity and knowledge to exploit this configuration. These capabilities relate with the realization of functionings. Functionings reflect functions of networks relative to environments (such as the function to sustain a military formation against an aggressor); they induce forms of agency in the sense of roles actors assume (such as military leadership). The power of an actor is also determined by how those functions are fulfilled successfully.

I propose to introduce a generic concept of 'power' to relate to this complex interaction between capabilities and functions in networks (figure 5.11). I argue that the phenomenon of trust is intrinsically related with the phenomenon of power. There are two different notions of power, however, 'power to…' and 'power over…': the term can refer to general capacities to achieve some goal, and to asymmetric relations of dominance between actors, with the former clearly being more general than the latter, which is one important determinant of the former. The more general one refers to the match between capabilities and functionings in networks, in the sense that the capabilities sustain proper functioning (which is also semantically prevalent in wordings such as 'empowerment'). Functions are mediated via the emergent patterns of intentionality in contexts of distributed agency. This corresponds to the classical sociological notion of a 'role', in the sense that power reflects the capacity to actively fulfil certain roles successfully, with the role relating to functions, and being behaviourally manifest in role specific patterns of agency. In network theory, this concept of role relates to induced forms of agency which relate with functions, thus define proper functioning.

The capability, seen in isolation, is not sufficient to establish a powerful network position, because capabilities can be mismatched with functions, and hence fail. This points towards the important question of how far actors are aware of their capabilities in relation to functions. Because the capability is a network phenomenon, this is by no means necessary. For example, an oppressed minority may not be aware of the capability to network collective action that can improve their position in society substantially. Yet, in their current position their perceived capabilities and their actualized functions may correspond. This match is an important precondition of the sustainability of the network pattern that includes discrimination against that minority. This includes the possibility analysed in great detail by Kuran (1995) that identity formation leads to the emergence of patterns of conformity (cf. Bernheim 1994) from which a dissociation of publicly expressed preferences and private preferences for action results. Because individuals need to confirm their identities, they accept power differentials which relate with respective network positions. Yet, this is a frequency dependent state, because if a sufficient number of individuals reveal their dissatisfaction with the current state, and capabilities for networked collective actions become common knowledge, the current power distribution can collapse within a very short time, also leading to rapid changes of publicly expressed majority views on political values and other convictions. As the dynamics of frequency–dependent processes is highly complex, such large–scale phenomena of social and political change ('revolutions') are difficult to predict for both internal and external observers, which feeds back to the probability of their occurrence.

5.5.3. Power as foundational category in evolutionary network theory

There have been many definitions of power in the social sciences, which remains an elusive concept, because most scholars acknowledge the fact that power is multidimensional and causally complex (for a thorough analysis, see Popitz 1985). The seminal definition had been provided by Hobbes: 'The power of a man, is his present means, to obtain some future apparent good', which is analysed by Kliemt (1985: 21ff). Hobbes refers to both 'power over…' and 'power to…' , that is the capacity for action. Power is seen as a stock, the value of which depends on its future uses, which therefore are conjectural. This definition is the most general and is equivalent to the concept of 'power to…' , as Hobbes has a general idea of controlling the environment in mind. As a result, power is not necessarily restricted to the social domain. Further, if power is conceived as an object of action, this implies a roundabout way to satisfying wants: Accumulating means does not necessarily lead to greater satisfaction in the present.

My approach follows the very simple and concise definition of power that has been proposed by Coleman (1990: 133): 'The power of an actor resides in his control of valuable events. The value of an event lies in the interests powerful actors have in that event.' This definition establishes an interesting recursive relation because in the second part Coleman refers to 'powerful actors'. It compares with Max Weber's (1922: 28) much-quoted definition that puts a lot of stress on the coercive potential and hence the 'power over…' notion: 'Power is the probability that one actor within a social relationship will be in a position to carry out his own will despite resistance.' Evidently, Weber also has a capability in mind, that is there is no exclusive reference to actually employed power. He restricts the use of the term to social relations (that is 'power over…') and defines a particular indicator of power, namely the capability to enforce some action on another actor. Many critics of this Weberian definition, however, have pointed out that a lack of resistance might not automatically imply voluntary agreement (as in the previously mentioned Kuran scenarios). Further, social relations also have implications for 'power to…' which might affect the coercive potential of an actor, too. Still, Weber seems to pinpoint an important empirical aspect of power, namely that it is related to the use of force in competitive social relations.

In contrast, Coleman introduces additional categories, namely interests and values. The important point is that power is clearly a structural category, that is, it cannot be simply reduced to a property of a single actor. As a structural category, power becomes an observable, because the actual potential depends on revealed interests. Power is an observer relative fact, and there is no way to refer power exclusively to internal and individual standards of value. This adds a specific feature to power as a relational category: If an individual is to maximize power, this presupposes a peculiar cognitive capability to perceive and to understand complex social networks of 'interested actors'. Hence, Coleman's definition seems to fit particularly well into network analysis. For example, network measures such as the centrality of an actor can be seen as partial determinants of the power of an actor relative to others, depending on the value of the resources that flow via that position, such as information (for a survey, see Hanneman and Riddle 2011). There are many results in network theory that network positions determine the relative success of actors in social interactions, such as the exploitation of 'structural holes' (Burt 1992), by which sparse connections between clusters of actors are created, which enable the use of resources (in particular, the newly opened network connections themselves are resources) that other actors cannot access. This one way to explain the performance effects of the utilization of 'weak ties' (Granovetter 2005).

This observation has an important theoretical consequence: Power is a foundational category in analysing human networks, in the line of approaches in the social sciences such as Foucault's. This is because all real-world networks are non-integral networks, thus manifesting the ubiquity of 'structural holes' and related phenomena. In other words, power is the dual of the incompleteness of networks. There are a large number of variants of this general argument. An important class of configurations refers to positions in which certain individuals control access to other individuals. There are different variants of this, such as 'gatekeepers' or 'coordinators'. For example, an actor who controls access to other actors can exert great impact on the success of others' transactions, and also improve the conditions for his own ones. These positions can emerge independently from interactions involving the actor. Although in many cases actors may strive to obtain such positions, there is also a strong role for network processes that are independent from their control. For example, if in a network access to a particular actor with important resources is controlled by two actors, and one of them passes away, the power position of the other is leveraged considerably because it turns into a monopoly. The value of a structural hole very much depends on alternative routes in the network and how costly their use is for the different actors.

However, one cannot simply deduce the power distribution in a network from network configurations, because the power of an actor depends on the valuations of the transactions with him by other actors, which is also independent from the actor's properties. Thus, power essentially depends on the recognition by others. This creates the paradox of power, which flows out from the deep relationship between power and trust. In fact, the general level of trust in a network is a reflection of the power structure.

The relation between power and trust results from the general aspect of power that awareness of power increases actor's expectations that transactions will be successful. In this sense, a powerful actor may show increased levels of trusting behaviour. But this effect is counterbalanced by possibly negative effects of power on the trustworthiness of the powerful actor. This is because precisely the increased capabilities of the powerful actor may increase uncertainty on the part of other actors about the success of their transactions, who switch to a lower level of trusting behaviour because of a lower degree of trustworthiness of the powerful actor: Powerful actors can always pursue their interest against the interests of others, which reduces their trustworthiness. There is a fundamental paradox of power, because the more power accumulates and concentrates in a network, the lower the general level of trust becomes, which in turn raises the interaction costs for the powerful actor: Because more power decreases trusting behaviour of others, this also means that the powerful actor loses trust into others, that is their trustworthiness shrinks from the perspective of the powerful actor. In the end, the powerful position collapses because of overwhelming costs of control which result from the erosion of trust.

Therefore, there are inherent limits to power, as the increasing level of power causes a decreasing recognition by others: This is a fundamentally Hegelian result of the analysis of power, which implies that power positions can only be maintained in the long run by sharing power with others who recognize one's power in turn. Ultimately, strong power positions need to resort to direct physical means of control, namely violence, in order to contain the forces driving this paradox. So, evolutionary network theory provides the theoretical foundation for the recent resurgence of interest in the role of violence on part of the economic theory of institutions (North et al. 2009).

The paradox of power underlies two phenomena in human societies that I will scrutinize in more detail in the next chapter: Firstly, the construction of more complex hierarchies of power was a major transition in human evolution, namely the transition from small group/tribe structures to large group structures in the early agricultural empires; secondly, the resulting hierarchical structures slowly evolved into the 'democratic' regimes of modernity that manifest a dispersion of hierarchical power, but result in higher degrees of recognition, so actually ending up with higher levels of institutionalized power. Modern democratic states actually manifest much higher concentrations of power than all earlier political systems (a fact which is emphasized in certain sociological approaches such as Elias's or Foucault's). Considering the primordial situation of human societies, that is the hunter and gatherer societies, one conspicuous phenomenon was the instability and functional specificity of power positions of single actors. In these human groups, there were many mechanisms that worked against the stabilization of highly asymmetric power structures, tending towards an egalitarian network structure (see Chapter Six in more detail).

As a result of this discussion, it emerges that power is a relational term like status in the general evolutionary approach to the individual (see Chapter Four, section 4.5.4). Therefore, we can relate power directly to biological categories, in particular inclusive fitness, in terms of an emergent matching concept on the level of networks. This is most evident in many societies in which power structures are dominated by families, directly or indirectly

(White 2011: 137). That means, the mapping of power into inclusive fitness of individuals should not be only determined by assessing direct differential reproductive success of individuals, because the original power measure would be highly context and reference group specific (for example, actors can be powerful in different reference groups, such as a powerful worker leader and a powerful military officer), such that the correlation with the simple measure of individual reproductive success is complex. Yet, there is much evidence beginning with Betzig's (1986) classic work that this correlation exists even in modern democratic societies, and certainly was highly prevalent in pre-modern and non-industrial human societies (on reproductive success of modern political leaders, see for example Betzig and Weber 1993). But the pattern that matters more is the correlation between power structures and the scope of resource control by kinship groups. The aforementioned evolutionary pattern of human societies reaching from more egalitarian primordial groups over strongly asymmetric agrarian societies to the more egalitarian democratic societies of the modern world seems to correlate with a matching pattern of symmetry and asymmetry of differential inclusive fitness of different social groups defined in kinship terms.

5.5.4. Social capital

My definition of power comes very close to the notion of social capital in economics, as far as it is used as a term related to the interaction potential arising from network relations (for general approaches close to network analysis, see Lin 2001 or Dasgupta 2005). So, I treat 'social capital' as a concept that is especially important in the empirical determination of power relations in networks (even though there are substantial issues in measurement, see Durlauf 2002). More exactly, I refer to all capabilities to transact as social capital, as a subset of all individual capabilities. The realized transactions are the functionings that are relevant for social capital. So, for example, social capital can refer to the capability to successfully conclude business transactions, or to the capability to mobilize support for one's political agenda.

We can distinguish between two kinds of social capital. One kind is the individually appropriable social capital, the other is the capital that is collectively shared by the members of a group (compare Burt 2000; this difference is treated in various terminologies, such as 'binding' versus 'bonding' social capital, see for example Putnam 2000). In both senses, social capital is a relational term, that is, it measures transaction capabilities relative to others. Individually appropriable social capital refers to relatively larger individual capacities to realize a transaction, which implies that social capital always exerts a negative externality on others in reducing their opportunities to transact. Collective social capital refers to collective capacities to transact. This translates into individual capacities, if the collective capacity leverages all individual capacities to the same degree. As a relational term, the collective capacity would refer to other groups. So, for example, if we say that a certain ethnic group has strong social capital, this refers to other social groups in society. Within the ethnic group, this shared social capital leverages all individual transaction capabilities to the same degree. At the same time, status differences within the group relate with different endowments of individually appropriable social capital, which creates individual differences within the group with a certain level of collective social capital.

Both are 'social' in the sense that they result from network structures and cannot be reduced to the individual level. Yet, in economic terms the former is a private good, the latter is a club good. As a club good, the latter is potentially precarious because of the free–rider problem. The former can be precarious because of the dissemination of information through perception and subsequent imitation. For example, the use of a network bridge might release the information about its possibility, and this might enable other individuals to establish bridges on their own. We can analyse these relationships by applying standard economic notions of goods characteristics (see table 5.2).

Table 5.2 Social capital and public goods

	excludable	**non-excludable**
rivalrous	private good (relationships)	commons (collective safety)
non-rivalrous	club good (associations)	public good (morals)

Individually appropriable social capital is a private good, as long as other actors can be excluded from its use, and if there is rivalry in utilizing it. So, a special relationship with another powerful actor certainly is excludable, as I can control its use by others, and the more that other actors claim that relationship together with me, the more it would be diluted. On the other hand, if I become a member of a lobby group, the results of the lobbying activities can increase my interaction capabilities, as I participate with the leveraging of the social capital of the group. This effect is non-rivalrous, because my utilization does not decrease the interaction capabilities of others. However, one can exclude members from the lobby group. This is important to increase the individual incentives to contribute to the production of social capital. Another possible combination can be illustrated with safety in a neighbourhood which results from mutual monitoring. A stranger who moves into the neighbourhood can enjoy this safety without actually contributing to it, thus even eroding the social capital. In this sense, it is rivalrous and non-excludable. Finally, there are genuine public goods such as public morals which appear to be non-rivalrous and non-excludable.

In common uses of the term 'social capital', all these aspects intermingle, but they should be clearly distinguished. Thus, social capital appears to be a complex and composite phenomenon in networks, which directly reflects the hierarchical nature of networks, that is the distinction between individuals and groups on different levels (compare Woolcock 1998); one practical illustration is the role of social capital in the formation of economic regions (Lorenzen 2007). What is essential for both individual and collective phenomena, is the role of boundary effects established by externalities, with collective phenomena manifesting positive in–group externalities and negative out–group externalities (Glaeser et al. 2002; Dasgupta 2005; this issue relates with the many difficulties to measure the aggregate effects of social capital on societal measures of performance, see Beugelsdijk 2006a, b; compare Alesina and La Ferrara 2005 on effects of ethnicity).

Figure 5.12 The accumulation of social capital

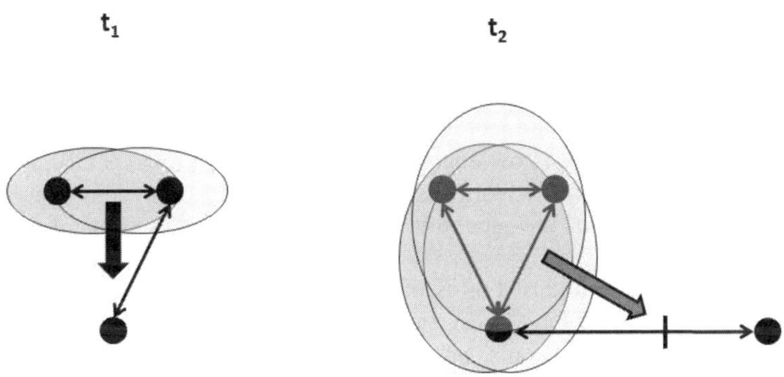

Note: Social capital accumulates via the recurrent formation of network interactions triggered by information externalities. In this abstract example, in t_1 a positive information externality causes an actor to interact in spite of limited access to information about the other actors. This interaction generates additional information, resulting into overlapping perceptual fields of all actors which support on-going interactions in t_2. This results in the emergence of a shared 'culture' which defines an in–group/out–group boundary that exerts a negative externality on other actors, thus inhibiting interactions. The boundary strengthens social capital further because of the emerging possibility of group–specific sanctions, in particular ostracism, that is refusal to continue interactions.

As I have already mentioned, one problematic aspect of social capital is the assumption that it can be accumulated, which also relates with the implicit assumption that an aggregate measure is possible (Solow 2000). In fact, all social capital indicators are only indirect ones. However, seen from another angle, this metaphorical use of the term 'capital' could be justified if it aims at grasping the diachronic nature of social capital (figure 5.12). Social capital always refers to past processes in which actors have accumulated capabilities for transactions. These capabilities are constitutive to distributed agency in the sense that they are embedded into specific network configurations. This is also true for individually appropriable social capital, as it essentially depends on network configurations. Therefore, the accumulation happens via the formation of network patterns which are sustainable through time and give rise to successful interactions. As these interactions actually confirm the capabilities, there are frequency–dependent effects such that on-going transactions do not consume social capital but increase it. This is the meaning of 'accumulation of social capital.' In other words, the mechanism of accumulation is the sequence of positive externalities between interactions through time, which work between same and different actors embedded into related network configurations.

This accumulation finds expression in positive externalities for actors who share the social capital and negative externalities who do not (thick black and grey arrows in figure 5.12). The increasing reach and scope of these externalities reflects the accumulation process. The driver of the process is the formation of network configurations which are bolstered by the emergence of common knowledge. I propose to denote this specific form of common knowledge in networks as 'culture.' In fig. 5.12, *A* and *B* evolve a culture that undergirds the accumulation of social capital in terms of network configurations.

This notion of 'culture' builds on the view of the individual that I have developed in Chapter Four. That means, culture as common knowledge does not refer to mental contents, such as beliefs or values, but relates to the identity of the individuals in externalist terms (compare Yamagishi's 2011 'niche construction' approach to culture which emphasizes mutual adaptation of actors and interactions, and rejects notions of culture in terms of 'values' or 'preferences'). It is a pattern in the distribution of transaction–related knowledge over individuals and configurations, which has the central function to determine the boundaries across which externalities work (on effects of culture on cooperation, see Gächter et al. 2010). This also explains why artefacts play an important role in culture, because the artefacts mediate network relations. For example, a network of actors may develop a set of shared ways to dress, which indicates their shared identity. A clear-cut example is the role of dress and other devices in networks of adolescents. So, we can expand the conceptual frame of capabilities, functionings and power to include the relation between social capital and culture. It is essential to recognize that culture does not relate with any specific functioning, but with the generalized functioning of transactions. Thus, it is not possible to reduce single cultural items to a particular function. In fact, only if cultural items are without function, they can operate as indicators of social capital and hence, boundaries in networks. I have analysed this basic fact in the previous chapter (section 4.5.2.).

Figure 5.13 Network determinants of social capital (modified after Lin 2001)

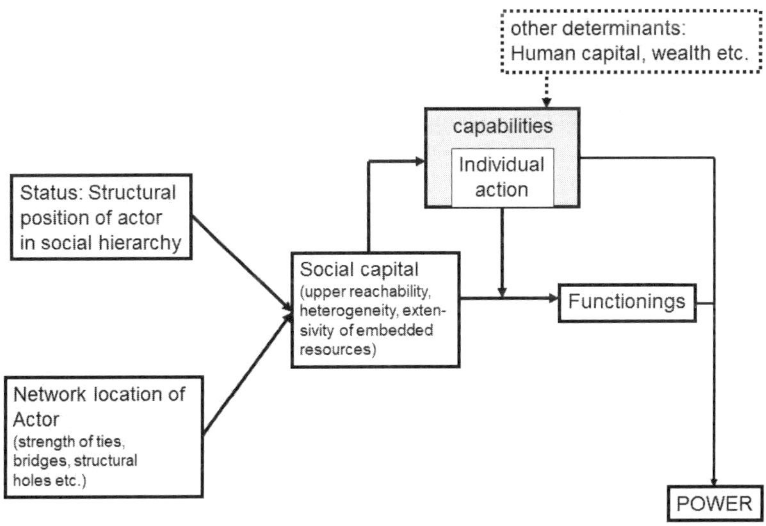

Note: Social capital is a central theoretical term in evolutionary network theory which, because of the complexity of its determinants, can only be approximated by existing methods of empirical measurement. The fundamental determinants are status in network structure and position in network configurations. Positions are determined by contingent factors such as the existence of structural holes. The resulting social capital can be described in different dimensions such as the scope of possible connections across social hierarchies or the quality of resources that are embedded in ego–centred network relations. Together with other types of resources such as wealth or education, social capital determines the capabilities for actions that result in functionings, relative to a network environment. Proper functioning and capabilities converge into certain positions of power in society.

Social capital can be analysed in terms of network configurations. If we focus on the individual actor and its embeddedness into network configurations, social capital determines its transaction capabilities in the following way (figure 5.13). Firstly, all human societies manifest structural hierarchies, so that status relates with hierarchies and therefore is a direct determinant of social capital. Secondly, independently from the hierarchical level there is a set of properties of network configurations that determine social capital, such as structural holes. These apply at both intra–level and cross–level. Thirdly, the determinants result in a specific endowment of social capital. This can be described along a set of dimensions, which include, amongst others, the scope and reach of the capabilities to transact, the heterogeneity of network relations and the resources that are embedded into the network configurations. Here, heterogeneity relates to a standard distinction in social network theory which we have already met when discussing information flows in networks, that is the distinction between homophilous and heterogeneous relations. Embedded resources refer to the functional value of transactions based on social capital, which is the accessibility of resources (having rich friends or poor friends). Social capital is one determinant of the capabilities to transact. There are other important capabilities, such as education in societies where some transactions require specialist knowledge, for example, or pecuniary wealth. The capabilities prepare the ground for the proper fulfilment of functionings.

5.5.5. Status and frequency–dependent network dynamics

It remains to clarify one final essential notion in network analysis, status. As we have seen, status is an important determinant of imitation processes. Imitation contributes to the enhancement of power of individuals. This relationship emerges from the simple fact that in the case of uncertainty about best behavioural choices, the most successful individual may be the one that should be followed. Evidently, this does not necessarily imply that all copied features also connect causally with the success of the individual. Many features may not be connected at all, so that biased transmission of this kind also contributes to the diffusion of non-functional features in a population. We can generalize over a certain class of signs that are status indicators. A status indicator is called a 'positional good' in economics (for seminal contributions, see Hirsch 1976 and Frank 1985). Positional goods need to be scarce, thus reflecting the scarcity of status, but they must be also transferable and possible to copy. For example, wearing expensive designer clothing is a status indicator which can be copied nevertheless. The partial diffusion of the status indicator in a population confirms the indexical role of that sign, because without diffusion the signalling function of the indicator would be hampered. Again, this statement needs to be seen in connection to reference groups and their hierarchical order in a given network. A status indicator in a high status reference group can be mainly relevant within the group, but is less significant in relation with low status groups. Expensive red wine might be a high status group indicator, but possibly meaningless relative to workers. The status distinction across the group is established by other indicators, such as cars. The causal interaction between status goods and consumption activities is complex and depends on the observability and reliability of status indicators. For example, poor people might invest disproportionally into conspicuous consumption of status goods, thus actually cementing their low income status, because they cannot rely on other easily observable status indicators such as human capital and professional position (Moav and Neeman 2012).

How does status emerge in networks? Status is the defining feature in all networks in which there is a preferential attachment mechanism working. As we have seen, preferential attachment is another expression of the homophily principle and can be triggered by any sort of similarity, attractive force etc. The important result of this sort of process is the emergence of hubs in networks, which is the ordering of elements in a network according to status. This is particularly important, again, to analyse the transition to large groups. In large groups, the preferential attachment process, under certain conditions, results into the emergence of network structures which are 'scale free', which means they manifest Power Laws (Newman 2010: 247ff, 487ff). Therefore, we can interpret the hierarchical distribution of status positions in human societies as an outcome of the more fundamental processes determining the dynamics of connectivity, as epitomized in the expression 'the rich get richer'. Power Law distributions result into very few individuals having high status (such as high income, in one dimension, or high levels of celebrity) and many individuals having low status.

This process does not require that initially there is the perception of high status based on intrinsic criteria (such as exceptional talent as a movie actress). For example, the scientific paper might be just of average quality, so that the only criterion to cite it even more is that it is just cited frequently. But the emerging status as a hub will ultimately also result in a high reputation of the paper as such, which remains even true if the majority still recognizes that it is average, but at least, because of the directed nature of quotation networks, it can claim priority. Further, a hub might not have high status in other respects, such as the hub in the transmission of sexual diseases (although that might possibly signal high attractiveness for sexual partners). Given the three–dimensional nature of networks, it is important to realize that these effects can interact. For example, a high status individual may not entertain many transactions within the network, but may stay in the centre of perceptual fields and communication processes, especially directed ones. For example, in the Web 2.0 many people might follow the tweets of a celebrity, who never transacts with them nor reads their tweets.

There is one important mechanism that turns into a self–selecting dynamics stabilizing status hierarchies (this argument generalizes Podolny's 2005 analysis of status on markets). Status has a direct impact on interaction costs in networks. All interactions are costly. Interaction costs result from generic uncertainty for any sort of network–bound agency. Therefore, we have already asserted that there is a general tendency to reduce the level of interaction costs in network evolution, which is an emergent network phenomenon that cannot be reduced to individual agency. Now, status may be seen as a signal that allows for the reduction of interaction costs. This is because status itself is interpreted as an indicator of successful action in the past. Individuals with high status can establish network relations with lower interaction costs than other individuals, and individuals who manage to manifest status indicators may achieve a similar effect.

Yet, if we consider the relationship between status and interactions, there is an interesting asymmetry. High status certainly lowers the interaction costs to interact with any other network member, because all other network members wish to interact with the high status individual. But high status also increases the interaction costs for all incoming connections to a substantial degree, because status requires selectivity on part of the high–status individual. So, the picture is that high–status individuals typically have a large number of incoming contacts but relatively few outgoing contacts. The function of this pattern is to reduce the erosion of status because of the overextension of the homophily mechanism: So, high–status individuals actively connect with other high–status individuals, such that status is also defining boundary markers, turning into an independent criterion for homophily across domains (so, high–status businesspeople comingle with high–status politicians etc.; in social network analysis, there is positive assortativity of nodes with different degrees, so well–connected businesspeople comingle with other well–connected ones, see Jackson and Rogers 2007). This observation is reinforced by noticing that actually exploiting the potential for a large number of interactions would certainly jeopardize the status position itself, which by definition implies limited access.

On the other hand, status is difficult to achieve, by definition. From this follows that a high–status individual can realize all possible interactions with lower interaction costs than low–status individuals. If the scope and value of interactions is a defining feature of status, this implies that low–status individuals face a fundamental barrier in invading high status positions: They would need to incur much higher interaction costs and would therefore be disadvantaged. However, high–status individuals cannot play out their absolute advantage across all levels of status, in spite of being able to realize all interactions at lower costs. This is because they would erode their status by adopting this behaviour. Therefore, status hierarchies are self–reinforcing and at least partly independent from external determinants of status. Status in networks perpetuates itself. Therefore, status typically manifests the phenomenon of evolutionary stasis, such as, for example, certain elite families maintaining their status positions even across major societal disruptions and changes.

To conclude, human networks feature many phenomena of structural stabilization, which result from endogenous hierarchical differentiation. These structures relate with functions, which are relative to environmentally selective forces. Since human networks always manifest the phenomenon of institutionalization, I postpone the discussion of the structure–function link to the next chapter.

This chapter has outlined the fundamentals of the theory of human networks, which adopts many insights and methods of established network theory, but adds the essential theoretical features of bimodality and information theory, combined with our knowledge about biological constraints on human network formation. Evolutionary network analysis of human societies is basically analysis of human distributed cognition and distributed agency. Both functions can only materialize in a sustainable way if evolvability of networks and constraints on network evolution co-evolve in a balanced way. This is visible even in the institutionally and technologically most advanced domains in the modern human economy, the financial markets. For example, trust in computer-mediated interactions still relies on small–group mechanisms and signalling specific to this level (Knorr Cetina and Bruegger 2002; for a classical analysis networks in financial markets see Baker 1984). So, one cannot say that the evolution of the modern economy overcomes those primordial mechanisms, but fuses them into new syntheses with novel technologies and institutions. This evolving fusion drives the evolution of markets, and is the subject of the next three chapters.

6. Institutions

> Instead of saying, the person behaves the way he does because he is following the rules of the institution, we should just say, first (the causal level), the person behaves the way he does, because he has a structure that disposes him to behave that way; and second (the functional level), he has become to be disposed to behave that way, because that's the way that conforms to the rules of institutions (John Searle 1995: 144).

6.1. THE MULTI–FACETED NATURE OF 'INSTITUTIONS'

6.1.1. Naturalizing institutions

The literature about the role of biological determinants in human life is mostly cast in terms of the biology/culture divide (for example Richerson and Boyd 2005; Mesoudi 2011). So far, I have referred to this notion, too, but I will now introduce a specification which completes the substantial revision of the use of the term 'culture' according to these views. I argue that humans are *institutional animals*, and assign a more limited place to culture. This more specific use of culture has already been introduced in the previous chapter: Basically, I refer the term to shared identities, that is, to the emergence of We–attitudes and We–modes, and to the emergence of group boundaries in networks. But shared identities only encompass a part of what makes human behaviour special in relation to other animals. I argue that this more encompassing phenomenon is *institutions*, following the arguments presented by John Searle (2005). Institutions are the core phenomenon that enables human phenotypic plasticity, in the particular sense of enabling humans to create entirely new forms of life which are not directly determined by their biological properties, though being subject to biological constraints, and being enabled by biological capabilities (see Boyer and Petersen 2012). These forms of life refer to life in groups, in particular, and how this life in groups changes individual behaviour.

I call this kind of behaviour 'Institutionally Guided Behavioural Patterns' (IGBPs). In this chapter, I will present a theory that explains this phenomenon, based on the principles developed in Chapters Four and Five.

With this term, I mark the difference to many current approaches in economics, and highlight allegiance to the so-called 'Old Institutionalism' (especially, Veblen 1899, 1914; overview in Hodgson 1999). Most economic approaches treat individuals as separate from institutions, which are seen as imposed constraints on behaviour, and rule–following is explained via the incentives that determine opportunistic behavioural choices (compare Smit et al. 2011, criticizing Searle). The early institutional thinkers assumed, in contrast, that institutions make up human nature, in the sense that there is a conjunction between external institutions and internal behavioural drives. So, Veblen famously defined institutions as 'habits of thought'. I follow this track, and additionally I refer institutions to regularities in networks which I conceive in bimodal terms, thus highlighting the role of signs in IGBPs; this relates with the theory of neuromemetics which I explored in Chapter Four, such that IGBPs are seen as emerging from causal circuits between signs and neuromemetic structures. By this, I refer institutions to behavioural dispositions, which contrasts sharply with the economic emphasis on choice. This argument amounts to a thorough 'naturalization' of institutional analysis (for a related approach, see Sperber 2011).

This approach can be put in the general framework of evolutionary analysis as deployed in Chapter Three. Then, as sketched in a most general way in figure 6.1, we can say that in a multi–level approach to evolution, IGBPs are population–level behavioural patterns which define the interactor relative to the environment in which human populations evolve manifesting certain institutions. Contrary to common economic approaches, these patterns are not reduced to individual–level choices and actions, but to a causal circuit that establishes the replicator of the institution. This circuit builds on the analysis of brain semiosis in Chapter Four (especially, figure 4.7) and connects the signs that are constitutive parts of networks among actors in a population with sets of neuronal states that result in certain dispositions to act. So, both replicator and interactor are distinct population–level phenomena, and the level of the individual is involved as the embodiment of certain mediating mechanisms. Therefore, what matters is not 'individual choice', but individual level mechanisms; the most important ones, as we shall see, relate with cognition, since cognition is what conjoins individual properties with external phenomena, as clarified in Chapter Four.

It should be emphasized that my approach also differs from non-cognitivist approaches that are also familiar from recent economics, namely in the context of evolutionary game theory (with seminal contributions such as Schotter 1982 and Young 1998). There, institutions are just seen as evolving rules in populations of agents representing rule varieties, without assigning a significant role to individual choice (for a critical reflection, see Sugden 2001). In contrast, I emphasize the cognitive mechanisms that underlie IGBPs, which also enable conscious reflection over institutions and active institutional design. That being said, I follow the line of thinking in Chapter Four and argue that these cognitive mechanisms are not confined to the individual body, but essentially relate with population–level phenomena. This highlights the central role of semiosis; in the context of institutions, one special sort of semiotic system looms large, namely, human language. Human language offers the blueprint for reconciling those two hitherto separated strands of thought in economics: On the one hand, language is a population–level phenomenon, on the other hand, language enables and is changed by individual human creativity.

Figure 6.1 Evolutionary framework for institutional analysis

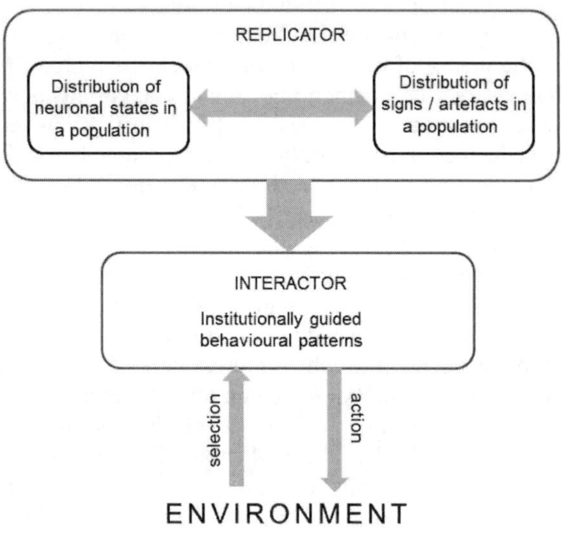

Note: In the evolutionary view, institutions can be analysed into the two levels of replicator and interactor which are both population–level phenomena mediated via mechanisms on the level of the individual. The interactor is the set of IGBPs in a population relative to a certain environment. The interactor is the causal circuit between external signs making up parts of networks in a population and sets of neuronal states that generate actions involving those signs. This framework will be completed and detailed in the summary diagram at the end of this chapter (6.15).

There are two essential aspects of institutions which need to be elucidated in the evolutionary analysis; both directly connect with fundamental aspects of human networks. First, institutions are cognitive structures, in the sense of the capacity to create new categorizations of behaviour and network interactions, to classify these according to those categorizations and to draw inferences based on these classifications. Secondly, institutions are intimately related with power structures, as they enable certain human actions, that is create interaction capabilities, and because they build on enforcement mechanisms. Again, this view defines principled departures from the standard approaches in economics which emphasize the role of institutions in raising the efficiency and efficacy of transactions. The analysis of power structures typically refers to macrosociological phenomena, whereas cognitive processes necessarily locate with the micro–level. Yet, insofar as we adopt the distributed cognition perspective, this also includes reference to collective structures of social cognition. The cognitive dimension of institutions has long been emphasized in some strands of the economics literature, which conceives institutions as problem–solving devices, in this regard again, akin to technologies (for example Mantzavinos 2001 for an overview of these approaches). In particular, institutions solve problems of social coordination in a complex world, especially complex social world, resulting from the so-called 'double contingencies' of mutual behavioural expectations (Luhmann 1984: 148ff; Blyth 2011). This view is even more plausible from the distributed cognition perspective. If everybody accepts an institution, and everybody possesses common knowledge, that this is the case, certain behaviours will be coordinated successfully. However, things are not as simple as that, which is also reflected in fundamental ambiguities in the use of the term 'institution' in the literature.

6.1.2. Diverse approaches to institutions

Most modern approaches start out from Game Theory. However, the immediate question arises whether the 'rules of the game' are the institutions or the observed behaviour in equilibrium (see for example Dixit 2004: 5ff). An influential definition of the latter type had been proposed by Schotter (1982: 11), who defined an institution as a regularity in the behaviours of a population, which is based on common knowledge of the underlying interaction structure. All individuals in the population know that everybody else knows that everybody will conform to the institution, and they know the underlying incentive structure. There are different incentive structures, which correspond to the standard definitions of equilibria in games. Finally, the institution refers to a recurrent situation. Thus, the situation as such and the game implied are not part of the definition. Schotter's definition is very different from the definition proposed by North (1990: 3ff) who treats institutions as constraints. As a constraint, institutions are not necessarily the object of agreements or choices of the agents, which is the assumption made by Schotter. Schotter's definition implies that institutions are not necessarily enforced by an exogenous party, even against the will of agents. North's approach directly relates institutions with the political process, where they are created and implemented. Whether agents agree or not, depends on the structure of that process. But once institutions are set, everybody has to follow.

Schotter's game–theoretic understanding of institutions has many ramifications in modern economic theory, as there are two alternative approaches of Evolutionary Game Theory and classical strategic interaction theory. However, the basic approach remains the same, which is to define an institution as an observed regularity of behaviour. The crucial difference is that the Evolutionary Game Theory approach does not introduce any assumption about the cognition of the agents, who can be just automata with a particular fitness function.

There is an entirely different definition of an institution which is given by Aoki (2001: 26). Aoki proposes that an institution is a self–sustaining system of shared beliefs about games. In a sense, this definition concentrates on what Schotter just takes for granted, namely common knowledge and the knowledge of the situation into which the game is situated. The fact that an institution is self–enforcing, given a particular incentive structure, is dependent on the evolution of these shared beliefs. So the cognitive dimension dominates the dimension of incentives. This position is akin to the position adopted by Greif (1994), who also argues that institutions depend on cultural belief systems, but on the other hand maintains the 'rules of the game' approach of North, who, in his most recent contributions, also emphasizes the cognitive dimension (North 2005).

In most of economic literature 'games' are considered, which are always interpreted in terms of specific cases of interaction, also as specific historical examples. However, if we talk about an 'institution', we normally do not think about a single case, but of a large number of cases, for which the institution applies. That is, one would at least need to distinguish between two levels of abstraction, a set of games and a more abstract, unique type of game. This perspective has been recently adopted by the 'mechanism design' literature (for a survey, see Myerson 2008a; also Hurwicz's 2008 Nobel lecture). This approach argues that institutions cannot be games, because institutions do not specify the preferences of the agents. Instead, institutions are conceived as 'game forms', which specify the set of players, the strategies and the payoff functions (see also Aoki 2007). From these game forms, one can generate games by means of specifying the preferences: However, in the parlance of Chapter Four, this means to fix the identities of players (section 4.4.2). In that perspective, institutions are seen as emerging from embedded games, in which enforcement takes place. Then, institutions are stable if every player expects all other players to conform to the larger enforcement game.

The mechanism design approach fits into the argument presented in this chapter, but with a different emphasis. There are two major conclusions: One is that the interdependence of embedded games and game forms implies that there is much space for the impact for cognition, which is essential to determine multiple equilibria; and second, the infinite regress in the enforcement problem implies that for the enforcers, different conditions may hold than for the other agents. In particular, as Myerson (2008b) argues, institutions for large societies might be enforced by a small group of political elites, in which relations of trust can be maintained; this directly connects with the layered networks perspective of Chapter Five.

Looking at this vast literature from a bird's–eye view, I propose to distinguish between three kinds of institutions and between three aspects of institutional evolution. The distinction of the three kinds of institutions is mainly based on their substantial differences in those three aspects. The three aspects are: emergence of institutions, enforcement of institutions and stabilization of institutions. Those three aspects come close to the three elements of the fundamental evolutionary VSR paradigm. Emergence relates to the mechanisms that lead towards institutional novelty, hence corresponds to variation; enforcement relates to mechanisms that favour certain institutions about alternative institutions, hence relates with selection; and stabilization refers to the maintenance and sustainability of institutions through time, hence retention.

The three kinds of mechanisms appear to work in different ways in three different basic types of institutions: conventions, social norms and formal institutions. I do not dwell much on discussing this view here, as they are as many different definitions of these terms as there are authors. For example, in using the term 'social norm' I combine pertinent thoughts by Elster (1989b) with the notion of 'informal institution' used by North (1990). Also, it seems to be rather unusual to subsume all three regularities in social interaction to 'institutions' as the more general term, but this sense follows the early institutionalist literature engendered by Veblen, for example. What is essential, however, is the fact that those three kinds manifest different phenomena in relation to the three aforementioned mechanisms. Basically, one can say that mechanisms of emergence mainly operate in different cognitive modes, such as inductive learning, which is familiar as reinforcement learning in psychology, and which directly allows to connect with the general theory of evolutionary mechanisms (Hull et al. 2001). This is what I will explore in the subsequent section of this chapter. Mechanisms of enforcement relate with mechanisms of stabilization, similar to the general role of selection in the retention of variants according to the general theory of evolution. The most important different types are individual commitment resulting from self–interest in following a regularity (such as driving on the left or on the right, the standard example in game theory); next comes *n*–order sanctions which are essential in enforcing regularities in network interactions, as we have already seen in Chapter Five, and hence are a defining feature of social norms; and finally there is the phenomenon of formal sanctions by formal organizations based on formal texts, which is an essential feature of more complex human societies building on cohesion among large groups (which is a major topic of the final section of this chapter). These enforcement mechanisms interact with mechanisms of stabilization that mainly relate back to the microfoundations of behaviour, whereas enforcement mechanisms mainly relate to the macro–level. I highlight the distinctive role of different kinds of individual interests, such as self–interest in conventions and generalized self–interest in other institutions, or the role of emotional commitments, which comes into play when considering the role of institutions in defining group identities.

The emergence of institutions is mainly a cognitive process; this remains an important criterion to distinguish the three kinds of institutions, as we shall see. For example, a convention is characterized by inductive cognitive processes that foster the emergence of behavioural regularities building on repetition and reinforcement learning (Cubitt and Sugden 2003; Sugden 2011). In comparison, formal institutions mainly build on deductive cognitive processes, that is, they involve abstract concepts under which certain behaviours are subsumed. Similarly, institutions differ in terms of stabilization mechanisms: Stabilization relates to all determinants that bias rule following on the part of the actors. So, I distinguish between specific and general self–interest: The former relates to the directly perceived benefits of following an institution, the second includes externalities of rule following on the collective level. Emotions refer to the analysis of the dispositions to follow an institution; finally, we have to take consistency across regularities as a major criterion which highlights the requirement that rule following has to be non-contradictory on the individual level.

Then, a typical pattern of *conventions* is that they are self–enforcing; hence involve commitment of actors, already on the basis of specific self-interest working as a stabilization mechanism. That means, they can emerge from simple patterns of reinforcement learning, hence induction. In contrast, *social norms* rely much more on *n*–th order sanctions, together with a strong root in emotional mechanisms, because the norms relate with individual identities. *Formal institutions* presuppose complex cognitive mechanisms, involving concept formation and deduction, and they often require a formal enforcement mechanism. Consistency is a criterion that is especially strong for social norms, because they are exclusively based on behavioural expressions, where individual identities count much. Formal institutions can be weaker in consistency, as this triggers conflict, in the first place, which has to be resolved by other mechanisms, including institutionalized mechanism of conflict resolution, as in the most advanced modern societies.

This brief sketch shows that one important difference between the evolutionary approach and established Game Theory approaches to institutions is that I will pay close attention to real–world network structures and mechanisms that undergird the evolution of institutions. One simple expression of this distinction is that the evolutionary approach does not concentrate on single and particular game structures in order to explain institutions but to network constellations of interactions; in game theory, that would translate into the analysis of networked games, in which the different game settings influence each other and mutually drive evolutionary forces that also change those structures (for a related view, see Bednar and Page 2007).

6.1.3. Institutions as network regularities

As a result of this brief reflection on the literature, we can say that institutions go beyond observable regularities in populations of actors, and that they manifest a higher level of abstraction, relative to cognitive processes of the actors involved. Cognitive functions of institutions emerge from regularities in networks, thus referring back to the more general ontological categories developed in Chapters Two and Five. As such, they relate to network structures, so that the general entropic analysis applies, which offers some interesting initial insights, especially that behavioural variety and structure are necessary correlates in institutional evolution, and that the information carrying function of institutions results from the fact that a range of possible behaviours is excluded: That is, institutions reinforce the property of structural incompleteness of networks. This is essential to define an important difference between the evolutionary and the standard economic approach to institutions, because the latter mostly approaches institutions as mechanisms of perfecting markets as networks, in the sense of universal connectivity.

What makes institutions different from other regularities that emerge in networks, as far as the cognitive dimension is concerned? One hypothesis is that institutions refer to large groups, hence basically involve a categorization scheme with a higher degree of abstraction. Typically, institutions define certain roles for actors, such as defining the role of a trader, a judge or a physician (what North et al. 2009 call a 'social persona'). An institution is a regularity that applies for these roles largely independent from the specific small group setting of interactions. Thus, a judge is expected to behave similarly in many different contexts. So, one cognitive effect of institutions is de-contextualization. The other side of the coin is that institutions define identities of actors in recurrent interactions. However, this introduces an ambiguity into the analysis of institutions because, as we have seen, identities of actors cannot only be defined via social categorizations: A judge also has a personal identity which is inextricably enmeshed with her social identity. In this sense, it is impossible to fully decontextualize any institution (for a related recognition of the complexity of institutions, see Mohr and White 2008). This is reflected in the fact that all institutions seem to be idealizations, in the sense that real world interactions vary within a certain range around this reference point.

De-contextualization is the major precondition for the cognitive performance of institutions, namely to save information costs. Now, the question is whether institutions themselves create costs. This is clearly the case: For example, in order to understand all the institutions that govern the behaviour of the judge, we would possibly need to study law. Actually, ordinary people who take part in a trial may have only rudimentary knowledge of the institutions that govern the behaviour of the judge. They just accept it, and this is what saves the costs. This point has been emphasized by several authors observing the Hayek tradition in analysing institutions, and matches with the distributed cognition view: Institutions can only economize on cognitive load if actors do not know the entire mechanism and the rationale of the institutions. But that means that there is no common knowledge, but only a partial one. This is an essential idea at the centre of Aoki's (2001, 2007, 2011) approach to institutions, that I will adapt to my evolutionary analysis: Institutions have an 'information compression function', which implies that there are no shared mental models (contrary to Denzau and North 1994) and whatever component of common knowledge as a necessary condition for the functioning of the institution.

These considerations imply that institutions need to refer back to the general framework of network analysis as deployed in Chapter Five, especially with regard to the interactions across levels related to group size. For example, social norms may originally emerge in small group settings and may continue to rely on small group mechanisms in enforcement; yet, via effects of actors' identities and corresponding semiotic mechanisms they can diffuse on the large group level, such that social norms, for instance, of large ethnic groups become constitutive of their identities. These norms may finally transform into formal institutions, for example, in the context of religion. Yet, this transformation does not imply that they only rely on formal mechanisms of enforcement and stabilization. Here, the consistency effect comes into play, as the formal institutions and the social norms mutually support each other on different levels of small groups and large groups.

Now, these considerations, based on the literature, reveal a certain bias towards the effects of institutions on behaviour and behavioural coordination, which is typically at the centre of attention in game theoretic approaches. This implies a serious neglect of the material dimension of institutions. In economics, this mostly comes into play when discussing the effects of institutions of economic performance. But this perspective only means that behavioural coordination has material effects; it does not touch upon the materiality of institutions. The inclusion of materiality into institutional analysis directly follows from the bimodal approach to networks deployed in Chapter Five: If all networks involve the role of material signs in an essential way, the same applies for higher–level institutions. All institutions build on material mechanisms involving semiosis. Mechanisms, however, are tantamount to technologies, if we intuitively refer this term to the rule-based handling of artefacts. Then, the standard economic approach to institutions and economic performance can be put into a fresh theoretical context.

6.1.4. Institutions and technology

Even a brief glance at the course of human history would suggest the idea that there was progress in terms of the propagation of institutions that increased human welfare, economic performance, life expectation, population growth or any other of the many indicators that have been designed to measure the advancement of human societies, and which are certainly expressions of the materiality of human life. This observation leads us to consider the relationship between institutions and technology, because as a matter of fact, the force driving those improvements was human technology. That means, if we want to assess institutions in terms of a performance measure, we cannot only focus on the effects of institutions on interactions in networks, but have to consider the simultaneous impact on technology. In the combination of the two, we can develop the notion of the 'productivity' of institutions, which is not the same as the 'efficiency' of institutions. We have already developed a general concept of productivity of networks, which combined the concepts of network throughput with the information structure of a network (Chapter Five, section 5.2.2). Since we can approach institutions just as a special kind of network structure, this idea directly applies in the context of institutions. Then, we refer institutions to both aspects of this ascendency measure: On the one hand, institutions impose a certain structure on the information flows in a network; on the other hand, they enable certain flows of resources through networks.

This two-sidedness of institutions is reflected in the fact that the transition from networks to institutions runs parallel to the transition from networks to technology. In a most simple way, we can conceive of this relation as in figure 6.2.

Figure 6.2 Networks, institutions and technology

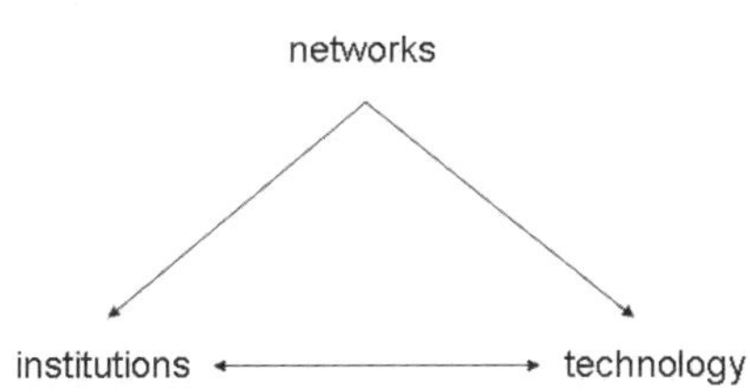

Note: Both institutions and technology emerge from networks, focusing on different aspects of their bimodal nature. Technology refers to the regularities in handling material artefacts, institutions refers to the regularities in interactions. However, technology and institutions are closely enmeshed in mutually determining their bimodal correspondents. That means, technologies are institutions as regularities in handling artefacts are also regularities in interactions, that is of communities of users of technologies; and institutions are technologies in involving the handling of artefacts, such as the material signs that accompany interactions, or enforcement technologies.

This simple diagram makes an essential point: Both institutions and technology emerge from networks, and institutions and technology mutually determine each other. This easily follows from my definition of networks, which includes artefacts. Then, technology is that aspect of human networks which focuses on the manipulation of artefacts, and, in a most general way, the matterenergy flows through networks. Institutions focus on the information flows in networks, viewed from the semiotic perspective. This was already made clear in the fundamental ontological analysis, where we locate technology in the observer relative and matterenergy mode, and institutions in the observer relative semiotic mode (see Chapter One, section 1.4.2.). However, institutions and technology are closely interacting phenomena, as technology is always embedded in institutionalized human action, and as institutions rely on technological means of communication and enforcement. In an even more general view, technologies are institutions, and institutions are technologies, just with different domains.

In this perspective, we can surmise the hypothesis that institutional evolution reflects the general principles of evolution that we have already referred to network evolution in general. This highlights the role of the Maximum Power Principle. So, I conceive of the productivity of institutions in terms of their contribution to the evolutionary trend towards the maximization of energetic throughputs. As I will discuss in detail in Chapter Seven, there are crucial stages in institutional evolution as highlighted in the next sections, which clearly followed this logic. In particular, the transition to agriculture and the subsequent formation of agricultural empires with the concomitant growth of institutions certainly increased the energetic throughputs of human societies, but did not realize efficiency in the sense of optimizing the relationship between energetic inputs (human labour) and outputs (for an overview of the quantitative evaluation, Smil 2008: 148). In a similar vein, the comprehensive changes of agricultural institutions during the industrial revolution certainly contributed to the growth of industrial output by the massive mobilization of fossil energy resources, but did not increase agricultural efficiency (Fenoaltea 1990; Allen 2009: 57ff). I will discuss these observations in more detail in Chapter Eight.

In the context of this chapter, there is one direct connection between technology and institutions that I will explore in detail in section 6.6.; this is that all institutions rely on enforcement technologies. This is one essential link between institutions and the physical aspects of evolution. That means, one essential criterion is the collective capability to harness and utilize energy resources, of which a part can be used in the context of enforcement. For practical matters, this refers to the use of energy in the context of the application of violence, that is leveraging the human capacity to violent action, which is the ultimate enforcement device. Then, we can submit a general hypothesis about institutional evolution, namely that it enables the more extensive and intensive use of energy resources, which feeds back to institutional evolution in terms of leveraging the capacity for violent action and hence rule enforcement. In plain words, I argue that the evolution of institutions is directly affected by the evolution of weapons technology, including the institutional patterns of its use.

However, this role of technologies of violence only comes to the fore under specific historical circumstances, such as civil wars of foreign invasions. Under normal circumstances, it is implied in the omnipresent threat of applying violence in general structures of social power, as theorized by influential writers such as Foucault. In this case means of violence need to be actively used in maintaining certain institutions: They mainly operate as signs that are part of a larger semiotic system which undergirds the operations of institutions. This is the most general aspect of the materiality of institutions that I will explore in the next section that transcends the more narrow aspects of enforcement: All institutions involve material expressions that impact on the behaviour of actors. For example, religious institutions often involve huge resource investments into religious buildings. This observation highlights the fact that all institutions involve signs (police uniforms, judges' robes, king's sceptres and so forth) in their behavioural practice. I will now argue that this role of signs is essential for analysing institutions and is constitutive of their materiality.

6.2. INSTITUTIONAL SEMIOSIS: EMERGENCE OF INSTITUTIONS FROM NETWORKS

6.2.1. The substantive view on institutions

In elaborating the semiotic aspects of institutions, namely institutional semiosis, I start out from one seminal analysis of institutions in the literature, which paves the way from the purely mentalist approach of standard game theory to a so-called 'substantive' view, which is most clearly developed by Searle (1995) who treats institutions as 'facts' in the real world. This is Aoki (2001) who defines institutions as summary representations of equilibrium paths in games. This role of a summary representation explains the durability and robustness of institutions in the sense that they are partly independent from environmental variations and changes in the actors. In game–theoretic terms, this argument requires that there is a mapping between the complete strategy space of the actors and a partition of this set into subsets, where one of which reproduces the equilibrium strategies of the larger set. The mapping between the larger set and this subset summarizes the information contained in the game for the actors, as they no longer need to consider the entire set of feasible strategies. The question is how this mapping can be stable. This requires that the mapping is related to a set of possible environments in a way that the variety of the environments does not change the mapping. This can be defined across a certain range of variations, such that the mapping breaks down if variations cross the fringes of the range. Finally, an essential determinant of the stability is the convergence of the mapping across all actors, which is not the same as common knowledge, because the mapping itself is not the object of the knowledge of the actors (otherwise, the information compression would not bring any advantage, because actors would need to know also the entire strategy set).

In more recent elaborations, Aoki (2011) has condensed his approach in figure 6.3, which I will take as a point of departure for later modifications. The essential point is that an 'institution' is the entire causal circuit involving the public representations as the key mechanism. In this view, the cognitive functions of the institutions result from the channelling of beliefs of actors that are caused by the public presentations. These channelling effects predetermine equilibrium selection in strategic interactions, of which one outcome is the generation of public representations. This is the pivotal point in which the semiotic perspective comes into play: The cognitive function of institutions results from the fact that all institutions involve signs, and that actors essentially rely on those signs in determining their behaviour. The sign is public and hence common knowledge: However, this does not imply that the meaning of the sign is public, as it is defined by the entire information that is implied by a certain institution. We use money, even though few of us understand central banks and the institution of money. That is, the public nature of the sign does not rest upon the common knowledge of the meaning, but the materiality of its use.

It is important to see that there is a fundamental distinction between a 'rule' and a regularity in network interactions: Regularities emerge with only partial common knowledge in networks; rules, in my definition would require full knowledge of the rule, and, in social coordination problems, shared common knowledge about the rule and that it is obeyed by everybody. The latter assumption typically inheres all social contract theories in which institutions are modelled at least 'as if' everyone had agreed on this role. The evolutionary view fundamentally differs in arguing that institutions evolve even without anybody overlooking the entire mechanisms of emergence, hence full knowledge of the institution, and still stabilize in recurrent social interaction. Hence, this approach comes close to Hayek's (1973) theory of institutions.

Technically, this analysis connects to recent efforts in Evolutionary Game Theory in analyzing signalling games, which are aptly overviewed and summarized by Skyrms (2010). They go back to an initial effort by Lewis (1969) who tried to explain the emergence of equilibria in pure coordination games. Then, the players can achieve a Pareto superior state if they successfully coordinate actions by means of sending signals, both receiving a positive pay off when the signal triggers the right action, and zero in all other cases. In this case, the signals are devoid of any meaning, so are purely conventional, and they are maintained in equilibrium.

Figure 6.3 Public representations and institutions (Aoki 2011)

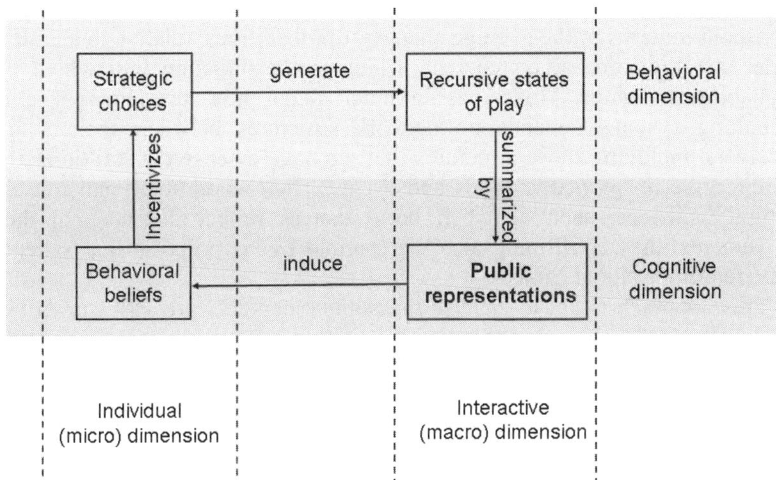

Note: The Aoki model of substantive institutions distinguishes between two dimensions of institutional analysis, the behavioural vs. the cognitive dimension, and the individual vs. the interactive dimension. In the behavioural dimension, micro and macro relate via the population–level interactions of individual strategic choices, mainly accessible to game–theoretic analysis. The resulting equilibria include the emergence of signals, which are public representations of certain equilibrium states of the interactions. These public representations 'summarize' the states in terms of compressing pertinent information. Therefore, they adopt a cognitive function, which is on the macro level in the first place, as the public representations are population level uses of signs. They induce certain beliefs of actors which are cognitive phenomena on the individual level. These beliefs incentivize choices which result in actions. Thus, an institution is the entire feedback circuit that is described in the two dimensions.

The more recent work in evolutionary game theory relates this structure with evolutionary analysis, that is, a replicator dynamics (see Chapter Three, section 3.2.2.). This refers to populations of senders and receivers which share a common interest in achieving joint positive pay–offs, that is moving to a Pareto superior state. This 'interest,' however, is not a mental state but reflects the directedness of the underlying VSR process. If payoffs are interpreted as fitness values, those pairs of senders and receivers who send matching signals and therefore reach the preferred state, will reproduce stronger than others. Thus, a signalling system emerges on the population level which can be also evolutionary stable, depending on parameters and game form. This signalling system does not relate to any speaker's intention to convey a meaning. What counts is information content, in the sense of environmental information (Floridi 2003). That is, the signalling game creates information in changing the probabilities of states and related actions. Skyrms proposes to distinguish between the quantity of information, measured in terms of the average change of probabilities, relative to an initial state, and the information content, which is the direction into which the probabilities change. He shows in much detail how this emergence of signalling systems depends on network structures between senders and receivers, including those structures that we have extensively scrutinized in ChapterFive, in particular triads and cycles. There is an additional role for natural saliences, such as when bees' dances reflect distances in their movements, thus confirming also the original Lewis proposal that salience may determine signal choices.

This approach is apt to analyse the population–level processes in Aoki's model. But it leaves open the precise cognitive mechanism that work at the interface between signs and the brain, as approached in Chapter Four. I argue that this requires enriching the game–theoretic perspective by more specific models of cognition. The question is how and which cognitive functions are involved in maintaining and creating institutions. Here, the semiotic approach matches with Searle's approach to the 'status function.' Searle argues that institutions build on status functions which involve a transfer of meaning, that is treating something as something else, such as treating a piece of metal as money. I will explore this cognitive function in more detail in section 6.3. In particular, I focus on one aspect that is less emphasized in the economics literature but essential in the Searlian view: Institutions are creative in the sense that institutions are infinitively recursive, like human language. And institutions can create other institutions. This recursivity becomes most evident if we apply the standard semiotic framework on institutions.

6.2.2. Institutional semiosis

In order to apply the semiotic analysis, we need to consider two different levels of analysis because we can analyse behaviour from two different viewpoints, as far as institutions are concerned. The first is the level of the individual actor whose actions manifest certain regularities. As I have already posited initially, this viewpoint would not grasp the important additional aspect that the behaviour is also followed by other actors in a population where following this institution is a fact. So, we also need to take the perspective of the IGBPs, which still refers to individual behaviour, but highlights the fact that, for reasons that we will explore in this section, the behaviour is also shared with others. In figure 6.3, this duality is reflected in the distinction between micro–level and the macro–level, that is the interactive level. The semiotic analysis aims at showing how these two levels actually are synthesized in the unitary fact of an institution.

Figure 6.4 Semiotic duality of institutions

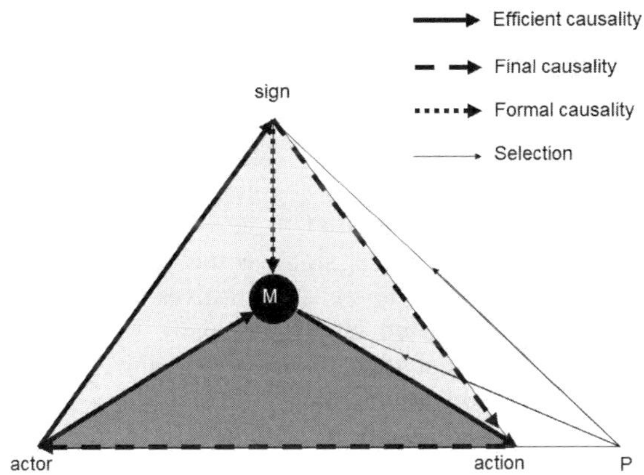

(a)

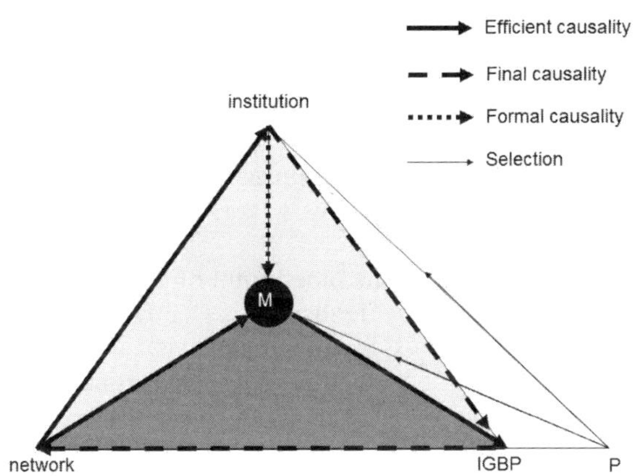

(b)

Note: The semiotic analysis of institutions proceeds on two levels. In figure 6.4a we consider the individual level. Here, actors generate actions via certain mechanisms that are categorized by intermediating signs. In figure 6.4b networks of actors manifest IGBPs that are mediated by institutions that operate as signs. The latter function results from the fact that the IGBP relate to perceived commonalities of actions on the individual level. This relates to certain mechanisms of information diffusion scrutinized in Chapter Five, such as imitation. The linkage between the levels results from the fact that institutions involve the signs that operate on the individual level, in the sense of Aoki's micro/macro relationship. This is shown in figure 6.3.

In a first step, we consider the individual actor (figure 6.4a). The actor generates actions via certain mechanisms; for example, the actor walks along a vegetable market, perceives an apple displayed on a stall and moves to buy one. In this process, we can directly identify certain mechanisms *M* that operate as in stimulus–response models in order to explain the action. However, following the cognitive counter–revolution against early behaviourism, the semiotic analysis highlights the role of signs in eliciting certain actions, which amounts to the cognitive categorization of certain mechanisms along the lines elucidated in Chapter 4.

Now, the question is where the signs come from. Aoki's approach suggests the important idea that the signs themselves are part and parcel of institutions. This idea is translated into figure 6.4b. Here, we look at the population level, hence the networks. Networks manifest mechanisms of interactions (such as buying apples) that result in shared or convergent patterns of actions in a population of actors. Again, these patterns are categorized via the semiotic intermediation that I identify as 'institution'.

In this analysis, we have two points where two diagrams interconnect, though relating to different levels. One is the actions: Actions in 6.4a are strictly individual; actions in 6.4b relate to these, but only in terms of their shared characteristics on the population level. This is the central idea behind the notion of IGBP, and it is ultimately based on the analysis of collective intentionality that I presented in the previous chapters: IGBP are individual actions in the We–mode, and therefore we can approach them analytically as population–level facts, in case we can show that there is a material complement. These are Aoki's 'public representations', which I equate with 'signs' in the context of semiotic analysis. It is essential to recognize that perceived IGBP are signs in turn.

Signs and institutions make up the other point of contact between the two levels. In this case, however, we realize an essential fact of ontological identity which will guide the subsequent analysis. This is that on the individual level, the institution becomes causally relevant because it is a sign; that means, for example, the actor's behaviour towards the police is caused by the material signs of police. On the population level, these signs are part and parcel of the institution as a population–level sign, referring to regularities of sign use. In terms of materiality, this involves the observable regularities of behaviour as being reflected in media which are involved in cognitive processing. For example, actors in a population observe similar behaviours of other actors towards police; the behavioural patterns themselves are translated into signs that are processed cognitively, resulting in fundamental network processes of information diffusion such as imitation. This is the point where the ambiguity in the literature about the nature of institutions comes into play, namely whether they are rules followed by actors or regularities that are observed by an external observer. In the semiotic view, these are just two aspects of the same fundamental process.

Figure 6.5 Unity of institutional semiosis

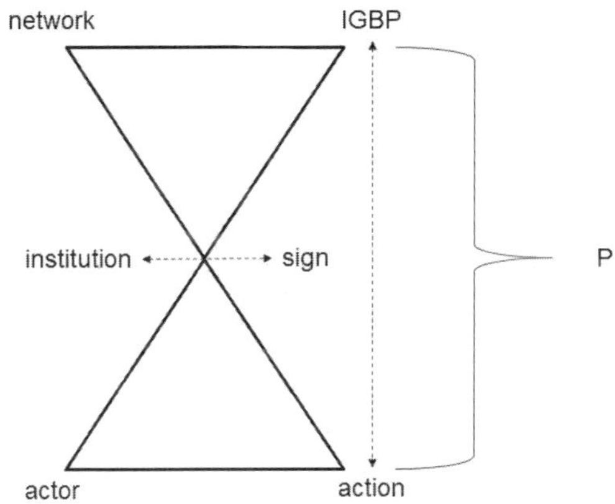

Note: Semiotic analysis allows making the mechanisms explicit that underlie the micro/macro relationship in the Aoki model of institutions. The mapping between individual actions and IGBPs happens via the intermediation of signs which are part and parcel of the institution. Individual action is impossible merely relying on internal mental states but necessarily involves signs which emerge from institutional evolution. At the same time, population level signs channel population level interactions into IGBP.

This is depicted in figure 6.5 which highlights the essential point in simplified form, namely that the mapping between actions and IGBP on the two levels of the individual and the population, the micro and the macro in Aoki's approach, occurs because of the ontological unity of the dual aspects of institution and sign. This dual nature stands at the centre of the analysis of institutions in this chapter. It is the manifestation of the fundamental principle of bimodality: One cannot explain the population–level regularities of behaviour without taking material signs into explicit consideration, that is by referring only to mental states of actors. Mental states of actors cannot result in action, unless mediated via signs; the signs are material complements to network processes on the population level. There cannot be police without the material signs of police, such as uniforms, weapons or seals. This role of signs is pivotal because it is the signs, and not the mental states, that are population–level phenomena. The same signs can trigger different individual beliefs and dispositions; what is essential is whether the interactions between the resulting choices end up in equilibria which reproduce the signs. Thus, for example, the material symbols of male dominance may relate with very different ideas and perceptions on part of the different genders, but they result into gendered behaviours that reproduce those symbols and hence, male dominance.

The semiotic analysis also allows for a deeper understanding of the information functions of institutions which is emphasized in most of the economic literature. Institutions carry information because the signs of institutions enable inferential processes. For example, if an actor perceives the sign of a policeman, she is able to infer behavioural expectations about the actors' actions. Now, as I have emphasized in the previous section, cognitive mechanisms play an important role in the emergence and stabilization of institutions. Therefore, I will now analyse different forms of inference that underlie the functioning of institutions. Again, the inferential processes happen on the two levels, which immediately qualifies them as manifestations of distributed cognition. Actors infer behavioural expectations via signs; collectives of networked actors infer collective behavioural expectations via institutions; both levels connect via the material entities of semiosis, the signs.

6.2.3. Induction and the primordial emergence of institutions

There are different kinds of cognitive processes that give rise to the function of institutions in categorizations with higher levels of abstraction. We cannot take this higher level of abstraction for granted, but need to show how this emerges from the primordial network processes. In order to achieve that I will use a simple workhorse with an economic background, namely a vegetable market in a setting where actors do not know each other well (this approach is similar to Fafchamps 2005, who, however, does not focus on the issue of institutionalization).

This market is just a physical place where some agents decided to set up vegetable stalls, and others appear on the scene as buyers. The different agents are not familiar with each other. People roam the place, considering where to buy. They face a fundamental quality dilemma, as they can only partly assess the quality of vegetables and fruits based on their outside appearance. Thus, the entire situation represents the Lemon's problem as analysed in Chapter Five. Let us assume that buyers have some previous experience with other vegetable trading places, so they start with a certain assumption about the probability distributions for different qualities, hence operating on the basis of assumptions about average quality. As we know, this situation easily leads to the unravelling of the underlying network configurations. As we saw, the reason for the Lemon's problem lies in a particular structure of categorizations in large groups.

I now consider the role of information externalities in networks of actors, thus showing how different patterns of abstraction can emerge. Let us assume that with others still roaming and observing, one buyer *B* decides to buy with one seller *A* based on purely idiosyncratic reasons. Let us further assume that the buyer checks quality, feels satisfied and that others observe this. Another potential buyer decides to follow up. This causal chain is depicted as the most inner feedback circle in fig. 6.6. The decision of the second agent *B* creates a positive information externality for the third agent *C*, who therefore decides to transact with *A* as well. *A* realizes this, but has no specific idea why another trade happens. There is now the possibility that *A* develops a commitment to future transactions with the same people, which corresponds to the simple game–theoretic analysis of repeated games. Agents develop mutual expectations, mainly based on reputation and trust, which create commitments. So, this stage refers to the emergence of small groups in networks in which mutual trust is bound to the individual identities of the agents, and emerges under the 'shadow of the future' (Dixit 2004: 57ff).

Figure 6.6 Emergence of institutions from network interactions

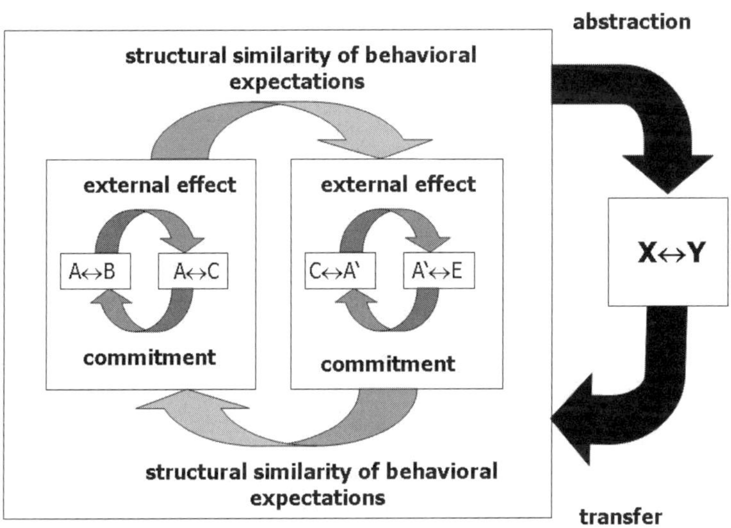

Note: Letters denote different actors or classes of actors. This diagram overviews the different cognitive mechanisms and types of interactions that drive the evolution of institutions in terms of the three types of conventions, social norms and formal institutions. Conventions or habits evolve originally via information externalities in small groups which also create commitment mechanisms such as reputation in on-going interactions. This is based on induction as a cognitive mechanism of inference. Social norms emerge from a higher level of abstraction which involves the perception of similarities of roles in different small group settings, resulting in structural similarity of behavioural expectations. This is based on analogy as an inference mechanism. Finally, the highest level of abstraction is achieved when those expectations lose their domain specificity, hence are transferred across domains of interactions (such as across different specific kinds of markets, resulting into a generic conception of markets). The pertinent cognitive mechanism is deduction. For more detail, see main text.

In this case, we observe an emerging regularity, such as that *B* will always trade with *A*. This regularity is certainly known by the agents themselves, hence is rule based. For example, the buyer might follow a rule, I always buy with seller *A*, or another rule, I always buy from sellers with a moustache, and this is the only one, or whatever sort of rule. The underlying regularity is more complex, if we look at it in more detail. On the surface, it is just the repetition of the transaction. But this also involves, for example, regularities of seller's behaviour, such as always offering a similar quality of vegetable, or maintaining the established signalling devices, such as not shaving the moustache. That means, the rule that is followed by the buyer does by no means reflect the entire regularities that actually underlie the repetition of the transaction through time. So, we have to distinguish between different kinds of phenomena. The first is the regularity, relative to the external observer. The second is the rule followed by the actors, who also know that they follow. In the simplest case, the rule directly states the regularity: '*B* always buys with *A'* also means that *B* states 'I always buy with *A*.' However, this rule following might, in turn, build on other regularities which are not known by *B*, but could be reconstructed by the external observer.

Now, an essential point for the further discussion is that this process is supported by the general cognitive mechanism of induction. Induction underlies the formation of mutual expectations based on previous experiences. *A*'s behaviour can only trigger information with regard to himself, and thereby create a group of buyers who share a behavioural pattern. This is a habit. It is essential to recognize that this first step in the emergence of an institution is non-Bayesian, because it is only based on individual perceptions of salience, such as idiosyncratic decisions to choose on seller (for example because the buyer reacts on the salience of the moustache).

I use a terminology that synthesizes the cognitive aspects with the philosophical dimension (surveyed by Vickers, 2012). The philosophical debate over induction gives many hints for the analysis of institutions. In the philosophical treatment, the topic of induction is dominated by 'Hume's problem'. Hume had stated that it is impossible to arrive at any kind of generalization by means of extrapolating past experiences, in the sense of establishing causal laws. Hume's scepticism has engendered a long and complex debate, which most recently converged with the literature on Evolutionary Epistemology. The reason is that in a certain sense, the VSR mechanism can be interpreted as an inductive process. In our context, the conclusion from the philosophical debate is crucial that induction is a 'singular predictive inference'. That means induction has the form:

1. $a_1, a_2, a_3, \ldots$.are all *F*s that are also *G*

2. a_{n+1} is also *F*. Therefore,

3. a_{n+1} is also G.

This formulation of induction does not fall under the scope of Popper's (1935) criticism of induction, because it does not state a universal law which would then build the basis of the conclusion. At the same time, the role of language is immediately evident, because induction is based on a proposition in which certain entities are assigned to certain classes which are denoted by the predicates, that is the properties.

Sugden (2011) presents a philosophical account of inductive reasoning that starts out from a pragmatist interpretation of the notion of 'salience', which is especially important for explaining the emergence of conventions, for example in coordination games. For instance, let us assume that there is only one seller with a moustache on the trading place, which appears to be a rare event to the buyer, hence as salient. This is a non-Bayesian inference based on priors about probabilities. In a convention, if such behaviour is generated, this triggers symmetry–breaking, such that eventually one single pattern of behaviour emerges (for a related discussion, see Skyrms 1996).

We can relate this with Schlicht's (1998) *Gestalt* theoretic approach to institutions, shared with Kubon-Gilke (1997). *Gestalt* theory posits that the brain generates regularities from sensory inputs, based on certain fundamental rules or cognitive laws, which all relate to the principle of *Prägnanz* (translated by Schlicht as 'clarity', by other authors as 'conciseness'). *Prägnanz* means that there are different mechanisms by which the brain completes incomplete sensory inputs to coherent and meaningful wholes. In particular, cognition tends to build collectives from single observations. For example, the 'Law of Proximity' implies that individuals tend to see things that are spatially close as totalities, or the 'Law of Continuity' implies that cognition tends to extrapolate movements etc. These *Gestalt* laws can also help to explain singular inductive inference, as the famous Goodman paradox shows. Goodman had argued that induction might support any kind of conclusion just by mixing up different properties which have different time indices. So, the statements 'emerald A is green', 'emerald B is green', and so forth, might not only inductively support the statement, 'all emeralds are green', but also, 'all emeralds are grue', which includes the case that the next emerald turns out to be blue. From the *Gestalt* theoretic viewpoint, this construction violates the Laws of *Prägnanz*, as 'grue' is just a haphazard combination of properties, and classes of colours are normally not divided according to time criteria. This corresponds to Sugden's (2011) analysis of the same Goodman example; hence *Prägnanz* is another way to refer to 'salience'.

So, in summary we can state that there are systematic cognitive mechanisms that nonetheless operate in a fundamentally random, which means singular, fashion in triggering the first emergence of regularities in interactions. Once a pattern emerges, we can say that particularistic norms of interaction are established, such as the habit of certain buyer always to buy from a particular seller. Both sides are aware of this, and there are subsequent mechanisms well-known from game theory that explain the sustainability of the habit in recurrent interactions: Actually, the famous 'folk theorem' in game theory states that any kind of interaction with positive gains for both sides can be maintained in sufficiently long interaction chains (Binmore 1994: 115ff). This highlights the essential role of non-Bayesian inductive mechanisms that can start and also maintain such interaction chains.

6.2.4. Metaphors and hypercyclic abstraction of regularities

Another cognitive mechanism is invoked when we consider the next possibility, which is that other sellers observe what is going on. For example, they might chat with *A*'s buyers to learn about their motivation. They would start to copy some features of *A*'s behaviour which they think that underlie the loyalty of his customers. If their presumptions turn out to strike the right chord with the potential customers, they might create their own group of followers, and, in particular, they might induce some *A* buyers to buy also with them. This is indicated in figure 6.6 with buyer *C* turning to seller *A′* as well. Once this situation occurs, in the innermost box the familiar mechanism of information externalities is triggered again, inducing other observing buyers *E* to buy with *A′*, thus creating new chains of habits, which lead toward an in increasing structuration of the population into small groups of customers with habitual buying patterns centred around certain sellers. In this process, the mechanisms that attract new customers and establish the role of new sellers and the actual procedures that guarantee a certain quality and hence the ultimate success of different transactions are by no means convergent. That is, a seller might adopt his own business practices in handling the vegetables and dealing with their suppliers, but might converge with others in the signals that she sends to the customers.

The important point about this stage in the evolution of the vegetable market is that another cognitive mechanism beyond induction is involved. For diverse reasons, buyers start to perceive different sellers *A* and *A′* to be similar in terms of the role they play as sellers. That is, structural similarity of behavioural expectations emerges over a larger set of actors. This is the cognitive mechanism of analogy, which differs from induction in one essential way, namely that the expectations are not based on past experiences about *A′*, but on the similarity between *A* and *A′*. This introduces a theoretical notion into the formation of expectations similar to concept formation: There is an emerging concept of a 'seller of vegetables' which goes hand in hand with certain ideas about reliability, trustworthiness, quality performances etc.

I treat this cognitive process as creating analogies, based on metaphorical relations between concepts. Most words that we use originate from metaphorical uses, and precisely the creativity and universal applicability of language resides in the possibility of transfers of meanings via metaphors.

Therefore, in a radical reassessment of established cognitive science approaches, Fauconnier and Turner (2002, 2008) argue that metaphor is the foundational cognitive function. As we shall see below, this applies for institutions in a general sense.

The philosophical debate over metaphors has produced competing approaches, which are insightful for our problem of institutional emergence (for a summary, see Lycan 1999: Chapter 14). The main problem is that metaphors build on similarities, which raises the question how these similarities are recognized, thus a problem very close to the problem discussed so far. If I say, 'This book is a gem', I do not really mean that it is a gem, literally. But I also do not mean that the book shines like a gem, or that it is as hard as a diamond, or whatever. So, just stating that there is a similarity between the book and the gem does not help to clarify the way the metaphor works. So, there must be a cognitive filter that determines which similarities count. One solution proposed by John Searle (whose theories we will follow closely) is to see metaphors in a pragmatic context. That means, especially, that the speaker and the hearer at least implicitly agree on Gricean standards of communication, that is, they agree that they wish to convey a meaningful message, and so forth. If this is true, even an entirely new metaphor used by the speaker can be understood by the hearer, if the two implicitly understand the context, or, in a more economic parlance, if they operate within the same frame. So, if we talk about the quality of a book, and the hearer expects me to give an honest assessment of its quality, she will be immediately able to trace the reference of the metaphor, based on some common understanding of the meaning. That is, the metaphors depend on the pragmatic setting of the communication. Searle argues that this functioning of metaphors is nothing special at all, because there is often a difference between the lexical meaning of words and the speaker meaning. That is, the meaning of 'gem' can differ from the information actually transferred in an utterance that involves the word 'gem'. This approach comes close to the so-called 'relevance theory' (Sperber and Wilson 2008), which views metaphors as a regular case of inferential communication, in which receivers infer the meaning of messages sent by speakers in taking the context into consideration. They emphasize that this semantic incompleteness is the hallmark of human language in general, and that this enables its generative powers.

This argument raises an intricate problem in our analysis of the vegetable market that we have conducted so far. If I argue that the emergence of the role of a seller happens via analogy, which is based on metaphors, the relevance of the similarities that are established among different sellers is determined via the frame in which all agents operate. From this we see immediately that the Gricean approach favoured by Searle might fail in our context because it cannot be taken for granted that the frame converges, and that even the most fundamental Gricean norms apply, in particular the norms of sincerity. After all, the original problem is that of cheating. This implies that only a co-evolutionary approach can explain the emergence of meanings, because this operates via the functionings. This also helps to clarify the argument on metaphors, which would always refer to some historical sequence of uses of symbols in certain contexts, which links up with the sequence of successful transactions. That means, there is no need to fully converge with the frame, but there is an evolutionary sequence of utterances and communications which are perceived as successful. This shows how the levels of abstraction actually build on one another, because the sequence of successful utterances is processed on the cognitive level via induction.

I argue that only in this stage can we speak about a network configuration in the abstract sense, because a particular configuration (the inner boxes) is replicated across a larger number of actors in a population, without necessarily involving the same actors. The configuration also unifies a certain set of habits: What is originally an individual habit diffuses among a population of actors as a collective habit. The convergence of roles of sellers marks the transition to institutionalization, because there is an emerging similarity of transactions across the population and through time. However, we cannot say that the configuration itself is the generating force of the repeated patterns. The generating forces are different sets of expectations that might be based on diverse perceptions of what makes up a reliable seller. That is, there is no necessary convergence of criteria for reliable sellers in the entire population, and no explicit reflection about that.

Yet, it is essential to realize that this emergent configuration shows the features of a hypercycle in networks. First, there is an important role of positive externalities that feed back onto previous buyers who would also observe the behaviour of other buyers, so would receive further confirmation about their expectations. Second, the emergence of sellers' roles implies that this causal connectivity is replicated across different actors such that they obtain the role of seeds that trigger the formation of further chains of information externalities. For example, a minimal cycle would be closed if buyer *E* also buys with seller *A*, without being aware that her decision to buy was originally triggered by an information externality caused by *A* and the transaction with *B*. So, finally the diffusion of the habit amounts to the establishment of a hypercyclic network configuration in the market in which information externalities come to full closure thus is supporting an on-going and successful trade activity through time.

6.2.5. Emergence of abstract rules as institutions

The transition to a full-scale institution occurs when actors start to form an abstract conceptual image of the configurations that are prevailing in the population. This may become evident in two kinds of phenomena. One is that actors who migrate across different places of vegetable trade transfer their expectations across those places and therefore trigger the emergence of similar configurations. The other is that those patterns can also be transferred on other markets, such as a textile market. Both processes are undergirded by communication about what constitutes a configuration in transactions that creates a context in which mutual expectations of buyers and sellers are confirmed. This case differs in terms of the cognitive mechanisms from the other mechanisms that we have scrutinized so far. We have reached a stage in which the abstraction over configurations entails the emergence of conceptual structures that allow for the deduction of certain properties of configurations under entirely new circumstances. Then, a conceptual structure would allow the inference that, if a certain configuration meets the criteria in the definition of a concept, certain expectations will be warranted.

Deduction implies the emergence of the concept of a vegetable market in terms of an institution. The institution of the 'vegetable market' will include certain details about the roles of sellers and buyers and certain transactional practices. These details can vary, but are also the object of explicit communication among actors, such that deviant phenomena are conversed about. Hence, the institution is deeply embedded into language, and it is language that enables the infinite creativity that inheres in the institutional process, which means that the institution can be applied over an infinite number of vegetable trading places, and even over trading places for other goods. Evidently, this mechanism of diffusion allows for the propagation of an institution across large groups of actors, even in different domains. This highlights the fact that the different cognitive mechanisms also manifest affinities with different levels of networks: Induction is mainly triggered in small groups, analogies establish connections across small groups (such as tribes) and deduction is affine to large groups. However, this is not meant to be an exclusive assignment. In particular, considering the different mechanisms of emergence, enforcement and stabilization, we can say that, for example, even though formal institutions come into existence based on deductive cognitive mechanisms, their actual operations are undergirded by inductive principles of actors' interactions under a formal institution.

To summarize, we have three steps in the emergence of institutions that reflect three different kinds of cognitive mechanisms. The first is the emergence of habits in small groups, which is based on induction. The second is the generalization of habits in interconnected small groups, which we might now identify as 'custom', and which is based on analogy. The third, in which fully-fledged formal institutions emerge, is the state in which explicit linguistic codes refer to configurations and enable the transfer of patterns across entirely novel contexts, relying on the cognitive mechanism of deduction. It is important to emphasize that the third step does not imply conscious handling of deductions, but refers to all cognitive mechanisms that involve hypotheses and predictions, which is a general approach in Evolutionary Epistemology. A hypothesis can be embodied, that is, be non-referential knowledge that does not involve conscious testing. This corresponds to the general distinction between induction and deduction. A fully-fledged institution generates behavioural predictions in the sense of anticipatory action that is not necessarily based on past reinforcement by induction, for the case of the individual actor who is acting. Against the background of the previous discussion of the relationship between kinds of institutions and mechanisms, we can relate the distinct role of cognitive mechanisms with three fundamental kinds of institutions. The inductively emergent and sustained interactions are conventions, of which habits are a particular kind. The analogically extended regularities are social norms, hence customs. The deductively propagated regularities are formal institutions.

The three different cognitive mechanisms also relate with different mechanisms of learning, which can be unified in a general evolutionary model of learning. In this context, induction comes close to different forms of reinforcement learning, whereas deduction relates to concept formation and hypothesis testing. Both follow a general model of variation, selection and retention. However, what is special, but also common to all the three mechanisms, is that the emergence of institutions goes hand in hand with the emergence of signs. This is because the perception of regularities implies the involvement of a cognitive mode which classifies phenomena according to certain criteria (such as the general features of a trustworthy seller). Hence, the behavioural response to an institution is semiotically intermediated. One essential difference between the three cognitive mechanisms is the increasing degree of separateness of the signs from the actors. In the inductive type, the signs are physically unified with the actors, such as the markers that identify the seller with whom the buyer usually transacts. In case of analogy, in spite of the fact that such markers are still unified with the actors, the metaphor itself is independent from the actors. In the case of deduction, the sign becomes fully independent from the actors, such as when a certain blueprint for market organization is created that can be used in different context. So, we can almost use the term 'abstraction' in a literal sense: signs become increasingly 'abstracted' from certain carriers of signs, and their independence allows for new forms of distributed cognition, such as the transfer of institutions via deduction.

6.3. INSTITUTIONS AND COGNITION

6.3.1. Institutions and language

In this section, I explore the role of signs in more detail; then, we have to analyse the relationship between institutions and language. My exposition follows the approach proposed by John Searle, but adds an important component, which is the theory of 'performativity'. I also depart from Searle's approach in taking an explicitly externalist view on meaning. This component is in turn related to a much more explicit treatment of the cognitive aspects of the institutional process, and thus directly relates to

Chapter Four. I will argue that sellers and buyers on a vegetable market which is institutionalized *perform* this institution, so that markets are actually performances. Signs are material means that enable those performances.

In this approach to institutions, the Searlian 'status function' obtains a central role. Status functions have the form: <*X* counts as *Y* in *C*>. *C* refers to a particular context, such as the vegetable trade. *X* is a certain object of any kind, including actors. *Y* denotes a particular item which establishes a new kind of functioning for *X*. So, for example, a piece of metal may count as 'money' in the context of trade, or a person might count as 'king' in the context of a certain body politic. If I refer to a functioning here, I directly connect the linguistic and the semiotic analysis. That is, the central point of the status function is the transfer of a particular meaning in the sense that an *X* as *Y* relates with a different set of functions in terms of network interactions. For example, if one treats a piece of paper with my picture as my identity card, this allows for certain actions that would not be possible without that transfer.

The status function minimally describes a metaphorical act on the cognitive level, because something is treated as something else, thereby creating a new function. But it is essential to recognize that this act is only possible because the status function refers to population level phenomena. This is because the metaphor is only valid in the context of a shared use in a population. That is, the metaphor is not only grounded in individual cognitive and ultimately brain mechanisms, but also in collective intentionality as established in Chapter Four. The status function is intended jointly in a population of followers of an institution in the sense that this shared understanding enables the functioning of *X* as *Y* in this population. Status functions involve We–attitudes.

Before I flesh out this picture in more detail, I need to add the other constituents of this Searlian approach to institutions. The most important one is the so-called 'power creation operator'. Again, this refers to a population of rule followers, in the sense of the underlying collective intentionality. It has the form of <We accept that (*A* has power (*A* does *a*))>. Power rests upon a social deontology which defines a set of entitlements and obligations. All institutions involve the assignment of power in the sense of marking a certain set of actions against all others, which might even be excluded from realization. So, the use of money implies a set of entitlements and obligations for the users of money, and it precludes certain actions such as forging money. This notion of power merges the social aspects with the purely causal aspects. Once an institution is recognized in a population, it generates social forces that cause other phenomena, especially changes of state of other actors. If a judge pronounces a sentence, the guilty person is put into jail.

In the current context, the most important aspect of causal power lies in the performative role of status functions. This is especially evident if we consider the difference between regulatory and constitutive rules introduced by Searle. A regulatory rule refers to a set of pre-existing activities, such as a local custom that governs fishing activities. This rule does not create these activities, yet it transforms their causal powers into networks of actors. For example, if an actor catches a big fish, the effect is different comparing to a state where there is no custom on fishing, or where there is a custom that big catches have to be shared in the community. So the causal powers of the action 'catch a fish' is substantially transformed by the custom. However, in the case of constitutive institutions, the creation of an entirely new social fact is possible, hence also the creation of causal powers that do not relate with a pre-existing activity (for a related analysis, see Holm and Nielsen 2007). For example, the creation of a court and the position of a judge may only very dimly connect with certain activities of third party intermediation and create new powers in the position of the judge. Institutions such as 'the legal person' go even beyond that, as there is no relation whatsoever with existing activities. However, this does not mean that there is no relation to what Searle calls 'brute facts'. So, the concept of a legal person still refers to the network of real persons that enact it, there is a long chain of possible physical consequences when deviating from the institution, and so forth (compare Tuomela 2011). Finally, the distance of many modern institutions from 'brute facts' results from the reflexivity of status functions, which can be infinitively recursive, thus building on previous status functions, which themselves do not count as 'brute facts'.

So, the distinction between the two kinds of rules relates back to the analysis of the three cognitive mechanisms in the emergence of institutions and the related role of language. Take the emergence of money, a topic that I will pursue further in later sections. If a certain item is used in triangular exchange, this does not yet imply the emergence of an institution but is a custom in a certain group of actors. In the incipient stage, this does not even qualify as a regulatory rule. If this item turns into a medium of exchange across small groups, and thus becomes a custom in a tribal network configuration, this qualifies as a regulatory rule. However, once the item is transformed into a coin, which implies certain standardized procedures to transform its physical appearance, we observe the emergence of a formal institution. This institution is based on a constitutive rule in the sense that the status of money as money is becoming independent from the underlying physical entity. This process culminates in the creation of fiat money, where the constitutive rule becomes most explicit.

So, constitutive rules are the most comprehensive expression of the creative role of language underlying institutions. Following my earlier adoption of Searle's approach in Chapter One, we can now say that institutions are observer relative facts. They have the status of facts because they have causal power in networks. They are observer relative because they only exist in relation to a certain population of actors who create the status function via collective intentionality. Further, they enable these causal powers because they operate in the semiotic mode.

In this context, it is of utmost importance to rely on all results of Chapter Four. Collective intentionality does not refer to any kind of aggregate set of individual intentionalities, in the sense of, for example, social contract theories where institutions are set up based on mutual consent. Collective intentionality emerges on the level of language, and it is also a foundation of language. Language is an exclusively population–level phenomenon, with Wittgenstein's impossibility theorem applying with full force. That is, even when actors explicitly reason in linguistic terms to express their individual intentionality, this still relies on population–level meanings that are not subject to any principled individual manipulation. In other words, an institution is not definable via the individual intentions that might relate with its existence, but only with the population–level functions that are causally empowered by its existence, formally homologous to the dissolution of meaning into function in the definition of rules of language. Yet, it would be also wrong to state that these functions are the cause for the emergence of the institution. These causes root in the cognitive mechanisms that we have analysed previously. Ultimately, the institutions rest on the population–level semiosis and the ontological separateness of the signs.

6.3.2. Status functions as metaphors

I will now detail the cognitive processes underlying the status function which links the signs with the dispositions. A most general concept that allows for that is the notion of 'conceptual blending' (Fauconnier and Turner 2002, 2008). The theory of conceptual blending can be put on a neurophysiological grounding by means of Lakoff's neuronal theory of metaphor, thus referring back to the analyses of Chapter Four (Lakoff 2008). Blending is a higher level cognitive function that reflects the basic connectionist mechanisms in the brain. Conceptual blends operate on different levels of complexity, but for the current argument it is sufficient to concentrate on the most complex one, so called 'double–scope blending' (Turner 2008). In this case, a conceptual blend happens if there are two different input spaces which are projected into a common frame of reference in a selective way, the generic space, such that a new concept emerges, the blend (see figure 6.7). It is central to see that this process has two different ways how to analyse its causal underpinnings. One is the neuronal level. On that level, conceptual blends correspond to particular patterns of neuronal circuitry, especially involving *Gestalt* effects and other forms of hypercyclic interdependence. On the other hand, the blend is a population–level phenomenon where the meaning of the blend only relates with the functions of the blend. For the empirical analysis of conceptual blends, it is sufficient to analyse the population–level phenomena, which supervene on the neuronal dynamics.

Figure 6.7 Conceptual blending and status function

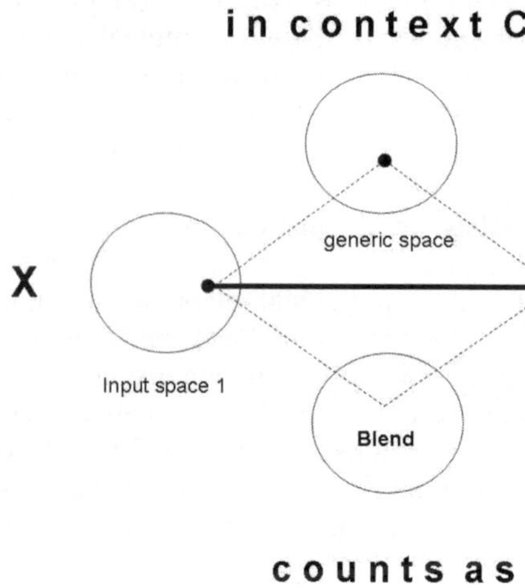

Note: Fauconnier's and Turner's diagram of double–scope blending can be directly related to Searle's status function. In a conceptual blend, two input spaces (such as 'time' and 'space' are projected into a generic space (such as 'motion') to generate a conceptual blend (such as cyclic conceptions of time, for example, the recurrent patterns of a year). This means that something (such as 'time' as a linear sequence of events) is treated 'as if' it were something else (such as a spatial movement) in a certain context (such as general conceptions of motions). The result, the cognitive blend, is the new function (such as being able to measure time in units of cyclical movements).

The structure of double scope blending directly corresponds to the status function, if only in a more specific form. This is because the notion of context boils down to a particular frame of reference that is activated in certain contexts. To give a particular example: Individuals from different countries who play the so-called 'trust game' may look at that interaction from the view of their different cultures (Karlan 2005). The game form of the trust game could be interpreted as an institution, and there is an underlying status function which determines how the pay-offs in that game are perceived. Now, it occurs that the game is interpreted in a different way as intended by the experimenters who conduct this research, namely as a gamble. This triggers entirely different responses to the setting of the game and to the different pay-offs, and may not allow interpretation of the results as indicators of trust.

Figure 6.7 reveals an important insight that is not obvious in the simple formula of the status function. This is that '*X* counts as *Y*' does not mean that *X* is simply substituted by *Y*, but that both *X* and *Y* are projected into the blend partially. That is, the metaphor is something new in relation to both input spaces, so that we can say that is equivalent to the entire status function, but not just the '...as *Y*' predication. This translates into the analysis of institutions in the sense that the signs that emerge from states of play are an essential part of determining those states, such that we cannot regard the states themselves as institutions. The institution transcends the states because it involves the signs, and we have to treat the entire causal chain as an 'institution'. This also constitutes the nature of the institution as a new social fact, which is reflected in new functions that are enabled by the institution.

Let us briefly go back to the example of the vegetable market. The different cognitive mechanisms correspond to different levels of complexity in blending. In the case of the inductive formation of habits, blends play a simple role, because they would just apply for the 'similarity' of different actualizations of the same persons in a chain of transactions. The analogical transfer of roles already involves more complex blends. In this case, there is an input space, the trader *A* and the related network transactions, which are taken as a template for trader *A'*, which, however, does not yet involve a reference to a generic space. This happens on the higher level of abstraction. In this case, for example, we would have an input space, the traders of the vegetable market, and another input domain, the traders on a textiles market. The two concepts are projected onto a generic space, which could be a generalized notion of trustworthiness in social exchange. In doing this, a conceptual blend emerges which is the concept of an 'honest merchant', which would apply across all potential markets, though possibly nowhere exactly. Then, this concept can serve as *Y* in the status function, implying that the notion of the honest merchant has been institutionalized. However, the more detailed view on conceptual blending shows that this is already a second level blend, in which the original emergent structure (in which *X* and *Y* are different kinds of traders) is now used to construct further blends.

To summarize, we can now identify the reason why and how institutions are ontologically creative, which transcends the more restricted meaning that humans are creative in 'inventing' institutions. The performativity of institutions means that human behaviour results into the creation of observer relative facts and thus creates new states of the world. As we have seen, this capacity of human behaviours does not relate or presuppose individual intentional action; yet, collective intentionality is accompanying institutions as facts. Institutions emerge from human action, but do not result from human design, to refer to an important early idea of von Hayek.

This view, however, clearly highlights the fact that we cannot confine the analysis of conceptual blending to the individual–level cognitive processes. Although we could present a neuroscience account of blending along the lines of Lakoff (2008) or Coulson (2008), this does not mean that blending occurs only on that level. Instead, we can say that it is enabled on that level, but proceeds on the population–level, or, that blending supervenes on the neuronal processes. There are many consequences of this fact. One consequence that plays an essential role in many theories about institutional evolution is that institutional change is path–dependent. Path dependence is a special property of the interactions between individuals in driving institutional change. Yet, in the Searlian approach we need to consider not only these interactions, but also the analytically separate dynamics of population–level cognitive processes. Institutional change also manifests the path dependence of distributed cognition. There are different mechanisms that lead towards this interaction across levels which were also shown to be essential for understanding the Aoki model. Especially important is communication which accompanies interactions (Schmidt 2008, 2011; there is an affinity to the 'cultural political economy' project which explicitly refers to semiotics, see Jessop und Oosterlynck 2008). Communication involves sign uses and interpretations of signs, and thus connects individual–level cognitive processes with emergent phenomena on the population–level.

For practical matters, this has recently been elucidated in the resurgence of research into the role of ideas in institutional change (Blyth 2002; Mehta 2011; Zweynert 2011). Ideas are signs and manifest abstraction, which implies they are handled independently from actors. Therefore, the emergence and diffusion of ideas partly follows an independent dynamic from the institutions in the narrow sense that relate with ideas. For example, the institutions of the vegetable market may be enshrined in a market charter which is a sign that can be handled by the actors in different ways, as in disputes. However, the wordings of the charter will depend on the interpretation of certain terms, which relates on connected ideas, such as general conceptions about what a 'fair' deal would look like. These general conceptions connect with other discourses in society, so that the ideas underlying the market charter may evolve partly independently from the market proper, though exerting impact on market practice in the end.

6.3.3. Cognitive path dependence of institutions

As a result of the previous considerations, we can distinguish between two different levels on which path dependence of institutions emerges. One is the level of the interactions between actors, such as the diffusion of a habit in a small group of actors of a vegetable market. The other is the level of the diffusion of cognitive phenomena related to these interactions.

As is well established in the literature, the stabilization of institutions is supported by critical mass effects (henceforth, *A*–type path dependence, following Ackermann 2001) which ground in the role of imitation in groups, thus giving rise to frequency–dependent effects, both locally and globally, depending on the way the institution is perceived. This is the most straightforward way that institutional evolution and cognition connect via the network dimension of perception. This is well known from the analysis of simple institutions, such as an institution that supports cooperative solutions in a prisoner's dilemma. If in a local neighbourhood individuals perceive the prevalence of cooperative behaviour, this can be stabilized and spread in a population globally (Hegselmann 1996). Critical mass effects are crucial in determining the effects of sanctioning, too. In many institutions, if people perceive a low efficacy of sanctioning, conformity breaks down easily. However, *n*–th order sanctions themselves depend on critical mass effects, such that these effects are self–referential, in turn. This is a major reason why institutions are very difficult to reconstitute, once they collapse. Especially, critical mass effects may cause hysteresis in institutional evolution (Schlicht 1998: 50f). This happens if the thresholds differ in two directions, institutional build-up and institutional decay. For example, tax compliance can be relatively high and only breaks down after a considerable number of people are perceived as deviating. However, rebuilding tax compliance can require overcoming a much higher threshold. This is also a major issue in the transfer of institutions via imitation.

These effects ultimately root in the cognitive *Gestalt* effects of institutions (analysed systematically by Schlicht 1998). That is, a critical mass point can also be conceived as a range of behavioural variations, which are reinforced in different directions, depending on the direction of the movement. In the case of tax compliance, if institutional change proceeds from the point of compliance, even imperfect compliance will always be 'complemented' into the institutional pattern of compliance. So, many institutions are seen as being valid and treated as social facts, even though at closer scrutiny there is a large range of variation in a population: Actually, action 'under the shadow of the law' can diverge substantially from the institution, in spite of achieving the coordinative functions (Ellikson 1991). Now, if the same range of a switching regime is approached from the point of non-compliance, even a similar pattern of realized behaviour will be complemented to the non-compliance picture. Thus, hysteresis of institutions is not simply an outcome of inter–agent dynamics, but also depends on the cognitive mechanisms.

The second, *B*–type path dependence refers to network externalities in the narrow sense (as in the literature on technological networks, with seminal contributions such as Arthur 1988, 1989). Institutions regulate network interactions. In this sense, they can be compared to communication technologies, that is, there is a requirement of compatibility of institutions across all members of the network. If there is a group boundary in a network, across which institutions diverge, this impedes successful transactions. This implies that institutions might be favoured just because they give rise to compatible transactions, and not necessarily because they are the most optimal ones for the transaction. In a situation of institutional choice, this might result in the dominance of an institution that has reached a broader diffusion earlier. This argument can also be related to a more complex one on institutional complementarities. As a result, single institutions might be difficult to change, unless larger sets of institutions also change, which is less probable or requires much larger effort and investment. Institutional complementarities can take the strong form of hypercyclic connectedness, such that different institutions mutually leverage their effects on the efficiency of network interactions. The conclusion is that institutions cannot be evaluated as isolated arrangements: The same institution can produce very different effects, if it is combined with different other institutions; for example, in a classical work, Aoki (1988) has shown that in the different economic systems of the US and Japan the institutions in the capital and labour markets manifest complementarities, such that one can only assess the performance of the system, which is revealed for example in comparative advantages of different domestic industries (Grossman and Maggi 2000).

Finally, in the *C*–type path dependence, all institutions relate with cognitive models that represent their functioning to the actors: For example, the institution of patents is reflected in economic theories about patents. The important conclusion is that the evolution of cognitive models is itself path–dependent in the three senses, with the third case of special interest, because this introduces reflexivity. That is, change of cognitive models is embedded into other cognitive models. This process is clearly evident in the important role of philosophies in determining institutional change in recorded written history of mankind, and is already reflected in the classical North (1981) argument on the role of ideologies in institutional change.

In sum, there are many reasons to assume that institutional change is path–dependent in a strong sense, or non-ergodic (North 2005). Against the background of the argument of this chapter so far, we can say that these path dependencies are mainly relating to the evolving systems of distributed cognition of which the institutions are part and parcel. Therefore, the notion of path dependence is essential to assess the scope and the capacity of actors to change the direction of institutional evolution, since agency is also distributed across networks of actors. If certain actors adopt intentional actions to change institutions, this is typically based on certain concepts, that is cognitive processes. These cognitive processes are distributed, that is institutional change cannot be simply imposed by a single actor on others, but requires population–level changes of the cognitive structures that undergird institutionalized behaviour. These changes happen via processes of communication, which are themselves population–level interactions and hence manifest path dependencies (compare Schmidt 2011). So, institutional change operates in a complex network environment, which can be summarized in figure 6.8. The two inner circles in the diagram indicate the fact that institutions refer to network interactions among different actors, including processes of communication.

I call intentional acts of institutional change 'institutional design'. Only under very exceptional circumstances, institutional design can project the intended state onto the real state of a network (for a related analysis, see Djankov et al. 2003 on the transplantation of legal regimes, extending on La Porta et al. 1999). It always interacts with type *A*–*C* path dependencies. 'Institutional path dependence' refers to the workings of *A* and *B* path dependence, where, for example, the *n*–th order sanctioning network externalities co-determine the actual diffusion of the institution. To this, cognitive type *C* path dependence has to be added, which refers to the embeddedness of institutions in prevailing cognitive models, and to the reflexivity of cognitive models. Cognitive path dependence roots in interactions among actors, which results into individual and collective patterns of action, conceived as distributed agency. Thus, institutional design becomes endogenous.

Figure 6.8 Institutional path dependence

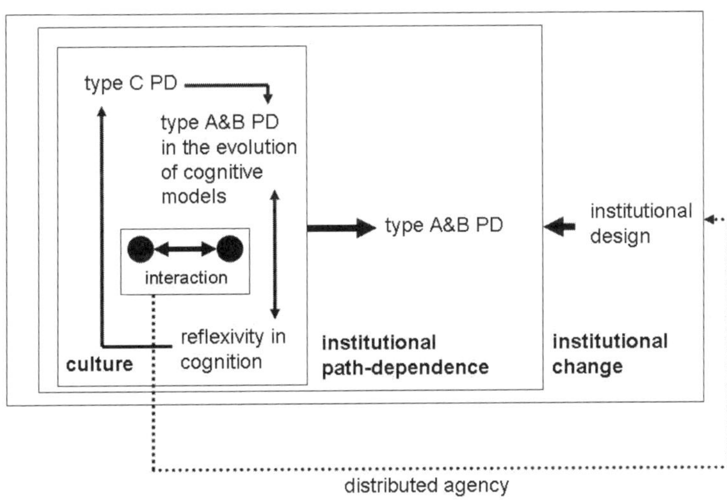

Note: In institutional change the two forces of institutional design and institutional path dependence interact. Even though institutional design is triggered by individual intentional action, it is an expression of distributed agency which is itself embedded into institutional change. Institutional path dependence is mainly based on critical mass effects (type *A*) and network externalities (type *B*) which also feature on the cognitive level, that is the emergence and diffusion of ideas; the latter embeds type *A* and *B* path dependence, thus resulting into type *C* path dependence. On the cognitive level, type *C* relates with reflexivity of cognition and gives rise to cultural phenomena in the interaction between actors that participate in institutional change, thus giving rise to distributed agency.

I relate cognitive path dependence with the notion of 'culture' (Djankov et al. 2003 include notions such as 'civic capital' here). In Chapter Five I have already proposed a notion of culture which emphasizes the role of culture in defining network boundaries and group identities. This role of culture is crucial, as it operates in a two-fold way. As we see in figure 6.8, culture is a central force of constraining institutional design in terms of path dependence. But at the same time, culture also affects institutional design, as it is normally also the culture of the actors who design the institutions. There are constellations where this is not the case, as in the example of occupation or colonization, where foreign rulers impose institutions on a native society. However, the more regular case is that of endogenous design of institutions. In other words, if the designers and the object population share a culture, there is a certain probability that institutional design will be pre-adapted to the path dependence, even if the institution is an innovation. The more divided a society, and the more cognitive models diverge among elites and the general populace (as, for example, in Russia of Peter the Great), the higher is the probability of frictions between the forces of imposed institutional design and path dependence.

Thus, it is essential to recognize that institutional evolution is the evolution of 'distributed cognitive blending', thus taking the perspectives of this section and the previous one together. This insight is of fundamental importance because it refutes one of the core ideas in many economic theories about institutional evolution, which claim that the fundamental driving force of institutional evolution is economic efficiency (especially in the context of the economic theory of property rights, for a critical overview and evaluation of the classical theory see Eggertsson 1990). That means, institutional evolution does not occur via any kind of mechanism that directly links the effects of institutions on the efficiency of economic transactions with the forces of institutional design and institutional path dependence, unless these effects are mediated via cognitive processes of actors.

6.3.4. An impossibility theorem on institutional evolution

In fact, there is fundamental reason why efficiency–based theories of institutional evolution must fail (for seminal related, though neglected arguments Schüller 1983 or Binger and Hoffman 1989; further, compare Furubotn 1991, 1998 or Hsiung 1999). I consider a most general impossibility theorem, which goes back on the impossibility theorem about interaction costs in networks that I elucidated in the previous chapter (Chapter Five, section 5.3.3.). It is most appropriate to interpret this in the context of the standard approach, which mostly refers to property rights when discussing institutions. In this case, the problem boils down to the question of whether it is possible to determine efficient property rights ex ante by endogenous actors. This is impossible, in the sense of a unique and correct anticipation, which means actors can only form hypotheses which are then confirmed or falsified ex post. The reason is that efficient property rights are defined via the costs of internalization and the gains that holders of rights can make, given competitive pressures on using them efficiently. However, the problem is that the two price vectors, before and after internalization are incommensurable because they represent two entirely different equilibrium points, with different institutional frameworks. That means, ex ante the costs of internalization can only be estimated by the prevailing prices, however, what counts for the efficiency assessment is the costs of internalization once the property rights have been created. These are unknown, unless the process takes place in a nirvana of perfect information. However, in this nirvana there would be no transaction costs at all, so the Coase theorem about the irrelevance of specific assignments of property rights holds. In other words, it is the existence of transactions costs in the real world which implies that those very institutions that evolve with the effect of possibly lowering those costs cannot be assessed ex ante in terms of efficiency. Therefore, if we accept the view that there is no exogenous causal force than the actions of the actors, mediated by perceptions, we cannot maintain the idea that efficiency drives the emergence of institutions.

This impossibility theorem is mainly based on Gödelian paradoxes of self–reference that occur if one tries to apply a particular criterion, namely efficiency, on institutions, which itself is dependent on institutions. So, what are the alternative determinants of institutional evolution that we need to scrutinize in the chapter? I distinguish neatly between the problem of the emergence of institutions and the diffusion and stability of institutions, and argue that the emergence of institutions cannot be explained on efficiency terms, but only as a phenomenon of power and powerful collective action in human networks. This question I will pursue in the final section. Yet, in the long run, only those institutions will be evolutionary sustainable which are productive in the economic sense, mediated by the co-evolution with cognitive structures. This is because the productivity of institutions is an essential determinant of the trajectories of group selection in human groups which differ in terms of institutions.

However, even when considering group selection, we cannot simply assume that the most efficient institutions will diffuse in the first place. Institutional diffusion in the real world seems mainly driven by three determinants. One is copying, along the lines of network analysis. Copying institutions need not be influenced by any kind of efficiency considerations, even if efficiency considerations may determine actual individual and collective learning processes, which is the second way how institutions diffuse. As we know already, copying can be biased in many other ways, such as status considerations. For example, a group of low status may copy the institutions of a group of high status. Further, if institutions also play a role in defining group boundaries, there is a constraint on copying institutions which might be efficient otherwise, but might undermine group identity. The third mechanism of institution diffusion is to impose institutions by force, for example, when annexing another group. Again, this might be driven by efficiency considerations on the part of the dominant group, but this will always be mixed with the need to maintain asymmetric network configurations of power. Even if institutions had direct and unequivocal effects on efficiency, we cannot reasonably assume that human actors have complete knowledge about the causality behind these effects. For many institutions, even modern economic science does not present unequivocal efficiency accounts: How can we assume that actors have this knowledge?

One important conclusion from this brief discussion is that it is this lack of a clear directional force in institutional change driven by unique efficiency criteria which implies a large scope for functional equivalences; that means, similar functions can be possibly realized by different institutions, and even forces of group selection may not weed out this institutional diversity. I discuss this point in some more detail on section 6.5. At the same time, this scope for institutional diversity implies that there is also much room for performative actions in the sense that even if more efficient institutions emerge from this process, the original forces of emergence may root in the unconstrained creativity of human action and imagination. In particular, this refers to actions driven by powerful actors, as scrutinized in the final section. Therefore, before we tackle the issues of institutional diversity and power we need to further elucidate the notion of performativity.

6.4. PERFORMATIVITY OF INSTITUTIONS

6.4.1. Performing institutions

I will now further detail the analysis of distributed cognition in institutional evolution by means of modifying the Aoki model as deployed so far. In this reconstruction, the status function obtains a central role in a circular causal process which links up the individual with the population–level, such that Searle's notion of collective intentionality can be shown to be an emergent property of an evolutionary dynamics. The central idea is that in institutions, individual and population–level processes intermingle in a specific way. On the population–level, we assume that there are complex processes that result in certain aggregate effects of the interactions in a network, and become manifest in path–dependent dynamics. All actors have leeway for action, and they take actions which interact strategically with other actions, in the sense of game theory. In this context, one should not have the seemingly archetypical examples in mind, such as oligopolies or environmental pollution. The most universal network interaction that involves strategic interactions is the production of information externalities. Here, a strategic aspect emerges from the effects of an action on the distribution of risks in a population. The actor who acts first takes higher risks than the actor who acts second and therefore can exploit the information externality created by the former. Thus, there is a strategic incentive to procrastinate action. These and similar kinds of choices happen on the individual level, and they work together to create certain population–level outcomes.

Now, I posit that one aspect of the outcomes of these population–level interactions is the emergence of certain sets of signs which relate with the interactions and their outcomes (see figure 6.9). The signs do not directly represent the outcomes, but they relate with them in a regular way. For example, the outcome might be that a certain person is treated as an arbiter, and this relates with a particular kind of dress or ritualized behaviour. Similarly, the signs that generate trustworthiness on the vegetable market also relate with outcomes, but they do not directly represent any particular aspect of the generating interactions. This is why in extreme cases the people that interpret the signs might have very different ideas of what they actually mean. However, what counts are the effects of the signs of the further actions of the actors. These effects are complex, because they are intermediated via the cognitive processing of status functions. I will detail this further below.

Figure 6.9 Circular causality in the emergence of institutions

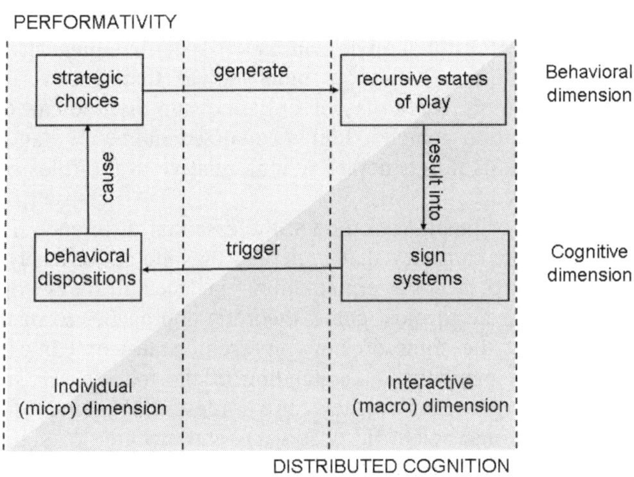

Note: The modified Aoki model (compare figure 6.3) recognizes the fact that public representations scaffold individual cognitive processes and hence are phenomena of distributed cognition; therefore, the micro and the macro–dimension merge. Signs trigger dispositions to act, which are not necessarily 'beliefs' as mental states. Dispositions cause choices, but not only in the sense of incentivizing them. Theoretically, this is tantamount to random generation of variants of actions the scope of which is constrained by the disposition. As a consequence, the individual choices are channelled in such a way that the recursive states of play are favoured; this manifests performativity of actions on the population level. Therefore, the dimensions of behaviour and cognition merge, in particular because population–level behavioural patterns are signs themselves. Thus, the two polar dimensions of the Aoki model reduce to the two aspects of performativity and distributed cognition.

What is important currently is that the signs directly trigger certain dispositions of the agents to act. A disposition is a neuronal state, ultimately rooted in neuromemes, which is efficiently–caused by the sign, without any necessary involvement of higher–level cognitive functions. Think of a soldier who automatically reacts on the hand sign of other soldiers in a platoon. Dispositions imply that the generated action is not deterministically caused. That is, the disposition relates with a range of actions which has a certain probability distribution in a double sense. Firstly, individuals have a disposition to manifest a certain action, which varies probabilistically through time. Second, within a population there is also a distribution of dispositions, which varies probabilistically (for example, some individuals may not have the disposition at all). However, the assumption is that the two probabilistic processes produce a set of strategic actions through time which interact so that a certain equilibrium position is generated which reproduces the signs that link up with the dispositions. In this picture, rule–following is not a sort of choice on the individual level, nor is it linked to any kind of collective intentionality as a mere aggregate of individual intentionalities. The collective aspect comes into play via the distribution of dispositions in the populations, related to the convergent use of specific signs. That means, the degree of variation of signs is much lower than the variation of dispositions. For example, there may be only one sign that indicates the role of a judge in a population, which is highly ritualized and hence standardized, whereas the dispositions that generate actions relative to the roles of judges can vary considerably.

Compared to the original Aoki model, the essential difference lies in the exclusively externalist causality that underlies the interactions between the different levels. There is no intermediation via 'mental states' of actors, which play a central role in most game–theoretic approaches to institutions. This also means that the signs do not 'represent' states of games, as this notion relates with a mentalist understanding of the meaning of signs (for example Brandenburger 2007) (they only 'represent' games from the viewpoint of the external scientific observer). The meaning of signs lies in the functions that are generated by them, which are, in this recursive structure, their effects on the actions of the actors (along the lines of Skyrms 2010). The externalist causality only relates with physical processes in the sense that signs trigger neurophysiologically embodied dispositions, these generate actions, which in turn play together on the population level, with one result being the emergence of signs.

So, in this view an institution is the entire causal circuit depicted in figure 6.9. An institution is a semiotic phenomenon which is rooted in neurophysiological dispositions that are shared in a population of actors via the interactions on the population level, which also result into the emergence and use of signs. This implies that the individual actions are performative with reference to the institution.

In figure 6.9, I also indicate how this process has to be conceived in terms of the fundamental duality of performativity and distributed cognition. The distributed cognition aspect comes into play because in real world network interactions, human cognitive capacities are by far too limited to process all the information that inheres in them and reach functional conclusions about strategic choices. Hence, sign systems assume an essential cognitive function in externalizing information processing such that the knowledge reflecting equilibrium states inheres both in the individual level (the disposition) and the population or collective level (the sign systems). On the other hand, because the signs trigger certain dispositions, there is a channelling effect on the individual level which entails the anticipation of equilibrium solutions on the population level. In this sense, the individual actions, ultimately triggered by the signs, perform the population–level phenomena. For example, the actors treat an individual as judge, irrespective of possible deviant strategies which lie at the fringes of the probability distribution of actions flowing out from existing dispositions in the population.

So, in the two notions of performativity and distributed cognition the micro/macro distinction implodes which is central for standard economics and is also introduced in the original Aoki model. Performativity implies a convergence between individual actions (micro) and population–level behavioural patterns (macro level), and at the same time the population–level sign systems (macro) scaffold, enhance and leverage individual cognition (micro). As a result, standard problems in explaining institutions facing certain dilemmata evaporate. In relation to Searle, it is important to emphasize that the proposed framework also explains how collective intentionality comes into being. In the externalist setting, collective intentionality is not a mental state, but in fact an ascription of intentionality by observers of the institutional causal circuits. In this sense, the proposed model treats actors 'as if' they had collective intentionality (the 'intentional stance' according to Dennett 2009). Searle distinguishes between agentive and non-agentive functions: Whereas the notion of collective intentionality would suggest an agentive functioning on first sight, in fact the institutional circuit is a non-agentive functioning. However, as we have seen, this does not preclude the possibility of reflection, which would project institutions into conceptual schemes which are handled on the level of consciousness. Yet, this phenomenon is not constitutive for an institution.

It is important to see that in this scheme, the 'as if' argument on collective intentionality also applies for the individual level, in the sense that performativity boils down to what I have called 'institutionally guided behavioural patterns' previously. The causal circuitry implies that the population–level aggregate results are embodied in individual dispositions to act. So, individual and collective intentionality converge into one concept, performativity. This is exactly the confluence of sign and institution in institutional semiosis as analysed in section 6.2.2. This view affects many other concepts proposed by Searle, which are maintained in terms of functioning, but changed in terms of causal explanation. In particular, the recognition of an institution and the implicated deontology does not imply that there is a mental state which results in this. The obligation to follow an institution is not necessarily reflected in a decision of an actor to follow the institution because she feels obliged to follow. This is possible, however, in the cognitive state of reflection.

I argue that Searle's status function is the causal link between the signs and the dispositions. This is because the actors treat certain entities as signs, thus producing certain actions that end up with a functioning by which those signs are reproduced. So, we have an externalist turn, again, because the functions prevail over the internalist assignment of meaning. This rests upon cognitive processes which are in turn supervening in neurophysiological structures. I argue that this causal circuitry defines 'Institutionally Guided Behavioural Patterns.'

6.4.2. Case study: The emergence of early money

It is important to analyse the interaction between the different levels of the revised Aoki model with the help one particular example which is also crucial for our analysis of markets in Chapter Eight. This is the example of money. As we shall see in Chapter Eight, I choose money because this institution stays at the centre of the functioning of markets. Money is an essential cultural artefact in the evolution of human economic systems, and it has very important feedback effects on cognitive mechanisms, such as enabling quantifications of values, commensurability of goods or enabling the perception of value through time. Beginning with Simmel (1907), researchers have recurrently argued that money cannot be simply seen in the light of its economic functions, but has important transformative effects on human cognition, such as enabling abstractions (for a survey, see Walsh and Lynch 2008). Thus, money is an essential example for structures of distributed cognition that feature the co-evolution and exaptation of artefacts with institutions in different domains; as we shall see, this also means that the institution of money builds on biologically evolved foundations (in the sense of Boyer and Petersen 2012). In this chapter, I attempt to show how this centrality of money can be explained in evolutionary terms, developing a co-evolutionary approach that assigns a central place to neuronal mechanisms, but does not reduce the institution to these (as envisaged by Glimcher 2011: 424).

As I have said previously, the essential question is when the transition from a mere use of an item in exchange for money as an institution happened, first in the regulatory, but eventually in the constitutive sense. There is a clear contradiction between established economic theories of the emergence of money and the historical facts (which often refer back to Menger's 1892 seminal account, such as Schotter 1982: 35ff). Purely theoretical accounts emphasize the role of money in enabling transactions, as in the triangular exchange paradigm. In these accounts a certain item evolves as (commodity) money for the pure function of serving as a transaction device. This also implies that basically, there is no conceptual transformation, in the sense of a status function, but only a growing functional salience of properties such as resaleability, storability and dividability. The institution of money would emerge as a purely regulatory institution, referring to commodity money.

This view clearly fits into the established economic theory of money, but contradicts the historical evidence (aptly summarized by Chavas and Bromley 2008; see also Ingham 2000). In fact, money emerged in the context of relations of power and authority, regulating hierarchical exchange relations and the production of public goods, and only the further evolution was intermingled with the more haphazard use of valuable items in barter. The historical data suggest that the transactional function of money tokens is in fact a derived function. This is an important observation, because it directly reveals the essential role of Searle's categories in analysing the institution of money. All institutions involve the power creation operator in the theoretical sense, and this implies that empirically, any explanation of an institution that fails to identify this component must fail, as in the case of purely economic explanations of the emergence of money, namely efficiency based theories. Further, the emergence of money also shows the essential role of cognitive transformations, which are summarized in the analytical notion of the status function. That is, there is a fundamental difference between 'money' and the simple use of some objects for exchange, which is the status function. This difference can by physically fixed in the distinction between those objects and the incipient use of a special kind of objects, 'coins' (for a general theoretical reference, see Hutchins 2005).

Historically, it is significant that money emerged at a cross–cultural interface, which separated different ways of functioning of proto–money and hence, cultural meanings, referring to different patterns of collective intentionality (my account follows Hutter's 1994 analytical summary of the historical facts). When money coins emerged for the first time in the Eastern Mediterranean (at least as far as Western civilization is concerned), this was an effect of cross–cultural merger of meanings between Assyrian culture and the Ionian peasant communities. In Assyria, gold served as an indicator of status and as a medium of wealth accumulation in a steeply stratified society; money as a unit of account had already existed much earlier in Babylonia, but as an abstract measure in a centralized bureaucracy controlling the economy (for a discussion of these essential differences, see Ingham 2000). In the Greek communities, silver was used for ritual purposes and occasionally for exchange, which was mostly mediated via a number of items with less value in barter. The first genuine coins originating from Lydia, however, were made from electrum, an alloy of silver and gold. Thus, they could be interpreted differently in the two societies, enabling cross–cultural exchange of signs and goods. Further, in order to test the quality of coins, people applied punches resulting in a punch mark, firstly unintended. Once the coins circulated, people discovered the possible use of the punch marks as indicators of origin. The question of origin was crucial in lowering quality uncertainty with regard to the actual metal composition. From this moment onwards, the custom of coining emerged, with the incipient use of the punch marks as signals. Soon, the new coins were integrated into the political and the religious realm when local regents adopted the institution of minting. Thus, the first coins appeared displaying the images of rulers and holy symbols. With this transition, we can say that the institution of money has emerged. The role of emerging collective intentionalities and of the corresponding deontology is most evident in the rapid fusion of economic and ritual aspects of money.

Figure 6.10 Conceptual blending and status function in the emergence of money

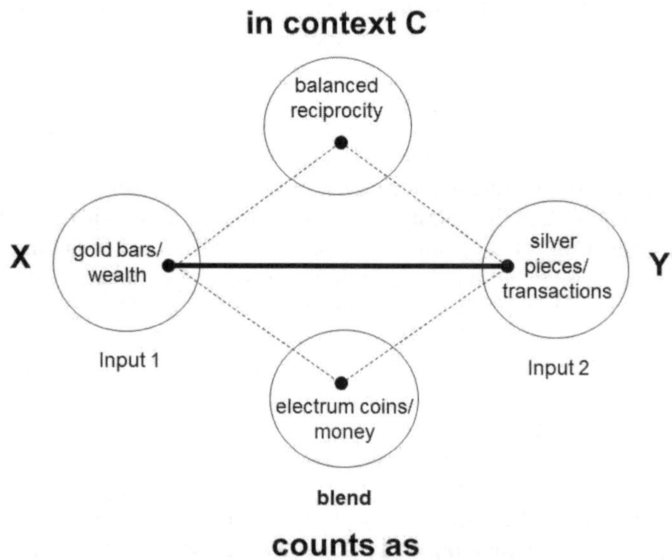

Note: The status function of early money resulted from a cross–cultural mapping of two different uses of metals as indicators of wealth (gold in Assyria) and as transactional devices (silver in Ionian Greece). The alloy materially carries the conceptual blend which results from the projection into the generic space of generalized reciprocity which encompasses both exchange within political hierarchies and markets. Thus, early coins diffused rapidly as transactional devices, but were also claimed by political actors as symbols of authority.

This account can easily be translated into the framework of conceptual blends. Simultaneously, we can apply the status function notion (figure

6.10). The central point is that two different artefacts with different uses in different societies merged into 'double–scope integration network', in which the two concepts are only partially merged. In the cross–cultural semantic ambiguity an alloy could be treated both as being close to a gold bar or a silver piece, thus also making those two artefacts commensurable, though only partially. In terms of the status function, in a double–scope integration network we can say that the status function in fact works in both directions, with 'gold' being treated as 'silver' and vice versa, in the context of cross–cultural exchange, and being related to the 'brute fact' of the physical entity of electrum, the alloy. In other words, the physical fact of an alloy enabled the creation of the status function that is in turn a conceptual blend. Once the status function was established, the institution of money, reified in the emergence of the first coins circulating in inter–regional trade, came into existence. The new coins were clearly different from the mere use of commodities in exchange, hence constituting new things as artefacts.

Putting this analysis into the context of the more general Aoki model, we can say that what emerged was the concept of money, based on the generation of a sign, a physical artefact, from activities that had no relation whatsoever to the intention to create coins. The merchants that checked for the quality of an alloy, and who eventually used the markers as indicators of origin, did not intend to create a 'coin'. This only happened after the use of signed metals had already spread in the multi–ethnic merchant encounters. Hence, we can also relate the transaction to money in the sense of the constitutive rule with the intentional marking of coins, that is minting with the use of religious and political symbols. These signs directly trigger certain dispositions.

In order to clarify this effect, it is important to include the neuronal level into consideration. Of course, there is no way to reconstruct brain level processes in historical times. But we can ask the question, what is the generic space that enables the conceptual blend, and can we present a possible connection with fundamental neurophysiological dispositions (so, basically following Lakoff's 2008 approach)? In figure 6.10, I propose to use the notion of 'balanced reciprocity', which is both an abstract notion underlying ritualized power relations and of early exchange across longer time horizons (Pryor 1977: chapters 4 and 7; compare Burkert 1996: chapter 6). That means, money and balanced reciprocity are deeply interconnected, which seems to be an acceptable intuition (interestingly, this idea underlies Simmel's approach to money as the embodiment of exchange, see Papilloud 2003b; Rammstedt 2003). As we shall now see, this connection can be supported by recent research on the emotional foundations of money use. Clearly, money is used as a mere transaction device, but at the same time it manifests very strong emotional reactions in other contexts, and can trigger strong drives of acquisitive and hoarding behaviour. It is these drives that were themes in the mythologies that emerged together with the early diffusion of money in the Mediterranean, recounting the fates of figures such as King Croesus.

As I have extensively discussed in Chapter Four, there is a strong presumption that the human brain is 'social', in the sense that humans are especially adapted to reciprocal exchange (Gigerenzer 1996; Cosmides and Tooby 2005; Ermer et al. 2006). This seems to be reflected in general emotional structures which do not only place high internal valuations on reciprocity, but also enable special cognitive performances in processing information about reciprocal social relations. This implies that these neuronal subsystems are also connected with the reward processing systems, as analysed in Chapter Four. From this it follows that there is also the possibility of dysfunctions, in the sense that the 'wanting' and the 'liking' systems may stay in tension with each other. In recent psychological theories about money, it has therefore been emphasized that money can be both a 'drug' and a 'tool', with the drug–like aspects emerging from its possible functioning as a 'perceptual drug' (Lea and Webley 2006). This means that a certain sign can hijack the underlying biological structures, thus activating the corresponding reward dynamics, but not realizing the pertinent biological function. From this, the hypothesis results that money as a sign triggers emotional structures related to social reciprocity, thus creating an especially strong anchor for following the institution of money. I propose to summarize this in the general statement that the use of money activates certain somatic markers connected to reciprocity. This hypothesis relates to the fact that money generates the same reward mechanisms as other positive sensory inputs such as beautiful faces (Camerer et al. 2005: 35; Phelps 2009: 240), which explains why money can be used a direct incentive in psychological experiments (Knutson and Wimmer 2007: 159f). One of the most conspicuous empirical facts highlighting this special aspect of money is money illusion, which invalidates the 'rational' distinction between nominal and real values: People tend to assign an independent value to merely nominal differences in quantities of money and value, and this disposition is anchored in neuronal mechanisms (Shafir et al. 1997; Weber et al. 2009). Further, monetary valuations of goods differ systematically from evaluations of expected rewards of consuming the goods, presumably the former directly relate with evaluations of the transactions involving the goods (thus relating to perceptions of reciprocity) (Amir et al. 2008). Dickhaut et al. (2009a, b) argue that general accounting principles (which are always based on monetary values) reflect basic neuronal mechanisms of valuation; accounting is essentially a representation of exchange processes.

To this relationship between money use and emotive structures we can add population–level dynamics in referring to the general theory of signal selection (see Chapter Three, section 3.5.6). The theory of signal selection implies that for arbitrary signs, the Handicap Principle may apply, depending on the selective context. As we have seen in Chapter Three, the Handicap Principle posits that the coordination of behaviour via signals may require the investment into costly signals which produces an adaptive disadvantage in the sense of natural selection (as opposed for example to sexual selection). Yet, precisely these costs make the signal functional, because otherwise it would be open to manipulation and cheating. That is, handicaps are truthful signals and because of that, are adaptive in terms of the universal currency of reproductive success. Yet, this implies the possibility of outright runaway processes which appear to be maladaptive, if only the pure engineering standards are applied.

So, consider money as a sign of reciprocity. If it signals the capacity and the willingness to enter relations governed by reciprocity, this means that it can be open to the Handicap Principle dynamics. So it is easy to explain why the emergence of money was immediately connected with the appearance of extreme forms of accumulative urges and wealth displays, as in Greek tyranny. In the original conceptual blend, money used for transactions and money used for storing and accumulating wealth were merged into one blend. This allows for a Handicap Mechanism to emerge, in the sense that the capability to hoard and display wealth is a marker of the capacity to spend limitlessly. The waste of wealth in useless displays is precisely the signal that communicates the capacity to enter into a limitless number of transactions, thus claiming the role of a hub with exceptionally high prestige in ever-growing networks of exchange. This account matches the historical data in the sense that the purely technical uses of money emerged as a side effect of the primordial uses. Later, the runaway evolution of money also supported its rapid diffusion as a tool for transactions. This blend was epitomized in the emergence of the coin as an artefact for trade, but at the same time as a symbol for power and authority.

6.4.3. Performativity of money

The detailed analysis of money gives an important case study for the performativity of institutions (figure 6.11). Historically, the emergence of money was triggered by the spread of new conceptual blends, which were related with the emergence of new signs, the 'coins', which were artefactual innovations compared to pre-existing tokens of value. Interestingly, this phenomenon also shows an important generic aspect of blends, which reflects a property of the original Aoki model, namely information compression. However, this does not refer to an allegedly 'representationalist' function of the money signs, but to their role in maintaining their functioning as an institution that is rooted in neurophysiologically anchored dispositions. Information compression is actually reflecting the distributed cognition aspect of the institution, which refers to the function of money as a medium of exchange, a value standard and so forth.

Figure 6.11 Pristine money as an institution

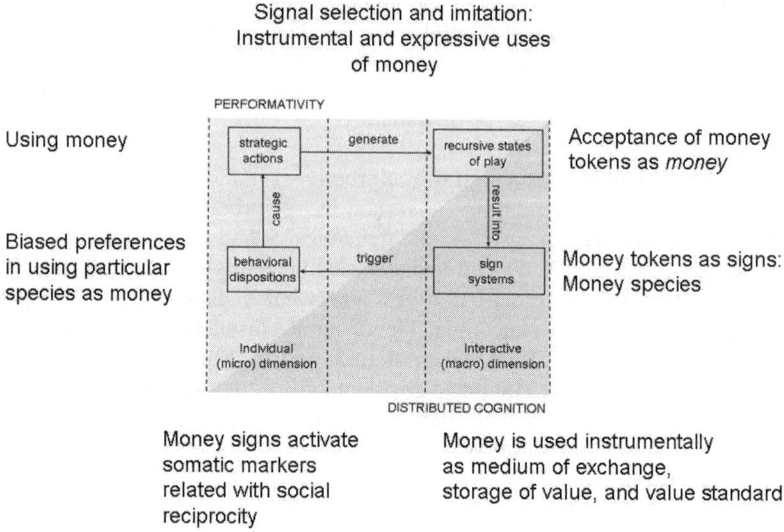

Note: The emergence of early money can be analysed along the lines of the revised Aoki model. This highlights the role of neurophysiological mechanisms in creating the dispositions to use money as a medium of exchange. The resulting actions are bolstered by the functions of money in expanding population–level exchanges. Once money emerges, it enables new cognitive functions: The artefact is an essential element of new patterns of distributed cognition, enabling, for example, valuations and calculations.

Based on this analysis, we can finally state that the institution of money is performative. The performativity of money is already reflected in the well-recognized fact that all conventional money is based in the general acceptance of its use, which reflects a basic trust in the institution (this is why money is also a favourite example in Searle's theory of institutions, also targeted by his critics, see Smit et al. 2011). In principle, this institution can implode at any time if trust is withdrawn (for a detailed analysis, see Chapter Eight). The analysis presented in this section reveals that performativity is a much more complex phenomenon. On the one hand, it is based on the self–reinforcing dynamics of money use, given certain constraints on money functioning, such as the preservation of value. On the other hand, reflecting the specific contexts of the historical emergence of certain money species, these are causally enmeshed with distributed somatic markets in a population that bias money use in a way that the population level dynamics is channelled and reinforced. This is the causality underlying the performativity of the single behavioural patterns.

We can now summarize and generalize this discussion in the following definition of performativity of institutions:

- An institution is performative, if it involves a conceptual blend across different domains, such that the pertinent action manifesting the institution is linked with particular somatic markers which generate a sustainable disposition to this action, and such that the action correlates with the regular occurrence of external facts, which operate as signs triggering the somatic markers. Hence, following an institution does not involve an intention to follow, in the sense of a mental fact, but results from a closed causal feedback loop between signs, internal neuronal states, and actions that are signs in turn. As the signs are shared in a population of agents, these patterns reflect collective intentionality supervening on the underlying causal patterns, and resulting from network processes such as imitation.

The example of money is also pertinent to demonstrate the role of the power creation operator, as introduced by Searle. The previously analysed mechanisms can also be interpreted as implying a deontology in the sense that the causal circuitry, as seen from the individual level, creates certain entitlements and obligations on part of the actors. For example, there is a general obligation to accept money as a medium of exchange. Further, as all historical trajectories of money use have shown, there is an intricate relation between money and power, which emerges from the conjunction of economic exchange and social exchange in the general notion of reciprocity. This linkage between power and money, however, does not directly emerge from the fundamental causal process, but results from a phenomenon that was enabled via the simple physical fact of the artefactual nature of money units. This is the accumulation of money tokens, and the fact that this reflects an increasing capacity for exchange. Once money came into existence, new forms of power emerged that resulted from the fact that the physical tokens have properties such as divisibility and fungibility to a degree which other media of power did not have. So, human societies faced an institutional innovation with widespread consequences for all areas of human life, because power is ubiquitous. This triggered the evolution of other institutions regulating the use of money as a new social fact.

Then, we can state that the fusion of money and power is also going back on a new conceptual blend, which merges the value dimension of money with the notions of status and power. Historically, these fed back into the process of institutionalizing money, such that political authorities started to get control of the minting process. Money and political power are almost always and everywhere closely enmeshed. So, this historical trajectory is a case in point for the role of power in creating and maintaining institutions. I come back to this insight in the final section.

6.4.4. Evolutionary microfoundations of the theory of institutions

I will now summarize the general analysis of institutions as deployed in the example of money, aiming at an overview of the different theoretical resources that play together in the evolutionary approach, as far as its micro–level aspects are concerned. I will further complete this theoretical rehearsal at the end of this chapter (figures 6.15 and 6.16). Figure 6.12 presents a summary map of the theoretical resources that I utilize in analysing those micro–level aspects. Institutions are conceived bimodally, yet it is important, in the line of semiotic analysis related to Searle's notion of status function, to highlight the role of artefacts in the functioning of institutions. Artefacts are essential in the context of distributed cognition, insofar as they are the media through which the status function operates. This transformative role of artefacts stays in the centre of detailing the cognitive mechanism of the status function in terms of cognitive blending. The other essential element of Searle's approach, as received in this chapter, is the role of dispositions which are anchored neurophysiologically.

The neuroscience perspective on institutions results from the fact that cognitive blending theory can be combined with Lakoff's theory of metaphor which makes the mappings in brain connectivity explicit that underlie the cognitive functions such as concept formation. This relationship was not treated in detail here, but means that the theory of conceptual blending, though operating on the semantic level directly, can be approached in terms of the analytical categories of Chapter Four. As we have exemplified for the case of money, dispositions on money use are rooted in somatic markers related to reciprocity, and these undergird the conceptual blends in the emergence of early money as cross–cultural mode of integration. These neurophysiological bases of money use can be empirically identified in many results of the neurosciences, such as neurophysiological correlates to money illusion. So, the cognitive aspects of money use can be explained in terms of sensorimotor feedback circuits which connect individual uses with population level patterns.

As I have discussed in detail in Chapter Four, these theories can be seen in the context of a generic Darwinian paradigm of the brain sciences, that is Edelman's Neural Darwinism. We have also seen that evolutionary approaches can apply both on the level of brain functioning and on the level of long-run structural evolution, as hypothesized by Evolutionary Psychology. We related these paradigms to Aunger's concept of the neuromeme. However, Aunger's approach goes beyond that, as it assumes the role of a conceptual bracket, because on the one hand, it conceptualizes the neuronal mechanisms, but also allows approaching the evolution of artefacts in Darwinian terms, a topic that I will pursue further in Chapter Seven. In sum, this combination of theories allows to add substantial detail to the framework established in figure 6.1; in particular, this applies for the mechanisms that connect the individual and the population level processes in the reproduction of institutions.

Figure 6.12 Evolutionary microfoundations of institutions

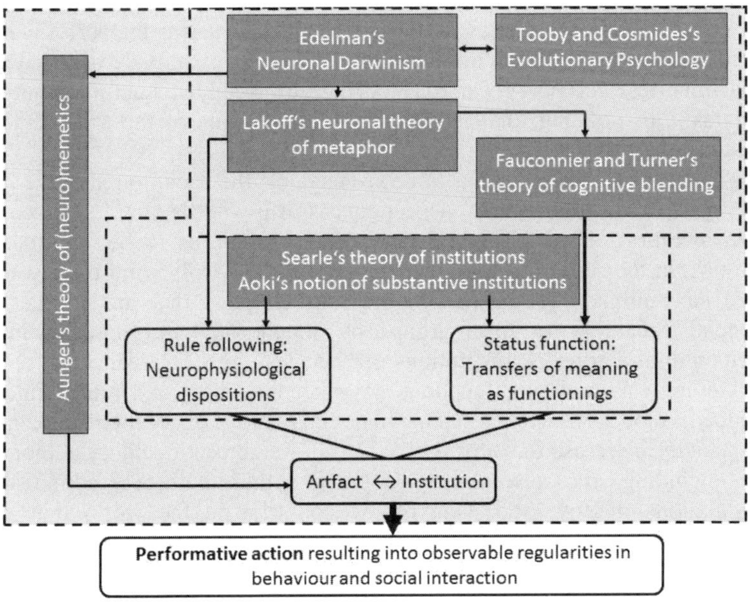

Note: This diagram overviews some of the theoretical approaches deployed in the evolutionary theory of the performativity of institutions. Searle's notion of the status function stays at the centre; real world status functions build on the bimodality of rules and signs, artefacts and institutions, as analysed semiotically. In the interpretation of Searle's approach that follows Aoki's theory of substantive institutions, two aspects receive particular attention. One is the view of 'following an institution' as a behavioural disposition, the other is the view of functional transfers as cognitive blending. It is possible to apply neuroscience theories such as Lakoff's theory of metaphors in both respects. Therefore, the entire approach can be embedded into general theories of evolution that connect different levels; especially, Darwinian approaches to neural connectivity and brain dynamics (Edelman) can be related with evolutionary theories about the structural properties of brains (Tooby and Cosmides). Finally, Aunger's theory conjoins the evolutionary analysis of neuronal processes with the evolutionary approach to artefacts, especially in the context of communication.

In other words, so far we have scrutinized the replicator function in institutions. So, we have a complex and encompassing view of the micro–foundations of institutions. If we use the term 'micro' here, obviously it does not only refer to the individual level, as we explicitly include population level processes. 'Micro' has to be seen as opposite to macro–level determinants of institutions which relate to generic features of network configurations and structures. These features connect with the micro–level via the signs: For example, the signs of police may represent structural properties of policing in a particular society. I will now turn my attention at those macro–level phenomena. This macro–level aspects relate with the interactor function in the evolutionary framework, that is the performance of institutions relative to environments which impact selectively on populations that manifest certain sets of IGBPs. One of the most important questions relates with policing, that is structural determinants of the enforcement of institutions.

This general argument has to be seen against the background of the notion of group selection. This aspect necessarily needs to be taken into consideration, as a defining feature of institutions is to be a property of groups, in the sense of group members collectively following the institution. We have already established in previous chapters that humans have the special capability to form groups by suppressing and policing internal behavioural variance. Institutions further leverage this capacity, and for achieving this, policing functions have become more and more important. Indeed, modern societies incur huge costs to police their populations, especially if we use this term in the sense of eighteenth century authors, that is including the government apparatus that enforces administrative regulations of any kind. One of the countries in the world that values individual freedom most, the United States, also has the highest levels of incarceration rates per population in the world, with the costs of prisons becoming a major burden for the fiscal system. At the same time, many thinkers have always highlighted the role of inter–group conflict in driving the evolution of human groups (for a collection of arguments, see Alexander 1979: 222ff; Bowles 2004: 463ff; or Corning 2005: 188ff; for a critical and dissenting view, see Holz 2012). War performance has always been driven by technological advances and the capacity for raising economic resources, with the latest example being the military race between the United States and the Soviet Union, after World War Two, in which different patterns of economic resource mobilization in both countries proved to be successful in fighting against the axis powers.

As we shall see in the final section, this role of military violence is closely connected to the emergence and the diffusion of formal institutions, such as in the domain of taxation. However, as I have discussed in the first section, different enforcement and stabilization mechanisms relate with different types of institutions, and we have also clarified that efficiency is not an immediate driver of institutional change. Therefore, it seems questionable to assume a simple evolutionary trend towards the preponderance of formal institutions and the related enforcement mechanisms. Indeed, there are good reasons to assume that relative to certain functions, different types of institutions might present functionally equivalent solutions, depending on the larger social, cultural and political context. This question requires some further scrutiny.

6.5. CULTURE, COGNITION AND THE DIVERSITY OF INSTITUTIONS

6.5.1. Functional equivalence of different kinds of institutions

The thesis of the functional superiority of formal institutions is sometimes connected to the distinction between formal and informal institutions (North 1990): Whereas formal institutions would require the existence of formal enforcement organizations and written rules, informal institutions would not necessarily show these patterns, but mainly rely on social sanctions in networks. The superiority thesis is mostly put on the grounds that formal institutions allow for the expansion of anonymous markets. However, as we have seen in Chapter Five, the maintenance of network configurations will always involve all levels of group sizes: For example, there might be a group of enforcers of formal institutions on the large group level which itself manifests internal enforcement of social norms by informal institutions. However, if formal and informal institutions co-exist in a particular domain of interactions, institutional conflict is possible: For example, a government would try to enforce a new marriage law, but people adhere to traditional behaviour. As I will argue below, this distinction results into the difficulty how to distinguish between social norms and informal institutions, because informal institutions manifest most properties of social norms (on the distinction between different concepts such as norms and institutions, see Elster 1989b). This may appear to be merely a definitional issue, but in the semiotic approach the distinction between formal and informal institutions mainly seems to be a distinction between different technologies in which the signs of institutions are cast, such as writing or oral traditions. At the same time, the difference emphasized in the literature seems to lie in the different structures of power that undergird enforcement mechanisms, which they share with social norms. In other words, considering these diverse aspects, it seems that the distinction between 'formality' and 'informality' is just ephemeral to the interaction between the more fundamental determinants of institutions.

The question is of interest, because there is the additional issue how to relate culture to the informal/formal distinction. The importance of this issue is best illustrated when considering a highly influential example of institutional analysis in economics that emphasizes the role of culture. This is Greif's (1993, 1994, 1997) comparative study of collectivist and individualist merchant communities in medieval Mediterranean trade, the Maghribi merchants and the Genoese merchants, which eventually developed into different institutional regimes. The latter established a framework of formal institutions which also allowed economic transactions with non-Genoese, whereas the former maintained segmented trading communities and mainly relied on *n*–th order sanctions for enforcing rules of trading. In the end, for complex reasons the Genoese pattern proved to be the more successful arrangement, but it is difficult to assess the different determinants, especially with regard to 'efficiency' (for similar problems in assessing the European guilds, see Gustafsson, 1991). During the period where both systems coexisted, there seemed to be no difference in efficiency terms, which transpires in Greif's analysis as the statement that both arrangements are subgame perfect and pareto–optimal equilibria in an efficiency wage based prisoners' dilemma about agency relations (see Aoki, 2001: 68ff).

The efficiency wage part of the story is straightforward. In medieval long–distance trade, merchants had to establish principal–agent relations with other traders, who might deliver deals at far-away places. Therefore, there were strong incentives to cheating. So, merchants had to define agency fees that would deter agents from cheating, considering the lifetime value of continued transactions. This defines the efficiency wage. Greif showed that the related equilibria can be maintained by two different systems of cultural beliefs about the behaviour of others. In collectivist settings, the actors care for the history of other actors, and they avoid employing agents who cheated in the past. In individualist settings, people do not care about past behaviour, but only rely on present contractual arrangements and their implications for future expected behaviour. The collectivist arrangement presupposes a particular information structure, hence network configuration, in the economy, which allows for the transmitting of information about past behaviour among the members of the community. The individualist arrangement can do without that. Both arrangements also differ in terms of the sanctioning mechanisms. The collectivist arrangement mainly relies on informal mechanisms and the possibility that cheaters can be expelled from the merchant community, after information has become available, for example, through the continuous communication among merchants via letters. The individualist arrangement requires formal organizations to settle disputes, such as courts. Greif shows that both equilibria are efficient. That means that the direction of institutional change will be influenced by the embedding social structure and the generated beliefs, but not primarily by the payoffs. Therefore, in the first place the two solutions seem to be functionally equivalent.

Greif's account contains another argument which is the crucial one in our context. The collectivist sanctioning mechanism requires *n*–th order sanctions, because the main mechanism of exclusion is to rescind the *n*–order sanction in the case of a cheater. That is, a cheater cannot expect that other merchants, who will cheat him, will be punished by the merchant community, in turn. This implies that he would need to pay a much higher efficiency wage to an agent, because that agent does not fear punishment in case of cheating him. So, cheaters will be driven out of business because of the resulting higher costs in arranging business transactions for them. This effect strengthens the collectivist institutions, with the implication that only the individualist societies allow for a growing integration of the economic system.

However, this argument cannot be fully proven within the model, because it is mainly a transaction cost argument. The collectivist traders overcome the obstacles to long-distance trade, such that integration in the sense of, for example, market integration via prices takes place anyway. Both regimes can approximate the 'law of one price', for example. So, the only crucial point would be to compare the different transaction costs involved in informal versus formal institutions, and then to relate this with the transformation costs resulting from the allocation of production activities in geographical space. On this case, our general impossibility theorem applies: There is no way to compare the efficiency of the regimes in a hypothetic general equilibrium setting. Against this background, it is important to notice that White (2011) argues that Greif overlooked the special structure of Arab kinship systems, which allowed for the extension of network configurations across a very large distance, because the marriage transactions allowed for many linkages across different lineages (White calls this 'kinship highways').

This example shows that there is equivalence between different mechanisms to realize functions, in this case the function to maintain long–distance trading networks. I argue that this renders the distinction between informal and formal institutions obsolete. Instead, we observe different ways to organize network structures on different levels by means of different semiotic systems (kinship versus contracting). Then, the efficiency criterion becomes meaningless because the economic actions under the different institutional arrangements are strictly performative. That means, the institutional arrangements in the narrow sense and the cultural context mutually leverage their functions: For example, the development of trading networks fosters the expansion of marriage networks, and the latter contribute to the expansion of the former. In other words, the 'informal institution' operates well in a collectivist setting, because it contributes to its stabilization, and the 'formal institution' does the same for the individualist setting. Efficiency considerations would only count relative to the settings, that is, transferring the informal institution to the individualist setting would be less efficient than the formal institution. But it is impossible to assess the efficiency of the institutions together and simultaneously with the cultural setting.

Figure 6.13 Hierarchies and triadic view on institutions

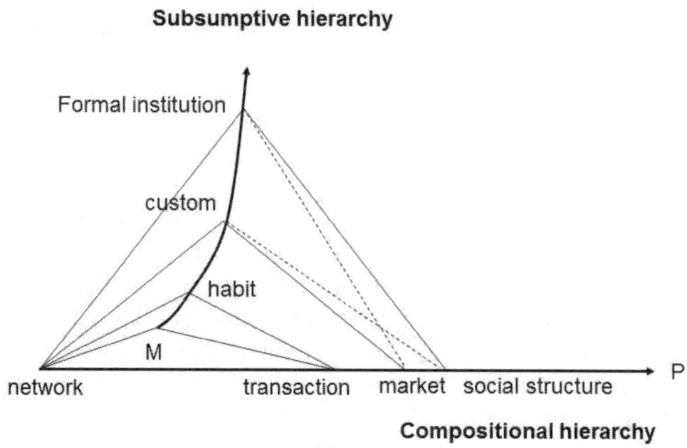

Note: The functional equivalence of formal institutions and informal institutions, that is social norms as custom, can be analysed in triadic terms when considering the compositional hierarchy of functions that puts transactions, markets and social structure in the sense of Greif (see main text) into an ordered sequence. Along the lines of figures 6.5 and 6.6, then we can refer to the sequence of habits, custom and formal institutions in the subsumptive hierarchy of increasing levels of abstraction. However, with regard to the compositional hierarchy, functional equivalence is reflected in the broken lines. That means, with reference to markets, custom may also obtain the function of stabilizing social structure, which further enables the function of custom in enabling markets, or, formal institutions characterize social structure, and thereby may also enable markets. The emergence of specific combinations will be driven by ultimate purposes of network evolution, which may emerge from larger contexts of group selection.

I propose to analyse this functional equivalence in terms of bimodal analysis of hierarchies, thus extending on the semiotic approach that was deployed in section 6.2. In figure 6.13 I refer this analysis to the distinction between compositional and subsumptive hierarchies in order to describe the evolution of types of institutions (see Chapter Three, section 3.3.1). Then, we can say that in the compositional hierarchy, we deal with nested functions in networks, which I term 'markets' in the context of our example. For example, there is the function to realize a single transaction in long–distance trade, and there is the function to maintain the business relationships with different actors through time, or the function to keep the merchant community sustainable. These functions are recurrently reproduced via transactions as mechanisms that make up the market in efficient–causal terms. At the same time, these transactions are classified in the subsumptive hierarchy according to different semiotic kinds, which I directly identify in terms of the distinctions made in the previous sections, and which relate with cognitive mechanisms, in turn. These mechanisms evolve in the way illustrated by our example of the vegetable market. Then, different levels in the subsumptive hierarchy project onto the different levels of the compositional hierarchy. Following the vegetable market example, this can imply that habits relate with a sequence of single transactions with the same actor, custom relates with a sequence of transactions with different actors, and institutions relate with transactions with different actors across different domains of business.

The point of this analysis is that similar functions can be realized by different semiotic mechanisms. As White emphasized in his analysis of Arab kinship and trading relationships, kinship connections can manifest a 'small world' mechanism that creates the possibility to expand the scope of information flows and enforcement mechanisms in the same way as the institutions of Genoese merchants. In other words, cultural variety means that there is no necessary evolutionary trajectory of institutions, relative to a criterion of efficiency. Functions emerge from the interplay of the two triadic modes, the efficient causal mechanism and the formal causal categorization scheme, which are orchestrated via final causality. Similar considerations have recently been made in other important cases of a supposed directionality and exclusiveness of particular institutional trajectories, such as the role of the corporation as legal person in Western capitalism as compared with functional equivalents, such as lineage organization in China (Zelin 2009). Again, this implies that the corporation is a performative institution, such that its emergence cannot be explained merely by efficiency terms as finality. Instead, finality emerges in the larger settings of path–dependent institutional evolution in the context of cultural settings.

6.5.2. A simple taxonomy of institutions

We can now combine the ideas of the two previous sections in fixing the simple classification of regularities in networks in terms of both the enforcement mechanisms and the cognitive mechanisms, thus completing initial cursory remarks in section 6.1.2. As a result of the discussion of different cognitive mechanisms in the emergence of institutions, we distinguish between conventions, social norms and formal institutions, depending on the nature of the enforcement mechanism necessary to stabilize them, and on the relative causal significance of different cognitive mechanisms in their emergence and actualization.

A convention is an institution which is self–enforcing, given the individual interests of the actors. The standard examples are regularities that emerge in coordination games, such as the drive left/right rules. In this case, it is always rational to follow the regularity, because deviance is dangerous, and because there is no intrinsic advantage to drive either right or left. Still, the convention must come into force, which depends on effects of salience or even a powerful act, which means that one party decides to establish the convention, and all others follow. This example shows that there are two different effects of power on institutions. One is that power is necessary to establish an institution, the other to enforce an institution. In the case of conventions, power may obtain the role of establishing salience. That is, a powerful actor in a network has a special advantage in setting up institutions because there is a higher probability that it is imitated. Once the powerful actor sets up the example, others follow, because it is in their individual interest.

It is important to notice that this argument also applies on different levels of aggregation. In all networks we have individual and group level power differentials, which we have grasped in the notion of social capital in Chapter Five. That means, in the same way as an individual can have a powerful position because of its network location, an entire group can have a similar position, which would be reflected in a most simple way in conflating the group into one node in the network (for example, a company relative to individual consumers). This implies that once a group sets up a convention based on internal power differentials, this group can impact on other individuals and groups if it has a positive power differential as a group. For example, a powerful country establishes right driving, and other countries follow.

The second type of institution is a social norm. The distinction between social norms and formal institutions refers to different forms of enforcement and the way institutions are embodied in artefacts. A social norm is a regularity that relies on *n*–th order sanctions in networks. A formal institution is enforced by a special set of actors, and which is often cast into formal documents. The classical case of a formal institution is the law, which is enforced by the government as an organization.

As we have seen in previous chapters, *n*–th order sanctions are rooted in certain neuropsychological patterns of human actors, which provide the emotional basis for spontaneous sanctions. This is important to recognize because all enforcement activities are costly. That is, an individual that enforces an institution produces an externality for others who refrain from enforcing but potentially benefit from the institution. This also provides a reason why powerful actors in networks might be especially inclined to enforce institutions if they also reap a higher benefit from the institution, given their power. The same holds true for institutions. A group of actors that form an enforcement organization will only gather if they can generate a benefit from this activity. In the case of government, this is the extraction of resources from all other actors.

The two different enforcement mechanisms come into play when compliance to institutions is not necessarily in the individual interest. This can happen on a universal basis or case specific, and with different scope as far as the number of individuals is concerned. So, deviance can result from principled opposition against an institution, or it occurs because under special circumstances it is not beneficial for an individual to follow. So, in fact we deal with a balance of power in networks, because the possibility of deviance itself is determined by network configurations of power. Since enforcement is a negative state for a particular actor or group of actors, those actors will try to counteract. This depends on their relative power, that is a powerful actor might continue with deviant action in spite of enforcement, or, on the level of groups, on their potential to organize counterbalancing collective action. This observation is essential to recognize that institutional evolution manifests the 'Red Queen Effect' that we have identified as an essential aspect of evolution in general (Baumol 2004). In our context, what is especially important is that enforcement power is driven by institutional evolution, but the counterbalancing capacity to deviate can also be enhanced by means of institutionalization.

This discussion shows that institutions also relate with the size of networks. Social norms typically prevail in small groups and tribes, because the reach and scope of *n*–th order sanctioning is wide enough, relative to the size of the network configuration. For example, in a group everybody is able to observe the sanctioning, so that imitation is also triggered easily. In larger groups, a problem of coordination of sanctioning emerges. It might be the case that in parts of the network, social norms are not enforced, which starts a process of imitative deviance. Therefore, the larger the group is, the more prevalent formal institutions are in sanctioning. This is the reason why formalization of institutions and increases of group sizes went hand in hand in human evolution. However, as our discussion of functional equivalences has shown, this needs to be assessed as relative to certain functions and hence final causalities.

In this context, the artefactual nature of signs comes into play, and the fact that the signs themselves are institutions, if we consider the production of signs. Signs are an essential constituent of all institutions. Many of those signs essentially depend on the artefact of writing, which involves the possibility of standardizing the physical artefacts, and also enabling the diffusion of institutions by the diffusion of artefacts that are not directly affected by this diffusion. For example, a book can be sent everywhere without changing its content. However, this does not mean that the activation of the artefact in certain institutional dynamics remains the same. This is the process of interpreting formal institutions in a particular cultural, political and social context. Yet, the production of signs can be institutionalized itself, which was a powerful leveraging mechanism of institutionalization in the past, with the emergence of special organizations that focus on the generation and administration of written texts.

In the case of social norms, the signs remain artefactual, but merge much more closely with the behavioural patterns. For example, a group may have certain customary behavioural patterns in social interactions, which can be activated in social ostracism to enforce an institution. These patterns cannot diffuse in a larger group or even across populations like a written document, because this would require direct imitation of the behaviour. This transition was already evident in our discussion of the vegetable market.

So far I have focused on single institutions. However, there are many interactions between institutions which relate with the same population. These interactions can be classified into synchronic and diachronic ones (a central distinction in Aoki 2001). Diachronic interactions refer to the impact of existing institutions on the establishment and enforcement of new institutions. Synchronic interactions refer to the mutual embeddedness of institutions. Both kinds of interactions go back to the more fundamental issue of consistency and coherence of institutions. This means that a set of institutions will evolve in a way such that endogenous tensions and contradictions between institutions are minimized, relative to the prevailing network configurations. At this point, individual actors obtain a special role, because the tensions between different institutions must ultimately find expression in cognitive dissonances on the individual level, such as tensions between different deontologies or behavioural drives.

As we have seen, there is the special issue of the relation between social norms and formal institutions, relative to network configurations. In a large–scale network, different small groups may follow different social norms, which interact with institutions on the level of the large groups or even the entire network population. One especially important aspect of this is that a group of enforcers follows institutions, in turn, in applying enforcement mechanisms. Then combinations can emerge such as that the internal enforcement of institutions within the group is based on social norms (a typical pattern in many political elites), which enables the enforcement of formal institutions beyond the group.

I summarize this discussion, which may appear to be a bit haphazard, in figure 6.14. But this circumstance reflects the simple fact that the determinants of institutional evolution are complex, idiosyncratic and highly context–dependent. Further, it is extremely difficult and even impossible to define a general benchmark for the relative assessment of institutions, as the discussion of efficiency has shown. This has been stated also in most general theoretical terms by Sen (2009) who argues that most economic and social theory adopts the perspective of 'transcendental institutionalism' which suggests that all institutions can be related to some final endpoint of ideal institutions, such as freedom, justice or other values. Sen proposes a methodology of 'realization–focused comparisons' in which the yardstick of assessing institutions is defined endogenously by the participant actors. As I will discuss in the next section, one central problem in this approach, however, is to account for the role of power, both within a particular society, and between different societies. This implies that internal and external benchmarks for realization–focused comparisons can differ; in terms of efficiency, what appears to be an efficient institutional state can fail to meet the challenges that result from competition between different groups with different institutions. One of the most interesting cases in human history is the comparison between China and Europe.

Figure 6.14 Types of network regularities and taxonomy of institutions

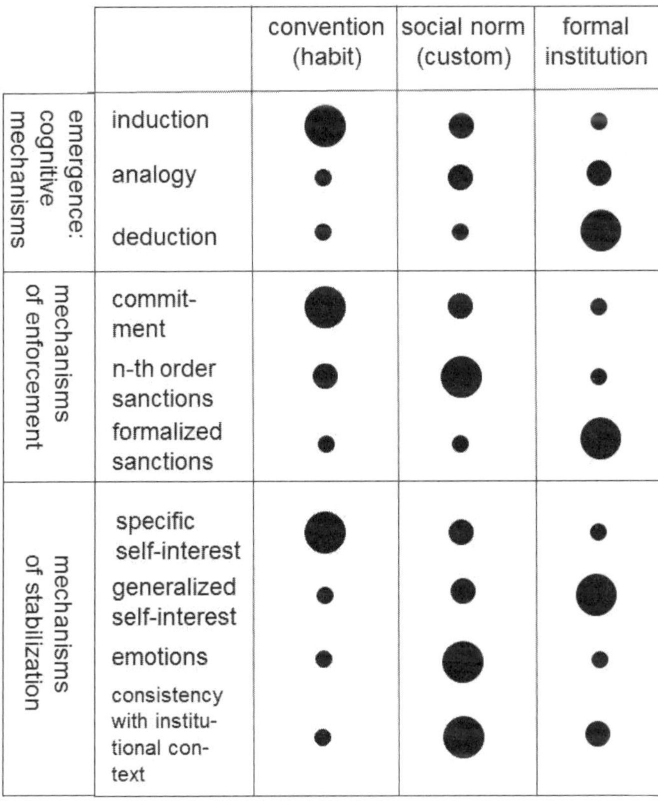

Note: This table presents an overview of types of institutions relative to the three mechanisms of emergence (variation), enforcement (selection) and stabilization (retention) (see section 6.1.2.). The size of the circles shows the relative importance of the mechanisms for the type of institution. The selection of aspects is by no means complete, but highlights important points in the discussion of the main text. For the explanation of the different categories, refer to the main text.

6.5.3. Culture and institutional diversity: China and Europe

The concluding analysis is important to extend the principled point on functional equivalence to the macroscopic level. We can say that macroscopic network structures always rely on the complex interplay on different kinds of regularities on different levels of networks, that is small groups, tribes and large groups. In this view, one cannot simply juxtapose one type of system which is supposed to be on the level of 'large groups' with other systems that mainly operate on the lower levels. The interplay between all levels leads to certain results that have to be sustainable relative to the forces of group selection that we will scrutinize in the next section. In other words, I believe that many accounts of the special trajectory of European countries towards modernity unduly overemphasizes alleged peculiarities with regard to internal network structure (in this sense, and 'institutional internalism') as opposed to external environmental conditions of group selection.

One of the most significant examples from world history is the comparison between China and Europe (tellingly, China is almost entirely neglected in North et al. 2009 who reiterate the story of Western separateness). China is the political entity with the longest unbroken history of the world, if one does not count the revolutions of 1911 and 1949 as a fundamental rupture, which corresponds with the perception of the Chinese people today. Until 1911, with a history of more than two millennia, China featured a peculiar institutional pattern that was evidently highly successful in maintaining the political integration of the country, but eventually failed to cope with the military pressure of Western powers and Japan. This military aggression was mainly building on technological means: China was always faced with military threats, and the last dynasty was an alien one. But the remarkable fact about earlier periods of military defeat and weakness is that there was no fundamental pressure on institutional change, to the degree that foreign rulers even adopted the Chinese institutions, such as the Manchu rulers of the last dynasty. Considering this structure, the most conspicuous feature is a peculiar combination of social norms and formal institutions, which is reflected in the state ideology of Confucianism. Two aspects loom large:

- Firstly, the institutions promulgated by different means by the government intentionally supported the social norms prevailing in kinship groups, even though these could stay in conflict with the central power (for a penetrating analysis, see Faure 2007, who argues that Chinese state ideology actually transformed traditional lineage structures into components of a proto–modern state, in the sense of North et al. 2009 on impersonal institutionalization). Thus, social norms were partly transformed into formal institutions, and some formal institutions were transformed into social norms. As a result, certain behavioural patterns for example of village social organization diffused across the country which provided the bedrock for government power, resulting into complex interactions between local culture and centralized civilizational institutions (for an overview, see Sutton 2007).

- Secondly, the same social norms also supported vast social networks among local and central elites (for a fascinating case study, see Clunas 2004), which were in turn monitored via the national education system which indoctrinated those elites with certain cultural beliefs. These cultural beliefs gave rise to shared identities of elites that reached beyond the scope of local identities. One important consequence of this system was a certain degree of openness of the central bureaucratic power structure.

This particular system of government reflects a peculiar power structure in Chinese society which was closely related with symbolic systems, in particular the dissociation between the spoken language and the writing system. This has been dubbed 'Culturalism' in China studies and compares with the emerging pattern of bureaucratic integration in Europe (for seminal studies on this sort of 'centralized minimalism', see Huang 2008). It is highly significant to notice that this system could operate on a much lower level of costs of government: The tax load was one order of magnitude lower than in Britain, in spite of the fact that the Chinese government was a stable centralized structure in ordinary times (Ma 2012). However, this integration was achieved by the special configuration of social norms and institutions, whereas the Western European model tended towards an ever increasing emphasis of formal institutions in different shapes. So, regarding the degree of formality one can notice telling differences, such as the creation of national civil laws in Europe, whereas China did not develop similar institutions, with formal law focusing on administration and the penal code. Or, whereas Europe developed professional bureaucracies, China relied on cultural leadership by scholar–officials, and so forth.

I will discuss the Chinese comparison again in Chapter Seven. In the current context, suffice to notice that the Chinese system supported a rapid expansion of the population until the twentieth century, almost parallel to the European one. China featured patterns that are often described as distinctly European, such as the spread of markets and the increasing social division of labour (Keller and Shue 2007). Therefore, recent scholarship (such as Pomeranz 2000), in a substantial revision of earlier views, argues that from the viewpoint of institutional performance, China and Europe compare even in details, although manifesting clear cultural differences in the institutional structures. However, as in the previous discussion of the Maghribi traders, this cultural diversity did not affect fundamental functions, such as enabling coordination in very large societies. This can even be traced back to micro–level structures, including distinct patterns of emotions and cognition in maintaining network configurations. As I have briefly sketched in Chapter

Four, East Asian and Chinese cognitive structures appear to manifest stronger field dependence than European and American ones, and emotions are handled differently in the context of social interaction (for a survey, see Herrmann-Pillath 2009a). This results in peculiar network configurations, with interlocking small–group structures that can achieve high levels of connectivity because of polycentric overlapping (therefore, the foremost twentieth century Chinese anthropologist Fei Xiaotong even coined a special Chinese terminus technicus for this social formation). These structures in turn enabled distinct mechanisms of enforcing social norms, but also formal institutions.

So, considering China and Europe, we can support the general approach taken in the first section, namely that institutional performance needs to be assessed in terms of productivity, and not efficiency. The larger productivity of the European institutions is strongly influenced by the capacity to generate certain technological innovations that allowed harnessing increasing energy throughputs, which also ultimately enabled the development of new enforcement technologies, in particular weapons; this part of the picture I am going to detail in the next chapter. The material symbol of this superiority was the steamship equipped with canon, and not the formal institutions of property rights. Both societies supported so-called 'extended orders' with open access and a high degree of competition; China even put the military under civilian control at a much earlier stage than Europe. Thus, cultural variety and functional equivalence are two sides of the same coin, which renders simple accounts of institutional evolution meaningless.

We have already noticed that the term that can conjoin these different theoretical perspectives is power. So, if there are different functionally equivalent institutions in terms of efficiency, power is the essential factor that determines the institutional trajectory chosen. From this view, power becomes an essential element of performativity, as it also reflects the creative potential of institutional design: Certain powerful actors have the capacity to design and enforce institutions, and if those institutions are performative, they can result in efficient institutions because of the mutually adaptive changes of behaviour of actors. Then, the question arises how the original positions of power emerge. This is the result of evolutionary forces which centre on the productivity of institutions, thus referring back to the fundamental laws of evolution, as analysed in the Maximum Entropy framework. In other words, the different trajectories of China and Europe may fail to demonstrate different levels of efficiency of institutions, but manifest different capacities for mobilizing power, both in the sense of network capacities and, ultimately, energetic throughputs, in the context of group selection, namely military competition.

6.6. THE EVOLUTION OF POWER AND THE EMERGENCE OF INSTITUTIONS

6.6.1. The 'specialization dilemma'

There is an illuminating coincidence in the use of the term 'power' in two seemingly unrelated domains. We refer to 'power' in the context of the capacity to generate physical work, as in Chapter Two, and we refer to 'power', as we have seen in the previous chapter, as the most general human capacity to realize interactions. If we extend the latter notion of 'power to do…' into the control of the natural environment, it is easy to see that the two concepts converge on a more abstract level, as all action taken towards the environment is physical work (on this semantic confluence, see Vermeij 2009 or Odum 2007: 290ff). So, we can speculate that the ascendency of human networks is bolstered by institutional evolution, and that this means that the mobilization of system throughputs is also accompanied by the accumulation of network power, that is the growth, the increasing scope and the growing intensity of power flows in networks. Institutional evolution is the manifestation of this principle.

The confluence of the two notions of power is manifest in the bimodality of institutions and technology, in the sense that the coordination of behaviour via institutions is reflected in certain matterenergy structures, namely technologies. We will put the different parts of the picture together in the next chapter; currently the focus is on one part of it which is essential for analysing institutions. This is the role of technologies in the enforcement of institutions. It results in an essential role of technology in determining the power balances between actors in designing institutions. This applies for both on the individual and the group level: As in the example of China versus Europe, European societies had evolved certain internal mechanisms of enforcement, and these mechanisms relate with the potential of collective enforcement towards China.

As far as institutions in the narrow sense are concerned, power is essential in two senses. First, the cognitive dimension of institutions must rely on power, because all institutions which solve a social coordination problem actually suffer from the same problem as the original problem, namely that there can be deviance. The taxonomic distinction between conventions and other institutions refers to different degrees of self–enforcement. Institutions that solve hard problems of social coordination need to rely on external enforcement mechanisms. This, of course, creates the next problem: How can these enforcement mechanisms be stable and reliable in order to safeguard the cognitive function of the institution? In fact, enforcement mechanisms are institutions on their own. We can refer these observations back to the analysis of the interdependence between trust and power in Chapter Five: Institutions can only fulfil their cognitive functions, if they are trusted; trust in institutions builds on trust in functional enforcement, hence the recognition of power that underlies enforcement.

The other aspect of power is that institutions create power in terms of capabilities to interact. This relates to the cognitive dimension, as my capability is determined by interaction costs, and coordination by means of institutions reduces these costs. Hence, my capabilities are enhanced. Beyond this, there is a direct effect of power: For example, if a certain coin is a legal tender, the seller has to accept it. So, I have a certain power relative to the seller if I own the coin. This aspect of institutions stands at the centre of the property rights approach in economics. However, I think that property rights are just a special case of institutions, which is useful in analytical terms as many propositions of property rights theory also apply for institutions in general. All institutions create entitlements and obligations (see Schlicht 1998), and this is what creates power. So, for example, we would not say that modern marriage creates property rights related to my partner, but yet, in the case of divorce my partner may have claims against me, for example regarding child custody.

Obviously, there is a feedback circuit between the first and the second aspect of institutions. Enforcement presupposes power. But a powerful actor might not be interested in enforcement, because it is costly. Why should an actor bear the costs of enforcement? One simple solution is that the parties themselves enforce the institution, which creates the problem that the power enhancing properties of the institution depend on contextual determinants of power relations in the momentarily prevailing network configurations: Who is powerful at the moment determines the degree of enforcement, which would actually erode the cognitive function of institutions. So, the solution lies either in binding commitments or third party enforcement. Third party enforcement requires a de-contextualized, that means exogenous power position and concomitant interest of the powerful actor to enforce the institution.

In the context of economics, this argument is a more general version of the so-called 'specialization dilemma' (compare Buchanan 1979; Kliemt 1986: 50ff). Consider two actors, Robinson and Friday, who agree to cooperate. They realize that there are efficiency gains in exploiting their comparative advantages in agriculture and fishing. Both need crops and fishes for survival. They could reach an agreement to specialize and later exchange their products. However, both cannot monitor the realization of the activities. If one side specializes fully, and the other does not, this ends up in an increased power position of the actor who did not specialize. If Friday fishes and raises crops, he is less dependent on Robinson than vice versa, if Robinson fully specializes. Therefore, there is a Williamsonian (1985) hold-up problem here, which might block full specialization, if both sides realize this.

Now let us assume that there is a third party, Saturday, who is especially strong. The three could agree that Saturday assumes the role of the enforcer of the specialization agreement. This implies, however, another specialization, namely that of Saturday on the application of sanctions by physical force. On the one hand, Saturday is dependent on Robinson and Friday for the provision of food, but at the same time he can just rely on physical force to extract food from both. This shows the fundamental dilemma of any specialization on enforcement: It creates a new position of power, which can interfere with further institutional evolution. This problem is especially important because it also applies in the case of institutions that contain physical force, such as property rights. All actors who specialize on the enforcement of property rights can also undermine them via the extraction of resources by means of violent actions. Therefore, the general problem of institutional evolution is that all enforcers have incentives for predation, which creates trade–offs with production (compare Skaperdas 1992 or Grossman and Kim 1996). More generally, institutional change always has a distributional impact that feeds back onto institutional change (for the case of property rights, see the seminal analysis by Libecap 1989).

Although this is a sweeping generalization, we can say that the institutional evolution of human networks followed a pattern that fundamentally reveals this dilemma (for an early and succinct economic statement on this, see Hicks 1969: Chapter 2). I have already pointed out in the previous chapter that we can discern a pattern that moved from the primordial small group and tribe structure over the millennia of agricultural regimes with stark power asymmetries to the modern societies with a more equal power distribution. In fact, the latter stage is not yet fully concluded in many developing economies, and in many cases the transition was only completed in the twentieth century. That means, the basic pattern of the specialization dilemma was the defining institutional phenomenon for most of human history. Considering this, we need to further acknowledge the fact that the alternative to production and cooperation, predation, is actually the application of violence towards others (Hirshleifer 2001). So, we can posit that the core function of institutions, in the sense of the evolutionary origin, is the coordination of violent action; this matches with the observation that one reliable measure of institutional progress is the continuous reduction of levels of violence in human societies (beginning with early seminal studies such as Knauft 1987 we know today that the myth of the peaceful savage was just that, a myth; for a comprehensive overview of this evolutionary trend, see Pinker 2011). As a result, the institutional patterns that shape predatory violence have been shown to deeply affect even the long-run development of societies, such as the impact of different colonial regimes across the world on basic institutions of property rights and ultimately levels of prosperity even today (Acemoglu et al. 2001; Acemoglu and Robinson 2005).

6.6.2. Power projection and scope of institutions

This pivotal role of violence has also been put at the centre of the theory of institutions proposed by North, Wallis and Weingast (2009), who ideal-typically distinguish between modern 'open access orders' and the 'limited access orders' that prevailed throughout most human history. Their argument can be cast into the simple terms of the group selection paradigm: The control of violence in human societies has to solve two problems at the same time; one is to maximize the capacity for violent action in order to ensure group survival facing external threats, the other is to contain internal violence in order to ensure economic sustainability and lower protection costs. Then, we can surmise that there are evolutionary forces that result in institutions that create or maintain external power balances or dominance patterns via internal power asymmetries; the latter emerge from an 'implicit social contract' by which actors with certain advantages in mobilizing violent actions restrain these action internally against the security of enhanced status, bolstered by highly asymmetric distribution of resource use which supports both the consumption of status goods and the maintenance of capacities for violent actions, namely the military. North et al. argue that this regime is highly stable and can only be overcome with violent disruptions, because the privileged actors need to give up their status. So, typically, these situations occur in the context of group selection, that is, if the society is under great external pressure, mostly a military threat (this is the unifying thread across as different historical events such as the French Revolution, the collapse of the Chinese Empire or the Communist Revolution in Russia).

Looking back on this period of limited access orders, there are several intriguing long-run evolutionary trends (for classical treatments of these facts, see Tilly 1975, 1990; these apply especially for Europe, which manifested a highly dynamic evolution and selection of political units, see the extensive overview by Davies 1996, highlighting the facts 1996: 456, 1268):

- Firstly, there was a tendency of increasing size of the reach of institutions, which is reflected in the secular decline of the number of political units;
- secondly, this trend was driven by recurrent military competition among those units;
- thirdly, there is a trend of increasing scale of military competition among this units, in terms of the mobilization of economic resources and the collective use of technology, and
- fourthly, there is trend of decreasing levels of violence within those units, which was accompanied by increasing levels of administrative costs.

So, in fact one trend that deserves close attention in the context of institutional evolution is the growth of government as a locus of power in the most general sense, which was taking place both in relative terms (growth of government as a part of a circumscribed network of interactions) and in absolute terms, namely the size of networks controlled by single governments ('state capacity' in the approach of Besley and Persson 2009). This raises one important question: Which forces determine the size of units with a set of unified institutions?

This depends on power projection, in terms of the reach and scope of enforcement mechanisms, but also in the sense of the feedback from the reach and scope of institutions on the projectability of power. Power projection is both a function of available technologies and of the institutions that undergird the application of technologies. In economics, this question is related to the theory of the optimum size of political units, which we can understand as units of enforcement mechanisms that stabilize a set of institutions within the scope of the political unit (for a succinct overview of the economic theory of size of nations, see Alesina and Spolaore 2003; for an extended treatment of the subsequent issues, see Herrmann-Pillath 2009b). This size can be theoretically explained via efficiency criteria, as there are a number of trade-offs, if we assume that the heterogeneity of a population increases with the size of the political unit. In a centralized political system, we can assume that increasing heterogeneity of the population means that the average dissatisfaction with a unified provision of institutions increases, such that tensions emerge that might lead towards dissolution of those entities, because internal conflict and coordination costs increase. This effect limits the size of a political unit. At the same time, however, many public goods can be offered with economies of scale. This is certainly also true for the setting up and the enforcement of institutions, such that with increasing size, for example, the costs of government decline, relatively speaking, thus enabling a decreasing rate of extraction. From these two trends, a fundamental trade–off in institutional evolution results.

Such arguments can be questioned, because, for example, increasing size means that individuals have less scope for leaving the system, such that coercive powers grow, as a result of circumscription (this notion is especially important in the analysis of early agricultural empires, see below). The general point that I wish to make here is that the size of the political unit in institutional competition is an institutional problem of its own sake, which, again, cannot be treated in terms of a universal measure of efficiency. In particular, we can go back to the problem of interaction costs, because generally, internal interaction costs will be lower, because of institutional homogeneity, than inter–group interaction costs, which add institutional diversity. Thus, one possible way to approach the issue of scope of institutions is considering the trade-off between external and internal interaction costs.

However, this is not feasible because of the role of conflict in inter–group interaction costs, and because these depend on the structure and size of the entire system of groups. In particular, institutions enabling larger size will be supported by selection, thus establishing multiple equilibria with regard to size (Alesina and Spolaore 2003: 128). This is because larger size can be a collective good in its own terms, as it enhances relative power of the agents operating under the pertinent institutional regime (for a related argument of relative size of countries in the context of the power distribution in international trade conflicts, see McLaren 1997). As relative power is a public good shared by all members of a group, heterogeneity of agents will not matter to a large degree, such that there is an internal positive feed–back mechanism fostering growth of groups with the same institutions. On the other hand, a large number of small groups will engender many small-scale conflicts, which require a corresponding level of the production of public goods, with a relatively high level of costs. As a result, there will be strong forces of increasing size of units with similar institutions.

We can therefore conclude that the interaction between power and institutions triggers the long-run evolutionary trend of an increasing territorial scale and scope of institutions, both in the extensive and the intensive sense (for a supporting theoretical model, see Besley and Persson 2009). So far, the high point of this development was the emergence of the modern nation state, which features large territorial scale of institutions and a high degree of institutional uniformity within its territories (for a classic analysis, see Gellner 1983). This compares with similarly large structures, such as the old empires, which features large scale, but much less internal homogenization (Mann 1986). As the recent history of colonial empires shows, the nation state also faced trade–offs which limited its territorial reach.

In this context, it is important to emphasize that institutionalization in the nation state does not only refer to the systems of law and formal enforcement, especially in the context of the monopoly of violence. The evolution of institutions in modern societies encompasses a much larger domain of the increasing homogenization of social norms as well, even including many aspects of the private sphere, such as sanitary and hygienic habits, which have been partly institutionalized (for example, the individual ownership of faeces to be used as fertilizer, governed by social norms in markets for faeces, was dispossessed via the institutionalization of hygiene, concomitant with the diffusion of certain technologies such as urban sewage systems, see Gleichmann 1977). This implies a deep integration of power structures with implications for the patterns of distributed agency in networks. Individualization in modern societies goes hand in hand with an integration of institutionally guided behavioural patterns, thus at the same time actually restricting the diversity of individual patterns, an observation emphasized by many researchers in the different traditions of Elias and Foucault.

6.6.3. Agriculture and formal institutionalization

In this chapter, I cannot deal with the fascinating details of these historical processes. I highlight one essential transition mentioned previously, namely the transition from primordial societies to the limited access orders, historically, the larger scale agricultural societies. This transition is the archetypical analytical case, because it means the transition from small group to large groups in expanding networks of interactions. According to the analysis of Chapter Five, institutions can be seen as the core phenomenon of categorizations that enable the viability of successful interaction in large groups. So, this early transition from social norms to institutions can reveal the basic interdependence between institutions and power, in the sense of mutual leveraging: power enables the emergence of institutions, and institutions enhance power (this view on early civilizations was seminally developed by Corning 1983, 2003).

Original human hunter and gatherer societies were pure network societies in the sense that they were characterized by fleeting and unstable network configurations. This lack of structuration resulted from the strategies of every member of the network to equalize the power distribution; status orders did exist, but they were not stable in the sense of exalting single members over a longer period of time (Binmore 2005: 130ff). This implies, at the same time, that no single member had a power position that was sufficiently strong to impose unilateral sanctions on others over an extended period. Therefore, these primordial societies did not manifest formal institutionalization, beyond social norms that might be supported by collective sanctions, that is *n*–th order sanctions, with the limit case of social ostracism, which could be a lethal punishment, given the harsh natural environment. This had a clear evolutionary consequence, namely limiting the size of groups, because of the limits to projections of group identity and workable sanctioning mechanisms, given the constraints of the human brain to process network dynamics. As we have seen in Chapter Five, the typical human group therefore is a tribe consisting of free–floating bands, in which kinship relations played an essential role for maintaining the social cohesion.

Historically, the transition to institutionalization proceeded via the intermediate evolutionary step of establishing chiefdoms, which in turn allowed for the emergence of more complex network configurations, because of the concentration of enforcement powers (for an overview, see Claessen et al. 1985). In the framework of Chapter Five, chiefdoms appear to be the result of the accumulation of social capital with certain members of the group, which triggers the emergence of self–reinforcing power differentials. However, in all primitive societies there were group reactions and norms containing those feedback loops. For example, the power of war chiefs, based on extraordinary strength and fighting prowess, might be limited to the time of war, or, the accumulation of resources following up the concentration of power was balanced by the social norms of regularly redistributing resources in the group, such as in the Indian potlatch. As a result, primitive human societies do not feature the high concentrations of power which are indispensable for formal institutionalization. Thus, from the evolutionary perspective, we can distinguish between human societies which are based on rank, which is a fluid, even ephemeral phenomenon resulting from the role of status in human networks, and persistently stratified societies, in which status is assigned to particular groups in terms of roles in network configurations, which are stable through time, and thus result in highly asymmetric power structures (Mann 1986: chapters 2–4).

The problem of how the threshold towards formal institutionalization was surpassed is mainly dealt with in anthropological and archaeological theories about the emergence of the early state (for a succinct overview, see Bernbeck 2007). It depended on the carrying capacity of the environment whether an incipient concentration of power was stable, because a central determinant would be the unequal distribution of resources. This is evident from the central significance of the Neolithic transition to agriculture, thus clearly manifesting the institutions–technology link that I have highlighted previously. Agriculture had far-reaching effects on network dynamics (for a seminal view, see Rindos 1984). Firstly, agriculture imposed a sedentary pattern, in which spatiotemporal relations between network members became fixed. From this, some functional requirement emerged to define the relations between networks and resources, namely land and crops. Second, through time agriculture allows for the emergence of more pronounced power differentials, as there are differences in the productivity of individuals and soils. These power differentials enhance the sanctioning potential in the network, and hence favour the emergence of formal institutions. Thirdly, agriculture fosters population growth, and given the sedentary pattern, this implies that group sizes can transcend the limits of network sanctionings, thus resulting in a functional requirement of alternative coordination mechanisms.

If a group stays closer to each other over an extended period of time, new needs for social coordination emerge. For example, closer proximity implies more opportunities for conflict, and generally speaking, social coordination becomes a more valuable public good. A crucial role in this process was played by the emergent technology of storage, which allowed keeping the advantages of higher productivity, and engendered early notions of possession. Storage had also been becoming more important much earlier on the short-term basis, as a consequence of cooking, which preserved food for a longer time (Wrangham et al. 1999). That means, the emergence of agriculture clearly supported the increasing complexity of networks, in all three dimensions: Firstly, there were more closer and recurrent transactions, secondly, the density and directness of perceptions increased, and thirdly, communication was eased. In all three dimensions, the sedentary patterns also implied that the role of third parties became more salient, for the simple reason that spatial closeness implies much higher levels of observability of actions of others, which substantially increased the scope and intensity of *n*–th order sanctions.

In sum, agriculture is an evolutionary stage with a ratchet effect, because the implied population growth means that either a mechanism of stabilization of network configurations emerges, which eventually forces everybody to conform to certain institutions that support the production regime of agriculture, or in the case of failure a breakdown happens, which would jeopardize the economic foundation for the larger population size. In this specific sense, agriculture is a hypercyclic phenomenon in human networks, which increased adaptiveness in the sense of biological fitness, without implying, as the empirical record shows, that general levels of the satisfaction of needs improved. That is, population pressure was a result of agriculture, which decreased the average availability of nutrients, but at the same time increased the average number of offspring.

Given this increasing complexity of networks, there was a high probability that a network dynamics occurred in which the endogenous formation of social capital was supported by external resource accumulation based on different sources, such as greater productivity in plant management, or, in the other area of human activity in the prior stage of development, that is hunting. Hunting success mainly depends on physical strength and agility, which is the main determinant of the capability to apply violence against others. Hunting, however, at the same time had fostered certain social skills which relate to the organization of collective action in hunting larger game. Thus, an emergent specialization occurred across gender, given certain physical advantages of males for hunting, but also regarding the success in hunting. However, hunting is an activity that is based on physical violence, and thus induces the possibility to direct violence also against other humans.

This is the fourth effect of agriculture which is crucial throughout human history, and exactly fits with the general argument on the specialization dilemma. Agriculture allows for the specialization among producers and ruler/warriors, with the latter role clearly being related to the function of hunting in more primitive stages (which therefore was also a privileged leisure activity for the ruling elites, see Betzig 2008). The classical expression of this pattern of socialization is that between sedentary agricultural societies and nomadic societies, which also preserve the hunting style of life, which shaped, for example, the evolution of the Chinese polity over two millennia. On a lower level of structural disaggregation, this separation of roles also appears in almost every agricultural society, with classical expressions such as the ‘three orders’ of the peasant, the knight and the priest in medieval society, or the Japanese warrior class, the Samurai.

It is easy to see that this emerging central role of violence in the emergence of power structures is the root cause of many of the fundamental patterns of human societies after the emergence of agriculture. One particularly important one is the inequality of the power distribution between genders. For reasons of space, I cannot detail these arguments about the possible role of the gender dimension in institutional change. In the context of agriculture the emerging institutional and technological complex changed the power balance between genders, which in traditional economies is also influenced by the tension between productive and extractive institutions. Generally speaking, the forms of agricultural production that emerged in the Fertile Crescent and that were evolving in Europe changed the power structure to the disadvantage of women. These effects were lasting, as has been shown by Alesina et al. (2011) who demonstrate the all traditional agricultural systems in which the plough played a central role, manifest more pronounced gender discrimination against women until today. Presumably, the reason lies in the fact that ploughing requires more physical strength, which favoured the role of males. As many of these agricultural societies also evolved highly stratified social systems, this effect worked together with the dominance of males in military activities.

This example applies generally: if a specialization pattern emerges, the sanctioning potential will concentrate with those agents who specialize on the means of violence. This evolution also depends very much on technological innovations, in particular iron and metal processing, which allowed for the construction of deadlier weapons, the handling of which also requires better skills. As a result, formal institutionalization essentially depended on the emergence of a stable and unequal distribution of power, because the default state with an equal distribution does not support sufficient sanctioning potential to maintain institutions over longer periods of time. This is the simple reason why, at the same time, institutions do not simply follow an economic rationale, but are strongly influenced by the interests of the agents who actually accumulate power resources.

The fragility of the incipient stage of formal institutionalization becomes evident if we consider the final evolutionary step towards the emergence of formal institutions, which is the emergence of early civilizations (Mann 1985: Chapter 4). For all these civilizations, a set of economic conditions, ideological frames and artefacts was central. As regards the latter, the emergence of writing was crucial, which allowed for the fixation of rules. At the same time, all these civilizations manifested the emergence of a ceremonial centre, in which basic meanings were fixed. All early civilizations relied on the exploitation of agriculture, while simultaneously offering protection. Finally, all early civilizations showed the feature of circumscription, that is, there was a natural boundary which stabilized the current distribution of power, as the opportunities to leave were very limited, under the conditions of induced population growth. This is tantamount to a hypercyclic closure, as the civilizational advantages contributed to the benefit of the majority of the population, relative to the status quo ante, either in terms of increased material benefit or greater population growth, that is differential reproductive success relative to individuals in groups with different institutions.

6.6.4. The biology of institutions

This brief account of the emergence of formal institutions serves the purpose to clarify the generic nature of institutions in historical–genetic terms: Institutions are network regularities of the expressions of power in human societies, across all domains, and in particular, the economic domain. The latter holds with special emphasis, as the differential mobilization of resources is a central aspect of asymmetric structures of power. This means, one cannot envisage a Whiggish history of institutions that would diagnose progress towards greater freedom and efficiency of economic interactions. This might be the case, but would be a process driven by unintended consequences for the societal struggle over power. Even in this process, the generic properties of institutions continue to hold, namely the tendency to formalization and the organized enforcement of formal representations of institutions, which defines an essential difference to social norms.

The essential phase of the transition to agriculture clearly shows how certain technological innovations interact with institutional evolution. They impact on two dimensions: Firstly, technology changes material conditions of enforcement and therefore power balances among actors; secondly, technology alters the mechanisms enabling distributed cognition among actors that undergirds institutions. Thus, the emergence of writing enables formal institutionalization, and the availability of new forms of weapons enables the increasing scope and intensity of enforcement.

We can also state how this evolutionary pattern matches with the biological criteria of group selection. Following the general theory of group selection, the main effect of increasing formal institutionalization is the coordination of group–internal behaviour resulting into the production of public goods; these public goods mainly emerge in the domain of inter–group violence, that is military competition, and partly in the domain of production (such as large–scale irrigation systems). The effects are also reflected on the biological level. One simple point is that the corresponding behavioural patterns will, in the average, converge to the inclusive fitness criterion, considering the hierarchical structure of human networks and the implied different degrees of genetic closeness of different constituent groups (Salter 2003: 135ff). This is directly reflected in Malthusian indicators, that is the relative growth of populations with different institutional regimes. Further, at least for the case of the limited access societies we can also posit that power structures tend to map into differential reproductive success of individuals, taking their different reference groups into consideration, and applying the inclusive fitness criterion, again.

Sociobiology had focused on the question right from the beginning whether political power in human societies also correlates with differential reproductive success (the classic is Betzig 1986). In almost all human societies, especially in the context of the aforementioned stratified agricultural societies, high social rank of males correlates with strategies to maximize the number of offspring. In this argument, the point made already by Veblen (1899) remains true that there is a trade–off between the investment in offspring and investment in all resources that are necessary to keep a certain status position, such as investment in conspicuous consumption. Resource constraints always work on complex reproductive strategies that include kin, in the sense of the classic inclusive fitness criterion. In all human societies, this is translated into family strategies in which genetic closeness is indicated by cultural constructs of family lines, though not necessarily in an exact way (consider the objective difficulties in tracking genetic closeness in complex families with high incidence of polygyny and partial inbreeding). For example, as shown in Boone (1983), in the European Middle Ages the emergence of patrilineal lineages serves the function to centralize control over scarce land resources. The new rules of inheritance forced a large number of young males with limited access to these resources to concentrate on military activities, which resulted in the crusades. Crusades were driven by bands of young males which were facing relative status deprivation at home, and for whom the anticipated spoils of war promised both access to resources and reproductive opportunities. Sadly, war and rape are close companions throughout human history, until today, in many places.

Even today, politics in many countries is shaped by family politics, although the immediate motives of differential reproduction stand in the background. For example, as Betzig and Weber (1993) have shown, in the United States there has been a convergence in patterns of serial polygyny between American politicians and the general population. In a nutshell, in earlier times more powerful men had more wives, and today the difference has been reduced considerably. However, this does not imply that the underlying biological motivation is no longer existent, but only that modern societies have developed a specific pattern of conflict regulation: Modern democracy is also a system in which access to reproductive opportunities is more equal among males. This observation needs to be put into perspective against the quantity/quality trade off: As Gould et al. (2008) have shown, if in a society the quality of females is more unequal, the occurrence of polygyny is reduced, because high status males will prefer high quality females, which is a requirement to generate high quality offspring. In modern societies, inequality between females is mostly driven by skill–differences, that is educational inequalities. Such factors contribute to the general decline of fertility, but this fact does not demonstrate the invalidity of the fundamental biological dimensions of human reproduction: What counts is not absolute availability of resources, but relative positioning in status competition. Only most recently empirical analyses of income distribution in the long run have recognized that relative income status on the household level tends to persist through several generations, that is, social mobility is constrained by the status hierarchy of families (Clark 2013).

Indeed, one conspicuous observation of the history of institutionalization before the modern period is the essential role of kinship structures in establishing the small group interactions that provide the glue to powerful groups in maintaining their cohesion relative to other groups in those large societies. Intra–group violence was often also reflected in inter–family conflict. It is essential to realize that many modern economic institutions emerged out of social conflicts over the allocation of power. In order to understand these mechanisms, it is necessary to adopt 'thick' historical analyses. One demonstration may suffice to make the general point.

Padgett and MacLean (2006), Padgett (2006) give an exemplary evolutionary analysis of these interactions for the case of Florentine history, based on network theory along the lines of Chapter Five. The starting point was the early medieval competition among patrilineal families, spatially organized in neighbourhoods, over relative status. This violent fight for dominance coalesced around the conflict between the papal and the imperial power, which divided the families into two groups. As the larger conflict was a European one, the papal alliances with the Pope in Florence started to play a role in the long–distance transfer of money to fund military activities. The reason for this was the more dispersed and spatially distributed network of members of the Italian nobility, which differed from the more circumscribed lifestyle of the French nobility. From this, the financial role of Florentine families emerged as a side–product. This was further extended into a central role in textile trade and production, as credit given to the Pope was repaid partially in goods, namely English wool, which was then further processed by Italian artisans, thus giving rise to the peculiar Italian tradition in textile manufacturing. This was also an effect of an existing institutional arrangement, namely the papal prohibition of interest payment. Out of this system a unique organizational form emerged, the patrilineal merchant bank that was partly based on kinship, partly on internal contractual relations, such that only a part of the male kin were involved in its management, but it was backed by the entire wealth of the larger family.

This constellation did by no means weaken the intensity of the violent strife among the patrilineal families, such that economic and political competitions were fused. Out of the emerging role of families as merchant banks catering the needs of the political system, new economic institutions emerged, with the bill of exchange being the most prominent one, which was used for long–distance remittances. In the beginning, these were just contractual arrangements among spatially dispersed stationary merchant–bankers belonging to the same network. This system received a major impetus for institutional development from political conflict, again, when the Florentine republic was born out of an alliance between some noble families and the guilds, that is lower–status citizens. This alliance built on the increasing differentiation among noble families, with some being economically active, and others sticking to their feudal roots. The former established an alliance with the guilds that organized lower–status citizens, which ended up with a transfer of economic self–organization into the political realm, thus defining the 'republican' structures. This kind of guild–corporatism was a cradle for the emergence of new economic institutions, in particular, the creation of a commercial court and the invention of the partnership system in merchant banking. All these processes were long-term, that is, evolving through decades, the partnership system emerged and stabilized at the turn from the 14th to the 15th centuries.

One of the major reasons for its development was another violent conflict within the polity, namely the Ciompi revolt, which had caused an influential group of major guildsmen to dismantle the guilds of their political functions. As a counter–movement, the more wealthy and powerful elites began to integrate lower–status guildsmen (especially, the so-called 'cambio' bankers) into their business models, which ended up in a much more individualized, loose and open network structure, as compared to the patrilineal merchant banks. They transferred their familiar organizational models into the new structures, such that in the end partnerships became the major institutional framework for the on-going globalization of Florentine commerce and banking. This fed back to the social and political power structure, as the new elites stabilized their position through marriage ties and other relations, supported by an imitation of the high–status life-styles of the elder patrilineal elites. A crucial channel was the individualization of credit, that is, the political and economic elites were deeply interwoven through a network of credit relations, which added a source of commitment to the underlying network structures of status. Thus, the tight patrilineal principle was substituted by the principle of clientilism. This system finally broke down in the face of external military challenge, especially by Milan, which exerted tremendous fiscal pressure, leading towards collapse and the eventual establishment of Medici rule.

This example clearly demonstrates the interaction between power struggles, violence and network dynamics, involving relative growth of groups, triggering the emergence of institutions often as an unintended by-product. Agents clearly perceive the functions of newly emerging institutions, but this does not suffice to explain their emergence causally. Further, the stabilization of those institutions strongly depends on the prevailing power structures, that is, it is not determined by the economic functioning of the institutions. Fundamental forces are conjunctions of inter– and intra–group conflict between groups which in these initial stages of formal institutionalization are still clearly recognizable as manifesting convergent interests on biological terms, too. Even fundamental economic institutions such as the notion of absolute private property of individuals emerged through social conflicts over power embodied in biologically grounded relationships: As Goody (1983) has shown in a classical work, the early Christian Church exerted a strong impact on the changes in conceptions of family and property in its effort to contain the power of traditional kinship groups, thus fostering in the long run the emergence of the distinct European demographic patterns that root in individualized notions of marriage, family and property, for example, differing fundamentally from the resilience of relative notions of property and extended kinship in China.

6.6.5. The general evolutionary model of institutions

I will now pull the different arguments in the chapter together in stating the general evolutionary model of institutions. This I do in two steps. Firstly, in figure 6.15, I sketch a general model of the macro–level determinants of the emergence and stabilization of institutions. Here, the concept of group selection stays at the centre of the evolutionary argument. Institutions relate to the generation of group–level functions, which work both intra–group and inter–group. In most general terms, the directionality of institutional evolution, namely its finality in the triadic model, results from inter–group functions that are deployed in group selection. This is a Hayekian model in essence, without its normative implications, that means excluding the idea that ultimately particular values such as 'liberty' become manifest in this finality. Secondly, in figure 6.16 I outline the micro–foundations of this model. These refer to basic concepts in evolutionary analysis, especially the replicator/interactor dichotomy, conjoined with the bimodal perspective, namely the necessary connection between the institutions as population–level behavioural regularities and their material manifestation in signs.

In figure 6.15, there is hypercyclic connectivity between different causal factors. The trigger of institutional evolution is the endogenous emergence of status in networks which are facing external forces of group selection. Forces of group selection work in the two dimensions of environmental group selection, that is, the production of public goods by cooperation, and inter–group selection, that is violent struggles over the control of valuable resources. Both forces intersect as cooperation to produce collective forms of violence (warfare) is a public good. Within the groups, one fundamental source of conflict is the production/predation trade–off, which is further accentuated by individual variations in the capacity for violent action, which includes small–group collective actions. As predation implies a non-productive redirection of resource use, and reduces the incentives for production, there is a second trade–off between the intra–group capacities to reduce this original trade–off in order to increase the capacity of meeting pressures of group selection. One aspect of this trade–off is the social maintenance of specialists in violence who are more productive in producing the collective goods of group protection and of predating on other groups; however, this creates a dilemma in further increasing their capability for internal predation. Therefore, a crucial transition in institutional evolution is the creation of stable structures which contain internal violence by means of enhancing the internal capacity of enforcement (policing), while at the same time increasing productivity and enhancing the external potential for violent action. This is a major condition for the possibility of group selection without direct determination by genetic closeness of group members.

Figure 6.15 Group selection of institutions

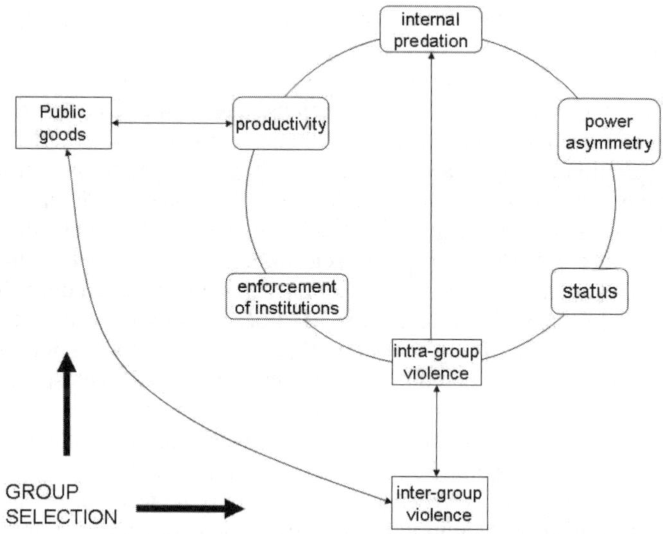

Note: The basic model of institutionalization in human groups is based on group selection as the fundamental force of directionality. Group selection favours the emergence of group–level functions. Most generally, these relate to the collective mobilization of violence in inter–group conflict and to public goods in economic production. Institutions emerge in intra–group conflicts over the distribution and resources and status, which we can model along the lines of the 'specialization dilemma'. Evolutionary contingencies result in the emergence of status differences that enforce institutions regulating intra–group conflict and enable the stabilization of collective functions in group selection. These contribute to higher productivity of groups, thus generating new opportunities for predation, both intra–group and inter–group. Under certain conditions, hypercyclic causal dynamics emerges, resulting into increasing scope and complexity of institutions, in particular formal institutionalization.

In this view, efficiency cannot be seen as the major yardstick to approach the evolutionary concepts of 'fitness' and 'adaptation', as it is mostly done in economic analysis. In contrast, we relate institutional evolution to the accumulation of power and power resources. This is the central measure of the 'productivity' of institutions, as compared to 'efficiency'. Efficiency in the economic sense is a by-product of the more fundamental forces driving the growth of productivity, because it contributes to the generation of surplus that can be mobilized for further accumulation of power. This conception allows for the theoretical integration between the analysis of institutions and of technology; once we include the latter into the picture (what we shall do in the subsequent chapter), we can show that power accumulation in institutions directly correlates with forces driving towards the maximization of energetic throughputs. Thus, ultimately figure 6.15 reveals the mechanisms in institutional evolution that are expressions of the general Maximum Power Principle, that is Lotka's Law.

Figure 6.16 Replicator and interactor in the analysis of institutions (the example of money)

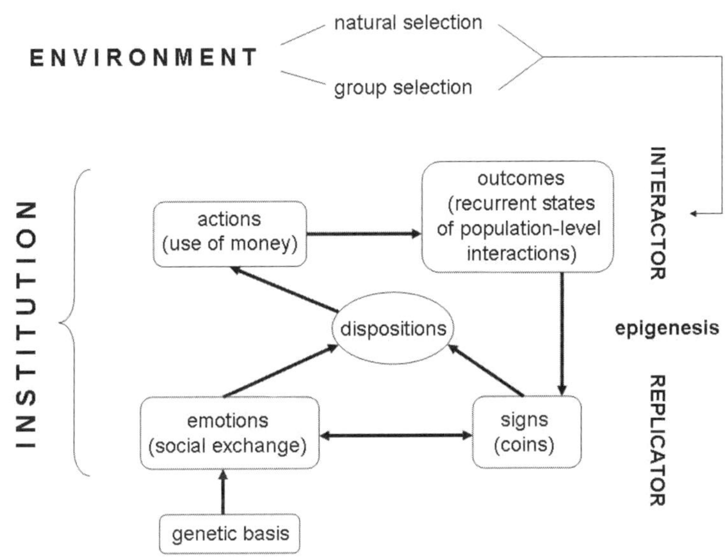

Note: This diagram embeds the Aoki model into the general evolutionary framework established in Chapter Three. In this framework, the term 'institution' refers to the entire feedback circuit between the population level and the individual level that is mediated semiotically, that is via signs (such as coins). The recurrent states of interactions lead to population–level phenomena which define the 'interactor' relative to the selective forces of the environment, as scrutinized in the previous diagram. The relationship between interactor and replicator is generated via the cognitive functions of signs which channel behaviours in the population. This builds on certain genetically embodied emotional structures (somatic markers) that causally interact with signs to generate dispositions to act. These causal circuits are the replicators, that is conjunctions of signs and neurophysiological states. The causal chain leading from dispositions to population–level behavioural patterns is epigenesis.

Next, I turn to the evolutionary view on the micro–level mechanisms of institutions. In figure 6.16, I relate the previous analysis to the generic evolutionary categories of the replicator and the interactor, thus coming back to the initial framework established in figure 6.1; I refer back to the example of money to illustrate the basic categories. This is straightforward, as we can identify the interactor as the population level regularities that generate certain functions relative to selective forces that we have identified in the analysis of group selection on the macro–level. These selective forces result from general determinants of natural selection, which refers, for example, to environmental conditions of economic productivity, and to the more specific forces of group selection, such as violent inter–group conflict. For example, as we shall see in Chapter Eight, the evolution of money was directly involved in war financing in the European state system, such that the roots of modern finance can be traced back to these functions in intra–group conflict. Further, money enables higher levels of economic productivity by many means, such as reducing the requirements to hold inventories of goods, and it enables more specialization of production, including geographic specialization, such that human niche construction capabilities are enhanced relative to diverse natural environments.

The interactor develops out of the actions of individuals, which are performative. That means, the actions are rooted in dispositions. We have seen how these dispositions, in the case of money, relate with certain emotional structures that enable social reciprocity in human interactions. Although these are genetically anchored, we cannot say that the institution of money is genetically represented, but only the generic emotional capacity on which dispositions to money use can build. Therefore, the relevant replicator function for institutional analysis is the conjunction between a sign, which is the coin, for example, and the neuromemetically embodied mechanisms of activating such generic emotional structures. Only via this causal conjunction can we approach institutions in evolutionary terms as phenomena which are emergent on the group–level; this is because the neuromemetics of dispositions could only refer to processes internal to the brain, and it is the signs and their population–level uses which enable the performativity of actions which are neurophysiologically mediated. Therefore, whereas neuromemes are replicators in the brain, institutional semiosis implies that the replicators of institutionally guided behavioural patterns on the population level are stable conjunctions of signs and neuromemes; this occurs via the recurrent generation of dispositions by the use of signs in populations. Thus, in the example of money, the use of money signs generates the dispositions that underlie that use. So, replication is essentially linked to semiosis.

To conclude this chapter, we can now show that institutions are part and parcel of the human extended phenotype, in the sense of enabling the integration of individual and collective behaviour in IGBPs. These patterns build on certain biological properties that humans have, in particular their brains, but they cannot be reduced to those properties. Institutions are new kinds of facts, and therefore expand the world ontologically. Human beings are institutional animals. We have already seen that this does not mean that a new sort of substance is emerging, akin to the old Cartesian dualism. Institutions are causal conjunctions of signs (artefacts) and neuromemes that we can observe via their expressions in IGBPs. This results into a specifically human form of niche construction. The central role of artefacts in this activity implies that institutions are also technologies, and that technologies also foster institutions. Technologies and institutions are essential features of the human niche carved out by evolution. So, we turn to the topic of technology in the next chapter.

7. Technology

These driving forces give us a broad picture of how technology builds out. Existing technologies used in combination provide the possibility of novel technologies: the potential supply of them. And human and technical needs create opportunity niches: the demand for them. As new technologies are brought in, new opportunities appear for further harnessing and further combinings. The whole bootstraps its way upward (Brian Arthur 2009: 176).

7.1. TECHNOLOGY AND HUMAN NATURE

7.1.1. Human niche construction by means of technology

In the previous chapter, I discussed the deep connection between networks, technology and institutions (figure 6.2). I will now turn to the analysis of technology proper. The core insight is that technology is an integral part of the human extended phenotype. Superficially, this seems to vindicate the standard approach to see technology as a 'tool', a means to achieve human ends, which is also congenial to Robbins' classical definition of economics that highlights the means/ends relationship (for example Arthur 2009: 28). I think that this 'tool view' is misguided for four reasons.

- Firstly, and most simply, actors do not have full knowledge about a technology when they use it. There are several factors that cause this incompleteness of knowledge, such as the disjunction between producer knowledge and user knowledge, and the unintended consequences of the use of technology. That means, if technology serves a human end, then individual actors are never fully informed about the means–end causalities and even the ends itself, if one considers the final results of technology use. We can only refer technological knowledge *in toto* to the human collectives that deploy technology.
- Secondly, therefore technology is the material expression of human distributed knowledge. This means that knowledge is distributed across both the artefacts and the collectives of actors who use a technology. In particular, technology enables cognitive functions that are not possible

without it (Levinson 1988: chapter 5). One of the most important functions is new ways of measurement: All applications of technology involve measurement in order to relate the use with the ends. It is important to recognize that this measurement function can include the human actor: For example, in order to use a hammer skilfully, the human body assumes the role of the measurement device; in acquiring skills, the body adapts to the tool in order to enable its functioning. So, distributed cognition of technology does not only mean 'out-sourcing' cognitive functions, but also internalizing technologies (what has been called the 'transparent' use of technology, following Heidegger see Clark 2010: 10).

- Thirdly, so we can say that human actors not only create technology, but also adapt to technology. This is the most radical argument why the tool view fails to grasp the essentials of technology. Technology changes the environment to which human evolution adapts. Therefore, the emergence of technological functions is a form of evolutionary niche creation (Odling-Smee et al. 2003). In other words, technology changes the human niche, and therefore cannot be regarded to be a tool that is just used to improve adaptation to a pre-existing niche. This has the important implication that the distinction between 'natural' and 'artificial' environment collapses (compare Mitcham 1994: 172ff; Perlman 2009).
- Fourthly, if technology is a defining part of the human niche, we also have to recognize that technology is an evolutionary force of its own because technological evolution is at the same time an adaptation to technology. That means, technological innovations mainly serve to solve technological problems (Petroski 1994). Frequently, the human needs that seem to stay in the forefront when considering innovation are in fact needs that reflect pre-existing technological functions. We can therefore say that the technological evolution of human wants is an essential part of technological evolution, insofar as many wants are derived from technological functions, and the fulfilment of wants also improves technological functioning.

This approach to technology can be dubbed 'ecological'. The principles of this view have been most extensively developed in the context of the recent developments in the literature on the extended mind and distributed cognition (see Clark 2007, 2011; compare Todd and Gigerenzer 2003). This approach makes the fundamental point that human cognition is always involving the environment in a systematic way: Organism and environment are systematically coupled in a way to reduce cognitive loads for the brain or generally, the neuronal structure of human bodies. Consider how difficult motoric tasks are resolved, such as catching a fly ball in baseball. The players do not build a complete model of the flight and calculate their optimal position after taking all data into consideration, but they constantly keep sensory contact with the ball, so that memory space is reduced. In this constant feedback with the position of the ball, they apply simple decision rules; one proposed rule is the so-called 'Linear Optical Trajectory Model', by which the player adapts her own position in a way such that the perceived trajectory of the ball is a straight line with constant speed. Thus, the cognitive subject uses the world to reduce computational load. Therefore, we adopt a radical shift of perspectives in stating that the external world itself is a technology that undergirds human cognition. Clark (2011: 81) summarizes these observations in a list of cognitive extensions, which shows that there is no clear line of separation between brain and environment; the borderline between the 'artificial' and the 'natural' collapses (a fascinating example is the artefact of writing, see Menary 2007).

So, I argue that technology does not entail a fundamental transformation of brain–environment interactions. The only difference lies in the circumstance that the environment is increasingly shaped by the results of human action. However, these results are non-intentional to a large degree: Human actors systematically fail to predict future technological evolution, and have only imperfect knowledge about the future consequences of technology used at present. If only for this simple fact alone, technological evolution is an autonomous evolutionary domain (a view emphasized in the early institutionalist literature, especially Ayres 1944).

7.1.2. Technological evolution, human intentionality and alienation

Interestingly, this raises some fundamental questions about the relationship between human intentionality and technological evolution, which have been classically discussed under the heading of 'alienation' in the Hegelian approach to 'Objective Spirit' that I introduced in Chapter One. Technology plays an essential role in enabling human work to be manifested in externalized products. The concept of alienation has been mostly received in the Marxian version; in the process of the technological division of labour, the producer becomes alienated from her products. Marx emphasized the role of ownership in the legal and economic sense, as the worker no longer owns her product in the capitalist manufacturing system, which was aiming at subverting Hegel's analysis of the civil society. However, considering the technological division of labour and knowledge, Hegel was right in emphasizing important aspects of externalization in general which match with the analysis of technology that I pursue.

In Hegel's philosophy of mind (especially his *Phenomenology of Spirit*, Hegel 1807), the subject can only develop into a fully elaborate structure of spirit if it externalizes itself into objects which it creates, and which therefore, in the first step, become alienated. If it further transcends to mutual recognition in the communities in which these objects are the object of interactions, the subject can ultimately realize full freedom in the sense of mutually accepting the collective uses of these objects. As Moyar (2008) elaborates in detail, the foremost example for this is human language, which in this respect would be homologous to technology. The subject externalizes its meaning into linguistic utterances, which is alienated in the first step, because that meaning becomes appropriated by the community of language users for the simple reason that meanings of words cannot be established by individual action alone. To the contrary, the individual only understands her own 'meaning' (taken as 'intended meaning') via this intermediation, such that, ultimately, overcoming alienation means to mutually recognize the meaning. This approach is different from its Marxian reception because it sees alienation as a necessary intermediate step towards a full realization of individual freedom. So, alienation in the Hegelian sense is immanent to technology because it establishes functions to which human actors have to adapt, and which they do not oversee and control. This lack of 'ownership' transcends Marx's analysis of property rights and can only be remedied by reflecting upon collective patterns of recognition, that is accepted uses of technology, but cannot be overcome in any meaningful sense.

The dual of the problem of alienation is the question of the autonomy of technology which plays a central role in the methodological debates over Science and Technology Studies (STS). In her survey, Wyatt (2008) distinguishes between four different kinds of technological determinism: justificatory, descriptive, methodological and normative. These different versions also differ in terms of the degree of generalization. The normative view mainly refers to recent historical developments and argues that the use of modern technology implies a particular stance towards rationality, such that technological imperatives become at least partly dominant in political and economic decision–making. In this case, one could reduce the hypothesis of determinism actually to the description of one particular pattern of society, which, however, may be a defining feature of today's global society. For example, technology is today a central feature of consumer culture (social networks, computer games etc.). One version of this normative position is to relate technology to the more universal phenomenon of modernity, which is a standard position adopted by many leaders in politics and business. Here, technological determinism would reflect a basic feature of being a 'modern' society, which precisely for being 'modern' places a priority on technological progress (compare Shapin 2008). This linkage between 'progress' and 'technology' also inheres those versions of the normative view which explicitly refer to competition, economic or even political. The imperative of technological progress is standard opinion in modern business, where technological leaders are expected to stay at the head of the pack, and partly politics, where 'high–tech' is perceived by many as the most important ingredient of military supremacy.

These normative views are different from to the descriptive approach, because this treats technological determinism as a universal factual feature of social change: Referring to the previously sketched positions, their 'technological determinism' would actually be seen as the outcome of a particular form of social organisation that emerged in Europe, but not, for example, in China. The descriptive approach would hold that technological determinism as an empirical phenomenon applies for both cases and actually explains the different tracks taken in social change. There are different versions of this position. One would simply state that technology evolves partly autonomous from other social changes, hence treating technological determinism as an aspect of technological evolution, but less of social change. For example, one would state that there was an endogenous technological dynamics in moving from the invention of computers to the internet, which was independent from other social forces. However, these forces would be considered to be autonomous, in turn, so that the actual social impact of technology would result from the particular balance of different forces. In comparison, strong technological determinism posits that technology is the core driving force to which other forces adapt. These different versions of descriptive technological determinism relate with the methodological view which moves to the theoretical level and presents arguments why technology is central to the analysis of human society. This position is often just reflecting a more fundamental analytical or even ideological stance, namely materialism. Materialists see technology as a response of human beings to material structures and forces in their living environment, and through technological evolution, technology also becomes a defining feature of this environment.

Historically, certainly the most influential author, again, was Karl Marx who introduced his distinction between superstructure and substructure and posited that technology is the driving force of the 'Produktivkräfte' which also generate the forces of social change (the 'Produktionsverhältnisse'), if the institutional structures of societies do not match with the necessities of social interaction that are imposed by technologies. This idea exerted a strong impact on all schools of thought that more or less relate with the Marxist legacy. For example, the theories of 'long waves' of economic development or the ideas about 'regulation' always assign a central role to the forces that result from the discovery and use of new technologies (Tylecote 1992; Boyer 1990). This also inheres the Schumpeterian notion of 'creative destruction': even though, ultimately, the entrepreneur is the particular social role that epitomizes the rise of a new technology, the 'destruction' results from the artefact itself and the substitution effects that occur during the process of innovation; the computer and the digital printer necessarily drove the typing machine out of existence (compare Freeman and Perez 1988).

These observations have led leading theoreticians of the relationship between technology and society to believe that entire epochs in human history and the corresponding social structures can be defined according to the most essential artefacts in use (such as the relationship between industrialization and the diffusion of the steam engine) (for a classical statement by a modern economist, see Heilbroner 1967, also Heilbroner 1985: 22f). For example, in the context of Evolutionary Economics one familiar approach is to generalize over the theory of 'long waves' and to partition the epochs according to lead technologies, understood in terms of technological systems, such as the conjunction of steel engineering and electrification, or the current ITC epoch (Freeman and Louçã 2001).

In sum, many contributions to the discussion about technology recognize technology as an at least partly autonomous domain of evolution. If this is the case, we need to reconsider the idea that is normally taken for granted in economics, namely that technology refers to production as being distinct from consumption. If technology shapes human niche construction as an autonomous evolutionary phenomenon, the distinction between production and consumption falls apart because both activities would be seen as being constitutive for adaptation in the context of technological niche construction.

7.1.3. The analytical irrelevance of 'consumption'

In the standard economic view, technology is mainly seen as 'technology of production', although one could also say that all production is a roundabout way of consumption. The latter view would at least draw attention to the fact that all consumption is also a technology, as we have seen in the earlier example of cooking and food consumption (Chapter Four, section 4.2.4.). This leads us to reconsider the role of human wants in driving techological evolution: Human wants are themselves endogenous to technology, and therefore we cannot simply say that they guide technological evolution. Then, the question emerges of how far technologically generated wants reflect underlying human needs (Cordes 2005; for example, modern food processing technology correlates with wants for food that seem to stay in conflict with needs, as reflected in obesity, see Cutler et al. 2003).

Considering the analysis presented in Chapter Four, I suggest that the philosophical notion of alienation reflects the differentiation between Object Self and Acting Self, with the latter being increasingly shaped by the evolution of technology and the resulting patterns of agency qua *agencements*. Then, on the one hand there is a mechanism that relates certain technological artefacts with needs that refer to the Object Self. So, we could relate technological artefacts with the realization of needs qua functions along the line of Corning's (2005: 283ff) list familiar from Chapter Four: 1. Thermoregulation; 2. waste elimination; 3. nutrition; 4. water; 5. mobility; 6. sleep; 7. respiration; 8. physical safety; 9. physical health; 10. mental health; 11. communication (information); 12. social relationships; 13. reproduction; 14. nurturance of offspring. However, this connection is mediated via technologically transformed wants of the actor, such that we cannot simply say that technology is an extension of organismic functions (on this view, see Mitcham 1994: 176f). One example is the transformation of communication by means of Web 2.0 technologies; these technologies fundamentally change the possibilities of communication, such as enabling instantaneous one-directional communication with large numbers of receivers. One cannot say that this particular kind of communication is a 'need' that pre-existed to this technology, but certainly can be conceived as a 'want' that emerges from it. Therefore, we can say that technological evolution transformed the ways how communication is conceived, thus endogenising the wants that relate to the generic need for communication.

Figure 7.1 Technological evolution of wants

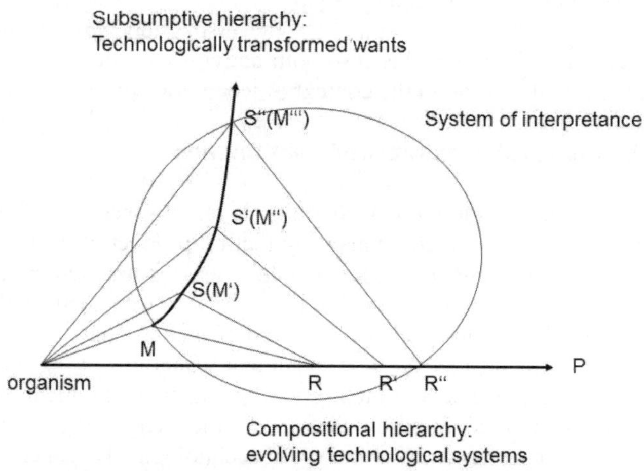

Note: Technology can be approached as evolutionary system of interpretance in two dimensions of hierarchy, the subsumptive and the compositional (see Chapter Three, 3.3.1.). In the compositional hierarchy we consider technological systems in terms of their mechanisms which interlock and embed a multitude of technological devices into composite functionings; these functionings are hierarchically ordered, such as a single car in a larger system of logistics. In the subsumptive hierarchy we consider the related hierarchy of goals which, as we shall see subsequently, refer to the role of design in establishing the relationship between usages of technology and mechanisms; for example, Henry Ford's 'Model T' transformed the role of early cars in American society in conceptually enabling its use as a multi–purpose vehicle in rural areas, whereas in Europe the notion prevailed much longer that cars are a luxury product. Thus, new wants were created that also changed the way how the larger technological system coevolved in which car use was embedded.

I visualize this important insight in fig. 7.1, referring back to the distinction between two kinds of hierarchies in evolution. Here we see that technology always involves two dimensions. One dimension is the embeddedness of technological functions in evolving compositional hierarchies of technological systems. For example, modern communication technologies have become increasingly complex technological systems which require huge complementary infrastructures and interlocking embedded technological devices in order to enable, for example, video communication over the internet. We can analyse these technologies in terms of their engineering characteristics, which means to understand the physical structures underlying the mechanisms of the technologically mediated actions. At the same time, however, these mechanisms are structured along the lines of the technologically transformed wants. Take, for example, modern journalism which has emerged as a special way to communicate news to an interested audience, and just compare classical newspapers with modern forms of online news communication. One cannot simply say that there is an organismic function, namely the need for information, and that this function is enhanced technologically. The challenge for business resulting from the new technologies in the news industry is that the wants themselves evolve with the enabling features of new technologies, which means that one cannot simply transform a newspaper into an online version.

Therefore, we have to conceive of wants as being part and parcel of technology (for a rare congenial view in economics, see Pasinetti 1981: 68ff.). Then, technology can be approached as a 'system of interpretance' on semiotic terms. One excellent illustration of this fact is the analysis of the 'industrious revolution' by De Vries (2008), which I highlight because we will touch upon the Industrial Revolution several times in this chapter. The standard view of the Industrial Revolution focuses on the innovations in the production technology and views the consumption side merely as passively adapting to the new opportunities. De Vries demonstrates that this is misguided, as the European proto–industrialization showed the emergence of a distinct pattern in the household economy in which the family emerged both as a unit of production in an increasingly differentiated division of labour mediated by the market, and as a unit of consumption of material goods produced for the market, ultimately by this household unit, with different members oriented towards different segments of the labour market. Interestingly, this view matches with Gary Becker's (1996) approach to analyse consumption as a production process, in which households use certain inputs to produce the ultimate goods that determine well-being. This view corresponds with my distinction between wants and needs, so that we can say that an essential element in the European Industrial Revolution was the emergence of a distinct pattern of wants, in the sense of the incipient modern consumer society. One important characteristics of this pattern of wants is the accumulation of consumption capital in terms of material goods, such as all items used in homes (furniture, porcelains etc.), very often in the context of signalling status. This was a shift from defining consumption in terms of leisure activities to consumption in terms of material goods, the acquisition of which requires market mediated pecuniary incomes to afford those goods.

I summarize the discussion so far in restating one of the major conceptual innovations that I developed in Chapter Five, building on the advances of

Actor–Network–Theory in sociology (Latour 2005). In Chapter Five networks were conceived as relationships between actors and artefacts which together establish patterns of distributed agency. Thus, people in the early Industrial Revolution desiring material goods were not simply aspiring at what was already part and parcel of their individual needs. They manifested evolving *agencements* in which both social relationships (such as emerging status orders) and artefactual innovations (such as watches) interacted to create evolving wants which themselves are novelties in the network dynamics of social and economic change.

7.1.4. Technology and multi–level evolution

Against the background of these introductory thoughts, I can now set up the analytical framework of technological evolution that uses the building blocks of the previous chapters (figure 7.2). The essential idea is to conceive of technology as a co-evolutionary phenomenon in human niche construction. This happens on different levels of evolution, with behaviour as a pivotal level in which the different forces interact and result in observable patterns of action, in the sense of the concept of 'institutionally guided behavioural patterns'. In this chapter, I expand the levels of evolution by including the level of artefacts. This level is closely intertwined with the level of institutions, because technology is impossible without the regularity of behaviour that is enabled by institutions. However, at the same time artefacts exert a causal force on institutions and behaviour, as they evolve partly autonomously; for example, a new kind of weapon changes power structures in societies and therefore destabilizes existing institutions. This feedback circuit is shown in figure 7.2 by connecting technological creativity with unintended consequences in institutional evolution. For example, certain institutions guide the diffusion of behaviour that drives the use of certain new artefacts; if in this dynamic setting a technological innovation happens, this feeds back on behavioural patterns and hence, institutional evolution.

In this picture of multi–level evolution, niche construction implies that adaptation happens on different levels. Via the creation of artefacts, niches are constructed that intermingle with the 'natural' patterns of change in the environment, ultimately blurring the borderline between the 'natural' and the 'artificial'; for example, human agriculture changes entire ecosystems in fundamental ways, such that this impinges in multifarious ways on different levels of evolution. A textbook case is human lactose intolerance which is genetically modified in human populations with a long history of livestock breeding and dairy consumption. In this case, we observe cultural adaptation in the first place, which results in the emergence of particular lifestyles and community organization matching with this agricultural technology. However, cultural adaptation is reinforced via culturally induced (Baldwin effect) genetic changes, hence biological adaptation (for an overview on cultural impacts on genetic evolution, see Richerson et al. 2010).

Figure 7.2 The co-evolutionary approach to technology

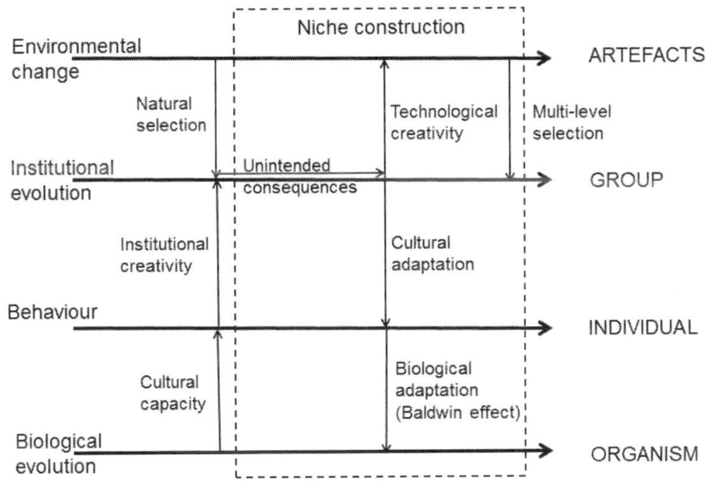

Note: Technology co-evolves with institutional, behavioural and biological evolution in constituting an essential part of human niche construction that fundamentally alters the environment setting the frame for adaptive processes. The human capacity for culture results in institutional creativity, that is phenotypical plasticity. Institutions leverage the unintended consequences of human action, including the possibility of technological creativity that results in the emergence of artefacts as part and parcel of the human environment. The evolution of artefacts triggers processes of cultural adaptation which ultimately channel biological adaptation via the Baldwin effect, among other mechanisms. Both institutions and technology are phenomena specific to the level of the group, which connects with the level of individual behaviour via the emergence of institutionally guided behavioural patterns.

The relationship between the biological level and the other levels is established via the generic human capacity for culture, which does not determine specific patterns of behaviour. Hence, this capacity for culture is also the precondition for technological niche construction. It is important to realize that technological evolution is therefore an unintended consequence of institutional evolution also in the generic sense. Technological artefacts may originally emerge in the context of the primordial need to demarcate groups and establish individual identities; in extension, they might have contributed to propel certain patterns of group selection. However, they also changed the human niche in more profound ways, such that complex adaptive processes also resulted into new expressions of the primordial patterns of behaviour. For example, Michalopoulos (2012) has shown that human ethnolinguistic diversity, a core feature of cultural diversity, reflects the diversity of land qualities across the world, presumably because of the interaction with the formation of location specific human capital, hence technological knowledge.

This co-evolutionary approach to technology understands technology as one of the channels in which human inclusive inheritance works. Therefore, it is appropriate to analyse technology as one form of knowledge that evolves in conjunction with other forms. In this respect, it is straightforward to interpret the generic naturalistic approach to knowledge championed in this book with reference to technology: Intuitively, technology is seen as ideas that are cast into the material shape of artefacts. All technology is embodied knowledge. This view builds the bridge between more common approaches in the economic study of technology (such as Foray 2004) and the evolutionary perspective deployed in the previous chapters.

7.2. TECHNOLOGY AS EMBODIED KNOWLEDGE

7.2.1. Artefacts and actors

One of the essential consequences of the co-evolutionary approach to technology is to see technology as a population–level phenomenon. This also transpires in the distributed cognition view of technological knowledge: Technological knowledge is not embodied in single human brains, but in complex evolving networks of actors and artefacts. These networks are patterned; technology and institutions are two sides of the same coin, the factory system was at the same time a pattern of artefacts and of social relations. In this section, I explore the question how far we can distinguish between different kinds of knowledge related to these patterns: For example, certainly engineers have individual knowledge about particular technological devices they create, but this knowledge differs from the knowledge deployed by users of the technology. The different kinds of knowledge are combined in the networks of interactions that constitute the usage of technology.

Further, there is a difference between specific network configurations that occur, for example, when workers cooperate in building a particular bridge, and the underlying generic features, which result from the use of certain standardized artefacts in the construction process, or the design principles underlying the construction of the bridge as an artefact. So, kinds of knowledge that is actualized in the use of technology also relate with the artefacts that are utilized in this particular network configuration, and with the kind of behaviour that is involved in using them. In other words, technology is embodied in both the artefacts and the human beings doing it (compare Lawson 2008). Technology is not a thing, but a pattern of action and a process, both on the micro–level of particular uses of technology and the macro level of its evolution.

Figure 7.3 Artefacts and actors: Affordances and IGBP

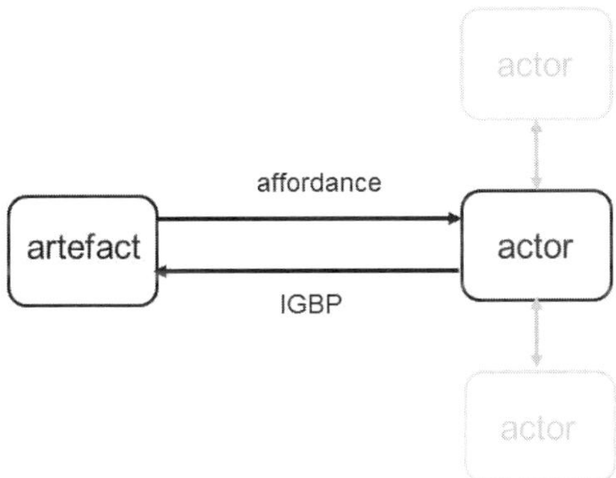

Note: Artefacts impact on actors via their affordances, which are causally triggered action tendencies (such as grasping the handle of a hammer). These actions are in turn reinforced by IGBP that are embedded into social relationships, such as imitation of Alters actions towards similar artefacts.

In more detail, I will argue that technology as embodied knowledge can be conceived in terms of the standardization of artefacts in relation with the institutionalization of behaviour. One important property of technology is that the artefacts undergo an evolutionary process that leads towards standardization of technological features. This is true even for the simplest forms of technology, such as the convergence of the shape of stone tools in the archaeological records. This standardization affects the usage of artefacts, which normally includes certain expert behaviours, such that the proper use of technology requires exercise, training and specific skills, which are different from the skills necessary to produce the artefacts. So, we can say that the usage of technology involves conjunctions of artefacts and institutionally guided behavioural patterns, IGPRs, on part of the actors. This picture matches with the general analysis of human 'grounded cognition' deployed in Chapter Four: If cognition is fundamentally based on sensorimotor feedback circuits involving external action, it is straightforward to realize that artefacts as objects of actions also exert a direct impact on cognitive processes. This interaction can be best understood by means of the Gibsonian concept of 'affordance' (see Chapter Four, 4.3.3.): In figure 7.3, IGBPs related with technology are deeply connected with affordances of artefacts, that is, behavioural tendencies that are triggered by the objects themselves. Further, we also see that these affordances are leveraged by the social embeddedness of IGBP, fore mostly carried on by the process of imitation, that is observing others in handling similar artefacts. Hence, we can posit that the use of artefacts follows the general model of semiosis that was established in Chapter Four (especially figure 4.7).

If we now ask the general question where knowledge is located that inheres the use of technology, we can say that this knowledge is partly embodied in the artefact itself. For example, the bicycle is a technological artefact that has certain physical properties that induce certain user behaviours in a way that a learning process is triggered which leads toward the proper use of the artefact. Then, we cannot say that all the skills on part of the actors are enshrined in their bodily features, or reflect some institutionalized knowledge that is external to the artefact, but we have to recognize that the physical structure of the artefact carries knowledge in the same way. In this sense, artefacts and embodied knowledge on the actors' side stay in a close symbiotic relationship. This view is essential to approach technological artefacts as an ontologically autonomous force in economic evolution, which is exactly the dimension missing in almost all mainstream economic approaches to technology, which leave the analysis of artefacts to the history of technology and engineering, and neglect important structural aspects of the production process (Metcalfe 2009). If we cannot separate the artefacts and the knowledge of actors, it is wrong to abstract from the precise properties of artefacts, and even more so to interpret technology as a set of 'ideas' (such as Jones 2002). This also leads me to question the view of technology as a social phenomenon in exclusive terms, as artefacts matter in an essential way (compare Latour 2005).

7.2.2. Kinds of knowledge, design and technological functions

All technologies, insofar as they are used collectively, involve skills and knowledge embodied in network configurations of actors, and not only knowledge located 'within' individual actors themselves. Technology is not just a set of ideas that are merely applied in practice, and which are carried by individuals, that is the inventors, innovators and entrepreneurs. Technology is a network configuration that systematically relates artefacts and institutionally guided behavioural patterns in collectives of actors. Ideas emerge in the process of technological evolution, partly as a simple effect of the deeper structural characteristics of technological networks. The evolutionary view of technological change assigns inventors to the mere role of generators of variations, which can be seen as a random process, ultimately (thus standing in the tradition of Ayres 1944 who saw technological progress as a distinctly cultural phenomenon).

Today, there are at least two different kinds of artefacts involved in the use of a technology: The technological devices and their descriptions, such as the blueprints, user instructions and so forth. This was by no means true for all technologies in the past. For example, the masters who built cathedrals may have relied on diagrams to explain certain steps in the work to erect the building, but most of the construction knowledge was embodied in their brains and the on-going network interactions in the entire group of artisans and workers doing the work (Turnbull 2000). Technological progress was also accompanied by the increasing importance of codifying technologies, which actually means that the complexity of the artefacts increases. Thus, it is important to distinguish between the artefacts of the objects which realize the function of the technology and the different physical means by which the knowledge is embodied; this includes a dual role for the technological devices, because they are the physical mechanisms that realize the function of the technology, but also embody the knowledge of the technology. In the previously mentioned example of cathedrals, the knowledge of building a cathedral was also embodied in the physical structure of its components which were then put together in the building, such as the famous case of the spandrels which evolved out of building practice and reflect physical design constraints (Gould 2002: 1249ff). For a more penetrating analysis, we need to distinguish between different aspects of this knowledge, namely the production knowledge, the reproduction knowledge and the user knowledge.

It is essential to recognize that producer and user knowledge are totally different phenomena, because the user does not need to understand the production process in order to use a technology. At the same time, however, the producer certainly needs to know some user knowledge in order to identify the function which the technology aims at fulfilling. When generating the technology, the producer partly has to assume the role of the user vicariously. In fact, we can posit that producer design operates just as a vicarious process of selection, which then undergoes the final test of real world selection by users. We can analyse this further in distinguishing between the artefact and the function, with the latter often referred to as services to the user. There is no necessary connection between the two, that is, the same functions can be fulfilled by totally different artefacts. For example, the function of indicating the time can be realized by mechanical and digital watches, hence entirely different physical mechanisms. This open relation between function and artefact expands even broader if we consider hierarchies of functions with different degrees of generality. For instance, if we consider the function of moving a person in space, there are today a large number of vastly different technologies, reaching from skiing to flying.

Hence, function and artefact are separate analytical categories. This is important to understand the relationship between technology and adaptation in the co-evolutionary framework. In general terms, producer design is about internal functions that make up the structure of an artefact, whereas the design of the artefact only relates with user knowledge, in the course of the evolutionary process. This distinction is homologous to the distinction between proximate and ultimate causes in biological evolution: Producer knowledge represents the proximate causes; user knowledge represents the ultimate causes.

One important effect of this dissociation is that, if we consider the factual course of technological innovation, there are many cases when either the user introduces uses of a technology that were not fully intended by the producer or when producers fail to link up with users' needs: This points towards an essential role of exaptation in the evolution of technology (Dew et al. 2004). The latter situation can happen even if the function could be fulfilled, in principle. Technologies might not be user friendly and so fail to disseminate. So, the question is how the relation between producer knowledge and user knowledge is established in technological evolution. I claim that this mainly happens via the semiotic dimensions of technology. There are, basically, three ways that user knowledge is embodied in technology. The possibly most important one is design: I will now use this term in the way how it is mainly used in technological practice, so that it does not indicate the intentionality of the producer, but certain structural features of the artefact that directly influence its usability (which differs from the emphasis on 'rational' design in Simon 1996). Next follows practice as a medium of embodiment, and finally all sorts of instructions.

Design is a field with a very large scope, especially if we include the practical dimension. However, there is a core meaning that is relatively precise and narrow, and which can be summarized in the meaning of Arthur's (2009: 98) statement that 'design is expression'. Arthur relates design with the intention to solve a problem, which introduces a different perspective into engineering than into science, because what ultimately counts is the capability to establish the solution, independent from the capacity to give a full explanatory account, and independent from whether the problem is artificial on its own count. This has been neatly elaborated on in Simon's (1996) classical approach to the 'Sciences of the Artificial'. Simon argues that design is the interface between the 'inner' and the 'outer environment' of systems. He thinks that most systems are simple, and that what we perceive as their complexity is actually the complexity of the outer environment that poses the problems the systems need to solve. Design relates the system to those problem solutions. Thus, design is actually the way the system fulfils functions. According to Simon, inner conditions only count when this fulfilment of functions fails, thus revealing the limitations of those inner structures. So, the role of design is always to restructure a system, given its constraints, to meet the challenges of the environment, hence to fulfil a function. It is important to notice that in this sense, all design is 'artificial', because it represents the results of a learning process. Artificiality implies structural equivalence of systems which fulfil the same functions. So, a computer can also play chess, with no difference to the human brain, if it is designed in a way to win the game in the same way as human players can do independent from how they do it.

In case of human design activities, Simon argues strongly in favour of scientifically based methods, especially computer–based simulations. Stankiewicz (2000) distinguishes between different design regimes that, on the most abstract level, relate a set of operands with a set of problems, thus creating structure–function assemblies as artefacts. However, in comparison to Simon, he thinks that the 'research regime' cannot be established as a universal regime, but is just a further development of the 'engineering regime' that uses symbolic systems to solve design problems. Aside of these two, the 'craft regime' as the primordial regime and the 'architectural regime' as the most complex one share important properties, such as manifesting a high share of tacit knowledge. The architectural regime prevails in problem spaces which require multi–functional adaptation of systems, and which therefore focuses even more on proper functioning, as trade–offs between different functions are extremely difficult to solve by theoretical means. In the context of technology, this means to focus on the user side, as I also argue. However, then there is even an Arrow–style impossibility theorem here, as Franssen et al. (2010) surmise, referring to social choices among different technological features united in one design. Basically, the architectural regime follows the logic of evolutionary processes (for a congenial modelling approach, see Frenken 2006). Today, this does not mean that there is no way to apply scientific method, because evolutionary principles can be applied, for example, in the context of computer–based simulations. Still, the emerging functionality could not be reduced from first principles, but would result from what Stankiewicz calls 'vicarious selection'.

So, we can say that design is central to technology, because it fully enables the function of the technology. Users will never comprehend all complexities of technologies, including the production process, unless they are guided by information compressing signs. Design is this sign. Design embodies user knowledge in the sense that users that process the sign enhance their capacity to use the technology, such that the function is fulfilled: Thus, the two notions of 'design' and 'affordance' as established previously are deeply connected (which is practically recognized in subfields of technical design such as ergometry). In other words, design is essential to change the environment of the use of technology in a way such that it embodies parts of the user knowledge. Take, for example, one of the most famous design examples in recent technological history, the iPhone. The acclaim for this technology is also based on its design which is said to guide users smoothly to its use, without the need for further instructions. The design is said to enable an intuitive use of the technology. But this is true for all technologies. There are different ways to build a bicycle, but only some designs are optimal in creating optimal synergies between the user and the artefact, also in the sense of channelling optimal uses of the technology. Design is the main medium through which technology becomes 'transparent' and assumes its cognitive functions.

7.2.3. Technological semiosis

I analyse this role of design in terms of the semiotic triad (fig. 7.4). In this perspective, there is an efficient–causal relationship between the artefact and the way it causes a function to materialize, which runs via the *OMR* line. It is important to emphasize the duality of artefact and mechanism here, which introduces a semantic ambiguity. All artefacts build on mechanisms, which, on the most fundamental level, are physical effects, such as gravity working along a ramp. However, because of the composite nature of almost all artefacts, those mechanisms mostly are also artefacts or modular devices (Arthur 2009: 35ff). Thus, both mechanisms and artefacts could assume the 'object' position in the semiotic triangle. The semantic ambiguity results from the fact that, once we consider the entire evolutionary process, the 'artefact' is actually the entire semiotic triangle, as the signs/designs themselves make up the new objects in recursively evolving systems of interpretance.

Figure 7.4 Triadic view on design

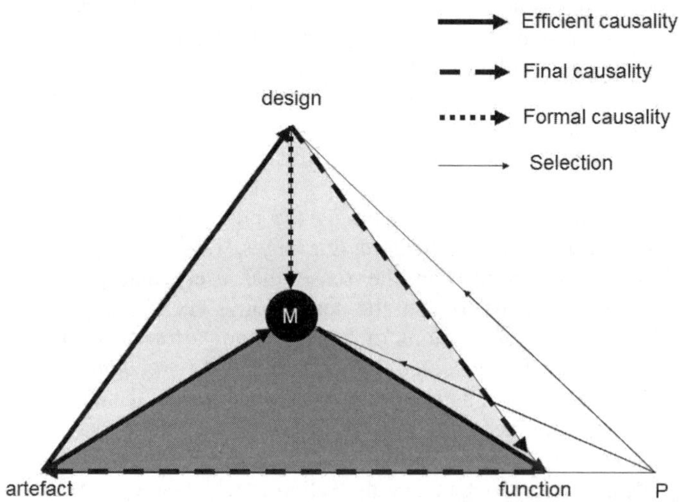

Note: Technological semiosis essentially involves design as mediating between artefact and function. Technological function is realized via mechanisms that operate in the efficient–causal mode (*M*). Function relates with purposes that drive the selection of technology; these purposes are proximately established by users of technology (final causality). The use of technology is guided by design. Design relates two different kinds of technological knowledge, producer knowledge that is embodied in the efficient–causal mechanisms of artefacts, and user knowledge that is embodied in patterns of usage, that is the previously analysed relationship between affordances and IGBP (formal causality).

As is evident from this view, I do not assume that the user is fully informed about the artefact. For example, the user does not know how it works internally, so she reads the time from the watch without knowing how its internal devices are crafted. However, some functions might need some knowledge of this kind. For example, in the earlier days of the automobile a driver might have needed to know how to do some simple repairs in order to be able to use the artefact in a proper way. In the earlier days of the personal computer technology users might have better had some knowledge about elementary programming to activate all functions of the artefact. Design plays the essential role to arrange this relationship between function and artefact in a such way that the information requirements on part of the user are minimized. This means that the user infers information about the artefact the structure of which is largely unknown to the user, yet in the semiotic view this implies that information is generated about the artefact (along the lines of Millikan 2009).

The evolutionary forces driving this result are the selection of different conjunctions of design and artefacts, for example, in market competition. Here, design is a central force in determining the composition of artefacts in the marketplace, as the actual efficient–causal mechanisms that result in functions are not necessarily the criteria that lead to the selection of artefacts in the first place, if users depend on the design features to actually discover the functions at all, or make it available at ease. Therefore, design channels selection, which results into a particular selection also of physical functions that are related with artefacts.

Design exerts formal causality on the physical mechanisms of technologies in the practical sense that design is a marker to classify artefacts. Again, the iPhone is an excellent example, as its design has driven the emergence of a new set of artefacts which are currently classified as 'smartphones' but which actually are not phones in the first place. Design communicates classifications of artefacts, such as what is a 'phone', what is a 'portable computer', or what a 'camera' is. Those classifications are important to channel technological evolution via user knowledge, in particular, but also via producer knowledge. For example, as long as a producer aims at producing mobile phones, the producer might select certain innovations of the artefact in a different way as when she aims at producing a mobile internet device that also serves as a phone. Hence, the design features also feedback on producer knowledge. On the other hand, if different designs trigger different relationships between users and artefacts, it may happen that what is seemingly a similar device – a mobile phone – emerges as a functionally different artefact because of the design, such as the smartphone.

This semiotic analysis has to be directly referred to the theory of the individual that I proposed in Chapter Four. In particular, the distinction between Object Self and Acting Self applies forcefully. We can relate the functions of technology with the Object Self, whereas the design of technology relates with the Acting Self. This distinction is implicit to marketing approaches assessing design in terms of attracting choices of users. But this relates only with the first decision, and overlooks the role of design in guiding the recurrent uses of a technology. Basically, these uses can be of two different types. One is that a technology has become transparent in the sense that its use is automatic. For example, we open the door with a key, which we do not really choose consciously when arriving at home. We drive cars absent–mindedly, listening to a news report on the radio etc. The other type is that we consciously activate the technology. Design is important in both contexts, but in the former it is the feature of technology that enables its 'transparent' use, finally, and for that reason becomes irrelevant in the emerging patterns of automatic uses. But in case of active choices, design guides the decisions of the Acting Self.

So, if we say that design guides users' behaviour in using the technology, then we can also say that it is part and parcel of the distributed knowledge of the user. The semiotic analysis implies that there are independent tracks of evolution of technologies which may work via different causalities. Design represents the force of formal causality, whereas efficient causality defines the physical workings of a technology. Therefore, we can generalize and argue that the triadic mechanism *OMR* reflects producer knowledge about creating the required function in combining certain technological artefacts into mechanisms that follow efficient causality, whereas user knowledge is embodied in the design, hence works via the triadic *OSR* channel, hence semiotic causation and ultimately final causality inhering in the evolutionary process.

It is important to see that the semiotic dimension can have an independent force in technological evolution. For example, the design of a stagecoach may have shaped the design of automobiles substantially, which may have imposed some constraints on developing the uses of combustion engines for transport. This partially autonomous evolutionary role represents the different role of design in producer and user knowledge. Design also plays an important role for the production process, of course. But we have to be careful in distinguishing those aspects of design which directly affect the physical functioning of a technology from those that affect its use. For example, changing the colour of cars from black to white to contain the heat impact of sunlight certainly changes the aesthetics of the car, but this is a side effect of the physical function.

The importance of design also results from the fact that it directly affects user practice, which is another important embodiment of user knowledge. User practice can be also analysed in semiotic terms against the background of our analysis of the individual. This is because firstly, the user herself learns about the technology via observing her usage patterns that are causally triggered by the design. User practice evolves via trial and errors in using the technology, with the fundamental split between Acting and Object Self being valid again. From this the important conclusion results that in technological evolution we cannot assume that users will manifest the preferences for a new technology simply because it enables improvements in certain functionings. Even though a functioning might be evident in advance, that does not mean that user practice creates the corresponding preferences. Again, design plays an important role in coordinating this process, which ultimately coordinates Object Self and Acting Self externally; hence, this coordination is a fact of distributed cognition.

7.2.4. Routines

User practice can lead to further novelties within the process of technological creativity, once it starts from the uses that were originally intended by the producers of technology. There are many examples in the history of technology when producers did not properly anticipate later uses of a technology. Thus, user practice is an autonomous force of technological innovation, which is partly underestimated in the heroic account of innovation which focuses on inventors and entrepreneurs, that is the production side (for an exemplary evolutionary approach to producer–user interactions, see Sandberg 2007). This is particularly relevant when considering the second aspect of the semiotics of user practice, which is that practice is observed by other users or potential users, and as such becomes a sign of actual practice, and thus triggering imitation (see figure 7.3). So, user practice determines both the diffusion of a technology and the potential innovations that occur during this diffusion. In some sense, user practice is much more important in establishing the functioning of technology than producers' actions, as user practice is the pillar of the stability and recurrence of the network patterns that actualize the technology.

Compared with the two physical embodiments of user knowledge considered so far, users' manuals are of much less significance, if only because most users actually complain about their deficiencies and obscure meanings. Indeed, the problems with user manuals in everyday life reflect a fundamental issue in analysing technology, namely that many actions involving technology are much too complex to be fully described in codified media (Foray 2004: 72ff). This complexity might not even result from the factual complexity of the actions, but from the complexity of the descriptions that would be necessary. Many technologies can only be properly used after a considerable time of practice, and this cannot be substituted by users' manuals. Actually, even most simple technologies such as the much–quoted hammer can be used on many different levels of talent and expertise, which need a considerable formation time. Most modern technologies require longer periods of training, such that there is an essential complementary relationship with human skills. Now, this sort of learning by doing mostly takes place in the context of organizations, if we consider the vast technological networks that only in their downstream part directly connect with the consumer. In these contexts, 'users' of technology are actors in complex organizational systems of division of labour, where no single actors overlooks the entire technological network, such as in a huge chemical plant.

In the literature about technology, this deep gap has been mostly grasped by means of the distinction between 'codified knowledge' and 'tacit knowledge'; with regard to the latter the notion of 'routines' has been introduced. Although this distinction is extremely important, the semiotic analysis offers a different view on the same issues. This is because the term 'tacitness' at least implicitly introduces a mentalist interpretation of user knowledge in the sense that there is something 'inside' the user which cannot be fully expressed in codified terms. In the semiotic and externalist view, this is wrong, because the practice itself is the embodiment of the knowledge, and there is nothing beyond it. 'Tacitness' would refer to the limits of describing the observed actions by linguistic means, but not to the knowledge proper.

This observation is essential for the analysis of closer forms of cooperation which happen if the use of technology presupposes cooperation in teams, as it is true for most industrial technologies. Actually, this is the defining difference between the artisan's workshop and a modern factory. Therefore, it is important to establish a connection with the use of routines in organization theory. My point is that routines are special kinds of semiotic systems scaffolding the use of technology. This requires paying attention again to the role of artefacts in creating and maintaining those routines. For example, certain artefacts in the workflow of technology use form sheets that serve as anchors for making routines stable through time. Somebody who controls a chemical process may have to fill in a regular report about certain observations which guides the behaviour of others who collaborate in the use of the technology. Therefore, the routine is essentially linked with the artefact, though not fully reflected in it. On the other hand, we cannot say that the agents are in full control of the entire process, as their actions in the entire process may only reflect the limited perspective of one single actor. This leads us back to the notion of *agencement*, in the sense of that via the emergence of routines the technology becomes an essential part of establishing the agency of the single actors (Callon 2008).

The concept of 'routines' was introduced into Evolutionary Economics by Nelson and Winter (1982), however, going back to the early research traditions in organization studies and administrative behaviour launched in the 1950s by the Carnegie School (for an overview of these historical aspects, see Lazaric 2011). Nelson and Winter established a direct relationship between routines and skills in stating that routines correspond to skills on the organizational level; that is, skills are seen as individual–level phenomena, and routines as collective–level ones. This also applies to concepts such as 'tacit knowledge', such that routines are seen as a kind of automatic behavioural pattern of collectives such as firms. Nelson and Winter also use the metaphor of 'genes' when analysing routines. Routines as firm–level programs are exposed to selection of firms on the marketplace, such that certain sets of routines emerge which are transferred across generations of firms, including, however, also Lamarckian transmission systems.

Based on this idea, Hodgson and Knudsen (2004) propose a strictly Darwinian approach to routines in which the firm is seen as the interactor and the routine operates as the basic unit of information storage and transmission, hence the replicator. This version of routine theory is seen in critical light by Nelson (2006) himself. Indeed, there is the principled question whether routines are generating forces or behavioural patterns. Considering the firm as a system of displayed behavioural patterns of individuals, the routine may just be one, possible even the most important pattern, but that would simply equate the form with the routine, hence the interactor. Regarding the interpretation of routines as generating forces, there are serious doubts whether one can directly apply the individual–level notions on the level of firms, such as 'tacitness', because many routines are in fact consciously designed and implemented. Vromen (2006, 2011) summarizes the empirical literature in this respect and offers an alternative approach to routines based on the notion of 'mechanism' in the context of multi–level systems. This view comes close to my one, because this reveals the nature of routines as artefacts. On the one hand, routines are observed patterns of behaviour on a certain level of observation, such as the firm or the team. On the other hand, it is possible to reduce those patterns to generating mechanisms. As in the analysis of artefacts, these mechanisms can be routines in turn, which then can be analysed into lower–level mechanisms, ultimately ending up at the level of the individual, where, in my context, routines can be interpreted as IGBPs.

In his definition of routines, Vromen also emphasizes the role of routines relative to physical environments. Indeed, the original Nelson and Winter model eventually boils down to a rule based formalization of firms as production functions, which would leave the artefacts out of sight. To the contrary, the role of physical artefacts has been elucidated recently by D'Adderio (2008, 2011) who offers a version of routine theory which directly matches with my one, yet without the evolutionary framework. D'Adderio draws on the sociological literature on performativity and argues that artefacts play a central role in establishing distributed agency. This is most obvious in the case of artefacts that directly represent routines, such as SOPs, where actual routines may differ, but interact with the SOP, but also with artefacts in general. Her discussion transcends technology, so that in the context of this chapter suffice to notice that therefore technological artefacts in the narrow sense, that is the physical entities, stay in a symbiotic relationship with human actors, such that the phenomenon of distributed agency actually runs in both directions. The technology also endogenizes human action in its regular reproduction, which sometimes even does not leave any further choices, unless the risk of disruption is incurred, as when working at an assembly line.

So, I argue that organization theory has to refer explicitly to the artefacts of technology, without implicating that the physical devices, as a sort of material substructure, would unequivocally determine the routines as a sort of superstructure. The relationship between devices and behaviour is multi–valued, but this also implies that we should not confuse the technology with the devices, again. In a sense, the technologies differ in the case of a combination of different artefacts with different routines. We have a variation in a population of technologies which go back to some shared point of origin and which branch out also in the dimension of the routines connecting with the device.

This view also implies that the collective level nature of routines does not refer to some emerging properties of the collectives as groups of agents, but to the fact that those collectives are networks involving stable artefacts through time. This is most obvious when we consider highly regular technical processes, in which the human actors mostly need to adapt to them. Routines emerge from collective practice, even if not directly embodied in written artefacts, but at least via the imitation of observed actions, and are essentially connected with the artefact. Although reproduction of routines takes place via individual behaviour, we cannot say that there is a replicator that directly relates with this behaviour. Instead, we need to recognize the essential role of the artefacts in replicating the behaviour. Hence, I argue that the artefacts of technology are the replicators of routines in organizations. This also implies that varieties of routines emerge in the epigenesis of organizational behaviour, in the sense of the emergent interactors.

With this insight, we have reached our first conclusions about how to relate the general evolutionary paradigm to the evolution of technology, as far as the reproduction of knowledge is concerned. Technological knowledge does not reside in minds, but in practices. These practices are outward manifestations of causal conjunctions between artefacts and behavioural patterns, which follow the same logic as IGBPs in the previous chapter. Therefore, we can analyse technology in the context of specific network interactions among actors in the same way as we have analysed institutions, that is in terms of the circular causality of the Aoki model. Then, it is straightforward to realize that the notion of routines dissolves into the conjunction between signs – which is design – and behavioural dispositions that result from the affordances of artefacts. So, we conclude that technology is performative in the sense established for institutions in Chapter Six. The performativity of technology rests upon the fundamental circuitry between affordances and IGBP that I analysed in figure 7.3: Artefacts are not simply objects of actors' actions, but transform actors in a way such that they perform the technology embodied in the artefacts. This is straightforward to understand if we come back to the familiar example of the hammer: The hammer is not just an object of our action, but requires skills to be handled efficaciously; these skills transform us, and ultimately the hammer and the skilled craftsperson merge into one conjoined entity, the technology of the hammer.

7.3. EVOLUTIONARY TRAJECTORIES OF TECHNOLOGICAL CREATIVITY

7.3.1. Artefacts as replicators in technological evolution

We can now state a very important homology between the semiotic analysis of design and technology and the generic semiotic model of the replicator/interactor in evolution. Comparing figure 7.4 with figure 3.9, it springs to the eye that design assumes the same position as the interactor, which fits intuition, as it is the design that mediates the interaction between the technology and the selective environment. Without proper design, technology will not diffuse because of failures in use. We can also emphasize once again that this also implies that design is on the level of the entire interplay of functionings of the artefact, which is homologous to the role of development in evolution. That means, successful designs also relate with a sustainable and efficacious process in generating the technology and its functions. This refers design back to the production of technology. Then, the replicator is on the same position as the artefact. This appears to be surprising because one standard idea is that the replicator of technology may be ideas and routines of its use or its production. On the other hand, the proposal that artefacts are replicators of autonomous ontological status has been ventilated previously by different authors.

There is an intensive discussion about the role of the notions of replicator and interactor in analysing technology, which relates with the debate over 'routines'. At this point, suffice to mention Mokyr's (2000) overview of the topic (compare Mokyr 1998). Mokyr introduces the general term 'technique' to analyse technology, which he distinguishes explicitly from the 'artefact'. A technique is a set of instructions on how to solve a problem by means of an artefact, thus, basically the rules governing the uses of artefacts. He also distinguishes between the technique and the information, such that both can evolve independently. Against this background, the notion of 'replicator' becomes very complex, in spite of the fact that Mokyr is inclined to approach techniques as units of selection and hence, in his view, replicators. Replication of techniques is very different from biological replication because techniques and information can be transmitted through different channels (for example, the same technique can be based on experiential or scientific knowledge), and because there is no clear notion of the life cycle of a technique. Even forgotten techniques can be revived on the spot, if necessary, and if the blueprints are accessible. The relationship between interactor and replicator is also complicated, because the replicator notion raises the question for the 'vehicle' that carries the replicator. Mokyr concedes that artefacts are important replicators of techniques, but that there are still too many degrees of freedom between the uses of artefacts and the structural features of artefacts. Other vehicles are storage devices, human memory and communication patterns. Finally, Mokyr ends up with a sort of confusion because he also argues that techniques can be 'interactors'.

I think that the triadic view helps to clarify this conceptual muddle, because what appears to be a 'technique' is the function, in relation to a design. Designs include all combinations of artefact and user patterns, such as clicking icons on the iPhone. The argument that the relationship between artefacts and user patterns is multivalued does not question the assignment of the replicator notion to the artefact, because also in genetics, the relationship between genes and gene expressions is multivalued and contextualized. Further, according to the approach sketched in Chapter Three, there is a substantial channel of information transmission which works via the selective environment, that is the adaptive niche. As we have seen, this results into a purely functional distinction between replicator and interactor, which is not bound to a particular ontological identification (such as identifying replicators with genes exclusively).

This approach is strongly influenced by Aunger (2002) and is very similar to Fleck (2000). Aunger applies a concise concept of the replicator which requires replicators to be physical entities that manifest a physical phenomenon, that of replication. Whether technological artefacts are replicators is a difficult question. Aunger argues that some artefacts assume that role, once they piggyback on memetic evolution (which is conceived along the lines of my Chapter Four). In this, signs play an essential role, that is, design related to artefacts operate as signs that coordinate brain activities (that is neuromemes), such that the replication of the artefacts results. This idea can be developed further in my semiotic view. Artefacts are replicators that use the brain as machinery of reproduction. This directly reflects the sensorimotor feedback circuits that connect actors and artefacts: It is the affordances that result in the exploitation of neuronal mechanisms for the sake of artefactual reproduction. This makes clear why design is different from user patterns. So, once the artefact of a bicycle emerged, its design operates as a sign that establishes functions in populations of user that also feedback on the reproduction of bicycles qua artefacts.

7.3.2. The problem of technological taxonomy

I notice that the role of design in the semiotics of technology is also akin to the role of the 'species' in biological evolution (see Chapter Three, section 3.4.3). This is an important observation, as it suggests that design plays a role in defining technologies as units of evolution. Again, this changes the perspective of established approaches also in Evolutionary Economics, where technological paradigms as technological kinds are mainly seen in the light of producer knowledge (for example Dosi 1982; Cimoli and Dosi 1995). But what effectively counts in the evolution of technology in the same way as in biological evolution, is the realization of functions in selective contexts. For this, the level of signs is essential, because it is the medium through which the evolution of knowledge about proper functioning is realized. Therefore, the grouping of technologies should be done via the functionings mediated by the signs, so that it is the design which defines 'species' of technologies.

As a consequence of the previous considerations, the semiotic analysis of technology suggests that there is the possibility of constructing the taxonomy of technology. All technologies relate evolutionarily to some common ancestors. For example, once the wheel had been invented, different ways to use the wheel for transport devices emerged which go back to the original version of the wheel, such as horse chariots or locomotives. I suggest that the taxonomy of technology may be seen as taxonomy of the embodied knowledge in artefacts. There is the principled question which kind of knowledge may underlie reconstructions of technological taxonomy. One approach would focus on the production side, thus highlighting different aspects of the technologies that are involved in producing artefacts, such as melting or grinding. Obviously, this would not result in an intuitive taxonomy, because very different products involve similar technologies. Taking the biological taxonomy as an example, the most appropriate approach would start out from the intuition that design and species are systematically related concepts. So, in the example of the wheel it does not matter how the wheels are actually produced, but whether certain applications of the most general concept of the wheel relate to each other. These applications reflect generic design principles of wheels.

In the past decade, there have been different attempts at designing technological or industry taxonomies following evolutionary principles (for an overview, see McCarthy 2005). This has a long tradition in engineering where taxonomies of manufacturing technologies had been proposed as early as in the 19th century. There are different difficult and fundamental issues here, which are increasingly discussed in considering the biological approaches to taxonomy. Originally, biological taxonomy had been created independent from evolutionary theory, but modern taxonomy is directly based on evolutionary theory in general, or even molecular genetics in particular. Modern biology is also a repository of special techniques to identify taxonomic relationships, such as in numerical taxonomy, that is, statistical approaches to cluster observed properties of objects.

The most general distinction in taxonomy relates with the distinction between synchrony and diachrony. This means, one can focus on a set of observed entities and their properties and investigate into similarities. This approach can refer to strictly synchronic phenomena, that is, comparing entities of a given population at a particular point of time, or to a set of phenomena which are differently dated, but are still treated as observations at a certain point of time, that is the researcher's present. A diachronic approach would concentrate on the genetic relationships between entities of different dates, which are the evolutionary taxonomy. The former approach is called 'phenetic' in biology.

There are two fundamental problems with a purely phenetic approach. Firstly, the question is which properties are relevant for classification, and which weight is assigned to them if there are competing possibilities of classification, and secondly, how can one distinguish between analogies and homologies in classification. In biology, both problems had to be resolved even in the phenetic approach in referring to evolutionary arguments, that is, to both genetic considerations on shared evolutionary tracks, such as common ancestors, and adaptationist reasoning. In the economic applications, these issues loom even larger because there is no direct and unequivocal role of evolutionary arguments. For example, McCarthy et al. (2000) proposed a classification of manufacturing systems that is based on evolutionary theorizing, but does not relate with adaptationist reasoning. They focus on a classification of production techniques, such as distinguishing between 'ancient craft systems' and 'mass producers', arguing that these different production technologies manifest a history of descendence and speciation. For instance, they distinguish between 'European mass producers' and 'intensive mass producers' as species in the larger taxonomic unit. This classification requires a list of more simple traits that can be combined in the different 'species'. For example, for the automotive industry the authors identify traits such as 'standardization', 'job enrichment' or 'automation'. Clearly, the problem is that such a classification does not directly reflect the selective environment, in which only the products are tested (the cars), hence the market, although these are important parameters to determine competitive success. Further, the classification of production techniques does not clearly distinguish between industries such as automotive and aircraft. Thus, the distinction is not deeply rooted in established conceptualizations of the history of technology.

The major concern in modern biological taxonomy is to support the classification by clear phylogenetic arguments. The strictest form of this is cladistic analysis that even aims at distinguishing between analogies and homologies in a common phylogenetic setting. An analogy is a similar pattern of change that happens in synchronically unrelated species which stem from a common ancestor, but develop the trait independently, given similar selective forces. A homology relates the shared trait directly to its emergence in a common ancestor, and takes this as a principle of classification. McCarthy et al. (2000) propose to adopt this cladistic approach, which can be applied on sets of traits by using the established biological tools, which includes software tools today. However, there remain substantial difficulties which relate to the differences between the domains. For example, at least according to the established mainstream view in biology, there is always a clear temporal ordering of descendence relations, whereas in technological evolution, lateral and synchronous transmission of patterns is possible.

Andersen (2002, 2003) develops an entirely different approach to classification which considers these differences. He proposes to apply biological tools on industrial Input–Output tables, arguing that there are genetic relationships between the knowledge bases of the different industries, in the sense of generating their outputs synchronically. So, if an industry relies on a number of inputs of other industries, this reflects a certain knowledge structure. It is then possible to treat the Input–Output characteristics as evolutionarily relevant properties and to cluster industries accordingly. This is a synchronic approach, which shares McCarthy's focus on the production side of the picture and does not classify technologies according to products, even though the difference results to be that inputs are products of other industries.

My own view is inspired by Saviotti's (1996, 2001) discussion of the notion of 'variety' of technology. Different from the aforementioned authors, Saviotti focuses on the artefact as the unit of analysis. Artefacts produce certain services, which can be analysed into a set of more simple and basic service features, and certain production techniques, understood as the ways how the service can be produced; this does not directly refer to the production of the artefact, such as a helicopter produces the functions of flying, with the special capacity to remain in the air without moving, which differs from the way how the helicopter is built, although this is also an aspect of producing the service ultimately (for an empirical application, see for example Windrum et al. 2009). Industrial taxonomies can therefore distinguish between different speciation patterns.

7.3.3. Branching out of technologies

So, the most appropriate way to approach the principles of technological taxonomy is to adopt the semiotic perspective and to analyse the recursive nature of technology (which Arthur 2009 refers to as 'autopoietic'; compare Witt 2009). In this view, recursive semiosis starts with the projection of a mechanism, that is an observed physical effect, into a design, that mediates the emergence of a function. This combination of design and function is the initial artefact. The initial artefact turns into an object that can be related with a new design to create a second artefact, which relates with a different function. In these three steps, the generic evolutionary processes of development, selection and evolution are combined. Evolution relates to the emergence of new functions in the process of creating new kinds of artefacts, which, however, build on primordial mechanisms. For example, the wheel, or, more generally, the realization of the physical effect of 'rolling' that appears with certain shapes of physical objects, is part and parcel of myriads of technological artefacts. In this sense, all these artefacts relate with the original mechanism. But the branching out of the technological taxonomy relates with the designs in which the mechanism is embedded. For example, the wheel of modern cars is a complex artefact which includes brakes or tires, which build on other physical mechanisms. This is one branch that directly connects with the early artefacts in the sense that the function, that is enabling movements of other artefacts, such as chariots or cars, remains the same, which is reflected in basic design continuities. The unfolding of the original design relates with the gradual emergence of solutions to particular problems that emerge in the use of wheels. For example, once the operation of wheels is improved, so that higher speeds can be achieved, brakes need to be improved, too. However, there are other uses of wheels, such as in clocks and machines, in which wheels assume other functions, which flow out from the different designs into which the original physical mechanism is embedded.

So, from this perspective we can finally reaffirm the notion that the replicator is the artefact, in the sense that it assumes a dynamic role in moving positions in the semiotic triad during the process of recursive semiosis. One of the most significant empirical evidences supporting this view is the fact that the international specialization of countries along traded product categories is strongly determined by the existing distribution of technological networks in terms of product classifications, which are essentially descriptions of artefacts (Hidalgo 2009; Hidalgo and Hausman 2009). There are strong path dependencies of the positions of countries in the international division of labour, depending on the previous technological specialization patterns in terms of products and the related technologies. At the same time, levels of development reflect the complexity of technological networks in terms of artefacts. Interestingly, this view on artefacts as replicators even applies in the sense of a direct correspondence between the technological phenomena and the role of genes in biological evolution. Gene and genome correspond to mechanism and artefact in my reconstruction. As in biological evolution, the same genes can have different expressions depending on the context in the genome. Mechanisms have different effects in different artefacts. However, in the course of evolution, the genes and genomes adopt different functions, depending on the stage of evolution that is considered. This is also true for mechanisms and artefacts. For example, an early stone tool could be conceived as a 'gene' in the sense of a primordial mechanism, and creating a design pattern that relates the mechanism with a function, such as cutting. That function can be put into a slightly different context once the stone tool was connected with a wooden stick, thus creating a sort of lance. This is a new artefact, which can turn into an object of subsequent semiosis, such as relating the combination of stick and stone to the notion of an arrow used with a bow. The point is that this transition turns the relationship between primordial arrow and the bow technology into one between newly emerging function and object: The artefact of an arrow becomes an object the properties which are explored in continuous trials and errors of improving the arrow, ending up in sets of designs, which clearly distinguish different kinds of arrows from each other (on this example, see Mesoudi and O'Brien 2008).

These observations can be summarized in understanding technological change in terms of categories from Evolutionary Epistemology. In particular, the state space evolves according to the emergence and diffusion of technological paradigms and dominant designs, which channel the search for problem solutions and hence the path of technological change (for an explicit modelling approach, see Frenken 2006). Technological innovations are problem driven, that is, they result from the search for improvements or perceived deficiencies in the existing technologies by means of combining existing technologies into new technologies (Petroski 1994; for an empirical evidence based on patent statistics, see Strumsky et al. 2011). For example, the car evolved into a dominant design, which refers to the existing general characteristics of combining certain types of engines with other technological features such as wheels, brakes etc. As we experience during the current experimentations and discussions about alternative designs of cars, this pattern exerts a strong directional force on further technological change. Electric cars may manifest important changes in the dominant design (such as introducing separate engines for the different wheels), and depend heavily on network externalities with other technologies (such as batteries and loading stations). It is still an open issue whether the shift of the technological paradigm of fuel–driven cars will happen, as there are alternatives which might substantially reduce fuel use (such as flywheels for energy regeneration from braking). Interestingly, some of these innovations would actually revive much earlier ideas (such as separate engines for different wheels in electric cars), which lost out in those earlier stages of the evolution of cars, thus revealing the forces in establishing the dominant design. So, once a certain design is established, search for improvements mainly happens within the scope of that design, and radical innovations may not occur for that reason.

I propose a conceptualization of these phenomena in terms of Evolutionary Theory as depicted in figure 7.5. The concepts of internal and external (environmental) selection are most relevant here (see Chapter Three, 3.4.4.). Problems create forces of external selection of technologies, which can be mediated via different contexts in the social organization of invention and innovation. This includes the well-known distinction between engineering and business in innovation: Engineering solutions may fail to pass the market test (and vice versa, success on markets does not necessarily imply optimal engineering solutions). However, all these are forces of external selection which result in the branching out of technologies into different functions. Given our previous analysis of routines, this also implies a particular pattern of the combination of artefacts with organizations (such as the 'Fordism' paradigm). This defines niches of technological evolution relative to selective environments, in which user–producer interactions play a central role in determining the direction of technological change (Malerba et al. 2007; on the concept of 'technological niches' see Schot and Geels 2007). I surmise that this can be related with the notion of interactors, which is most appropriate as the connection between artefacts and routines or practices defines the actual pattern of interaction between the technology and its environment. Then, the dominant design may be assigned to the function of replicator, which, as we already surmised, boils down to the technological artefact. However, considering the example of the bicycle, this certainly cannot be equated with the earliest ancestor, but to a recurrently embodied pattern of design principles of the technology, which actually might only fully emerge in the course of evolution, and which can be extracted from the channel that is followed by it.

Figure 7.5 Selection of technologies

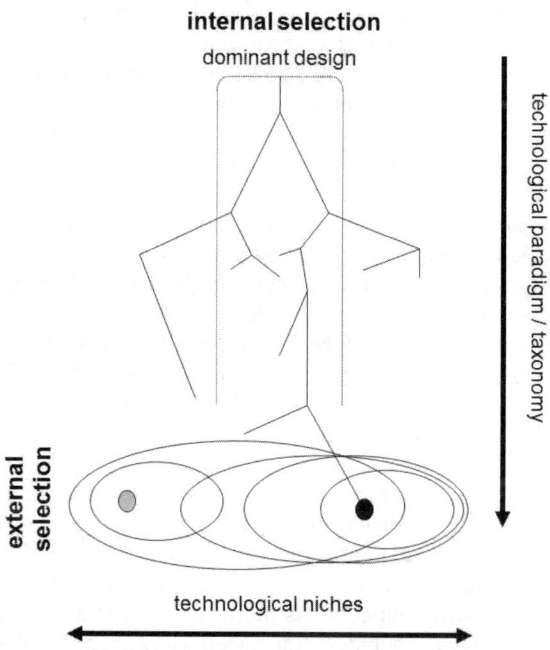

Note: Technological evolution proceeds under both internal and external selection. External selection occurs via problems posed by the environment and carves out technological niches for different technologies or variants of technology, relative to specific problems (such as racing bicycles, mountain bikes etc.). Internal selection refers back to the dominant design that originated in the past and which is embodied in certain stable design patterns of the different variants (such as two wheels of bicycles). The interplay of the two forces is manifest in the taxonomy of technology, that is the historical branching pattern of variants.

The duality of internal and external selection of technology refers back to a classical idea ventilated by Veblen (1899, 1914) who argued that there is a dualism between selective forces resulting from instrumental uses of technology and from market competition. This dualism was epitomized in two different kinds of actors, the 'engineer' and the 'captain of industry'. Indeed, technological evolution in recent times is increasingly driven by the logic of markets. This seems to vindicate the belief of many modern economists that markets are the most effective environment to drive the growth of knowledge. However, there persists considerable leeway between the range of possible technologies and those selected by the market. This is one important reason why the essential property of the performativity of technology can find full expression: It is less a question of efficiency or superiority, but of performative action, which technology will prevail under concrete historical conditions.

7.3.4. Technological creativity

The branching out of technologies happens via its diffusion in a population of users. There are two fundamental processes that are involved here. The first one, considered briefly in this subsection, is the process of technological creativity which defines the points of branching out. The second is the topic of the next subsection, namely the standardization of technology, mentioned previously; this refers to the forces that determine the dominance of certain design patterns. In principle, this does not imply that users have to cooperate, even though, as we shall see later, many technologies indirectly imply cooperation, such as in the context of technological networks which need to rely on standardization. Yet, even in the case of isolated adoptions, the role of perceptions of usage by others and hence imitation highlights the fact that technologies share one important property with institutions, namely, they relate with collective intentionality. This results from the fact that technologies also involve status functions in the sense of Searle's. This is straightforward to see if we consider that technologies build on transfers of meanings, that is metaphors in the sense that a physical item is used for a new purpose, after a manipulation, relative to the original generic function that a technology is intended to fulfil. For example, there is the function of moving my body and carrying a load. If I discover the use of a wheel for moving things, this involves a status function in the sense that I use the artefact in a certain context to realize the function of transport. Technological imagination starts on a metaphorical level, as when imagining marvellous devices of flying 'like birds'. What turns technological inventions into practice is to relate a physical mechanism that is observable with a new field of application, that is a function, such as using the physical effect of light emissions by certain metal objects when exposed to electric currents in order to produce light in human dwellings. This creative act corresponds to

Searle's status function: Using *X* (the physical effect) as *Y* (light, like a candle) in context *C* (human dwellings).

We can generalize over this observation in particular if we consider the gradual process of innovation which always consists of putting different existing elements together to realize a new coherent whole with an entirely different function. In this case, we observe double or multiple scope networks of blends, in which different artefacts obtain a new meaning with reference to a new function that refers to their combination (for a related analysis of novelty, see Witt 2009). This mechanism applies for both the population level and the individual level processes and thus manifests the role of performativity. For example, considering one of the most famous 'heroic' inventors of human history, Edison, it is clear that his immense productivity relied on the conscious exploitation of these processes (on the following, see Carlson 2000). In creating the modern system of lighting, his long list of patents involves one for a long–lasting carbon filament, which was the only one retained after a patent litigation over his claims on the incandescent light bulb. Indeed, Edison was able to build on a long history of variations of similar devices, which, however, did not have the most optimal properties. He digested a large number of blueprints, reports and other sources about inventions and continued with a tinkering process, changing and reshuffling single elements in order to create new combinations. This does not only apply to the single artefact, but even more important, to the network of artefacts that ultimately constitutes the technology. For example, the light bulb as such is an interesting technological device, but its practical and commercial use depends on its embeddedness into larger technological networks which includes cheap and efficient production technologies and the whole system that connects light bulbs with electricity supply.

Edison's example shows that even seemingly simple looking devices such as the light bulb are material complements of a complex evolutionary process which relates certain functions with a sequence of status functions in which different existing elements are combined in order to achieve improvements of these functions (this matches with Simon's 1996: 108f emphasis on the role of representations in searching for problem solutions). In the case of the light bulb, the general idea emerged with the discovery that a filament of metal can emit light. After that discovery was made, people started to think about how this physical effect can be used practically. The entire sequence linking the mechanism with the final shape of the light bulb is a history of improvements (in general, see Petroski 1996). For example, one problem that emerged early is the fact that chemical reactions with the air would reduce the longevity of the filament substantially. So, methods to create a vacuum while retaining the visibility of the light were tested continuously. Several entirely different technologies were combined, such as the technologies of pumping and the technologies of glass production. We can analyse this combinatory process as a process of conceptual blending, which is arranged into a system of interpretance, relating with the hierarchies of functions involved in technology.

Figure 7.6 Conceptual blends in technology: Example of light bulbs

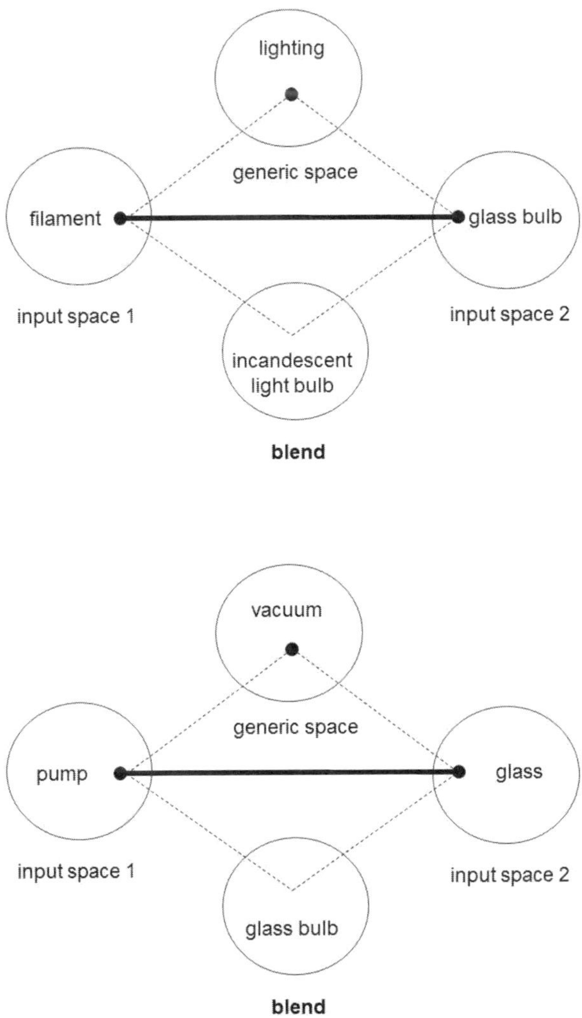

Note: The artefact of the 'incandescent light bulb' results from nested conceptual blends that involve two projections into different generic spaces related to the modular components of those bulbs, that is the filament and the glass bulb. The two connect via the cognitive projection that rapid oxidization of filament can only be avoided in a vacuum. The conceptual blends establish technology as a Searlian status function, shifting the contextualization of existing artefacts via projections into new generic frames, such as from the original experiments with electric currents in filaments into the frame of lighting (for further discussion, see main text).

I show the fundamental structure of conceptual blending in this case in figure 7.6. In the upper diagram, we see how two notions were blended with reference to the generic space, which is defined by the function of 'lighting'. If lighting by a filament should be usable for practical purposes, it needs to be combined with some other device. Based on the physical and chemical knowledge of the nineteenth century, that could be a vacuum. This concept was connected with second order conceptual blends, shown in the lower diagram. Here, the notion of vacuum was related with two other notions, the pump and the glass bulb. Vacuum can only be created in a container, which had to consist of transparent technology, and one needs to use a pump. So, the two concepts of a lighting filament and of the vacuum were blended in the generic space of 'lighting'. Thus, two input concepts, 'pumps' and 'glass' were related to the generic notion of 'vacuum', resulting into the new technical device of a glass bulb. That vacuumed glass bulb was blended with the notion of the heated filament, resulting into the final blend of the 'incandescent light bulb'. This analysis could be extended to include the network effects, such as the devices that feed the bulb with electricity. So, in the end we can deconstruct the technology of light bulbs into a large number of networked conceptual blends that are embodied in the actual physical network of the technology that mediates all causal processes that ultimately result in the use of light bulbs in human dwellings.

In the case of technologies, status functions directly involve the manipulation of physical entities that embody the original meanings as functions of the concepts that are used in reference to the entities (compare Hutchins 2005). So, for example, when Humphrey Davy used a filament of platinum to demonstrate the strength of his battery to a British audience in 1802, the function of this experiment was entirely different from the function that was discovered by this action, namely that light could be produced as a side effect. The discovery is a status function in the sense that there was an original context, the experiment of testing the power of batteries, and the new context, the lighting function. Similarly, the notion of vacuum was put into another context than in the original contexts.

Clearly, this role of status functions in enabling certain technologies implies that collective intentionality is also central in establishing those functions, which reflects the underlying semiotic nature of technology. The simplest example of collective intentionality is the coordination between producer and user knowledge in manifesting the technology as a social fact. As we have seen, this does not mean that the two sides manifest the same knowledge, but it is essential that collective intentionality applies for the use of the technology. In our case study of lighting, this is the evolution of the myriad ways that light bulbs can be applied in different environments.

Coming back to my previous semiotic analysis of design, the example of the light bulb also clearly shows the role of design in defining technological species. Even though the emergence of the technology can be analysed in the different steps of conceptual blending, these steps do not count for the final result, the blend. The incandescent light bulb as the final conceptual blend is defined via its design, and few users may even know how a light bulb is constructed and produced, even though it is an everyday technological artefact. So, the design is the conceptual blend which relates with the proper functioning, in this case lighting rooms. Once this blend is established, numerous alternatives emerged by means of varying certain parts of the technology, such as halogen lamps. But all these fit into the generic conceptual blend. Only very recently an alternative developed, the LED. This development has re-opened the design process, and there are still many ways that this technology can be actually used to light rooms. But without a final design which also reflects the central conceptual blend, the process of substituting the light bulb by LEDs is unfinished.

This analysis further supports my previous argument that technology is performative. One cannot say that the technology is just the artefact that embodies the physical causality of its function. On the one hand, as we have seen previously, technology is essentially involving performative acts of human actors who realize the routines which are complementary to the artefact, and which are emerging from its design. Without the performative action on part of the human actors who share collective intentionality, technology does not materialize its function. These performative acts are conditioned by the complete semiotic process involving the technology. We have now seen that semiosis also underlies the process of technological creativity in terms of the Searlian status function and the related conceptual blends.

7.3.5. Standardization and the evolving state space of technology

The other essential force in channelling the branching out of technology is standardization. Standardization is an essential property of all modern technologies, but also played a role in earlier technologies, such as when the first Emperor of China standardized chariots and street width. All standardization is a semiotic process even in the narrow sense of activating representations of technology in order to define and impose standards; then, a standard is a description of certain features of a technology which defines a fit with real world manifestations. There is a range of economic forces that determine the emergence of standards in networks independently from such representations, which have a direct effect on the state space in which technology evolves. So, in order to understand standardization we need to take a closer look at this state space.

This state space is itself a semiotic phenomenon in the sense that it is structured via the interactions between functions and design. Standardization most generally affects design features of technologies, which then affect the combinatorial possibilities and hence the structure of the evolving state space. To go back to the light bulb, standardization was involved in many different steps, such as the standardization of the materials used for the filaments, or later with the standardization of sockets and caps, and, of course, in the entire process of mass production of bulbs. In the original state, there was a huge variety of possibilities of producing light bulbs of different materials and shapes, which ultimately was reduced to a number of specific combinations. So, two different processes of changing the state space were involved. In the initial invention, existing elements were combined in creating an entirely new thing, which is a state of the world, namely the light bulb. This new thing allowed for the branching out of the state space, again in two different senses. One is that there are many different possibilities for designing this artefact; the other is that new combinatorial possibilities emerged linking this artefact with other artefacts. All these combinations are new states of the world, in one sense, though possibly being just related to existing functions. For example, lighting the home with candles or with bulbs is not a new function, but still involves a new state of the world.

Once a new configuration of the state space had emerged, a process of standardization started. Consider, for example, the history of the bicycle. In the early days, many variants existed, for example, with a large diversity of wheel sizes. Many of these variants have vanished, though remaining possible states of the world, which are rarely manifest. At the same time, today we have another expression of the diversity of forms, which mainly refers to the specialization of functions of different kinds of bicycles, such as regular bikes, mountain bikes etc. Although these bikes also show a huge variety, there is standardization of forms within the different types, relative to specialized functions, and there is still a shared basic standard, such as that most bikes have two wheels of the same size.

Considering the causes of standardization, we can identify a number of different economic forces (for comprehensive surveys of the literature on standardization, see Swann 2000, 2010). The first is economies of scale in the production and the uses of a technology. For example, if there is a standardization of screwdrivers and screws, there is the possibility first, to exploit economies of scales in producing screwdrivers with a particular size, if there is a standardized set of screws with this size. In turn, standardization of screws also allows exploiting economies of scale in producing screws. In principle, the two economies of scale are independent from each other. But if there is additional coordination, the effects are further enhanced. So, apart from economics of scale, standardization creates economies of coordination. Both are already sufficient to establish the systemicity of technology. Systemicity is a semiotic phenomenon in the sense that the match between the representation of design, the standard, and the manifestation in the technology creates the conditions for systemic connectivity in networks of technology.

The two aspects discussed so far relate with the reduction of possible variety and the enhancement of compatibility. The former is essential to activate critical mass effects and to exploit economies of scale, the latter enables network externalities. The former is an essential aspect of the transition from artisan work to industry, and the latter in establishing technological systems. Network externalities are particularly strong in technologies which themselves have network structures, such as transportation (for example standardizing railway gauges) or communication. There are two other forces of standardization that I do not emphasize much in the current context, because they only become important in the market context. These are minimum quality standards and information standards. Both overcome information asymmetries in market relations.

If we concentrate on the former two forces here, we can already draw some principled conclusions about the relationship between the state space evolution and standardization. Basically, this can be depicted as in figure 7.7 (from Swann 2000). We distinguish between vertical technology differentiation and horizontal technology differentiation. Vertical differentiation is functional specialization relative to certain performance standards; horizontal product differentiation is differentiation according to functional diversity within a certain class of functions. For example, if we look at early versions of the car, later versions distinguish themselves vertically (higher speed, higher safety etc.) and horizontally (trucks, sports cars, vans etc.). In all horizontal lines, vertical change is possible.

Standardization is essential to realize both the economic advantages of economies of scale and the coordination benefits in the evolving state space. For example, in figure 7.7 the right hand side shows two different patterns that can emerge in state spaces of technologies. In the upper pattern, specializations take larger steps of improvements, that is branch out later, and result in a selective exploration of the state space. In the lower pattern, after an initial technological push, the state space branches out into a large number of idiosyncratic specializations which do not manifest further innovation dynamics, for example, because of a lack in economies of scale. The difference between the two patterns lies in the degree of the abstraction of new sub-functions. In the lower pattern, the design of products would adapt to individual idiosyncrasies, like a tailor-made suit. This is a typical evolutionary path in product classes where there is less space for fundamental innovations. In the former pattern, products evolve into broader functional classes that specify classes of patterns of use, such as when a special kind of aircraft evolves out of the general type of aircraft, which can be used in a larger number of instances of application (for example a fighter jet).

Figure 7.7 Evolutionary patterns of standardization in the technology state space (Swann 2000)

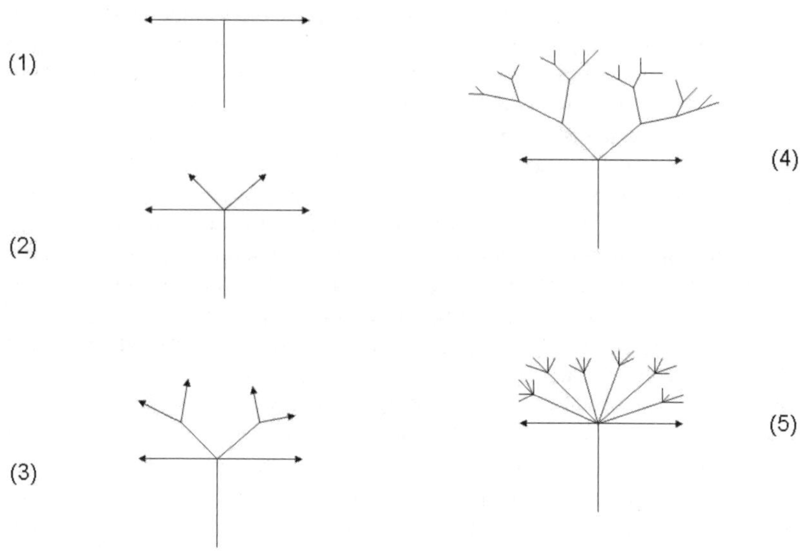

Note: These diagrams give a simple diagrammatic idea about the dynamics of the evolution of the technological state space. (1) depicts horizontal differentiation of standards, such as into types of automobiles for different purposes. (2) shows vertical differentiation in terms of different performance standards (such as speed of automobiles). Technological evolution proceeds in both dimensions (3), involving different steps such as creating new types of cars with new performance levels (such as SUVs). (4) and (5) show different branching patterns that involve distinct forms of technological progress. In (4) branching involves substantial steps in both horizontal and vertical differentiation, whereas in (5) branching occurs via the creation of a large variety of individual manifestations of technology that do not involve much vertical differentiation (such as in fashion).

In this context, it is interesting to notice that the former pattern of branching is more probable in the case of composite artefacts. For example, a suit may not offer many opportunities to implement new combinations of components that would offer to realize new classes of functions. However, once the technological possibility emerges to include sensors and digital devices in the cloth, this evolutionary track may switch to the mode depicted in the upper right part of figure 7.7.

The previous discussion shows that we cannot say that the state space of technology is an exogenous given, but that it is endogenous to technological evolution. This matches with the general analysis of evolution in Chapter

Three. Especially, we can state that technological evolution is path dependent, thus making the state space non-ergodic (this is a standard topic in the Evolutionary Economics of technology research, going back to Arthur's 1989 seminal article). Standardization is the most important force that creates path dependence, and the analysis of institutional path dependence in Chapter Six applies here, too. So, we can distinguish between effects of frequency dependency, network externalities and the interaction between the semiotic and the matterenergy modes. Frequency dependency shows up in critical mass effects in the diffusion of technologies, yielding the typical *S* shaped logistic curves in many cases (Andersen 1999). Standardization supports critical mass effects, as the possibility of fragmented and isolated diffusion trajectories is constrained. Network externalities create the aforementioned effects of systemicity of technologies and therefore impose constraints on the coevolution of trajectories in the state space of technology. The interaction between the semiotic and the matterenergy mode includes, for example, the interaction between the diffusion of ideas about technology and the actual artefacts.

This is not the place to investigate into these observations in more detail, which are the topic of much of applied research in Evolutionary Economics and innovation studies. In the current context, it is important to conclude that because technology is performative in essence, it is not possible to define an external benchmark to assess technological 'progress' of any kind, as long as we consider single trajectories of technologies. However, we can identify one most general criterion of change that relates technology with general evolutionary principles. This is the role of technology in harnessing energetic resources to generate physical work.

7.4. TECHNOLOGY, PRODUCTION AND ENERGY

7.4.1. Consumption as production

In subsection 7.1.3 I have argued that in the evolutionary approach to technology there is no separate role of the notion of 'consumption' as external objective of technology. Wants evolve as an integral part of technology. This view has a radical implication if we apply it on the aggregate level. In the traditional economic approach, technology exclusively relates with the production side of the economy, such as in the shape of the production functions deployed in growth theory. The autonomy of wants is implied by the idea that production only serves consumption. If wants are endogenous to technology, we can no longer maintain the separateness of consumption. Instead, we have to approach consumption as part and parcel of 'production', now approached from an entirely different angle. In this section, I explore the implications of this view on the aggregate level.

Figure 7.8 Traditional versus evolutionary view of production

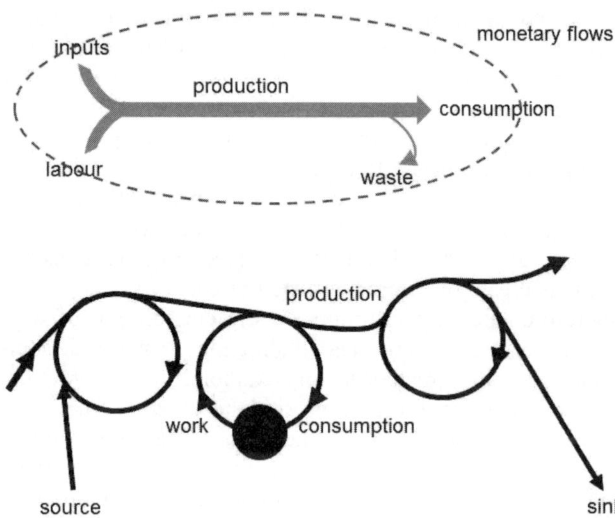

Note: In the traditional view on production and consumption (upper part), consumption is the exogenously set goal of production; production is a linear process combining inputs and labour and resulting into wastes and consumer products. Only the monetary flows connecting consumers and providers of factor services are circular. In the evolutionary view (bottom), production is a sequence of circular processes which involve sources of matterenergy and results into wastes that stay in sinks of the system. Production is driven by human actors who consume in order to generate the work necessary to sustain the system. The different steps apply for each cycle and are only distributed across different cycles in the diagram to avoid cluttering.

The traditional production function framework follows the idea that the human economy is closed with the ultimate act of consumption, which is accompanied with monetary payments that feed back to the producers (see figure 7.8). Both consumption and wastes are final states of a linear flow of production activities. Human labour is just one of the inputs to this production process. The material flows are seen as being terminated with 'consuming' the products; circularity is only implied by the monetary flows. This view results into a strange conceptual tension: On the one hand, the economy is conceived as a circular flow of goods and services, but this only reflects the accompanying monetary flows; there is nothing that motivates the acts of consumption causally within this flow. In fact, we can say, anticipating thoughts developed in the next chapter, that this tension expresses a peculiar way to perform the economy, based on basic metaphors and ideas which are partly disconnected from the empirical patterns that we observe, and which emerged together with the transition to the modern market societies in Western Europe (Gudeman 1986).

In the alternative evolutionary view, production involves energy throughputs stemming from a source of energy, and ultimately involves the joint production of waste, which, however, does not leave the system but remains in certain deposits or sinks. Consumption relates with functions, and in this general sense it is just a special kind of human work, which supports the general human capacity to work, that is to partake in production. In this sense, consumption is just one aspect of the production process. This reinstates certain views of classical economists which approach consumption of the working class as the means to reproduce its labour power, whereas only the rentiers or capitalists can indulge in luxury consumption. In the modern view on consumption, highlighting the role of consumer sovereignty, essentially every economic actor is equated with this role of an autonomous consumer of surplus. In the 'consumer society', apparently economic actors are not driven by the need to produce and reproduce themselves and their capacities for productive work.

I claim that the classical view partly presages the more comprehensive perspective of a generalized evolutionary theory which approaches technology in terms of multi–level adaptive processes. Then, consumption cannot be treated as an exogenous goal of the evolutionary process. Instead, consumption is a production process of its own kind, related to the production and reproduction of the human networks that maintain the entire economy as part and parcel of the larger ecological systems. This network perspective allows, for example, to interpret seemingly autonomous consumption acts such as status good consumption in terms of their embeddedness in those larger network structures which in turn provide the framework for the production process.

The idea that I am going to develop in this section is that the entire circular process of production reflects evolutionary principles, and in particular the Maximum Entropy Principle; this implies that the human economy only operates on the basis of increasing the entropy of the entire economy/environment system. In this view, technology is seen as the physical mechanism that carries these processes onwards. This observation implies that the entire technological system evolves in such ways that the fundamental evolutionary principles of MPP and MEP are fulfilled.

This idea was essential for establishing Ecological Economics as a special discipline in economics, based on Georgescu-Roegen's (1970) seminal work. It revives approaches by classical economists, with Marx as one of the last representatives, to see consumption as reproduction of labour. We can now say that this conceptual revival is primarily driven by the idea that consumption is just one aspect of the general energetic transformations that proceed in the economic process.

7.4.2. Technology and entropy

Thus, in this section I explore the role of technology in the processing of energy through the economy. This is the macro–level view on technology, and actually refers to the global technological system (what Garrett 2011a calls 'civilization'). This is an essential distinction, as many analyses of technology focus on single artefacts or certain 'technologies' in the sense of partial technological systems. However, if we want to understand the impact of technology on energy throughputs in the human economy, we can only take the global perspective, because all partial technological developments always have global complements, side-effects, externalities etc. This is a truly global view, as it approaches technology in its relationship to the Earth System; this means, for example, that even national perspectives on technology are irrelevant since technological change in national economies is closely integrated with global developments via international trade.

On the highest possible level of conceptual abstraction, we can define technology as a means to transform energetic throughputs into functions that further enhance energetic throughput (compare Mitcham 1994: 183ff): This captures the aspect of self–referentiality of technology that is also emphasized by Arthur (2009). In order to justify this most general definition, it is important to distinguish between single 'technologies' and 'technology'. The definition applies for the entire system of human technology, that is the complete set of technological artefacts, but not necessarily for single technological artefacts. Technological artefacts manifest a division of functions. Most generally, we can distinguish between information processing functions and energy transformation functions. These functions are merged in the design of technology: The specific form of artefacts carries information that underlies the function. This embodied information relates with the information that is embodied in the activities that result in the creation of a technological artefact. On the other side, technology leads to information flows that accompany the energetic transformations.

Ayres (1994, chapters 9 and 10) has an extensive discussion of approaches to measure the information content of technology. The general statement is that the information content of a system H is proportional to the available useful work A in it, relative to an environment with temperature T_0, as we have seen in Chapter 2 (2.2.3.):

$$H = \frac{A}{T_0}$$

However, as he shows, it is very difficult to measure information directly that is embodied in technological artefacts, because the issue of the relevant state space is perhaps impossible to resolve (given its endogeneity). However, Ayres is able to present a more specific interpretation of the generic ontological principle, which is the 'principle of minimum morphological information' in design. This principle states that if a certain object contains a large amount of Shannon information, this is the result of a large number of activities that create this information content. Consider a sculptor who designs a complex object: she will apply many more activities on shaping a complex object, in terms of comparisons with other objects, than in the case of a simple object. So, information content in complex manufacturing objects is created by labour inputs which are exergy flows. Further, all these operations create waste, such as the residuals from cutting and grinding. So, we recognize the duality of information content and information capacity that reflects the interaction between MPP and MaxEnt in the MEP principle. There are interesting applications of this idea in engineering (for example Zhirnov and Herr, 2001) which refer to the resulting imperative to reduce the extent of activities that create morphological information by exploiting self–organizing principles of matter.

Figure 7.9 Technology and Maximum Entropy

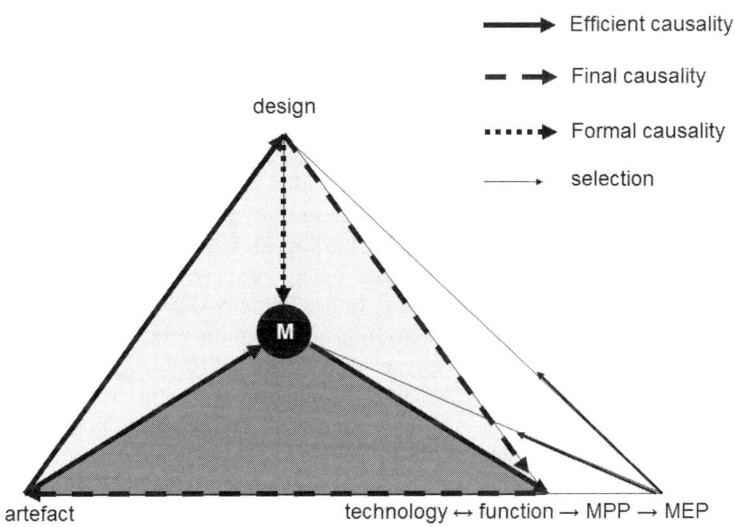

Note: On the population–level, technology evolves functions that manifest MPP and MEP through time. Energy dissipation is efficient–causally realized by the mechanisms of technology. The evolutionary trajectory is driven by the interaction of the other triadic causal modes. Design formal–causally patterns mechanisms such that usages in functionings emerge that manifest entropic principles; final causality establishes the directionality of technological change.

As a first approximation to this entropic view, I propose the triadic analysis of figure 7.9. Here, I distinguish between the artefact and the technology.

Technology is a function that realizes energetic transformations. In the triadic analysis, this implies that technology follows the MPP principle. This does not mean that single technologies always realize the state of MPP but that the evolution of populations of artefacts realizes MPP. This is an essential statement: For example, even if single artefacts realize energy–saving efficient mechanisms, this does not mean that the entire population of evolving artefacts realizes these savings in absolute terms, but increases energetic throughputs. On the one hand, there are the energetic transformations that happen via single artefacts, such as an engine; on the other hand, the population of engines evolves, such that the construction and the increasing diversification of engines is a process that involves energetic transformations, too. The MPP only applies for the conjunction of these different processes. This corresponds to Odum's (2007) approach to embodied energy, which is to consider both the energetic transformations of an artefact and the energetic transformations that result in the evolution of this artefact. The realization of MPP is governed by the more fundamental MEP principle, in turn.

In this analysis, I assign a central place to design, thus vindicating the pivotal role of design in the previous analysis of the relationship between technology and knowledge. Design is the causal force that arranges the relationship between populations of artefacts and aggregate functions in the evolution of technology. The term corresponds to the general notion of 'Bauplan' in biology, which is actually taken from technology, in turn. Design arranges technologies into larger patterns of shared characteristics, as we have seen in the analysis of technological taxonomy; the important role of design results from the fact that design governs human action involving technology. So, similar to the biological notions of species and related 'Bauplan' features, we can say that design both relates with the process of development of technology, in the sense of guiding the production of technological artefacts, as well as demarcating the niches of different technologies in the entire state space of evolutionary possibilities (for a related approach, see Arthur 2009: 76ff. 167ff). That is, the semiotic dimension of design links artefacts with human behaviour, thus establishing technologies as patterns of distributed cognition that conjoin artefacts with human behaviour, the latter conceived as IGBP. Correspondingly, we cannot analyse technology only in terms of engineering characteristics of artefacts, but always need to take the usage patterns into explicit consideration. For example, a device that is energy–saving in the engineering sense may not lead to usage patterns on the population level that also reduces aggregate energy consumption. This comprehensive view is essential to understand the relationship between technology and entropy.

7.4.3. Hypercyclic leveraging of energy throughputs by technological evolution

We have already gained important insights into the general principles of technology in analysing the case of fire and cooking in Chapter Four (subsection 4.2.4.). This example illustrates the role of technology in niche creation and human adaptation: The technology of cooking turns fire into an artefact (that is controlled fire in different artificial environments, such as a fireplace or an oven) thus allowing for harnessing energy for a specific function, which is preparation of food and ultimately eating. This function resulted into a higher energetic throughput per unit of time and thus triggered adaptations of the human body, responding to selective pressures to use time for other purposes. As a result, hypercyclic connectivity emerged, such as the possible intensification of hunting activities resulting from the availability of time, the possibility to preserve food etc. We have already seen how this co-evolution of technology and organism was accompanied by the emergence of new institutions governing human behaviour, with the transformation of the social brain also co-evolving to generate the capabilities to follow such institutions.

Figure 7.10 The Salter cycle

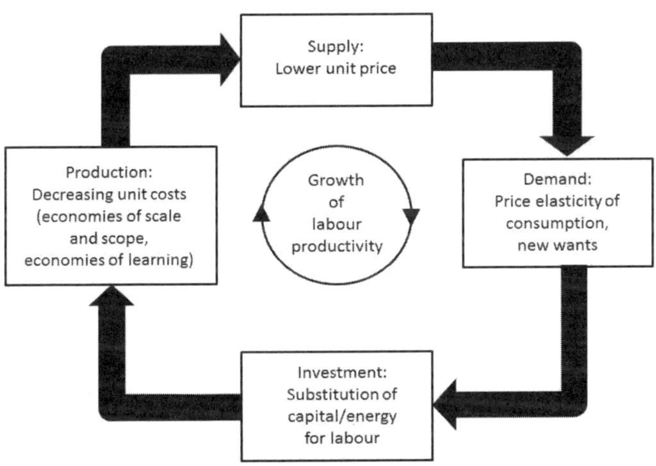

Note: The Salter cycle shows the hypercyclic interdependence between consumption and production in the context of markets, hence in terms of standard economic concepts. Technological progress drives the growth of labour productivity; this results into decreasing unit costs of production that triggers the expansion of demand and the generation of new wants. The Salter cycle is one application of the general notion of hypercyclic leveraging of energy throughputs by growth in evolutionary technological systems.

In the context of economics, this hypercyclic interdependence has been termed the 'Salter cycle' (Ayres and Warr 2009: 8ff; Ayres 2005: 147 pinpoints its autocatalytic structure). The Salter cycle refers to the interaction between the supply and the demand side in the growth process, given market systems (for a congenial economic approach neglected by Ayres, see Pasinetti 1981). Continuously increasing labour productivity stands at its centre; this is caused by the expansion of the demand that results from certain patterns of price elasticity, such that lower unit prices cause a more than proportional expansion of demand. The latter requires non-satiation, which, in my framework, can be explained by status good consumption and endogenous wants. In the market context, if demand grows, there are incentives to invest. Investments result into increases of labour productivity if capital substitutes for labour. We shall see in the course of this section that this in fact means to increase energy throughputs by technological progress. This is one determinant of decreasing unit costs, which is further driven by economies of scale and scope and movements down the learning curve.

So, the Salter cycle is one conceptual means to grasp hypercyclic dynamics by standard economic concepts. The interaction between production and consumption, hence endogeneity of wants, plays a central role, but if we look at the central enabling causal force, then we need to concentrate on energy. In most general terms, technology is the mechanism that underlies the human self–referential heat engine as analysed in Chapter 2. That means, technology evolves and thereby shifts the interface between the human economic system and the potential sources of energy. As we have seen in Chapter Two, from this it follows that the economic system grows, because technology ultimately intermediates the use of energy to harness and utilize energy. Let us analyse this generic structure in more detail.

The perspective on technology that I am going to deploy is a thoroughly naturalistic one and differs from the conventional approach of economics to production which highlights the role of knowledge and of social coordination among 'factors of production'; instead, I highlight the role of production systems that centre on different ways how to harness and transform energy (Witt 2005; cf. Hall et al. 2001).

We can focus our understanding of technological change on the use of energy in three major episodes. The first stage is the emergence of technologically enhanced food processing, that is the use of fire and the invention of cooking, the second stage is the transition to agriculture, and the third is industrialisation. The three stages differ in terms of the internalisation of the environment, in the sense of the culture/nature divide, and in the focal source of energy: That is, we can distinguish between three different stages in human niche construction.

- In the first stage, technology remains a part of general biological niche construction; that means that human technology does not substantially alter the evolutionary processes in the environment. The focal sources of energy are diversified across plants and animals. There is no independent production process (hunting and gathering).

- In the second stage, human culture and nature evolve into a symbiotic relationship via domestication of plants and animals, thus creating a new ecological niche which essentially depends on the agricultural technologies applied by human beings, and which could substantially change the natural environment, such as when creating irrigation systems. The focal source of energy in this stage is photosynthesis, that is sunlight harvested by plants, which are the either consumed directly or indirectly via meat consumption by humans. The main source of work is human labour, gradually being enhanced by technological means.
- The third stage makes many technologies independent from symbiotic relations with the ecological system into which they are embedded, ultimately leading into the 'Anthropocene', where the natural environment is transformed into a technological artefact in the broadest sense. Industrialization has turned fossil fuels into the focal source of energy, and enabled the more comprehensive substitution of capital and technology for labour. The historical stage of the Industrial Revolution just appears to be the incipient stage in the transition to the Anthropocene. The central point about industrialization is that energetic resources could be harnessed that expanded the reach and scope of the evolution of artefacts, ultimately transforming most of the surface of the Earth into an artefact (Mitcham 1994: 175).

7.4.4. The transition to agriculture

The transformative forces of human activity in the biosphere were already released with the transition to agriculture. Given the relatively short evolutionary time that has passed since the transition to agriculture, similar genetic adaptations as in the case of cooking could not happen, even though there are important examples such as the lactose intolerance of certain populations that did not practice livestock breeding (Swallow 2003; Burger et al. 2007). The main characteristics of agriculture as a technology is that it consists of a number of techniques which generate co-evolutionary changes in living systems that are part of the evolving symbiotic relationships. Thus, vegetables become dependent on human weeding and other forms of support, and they are an object of breeding techniques, as it is also the case for all kinds of animals. This is not the place to go into details here, as we would need to further distinguish pastoralism and agriculture etc. Yet, the fundamental point applies, namely the co-evolutionary linkage between human and other living systems in the first emergence of human technology.

As has been noted by many observers, in most circumstances the emergence of agriculture implied a decline of individual well-being. Smil (2003, 2008) gives a very detailed and careful account of the evolutionary forces that drove the transition from foraging and hunting to agriculture, which I subsequently follow. The basic energetics is determined by the needs of the human body that is involved in different activities, the technology of harnessing energy, which is mainly determined by environmental factors and social organization, and the energetic harvest. One important aspect of all pre-agricultural regimes is the need to move across space, which automatically puts constraints on the evolution of more complex forms of social organization. However, especially with regard to hunting, there is a minimum size of human groups that is necessary also to ensure individual survival, which is about 30–40 (compare Chapter 5, 5.4.1.). So, transition to agriculture is an improbable event, as there are two alternative scenarios: Either the traditional economy is sufficiently productive in order to make adoption of agriculture superfluous, or there are constraints on adopting a sedentary lifestyle.

It is a universal pattern in agricultural societies all over the world that they lived a very precarious existence, with a frequent occurrence of famines. The reason is that agriculture implies sedentary patterns of behaviour, and these affect the rate of reproduction. That is, the emergence of agriculture caused population growth, and, following the classical Boserup hypothesis, population growth increased the adaptive pressure towards further agricultural innovation. These innovations can always be sorted into different classes, with three possible distinctions, that one between living and non-living entities in the first place, such as the emergence of the plough and the breeding of new variants of seeds, and the third one which is the evolution of new forms of social organization in which the use of the other entities is embedded. All agricultural societies manifest the regularity that the growth of the population always exploited the carrying capacity of the agro–ecological niche. Compared to hunter gatherer societies, agricultural societies can maintain a much higher population density. Correspondingly, the exploitation of human labour drives reproductive behaviour, with children being the cheapest sources of labour input, especially also considering the costs of monitoring their work.

The energetic needs of humans vary substantially relative to the environment and the tasks to be accomplished. However, there is always the need to balance energetic inputs and energetic outputs, taking certain constraints on the chemical composition of foods into consideration (such as amino acids etc.). If we consider only the energetics here, labour inputs are substantial in either of the regimes, hunting and gathering and agriculture, especially with regard to high energy content food, namely meat. For example, hunting large game may require the energetic costs of running marathons for a group of hunters, thus reflecting the central role of running in the biological make up of humans. Since hunting may require high levels of mobility, the additional energetic advantages of agriculture may be not very large, which explains the coexistence of both technological regimes in many areas, or the late adoption in Northern Europe.

It should be emphasized that in hunter gatherer societies status good consumption may also have played a role in determining technological patterns, which explains the exalted role of hunting even in the early large agricultural empires, where hunting evolved into a special activity of the power holding elites (Betzig 2008). That means, meat partly played the role of a status good, which also contributed to the development of weapons technologies such as archery. I come back on this point in the next section. The role of meat as a status good is discernible especially under conditions where the transition to simple forms of agriculture took place, such as shifting farming. In some cases, raising pigs is in fact energetically a loss, but allows consuming prestigious fat.

The emergence of agriculture clearly reflects the Maximum Power Principle, directly expressed in population growth, as this is a direct measure of energetic throughputs in pre-industrial societies, resulting in increasing output of work. In terms of efficiency, hunter and gatherer societies coexisted with agricultural societies until most recent historical time. The living standard in terms of nutritional status deteriorated in most agricultural societies. Yet, on the population level the combination of population growth and territorial expansion implied a maximization of power generation, as compared to the maximization of exergy returns, which would have been reflected in improved physiological functionings. To this, the utilization of animals in agricultural production needs to be added. This leads to a trade–off, as draft animals consume agricultural production at the same time. For example, at the beginning of the twentieth century an estimated 20 per cent of the entire US farmland was used to maintain the draft animals, mainly horses. This relation was impossible to achieve in other agricultural regions such as China, which also explains that in some agricultural regions draft animals were even more expensive than human work, as in this case there was no direct competition over energetic throughputs, only in the sense of higher energetic needs of intensive manual work.

However, once agricultural societies came into existence, they operated under the relentless pressure of increasing the availability of exergy, again, in the two dimensions of power, that is amount of work and time savings. This is the driving force of the evolution of agricultural systems, which, depending on climate and soil conditions, could develop into extensification or intensification. Intensification requires increasing exergy inputs, both in the form of human work and the construction of artefacts (terracing, tools etc.). Comparing agricultural systems across the world, the climate imposes one particular constraint which is crucial for the most general analytical level (for a seminal approach, see Hesse 1982, building on Georgescu-Roegen 1971: 211ff): Intensification can face a time constraint in all locations which manifest frost during the winter period. The beginning of the frost period marks an abrupt ending of all harvesting activities, which implies that even if the production can be further maximized during frost-free seasons, there is an upper limit to the harvested quantity, unless there is the possibility to save time in the harvesting period.

Therefore, agricultural intensification processes differ fundamentally between Northern and Southern regions. If soil qualities and the general climatic setting allows for it, in frost-free locations there is a strong incentive to intensify the utilization of land and to maximize the input of labour, and there is no incentive to save labour time. In northern locations, there are strong incentives to save labour during the times when harvesting and seeding are pressing tasks, and losses of a few days of labour might lead to serious disadvantages. Additionally, idle labour in winter time can be set free to do other work, such as on tools. Different agricultural conditions also set different incentives for population growth. In northern regions, there were incentives to adapt population growth to the carrying capacity of agriculture, given temporal constraints, until the industrial revolution released the essential constraint on agricultural productivity.

It is important to notice that technological innovation in agricultural economies focuses on either the domestication process, such as the introduction of new seeds and animal varieties, or methods to improve the energy conversion process. Important examples are the plough and the harness for draft animals where new technologies could improve the productivity of animal work substantially. These systems support extensive agriculture, where human labour increasingly morphed into controlling activities, such as guiding the horse and the plough. Under different agro–ecological conditions, the direction of technological change may be different, such as in the irrigation agriculture in uneven territory, where terracing and water pumps play a central role. Moving water is extremely costly in energetic terms, if that would rely on labour input alone. So, many ingenious devices were developed in agricultural societies to deal with this challenge.

7.4.5. The modern carbon–based economy

The substitution of human labour with draft animals and agricultural tools created the conditions to leverage the animal energetic input as far as possible. In other words, this pattern established a technological paradigm in which, firstly, a demand for tool improvement was created, and secondly, a general pattern was emergent in which the role of draft animals could be easily substituted by machines. This connection is most obvious in the case of the United States, where the first mechanical harvesters, drawn by up to 40 horses, were developed in the second half of the 19th century. This trajectory could integrate fuel–powered machines easily. A similar preformation of technological trajectories results from the high energetic returns of fertilizers, which links up with the emergence of modern industrial chemistry.

This analysis shows how the crucial historical phenomenon of pre-industrialisation is deeply embedded into adaptive processes in agricultural production, which in turn reflect the more fundamental processes of energy conversions. In the context of world history, this explains the bifurcation between Asian growth and European growth, and the divergent path of technological evolution. In both cases, the Maximum Power Principle holds, which translated into strong population growth in Asian societies, only kept in check by the frequent occurrence of wars. In European societies, agricultural conditions caused the search for labour–saving technologies, firstly in the shape of simple tools and devices, used in production and transport.

It is important to notice that in the preindustrial societies of Europe many technological innovations already happened before the advent of full-scale industrialization because technological artefacts could rely on alternative sources of energy. Over centuries, important classes of artefacts widely in use related with mechanical devices that leverage power of humans and animals, especially levers and wheels (tread wheels). Wheels were also connected with non-living sources of energy throughput, wind and water. Slowly the mechanical knowledge was converging with developments in artefact construction that resulted from the use of iron and steel for constructing tools and machines. The central bottleneck in developing those technologies was the supply of carbon that is necessary to reduce ores, which could only stem from charcoal. Charcoal production put heavy pressure on wood supply and triggered deforestation processes. Therefore, the supply of wood was a major constraint on the transition from pre-industrialization to industrialization, especially because there were always competing uses for cooking fuel and construction.

This observation puts emphasis on the central significance of coal for industrialization, as I have already pointed out previously. Only coal could provide the necessary energetic throughputs and chemical potential to kick-start the industrialization process, once a peculiar type of artefact came into existence, the steam engine. Steam engines were an essential part of a complementary industrial structure in which steam engines were also used in mining, such that the costs of coal declined. In Britain, this complementarity was leveraged by fortuitous geographic factors, because coal mines were close to emerging centres of industrial production. The diffusion of coal preceded other countries substantially, which explains much of the head start of Britain in industrialization (for a detailed analysis of the role of coal and energy prices in Britain, see Allen 2009: 80ff). So, the most important feature of industrialization was the hypercyclic interdependence of different technological applications, which is driven by the MPP principle, and represented by the Salter cycle in economic terms, under the conditions of already well-developed markets. The steam engine became a universal purpose technology, once combined with the existing mechanical knowledge about levers, wheels and other devices, and could be used over a wide range of applications in manufacturing, also triggering organisational innovations because of the centralization of the power source in manufacturing processes (Allen 2009: 156ff).

Coal continues to be a major source of energy throughputs in many countries of the world, enhanced by the use of hydrocarbons. So, the diffusion of industrialization was mainly driven by the fact that those reservoirs of past solar energy throughputs allow to activate energetic reservoirs that had needed a much longer time to result from the yearly throughput of solar energy. This fact is mainly hidden by the seemingly small share of energy production in GDP. However, this small share does not justify the conclusion that energy is not a central sector of modern industrial economies, a fact that is evident if one adopts the network perspective and looks at the significance of energy from the viewpoint of input–output relations which grasp its role as a complementary throughput factor for which there is no substitute. In this case, the importance of energy springs to mind because it is an input that is complementary to all other inputs, such that, for example, price hikes in energy lead to strong effects in all sectors of the economy (for a detailed discussion of this issue, see Kümmel 1998; Ayres and Warr 2005; Lindenberger et al. 2008).

For assessing the significance of energy throughputs for modern economic growth it is useful to expand the perspective firstly and to include all flows of exergy into the picture. This means to adopt the 'industrial metabolism' view, which looks at the entire input side in terms of mass in the first step and converting these into exergy in the second step (surveyed in Ayres and Ayres 2002).

The mass flow view is directly equivalent to a network analysis of the economy, which can be broken down to the flow of fundamental chemical substances for which the law of preservation of mass holds (Bringezu and Moriguchi 2002). Substance flows can be considered on different levels of aggregation, reaching from single chemical substances to different larger groups, such as fuels, metals or biomass, and to the total value of mass of inputs. This view corresponds to Input–Output analysis in economics (Strassert 2002). If one considers a single economy, this means that imports and exports are also taken into consideration, and all the direct relations with the natural environment, so that on the one hand extraction processes dominate the input side, and waste generation dominates the output side, beyond final consumption and exports. In modern economies, reflecting the significance of carbon inputs, the emission of carbon dioxide has become one of the largest final outputs in terms of mass. For example, in Moriguchi's (2002) material flow analysis of the Japanese economy in 1990, CO_2 emissions amount to 1170 MMT, whereas exports amount to 70 MMT or industrial wastes to 395 MMT. Extraction is a very broad term and corresponds to the first sector, broadly speaking, in the traditional industrial classification. Thus, agriculture is an extractive economic activity in the sense of transforming sunlight and nutrients in the soil into usable products. The industrial sector refers to all activities by which primary inputs are further transformed technologically, before they reach the final consumption or waste production stage.

Now, considering the aggregate material flows in modern economies, one can state three observations (I summarize the detailed empirical observations in Ayres and Warr 2009: Chapter 3; see also Ayres and Warr 2003, 2005). The first is that the total mass of all inputs grew consistently over the last century, and reflects the major events in the development of the GDP, such as major crises. Secondly, there is a clear trend for total mass, but also for more disaggregate categories, of a declining ratio between mass and GDP, which, on first sight, reflects the improvements in the technological efficacy of transforming material inputs into economic value. Thirdly, if one considers the values of mass per capita, there is also a very clear continuous upward trend, which masks a certain variation, such as the upward movement of fuels per capita versus the more recent reduction of metals per capita. There are many important other observations on a more disaggregate scale, which I leave out here. Just to mention one, namely that technological outputs have been increasing much stronger than other outputs, for example non-renewable outputs from synthetic chemistry.

This picture needs to be further specified in taking the energetic perspective. In this case, one first step is to transform the unit of mass into the unit of exergy that is embodied in all material products. Then the astonishing picture emerges that in the mass view, fuels grow in a similar way as other categories such as construction materials. But in the exergy view, fuels do not only dominate the growth of inputs by far, but also drive the expansion, with all other categories only manifesting a slow rate of growth. This also applies for the per capita calculation. In case of fuels, the mass per capita and the exergy per capita view produce a very similar picture, whereas, for example, in case of construction the mass values go up, whereas the exergy values remain stable. The relationship between inputs and GDP shows the same trends for the mass and the exergy view, namely that there is a clear downward trend. This is especially important to recognize for fuel inputs: Exergy per unit of GDP has been declining consistently during the past century, thus certainly reflecting technological progress in transforming exergy into economic outputs.

From the viewpoint of the MPP/MEP approach, these observations match with the fundamental assumptions: In spite of the fact that the entire economic system improves the efficiency of conversion processes, this does not imply that there is an absolute reduction of throughputs. On the contrary, the energetic throughputs grow consistently. Obviously, this has been driven by the consequences of the major transition of the Industrial Revolution, that is, the emergence of a carbon based economy that activated the embodied energy of fossil fuels.

7.4.6. Technology, energy transformations and MEP

The essential role of energy for modern industrial civilization can be further detailed in considering improvements in energy conversion efficiencies as the core aspect of technological progress (again, summarizing Ayres and Warr 2009). This means to abstract from all specific uses of technology, so that technology only appears as a device to expand work output in the physical sense. One can distinguish between primary and secondary work. Primary work is generated by primary processes of exergy conversion, such as when a heat engine is used to generate electricity. Secondary work is work generated by devices that use that electricity. So, on the most general level of analysis only primary work is relevant to assess the role of energy in the economic system. Primary work can be further differentiated into work generated by so-called prime movers, that is mechanical devices of any kind, and heat generation (including cooling).

It is then possible to relate exergy and useful work generation in terms of a measure of conversion efficiency. Exergy is a measure of potential work, so that one can compare measures of exergy input with the flow of useful work in the economy. This includes work by humans and animals, in terms of the exergy used in creating their physical work output (such as manifested in different caloric needs of different kinds of workers). However, the hallmark of industrialization is that this kind of work has been declining to a very small share of total useful work generated in the economy. Therefore, it is feasible to focus the analysis on the prime movers and heat generation. In this view, the prime movers also include the generation of electricity, which results from the use of certain prime movers such as turbines. Heat generation is a very important aspect of many industrial processes, such as metals production and chemical processes, apart from the use of exergy in human dwellings.

These measures of primary work relate with measures of secondary work, which is important when considering the final result of economic activity. The efficiency in generating this final economic output is determined by the efficiencies of the energetic conversion processes on both steps, that is generating primary work (such as using sunlight to produce electricity by photovoltaic technologies) and converting primary work into secondary work (such as using electricity for an industrial tool). This also implies that one can estimate the amount of total useful work in an economy by means of calculating the exergy inputs and the conversion efficiencies of different technological means, such as the use of fuels to produce transport output in combustion engines. However, as primary work drives secondary work, one can also focus on primary work, where the calculation of conversion efficiencies is straightforward by considering the efficiency of water turbines, combustion engines etc.

The central observation here is that the continuous growth of exergy throughputs is also reflected in the continuous growth of primary work generation, in spite of similar improvements in the primary work/GDP ratios. Until the 1970s, the primary work/GDP ratio was continuously moving upwards, and was declining thereafter. But this did not stop the increase of primary work throughput in absolute terms.

One way to further analyse this relationship between work and GDP is to adopt a production function approach. In this approach, the traditional economic production function which only regards energy and capital is enhanced by adding a third production factor, useful work (for instance, in Warr et al. 2008). Statistically, it is possible to calculate this by using data on exergy inputs and an aggregate conversion efficiency value that considers both steps, primary and secondary. The important result of this approach is that useful work is an essential input driving economic growth, and that what has been regarded as 'technological progress' in the past can be identified as the aggregate improvement of conversion efficiency. This is an essential result, because it directly vindicates the view that the knowledge embodied in technology is control information in the larger thermodynamic processes. Technological progress directly enhances the energetic productivity of the economy.

So, a central question is how to reconcile the two observations, namely about the growth of absolute throughputs and simultaneous efficiency improvements. One central notion is the so-called 'rebound effect' (surveyed comprehensively by Sorrell 2009, Sorrell et al. 2009). The rebound effect can be related to the more general view on economic growth which in turn reflects a hypercyclic conceptual framework. The theory of the rebound effect goes back to Jevons' classical analysis of the 'coal question'. Jevons already had all necessary ingredients in place. He analysed the effects of steam engines on coal use in the entire mining industry and argued that improvements in the design of steam engines led to many direct and indirect effects ultimately increasing the demand for coal. Firstly, if steam engines are more efficient, this makes steam cheaper and thus increases demand for steam engines. But steam engines can also be used in steel production which thus leads to price decreases of steel. That makes steam engines even cheaper and better, thus leveraging the first effect. Both channels work together in propelling the mining industry. Cheaper steam engines improve productivity of mining, cheaper steel also supports the expansion of railways which also use steam engines. With transport costs down, the demand for coal increases further. In the end, efficiency gains in energy transformation lead towards an increase in the demand for coal. In this view, economic growth is a positive feedback cycle which is driven by two main forces, as stated in the Salter cycle. One is the improvement of the knowledge base that underlies the use of technology in production. The other is the interaction between the resulting effects on the costs of production and demand expansion. That is, the demand expansion is a central mechanism that directly affects the continuous growth of energetic throughputs that generate the useful work necessary to realize the productive activities.

Against this background, the rebound effect is a complex phenomenon because it includes direct and indirect effects in the entire network of economic activities. The general idea is that improvements in energy efficiency directly drive the expansion of the demand for energy. For example, a direct rebound effect would occur if improved energy conversion of cars leads to increased personal transport. The indirect rebound effect would occur if the lowering of expenditures for fuels used in personal transport results into demand increases for energetic inputs in other services. Clearly, if we want to know the general effect of improvements in energy efficiency we would need to consider the total effect, hence adopt a general equilibrium view in the economic context. Direct rebound effects tend to be relatively small, although they clearly exist. For example, improvements of fuel efficiency in cars seem to lead to a 10 per cent increase of fuel demand, relative to the achieved reduction.

However, this result is certainly too narrow, as it only focuses on single technologies. Even in this case, there are technologies which manifest rebound effects that might even be larger than one, such as in lighting. But if we adopt the framework of self–referential heat engines that I outlined in Chapter Two, the indirect rebound effects matter much more. Indirect rebound effects occur via many different channels, such as related to the exergy that is embedded in the energy saving technologies, the aforementioned indirect spending effects, or the price effects in the aforementioned general positive feedback models of economic growth. These indirect rebound effects are particularly strong if one considers general purpose technologies which have broad cross–sectorial applications, such as the steam engine. Further, it is necessary to consider world-wide effects. For example, the introduction of energy–saving devices might increase costs for certain products in the advanced industrial nations, which are then imported from other less–developed countries which use more energy intensive techniques. These total rebound effects are very difficult to estimate empirically, but it is possible to analyse them in the context of theoretical models of growth. These models translate the general feedback model of growth into a feedback model for energy throughputs, which simply argues that the growth of total factor productivity increases demand for economic output that feeds back to energy demand.

One most recent example which directly relates with the general entropic approach in Chapter Two is the rise of information technology. There is now increasing awareness that the spread of computer technology has serious effects on the demand for energy which directly results from information processing (heating and cooling of computers). This is a general purpose technology that certainly contributes to energy efficiency, but increases the demand for energy, too. So, we can conclude that one central fact of economic growth since the Industrial Revolution, that is the simultaneous improvements of energy efficiency and the continuous growth of energy throughputs, seems to vindicate the existence of strong rebound effects, which can be explained in turn by the general principles of MPP and MEP on the level of the global economic system. In other words, MPP and MEP find expression in the mechanisms of rebound effects.

This means that the entropic approach to technology can never apply for single devices, but only for the system of technology *in toto*. MPP and MEP work on the level of the global technological system. Therefore, assessments of energy efficiency are not relevant as long they argue with reference to single devices or even single clusters of technology. Practicable alternatives can be very simple, such as the EROI indicator that directly compares energetic output of the entire energy generation system with the energetic outlays, which means the investment needed for harvesting energy, which is also a valid perspective for single technologies (for an overview, see Murphy and Hall 2010). This is of particular interest for analysing general purpose energy transformation processes, such as comparing coal with biofuels in the transport system. Then, the significant observation can be made that there is an overall trend of moving from high EROI technologies to low EROI technologies, which means that the additional energy gained by new technologies is very low. Hence, in the energetic perspective it seems that a sort of 'law of diminishing returns' applies for the evolution of the entire technological system. However, this implies at the same time that the energy embodied in the energy transformation mechanisms grows.

Considering the embodied energy in any kind of product implies that one could move back even to the primordial source of energy, that is solar radiation (apart from nuclear energy) (for a systematic approach, see Odum 2007). All fossil fuels and all renewable energies ultimately go back to solar radiation. Then, the view on single technological devices is misleading if one does not consider embodied energies. In this context, one needs to distinguish between the economic and the physical effects. For example, introducing hybrid cars may induce fuel savings. However, hybrid cars need many new technological inputs, such as rare earths, which embody large amounts of energy. Given certain price relations, this diffusion of hybrid technologies may last for a certain time, that is, it is economically profitable. But this is precisely the factor that ultimately generates a global rebound effect via the embodied energies. Thus, ultimately energy throughputs increase, including the embodied energy. This view directly reflects the hierarchical nature of the energetic flows that we have already scrutinized in Chapter Two. In the embodied energy perspective, this means to focus on the mechanisms how certain energetic investments result in certain power outputs in the sequence of the hierarchy, with the empirical regularity that the so-called 'transformity' increases, namely the ratio between original embodied energy (solar energy) and power generation increases. In my view, this corresponds to a reverse process in which those power outputs mainly assume the role of control information that channels the original energy flows.

7.4.7. The Anthropocene

As a result of the emergence and unfolding of the modern carbon economy, human niche construction has become a global phenomenon, implying that human networks encompass the entire Earth System (McNeill and McNeill 2003: 319ff.). Geologists have therefore coined a term for what seems to emerge as a new geological epoch. The aforementioned notion of the 'Anthropocene' has been proposed by Crutzen (for a short statement, see Crutzen 2002). With this term, Crutzen aims at catching the fact that the human impact on the Earth System has been increased dramatically since the Industrial Revolution. As such, this idea is not entirely new, as the Russian scholar Vernadsky already had developed the notion of the 'biosphere' in analysing the Earth System, which refers to the pervasive impact of life on the biochemistry of geological processes (for a survey, see Smil 2003: Chapter 1). Vernadsky also adopted the term 'noosphere' which referred to the idea that mankind represents the transition to a new phenomenon transcending the biosphere.

In comparison, the 'Anthropocene' notion is a strictly geological one that directly refers to the issue of stratigraphic criteria to distinguish epochs in the evolution of the Earth system. The geological present is part of the Quaternary that spans 2.5 Ma roughly and thus includes a number of interglacial epochs of which the Holocene is the most recent and distinct one. The Holocene only spans about 12,000 years, thus the period of the emergence of human civilization, especially with regard to the transition to agriculture and the speeding up of technological change. The Holocene is a distinct stratigraphic unit because there were very pronounced geological changes that resulted from the increases in global temperature, such as the rise of the sea level and the increase of atmospheric carbon dioxide. Thus, the Holocene is already an extremely short geological period, and the question is whether the identification of a new period is warranted, the Anthropocene, even considering the possibility that this does not only represent a transition from the Holocene, but from the Quaternary (for an overview, see Zalasiewicz et al. 2008). There are many convincing reasons why this view can be justified. They all relate to the tremendous impact of human technological activity on the most recent strata: For example, sedimentation caused by human hydro–engineering is already much more significant than natural sedimentation. Further, the changing carbon dioxide levels in the atmosphere already cause very substantial changes in all geophysical and biological processes that are influenced by this, such as the capacities of carbonate–secreting organisms (such as coral reefs). The human environmental impact is also clearly leading towards a major extinction event across all ecological systems which will soon leave also stratigraphic traces.

Some geologists believe that these changes are already large enough to justify even the claim that a transition from Quaternary to Anthropocene is going on because the last geological epoch when comparable levels of temperatures etc. were realized in the average was the Mid-Pliocene, 3 Ma ago. However, it is difficult to assess the long-term consequences of the contemporary conditions reliably. In the context of this chapter, suffice to notice that geologists almost take it for granted now that human technology is a geological force, and no longer just a biological phenomenon with partial impact. This is confirmed by estimates of the energetic flows in the Earth System: Kleidon (2009, 2010, and 2011) shows that the annual energetic flows of human activity amount to 50 TW roughly, whereas geological forces only amount to 40 TW; this compares with the entire biosphere, which processes 150 TW. In this account the fact is even left out of sight that many energetic flows resulting from human activity actually impact on the biospheres' flows and even geological flows, in the sense of 'control information' as elucidated in Chapter Two.

These observations suggest that the evolution of technology as a system follows the principles of MPP and MEP, as posited in figure 4.9. This finds expression in the energetics of technology induced growth. Technology has become the driver of growth since the Industrial Revolution in one particular sense: Namely, mobilizing stocks of fossil resources to rapidly increase energy throughput and useful work. In this, technology is a hypercyclic system which manifests the same features as autocatalytic cycles in physics and chemistry: Technology manifests mechanisms which increase energy throughputs via mutual leveraging of productivities, as stated in the Salter cycle. Technology furthers the growth of free energy rate intensity via the creation of new layers of information that further enhance energy throughputs, thus staying in line with earlier major transitions in 'Big History' (Aunger 2007; see Chapter Two, 2.5.3.). In this view, human technology operates in a similar way as large predators operate in ecosystems: The existence of large predators actually leverages energy throughputs, and extinction events affecting large predators typically reduce the entire biological productivity of an ecosystem (Vermej 2004: 111ff.). The same applies for human technology. This does not simply mean that human activities consume more energy: For instance, in agricultural systems the entire productivity of plants and animals is also increased, which enables population growth of the 'top predator', the human beings. This view leads us to reconsider technology in relation to one important hypothesis in Ecological Economics, the Gaia hypothesis.

In Chapter Two I presented the original Gaia hypothesis which states that the Earth System is a self-regulating system in equilibrium. In this view, human technology is a subordinate phenomenon in the larger system. That would imply that the energetic dynamics of human technology is ultimately a disequilibrating and disturbing factor, as evident in phenomena such as global warming. According to the new Gaia hypothesis as presented in Chapter Two, the MPP/MEP holds for the entire Earth System, such that the Earth System *in toto* is in a disequilibrium steady state of continuous growth of energetic throughputs driving the Earth System farther apart from equilibrium. Then, it is the biosphere that regulates the geosystem via its strong impact on chemical and other physical processes, and it is the emergent technosphere that regulates the biosphere, with the transition to the Anthropocene. Both the technosphere and the biosphere manifest MPP/MEP, such that there is no inherent contradiction between the two. The biosphere drives the Earth System away from equilibrium, and the technosphere works in the same direction, and even leverages the disequilibrium forces in the biosphere. However, even though the energetic transformations have already achieved huge scale, as mentioned previously, this does not necessarily imply that human-induced entropy production of the entire Earth System as measured at the interface to the outer cosmos has already achieved substantial weight, which is the only criterion for assessing sustainability on this level of aggregation (Kåberger and Månsson 2001). This view is a radical move in reconsidering the relationship between nature and culture, or technology: Technology appears to be an emergent phenomenon in the biosphere, and the technosphere co-evolves with the biosphere according to the same underlying principles.

I summarize this view on the conceptual integration between Chapter Two and this chapter on technology in figure 7.11, which reproduces figure 2.21, with minor, though essential changes. The general claim is that the entropic processes are driven by physiosemiosis, which manifests the generic mechanisms of emergent hypercyclic structures. This basic process was operating in the most fundamental event of the origin of life, thus establishing the principles of physiosemiosis, as elucidated in Chapter Two. Life shows the feature of autonomous agents, namely agents with teleonomy, which are, from the thermodynamic view, self–referential heat engines that generate work in order to increase the throughput of useful energy. As we have seen in Chapter Two, this mechanism essentially implies the accumulation of information, as this mediates the energy/work link. This link applies for technology in the same way.

The physiosemiotic process causes the emergence of hierarchies in which higher level energy flows control lower level energy flows, which together follow the MPP. An essential aspect of the physiosemiotic process is the emergence of hierarchically ordered niches. Technology is an essential part of human niche construction and hence human evolution. Human technology controls biological processes, and, after the process of the Industrial Revolution has unfolded, the entire biosphere, especially via climatic effects. This is what I call the 'technosphere'.

Figure 7.11 The technosphere and Gaia

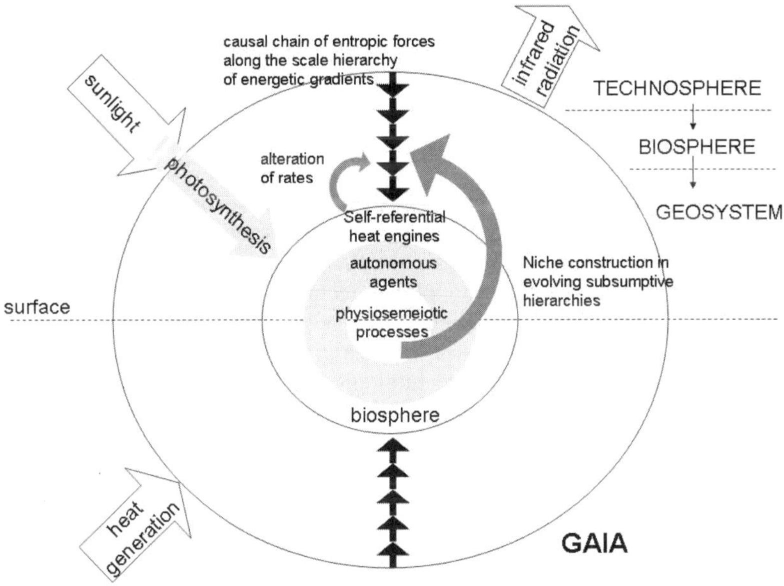

Note: For a detailed description of this diagram, see figure 2.21. This version includes the view on the hierarchical control information that emerged during the evolution of the biosphere. The original Gaia hypothesis emphasizes the biosphere as regulator of geological processes and integrates human activity in the biosphere. In the view proposed in this chapter, the technosphere emerged from the biosphere and accumulates control information that encompasses both technosphere and biosphere. The current developments regarding climate change manifest this fundamental change: Human technology does not only change the entire geosystem, but solutions to climate change can only build on further technological evolution.

7.4.8. The technosphere

On the aggregate level, the technosphere follows the same fundamental evolutionary principles as the biosphere. One central notion is the Constructal Law (for an explicit reflection upon the relationship between the Constructal Law and technology, see Bejan 2009). The Constructal Law is the most important single hypothesis that relates design principles of technology with the principles of MPP and MEP. Although it is still mostly applied on technology in the engineering sense, that means on single artefacts, I venture the hypothesis that it applies also for the long run evolution of technological design. That means, if we consider the Gaia hierarchy, then there is the efficient causal chain of entropic forces that ultimately drive the energy transformations in the biosphere and the human economy. On the other hand, the physiosemiotic process results in changes in the rates of those causalities, thus ending up in a control information hierarchy, in which energy throughputs are leveraged. The interplay of these two dimensions is reflected in the Constructal Law. The Constructal Law, as introduced in Chapter Two (section 2.4.5.), states that flow systems will always evolve in a way to improve access to the flows, which means, to increase throughputs. This can be applied on single devices in engineering, for example, such as heating systems. However, if we consider technology as a system, the Constructal Law would refer to the entire network structure of technology, and energy flows as the relevant flows. Then, it is straightforward to see that the global technological network will evolve according to the MPP and MEP principles as stated in Chapter Two.

The general interdependence between network evolution and flows, resulting into directedness of technological change, and concurrently the evolution of knowledge, can be observed in the validity of scaling laws which hold for biological organisms in a same way as for larger-scale networks in human societies (see Chapter Three, 3.5.7.). Scaling laws have been observed to apply especially for the emergence of cities, which are the most essential large scale network configuration in modern economies. They have been well-known in terms of 'Zipf's Law' for long, which refers to the size distribution of cities that reflects a Power Law (Krugman 1996: chapter 3). Cities can be seen as the most concentrated expression of human niche construction by means of technological evolution, because all important human technologies evolve in the context of the growth of urban agglomerations. For example, the transition to the modern carbon economy was driven by the huge demand of cities (especially London in the British head start towards industrialization) for cheap energy supplies and the corresponding transport logistics (Allen 2009: 84ff). Urban growth was also the main driver of agricultural productivity via the demand–induced pressures for technological progress (Allen 2009: 74ff).

There are more specific scaling laws for human and urban networks which are similar to the scaling laws that relate resource flows and energetic flows in biological organisms (Bettencourt et al. 2007). The regularities that emerge in city growth have been in focus of geographers for long and have also attracted the attention of economists (Fujita et al. 1999). There is a clear connection to general network mechanisms, especially power laws emerging from preferential attachment (overview in Newman 2006). Bettencourt et al. introduce a very simple formula that allows arranging many different empirical phenomena:

$$Y(t) = Y_0 N(t)^\beta$$

where Y denotes the quantity in question (ranging from GDP over electricity consumption to road length), N the size of the city in terms of population and

β the scaling parameter which allows us to distinguish between sublinear, linear and superlinear processes.

The ultimate source of superlinearity, hence increasing returns is the growth of knowledge which is vastly increased in cities (Glaeser and Gottlieb 2009). We can analyse this process in terms of the general entropic approach to networks developed in Chapter Five (5.2.1.). A major feature of cities is that the state space of possible combinations of actors and their properties increases very fast, both in the sense of the growing diversity of elements and the ways in which to combine them, which matches with the analysis of Boolean Networks. However, at the same time the gap between the possible and the realized combination increases, as the specific dynamics of small and large groups is maintained, because the cognitive capacities of individuals define principled limits on the formation of small groups (Glaeser 2011: 38). Hence, modern urban life manifests the combination of small group structures with growing connectedness in vast larger configurations, which means that information accumulates on the aggregate level, while increasing information capacity at the same time.

Cities are the most important driver of energetic flows in the modern economy. One illuminating observation is the increased 'speed' of city life, which has always been identified as major characteristic in literary and popular culture descriptions of urbanism (Simmel assigned a central role to this in his analysis of 'life styles', see Papilloud and Rol 2003). Speed is expressed in phenomena such as higher crime rates, more rapid spread of infections and even higher speed of walking. One literally enlightening empirical manifestation of these increased energy throughputs is the reflection of GDP growth rates in changes of the night lighting intensities across the globe (Henderson et al. 2012). Night lighting is a response to prolonged and intensified activity rates in urban areas, such as the extension of working hours. Many consumption activities during night-life reflect corresponding production of services. Further, lighting is one of the most conspicuous expressions of the rebound effect in energy use, as I mentioned previously. Therefore, the varying intensities of night lighting directly reflect the dynamics of growth. This applies generally for the rising trend in absolute and relative energy consumption in urban dwellings, that is including heating, cooling and others (Pérez-Lombard et al. 2008).

At a closer look, different aspects of urbanism follow different power laws, some sublinear (infrastructure such as roads), some linear (individual consumption), some superlinear (wealth, energy). In general, all aspects that relate with the growth of knowledge scale superlinearly, which matches with the conceptual connection between urbanism and the creative industries concept which especially highlights the role of cities in generating new knowledge (Florida 2002). The interaction between these different effects results into the hypercycle of urban technology; from the perspective of this chapter, urbanism is the core phenomenon of evolving human technology, as it conjoins most elements of technology in a pattern that is manifest in increasing productivity and rates of innovation. This has been most succinctly elaborated recently by Glaeser (2011: 36ff) who argues that a generalized Jevons 'paradox' (which means rebound effect in my parlance) applies for urban growth: Since urban growth centres on the accumulation of information, increasing efficiency of information processing in cities directly increases the demand for information more than proportionally. In the bimodal view of network growth, this corresponds to the leveraging of energy throughputs.

So, following McNeill and McNeill (2003: 317ff) we can identify the 'cosmopolitan web' as the ultimate physical expression of human technology being the shaping force of the technosphere emerging from the biosphere. Ontological continuity continues to hold across these evolutionary domains in terms of the common fundamental entropic principles. However, so far we have neglected one particular aspect of the evolving technosphere: This is the fact that it relates artefacts with human social interaction. Considering the semiotic aspect in bimodal human networks, we have elaborated in Chapters Five and Six that those networks manifest the pervasive role of group boundaries. Group selection is a major force in general evolution and in human evolution. I turn to this question in the final section of this Chapter.

7.5. POWER AND GROUP SELECTION OF TECHNOLOGY

7.5.1. The role of the military in technological innovation

As I have argued in Chapter Four (4.5.2.), group selection implies that the diffusion of artefacts is determined by a fundamental functional dualism: Artefacts fulfilling certain purposes of efficient and efficacious action will diffuse across group boundaries, whereas other artefacts that establish group boundaries will only fulfil this function if they are devoid of such purposes. Clearly, we can consider technology also under this aspect, as in the case of canoes considered in Chapter Four. This observation provides a general reason for the dualism in technological evolution that Veblen stated originally and that I already alluded to (7.3.3.), namely that there is always a mixture of functional and non-functional aspects in technological evolution. For example, in the case of the early 'industrious revolution' as analysed by De Vries (2008) (see 7.1.3.) there is the example of expensive watches which served as a status symbol even for poorer groups in English society before the need emerged for them to measure time exactly. One can even say, as in the example of money considered in Chapter Six that the emergence of many artefacts is first driven by non-functional determinants, and only once the artefacts exist, efficacious uses are discovered.

There is one important class of artefacts where these two aspects intermingle: weapons. Weapons fulfil the function to leverage physical violence and at the same time directly operate as mechanisms that enforce and signal group boundaries, and they simultaneously serve as tools and signs of status. In this final section of the chapter I explore the role of technologies of violence in more detail. The general idea is that the network mechanisms that drive the manifestation of MPP and MEP are directly and indirectly connected to the use of violence in human societies, because enhancing the energetic power of means of violence is one important driver of technological progress in human societies, apart from market competition, which is the exclusive topic of Chapter Eight.

Many technological innovations have occurred in the context of competition between territorial units, such as empires, states or nations, and therefore directly or indirectly connect with the military and weapons technology. This is not the place to go into the historical details, as this observation is well established in the literature (for a survey, see Constant 2000). However, in economics this point has not been considered as a central aspect of technological evolution, which concentrates on economic growth. But even in this case, we can safely assume that many path-breaking innovations have been connected with military uses. This is certainly true, for example, for milestones such as the development of the computer and the creation of the internet, but also for many pharmaceutical innovations, in earlier times. These examples show that we certainly need to distinguish between the emergence of a technology and its predominant uses afterwards. A case in point is the telephone, that was originally seen (similar to computers) mainly as a device used by the military, government and large scale business organizations, but rapidly evolved into a consumer good with widespread uses in the general population. The same is true for another communication technology that shapes our modern world, the radio: The radio was initially perceived to be a point–to–point communication technology, and only a 'maverick' application discovered the technological possibility of broadcasting. It is important to recognize that very often the technologies might have never crossed the initial barriers to entry without the push and pull of military needs, even if the main use afterwards has been civilian.

If I introduce the term 'military' here, I do not refer to uses external to political entities only, but to the general role of violence in society. As we have seen in Chapter Six, technology plays an essential role in all enforcement mechanisms of institutions, also beyond its use in the context of punishments. A primordial example are means of communication, which are essential to detect and track deviant behaviour in the context of institutions of enforcement, and also to use non-violent means of securing compliant behaviour, such as communicating ideologies. For example, the radio played an essential role in spreading ideology and behavioural norms across villages in early Communist China. It is also necessary to recognize that technologies of violence may not be used widely in a society, and nevertheless influence the behaviour of all actors via their perceptions and expectations of potential enforcement actions.

In that regard, one particularly important aspect of the relationship between power and technology is the role of the latter in the design and the creation of artefacts that directly reflect the power structure of a society. From the viewpoint of economic analysis, this can be summarized by the role of technology in the creation of status goods. An especially important case in point is the relationship between construction engineering and power: Many advances in construction technology were related with the creation of architecture which expresses supremacy of power holding elites, both in the political and the religious sphere. However, it is important to notice that in this field the role of standardization is very weak, as status goods may necessarily manifest the feature of singularity. The skills in erecting cathedrals may not diffuse widely in society, because this sort of building is unique, and requires lots of tacit knowledge and routine–based technological solutions. This is different for the case of military technology, which, apart from certain stages in history, such as the first applications of nuclear bombs, normally would require a high degree of standardization in order to create the necessary critical masses to establish dominance, and very often presuppose technology use in larger groups of actors, such as standing armies. The most famous example of this effect is the fact that the modern factory system was created in the context of weapons production for the US Army. Further, the role of technology in enforcement is not only limited to political bodies. For example, writing and calculation devices may have evolved in the context of taxation and resource extraction, but may also be used in the context of contract enforcement among economic actors.

My final observation relates to the fact that military power always involves the concentrated mobilization and application of energy. Not without reason was Hiroshima regarded to be an ultimate expression of military power. Modern tanks, fighter jets and battleships mobilize enormous amounts of energy, and destructive weapons are ultimately transformers of that energy into deadly results. But this applies for all earlier technologies as well. The most straightforward observation refers to the maintenance of supply lines for armies, which needed food and other equipment. Building fortresses and walls required huge energetic outlays, and crushing them as well. It is essential to notice that this mobilization of energetic throughputs is often not efficient unless economies of scale are achieved, and that therefore demand for military purposes often provides the drive to achieve those economies. For example, almost all modern transportation technologies such as the aircraft would have never emerged as economically feasible items in civilian uses if the great wars of the twentieth century had not propelled technological and organizational advances in mass production. In between the two world wars, the development of civil aviation slowed down again, only to be speeded up by the immense efforts to create flight infrastructure during WWII, such as airports. Not without reason is aviation still an important exception to the general rules of the modern system of international trade (ominously, together with energy trade), because countries aim at controlling the institutional conditions for keeping military uses of aviation possible (the same applies for shipping, see Strange 1994). The modern passenger aircraft would still be a luxury toy without this effect.

7.5.2. Power projection and social organization of means of violence

I summarize this discussion in the notion of 'technologically enhanced power projection'. Power projection refers to the original dimensions of power in the biological context, that is, to create larger units in terms of different dimensions, such as relative size, sustainability through time, speed and number of actions and so forth (Vermeij 2004). Power projection applies both internally and externally to the units which are institutionally integrated via a power structure. So, internal power projection applies to the notion of the monopoly of violence in modern nations, in which internal pacification means that a central institutional structure is maintained by a strong asymmetry in the distribution of capacities of violence. Accordingly, recently, political revolutions such as in North Africa and the Middle East often depend on a rearrangement in this asymmetry, such as in Libya. External power projection mainly refers to military competition between political units. Therefore, we can expand on figure 6.14, resulting into figure 7.12: The process of group selection that drives institutional evolution is essentially supported at critical junctures by technological artefacts. This is the direct manifestation of the bimodal conjunction of institutions and technology in human networks.

In this context, it is important to notice that we observe a direct manifestation of the bimodal nature of technology, as it is not simply the availability of artefacts in the matterenergy mode which determines power projection, but also the corresponding institutional and organizational patterns. Even the simplest weapons change their efficacy if accompanied with particular patterns of social organization. This is by no means only a question of organizing the particular actors who apply the technology, that is, in the sense of military leadership and organizing combat units. The possibilities of effective military organization depend on the embeddedness of network structures into larger societal patterns. There are many examples of this, such as the superiority of the Swiss pike phalanx over mounted armoured warriors of medieval Europe, which depended on the strong commitment mechanisms that emerged from the more egalitarian small-scale proprietor structures in Swiss peasant society. The pike as such was a newly designed weapon, but without any additional technological sophistication. So, its efficacy depended on military organization and the resulting organizational capabilities, which are embedded into larger societal network configurations: There is a complementarity between military technology and certain forms of social capital. Modern guerrilla wars are another case in point, as it was the rise of modern national armies triggered by the French revolution.

Figure 7.12 The role of technology in group selection of institutions

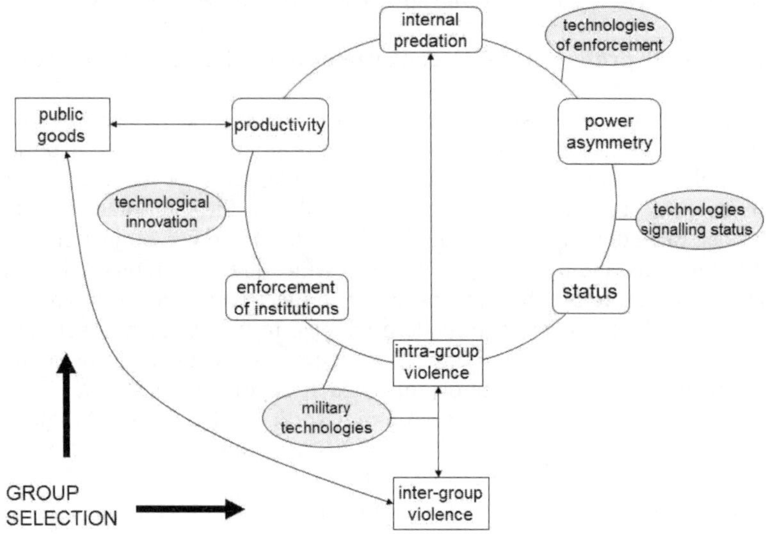

Note: Extending on figure 6.14 (see the pertinent note) we can identify five critical junctures where institutional and technological changes interact. Internal predation establishes power asymmetries depending on available means of enforcement; power asymmetries are stabilized by means of status signals; military technologies affect both patterns of intra–group and inter–group violence; both result in the enforcement of institutions that determine technological innovation, which in turn impacts on productivity changes.

This perspective has been systematically explored by Mann (1986). One of his important case studies is the Greek hoplite phalanx (Mann 1986: 198ff). The phalanx is a form of military organization that presupposes unique psychological features of the single soldiers, because it requires very strong discipline on the outer lines of members. Consider the structure of the phalanx: Every single soldier protects his neighbour with the shield, and the entire group moves in coordination, like a turtle. This had implications for weapons technology, because weapons and armoury could be made much heavier than compared with the case of individual and flexible combat. This is only possible via very long training of soldiers, and presupposes that the individuals are ready to sacrifice themselves for the others, especially when standing on the outer lines of the phalanx. Mann argues that the phalanx was only possible because Greek peasant societies evolved into the first democratic societies which had a class of small landholders at its core. This made a relationship between political and military organization possible that repeated itself throughout history. The Hoplites were relatively wealthy landowners who could afford the heavy weaponry economically and at the same time were highly motivated to protect their community against foreign invaders, because their individual wealth was at stake. So, in modern terminology, they developed a sense of 'ownership' with regard to the military organization which was mediated by the political organization of the polis. A similar connection between wealth and military technology emerged during European feudalism, epitomized in the figure of the heavily armoured knight, but this time based on the peculiar class structure with peasant serfs. The Swiss pike phalanx played a similar role as the Hoplite phalanx in linking individual ownership with military technology, thus regaining a balance of power in the feudal system.

However, such relationships are always embedded into the larger institutional patterns, if only because military advantage is always multi-dimensional, such as in the Greek case, and exemplified in the military competition between Sparta and Athens, when ultimately naval power was crucial. Rome's military dominance over Greece was created by important innovations in military technology which were mainly logistic in nature and enabled power projection to a degree that was unknown in the Western world previously. Again, Mann (1986: 272ff) offers a penetrating analysis of what he calls the 'legionary economy': the major innovation was to equip the soldier with the tools to enable him to build fortifications and other military infrastructure quickly and efficaciously. This military infrastructure, such as roads and bridges, also supported economic development and trade, thus leveraging the accumulation of wealth by the Roman people.

In other words, the relationship between technology, military power and institutions is determined on different levels of societal network configurations, including also the most aggregate and general properties of these. This is because the organization of warfare requires the mobilization of large numbers of people, both on the battlefield and in the logistic support. Therefore, the analysis of military technology and its social organization always requires reference to generic institutional features of the competing groups (for an illuminating comparison between the frontier challenges in early modern Russia and America, also related to geography, climate and other factors, see White 1990). Again, this does not imply that the military factors are the prime movers. There are examples for many different causal patterns. For example, two central innovations that changed military power in Europe substantially was the simultaneity of the introduction of the stirrup and of the mould–board plough. The stirrup is not directly connected with the use of the plough, but the plough enabled people to increase the productivity of the heavy North European soils. This provided for the possibility of agricultural surplus that could be appropriated by a class of land–holding elites, provided that they controlled a military technique to suppress the peasants (very much along the lines of the specialization dilemma as analysed in Chapter Six). Amongst others, this was enabled by the stirrup, because it made the use of strong war horses feasible. So, two technological inventions worked together to support the Northern European institutional regime of feudalism. Without those innovations, this regime would not have been possible. That is to say, in the conjunction of military technologies, general economic evolution and institutional change, it is certainly impossible to identify the prime movers unequivocally, but there is still clear evidence of a strong co-evolutionary connection between military developments and technological change. In many cases we can assert that certain evolved institutional structures have unintended effects on military power structures. That being said, we have to recognize that the institutions regularly emerge in internal conflicts about power that also involve the use of military means.

7.5.3. Red Queen effects in institutional group selection

Generally, we can say that military competition among groups creates strong Red Queen effects in group selection; yet, because of the multidimensionality of military competition there is no unique directionality that links up technological change on the level of artefacts with the results of military competition. For example, guerrilla warriors might be able even to overcome technologically most sophisticated enemies, depending on the natural and social environment, such as in the Vietnam War.

Yet, there are some generic conclusions regarding the relationship between power projection and technological change which result from the fact that the Red Queen effects strongly support a positive feedback mechanism between the size of political units and technology, which results from the simultaneous role of power projection both internally and externally (for a pertinent result in experimental economics on group conflict, see Abbink et al. 2010 who show that inter–group conflicts drives the escalation of conflict expenditures). If certain mechanisms of power projection work towards internal integration and sustainability of a political unit integrated via a certain power structure, it is also challenged by external selection pressures, such that the relationship between internal and external projection mechanisms determines the entire result of the emerging trajectories. One of the linkages between the two is the fact that external power projection depends on internal generation of economic resources, which in turn depends on internal power projection. Thus, technology plays an important role in determining the size of institutionally integrated groups.

For example, the military competition between the Soviet Union and the United States after WW II certainly depended on the respective possibilities of global power projection, both in the field of nuclear weapons and conventional weapons. However, at the same time the degree of resource extraction was determined by the nature of the economic system. Although in the initial decades the centrally planned economy proved to be conducive to the build-up of external power projection mechanisms, at the same time it caused economic inefficiencies and a decline of innovation dynamics, which led to an increasing contradiction between resource extraction and the availability of internal resources. In the end, relative economic decline was even a factor in the collapse of the larger political unit of the Soviet Union, also reflecting the increasing weakness of the internal power projection mechanisms, given the weakness of the economic base. In other words, the strength of the centrally planned economy as a resource mobilization mechanism was manifest in the war economy, but turned into a weakness afterwards.

There are similar systematic patterns of power projection throughout the history of the relationship between power and technology. Very often the nature of the military challenges impacts on the trajectory of technological change, at least indirectly, which in turn feeds back on economic development. A foremost example is the role of navies in the build-up of colonial empires on a global scale in the 19th century, which was accompanied by the increasing relevance of industrialization for relative military strength, especially steel production and precision manufacturing, ending up in the naval competition of WWI. The global dominance of the European navies shaped the global power structure for centuries, maintaining a peculiar economic division of labour, which in turn affected technological change, possibly even until today, as the focus on resource extraction is one of the enduring legacies of colonialism in many countries after de-colonization. In this historical development, Britain played a central role, because of its peculiar geopolitical situation and the results of its political evolution, which created a particular combination between patterns of a strong domestic potential for resource extraction, and the decisive role of the navy in protecting its island location.

The classical analysis of these relationships is the 'World System' approach that was seminally developed by Wallerstein (1974) and completed over the decades into a fully-fledged theory of the world economy as determined by the political context. In his first book on the topic, Wallerstein argued that there was a relatively small head start of certain European countries in terms of economic development and military power which enabled them to build colonial empires that institutionally manifested the divergent development into centre–periphery structures (for a related, more recent analysis with a different theoretical focus, see Acemoglu et al. 2001; Acemoglu and Johnson 2005). Those structures created path dependencies in several respects. On the one hand, peripheral regions were shaped by the repressive institutions of colonialism, but also the resulting social structures with intermediating elite; on the other hand, the creation of specific agricultural regimes such as the plantations for sugar production also affected the agro ecology, which fed back to the evolution of social structure (such as slavery).

This viewpoint is further supported by Findlay and O'Rourke's magisterial history of world trade (2007). The authors collect overwhelming evidence that the division of labour in the modern world economy was driven by a trade–military nexus and cannot be simply explained by merely economic factors of comparative advantage. Trading activities were always accompanied by activities of power projection. This is most relevant in the British case, because Britain stood at the centre of the Industrial revolution, hence the single crucial step towards the emergence of the carbon economy. With hybrid institutions such as the East India Company, British overseas trade directly merged economic and military organization. The build-up of colonial empires proved to be also a decisive force in determining the European balance of power, especially between France and Britain. Economists tend to tell a Whig's history of the Industrial Revolution in emphasizing the role of property rights and political freedom. But even economists such as Findlay and O'Rourke today concede that this picture is wrong (2007: 346ff). Britain was not only a highly taxed economy, but also the vast majority of revenue was invested into the military and especially the navy. As has been demonstrated forcefully by Pomeranz (2000), the build-up of the colonial empire and the mobilization of resources for British economic growth was the necessary condition for pushing the Industrial Revolution, and not the economic factors in the narrow sense, that is certain institutions such as patents and certain technologies. This becomes evident, as in the Findlay and O'Rourke study, by comparing different regions at that time, such as China and Britain.

If I argue that the modern world economy has been fundamentally shaped by military technology, it is important to emphasize again that the causality is complex. Mere technological advances are necessary but not sufficient causes of the emergence of particular economic structures. At Columbus's time, China was far advanced in naval technology than Europe, but because of the interaction between internal and internal power projection the Ming Emperors even deployed a policy of prohibiting seafaring. Presumably, this policy emerged from the concerns about the security of coastal areas, and the perceived need to concentrate military resources to the protection of the continental borders. The weakness of Chinese naval power compared with the British navy was crucial for determining the outcome of the Opium wars in the 19th century.

There is one intermediate factor that establishes a connection between the analysis of military factors and the more general aspects of power; this is the role of resources in general and of energy resources in particular. Considering the ultimate goals of military competition, it is obvious that asymmetric control of human labour and resources is the central motivation of aggressive or of pre-emptive actions. In most pre-industrial societies, military competition also centred on the control of human labour as a source of energy, for example public works. Reflecting upon the history of international trade and the implied division of labour, it is evident that in earlier stages control of land and people were main motivations, enhanced by the specific demand for status goods. In the context of agricultural economies, land stands for the entire agricultural system through which the inflow of solar energy is transformed into resources that can be consumed by human beings. This was an integral part of the world system until the 19th century in the institution of slavery: In 1800, up to 5 per cent of the global population were enslaved (McNeill and McNeill 2002: 206). This is a most direct expression of the mechanisms of group selection elucidated in figure 7.12, considering the role of internal policing both in terms of controlling labour resources and mobilizing military capacity in order to establish military dominance relative to other groups.

7.5.4. A natural *experimentum crucis*: China vs. Europe

The relationship between resource endowments, human labour, technological change and military competition can be analysed by considering one of the most important cases in human history: the divergent patterns of economic development between China and Europe (there are other related cases, such as Japan, see MacFarlane and Harrison 2000). This example deserves close scrutiny on the theoretical level, because China was ahead of Europe in terms of technological and economic sophistication at the eve of early European industrialization. Since there is only one single case of endogenous industrialization in human history, the European one, the comparison with China is central to understand the specific factors that contributed to this landslide change in technology. From the viewpoint of Evolutionary Economics, one central question is whether this 'punctuated' change, taking place within just one century, was mainly driven by institutional factors, often emphasized by the economics literature (such as property rights, or, more recently, culture, see Landes 2006), or whether other factors counted more, such as resource endowments and the patterns of their control, fore mostly also including aspects of power structures and military competition. Actually, in recent thinking about this issue, theoretical lead thinkers such as North moved from the first to the second view (compare North 1984 with North et al. 2009).

Industrialization started out from certain economic structures which were common between the agricultural economies of China and Europe, interacting with certain institutional patterns and power configurations. From the evolutionary point of view, the important question is which selective forces drove the two systems into different directions. As we have seen in the previous section, the essence of this difference is the evolving European capacity to harness new energy resources and to transit to a full carbon economy, whereas China continued to rely on a solar economy until the mid of the twentieth century. It is the carbon economy that also provided the basis for European military dominance in terms of steel production and steam engines, combining into advanced naval forces and strong artillery powers, especially with regard to crushing fortifications.

That being said, it is important to emphasize that this view also points to essential differences across Europe (Allen 2009). Precisely because of the central importance of energy, Britain's special role can be explained, given the unique interplay between coal mining and technological innovation in this country, which did not happen in other countries. After its launch in Britain, European industrialization was strongly driven by geopolitical interests, hence forces resulting from the competition for power in the European state system, with Germany being one of the foremost examples. Hence, the analysis needs to distinguish neatly between the original emergence of the phenomenon of industrialization, and the forces driving its diffusion. For the latter, generic patterns of group selection played an essential role, related to internal control of human resources and external military capacities.

The most fundamental difference between Europe and China were the climatic constraints on agriculture that we have already highlighted in the general role of agriculture and climate for the transition to industrialization. China's climate is shaped by the Monsoon wind systems which impose a distinct climatic pattern in winter and summer times. Whereas the isotherms run in the East–West direction in winter, they run North–South in summer. Therefore, in winter times there is a zero degree isotherm roughly coincident with the Yangzi River that separates the agricultural regimes into the Northern and the Southern one. This observation can be combined with considering the Monsoon system; precipitation patterns differ between the seasons and between North and South. In the northern part of China, winters are extremely dry, and rainfall concentrates in summer, often causing floods in the plains through which the Yellow River searches its way. In the southern part, rainfall is plenty and more equally distributed across the year. The different patterns created different needs for developing hydrological management systems. In the North, large scale dam building was necessary to control certain stretches of the Yellow River, whereas in the South water management focused on the distribution and transport of water in an increasingly intensively exploited agro ecology. Finally, both regions differ in land/labour ratios, as a result of secular trends of migration and war which led to a growing population in the more productive Southern areas.

The Chinese pattern is very significant against the background of one potential explanation for European proto–industrialization that highlights the effects of climatic conditions on technology choice, as mentioned previously (Hesse 1982). Agricultural activities can be arranged into a sequential pattern of elementary processes which cannot be further subdivided. Now, if there is a climatic constraint on sequencing, as with the beginning of the frost period, a particular constellation emerges in the demand for labour. Once the frost period approaches, a huge effort is needed to complete all harvesting activities in time. This creates a demand for all technologies that may support higher productivities of labour and save time. By comparison, if there is no climatic constraint, it is possible to arrange the elementary processes in other ways, because they do not need to be completed at a certain point of time. Given the conditions of southern Chinese agriculture, this enabled the development of complex horticultural techniques, which often involve the simultaneous management of different crops at different stages of maturation, and the maintenance of all means to intensify the utilization of scarce land. It is straightforward to see that the European pattern creates a demand for leveraging human labour by means of tools, whereas the Chinese pattern increases the demand for human labour, without the need of leveraging productivity and especially time economy. The horticultural production technology also implies that certain patterns of land use, namely the partitioning of land into increasingly smaller plots, responding to population growth and the division of families, were much less a constraint on productivity growth in China than in Europe.

However, this argument only applies for the southern part of China. Thus, institutional structures of internal enforcement at large come into play. In the literature about the so-called 'European Miracle', since Max Weber many researchers have emphasized the role of political fragmentation in driving institutional innovation in Europe (for example Jones 1988). Clearly, this directly relates with military competition, thus referring the military dimensions to the dimension of economic change. During the past 2000 years, to a substantial degree China also experienced fragmentation, but maintained the strong tendency towards unification, which also prevailed in the last two dynasties which correspond to the periods of proto–industrialization and industrialization in Europe. Unification was accompanied with two important fundamental trends in military organization and strategy: Firstly, China abandoned systematic attempts at expanding its influence over the Pacific and gave up further development of seafaring activities and navy construction; and secondly, China concentrated on internal pacification and the control of the continental borders by means of standing armies and fortifications. Both trends supported the reliance on traditional military technologies and the development of logistic and organizational skills (Elvin 1973).

The high costs of standing armies also made a significant difference between the developments of continental Europe as compared to Britain. Nevertheless, a remarkable fact about China is that internal and external stabilization of the Empire was possible at extremely low levels of taxation, which contributed to the strong economic growth under the last dynasty of the Qing. There are several explanations of this remarkable circumstance, and I cannot deal with these in the context of this chapter (Ma 2012). However, it is important to state that political fragmentation in Europe certainly triggered special developments in the context of state administration related to resource extraction (for a number of seminal contributions, see Tilly 1975; there was distinct Red Queen effect here, see Baumol 2004). Therefore, contrary to earlier views of a stifling bureaucracy in China, in fact we need to notice that partly there was a lack of state initiative in directly driving economic development (for example infrastructure development, development of industry). Further, a distinct phenomenon of European capitalism, the emergence of capital markets, was mainly driven by the expansion of government debt, resulting from the fiscal needs of military competition, whereas in China fiscal conservatism prevailed even to the extent that newly emerging economic activities were not taxed.

The distinct institutional foundation of the Chinese Empire has been coined 'Culturalism', which refers to the active policy of unifying the cultural frames of educated elites by means of classical teachings and humanistic education. One essential element of Chinese Culturalism was the quasi-religious role of the family, which differs from Europe in essential respects. So, one explanation of the long run stability of the unified Empire refers to the special combination of bureaucratic rule and societal self-organization in the context of familism as a cultural orthodoxy (Eastman 1988). This is an important observation also in the context of this chapter, as familism is also a central feature of the organization of agricultural production in the traditional regime. In other words, I argue that the differences in technological development between Europe and China also result from differences in the cultural embeddedness of technology use, which is directly reflected in economic parameters, too.

A central determinant of the choice of technology under the familistic institutional framework is the fact that families are both units of production and consumption. If there are economies of scale of consumption in families, which is a standard assumption in economics, this allows for the possibility that workers can offer their work below a wage that matches with their marginal productivity (Chao 1986). For example, children can work at a wage that would normally fail to cover subsistence. This pattern supports a technological regime in which labour input is intensified. In China, such a model matched with the special agro–ecological conditions in the South, with a tightening supply of arable land and the possibility of complex horticulture which is conducive to the intensification of labour. By implication, this supports high labour demand in families and therefore, a high rate of reproduction.

Indeed, one of the remarkable patterns in comparing China and Europe is that both institutional and technological regimes supported a similar expansion of population, however, in Europe that was finally achieved via the increasing use of industrial inputs in agriculture, whereas China experienced technological stasis or even involution, for example, in substituting draft animals for humans. The substitution of animals for human labour is one of the most significant indicators for energetic constraints, taking also the role of animals in manure production into consideration. Draft animals can be extremely expensive in energetic terms if there are acute trade–offs between cropland and pastures. Under the conditions of horticulture, feeding human workers is more efficient because they can fulfil many more different functions, compared to draft animals. Thus, the peculiar pattern of Chinese agriculture emerged in which meat and manure production focused on poultry and pigs.

Family production directly impacts on technological change because it is handicraft production. So, the question is whether manufacturing can outcompete family production. China had developed an elaborate system of markets in which most civilizational artefacts were produced in family side-line activities (Elvin 1973; Keller and Shuie 2007). In other words, there was a synergy between market development and family production, through which the costs of manufacturing, especially as long as there were no substantial economies of scale, remained above the costs of exploiting family labour with economies of scale in consumption. As a result, both in agriculture and in traditional crafts a knowledge structure emerged that was not conducive to structural changes that would have pointed towards the emergence of industrial technology (dubbed 'involution' by Huang 1990).

Demographic expansion also increases ecological pressures on scarce land, which strengthens the familistic institutions as intensification of labour also requires effective governance of labour input which is increasingly difficult in horticulture. Familistic authority and strong moral commitments solve this problem and hence safeguard sufficient levels of labour effort. However, demographic expansion also implies increasing competition over resources. Given scarce land, one important aspect is the trade-off between uses of wood for energy generation, especially cooking, and for other purposes, such as steel production using charcoal, or tool production. There are strong indicators that the increasing scarcity of wood also impeded proto–industrialization because of the implied high opportunity costs of wood used as fuel. Although this development also took place in Europe, the general constraint applied.

However, this constellation still defines an essential difference to Britain, where coal substituted for charcoal during early industrialization (Pomeranz 2000). In China, there are rich coal deposits which have driven economic growth up to the present, but which could not be used widely in a potential take-off of industrialization, because deposits were far away from poles of economic growth, resulting into prohibitive transport costs. Further, the technological challenges of mining differ fundamentally in China from Britain: In China, the danger of combustion loomed large (even today), whereas in Britain, water inflows had to be managed. For solving the latter problem, pump technologies were required, which were basically known from water management in different areas, and for which the core invention of the Industrial Revolution, the steam engine, could be directly applied. On the contrary, in China there was no direct match between incipient technological changes and the needs of coal mining.

Therefore, we can restate that the truly special aspect of the British development was relieving the energy constraint via the exploitation of coal as a resource (Allen 2009). This fundamental ecological effect was leveraged by another effect that was directly related to military developments, namely the build-up of the colonial empires of European powers, especially Britain. Again, this is a complex story, but in the context of this chapter it is of utmost importance to emphasize the distinct effects of colonialism on global eco-technological change. One essential effect of colonialism was the change of eating habits in Europe, especially raising the consumption of sugar tremendously (Ruprecht 2005). Sugar was one of the most important export items of the plantation economies in the colonies, which represent a distinct agro–technological regime that also had lasting effects on the local ecologies (McNeill and McNeill 2002: 204). The cheap production of sugar was enabled by the importation of forced slave labour into the colonies, thus creating a pattern that directly affected technological development.

So, colonialism supported European industrialization in the specific sense of alleviating agricultural constraints that were basically similar to China. Further, the classical argument applies that the expanding colonial empire also provided for the growing markets that allow exploiting industrial economies of scale. However, this development cannot be simply seen as the unfolding of economic factors in the narrow sense. As I have pointed out previously, international trade and military activities were deeply interconnected until the twentieth century, and the role of China is only a case in point. The main motivation for the military conflicts between China and Europe in the nineteenth century was the drive for commercial expansion on the European side, aiming at opening up the vast Chinese market.

So, to summarize a complex story, any explanation of European industrialization has to concentrate on the interaction between institutional and ecological factors that produced a singular constellation that drove the emergence of a new technological regime which was based on fossil fuels, at this stage, coal. Institutional factors are factors that have economic consequences in the narrow sense, but mainly relate to the establishment and maintenance of particular structures of power, which interplayed with the deployment of military technologies. In the course of industrialization, these military technologies were directly affected by innovations related with the carbon economy, such as steel production and the steam engine, thus resulting into a military dominance of Western powers across the world. This enabled the rise of colonial regimes, which fostered a particular technological divide between the European regions and the colonies that also impacted on the local ecologies.

The detailed comparative study of China and Europe shows how power and technology are deeply enmeshed in driving the process of technological evolution. This generalizes on a previous observation that the demand for status goods is an important determinant of technological change. Power is essential to maintain institutional structures, and it relies on technology. At the same time, the use of technologies in enforcing dominance depends on institutional structures. Against the background of the previous section, it is important to notice that in this Red Queen dynamics of human group selection, a strong force emerges that manifests MPP: This is because power projection requires the capability to harness maximum power in activities that involve the application of violence.

In other words, considering the entire technological system, the pivotal role of the production of violence determines the evolution of capacities of maximum power generation; this also implies that under normal circumstances, these capacities need not materialize regularly. This corresponds to the analysis of MPP for evolutionary systems in general: The MPP firstly refers to the evolutionary trends of the structural capacities, and only secondarily to the factual generation of maximum power under any environmental condition. Yet, the capacity is the relevant fact that shapes the outcomes of competition among human groups. In this sense, technological evolution is strongly influenced by political factors. In the past, most advanced technologies emerged in the context of enforcement internal and external of human groups, if one includes the role of status goods. The only domain where purely productive uses of technology dominated, agriculture, was typically shaped by slow technological progress, often also driven by elite interests to increase surplus. This pattern changed gradually, though substantially with the increasing roles of markets in determining economic decisions. Therefore, in order to fully understand technological evolution in the Anthropocene, it is necessary to shed more analytical light on this most important institution in the modern economy. This is the task of the final chapter of this book.

8. Markets

> We are then charmed with the beauty of that accomodation which reigns in the palaces and the oeconomy of the great; and admire how every thing is adapted to promote their ease, to prevent their wants, to gratify their wishes, and to amuse and entertain their most frivolous desires. If we consider the real satisfaction which all those things are capable of affording, by itself and separated from the beauty of the arrangement which is fitted to promote it, it will always appear in the highest degree contemptible and trifling. (…)
>
> And it is well that nature imposes upon this in this manner. It is this deception which rouses and keeps in continual motion the industry of mankind. It is this which first prompted them to cultivate the ground, to build houses, to found cities and commonwealths, and to invent and improve all the sciences and the arts, which ennoble and embellish human life; which have entirely changed the whole face of the globe, have turned rude forests of nature into agreeable and fertile plains, and made the trackless and barren ocean a new fund of subsistence, and the great high road of communication to the different nations of the earth (Adam Smith 1759/1976: 183)

8.1. PERFORMING THE ARTEFACT OF MARKETS IN HUMAN NETWORKS

8.1.1. Markets as evolving networks

This chapter is the capstone chapter of this book. I pull together all established concepts and ideas in order to explore what markets are. The precise definition of markets will be the outcome of this chapter, so I only start with a rough idea right now. This is that markets are special kinds of bimodal networks which realize transactions involving peculiar institutions and artefacts, in particular money. These networks are usually the object of the science of economics. In other words, I follow the 'markets are networks' view proposed by economic sociologists, in particular, but which is also advocated in management science and organization studies, and in certain areas of economics (for example Forsgren and Johanson 1992; Ring 1996; Rauch and Hamilton 2001; Granovetter 2002; Earl and Wakeley 2010; Goyal 2011), but add the bimodal perspective developed in Chapter Five by extending the semiotic approach to the analysis of markets; this dimension inheres the special role assigned to the artefact of money which entails viewing prices as material artefacts.

This approach is at the same time narrower and broader than conventional economics. It declares economics to be the science of complex systems called 'markets.' Normally, the scope of economics would include organizations or individuals, among other phenomena. For example, consumer choice is the object of economics as it stands. One of the major consequences of the approach of this book is that economics would not include consumer choice as an object of its domain–specific theories, if consumers are seen as real world beings (compare Ross 2007a). This directly follows from the results of the previous chapters: Consumer choice is the object of evolutionary sciences in general, such as evolutionary psychology or neuroscience. Yet, consumer choice becomes an object of economics if networks of money–intermediated exchange transform the nature of consumer choice, such as in the context of the creative industries, where individual preferences directly depend on networked valuations of others (Potts et al. 2008). Or, as we have seen in Chapter Four, sequences of realized transactions on markets directly impact on the valuation of goods by the economic actors (Ariely et al. 2006); thus, preferences become adaptive in the market context. Considering the role of distributed cognition in human action, markets can become part and parcel of consumer choice, such that the latter also turns into an object of economics. However, this view would not build on foundational economic theories about consumer choice such as the constructs of subjective utility functions; to the contrary, the role of economics is justified and framed by the insights of the other evolutionary sciences. Vice versa, economics is only one of the different scientific disciplines that contribute to our understanding of consumer choice.

My approach is also broader than conventional economics because I regard economics as being embedded in the transdisciplinary relationships and in particular, because markets are seen as networks of human actions. Networks as defined in Chapter Five are more general structures than markets, and economics has to include them into its approach to markets. This is particularly true if we consider the three dimensions of networks; then, economic transactions on markets involve the two dimensions of perception and communication, which to a large extent cannot be directly analysed by standard economic theories, yet need to be explicitly included in the economic approach. For example, the distinction between groups of different size and its implications for the configurations of perception and communication implies that the economic analysis of the pertinent transactions has to consider specific technologies of perception and communication. As we shall see, this view has interesting consequences, such as exploring whether the law might be less important in enabling large scale markets working effectively than firm–specific knowledge how to overcome information problems in such markets.

Economics is a very rich and well-developed science. In this brief chapter, I will not be able to pay due respect to this richness. I will only discuss a selected number of foundational issues, which, however, will have large effects on all special fields of economics. In doing this, I will be deliberately simple and will not reflect the sophisticated state of modern economics, but go back to the roots. For example, I will argue that core prices in markets, the interest rate and the wage rate, are institutions that cannot be modelled along the lines of the standard supply and demand model. This means although those prices play a pivotal role in the causal processes on markets, they cannot be explained by means of the conventional market model. This argument is simple and can be made by reference to the freshperson's course of introductory economics. At the same time, my aim is to show that economics indeed deserves an autonomous place in the evolutionary sciences, because markets are emergent phenomena with a number of properties that are novelties in the process of human evolution. These novel properties require the deployment of new analytical tools which are well-developed in economics as it stands.

If I define economics as the science of markets, this means that I also show why it has evolved in the way it has done (for a survey of definitions of economics, see Backhouse and Medema 2009). My approach does not contradict with the basic tenets of economics, though it also questions many of its foundational assumptions; in curtailing its scope, I also provide a rationale of the autonomy of those theoretical elements which remain valid. Thus, the explanation of markets rests upon general evolutionary principles which are not 'economics' in the narrow sense, but markets also represent an emergent level of human evolution. This entails the possibility that markets, once in existence, operate like economics claims it to be the case. That means, more exactly, I ask how certain institutions and technologies co-evolve in a way such that entities called 'markets' by the participants emerge in which actors and their interactions can be analysed in terms of economics proper, such as it is done in macroeconomic modelling, for example. This means, in particular, I ask how markets give rise to peculiar forms of agency, whereas economics proper normally presupposes these particular forms. These forms of agency should not be confused with agency related to physical human individuals, that is human organisms (along the lines of Ross 2005, 2007a). We need to expect right from the beginning that there are fundamentally different forms of agency involved in market evolution, depending on whether the conditions for applying economics proper come into existence. For example, there is the possibility that firms manifest agency according to economics proper, but consumers do not, because firms operate under the institutions of money–intermediated exchange with the implicated valuation principles.

More generally, I treat markets as special kinds of human systems of interpretance, following the structure of figure 4.2. This implies that markets are specific conjunctions of networks, institutions and technology, and hence special kinds of 'extended minds'. In this conjunction, the artefact of money can be seen as a technological innovation which enables certain network configurations of transactions, and which has been made possible by certain institutional evolutions which I have already scrutinized in Chapter Six. This view has been presaged in many contributions on the cross-disciplinary research on money, which, for example, have argued that the emergence of money affected human cognitive modes in interactions in a fundamental way, such as by making sets of qualitatively different transactions commensurable and hence enabling to adopt an abstract view on network relationships (for an overview, see Walsh and Lynch 2008). Following early approaches such as Simmel's (1907), researchers have even argued that the emergence of money produced side-effects on the development of philosophy and the sciences in early civilization. These views clearly reveal the functions of money and markets in human distributed cognition. Hence, one task of the chapter is to analyse certain basic properties of this system of interpretance. One important immediate consequence of this view is to analyse the evolution of markets in relation to the functions markets have in the larger human systems, and therefore to relate markets with proximate and ultimate processes of general evolution.

8.1.2. Performativity of economics and 'marketization'

As I have already pointed out in Chapter One (section 1.4.2.), viewed in bimodal terms, markets relate with different phenomena, depending on how we analyse them in the different modes. Conventional economics very often adopts the observer independent semiotic mode, in terms of mathematical modelling of certain aspects of markets, and neglects, for example, the matterenergy aspects of markets, which specify in terms of ecological relationships (observer independent) or technology (observer relative). This standard mode of economic analysis is certainly justified and yields important insights, but remains incomplete. If we ask for the reasons why economics adopts this attitude, I submit that this overlooks the fundamental fact that economics is endogenous to the object of its study (Witt 1992; O'Flaherty and Bhagwati 1997; Dixit 1997). Economists normally adopt the position of an external observer to analyse economic phenomena, but factually they are participant observers, even if they are not directly involved in activities such as advising policy-makers. If we treat economists as participant observers, this has the important implication that economics has to be seen as being performative: Economics as a science contributes to the formation of its object, markets. In other words, economics is part and parcel of the system of interpretance evolving with the emergence of markets.

This insight goes beyond the mere fact that there is 'applied economics', such as the economics of health care systems, or more recently the shift towards 'market design' as a foundational approach (Roth 2008). Fundamental notions of economics are performative because they influence the way how actors act in networks of exchange. For example, it makes a fundamental difference whether a real-world wage rate is seen as the price for human labour services, or as an enforced means of redistributing wealth among different social groups (as in Marxian theory). Once it is seen and 'done' as a price, all analytical tools of economics apply, resulting in an 'economics of labour markets'. The performativity of economics has driven many classical ideological controversies about what is essentially a question of theorizing and scientific argument (such as the Cambridge controversy about the notion of capital, which seems highly technical, from one point of view, but involves the possible interpretation of the interest rate as a purely redistributive mechanism; see Cohen and Harcourt 2003).

This approach is strongly influenced by the notion of 'performativity' as expounded by Michel Callon, and which I have already invoked in the earlier chapters. Çalışkan and Callon (2009, 2010) have embedded this concept into a general research program on 'economization', which encompasses 'marketization' as a special phenomenon. The former notion refers to the question how far 'the economy' is recognized as a separate domain in the larger societal system, which is strongly influenced by the theories that actors maintain about 'the economy', hence economics in particular (compare Callon 2007; for an early anthropological view see Gudeman 1986). Çalışkan and Callon have an extended discussion about how and why this differs from earlier notions such as the formalism vs. substantivism debate (for a classical overview, see Schneider 1974). In anthropology, formalists apply the rational choice paradigm in analysing societies of any kind; they refer to the notion of 'culture' in defining the specific ends that rational actors pursue in cultural terms. Substantivists, with Polanyi as a most famous representative, adopt an institutionalist perspective and argue that 'the economy' is the expression of certain historically rooted institutional arrangements. Clearly, this distinction is also closely related to the German 'Methodenstreit' and the clash between the Historical School and the rationalist Political Economy that had emerged in Britain, but also had strong advocates in France and Austria. The position that is proposed by Callon and his collaborators goes beyond this dichotomy because it tries to overcome the tension between the 'individual' and 'society', which, according to them, still haunts the so-called 'New Economic Sociology' (for an overview, see the volume edited by Guillén et al. 2002). The core term in this field, 'embeddedness', still seems to suggest the autonomy of 'the social' from individual actions. I argue that the new view corresponds to the distributed cognition approach that follows from general evolutionary analysis.

One most important application of this view is the study of 'marketization', which is also reviewed by Çalışkan and Callon (2010). Marketization takes place in the economy via the assembling of artefacts, actors and skills in order to make money-mediated exchange possible. This differs considerably from the view of institutional analysis in economics, because research includes all the so-called 'technical' aspects of markets, such as the use of certain technologies, standardization etc. (the 'market devices' along the lines of Callon et al. 2007). All these arrangements are 'prosthetic' in the sense of Callon (2008), that is, they enhance the capacities of actors in terms of establishing more complex *agencements* which create the patterns of market interactions. I relate this idea with my analysis of capabilities in Chapter Five: Then, we can speak of market relations as a particular kind of network transactions, and trace these back to expressions of certain capabilities of actors. This capabilities enable actors to generate transactions that make market transactions possible, which I call 'transaction enabling transactions', TETs. As I will argue, there are important classes of market related actions that are TETs, such as the creation of firms. This idea allows for a simple focus of all economic analysis on markets, and view non-market actions such as network interactions in general in terms of their potential function as TETs. Hence, I re-interpret the sociological notion of 'embeddedness' in terms of the functional transformation of non-market actions in relation to markets. Thus, I do not expand the scope of economics to include these non-market interactions, which remain exogenous determinants of markets in terms of disciplinary approaches, but at the same time define the specifically economic context for the functional transformation that is driven by the evolution of markets. In other words, TETs are essential to explain the operations of markets, but they cannot be merely explained as expressions of market–mediated causalities: The firm is a constitutive element of modern markets, but it cannot be explained by causal determinants of markets exclusively, neither with reference to its historical emergence nor with regard to current choices between firms and markets as regimes of transactions. So, the firm is a non-market kind of artefact that is an important determinant of the evolution of market kind artefacts.

The approach outlined so far means that there is a fundamental difference between markets and exchange in general. Exchange is a universal biological and behavioural category, and there are strong reasons to assume that human actors are specifically adapted to this, as we have seen in Chapter Four. Markets introduce a new dimension with the use of money in exchange, as established in Chapter Six. So, I claim that money is the most important artefact that defines markets. This also means that exchange and markets are not related to each other as the more general versus the more special category. Markets evolve out of exchange, but they have properties that are emergent in relation to exchange. These properties relate with the textbook functions of money, especially with its function as a standard of value and its function as a store of value. Again, this refers to real world phenomena, which implies, in particular, that the evolution of markets does not mean that markets become ubiquitous. Markets and exchange co-exist in all human societies, and there was a long time of transition until markets assumed a dominant role as in modern societies. This transition is accompanied with the diffusion of money as an intermediator of network interactions. If the two domains, exchange and markets are conflated theoretically, this leads towards a distorted view on the actual dynamics of the evolution of markets.

8.1.3. Markets in the context of general evolution

So, markets are part and parcel of general evolution, and they also represent novel emergent properties in bimodal terms. These different dimensions result in a new analytical stance towards markets, which I summarize with an overview that follows the chapter sequence of this book.

- Firstly, I approach markets in terms of social ontology, which means that I apply the fundamental principles of bimodality and observer relativity versus independence. We have already seen that the notion of observer relativity applies even on economics proper. Bimodality means that I treat markets as specific forms of semiotic systems, which also implies that I make the materiality of markets explicit. For example, prices are constitutive of market relationships. In standard economics, a price is a theoretical term which relates with certain implied relations of scarcity in demand and supply systems, and that needs to be distinguished from the real world prices; so, economists can calculate shadow prices which are not quoted in real world price lists (on the status of prices as theoretical terms see Balzer 1982). In evolutionary ontology, a price is a sign with a material form, and hence an observer relative fact (extending on Beunza et al. 2006 or Çalışkan 2007). Prices are what we read on price tags in the supermarket, or what we watch on the computer screen when trading stocks. This view leads to a fundamental change in the theory of prices: Whereas the standard view on prices treats them as relative prices, the evolutionary view treats absolute prices as fundamentals, and relative prices as derivative phenomena. Relative prices are emergent phenomena in market–enabled distributed cognition.
- Secondly, as a consequence of bimodal analysis, markets obey to evolutionary principles, in particular in manifesting the interaction between triadic causal modes. Markets are a special form of physical knowledge systems, that is, they create and process information, and they relate with physical processes of energetic transformation. So, markets organize physical causalities (especially, technologically mediated ones) in relationship to emerging systems of interpretance (such as classifications of industries, products, etc.) and in response to environmental selective forces determining their functions on the aggregate level (such as stabilizing the food supply for human populations). In this view, markets are a specific form of organizing control information in complex human societies, and they are a most developed form of distributed cognition (for a related view, see Mirowski and Somefun 1998); this partly extends on Hayek's (1945) classical view of distributed knowledge in markets, but adds the material dimension, especially in the sense of entropic analysis seminally launched by Georgescu-Roegen (1971). This is especially important for understanding the relationship between technological evolution and markets.

- Thirdly, markets also obey to evolutionary principles on a more detailed level. Markets are historical phenomena in the sense that there is no essentialist definition of markets. Markets evolve out of previous constellations of complex human systems, and we can analyse this evolution by means of generic concepts of evolutionary theory, especially in the sense that markets are a fundamental element in advanced human niche construction. The relationship between these principles and markets is mediated via the other levels of evolutionary analysis, as reflected in the chapter structure. For example, networks exert a substantial impact on the mechanisms that are specific to markets. However, there is one concept in standard economics that is directly pertinent on this level, namely 'scarcity'. Scarcity is not an economic category, but an evolutionary category (contra the classical view of Robbins 1945). Scarcity is a shorthand notion for all selective pressures that operate on human behaviour, also in the context of markets, but scarcity is also endogenous to evolutionary niche creation. Hence, scarcity is essentially related with novelty. Then, the most widespread definition of economics is actually misleading which relates scarce means to ends, because the essential question is how means and ends co-evolve. Neither means nor ends are givens in economic evolution.
- Fourthly, one major implication of this view is that we cannot separate individuals and markets. We cannot conceive of autonomous individuals just coming together, and a market spontaneously happening. The specific historical forms of markets are also constitutive of human agency in markets. This is especially true for the notion of 'rationality' (thus following Max Weber's classical approach). The rational agent of economics proper is endogenous to market evolution and cannot be regarded to be an exogenous given. Further, we cannot simply treat markets as certain media that serve the fulfilment of human needs. In fact, human wants are endogenous to market evolution, which is the essential condition for the insatiability of growth of markets (Witt 2000). Finally, and to re-emphasize, markets are an essential feature of human distributed cognition. All this converges in the idea that markets are essential for defining distributed agency, that is the *agencements*, especially in modern societies. But this also implies that persons, in the sense of the unity of the human individual across different domains of interactions, cannot be analysed on market terms alone. This is especially salient in one particular market domain, labour markets.
- Fifthly, markets are a specific form of network interactions. In recent research, this is the dividing line between economics proper and economic sociology. In my view, markets are a specific form of bimodal networks because they relate with specific artefacts, money and prices. This is essential to deal with the problem of observer relativity and the endogeneity of economics in empirical terms. Whether marriage is a

market or not, depends on whether the network interactions are mediated by money and prices (such as bride price). This view clearly demarcates my approach from many other economic approaches which would argue that scarcity is the defining feature of applying economic analysis. Scarcity is a generic evolutionary concept, and whether it is relevant for economics proper depends on whether in real world systems, scarcity drives the emergence of markets and their related artefacts, namely prices. Once prices do not emerge, network interactions are of a different kind, such as customary, hierarchical and so forth, yet continue to deal with the problem of scarcity. Further, it is not possible to neatly separate all kinds of network interactions from pure market interactions unless there are special institutional arrangements, which, for example, create a certain status for actors. This reflects the unity of persons across different domains of networks interactions. For example, there is a job market for scientists, but this does not necessarily imply that research aims at maximizing pecuniary remuneration.

- Sixthly, markets are institutions. This is essential to recognize the limitations of economics proper, epitomized in the standard supply and demand diagram which is supposed to show a 'market'. This diagram only shows a certain price mechanism resulting from certain institutions which create the pertinent market. Such a view has become almost commonplace across a broad range of economic research, such as Law and Economics. The evolutionary approach makes best use of all these insights. However, there are also differences which relate with two points, in the first place. One is that market institutions are knowledge structures, and these structures cope with fundamental challenges of ignorance and uncertainty. The other relates with the role of power in market institutions. All institutions are also power relations, but power relations do not obey to the narrow logic of markets in terms of economics proper. This role of power covers extremely important phenomena, in particular the relationship between governments and markets, or between firms and markets. In other words, once markets are recognized as being institutions, this necessarily implies a primordial role for non-market determinants in their evolution.
- Seventhly, as I have stated previously, markets can be seen as control information relative to technological evolution. But markets are also technologies of their own kind. Technological evolution directly affects markets, or, even more so, markets evolve as a form of technological evolution. Market evolution occurs via the technological evolution of tools, devices and artefacts that enable market transactions. This view can be further vindicated if we reflect upon the interpretation of institutions as technology. Markets are technologies of social interaction. This leads us back to the network perspective, in the sense that markets are technologically enhanced network transactions, which have to be treated in the bimodal view. The term 'technology' should not be biased to

notions of advanced technological devices. For example, a regular market at a particular physical location, with numerous booths, is a simple market technology. The perspective on technology is absolutely necessary to establish the most general connection between the theory of market evolution and the foundational principles of MPP and MEP, as we have seen. This link lies in the connection between markets and growth, with growth being conceptualized as the economic manifestation of increasing energetic throughputs.

These perspectives on markets result in substantial differences to the standard economic methodology. To a certain extent, these amount to a thorough empiricism which follows from the emphasis on the materiality of markets, and leads towards eschewing any kind of 'model platonism' (see the classical critique of Albert 1972). On the other hand, in so far as markets are emergent phenomena in general evolution, the systems perspective justifies approaches that abstract from many real world properties of the empirical referents of economic theories, such as concrete human individuals. The linkage between the different levels and perspectives must be provided by the thorough analysis of institutions, as these establish the regularities of market interactions that can be the object of economic theorizing in the narrow sense. Insofar as economics influences institution building in the real world, this implies that economics partly determines the conditions of its application, which means it is part and parcel of the performativity of markets (MacKenzie 2006).

8.2. MARKETS AS INSTITUTIONS: UNCERTAINTY AND NETWORKED VALUATION

8.2.1. Trust and the asset specificity of specializing on market opportunity

Markets establish complex interactions between economic actors in networks in which those actors take decisions based on imperfect and incomplete knowledge about those interactions. As such, this problem is by no means unique to markets, but also applies, for example, for acting in the context of ecological systems. The special nature of markets results from the fact that there are specific mechanisms that lead towards the generation and storage of knowledge about those complex interactions. In this chapter, I put much emphasis on two phenomena without implicating that these are exclusively relevant, money and firms. Both phenomena relate with a distinct property of human niche construction on the evolutionary scale which has already been put at the centre of attention by Adam Smith, which is the division of labour. Markets are the institutional setting in which the division of labour can be sustained and expanded, such that human groups collectively can generate adaptive functions that are not available at the individual level. The precondition for this specialization is the reduction of uncertainty about future opportunities of exchange, which relates to the discussion of the 'specialization dilemma' in Chapter Six (6.6.1.). A more general version of the specialization dilemma implies that there is a fundamental problem of specializing in complex systems of division of labour that results from two determinants: One is the fact that specialization needs to be initiated by single actors who have limited knowledge about the systems level determinants of the optimal degree and direction of specialization; the other results from the possible changes in the distribution of capabilities of actors in terms of the distribution of power in collectives that manifest division of labour.

The solution of this fundamental problem is the main evolutionary novelty of the institution of money. Evidently, we cannot say that money evolved in order to solve this problem. But given the emergence of money as analysed in Chapter Six, the existence of money results into new forms of network interactions by which the problem can be overcome. This relates closely with the standard economic analysis of the functions of money in multilateral exchange relations (such as Schotter 1982). Money enables multilateral exchanges because it allows eschewing the need to find specific exchange partners for all single goods on offer. With a generic medium of exchange, actors can exchange their goods against this generic medium and can find other partners who are ready to accept this medium as well. There is no need to clear all single market transactions, because money allows carrying over balances to other transactions. However, in the standard economic treatment of this problem the specialization dilemma is not given due attention.

Continuing with the discussion in the previous section, I propose to distinguish exchange and markets in another respect, which is the willingness of actors to produce goods for the sole purpose to be sold on markets in order to generate monetary income flows. In other words, we need to distinguish between the division of labour in general and the market oriented division of labour. In exchange relations, actors own certain goods which they produced anyway, or for which they perceive a purely contingent surplus (for a pertinent analysis of the origin of market exchange, see Ofek 2001). That means, if they fail to find an exchange opportunity, they do not realize a loss beyond their expectations. But if they actively and exclusively produce for the market, the products may become even worthless if they do not find an opportunity for exchange, such that their expectations fail to materialize. Thus, I claim that markets systematically involve a sunk cost phenomenon that relates with the asset specificity of the production for the market (thus applying an important notion from Williamsonian New Institutional Economics, see Williamson 1985): Specializing on market opportunity typically involves a previous investment into the generation of offers (compare Mailath et al. 2004). Here, 'asset specificity' refers to specificity with relation to opportunity, or, specific time and place of the exchange opportunity. Even if there is the possibility of aggregate market clearing, this still does not guarantee that these specific expectations are met, meaning that the specific opportunity is realized within reasonable time. Of course, the degree of asset specificity depends on the extent in which new opportunities can be found, if the products can be stored, but in general, the point holds that market oriented behaviour is always specific to opportunities of exchange, which is fundamentally different from generic exchange relations.

The problem of asset specificity in market exchange gives rise to the specialization dilemma which even applies for bilateral exchange, once there is a temporal sequence of steps of specialization and exchange which allows actors to take unobservable actions. Then, if specialization is based on a mutual agreement to exchange the products in the next period, it is possible to cheat by specializing to a lesser degree than agreed upon, which changes the relative scarcity of the products and hence the expected prices. The less specialized side gains in power relative to the more specialized side. From this, a generic hold-up problem emerges that would lead to a low degree of specialization, as this is necessary to maintain power balances through time. Hence, the transition from generic exchange to specialization of production for exchange is an improbable event. So, the emergence of markets implies a fundamental paradox of power: On the one hand, markets vastly enhance the action capabilities of actors, hence their power in the sense of Chapter Five (5.4.3.); at the same time, however, the necessary specialization creates dependencies which can translate into losses of power in the individual case. This is one of the major reasons why markets and other domains of exchange continue to co-exist even in modern times.

Many anthropological analyses of exchange relations employ an abstract definition of spheres or domains of exchange, such as comparing gift versus market exchange. At a closer look, there are smooth and complex evolutionary trajectories in which the different spheres overlap and intrude into each other, and actors manage these fuzzy boundaries actively (for an analytical summary of this literature, see Çalışkan and Callon 2010). Köhler (1985) gives a systematic account of different forms of early trade and argues that markets have the essential property to rely on a generalized medium of exchange and to involve specialization on market opportunity, mostly in the shape of specialized traders. Then, there are different degrees of involvement into markets possible, which show up in the price sensitivity of economic decisions. So, many transitional forms of exchange in subsistence based societies may manifest a role of markets, but the production decisions are still not crucially affected by market prices. Further, in analysing emergent markets it is also important to notice that all types of market transactions can rely on certain incipient forms of exchange that existed without money. For example, even in long-distance exchange credit could be given between trading partners without direct reference to money. Or, even in the context of families certain exchange relations could be based on the direct calculation of individual interests, without emphasis on the embeddedness into the kinship relations. But all this does not imply that the entire network configuration is that of a market.

One indicator of the emergence of genuine markets is the existence of market places, that is central places where traders meet, as this also manifests the artefactual nature of markets, in the bimodal sense. Market places are important for several reasons: Firstly, they extend the scope of accessible multilateral exchanges via spatial proximity and temporal coordination ('thickness' of markets in the sense of Roth 2008); they enhance the observability of market activities and hence create information externalities (see Chapter Five, 5.3.2); and finally, very often central markets enjoy the protection of powerful leaders, thus increasing the physical safety of traders, and since market places often compete against other places in attracting traders, this competition creates a constraint on the abuse of protective power for extraction (so, solving the original specialization dilemma as discussed in Chapter Six). Hodges (1982: 15ff) emphasizes the role of spatial, hence physical structures in indicating different forms of exchange. In most tribal societies, commercialization does not happen, and therefore central places do not exist which specialize on exchange. Once the transition happens, different kinds of centre/periphery systems emerge, where in the incipient stage the relationship between market places and the centres of power is strong (administered markets in early empires, for example). A fully developed market system, such as it has been classically analysed by Skinner (1964/65) for the case of China, features the coexistence and even competition between different central places in a hierarchy of markets (which is an early idea of economic geography, especially Lösch 1945, which was only rediscovered recently in economics, see Fujita et al. 1999). Hence, the geography of markets is perhaps even more important than certain institutional features for defining the essentials, because it provides the physical setting of the hypercyclic emergence of institutionalized market interactions, as in my exemplary analysis of the vegetable market in Chapter Six. Obviously, these observations directly connect the evolution of markets with the emergence of urban places and the process of urbanization in general. This establishes a direct connection between market-based economic growth and flows of matterenergy that sustain the on-going urbanization process (in the sense of Chapter 7, section 7.4.8.).

To summarize, it is obvious that any sort of exchange which would lead to an intermediate possession of goods for which the actor even does not have an individual use leverages the risks of asset specificity, and that the introduction of a generic medium of exchange and store of value, money, reduces the risks substantially; this effect is substantially leveraged in the context of certain material market infrastructures and networks. Money enlarges the opportunity set of markets in the order of magnitudes, because the opportunities to exchange money are universal (actually, this is an essential part of the definition of money). This multilateralization also levels off power differentials that might result from the specialization dilemma. Yet, there is one essential condition: There must be confidence that money is indeed universally accepted. For this reason, trust into money is a fundamental condition for the unfolding of market relations in general. Money is the institutional solution to the high degree of asset specificity of market oriented behaviour. Without money, markets implode, as we know from many historical episodes of monetary crises, hyperinflation etc. This pivotal role of money for markets will be further explored in the next section.

8.2.2. The fundamental problem of the uncertainty of comparative advantage

Thus, the most essential aspect of markets, which is the division of labour, cannot be seen as the starting point of their evolution. The emergence and the diffusion of money as an artefact is the necessary condition for the unfolding of the division of labour, because only money can solve the problem of asset specificity of market opportunity. This drives further specialization processes. One can make this general point with reference to the notion of 'comparative advantage' in the context of international trade, which is actually the most fundamental economic theorem about the division of labour in general. Then, the question is how actors can discover their comparative advantages in complex systems of the division of labour which they cannot oversee; this is a simple, yet fundamental problem: How can one compare oneself with others that one does not know?

The traditional view sees comparative advantage as a driver of the division of labour. The evolutionary view argues comparative advantage is not known to actors unless real transactions happen that reveal the potential of specialization, but only rely on realized advantages in past transactions. In the theory of international trade, the standard argument runs as follows (figure 8.1, A–E). There are given comparative advantages in production which result from factor endowments and productivity differences in influential theories of international trade (Heckscher–Ohlin or Ricardian). In these theories, those comparative advantages are actually observer-independent facts (such as proportions between factors of labour and land). They are directly reflected in price differences, as they give rise to differences in opportunity costs of resource use. These price differences trigger arbitrage activities which result into realized trade transactions. There will be corresponding factor movements that lead to adaptations of production structure. As we see in this model, evolutionary changes in the economic structure of economic systems root in exogenously given comparative advantages.

Figure 8.1 Two ways of conceptualizing comparative advantage

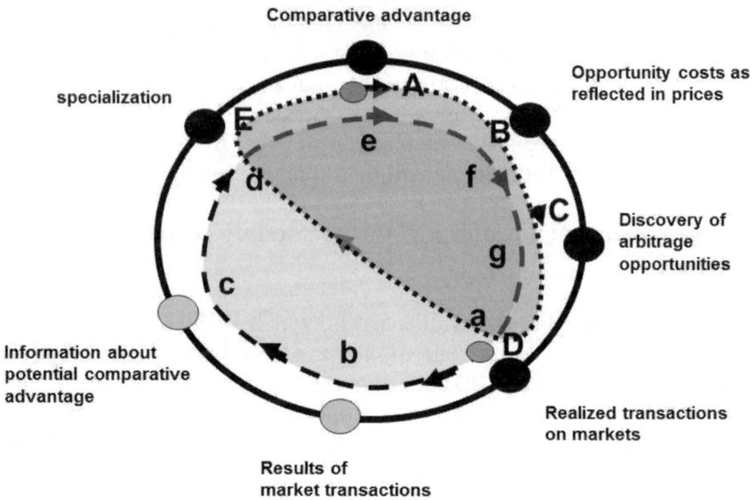

Note: The diagram distinguishes two different economic conceptualizations of the causal processes that drive the division of labour. Basically, the division of labour reflects differences in comparative advantage across sets of actors. The standard approach (A–E) takes comparative advantages as a given and assigns the role of primordial causes to them. The causal chain operates via prices that reflect the implied opportunity costs of economic actions, and the resulting arbitrage once market transactions takes place, driving specialization according to comparative advantage. In the evolutionary view (a–g), transactions start at arbitrary prices that do not necessarily reflect comparative advantage. The results generate information about potential comparative advantage which causes specialization processes; the latter generate comparative advantages which are reflected in opportunity costs and prices, generating further transactions.

The conception of the market as outlined in this chapter presents an entirely different picture (a–g). Here, we start with realized transactions in markets, which have been triggered by price differences of any kind. These transactions reveal information about economic opportunities, which ultimately refer to potential comparative advantage. In the next step, economic actors invest into the creation of capabilities in order to exploit those perceived advantages. These investments result in realized comparative advantages which drive market transactions in the next steps. It is essential to realize that this discovery process is impossible without the function of money as an intermediator that reduces the uncertainty related with specialization according to potential comparative advantage. This is easy to see when considering two parties that specialize under uncertainty and commit errors: If they realize pure exchange, they would end up with a stock of goods that ultimately does not reflect factual comparative advantages on both sides; if they exchange goods against money, the acquired stock of money is immune against this sort of failures. This implies, further, that they are also more willing to specialize under uncertainty even if there is a high probability of error, because they expect to gain a universal medium of value.

In this view on markets and the division of labour, the notion of market clearing obtains a central role, which has to be neatly distinguished from 'equilibrium' in the standard sense. In an evolutionary approach, equilibrium would be a state that does not allow for novelty which is by definition equilibrium–breaking. Market clearing is a much simpler notion and refers to the idea that economic actors who specialize on market opportunity will form certain expectations about the stock of goods and money that they will hold after transactions have taken place. Markets do not clear when those expectations are violated, such as when an actor offers too many goods and is forced to hold them on stock, thus accumulating sunk costs (for a detailed analysis, see Mailath et al. 2004). Again, it is straightforward to see how money introduces an essential difference, because money is the only good where stocks have no intrinsic upper limit.

8.2.3. Prices and market clearing

From the viewpoint of distributed cognition, the emergence of money enabled an entirely new cognitive function, namely the measurement of value independent from individual valuations: the price. Prices are valuations denominated in money terms, as far as markets are concerned. Traditional barter relations are not markets, in this view, as they do not refer to a socially constituted standard of value, embodied in an artefact, apart from the direct valuations of the goods (however, modern barter such as in countertrade refers to prices, hence is a market). To a certain extent, this notion is also represented in standard economics, namely in the concept of the 'price taker'. As is well known, this assumption is a defining feature of perfect competition in equilibrium theory, which has also raised the intricate question very early who sets the prices and why, if the original Walrasian construction of the 'auctioneer' is given up. This problem corresponds directly to the discussion of comparative advantage in the previous section: If prices reflect comparative advantage, how can this relationship be established with firstly setting prices without knowing comparative advantage? Yet, once certain prices are set and therefore known, actors can know and compare the value of goods that they own, consider alternative uses beyond the confines of their immediate space of action, and can aggregate over all the possible transactions to evaluate their total wealth, both actual and expected. All this is impossible if they cannot refer to prices that are recognized as social facts by a certain community.

Thus, one essential aspect of markets is the institutions and norms governing the creation of prices. Then, we can realize that the notion of 'price taker' actually means that prices are phenomena of collective intentionality, implying a fundamental ontological gap between market prices and individual actions of price setting. This gap is reflected in the colloquial reference to 'the markets', as if these were agents of their own. In this view, prices do not relate with the notion of equilibrium but with the more general and empirical notion of 'market clearing'. There are prices which clear markets and others which do not. Failure of market clearing is observable via many empirical facts, such as unsold goods or people registering as unemployed and searching for jobs. Now, one of the celebrated results of economic theory is the Sonnenschein–Mantel–Debreu (SMD) theorem which states negatively that it is impossible to reduce aggregate excess demand functions to one set of properly behaved individual demand functions ('anything goes' here), but also confirms positively Walras's Law which establishes the universal connectivity of all markets; then, market clearing in all but one market implies market clearing in the remaining market (for a recent survey on the SMD theorem, see Rizvi 2006).

In our context this implies that certain hypotheses about networks that hold together with the SMD theorem could suffice for explaining processes of market clearing with prices independent from the notion of equilibrium. For example, Kirman (2001) argues that markets presuppose a particular kind of collective behavioural coordination in order to make price adjustment work (for a related view on 'market order', see Nelson 2013). Only as a result of this, markets manifest market clearing in the sense of the SMD theorem. His case study of a fish market is representative of this kind of thinking. Fish markets are of interest also in the context of this chapter as they manifest sequencing between production and trading: Since fish is perishable, the supply is prepared on the basis of expected prices, whereas the trades take place with a fixed supply which meets the actual demand, with market clearing as the goal. Kirman shows a remarkable empirical result about the Marseille fish markets: Although the market is not organized as an auction, and highly individualized negotiations with price discrimination take place, the resulting distribution of prices is stable through time and results into market clearing. He shows that very few assumptions are needed to explain how market clearing happens through time, as a result of on-going sequences of individual transactions within one day. What is especially important are loyalty relations between customers and sellers, and very simple rules of thumb which relate the prices on the fish market with the past retail prices of fish (thus indicating expected profits for the intermediaries that operate on the fish market). Kirman (1992) directly relates this sort of research to the SMD theorem and therefore criticizes one fundamental assumption in modern equilibrium analysis, the representative individual approach, which implies that the dynamics of network interactions in markets is directly ruled out from the scope of economic analysis.

It has been well established by numerous results of experimental economics that market clearing is entirely independent from any assumptions about the cognitive complexity of actors, but only dependent on the institutional set up of those experimental markets (for an overview, see Smith 2003; Plott and Smith 2008). That means, if we substitute 'equilibrium' by the criterion of 'market clearing' we do not need the analytical apparatus of equilibrium analysis (for an entirely different formal framework of markets that matches with my view, see Sugden's 2004 approach to markets as arbitrage–driven 'money pumps'). So, I present an Occam's razor argument based on empirical research in experimental economics, which also underlies much of recent research on market design. Market clearing is a question of market design, which can be both evolutionary and engineering based. This implies that we cannot just state that price movements establish market clearing, as these movements only lead to clearing if certain institutional conditions are met. This is the most fundamental reason why markets need to be conceived as institutions, beyond the commonly accepted proposition that markets build on certain institutional frames; market clearing as a fundamental function of markets is an institution. This means, market clearing is a regularity in network configurations, and one function of markets is to establish market clearing as a recurrent, hence steady state in economic evolution (meaning that in the dynamic flow of economic actions and events, particular markets clear normally through time, which is not trivial) (this matches with Pott's 2000 network approach to microeconomics, also see Earl and Wakeley 2010).

If we observe a market, supply and demand will always meet in terms of realized transactions. In this sense, markets always clear, if the transactions are voluntary. So, failure of market clearing can only relate to the mismatch between the planned supply and demand, for example resulting into a stock of products which is larger than expected. However, this implies that the necessary condition for market clearing to hold in reality is the coordination of plans, hence expectations. Market clearing is a process that takes place in real time and involves a sequence of decisions, in particular the sequence of producers' decisions to create a certain supply on the market, and the subsequent decision of consumers to buy at a certain price. That means, the standard supply and demand diagram is misleading because it suggests that production decisions and buying decisions take place at the same time. Once we consider the process in real time, the coordination of expectations becomes the core process in market clearing. Obviously, this is a level of analysis which is totally different from the level of market transactions, as we cannot conceive of the coordination of expectations as being realized via supply and demand relationships that are co-extensive with the relationships of the pertinent transactions. That being said, there is the possibility that past transactions influence the expectations about future transactions. Then, we arrive at a theory of market–mediated learning of actors how to clear markets. As a result, the category of market clearing becomes a very powerful analytical category, which, to reemphasize, is independent from standard equilibrium analysis. Market clearing becomes dependent on the knowledge structure in the economy, which is in turn deeply determined by its institutional structure.

8.2.4. Asset valuation, markets and networks

We have already stated that the existence of money implies the possibility of public valuations of goods. For market clearing, it is essential to value stocks of goods, that is balances in exchange. Historically, the transition to fully-fledged markets of modern capitalism was essentially dependent on the evolution of bookkeeping. Valuation of stocks results into measures of wealth, hence identifying the wealth constraints of actors on markets. Wealth is an important analytical category as wealth is a direct determinant of actors' capacities in networks, which means it is a determinant of relative power. In comparison to other determinants of power, wealth is defined via its fungibility in exchange with money. The degree of fungibility is determined by the institutional structure of the particular societies in which markets are embedded: For example, a high degree of corruption reflects the fact that political power is partly fungible. I do not consider these intricacies here.

Wealth constraints result from different sorts of assets. One is simply the money stock. Another is the stock of goods in a most general sense that can be traded via markets, because only those goods can give rise to monetary flows. In this case, the valuation of the stocks directly depends on the prices that result from current flows. The failure of the individual transaction does not necessarily imply that the asset is worthless, as long as there is a market price. For example, I might fail to sell my used car, so hold a stock that I do not desire, but yet there is a price tag on it, and hence the car contributes to my wealth. However, this also means that the value of the asset is determined by those market prices and can hence change without any action on my side. This introduces a fundamental wedge between individual valuation and collective valuation. In other words, we realize that the 'market price' is in fact a collective phenomenon, as far the market valuation is concerned, and it is not identical with the price obtained in the individual transaction.

The third kind of asset plays a most important role in the evolution of markets, which are the claims that actors have on other actor's wealth. I call these claims 'credit'. Credit is an emergent property of markets if monetary flows do not clear: For example, a trader gives credit to a customer who cannot immediately pay the bill. The possibility of credit is another reason why money is essential for expanding the division of labour, because it allows for smoothing out coordination failures in exchange. It is straightforward to see that credit involves the dimension of time, as the value of claims rests upon expectations about the possibility to realize those claims in the future.

This introduces an entirely new dimension into markets, as there is now the possibility to evaluate those claims, which are monetary values, in turn. This is the root of the emergence of a special kind of market, financial markets. Financial markets manifest certain properties that other markets do not generally have, and which relate with the fact that they trade monetary assets in the broadest sense. This new property is that trade in financial assets depends on differences in the expected value of those assets. If we consider a certain distribution of assets over a population of actors, trade will only occur if expectations about future value will diverge, independent from the current market valuation. If we reflect upon this, how can actors access those differences in expectations? – only via the perception of market prices. But if differences of expectations drive current market transactions, then these future transactions will determine the future prices and hence the values of those assets tomorrow. These transactions will be determined by the future differences in the expectations about the next period values of assets, and so forth.

So, we realize that in financial markets, it is not simply differences in current expectations that drive transactions and hence values of monetary assets, but differences in expectations about future differences in expectations about future differences, and so forth. This results into two fundamental paradoxes of financial markets. The first one was recognized by Keynes in his notion of the 'beauty contest', namely that for the individual success of transactions the anticipation of collective expectations only matters, and not intrinsic properties of the asset. The second one is that the Gödel theorem applies for the formation of expectations, because the future is actually a meta-criterion for previous period expectations, yet the future is open in a fundamental sense. This means that the ultimate root of valuations cannot be in the markets, but must be exogenous. The determinant of the value of monetary assets is external to the market process, that is, depends on institutionalized factors in the most general sense, including institutionalized patterns of changes of expectations. In other, very radical terms, it is misleading to analyse financial markets in terms of the supply and demand paradigm, and hence interpret 'market prices' as equilibrium phenomena. The prices that are observable on financial markets are directly determined by the state of expectations, which is triggered exogenously, and they are further processed via market dynamics including the generation of certain supplies and demands via prices that are determined exogenously.

Indeed, one of the celebrated results of the equilibrium analysis of financial markets is the 'no trade theorem', which is basically a paradox about information processing in these markets if they are analysed only endogenously (for a concise analysis, see Samuelson 2004). The 'no trade theorem' follows from the idea that the announcement of the willingness to trade an asset gives information about the private information that the trader has about this asset. Now, consider a state of equilibrium in the financial market: Traditional theory assumes that market prices would perfectly process all available information, which is reflected in the market prices. But that means that this information is public and is common knowledge (Geneakoplos 1992). Now, if one trader announces the willingness to trade that would imply that she has private information that has not yet been reflected in the market. But in fact, even the announcement already makes this information public, leading to corresponding changes of market prices, such that the original incentive to trade would vanish. So, the 'no trade theorem' follows. In my view, the 'no trade theorem' is just one instance of general propositions about the logical complexity of markets, which ultimately fall under the general scope of the Gödel theorem and related theorems (compare Knudsen 1993; Koppl and Rosser 2002; Markose 1998, 2005).

My argument stands in the line of the numerous readings offered of the famous 'chapter twelve' of Keynes' 'General Theory' (Weintraub 1979). This chapter deals with the state of long-term expectations, which Keynes distinguishes from short-term expectations in a way that is also very useful in my context (1936: 148). Short-term expectations are the expectations about the market conditions once a production sequence is completed and the product will be offered on the market. Hence, long-term expectations come into play if, for example, production capacity is changed, that is investment. Keynes (1936: 152) proposed that this state is a 'convention'. Evidently, conventions do not imply stability as Keynes emphasized the possibility of sudden changes of conventions in larger populations of actors who decide interdependently. I subsume the term 'convention' in the general notion of 'institution' in the sense of a regularity in networks.

I generalize these observations in analysing markets as 'social network markets', thus taking into explicit consideration the fact that all markets are networks, and hence the formation of expectations on markets is a network phenomenon (Potts et al. 2008; Herrmann-Pillath 2010/11; this view can be traced back to Simmel's relationship based theory of value, see Papilloud 2003a). Social network markets are markets where the valuation of an asset depends on the valuation of other actors, with no direct relation to any sort of other function of the goods traded on the market. For example, consider a hammer. If a hammer is traded via a market, and even if a producer fails to anticipate the future demand for hammers and creates oversupply, this does not affect the function of the hammer, such as fixing nails. This is entirely different from assets which depend on the collective valuation exclusively. It is not without reason that in the history of financial crises and manias, the early examples do not only refer to financial assets in the proper sense, but to items such as tulips, too. In the Dutch tulip mania, the value of the assets was exclusively driven by the perceptions of the valuations of other actors, and entirely disconnected from the function of the tulip, which, after all, can only lie in the joy to watch it. Social network markets emerge in all cases where there is a high degree of intrinsic quality uncertainty, such that the perception of quality entirely rests upon the valuation of others. This is also true for other important markets in modern economies, such as creative goods and innovations. In our current context, the intrinsic quality uncertainty results from the complexity and uncertainty of future determinants of the value of present claims on future income, that is financial assets.

However, this definition of social network markets can be further generalized when considering asset specificity of market opportunity with a market–centred division of labour; in this case, supply to the markets does not have an intrinsic value for the supplier. Then, the problem of uncertainty applies for market opportunity in general. In a social network market, there are very strong externalities between the formations of individual expectations about values. This is because if Ego perceives that Alter does not appreciate a good, this immediately implies that the value of the good also goes down for Ego, because the only value that counts is the external value judgment of others, which creates the market opportunity. Ego can only make use of the asset with relation to the market and other actors. This means that the value of an asset is a phenomenon of market mediated collective intentionality.

In this sense, markets are strictly performative. This should not be confused with self-fulfilling prophecies. For example, in the tulip mania people at some time realized that tulips do not have that intrinsic value that was suggested by the market valuations. In the same way, the value of financial assets may be determined by general economic and financial conditions in the economy. Finally, in a so-called bubble it is a sure event that the bubble cannot expand forever and will have to burst at some time. But in social network markets, given the strong externalities, there is a fundamental incentive problem in realigning values by individual action. As long as values go up, individual actors would have to forego expected profits in order to start proper re-evaluation. In other words, only the realignment of the collective expectations can lead to the sure re-evaluation from the individual perspective. The prices of financial assets depend on the collective state of expectations, and individual expectations can only be determined in dependence from this state of expectations. This does not mean that individual expectations are the same as the collective expectations, but that they are defined and made operational relative to those collective expectations. This is what practitioners in finance refer to as 'the markets'.

The previous discussion can be also summarized in the proposition that social network markets are strictly performative in the sense that the valuations on these markets are performative. The performativity of financial markets is also reflected in the essential role of all artefacts that are used to fix the prices of assets. In this regard, it is important to notice that economics also plays a big role in this context, as its branch of the 'theory of finance' has been crucial to solve the problem how to calculate the risk levels of certain assets (MacKenzie 2006, 2007). This is another reason why financial markets are not simply based on self-fulfilling properties. A financial market is a complex system which certainly has certain aggregate properties which relate to its system performance. One important aspect of such properties is statistical properties (Mandelbrot and Hudson 2008). Those statistical properties have to be identified by means of data, but also by means of introducing certain generic theoretical assumptions, such as assumptions about the nature of the fundamental statistical distributions. These assumptions are uncertain by themselves. Once certain tools for estimating values are established, however, they feed back on the behaviour of the actors. Then, even if some of the assumptions might be actually wrong, there is also the possibility that within a certain range of system performance, the behaviour actually produces the expected performance because it follows the valuations that have been deduced by the economic models. Once events happen that lie beyond the scope of the underlying assumptions (for example, extreme valuations might happen more frequently than in a normal distribution), this connection breaks down.

This analysis of financial markets as social network markets extends to the general analysis of markets because credit is just the primordial form of finance. If we consider the network of credit relations, one essential problem is how to assess the creditworthiness of borrowers by means of assessing the value of their assets relative to the credit give (which means, assessing their leverage, see Geanakoplos 1997, 2010). This value can be determined by different means, as it is itself dependent on the expectations about the future possible uses of an asset. For example, the value would depend on adopting a short-term or a long-term view about the future development of the economy. From this follows that in markets, institutions and social norms that govern the network–mediated evaluation of assets play an essential role in shaping market dynamics.

8.2.5. The institutional nature of market valuation

The previously noticed fact results into another form of performativity in markets. Markets can be performed differently depending on which way to evaluate assets is adopted. It is important to emphasize that there is no 'correct' way to fix the values of a magnitude that is fundamentally uncertain. Now, consider a network of transactions, and just compare two cases that differ in the dimensions of perception and communication. One case is a network in which relationships are relatively close, and information about the behaviour of actors is at least easily available for a set of other actors who might be willing to extend loans. In this case, the credit relationship can be based on relational network connections, which implies that asset valuation will include many complex determinants that relate with past and future behaviour of borrowers. The other case is one in which borrowers do not have detailed knowledge about the behaviour and context of lenders' activities. In this case, they would need to rely on valuations of assets which are accessible via public media of information, and would tend to build generalizations over classes of borrowers. Basically, the latter valuations are abstract market valuations. So, two fundamentally different institutional frameworks for valuation emerge, one relational and one market–based. The frameworks relate with different network levels and group sizes: The former builds and small groups and tribes, the latter focuses on large groups. The pertinent institutions that establish these performatives in different network contexts are the accounting systems used in business.

For example, the first kind of accounting system was the one prevailing in Germany before the adoption of International Financial Reporting Standards IFRS. In this system, stakeholders, especially banks, have more detailed information about a lender's status because they also maintain a long-term relation with them ('Hausbank'). Then, stakeholders will have a prime interest in stabilizing the operations of the lender and in adopting a precautionary attitude towards valuations, resulting in hidden reserves, which might be mobilized in terms of economic distress. This implies that accounting values and market valuations are not the same, and might even diverge considerably. The second kind of accounting system is prevailing in the Anglo-Saxon world and interprets the relationship between borrower and lender as an arm's length relationship. In this relationship, what counts for the borrower, or more generally, the investor, is whether the investment of her own assets will increase its monetary value. This results into a more short term perspective in which a lender is perceived as a portfolio of assets, and borrowers invest into those assets (including the equity owners relative to the firm, in this view). Then, total profitability depends on the changing values of these assets, as determined by the market valuation. The major effect of this view on asset valuation is that the financial position of the lender will always be assessed in terms of the net value of assets, and not simply by the balance of monetary flows. So, a lender who realizes a positive value of flows may nevertheless incur an accounting loss if the market value of its assets decreases more than this flow balance. In this view, profit is ultimately measured as a change of total wealth.

A classical economic analysis of the two different ideal typical schemes in relating the financial system with the productive sector is Aoki (1988, 2001). Aoki distinguishes between arm's length financing and relational financing. The former is a purely market based approach in the previous sense. The latter is economically feasible and also efficient if, as I have discussed previously, the extension of funds needs to be based on highly specific and even tacit knowledge of the project in question. These are two fundamentally different ways to perform markets, especially in the way the systemic borders of markets are drawn. In the second case, these borders are more open in the sense that the embeddedness of markets into other social relations is explicitly recognized. Especially, there is no clear cut separation between the market actor and the individual that this actor represents. For example, in the market based accounting scheme, the family owned company is treated as being separate from the family beyond the notion of limited liability. That means, equity owned by the family is treated as a liability, because the family is considered to be a generic investor who would focus on the profitability of its entire portfolio. To the contrary, in the relational accounting approach, equity would be just evaluated by historical values, that is the initial investment. The firm is seen as a family firm, with the possible modification of limited liability, which, however, does not transform the relationship between family and firm into an arm's length market relationship.

The role of accounting systems in the social ontology of markets is rarely recognized by standard economics on a theoretical level. Recently, it has received much attention by political scientist and heterodox economists in the context of the 'financialization' paradigm (Krippner 2005; for a lucid overview, see Perry and Noelke 2006). This continues with long-run historical trends involving the emergence of new patterns of agency, such as the 'investor' (Preda 2005). The contemporary case in point is the transition to the IFRS accounting standards which are clearly based on standard economic theory, especially in the context of the evaluation of assets. A central observation is that the new accounting standards move from a 'stewardship' approach to management to the emphasis on the investors' perspective. The clear difference is that in the stewardship approach, the more specific goals and interests of the particular business weigh heavily, such that the historical cost accounting intends to show whether the manager has used investors' money in a responsible way; in the investors' perspective, what counts much more is the question whether this particular investment offered the highest possible returns of the financial funds owned by the investor, compared to the alternatives. That means, in the investors' perspective the return on the monetary investment counts exclusively, independent from the specific object of investment.

I generalize this analysis along the lines of the recent 'varieties of capitalism' literature (with seminal contributions such as Berger and Dore 1996), but make the more general point that markets are performative in the particular sense that all the underlying monetary functions are performative. This is a direct consequence of the performativity of money. Because money is performative, the way that monetary valuations are realized is performative, too. This happens mainly via the accounting systems that are adopted in different market systems and via the tools and devices that are used to deal with the uncertainty of future values of assets, especially in the context of financial markets. It is a misconception to argue that the market based valuation scheme is the 'better' one in terms of any indicator of economic efficacy, such as firm performance, growth or innovation. This is evident from the fact that on the systemic level, countries with very different financial systems can manifest high levels of economic performance in this sense (World Bank 2008). Yet, this does not mean that particular kinds of performing markets do not have real consequences.

Therefore, we can extend this analysis towards a general approach to the taxonomy of market–based systems. Again, the case of China is useful to illustrate this point. As we have seen in previous chapters, China's historical economy featured a wide diffusion of market institutions that enabled the rapid economic growth of the past centuries, as being expressed in population growth. In assessing this institutional setting, historians led an intense debate over the question of whether China already featured the transition to 'capitalism'. In earlier views, China was seen as being distinct from the West in terms of bureaucratic rule, but today the revisionist economic history clearly shows that China even was a market based society to the extent that major social institutions were embedded into the market (Skinner 1964/65; Keller and Shiue 2007). So, China was clearly a market economy in the sense of a 'Smithian economy' based on the division of labour and market exchange (Arrighi 2007). Then, the distinction between the market economy and capitalism can only be established via identifying certain performatives, relying on Searle's distinction between regulatory and constitutive rules (compare Barnes 1995: 191). Many market institutions are regulatory in the sense that they emerge as functional solutions to certain technical problems in organizing markets, such as structures of intermediation. However, there are also constitutive rules which create social facts that did not exist previously in the context of market exchange. In comparing China and the West, we can identify at least two constitutive rules that did not evolve in China: Credit–based money created by the banking system and the corporation as a legal entity. Both institutions therefore might define the difference between capitalism and the generic market economy (compare Kuran 2009). Ultimately, China's economic growth was limited by the money supply and the impossibility of creating money from credit, and there were no institutions to value assets independently from the individuals as owners of the assets.

As we have seen previously, this argument can be extended to more recent evolutionary trajectories of markets: We can identify 'financial capitalism' as a variant of capitalism that employs the valuation principles and the resulting management practices that relate with the emergence of investor–focused accounting systems (for more detail, see Herrmann-Pillath 2013). Capitalism as such shows a considerable diversity of forms, which also relate with other performative functions that I will scrutinize later, such as the organization of labour in firms and labour markets. So, it seems possible to elaborate on a taxonomy of markets in terms of the performativity of certain central institutions: Market economies manifest the pervasive role of markets, capitalism adds peculiar institutions such as the corporation and credit–based money, and financial capitalism differs from continental European versions of capitalism ('Rhenish capitalism') in terms of the role of market–based systems of accounting, among other criteria.

8.2.6. Market states as institutions

I summarize the results of this section in figure 8.2 which casts my argument into the framework of the Aoki model of institutions. This highlights the essential idea that markets are not social entities in which supply and demand achieve an equilibrium via price movements; instead, I argue that states of markets, even if dynamically changing through time, are institutions of their own kind ('market orders' dubbed by Nelson 2013). This institutional nature of markets is most visible in their regular operations which mostly tend towards market clearing, as in the case of the fish market that we considered briefly. In the first place, a market is a closed circular feedback loop which connects transactions, clearing, prices and expectations. The four poles are embedded into larger social environments shaped by the forces that I have analysed in the previous chapters.

Figure 8.2 Markets as institutions

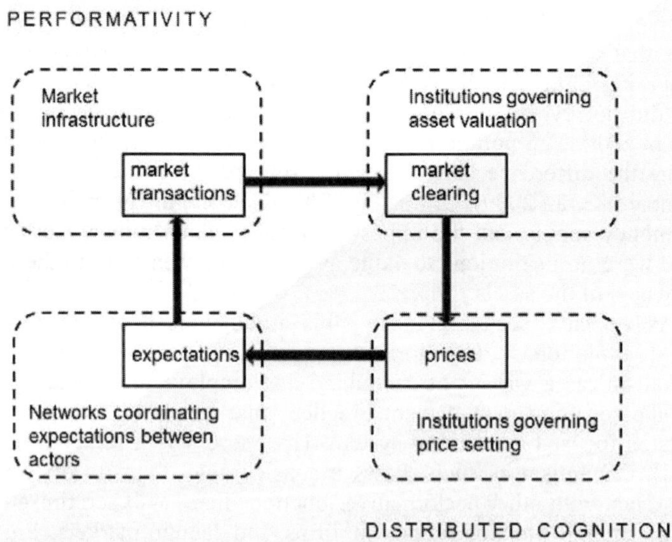

Note: The diagram applies the modified Aoki model of institutions (Chapter Six, figure 6.9) on markets as institutions. Market clearing is a state of markets which includes the emergence of prices as signs which cause certain expectations of economic actors. Expectations result in transactions which cause market states. The four poles of the institutional circuit are embedded into exogenous determinants of their functioning (see discussion in main text). In this analysis, distributed cognition is mainly realized via the prices–expectations link, thus vindicating Hayekian and Austrian views of the price system, and performativity works through the transactions–market clearing link.

To begin with the transactions: market transactions are triggered by states of expectations of actors, thus are intrinsically uncertain and future–oriented. These transactions are embedded into a technology of transactions, that is a market infrastructure. In its most general form, this is a physical market place, such as an urban central place or an electronic auction site. Technologies of transactions play an important role in determining the outcomes of transactions, given certain specialization patterns, for instance, because they determine market density. The transactions result in states of markets which are reflected in degrees of market clearing, which is balances of actors that may or may not match with the original expectations. These states are also determined by the institutions that govern the valuation of assets; as we have seen, economics can play a direct performative role at this point because valuation principles have to be based on conventions which can be theoretically justified, but not ultimately proven. As these conventions are known to the actors, they adapt their actions to these environments. Hence, this part of the feedback loop is performative in the strict sense.

The states of markets include the generation of signs that also underlie the valuation of assets, that is prices. Prices are signs in the strict sense, which means they correspond to the absolute prices of standard economic theory, and they are materially embodied. They are not equilibrium prices but emerge from realized transactions (including so-called 'false trading' of the standard approach) and they relate to institutions governing the setting of prices. In this sense, prices are institutional in nature. This will be shown in some detail subsequently for two fundamental prices in modern markets, interest and wages. The institutional determinants of prices are multifarious and include individual–level regularities (such as firm–specific cost–plus rules) or social norms (such as fairness norms).

Given prices cause expectations of actors about the results of further transactions. Therefore, prices are essential for the distributed cognition function of markets. Prices are publicly observable and compress information about the realized states of markets. Expectations of actors do not simply follow prices, though, because prices need to be interpreted (for instance, a rising price can indicate both rising prices in the future or falling prices, depending on the assumptions about the ceiling, given general market conditions). Actors' expectations are fundamentally shaped by social networks and transmission of market information, including transmission of information about expectations of other actors (for instance, networks transmit information about whether other actors interpret rising prices as indicator of further price increases). Therefore, the ultimate causation of transactions indirectly rests upon both the networked expectations and the institutional determinants of price formation.

This picture of markets as institutions differs sharply from conventional treatments of markets in relation to institutions. Conventionally, markets are seen as being shaped by or embedded into institutions such as the law. In the naturalistic view deployed in this book, markets are institutions in the sense that states of markets and essential market parameters, in particular prices, are institutions.

8.3. POWER AND THE INSTITUTION OF MONEY

8.3.1. Money and credit

In Chapter Six, I have developed the fundamentals of the theory of the institution of money. We saw that money is a special artefact which emerged from conceptual blends that are projections into the generic domain of social exchange. Hence, this analysis exactly reflects the distinction between exchange and markets. In markets, money is an institution that represents future opportunities of exchange, in a generic sense. Thus, in real world societies, money is not only a technology in markets, but also a status good that causes a manifold of emotions in using and owning it. In this chapter, I abstract from these emotional aspects of money, and mostly refer to only one important aspect, that is the role of trust. Indeed, one of the crucial aspects of the evolution of money lies in the fact that the resulting possibilities of calculation, aggregation and evaluation make the use of money partly independent from the original emotions underlying its emergence and primordial uses. Yet, as I have already shown in Chapter Six, this does not mean that they are irrelevant even in the context of the most sophisticated modern markets, that is financial markets (Tuckett 2009).

As we have seen in the analysis of the performativity of money, an essential aspect of the emergence and the stabilization of money is to refer to the collective intentionality of a population of money users. This means, we cannot treat money as an abstract institution related to markets in general. It is a defining property of money to be bound to concrete user communities who share the intention to use certain artefacts, such as species, as money; following Richter (1987), I call these 'primary monetary communities'. The function of money does not rest upon abstract and generic principles, but on the trust that this community puts into a concrete form of money. This fact is well recognized in general opinion, but is not put at the centre of standard economics which analyses money merely under its technological aspects, that is, the functions of money in enabling new forms of economic transactions (for a related critical assessment, see Ingham 2000). However, if we recognize that trust is essential for the institution of money, this has the important implication that trust also affects the scope of all transactions that are conducted with specific money. Trust into the institution of money and the formation of expectations in the network of market transactions, which I already scrutinized previously, are therefore deeply interconnected; in most general terms, the rationale of the institution of money can only rest upon the fact of fundamental uncertainty in economic relationships (for a concise elaboration on this essential point, see Goodhart 1977).

Money enables the de-contextualization of the valuation of transactions in terms of a commensurable standard of value, and it allows for the operationalization of aggregate values. Money is also an object of network transactions. This includes one sort of transactions which is essential for understanding the evolution of markets in the sense of the interaction between market dynamics and economic evolution, seen as one expression of evolution in general. This sort of transaction is credit: Once money comes into existence, it can be the object of market–based transactions which refer to a price of money in terms of funds transacted among different actors, which is interest.

However, it is important to emphasize that credit is also more universal than money because all network interactions refer to the future and include credit in the sense of future–related entitlements and obligations. Generic social exchange also involves credit relations: For example, I might help my neighbour today, but expect something back tomorrow. Actually, all human societies have complex norms in governing credit relations in social exchange, which partly overlap with the social norms regulating gift exchange. With the emergence of money, the possibility emerged to delink these primordial credit relationships from particular network relations. So, the role of money in credit finds specific expressions in terms of valuations of credit and instruments of credit; and this includes the self–referential extension of credit to money. The shared universal property of all credit relations is that their stability and sustainability rests upon the sustainability of the mutual expectations about the future fulfilment of the mutual obligations.

There are four essential aspects of credit in relation to markets and money.

- Firstly, credit introduces uncertainty about the future value of claims from credit relations, if prices change, in terms of the valuation of money relative to other goods obtained in future transactions. Hence, credit activates a special kind of expectations about the future value of money proper, and about the certainty of repayment promises.
- Secondly, considering the history of markets, credit stands at the centre of the relationship between power and markets, in the shape of sovereign debt. Sovereign debt was the single most important institution in the emergence of modern capital markets, because there are special presumptions about the safety of sovereign debt.
- Thirdly, credit creates the possibility to delink money from any physical assets in the economy, as credit instruments can be treated as money, once they come into existence. This opens up the possibility to create credit 'from nothing', a possibility which relates with one of the central institutions of capitalism, the banking system. This implies that credit

creates money, under certain institutional conditions which are universal in modern markets.

- Fourthly, once credit instruments came into existence, the possibility of derivative instruments emerged. However, this is only one path how markets create derivative institutions based on the institution of money, and, ultimately, the implied possibility of universal representation of value. All these institutions relate with modern financial markets.

The important consequence of these four developments is that the function of expectations in market dynamics is leveraged considerably. All those institutional derivatives of money relate with the future, and hence imply the formation of expectations. In particular, as all derivatives can be held as a stock, they imply the possibility of expectations of their own value, which is essential for enabling the emergence of markets for those derivatives. This is because markets for derivatives of money are only possible if there are divergent expectations about the future value of the derivatives; this implies that the scope of performativity of markets is further expanded, especially in the sense of creating new forms of markets (Millo 2007).

8.3.2. Government and trust into money

Conventional economic explanations of the evolution of money fail to pay proper attention to the fact that money is deeply related with political institutions. Almost all advanced forms of money have been issued or controlled by political bodies of all sorts (for a brief summary of the historical record, see Ingham 2000). I claim that this is essential to establish trust into money, however, in terms of an unintended consequence of another institution, namely taxation. This is a foremost example for the essential role of non-market determinants in the evolution of markets.

For the definition of markets, voluntary exchange is essential. However, from the earliest stages of human political evolution onwards, exchange relations also involved the dimension of power, hence forced exchange, as I have discussed in Chapter Six (section 6.6.). Once more complex political organizations emerged, forced exchange took the shape of taxation in different forms. The evolution of taxation and the evolution of money are closely related phenomena, as taxes can be paid in money. Now, if the issuer of money and the recipient of the tax are identical, this is a major determinant of trust into money. In all human societies, the tax burden has been substantial, so that confidence that money can be used to fulfil that obligation provides the ground for basic trust into money, which reduces other possible risks in market exchange. In other words, if the issuer of money promises to accept money as a means to pay taxes, and keeps this promise, this creates a basic level of trust into money. From this follows, that in the course of the evolution of the institution of money, the original evolutionary force of stabilizing the institution, emotions related to social exchange, were supplemented by another force, namely political power. I argue that this is the major reason why ultimately a purely market based provision of money is not viable, because that would lack the external anchor in power relationships.

My argument builds on the ideas developed by Chavas and Bromley (2008). Chavas and Bromley argue that the historical origins of money do not lie in enabling market exchange, but in solving certain incentive problems in collective action, though in the context of vertical power relations. This fits into my view that money enables markets, but markets do not create money. Their point is that money is mainly an instrument of debt, and via relations of indebtedness results into the coordination of activities which have a strong public good character and manifest externalities. This applies, for example, for the creation of large scale infrastructure in early kingdoms and religious communities. I think that this view captures well the fact that there is a strong relation between money and communities, which is emphasized by the term 'primary monetary communities'.

This argument is different, though compatible with the Chartalist theory of money which has a certain impact on Postkeynesian thinking today, and which goes back to Knapp's 'statist theory of money' (for an interpretation based on Simmel, see Monthoux 2003). However, I do not posit that money can only be created by the state, but only argue that the primordial trust into money is bolstered once money is used to fulfil obligations to the state, which is an important part of exchange relations in general. Yet, I follow modern interpretations of Chartalism in emphasizing the interaction between vertical and horizontal relations in shaping the specific forms of the institution of money. One common criticism of these interpretations is that they take accounting balances as causal explanations. Yet, the special position of government implies that certain accounting relationships acquire special economic significance. This is clearly recognized in standard practice when government bonds are treated as the risk–free referential asset for financial markets: This practice is based on the vertical relationship between government and markets, and can collapse if trust relationships break down, as in the recent Euro crisis. That means, if modern Chartalists argue that government deficits are a net financial asset for the private sector, this is true relative to a certain state of expectations. Evidently, if this is governed by market relationships, the Ricardian equivalence holds. But it is not possible to identify one particular state as the 'rational' or 'true' one. If the owner of government bonds regards these as the least risky asset in her entire portfolio of assets, this is net wealth, irrespective of the fact that in the future taxes have to be raised for repaying the debt. There is no real world alternative. Clearly, under these circumstances the status of government debt is performative, since it depends on the nature of expectations that are generated via the theories about money and debt that the actors in the economy maintain.

However, again we need to distinguish between the causal forces driving the emergence of institutions and the emergent properties of the institution once diffusion takes place. Although trust into money ultimately is a form of trust into the producer of money, it also depends essentially on the fact that other actors accept it as a means of payment. The diffusion of money as a means of payment implies that the primary monetary communities can be entirely independent from the reach of the political body, in the sense of the reach of network transactions, but also and importantly in terms of the territorial scope of the diffusion of money. The US$ today enjoys a substantial degree of trust, which does not result from the fact that the users of the US$ pay taxes to the U.S. government, but from the circumstance that it is a globally accepted means of payment in international business transactions. That means, even if there were reasons to mistrust the producer of the US$, because it might adopt an inflationary policy, these reasons might weigh less than the fact that the currency is used globally as a medium of exchange.

The causal force that drives this emergent property of money is the existence of strong technological network externalities, which are formally equivalent to network externalities in all technological means of communication (compare the treatment of standardization in Chapter Seven). The individual benefit of money, namely reducing the asset specificity of specializing on exchange opportunities, depends on the number of other actors who accept money as a means of payment. Therefore, markets create the tendency that one currency might obtain the position of a close–to–natural monopoly. This has an important side effect, namely that in principle, even sovereign producers of money stay in competition with each other, because markets can produce tendencies towards the expansion of the reach of primary monetary communities beyond the borders of the political unit. However, this entails the possibility that the voluntary use of money is subdued by the forced use of money, if political actors enforce the convergence of monetary communities and political borders (such as controlling capital flows etc.).

This evolutionary convergence has led towards an important phenomenon in markets, namely the co-evolution of markets, primary monetary communities and political bodies, ultimately epitomized in the emergence of 'national economies'. The modern notion of a 'national economy' essentially depends on monetary artefacts, such as the unity of the means of payments as a legal tender, but also the use of this money as a means to construct all nominal values in the economy, individual and aggregate, such as in national accounts. The spatial diffusion of different currencies interacts with the reach and scope of markets, which certainly extend far beyond the reach and scope of political bodies. But at the same time, this diffusion also depends on the perception of these political bodies outside their communities. In the global economy of modern times, these are the complex forces that determine the emergence of global reserve currencies and global means of payment.

I summarize the discussion so far in figure 8.3 which elaborates on figure 6.10. In the centre of the diagram, we find the circular causality underlying performativity of money. As I analysed in Chapter Six, the performativity of money rests upon the activation of somatic markers related with the generic emotion of social exchange which creates behavioural dispositions to use a certain emerging artefact, the money sign, as money. Already in this analysis, I have referred to the role of exchange in general, which in balanced exchange encompasses both market exchange and all forms of reciprocal exchange, including forced exchange which maintains reciprocity across power differentials.

Figure 8.3 The evolutionary trajectory of money

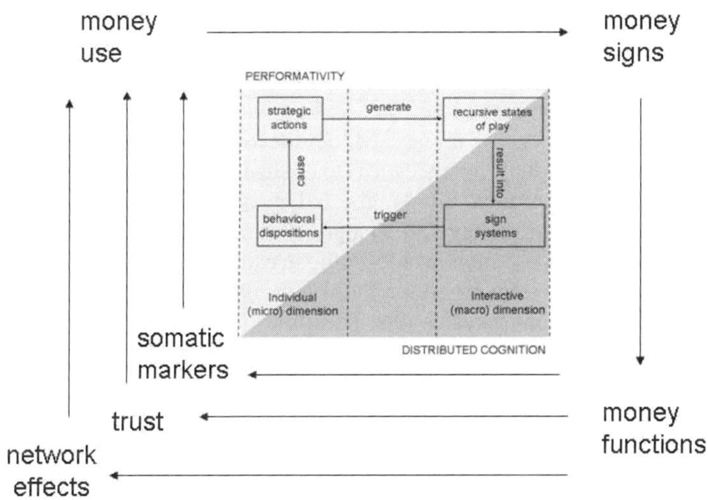

Note: Building on the analysis of the institution of money in Chapter Six (figure 6.10) this diagram shows the evolutionary ratcheting of money use after its primordial emergence. In this initial stage, the relation between the money sign and somatic markers of social reciprocity matter much to anchor money use in particular communities of exchange. Once political power usurps the money sign, and exploits money in the context of resource acquisition (taxation), an unintended effect of this is the strengthening of trust into the money institution, hence leveraging emotional commitments to a specific pattern of money use. With expanding scope of money–mediated transactions, this is further leveraged by network externalities of money use, which increasingly put the purely instrumental aspects of money in the foreground.

Thus, I introduce the role of trust as another determinant of individual dispositions to use money. Trust which is created by certain institutional settings in which money relates with government is different from trust resulting from primordial relations. In fact, what we consider here is a more detailed analysis of the population–level processes (upper part of the diagram), which I do not make explicit here. The population–level processes are strongly influenced by behaviour that is in turn neurocognitively embodied, in particular imitation. Therefore I put the term 'trust' into the same place as somatic markers. In the case of trust and power, the original emotions are supported by emotions related to power and authority. Finally, as I argued above, the population–level processes activate network externalities, which drive the diffusion of money even beyond the scope of emotional anchors. So, figure 8.3 shows a spiralling evolution of money that increasingly puts the technological functions in markets in the forefront, and drives the emotional anchors into the background, without however making it fully obsolete, as we have seen in Chapter Six.

8.3.3. The institution of credit

Turning back to the essential role of money in extending the scope of markets, money introduces a new possibility, namely to keep balances via the accumulation of stocks of money. Money decouples the flows of particular goods from individual balances of exchange. There are two important consequences of this fact. Firstly, the balances are turned into aggregates, measured in terms of money and changes in the individual stocks of money, and second, if there are money stocks, those can be exchanged, too. The first consequence is essential to create the micro/macro distinction in economic processes; the second creates the possibility of credit, which I already introduced in section 2.

Standard economic theory treats credit as a market phenomenon, with interest being conceived as the price of credit, and a market for credit (in the most simple textbook version, the 'loanable funds' model. However, the empirical facts about those markets reveal that this picture is seriously flawed (in the subsequent analysis, I follow Stiglitz and Greenwald 2003). The reason is that it pays insufficient attention to the role of uncertainty in credit relations. There is a double uncertainty in all credit relations. One relates with the confidence that the value of money is stable during the period of the credit relation. The other is that the borrower will keep the promise to repay the loan. I concentrate on the second source of uncertainty in the current context.

In the real world, there are three issues with assessing the individual creditworthiness of an individual borrower. The first is that the lender can never know all the individual circumstances which determine the repayment capacity. There is a fundamental information asymmetry between borrower and lender which turns the relationship highly specific. This is even true for the case that the individual borrower is honest. If the borrower is just optimistic about the future repayment capacity, the lender would still need to collect all the relevant information to reach an independent judgment of the situation. The second and the third issue emerge in the context of markets. In a market for credit, the first issue is leveraged to a substantial degree, because lenders will never be able to collect all the information about all possible borrowers to optimize their returns from given volume of credit. The market for credits is a classical 'Lemons market' in the sense that lenders will only be able to assess the average creditworthiness of a certain class of borrowers. As the textbook analysis of 'Lemons markets' demonstrates (Akerlof 1070, see my extension in Chapter Five, section 5.5.1.), this implies the possibility that credit markets do not come into existence at all, even if there are objective possibilities for mutual gains (which is an empirical fact which stood behind the emergence of the microfinance industry recently). There is the risk that bad borrowers tend to dominate over good borrowers, and if this tendency is recognized by lenders, they will refrain from extending credit at all. However, this relates with the third issue in credit markets.

The third issue results from the fact that the capacity of repaying loans is not fully determined by the actions of the individual borrower, but also by other borrowers. An essential feature of markets, once balances exist between actors via connected market clearing, is the interdependence of credit relations in the following sense. If there is a low quality borrower who defaults, he might jeopardize another actor who trusted into the exchange relations with this borrower. That means, a bad borrower can reduce the repayment capability of a good borrower with whom she maintains exchange relations. In other words, networks of markets in general, but especially in relation with credit markets, manifest a high level of negative externalities between actors. This further leverages the uncertainty facing the lender, because he would need to assess not only the creditworthiness of the individual borrower, but also the creditworthiness of all borrowers with whom the borrower maintains exchange relations. In other words, all individual credit relations have a systemic or collective dimension. Basically, this is hypercyclic interdependence: A good borrower can bolster the repayment capacity of a lender who is a borrower towards another lender, thereby causing a positive externality via triadic network connectivity.

The information asymmetries and externalities in networks of borrowers and lenders could be partly overcome via the institution of collateral (Geneakoplos 2010, 2011); however, this creates another mechanism of externalities at the same time, because the value of the monetary claims is linked with the value of the assets used as collateral. In case of default, market clearing on the markets for these assets will be affected (such as imploding housing prices during the recent financial crisis), which in turn deteriorates the financial status of other borrowers. In other words, externalities are also indirectly channelled via the leverage mechanism, which automatically enhances the collective effects of defaults.

I claim that these three issues suffice to show that the credit market does not operate along the lines of the standard price theoretic model of markets (even without such a radical conclusion, standard macroeconomic theory requires a substantial rethinking in terms of making the role of financial intermediation explicit, see Woodford 2010). Interest is not a price that balances the demand and supply of credits. The standard model is misguided, as it does not reflect the fundamental fact that unifies the two institutions, money, and the derivative institution, credit, namely that trust is the single most important determinant of the aggregate performance of the institution. This can be put into the context of standard models by means of the notion of 'credit rationing': Credit rationing implies that the market for credits is cleared via the explicit constraints on quantities of credit, such that quantities also obtain a central role in the information processing of credit markets.

Figure 8.4 The credit market (Stiglitz and Greenwald 2003: 47)

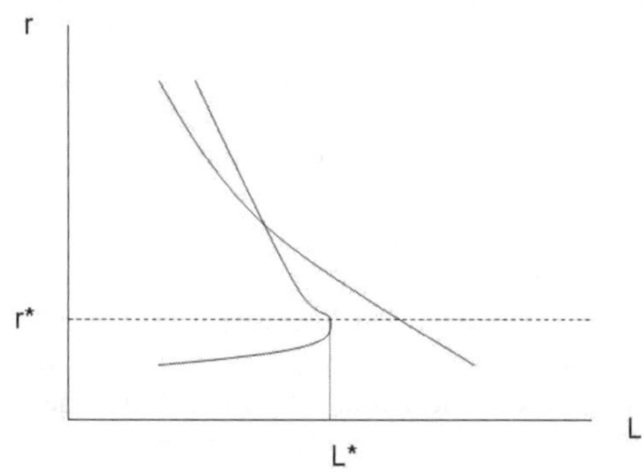

Note: This is a simple diagram of the loanable funds market with credit rationing. The basic assumption (elaborated in detail in the main text) is that higher interest rates signal increasing levels of risk. There is a threshold where lenders are not willing to bear that risk, independent from the level of interest, because they expect complete default of both principal and interest. Thus, the supply of loans actually shrinks with higher interest rates beyond that threshold. As a result, the market equilibrium is determined by the state of expectations in the economy, which is in turn influenced by the determinants highlighted in the general analysis of markets. Therefore, one cannot say that the interest rate is a price that equilibrates supply and demand of loanable funds.

So, the Stiglitz and Greenwald theory is based on an adverse selection argument with reference to the role of the interest rate: The higher the interest rate, the more risky the projects chosen and the more difficult to monitor the projects. This implies that an increase in the interest rate will lead to abnormal market behaviour: Credit supply will not increase, but may be simply blocked at a certain level, which is credit rationing. As a result, the standard supply and demand model is presented as a loanable funds model in which the demand schedule is regular, but the supply schedule is irregular (figure 8.4). There is a certain interest rate r* at which the lenders extend a certain quantity of credit. In this scenario, what matters most are the expectations about the probability of defaults in the economy. Worsening expectations just reduce the credit supply without affecting the interest rate at all. Again, following Geneakoplos (2010), this also applies when considering collateral and leveraging. Then, negative externalities directly affect the state of expectations about future defaults, rendering the interest rate almost irrelevant for market clearing (vide the 'credit crunch' after the recent financial crisis in spite of historically low Central Bank interest rates).

All credit markets manifest the phenomenon of credit rationing, which means that there are certain behavioural norms that guide the actions of borrowers, who do not follow a simple price scheme. Borrowers will have certain expectations about the level of creditworthiness of possible lenders, the general economic conditions and so forth, which will lead them to adopt a certain exposure to credit risk which cannot be changed by mere movements of the price of credit, interest. This fact is most obvious in the duality of credit markets in early stages of economic development: A typical phenomenon is the coexistence of a formal market with constrained credit, and an informal market with extremely high interest rates ('usury'). Apart from the fact that usury certainly results from market imperfections as well, it is also reflecting the fundamental issues of emergent trust in credit markets.

In most general terms, I posit that money and credit are institutions in the strong sense; that means, even if market–like relationships exist between the two sides of the credit market, the transactions are determined by institutionalized behaviour, which includes the possibility of changing institutions, dependent on external determinants of trust into money and credit. Hence, I propose to distinguish between primary and secondary monetary communities, again following Richter (1987). The secondary monetary community is the community of actors that is connected via trust–based credit relations. In advanced economies, these are banks and their clients. This results into a two–layered structure of markets which is shown in figure 8.5 (extending on Stiglitz and Greenwald 2003: 139).

The essential observation in this model is that the flow of transactions is dependent on the universal use of money as a means of payments which makes the indirect trade along the circle possible (so, ideal–typically, market clearing is only possible via the full closure of the circle). However, this also implies that if one single link in the circle is broken, this leads to the collapse of the entire structure. This very strong negative externality of single failures is avoided by credit relations. Then, the credit supply and the secondary monetary community obtain a pivotal role in embedding the entire flow system. As a result, we can say that markets essentially depend on credit in order to be sustainable with the increasing division of labour and hence the increasing length and complexity of indirect exchange relations in the market. Astonishingly, this simple fact has been neglected in recent mainstream macroeconomic modelling that has been used to design monetary policies in most advanced industrial countries and only had been highlighted in dissenting traditions of thought, such as Minsky (1982) and the different streams of Post-Keynesian thought (as an example, see Keen 2010).

Figure 8.5 The basic structure of markets, money and credit

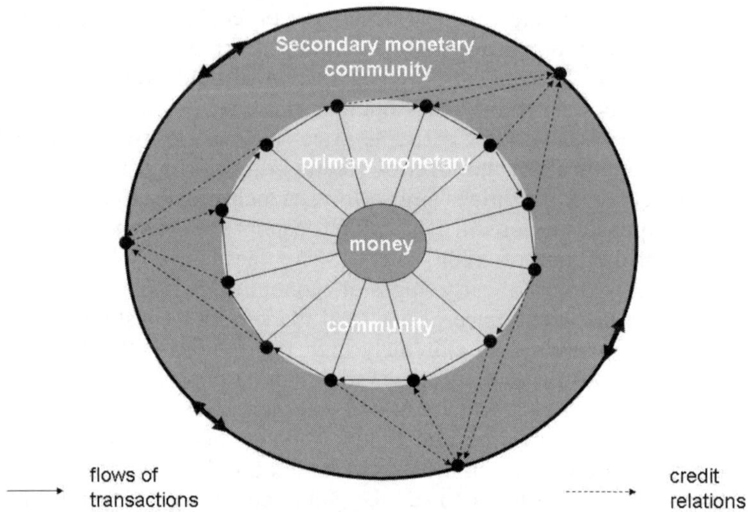

Note: The basic structure of a financial system based on money and credit relates two kinds of communities with each other; the secondary community is a subset of the primary community consisting of financial intermediaries. The primary monetary community is the set of actors who accept a certain currency as a means of payment. The actors are connected via a closed chain of transactions in which the acceptance of money obviates the need to match goods supplied and demanded in barter relations; as such, money established a primary credit relationship because it presupposes trust into its subsequent uses to buy goods. The secondary monetary community of financial intermediaries enables the possibility of credit in monetary terms, that is borrowing and lending which allows smoothening temporary coordination failures in balancing the chains of transactions in the primary community. There are different mechanisms linking the values of assets between the two communities, such as the value of claims resulting from credit and the value of assets used as collateral in credit.

8.3.4. Trust and status in monetary evolution

One important feature of secondary monetary communities is the role of status in creating trust. This is just an application of the general principles of trust in networks. As we have seen in chapter Five (5.4.6.), status in networks has the special effect to partition networks into groups of transacting actors. In the context of credit markets, this has the following implication. Consider a high status borrower. This borrower will be able to get loans at better conditions than low status borrowers. That means, in principle, that the high status borrower can exploit arbitrage opportunities if there are lenders who do not want to extend credit to less than high status borrowers. The high status borrower can reap an economic gain in extending her loans to low status borrowers at a higher price, provided that she has some informational advantages that allow the high status borrower to assess the creditworthiness of low status borrowers better that ordinary lenders. So, status differences on the market for credit imply the possibility for the emergence of financial intermediaries.

The question is who is a high–status borrower? There are two most general cases. With the existence of money, a high status borrower is somebody who owns a number of assets that have high exchange value, especially relative to money. In most simple terms, 'rich' actors are high–status borrowers. The second case is the case of borrowers who control a safe access to income, which is especially true for all borrowers who can apply coercive power on other actors. It is straightforward to see that this is the network configuration that undergirded the early evolution of finance during the late medieval times and the Renaissance, with rich merchant families providing loans to political actors (for an analytically congenial network analysis, see Padgett 2006, summarized in Chapter Six, section 6.6.4.). Far into the 19th century, the relationship between private bankers and governments assumed a pivotal role in the evolution of the financial system, and the former stayed at the core of that system until the modern shareholding banks emerged (Born 1976: 48ff). In later stages of the evolution of the credit market, the special role of governments remained influential, until modern times, when government bonds set the reference interest rate for the financial market. As regards the first kind of high status borrowers, the generic kind of financial intermediaries, which are banks evolved out of their position in credit networks.

It is important to notice that status continues to be a significant aspect of credit markets until today, although there is a complex influence by regulations and financial innovations. There is a clear hierarchy among financial institutions, especially in investment banking, which reflects levels of network relationships between lenders and borrowers of different status (Podolny 1993, 2005). For example, today certain corporate actors have obtained the high status borrower position, and they relate with high status lenders/borrowers in the banking industry. At the low end, especially in the developing economies, we observe the level of low–status lenders and borrowers (usurers and farmers). So, the role of modern microfinance is essentially to break apart the status order in the credit markets by means of entirely new business models. However, the general hypothesis continues to hold that status is a major determinant of trust in credit networks.

This role of government in markets can be further detailed in analysing the relationship between government debt and money. Among the large number of pertinent approaches, one especially interesting one has been proposed recently by von Weizsäcker (2011) that takes up an early contribution by Paul Samuelson. In this contribution, Samuelson argued that in an economy without the need for accumulating real capital, the only way to solve the problem of provisioning for old age is to hold a stock of fiat money. In a world with real capital, capital accumulation can serve this purpose, and in a world with different national economies, also capital exports. Now, von Weizsäcker argues that this problem retains its bite if the need for real capital accumulation results into a stock of capital that is too small to solve the provision problem. This depends on demographic variables and the general standard of living which determines the needs in old age. Von Weizsäcker argues that today there is indeed a growing gap between the two magnitudes, reflected in historically low real interest rates which manifest the limitations of the demand for real capital investment. Interestingly, these limitations are seen as resulting from the Second Law (compare Kåberger and Månsson 2001), because a growing stock of real capital continuously increases the costs of maintaining this stock in face of the forces of obsolescence, thus defining an upper limit to extending the capital stock.

On the other hand, because of population growth and rising standards of living the demand for the accumulation of financial means for the provision for old age grows continuously. If this demand were simply funded by the expansion of the money stock, this would create inflationary forces that hamper the attainment of the original aim. Therefore, the only way to close the capital gap is government debt. Hence, the optimal level of government debt is one which keeps the real interest rate at zero, thus avoiding negative interest resulting from inflation. In other words, the combination between a certain money supply and a certain level of government debt is the only way to meet the demand for real savings on the part of the population. This analysis implies that government debt is net wealth, and therefore refutes the Ricardian equivalence theorem which is exclusively based on market relationships. Ultimately, this solution depends on the state of expectations of the economic actors who recognize the non-market nature of government, that is its institutional nature of being the ultimate holder of means of violence in modern societies, namely forced exchange in the shape of taxation. By conclusion, all modern markets manifest the conjunction of the expansion of financial markets and growing government debt. This analysis is close to paradoxical for conventional economic analysis, which perceives increasing levels of government debt as detrimental to the stability of the monetary economy. To the contrary, government debt is the essential non-market determinant of the stability of the market institution of money, considering the fundamental problem of provisioning for the future. The root of this function rests in the surplus of trust that is enjoyed by the holder of ultimate means of violence. This observation finally confirms our analysis that the institution of money is deeply rooted in network phenomena of power, thus referring back to evolutionary forces transcending the scope of markets.

8.4. PRICES AS SOCIAL FACTS

8.4.1. The fundamental incompleteness of arbitrage

The role of money in defining the essence of markets is also evident from the pivotal role of prices. In standard microeconomic theory, money is treated as a 'veil' in the sense that the quantity of money only affects the general price level, but does not affect relative prices, which are seen as the determinants of choices and allocations. The question of 'real' effects of money is only debated in the context of macroeconomics. I argue that this is fatally wrong, because in the evolutionary view, prices are artefacts in the same way as money is an artefact. Prices are a special kind of monetary artefact. This is a definition that differs fundamentally from the notion of relative prices as indicators of scarcity.

This approach is based on two very simple observations. Firstly, actors have to set prices, and prices have to be made public. A price is a public representation of value. Secondly, the public nature of prices essentially depends on the technology of expressing and disseminating prices.

The first problem is partially recognized in the standard approach in the context of the tâtonnement problematique. There need to be actors who announce prices, and who conduct transactions at these prices, in order to enable the function of prices at all. The (in) famous theoretical construction of the auctioneer actually prevented the analysis of this fundamental process in due detail in the early stages of developing equilibrium theory. Clearly, once prices need to be set and transactions need to be realized, the original notion of equilibrium is meaningless as the composition of the excess demand and supply functions would change continuously. Some actors leave the market because they already realized the transactions that they wanted to realize at prices which might be equilibrium prices only by coincidence. However, this seemingly negative result is actually a positive result about the role of prices in markets, as it is now well-proven by numerous empirical results about experimental markets (Plott and Smith 2008): Those actors who take the first step and announce prices provide an essential information to all other actors who can now start to calculate their own decisions about buying and selling. Therefore, arbitrage is the essential process in markets, as far as prices are concerned. Arbitrage relates with two fundamental theoretical notions that are independent from the standard equilibrium notion, which is market clearing and the so-called Law of One Price. However, as I shall show, the latter only counts in the negative sense, that is the impossibility of the Law of One Price.

Arbitrage is based on public prices which are absolute prices in terms of conventional economic theory. Therefore, trading is an essential activity in markets (for a matching formal model, see Sugden 2004). I treat this as a very broad category, so, even if somebody produces the traded goods in the first place, I treat this as 'trading', too, as this actor wants to trade the goods, taking price differences into consideration that result from a divergence between input prices and output prices in the production process that leads to the possibility of accounting profits, that is changes in monetary balances. In this sense, the zero profit condition in standard equilibrium theory just reflects the Law of One Price, that is, the convergence of the valuations of a good in terms of input and output prices. Trading exploits differences in public prices, so one does not need to refer to internal valuations. Actually, these internal valuations are expressed in the publicly announced prices. So, the artefact of prices allows for this expression. But arbitrage means that ultimately those prices will converge to a certain degree, because arbitraging actors will drive up prices in offering higher prices at the lower boundary and lower prices at the upper boundary. This process continues until the spread of public prices will have narrowed down to a degree so that no further arbitrage activities are triggered. This situation is the clearing of the market.

Evidently, this activity depends on the willingness of actors to conduct arbitrage. This is not only based on the information about price differentials. There is always the problem how price information relates to the intrinsic quality of the goods. So, one source of uncertainty relates with quality uncertainty. The other source of uncertainty relates with the uncertainty about the costs of arbitrage. These costs relate with the first source of costs as they are created, amongst other determinants, by the information costs of reducing quality uncertainty. As we shall see, other costs relate with the costs of reducing the uncertainty about the partners of the transaction. From this follows that there are certain limits to arbitrage, which also means, limitations to the validity of the Law of One Price, which ultimately relate with differences across the set of actors in terms of their capabilities to reduce the uncertainty with regard to arbitrage activities. In other words, the Law of One Price fails to apply under the condition of heterogeneity of actors (also emphasized by Geneakoplos 2010).

Now, considering that these capabilities clearly are an economic asset, because they are a source of profits, the question results of whether there can be a price for this particular asset, which is actually a form of social capital as elucidated in Chapter Five (section 5.4.5). For example, an actor who perceives a price differential, but does not trust in her own capability to exploit this for reasons of uncertainty, might hire a more capable actor as an intermediator at a price. Then, we realize that markets will always manifest an evolutionary trend of emergent higher–order markets on which the capabilities to trade are traded, in turn. Now, the question is whether it is possible to end up with perfect arbitrage over all these markets, given the fact that the costs of hiring an intermediator are the costs of arbitrage on the first order market. For answering this question, we can go back to the fundamental impossibility theorem on interaction costs established in Chapter Six (section 6.3.4). It is impossible to evaluate idiosyncratic capabilities to trade or transact in an open state space of the world which manifests the possibility of novelty. The ultimate reason for this, however, is endogenous to the market: The superior capability to trade will never be offered as a service to others because that would imply giving up profit opportunities for the owner of that asset. In other words, the ultimate asset of entrepreneurial capability will not be traded on markets; this also applies for entrepreneurial agency distributed across network configurations (see Storper 1995 in the context of economic regions). This implies that there is always a wedge in establishing the Law of One Price across all markets, and hence there will always be profits in markets.

These profits are also a necessary reflection of the non-tâtonnement in establishing prices in the first place. There will always be transactions at prices that are higher than the prices towards which the arbitrage process gravitates. The resulting profits (actually, monetized rents in the standard model) set the incentives for arbitrage. That means, a fundamental error in the auctioneer model is that it does not recognize the role of non-equilibrium profits in putting the incentives into place to set prices at all. In order to establish market clearing prices, non-equilibrium prices, which are public in terms of realized and observable transactions, are a necessary condition. That is why evolutionary conceptions of markets are always non-equilibrium conceptions. This argument is more fundamental and a principled refutation of the LOP compared to the long series of empirical works in international trade which shows the empirical limitations to the LOP (Froot et al. 2001 is a classic; Herrmann-Pillath 2001a surveys the arguments): The LOP does not hold because there are non-pricable inputs to the arbitrage process. It is closely related with the analysis of incomplete contracts proposed by Anderlini and Felli (1998a, b; 1999). Perfect arbitrage must fail if there are inputs to the process of contract formation which are not contractible by themselves. The empirical literature matches with this result as it also emphasizes the role of non-tradable goods in limiting the role of the LOP for tradables, such as recently in Alessandria's and Kaboski's (2011) argument that 'pricing to market' is a permanent feature in international markets because of the role of non-market local search activities on part of the buyers which are complementary to the realization of the final transactions and which relate to different opportunity costs of search across countries.

8.4.2. The complexity of collective price-setting

We can treat the previous argument as another proof of the ontological separateness of prices in the bimodal sense. Prices are artefacts in a very down-to-earth sense, which is rarely analysed in standard economics (one exception is the notion of menu costs). Prices need to be expressed in material terms, as price tags, price lists, ads or signals on the computer screen. Thus, prices are signs. These signs directly cause monetary flows once a transaction is realized, unless contracts are violated. Therefore, prices and changes of money stocks of individual actors are directly related. Establishing a price is a complex procedure involving a collective of actors. Consider a traditional vegetable market and a modern supermarket. In the former, actors might haggle over the price. They might move from one booth to another, until they might feel satisfied with a deal, on both sides. In the supermarket, prices are announced one-sidedly, and consumers are left to take it or leave it. They can move between different supermarkets, but normally they do not haggle over the price. That might be possible when buying larger items, such as furniture. Comparing the cases, there is a very different degree of publicity of prices. In the traditional markets, realized prices are only public to a limited degree, whereas in the supermarket they are entirely public.

This role of prices as public entities is much emphasized by Shackle (1972) who treats prices as conventions in general, along the lines of Keynes; this view can be traced back to Simmel's theory of value as externalized embodiment of exchange relations (overview in Rammstedt 2003; for a theory of value that takes a similar position based on a modern neuroscience reading of Hayek, see Basso et al. 2010). Prices as material objects have only been scrutinized recently by economic sociologists, especially in the context of arbitrage on financial markets (such as Beunza et al. 2006). One exemplary study is Çalışkan (2007) who analyses price formation on Turkish cotton markets. He shows that on the official Turkish cotton exchange, where traders still meet in a pit, the daily price is actually constructed from the interaction between traders across different phases of the trade, including the price formation on the futures market. In this process, traders represent both sides of the demand and supply schedule during the trading day, and the resulting prices are not perceived as the 'market price' of that day. For the traders, this physical activity at a particular place 'is the market'. In the pit, the traders try to get information from many sources, even the physical appearance of other traders, about the unknown supply and demand. Interestingly, everybody is aware of the fact that there will be a 'market price' at the end of the day, but during the trades they aim at finding out their own position towards this unknown reference point. The brokers at this cotton exchange actually know and feel that they 'make the price' and they perceive this as their individual responsibility, especially in the sense of keeping the market sustainable and viable. Çalışkan calls these prices 'prosthetic' prices in the sense of Callon (2008) as those transaction prices mainly serve as indicators for the post-pit trading process, where pairs of buyers and traders fix the final deals of the day. Therefore he gives a special name to these prices, 'rehearsal prices', as they only cover a minor part of the entire volume traded on a day. These prices are public, whereas the post-pit trading prices are not necessarily public. In post–pit trading, compared to the trading in the pit, social relations between traders play a more significant role, such as reputation. The actual transaction prices are oriented towards the rehearsal prices, but they vary across the particular deals. But this is not yet the 'market price' of this day. This is fixed at the meeting of the Closing Price Committee. The Closing Price Committee reflects status distinctions among traders via the selection of its members. Those members rely on the data about the prices of the day, as far as they have been registered, in order to fix a final 'market price'. For example, they might exclude certain deals from this process if the deal appears to be influenced by collusive activities. Finally this price formation process is embedded into a political coordination mechanism, the Permanent Working Group on Cotton, which assesses the longer-term structural determinants of cotton supply and demand and develops pricing benchmarks, for example, via official estimates of production costs.

I discuss this example in some detail because cotton is a commodity. Even in this case, the simple supply and demand diagram does not catch the complex structure of the market in which the different actors interact in performing the price. There are many other examples for essential prices in the economy which are set by similarly complex processes of establishing collective valuations, such as the prices for oil and gas, and where the supply and demand paradigm fails to grasp the essentials of this process, even though there is minimal quality uncertainty. This corresponds to the theory of markets that has been proposed by Harrison White (1981, 2002). White argues that the supply of firms is constituted by a schedule that relates revenues with volumes, and not prices and quantities. The reason is that they need to explore an unknown demand side, which is an aggregate phenomenon, in order to establish a sustainable position in the market through time, which is their individual niche. The most important source of information is the observed behaviour of other firms, so that White defines 'the market' as a clique of firms that define the industry and stand in a collective relation with the demand side. From this, many different forms of market structure emerge, depending on the effects of cost structures and product qualities on the fundamental revenue/volume relationship. This analysis mostly applies for industrial firms, which do not operate in the context of a physical market such as the trading pit for cotton. It is illuminating to notice that this view receives support by economic research on price formation (for example Greenslade and Parker 2012). The vast majority of firms orient their pricing towards the prices of their competitors, and only a minor share points to their customers as forces determining their price.

One fundamental consequence of this analysis is that on the one hand, prices carry essential information about the economic process, but at the same time they do not carry all information that is needed to clear markets.

There are two aspects here. One is that prices have a strong habitual component, which is reflected in the so-called 'stickiness' of prices. The other is that there is a core informational role of quantities, independent from prices. So, as we have already seen in the context of credit rationing, we can say that a core mechanism in market clearing is price–quantity coordination, and not just price coordination. The most straightforward example for this is the role that profits play in guiding economic decision making, with the counterpart played by bankruptcies and defaults. Both are quantitative signals, and not price signals. The same holds for general perceptions of demand and supply. For example, if producers perceive a decrease of demand, this can happen without any change of prices, as long as there is no collective behaviour towards this. Price setting is a complex procedure, which even on almost perfect financial markets is driven by experts, the 'market makers'.

8.4.3. Reconsidering the simple supply and demand framework

The previous thoughts lead to a reconsideration of one of the simplest concepts in economics, the Marshallian partial analytical framework of demand and supply. Consider the standard textbook model. In this model, the market equilibrium results from the intersection of demand and supply schedules which depend on the current market price (figure 8.6a). In the standard textbook, this diagram is interpreted as follows. Supply increases with price, because there is a sequence of producers with increasing marginal costs of production which will post an offer on the market if the price covers the costs of this additional quantity. Producers that cannot cover their costs will not offer anything. On the consumer side, what counts are the opportunity costs of paying the price in terms of marginal utilities. Consumers who cannot cover these opportunity costs will not buy (reservation price), and all others will reap a consumer rent because their willingness to pay is larger than the equilibrium price.

This picture neglects the time dimension and the sequence of economic decisions, as well as underlying information flows (which, certainly, are made explicit in industrial organization models, however, the standard model remain a basic reference). My approach to the supply and demand diagram owes much to Binswanger (2013: chapter 5). Binswanger argues that firms orient pricing towards a 'reproduction price' which covers costs and a certain minimum profit. The demand that actually comes up at this price is called 'effective demand'. The market price can diverge from this reproduction price, if demand diverges from expected demand. Then, the price difference generates gains or losses in the profit position which give signals to the firms to adapt their decisions. In this process, what is crucial is that the changes of the profit position depend on the activities of other firms, so that a fundamental driving force of the market is to anticipate pricing decisions of other firms. This is crucial because the individual supply curve is fixed on the present market, as it was created by the decisions of firms in the previous period, given certain price expectations. Therefore, Binswanger argues that the actual supply curve is always vertical.

Figure 8.6 Supply and demand, reconsidered

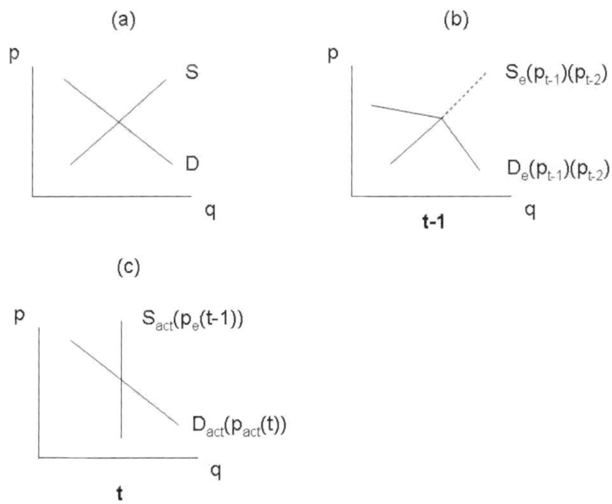

Note: We compare the standard supply and demand diagram (a) with the complex reality of price setting in markets. Diagram (b) describes the market from the perspective of the suppliers who set prices. They construct the schedules based on expectations formed in the previous period *t-1* which use data of *t-2*. Their supply schedule is truncated above the expected market clearing price because they would not be willing to make offers which do not result in transactions. The demand schedule is kinked at the expected equilibrium because suppliers expect asymmetric reactions of the demand side. Based on this construction, the realized market transactions can be graphed like in 8.6c: The supply based on 8.6b is fixed in the short run, realized transactions occur with demand reacting on the actual price offers. For a full discussion, see main text. In this view, the standard diagram 8.6a describes the market as a steady state, but not as an equilibrium; this reflects the nature of markets as institutions, and only builds on historical observations on this steady state.

I relate this analysis with the concept of perceived demand developed by Negishi (1979). Negishi argues that models of imperfect competition are the only realistic models of markets because only these can include the process of learning into the analysis, especially with regard to the demand side. In this he builds on the notion of perceived demand firstly developed by Chamberlin. Perceived demand is a construction that is made on the basis of observed reactions of demand on prices, which leads towards certain assumptions about the future demand. This theory was expanded by Sweezey to the theory of the kinked demand curve for oligopoly. However, one can argue that this does not only apply for oligopoly but for the more general case of monopolistic competition with price differentiation. Then, a fundamental information problem emerges, as the firm does never know whether the perceived demand curve and the actual demand curve coincide: The firm only knows the observed price–quantity combinations, in which the two schedules meet. But all other possible combinations are only conjectures.

Of course I am aware of the fact that this is a simplistic view of markets if we compare this with the state of the art of modern industrial economics. But on the other hand, Marshallian partial analysis is still the reference in establishing the textbook basics of markets, and the more sophisticated versions are seen as adaptations to a more complex reality. My point is that even the most basic conceptualizations of markets have to take the fact of decision sequencing under uncertainty seriously. Marshall (1890) himself was well aware of this fact, as in his 'Book Five' he puts a lot of emphasis on the different time horizons of adapting supply to market conditions, and the dynamics of expectations. Binswanger's 'reproduction price' bears close resemblance with Marshall's 'normal price', which can be seen in different temporal reference frames, but ultimately refers to the cost conditions and the implications for profitability and hence the survival of the enterprise.

So, turning back to figure 8.6, consider the supply schedule (8.6b). Producers who decide to put an offer on the market in the real world (that is without an auctioneer) will not decide on the basis of actual prices but expected prices. That means, the supply schedule in t depends on expected prices in t-1, not actual prices that result on the marketplace in t. Even if we accept the marginal cost calculus as a frame of reference, this means that the standard analysis only applies if the expected prices in t-1 match with the realized price in t. We can assume that expected prices depend on realized prices of previous periods, however. This argument immediately shows why expectations are of central importance for even the simplest conceptualization of markets. Thus, we end up with a supply schedule which is based on the most general function of $q_s = q(p_{e(t-1)}(p_{act(t-2)}))$. This is the correct and most simple definition of the supply schedule on markets.

There is an additional problem once we consider the possibility that expected prices underlie the fixing of prices by the single firms. The expected prices reflect different expectations; which means they all represent expected market equilibria. Thus, there are underlying assumptions about the demand schedule. Now, consider t-2. Firms might just accept this as a given, which would imply that the supply curve is actually truncated above that market clearing price. No firm will post an offer if they know that they cannot cover their costs at all, and given uncertainty about the currently prevailing costs of competitors; this implies that the market supply above the previously realized price is not observable (firms would only know their own potential supply). Now, the question is whether firms consider changes in prices, given $p_{act(t\text{-}2)}$. This means that they figure out the demand schedule.

The construction of the demand schedule can be based on past experience again. But the fact still remains true that in *t-1* this is a perceived demand schedule based on $p_{e(t\text{-}1)}$. This demand schedule will not be the same as in the standard model because there is a fundamental asymmetry in the price elasticity of demand right and left of $p_{e(t\text{-}1)}$. If a firm raises its prices, it will reasonably expect that potential customers will leave for firms who offer a lower price. The difficulty is that the firm does not know which prices the other firms expect, and does not have any information about those expected prices. Even worse, if other firms would announce their estimates in advance, and their corresponding price notations, the single firm cannot trust this information because there are very strong incentives to cheat about the true expected future price. On the other hand, if the firm lowers the price, there is no immediate effect on the demand side because the firm cannot assume that the information about this price will spread instantaneously across the market. As a result, the perceived demand schedule will have a kink at $p_{e(t\text{-}1)}$, with different perceived elasticities of demand right and left of the kink (this is standard analysis of oligopoly, but applies as well for the general case under realistic assumptions about information). From this follows that at the point $p_{e(t\text{-}1)}$ there is no mathematical solution to the optimization problem of the firm. The resulting supply and demand diagram is shown in figure 8.6b, with a truncated supply schedule and a kinked schedule of perceived demand. This is how the market looks like in the moment when sellers and producers take their decisions about their offers, that is from the perspective of the participant observers; the standard diagram 8.6a describes the market from the perspective of a perfectly informed external observer. To the contrary, figure 8.6b depicts the market conditions under uncertainty, which also results into the phenomenon of asset specificity of market opportunity that I analysed previously.

This is one of the most important reasons why prices tend to be sticky. Even in the simplest conceptualization of supply and demand, information structure and flows matters, and expectations result in strategic coordination problems in setting prices. We can even conclude that for the single sellers, what matters most is what they observe about the behaviour of other sellers, and not so much what buyers do. Thus, price setting is an activity that can reveal important information among the group of sellers, but therefore also involves free rider problems and cheating about truthful information. As a consequence, in real world market design, such as designing auctions, the most important problem is how to establish institutions in the market which cause actors to reveal truthful information about price expectations and price settings.

Now, consider the situation at *t* (figure 8.6c). At this time, the firms have already produced their supply and offer this on the market. This means, the short-term supply curve at *t* is vertical and inelastic with reference to price. Price will only adapt to actual demand, given the price offers of different firms. The crucial question is whether firms would be able to discriminate among consumers with a different willingness to pay. If we assume that the information about the price is public and available to everybody, rational consumers will certainly not pay a higher amount than market clearing implies. However, it is straightforward to see that without an auctioneer even this is a tricky problem. Suppliers might meet different customers with different reservation prices. So we are back with the problem how to elicit truthful price information via market design. This problem is one of the reasons why markets show a tendency to price discrimination via product differentiation. On the buyer side, there is a similar strategic problem as on the supplier side in the previous step, because buyers willing to buy at a certain price might consider waiting until lower price offers are made. This depends on the behaviour of sellers who wish to sell their fixed supply.

The consequence of this analysis is that those producers who expected a price that is above the realized price will only be able to fix a deal at a loss. That means, market clearing and equilibrium are not the same notions, because market clearing implies the possibility of losses, unless the sequence of actual prices is static through time. In a market where no changes of data take place and all actors just repeat the same behaviour under the constraint to avoid losses, a certain price will emerge at which these losses do not occur. In this sense, the standard neoclassical assumption of the no-profit condition applies. However, it does not reflect equilibrium, but a steady state of the market. This steady state of the market is an institution in the sense of a recurrent regularity, as analysed in section 8.2. Hence, we can conclude that the standard supply and demand diagram actually describes this steady state, based on historical data about the market, but does not describe the current market conditions under uncertainty resulting from the possibility of novelty. The steady state is a recurrent sequence of market clearing with prices as conventions, or, in my parlance, as institutions.

8.4.4. Market clearing across many markets: Macroeconomics

One consequence of this analysis is that failure of market clearing has aggregate consequences on market clearing in other markets. In Evolutionary Economics this point has been emphasized Potts's (2000) network–based approach to the classical macroeconomic theories of Clower and Leijonhuvfud (for an excellent overview, see Snowdon et al. 1994: 112ff.). Clower formulated the so-called 'dual–decision hypothesis' which is based on the distinction between effective and notional demand. If actors are constrained in one market, they can only express their effective demand on other markets which is backed by the pecuniary income generated in the constrained market. So, if workers are constrained on the labour market, they can only express the demand backed by actual wage income. This would be below the market clearing demand on the goods market. However, the firms would not sell their products based only on the notional demand that would correspond to a non-constrained labour market. Hence, firms perceive a constraint on the goods market, which, for example, would then result in a low demand for investment goods. Leijonhuvfud had emphasized the point that this is only possible in a monetary economy in which balancing of money flows is possible without clearing the markets in the sense of coordinating the notional demands, that is the plans of the different economic actors. Ultimately, it is money and the money balances that lead to the breakdown of Say's law in the market (compare Weintraub 1979: 76ff.). This implies that prices cannot play the role of a coordination device on the aggregate level anymore. By implication, and essential also for evaluating more recent trends in macroeconomics, this also means that price rigidities do not matter, an argument that was already found in the original position of Keynes, with reference to nominal wages.

The dual–decision hypothesis is central for establishing a relationship between Keynes's thought and evolutionary approaches to markets. The dual–decision hypothesis shows that there are two fundamentally distinct signals in markets, prices and quantities, and that quantity signalling can become the most important mechanism in market coordination as market clearing (so, as Witt and Brenner 2008 emphasize, the corresponding equilibrium notion would be a 'flow equilibrium'). As it is emphasized in Potts's (2000) elaboration on the dual decision hypothesis, quantity coordination is one expression of the more fundamental fact of non-integral networks. Thus, we can also subsume all sorts of network communication under the heading of 'quantity signalling'. For example, maintaining customary relations between sellers and buyers in Kirman's case of the fish market creates a structure of established quantity signals (that is past volumes of sales) which support the pricing process.

The notion of market clearing is intimately related with the notion of accounting balances once we refer to monetary magnitudes. The intricacies of aggregation in equilibrium theories lose all of their bite if we regard aggregation just naively as summing up over individual balances. In this view, markets create the possibility of treating segments of networks of transactions or entire networks as aggregates. Stated in this way, this purely arithmetic procedure seems innocuous, but in fact it has the important implication of making the micro/macro distinction possible in economics, which is essential for modern economic theory, though presenting a major headache, as long as the demand is raised to reduce the macro–dimension to the micro–dimension. One essential idea in Keynesian economics that markets manifest emergent properties which to a large extent result from the fact that the use of the artefact of money necessarily implies a set of accounting balances over a certain arbitrarily defined set of network transactions. Accounting balances are constitutive for the distinction between the microeconomic and the macroeconomic dimension of markets, because they introduce the possibility that the mere aggregation over individual decisions does not end up into an aggregate state of the market which reflects the goals of these individual decisions, but results into a different state. The classical statement of this phenomenon is Keynes's 'paradox of savings': If actors on one market try to reduce their monetary expenditures in order to save more, this will affect incomes in other markets, and hence, following Walras's law, ultimately the income of the actors initiating the reduction of expenditures. Thus, all actors as an aggregate group will attain their savings goal only via the reduction of income on the aggregate level.

This approach to the micro/macro distinction goes back to the early work of a German economist, Wolfgang Stützel (1953/1979; 1958/1978). Stützel already anticipated later developments in macroeconomics that relate with the dual decision hypothesis, as he emphasized the role of accounting balances in the economy (which he called 'Saldenmechanik' in German, 'accounting balances mechanics'). Stützel argued that accounting balances stay at the core of macroeconomic theory as monetary theory because they give rise to systematic discrepancies between what he called 'partial propositions' and 'global propositions'. He believed that many economic problems actually result from fallacies of composition in which partial propositions are extended to global propositions. These fallacies underlie many propositions of standard equilibrium analysis, in his view. For example, he (1953/1979: 146ff) debunked Say's law by showing that this is based on a partial proposition for the accounting balance of a single economic unit which can only spend what it can sell, given a monetary economy. On the global, that is macroeconomic level, and given a monetary economy, according to Stützel, a neat distinction must be made between monetary flows at a certain point of time and the sequences of transactions between different points of time (a view that vindicates Simmel's early insights into the fundamental difference between a synchronic approach to money and a process–oriented view, see Flotow and Schmidt 2003; compare from a different perspective Witt and Brenner 2008). If modern extensions on Say's law states that a general surplus production is impossible because increased savings would lower the interest rate and hence increase investment demand, this is an argument referring to simultaneous flows at a certain point of time. Stützel argues that general 'over-saving' is impossible on mere accounting grounds, because this always needs to be done via changes of monetary stocks ('Geldvermögen', which he distinguished from 'Zahlungsmittelbestände'), which automatically lead to corresponding changes of stocks held by other actors in the economy, given the closure of the accounting system. Hence, in his view, violations of Say's law can only happen because of the temporal structure of economic decisions, in which expenditures can decrease relative to the expenditures in previous periods, such that planned transactions at planned prices cannot be realized. Evidently, this is exactly Clower's point, and also implied by the analysis in the previous subsection.

The pivotal point in Stützel's approach is to distinguish between changes of monetary expenditures and income relative to each other and relative to previous levels on the one hand, and the accounting balances at a certain point of time. Further, he distinguishes between wealth as measured in monetary terms and stocks of money as a means of payment (hence, liquidity in the Keynesian sense). Then, for monetary wealth strict global accounting balances hold, and fluctuations in economic activity occur via the de-synchronization of expenditure and income flows (his 'Nachhinken' versus 'Gleichschritt' etc.). He claims that most problems with equilibrium theory result from the fact that at least implicitly it always assumes synchronicity of flows. If there is de-synchronization, which is only possible if money exists, and also derivative credit, changes of stocks can happen at different levels of absolute flows, if balances hold, and vice versa, that is changes of stocks require changing balances through time. In this view, equilibrium of flows is defined as a situation where there are no involuntary changes in the stocks of monetary wealth, namely deviations of realized from planned flows.

Schelling (1978: 75ff) gives a generalized account of the properties of systems that manifest a dissociation between what he calls 'micromotives' and 'macrobehavior', and which neatly fits to Stützel's framework. His list includes the following items, which ultimately all relate to systems which manifest certain 'accounting' interdependencies. Firstly, events and phenomena always occur pairwise (every payment is also a receipt) and often involve complementary groups in a population of actors (such as actors who save and actors who invest); secondly, there is a principle of conservation that corresponds to system closure (e.g. the quantity of money is fixed and flows through the system without any leakage); thirdly, flows run through different systems states; fourthly, there is a number of arithmetical relations between rates of changes and state and of statistical properties that relate independent and dependent variables (the decision to invest may depend on how many others decide to invest, my decision to invest more drives the average investment up etc.). It is important to emphasize that such accounting systems are entirely based on public information, hence sign systems, as in macroeconomics defined by monetary quantities. Thus, the 'Saldenmechanik' is actually a naturalistic macroeconomics in terms of the underlying ontology.

So, to sum up, given the complexity of markets and the corresponding formation of expectations, we have to recognize that prices on single markets are social facts in the sense of having an institutional nature which relates with the history of sequences of market clearing. This history is reflected in the expectations of actors and hence drives the dynamics of expectation formation in social networks. The existence of money introduces the possibility of two fundamentally different states of a system which consists of many markets. One situation, conventionally labelled a global equilibrium, would connect markets which all clear. However, with the existence of money and credit it is possible that single markets do not clear, even though the entire system of accounting balances is closed, this must result into 'market clearing' in the accounting sense, including the covering of losses resulting from failed transactions by means of credit. Therefore, in the monetary economy it is possible that failure of market clearing in the aggregate coexists with a sustainable network of money–mediated transactions maintained by credit. This fact is recognized by the standard distinction between microeconomics and macroeconomics. However, the evolutionary approach does not see any merit in attempts at reducing the 'micro' to the 'macro,' because the separate analytical role of the 'macro' results from an exclusively system level phenomenon, namely the role of accounting balances in the monetary economy in closing the flow of money in networks of transactions.

8.5. TRANSACTIONAL CAPABILITIES AND FIRMS AS MARKET REPLICATORS

8.5.1. Social capital and transaction enabling transactions

As a result of the previous analysis, we can state that eschewing the standard supply and demand diagram and the implicated equilibrium notion is the most principled step necessary to be taken in an evolutionary approach to markets. The essential activity in the economy is setting prices, which is determined by a vast manifold of factors. These prices are absolute prices and social facts. Once they come into existence, they trigger the fundamental market process of arbitrage which results into market clearing. However, one cannot assume that this is a process that erodes all price differences, because arbitrage builds on capabilities to create, discover and exploit those opportunities, and which cannot be an object of market valuation, following fundamental impossibility theorems. Therefore, understanding markets requires investigating into those capabilities. In other words, in the evolutionary perspective, markets are processes of money–mediated network transactions which are enabled by sets of transactional capabilities which generate transaction–enabling transactions TETs. So, we can differentiate any kind of market transaction into two transactions; one is the transaction that results into certain changes of states of actors, and the other is the transaction that makes this transaction possible. This differentiation is evident from the fact that it can be a part of the division of labour: For example, if I buy a good via EBay, this transaction is enabled by the services that EBay offers to both sides of the transaction. However, this analysis also applies for simple transactions: If I buy an apple on the vegetable market, the TETs are my screening activities or the advertisements of the traders. In other words, the notion of TETs refers to all activities that change interaction costs (transactions costs in the NIE parlance).

The notion of TET provides the bridge between the analysis of markets and the analysis of networks. All market transactions are embedded into networks of relationships through which information is transferred. This fact has been recognized by economics in emphasizing the role of social capital for markets in the past three decades (Dasgupta and Serageldin 2000; Sobel 2002; Dasgupta 2005). I posit that social capital is a central theoretical element in analysing markets. In understanding this concept, I draw on the results of Chapter Five (5.4.5.). There, social capital is a concept that extends far beyond markets, as it also affects, for example, the production of public goods in communities. In the context of markets, social capital is a central determinant of transactional capabilities of actors. This works both via ex-ante and ex-post channels. Ex-ante social capital leverages individual capabilities to collect and process information about other actors and transaction opportunities. Ex post, social capital enables the individual capabilities of actors to sanction other actors. So, social capital reduces information asymmetries among actors and creates incentives against cheating.

The mechanisms are well documented by the rich research on social capital. Ex-ante social capital is embodied in network relations that enable an actor to access information about another actor via other actors. It is of central importance that both actors in a transaction know about this fact, because this implies that the actor who would have the possibility to cheat knows in advance that the other actor has access to this information. Further, social capital does not only inhere in close network relationships, but also in all kinds of weak ties, as weak ties also enhance the accessibility of new information. This is particularly important for expanding the scope of market transactions. In this respect, there is an issue of assessing the quality of this information in turn, so again, a problem of reflexivity and recursivity between different items of information arises. If I receive information via a weak tie with another actor, I have the derivative problem in assessing the quality of this information. However, the point is that information flows via network relations which are independent from the original transaction mostly are not directly influenced by the interests of the actors in gaining an advantage in a market transaction.

Further there are multiple checks possible in comparing information from different sources. As we have seen in chapter Five, these comparisons between different sources include a whole gamut of differentiations between network positions, such as, for example, status distinctions between actors which can result into different degrees of the reliability of information provided, or different weights assigned to the value of the information. This constitutes the central importance of all kinds of intermediators or advisers in the unfolding of market relations. This notion includes both the professional consultant and the friend who gives an advice about 'best buys'. So, in spite of the fact that network relations never guarantee that information is reflecting the true state of the world, the fundamental point remains that networks create a web of positive information externalities among actors which are supported by the underlying social capital, that is the accumulation of reliable network connections between actors.

The same holds true for the ex-post sanctions (compare the analysis of Greif's case of medieval trading discussed in Chapter Six, 6.5.1.). The ultimate and simple sanction against all members of a network is exclusion from the network, which can be realized in degrees, which means that the costs of transactions might depend on the degree of inclusivity. In other words, cheaters might be sanctioned via the collective constraining of their future transaction opportunities. This is a generic constraint, which means, that the type of transaction possibilities need not be the same. In particular, there is also the possibility that all network relations outside the market proper are affected. For example, if I know that an entrepreneur cheated me, I may spread this information among my friends, and they might shun him at the sports club.

This brief analysis shows that the same problem applies in ex-post sanctions as with the ex-ante relations. The issue of sanctions is more difficult, because sanctions can imply costly behaviour, and include a collective good problem. That is, if an actor was cheated, sanctions that work via the network require that other actors act upon this information, even if they are mere bystanders and do not have any direct stake in the relation with the cheater. This is a collective action problem, as the sanction will only work if a sufficient number of other actors adopt punishing behaviour, and it is an individual rationality problem, as the individual has to invest some costs, depending on the circumstances. Therefore, social capital needs to have specific configurations and content in order to enable this kind of behaviour.

This is evident if we look at the empirics. The two issues that I have described briefly lie behind the phenomenon that in early stages of market evolution trading communities play a central role (Landa 1994; Rauch 2001). This is especially true in global trade, where, for example ethnic trading communities are important until today. But similar principles, if only with a lesser degree of social differentiation, apply for local trade, such as when transactions are mediated via friendship networks. An example for the latter are the networks that underlie the hiring of service providers in small trades, where there can be considerable problems with quality uncertainty (for instance, building a roof, which cannot be inspected directly after the completion, but might only reveal deficiencies much later, after a tempest). Very often, this is mediated via recommendations in social networks such as neighbourhoods.

8.5.2. Dimensions of networks and scope of market transactions

We can generalize over this observation in relating the theory of markets with the general conception of levels in networks. We have distinguished between groups, tribes, large groups and society in general. The previous example of trading communities relates with the level of tribes, mostly (Kotkin 1992). So, typically an ethnic trading community might be differentiated into tribes which concentrate on particular industries. Small groups can play an important role either in local trade or in regulating the internal operations of the larger networks. For example, considering large deals of investment banks, we can typically discern a small number of highly influential actors who work 'behind the scene' to fix the deals. So, we can repeat the same statement: In modern corporate networks, we observe tribes of 'CEOs' who differentiate along industry lines to a certain degree, and in which a more constrained number of very influential individuals plays an important role in regulating the behaviour of those tribes.

However, there is an inherent contradiction between the evolution of social capital as embodied in networks and market evolution, which has been always emphasized in the economic literature (such as North 1990). This is that once the scope and reach of markets grows, transactions will be done increasingly between actors who do not have any direct connections, and who are only very thinly related via indirect connections. This is the standard description of modern market relations as being 'anonymous'. The argument is presented that this transition is only possible with the emergence of formal institutions, that is the law, which is implemented by the government and an independent judiciary. Although I do not question the role of the law in principle, it is necessary to reconsider this argument. However, there is one aspect which is certainly important to recognize, but which still differs from the standard argument. The standard argument opposes two entirely different regimes, namely a personalized one and an impersonal one. This is certainly empirically wrong, as we observe a strong role of personalized networks all over modern business, on all levels of transactions. The real issue lies in the fact that precisely because of the existence of those networks, the anonymous relations that are driven by markets growth, will manifest a particularly strong sort of defect, because they might accumulate all cheaters (Kranton 1996; Bowles 1998). So the real issue is how the two domains relate with each other.

I argue that the interaction between the domains works in both directions. One is that personalized relations will increasingly work 'under the shadow of the law' (see Dixit 2004: 25ff), and the other is that networks create new forms of information processing that transform the traditional functions, but keep their essence. Dealing with the first issue firstly, I argue that most transactions in markets succeed without explicit reference to the law (for a classical related research on conflict resolution in communities see Ellikson 1991). This is possible because the evolution of markets happens alongside the evolution of technologies of network organization, which, in the context of markets, coalesce into TETs. For example, the recent emergence of the social web considerably expands the scope of personalized network relations in making them more transparent and increasing the speed of information transmission. But the notion of network technologies does not only include technical devices but all sorts of behavioural innovations. These innovations mainly refer to the organization of markets in terms of industries which focus on particular categories of goods. My general point is easy to see if we consider a case such as online auctions: They operate 'under the shadow of the law'. But if cheating would only be contained via the threat of legal disputes, the market would never come into existence, as the costs of legal disputes are by far too high for actors who might just trade small-value items. The market is enabled via a conjunction of technological devices and certain design patterns (such as public evaluations of traders) which increases the trust into the future transactions, even though they remain anonymous in essence. So, one cannot say that the transition to the regime of anonymous markets is essentially dependent on the formal institutions of the law. In order to understand this phenomenon, it is necessary to go back to fundamental network properties. This is the distinction into the three dimensions of perception, communication and transaction.

Standard economic theory only focuses on transactions, and in this context only concentrates on prices as a medium both of communication and perception. Certainly, perception also includes the perception of the goods in question, but this is not the object of the theory, only in very abstract generic terms of 'quality uncertainty' etc. In fact, markets operate in all the three dimensions, and for solving problems in the transaction dimension, the other dimensions are essential.

Beginning with the dimension of perception, the transition from small to large groups in markets is related with the emergence of standardization and 'labelling'. That means, all markets are differentiated along industries and product groups, which carry certain labels (Carroll and Hannan 2000). Labels are important because they standardize certain properties of goods and mostly also certain properties of producers or traders in those industries. So, labels define certain default options which commit the actors because if they do not meet with the resulting expectations, their costs in realizing transactions will be higher.

A central phenomenon in modern, large scale markets are the 'brands'. Branded goods create certain expectations about the characteristics of the particular goods, and these expectations are supported by large investments on part of the producers that create those commitments. This is the basic element of the theory of advertising: If a producer invests a lot into advertising for a particular branded good, these investments are highly specific because they are lost in case of failing to meet the expectations. Buyers know this, and hence might trust the brand even if there were no other social network mediated sources of information. However, these sources even leverage the brand effect as communication about the products is made much easier, given the strong standardization. So, for example, if there are several individual fast food shops in a neighbourhood and one branded shop, the business of the former might depend on local networks and recommendations. The business of the branded chain store depends on the advertisement and the resulting commitment to the quality promises, but is further leveraged, if the information transmitted in local personalized networks converges with this information.

So I argue that labels, such as brands, play a central role in enabling the increasing scope of markets. They operate in the dimension of perception, that is, all markets are supported by evolving semiotic structures which shape the perception of the product space and the expectations of buyers and sellers (Mick et al. 2004). The latter happens because particularly successful sellers and producers are highly influential in setting the industry standards that are eventually designated by the labels (the default modes in the sense of Hannan et al. 2007). This effect requires looking at the other dimension, communication. The crucial difference between the small group and the large group level in network mediated markets is that large groups constitute 'audiences' (this approach is well developed in the context of organizational ecology, see Hsu and Hannan 2005 for a survey). Standard economic theory only considers the two sides of transactions. An audience includes a much larger group of actors, beginning with those potential buyers who do not realize transactions at present, but also all other actors that have a stake in the product or industry, such as suppliers, creditors, trade unions etc. One most important part of the audience of a single firm is the peers. Audiences are stakeholders in a most general sense, and as such they are also 'experts', in the sense of being motivated to collect and assess information about the industry and the products. Processes of labelling always take place relative to those audiences. For example, in modern markets NGOs that focus on working conditions in supplier industries have become a part of the audience in certain product segments, whose opinions may affect the brand reputation even if the members of the NGO are not buyers of the products in the first place.

Audiences are not simply collections of actors, but are organized in a particular way, and they are strongly influenced by the prevailing technologies of communication. For example, a most influential audience in the modern financial industry are the 'markets'. By this, observers refer to the financial markets. Evidently, markets are no actors. The actors behind the markets who constitute the audience are investors, analysts and traders, to name the most important ones. Looking at the evolution of modern financial markets, technological innovations were essential to create the modern global financial markets, such as in early times the ticker, or more recently the computer. However, the audience is not simply structured by those innovations. For example, when the ticker was created, this innovation linked up cross–continental audiences with high speed (cf. Preda 2008b). But the ticker could only be observed by very few actors standing close to it. So, the local audience had to be organized in a particular way. That means, market organization includes a whole gamut of communication technologies and processes, reaching from the personal communication in clubs close to the financial district to newspapers and to computerized data mining techniques. All these activities work together in shaping the collective behaviour of the audience. If today the 'discipline of the markets' is often invoked, this means that the collective behaviour of the audience cannot be directly influenced by any single actor, and that it cannot be predicted by any single actor with certainty. All these modern markets are social network markets.

So, I argue that in modern markets, large group network relations operate as a medium of securing transaction success via arranging audiences that operate in certain semiotic domains which process labels related to industry standards and quality characteristics of goods, and which create commitment mechanisms that contribute to containing cheating behaviour. It is essential to see that this is not 'anonymous' in the strict sense, but just the other way round, we observe a very high degree of publicity of information which relates to clearly identifiable actors. However, these actors are mostly firms, not individuals, even though in particular industries firms are often personified by people relative to the audience (such as Steve Jobs). Thus, the hypothesis of the transition from personal to impersonal exchange does not pay sufficient attention to network mechanisms that work in large groups. The so-called 'anonymous markets' are in fact markets with a large–group network structure.

8.5.3. Firms, markets and networks

Then, it is necessary to recognize that in these large groups, corporate actors play a central role. I propose a theory of markets in which firms and markets co-evolve because firms are special kinds of arranging TETs into one organizational structure which is represented towards audiences via a common label, the firm. This has one important theoretical consequence: I argue that the standard view is wrong to think of markets and firms as being substitutes, in the sense of choosing between the market and the firm as alternative transactional regimes. To the contrary, a firm is a set of TETs; hence firms and markets are complementary. The growth of the complexity of markets is only possible via the growth of the complexity of firms. As we have seen in the previous argument, this role depends essentially on the fact that firms and large groups interact via the formation of audiences. It is a misplaced conception to view the market just as an abstract entity on the level of 'society' (or even the global economy).

It is highly significant that the emergence of modern capitalism was intimately connected to the invention of the corporation. Kuran (2009) is most explicit in treating the invention of the corporate actor qua legal person as the essential difference in determining the divergent evolution of economic systems, in particular China and the Middle East. For example, only the concept of the legal person would have enabled corporate entities to persist after the death of entrepreneurs who otherwise rely on a network of personalized contracts to design and shape a large–scale business venture. So, the difference between the evolutionary tracks of Europe and China or the Middle East does not lie in phenomena which relate to markets, such as the entrepreneurial spirit, the role of prices or of property rights in the generic sense, but to corporations as a defining feature of the culturally specific social ontology. However, as I have already emphasized in Chapter Five (referring for example to Zelin 2009), this view overlooks the role of functional equivalences in organizing economic action. But this criticism mainly shows that firms have to be conceived as special kinds of TETs, for which other TETs can functionally substitute. This is most obvious from one of the most outstanding characteristics of recent market evolution, that is the growth of global production chains where branded firms may outsource all production activities and operate as mere coordinators of transactions among functionally integrated firms (Gibbon et al. 2008). In this case, the technology of production is entirely separate from the technology of transactions, and firms exclusively focus on the latter.

The theory of the firm vacillates between two different poles, the transaction cost view and the competence view (for lucid comparisons from the perspective of Evolutionary Economics, see Foss 1993; Hodgson 1998). The former view originates in Coase's classical contributions and is well developed in the Williamsonian paradigm (Williamson 1985). The main difference between the two perspectives is that the former view approaches markets as a sort of default forms of economic organization, such that firms enter when market failure occurs. However, given the ubiquitous phenomenon of contractual limits in face of information asymmetries and opportunism, firms need to develop special governance schemes to deal with them, too. In contrast, the competence view approaches firms as repositories of knowledge, independent from transaction cost problems. Especially, routines may contain knowledge which cannot be codified; this constitutes a limit to contractability that is not is caused by opportunism and information asymmetries. The competence view has been very influential in Strategic Management, as it focuses on the development of specific capabilities of firms which result in sustainable competitive advantages (with seminal contributions such as Barney 1991). Solving problems of transactions may be a minor factor in generating this.

To a certain extent, my approach unifies the two theories as I focus on capabilities to solve problems of transactions. But these transactions are both internal and external to the firm. This approach owes much to the theory of the firm that has been proposed by Casson (1997). Casson treats firms as 'market makers' in the sense that the firm combines knowledge about market conditions and opportunities that is dispersed over a number of actors that need to collaborate in order to create the market. In this collaboration, and basically following the standard logic of property rights theory (as outlined, for example, by Barzel 1989) the person who controls that part of the information that has the highest degree of non-tradability will obtain the position of the owner and hence the residual claimant. Casson emphasizes very much that this approach does not correspond to the transaction cost approach because information costs is a much broader category, including for example, technological knowledge related to market opportunities. However, some of these aspects can also be integrated into a transaction cost approach, such as Hallwood (1997a, b). Another aspect of the firm is that the organization also serves to contain information dissipation which would otherwise be possible if the transactions are organized via markets, and to provide the conditions by which, for example, product quality signalled by branding can be maintained. An interesting conclusion from Casson's approach that matches with my analysis is that in the long run, firms and markets will co-evolve, as with rising incomes, the products will become more and more information–intensive, for example in the sense of matching with more specific consumer needs. This implies that information processing via markets causes increasing complexity of firms, and more complex markets can only be sustained by more complex firms.

This discussion can be related to the important question about the role of firms in knowledge generation and processing on markets. I argue that this mainly refers to two kinds of knowledge; one is the previously mentioned capabilities to transact, that is the production of TETs (which are called 'business models' by management sciences), and the other, of course, is technological knowledge. Regarding the latter (but also applying on the former), the standard view that firms are generators of technological knowledge stands in sharp tension with the analysis of Chapter Seven which shows that technological evolution is a population–level phenomenon. This tension is most obvious in the fact that the patent system underwent secular changes towards the identification of the firm as the main holder of patents (and not individuals as members of firms) (for a detailed discussion, see Coriat and Weinstein 2005). In this case, we can clearly speak of another expression of the performativity of economics in establishing markets, as the standard theory of property rights is applied to create markets for knowledge which follow the standard logic, with the firms as suppliers of technology. But based on the analysis of Chapter Seven, we cannot say that new knowledge is created by corporate actors and then sold to other actors. The innovation process as a whole also requires active participation by the user, who, for example, has to be ready to give up acquired knowledge (hence, avoid the sunk cost fallacy). So, why does the user do not have similar claims on the benefit of a new idea? In fact, the interaction between producer and users in innovations is already well recognized in industry collaboration across supplier networks. Especially, if firms contribute to the formation of standards, industry communities have developed norms about the 'fair' social exchange of standard setting patents that do not follow the market logic in the narrow sense.

Further, we cannot assume that the traditional market model will continue to apply in the future even in consumer industries. In the traditional model, there is a linear sequence from the producer of an innovation to the consumer. However, recently the concept of 'prosumer' has gained attention, which highlights the fact that consumers are increasingly involved in the production of a good (Bruns 2008). This is a consequence of technological evolution, in turn, which allows for different ways how consumers can be directly involved in the design of goods, or can directly order highly individualized versions of goods, for which, if they are also appreciated by other consumers, no IPR exists, but consumers share these innovations as a group.

Figure 8.7 Firms and networks: Linear and evolutionary models (after Hartley)

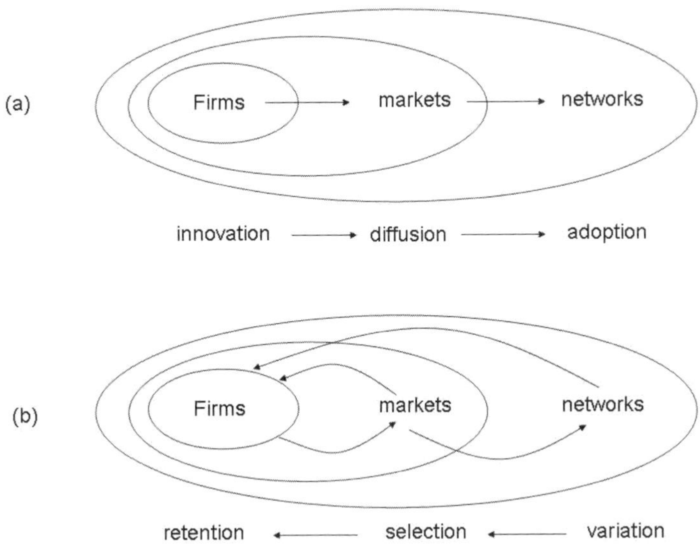

Note: The traditional concept of the firm posits that firms are sources of innovations which diffuse via markets and are adopted by actors in networks; hence, the user side plays the role of retention in the evolutionary process. The approach in this chapter, building on Chapter Seven, reverses this idea based on evolutionary principles: Innovation is caused in networks of actors (which include firms). Firms test those innovations in markets (that is they connect innovations with business models) where selection takes place. Ultimately, the new knowledge is stored and transmitted by firms, for example, by creating sustainable product designs, corresponding labels etc.

So, we need to distinguish between different forms of the embeddedness of markets into the general network structures of knowledge evolution. In this context, it is possible to assign the proper analytical position to firms and holders of rights. In the standard model (figure 8.7a), the assumption is that of a linear flow of causation. There is a producer of innovations, and those are adopted in a population of users. In the new evolutionary model, we apply the idea of the coevolution of firms and markets (b). If we extend this into the generic network model, what we observe is a process in which new ideas are actually generated on the population–level. These ideas are then put into use in the context of firms. Firms turn the ideas into products which are viable in the market context, thus allowing for the evaluation of ideas in terms of market prices. This process leads to the final adoption of innovations on the population level. What we realize in this picture is that the firms obtain a crucial role in the retention process of the economy, hence obtain the status of replicator of knowledge.

This analysis has direct implications for the generic approach to the co-evolution of firms and markets. The central observation is that markets and transactional capabilities co-evolve. Markets are impossible without those capabilities. In the modern economy, this is mainly epitomized in the co-evolution of firms and markets. So, knowledge evolution happens via both channels: Firms creates niches in the market system, and these niches evolve into markets via the attraction of other firms, and the emergence of particular audiences. So, the niches establish patterns of selection which impact on firm evolution. Firm evolution feeds back to niche evolution. So, for example, there has been a niche for mobile phones in which certain firms were active and defined that niche. However, when firms developed new products, the niche changed into the smartphone niche, thus creating a strong selective force leading towards change in the composition and the strategies of the firms. Even though particular firms can be dominant in certain stages such as Apple, competition creates forces through which knowledge transmission will take place on the industry level. This is because the niche carries essential information such as about standards and consumer preferences.

As a consequence, one cannot equate firms with the conjunction of organization and technologies, although both play an important role. Technological evolution happens on the population–level and hence involves the conjunction of firms and niches. The essence of firm evolution lies in the evolution of the TETs that are enshrined in the organizational structure, and which relate the firm with a specific pattern of market processes. Hence, if we think in terms of the replicator/interactor dichotomy, we can say that the firm can be seen as the replicator that steers interactions of actors within the industry. The interactor has to be seen as a multi–level configuration in the network of firms and audiences from which the niches emerge in which and across which the firms compete. This view comes close to Aldrich's (1999) approach that analyses organizations in the context of populations of firms in certain market environments. Aldrich puts the organizations at the core, in the sense of being unique combinations of routines, knowledge and skills, created by individual entrepreneurs. But he also emphasizes the role of the embeddedness of organizations into environmental configurations, such as social networks. This broader view is most appropriate to grasp the fact that firms compete against similar firms in a particular niche, but those populations compete as a higher–level unit against other populations in related niches, and so forth. The routines of a single firm may in fact be routines that are shared by all firms in a niche, and which emerge from the movement of workers between the firms, for instance. I think that a multi–level view on the interactor function is the best approach to deal with this complexity. On the other hand, focusing the replicator function on the firm emphasizes the ontological centrality of the firm as the entity where the market interactions coalesce into material structures. Especially, this applies on the technological aspects, and correspondingly to the specific combinations of actors using the technology, thus constituting specific forms of *agencement*, as analysed in Chapter Seven.

I think that this strong role of material structures in firms is the major reason which justifies the view that the firms are the replicators in the larger market system. Then, following Vromen (2011), we can connect this analysis with the analysis of technology and organizations in Chapter Seven and identify multi–level evolutionary mechanisms. There, we stated that artefacts are replicators, with designs and routines of firms as interactors. These interactors co-evolve with the market niches that they create. Relative to markets and their recurrent patterns of market processes, this interactor turns into the replicator of these structures. Then, markets are seen as being organized along 'industries'.

Industries manifest complex patterns of distributed knowledge beyond the boundaries of the firm, such as shared standards. These are essential in enabling the emergence of markets, for example, because standards relate with labels that support the interaction between firms and audiences. Industries and markets are not co-extensive, however, thus reinstating the standard economic distinction in this regard. More specifically, we can distinguish between, for example, the automotive industry on the one hand, and the markets with different geographical scope. Then, we end up in relating the 'global automotive industry' with the 'global market for automobiles', with complex mappings on lower levels of the hierarchy. This analysis makes clear how knowledge is structured in the co-evolution of firms and markets, thus connecting technology and markets via the pivotal role of firms. On the lower level (8.8a), firms are part of industrial organization with relation to a particular market niche; on the higher level (8.8b), industries are parts of the more encompassing industrial taxonomy (such as special chemicals as parts of chemical industry). This complex mapping reflects the evolving knowledge structure of markets.

Figure 8.8 Multi–level replicator–interactor relationships in market evolution

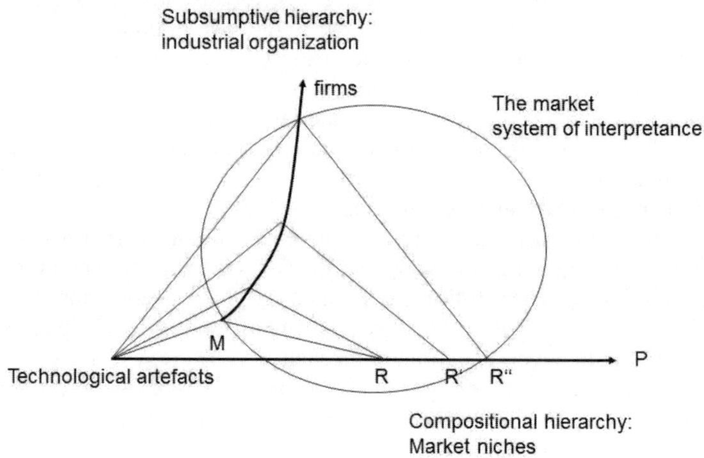

(a)

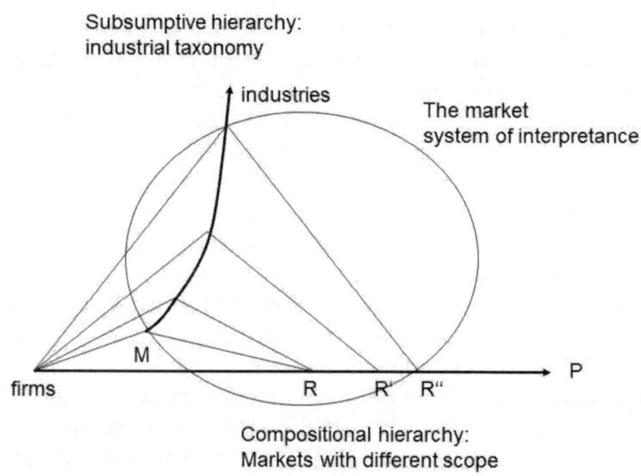

(b)

Note: The upper diagram (a) shows the role of technological artefacts as replicators of firms; firms are interactors (made up by designs, routines and so forth) which relate to market niches that co-evolve with firms. The subsumptive hierarchy relates to the pattern of industrial organization in the context of a particular technology (such as relationships between suppliers and main producers); the compositional hierarchy relates to the embedded structure of market niches (a supplier of brakes has its market niche, which is embedded into the market niche of the main automotive producer, and so forth. The lower diagram (b) shows the higher–level role of firms as replicators of markets. The interactor is the industry, which is reflected in complex patterns of industry–specific knowledge (such as skills of workers specializing on the industry, industry–specific standards etc.). The subsumptive hierarchy refers to the embeddedness of industries (such as computer chips in the larger computer industry). Industries enable the emergence of markets with different scope, in particular geographic. These layers of markets manifest the complex forces of selection operating of firms relative to the proximate goal of profit generation.

8.6. FIRMS, MARKETS AND HUMAN LABOUR

8.6.1. Firms and the measurement of entrepreneurial input

The previous analysis of the co-evolution of firms and markets can be further enriched by considering the firm as a nexus that connects input with output markets. I suggest that the connectivity of markets can only be established by means of a non-market network configuration. This point applies with special force to the organisation of human labour. Labour is an input to the firm that contributes to the production of the output, and it is essential as this includes most, but not all of control information operative in the firm. However, see from the perspective of general network analysis in Chapter Five, the problem is that firms only integrate partial aspects of actors in networks (the 'labour services'), though including entire individuals qua persons. This raises the important issue how labour in firms relates with identities of actors.

In this context, we observe a strange split in standard economic theory. On the one hand, there is a very rich and substantial literature on the role of wages as incentive devices in firms, which certainly also influences the analysis of the labour market, and which explicitly recognizes the relationship between the actor as a producer of 'labour services' and its identity as a person. But at the same time, in many contexts, especially macroeconomic analysis, the labour market is treated as a simple arm's length market, with the central hypothesis that the wage is a price that equilibrates the labour market (for a critical review, see Akerlof and Shiller 2009: 97ff). I contend that the wage cannot be seen as a price in the standard sense. The wage is not a price that indicates scarcity of labour services. That being said, it is certainly a price in the sense advocated in the previous sections, that is, a monetary tag that is assigned by market actors to certain goods, in this case, labour services, which affects market clearing on the labour market. Therefore, it plays a central role in establishing the global balances in market relations. But it does not equilibrate the 'labour market' in the standard sense (for a related view in macroeconomic terms, see Pasinetti 1993: 15ff).

This is straightforward to see if we consider the role of uncertainty. Wage contracts have the function to reduce uncertainty for the suppliers of labour, who could otherwise be independent entrepreneurs. Therefore, it seems plausible to assume that the need for uncertainty reduction also played an essential role in the emergence of the firm. From this perspective, the firm expresses a temporary guarantee of a certain income flow to its employees. This entails a considerable economic risk for those actors who guarantee those flows, because they have to be covered by the future income generated by the firm. So, we are back with our temporal analysis of the market process: A firm has to conclude contracts on the input side and even pay certain inputs, in particular labour, before it generates any income from selling outputs on the market. So, a firm shifts and aggregates risks at a particular point. These are the owners of the firm. Typically, the owners of the firm are those actors who claim the residual profit which remains after deducting all guaranteed income flows. This includes wages and interest, in the first place, and all other long–term contractual commitments in purchasing inputs.

This arrangement creates an intricate problem: How to determine the level of those certain income flows? There are two issues here. One is the problem of measurement; the other is the problem of the uncertainty of future productivity. The two are related. Regarding the measurement issue, we can gain one principled insight in considering the relationship between the possibility of measurement and the contractibility of a service. The assignment of a price tag to a service requires that the output can be measured in some way. There are two ways of measurement. One is to measure the output in terms of the contribution to the firms output, for example a piece rate system. However, this does not directly relate the input with the monetary evaluation of the output. In fact, relating monetary inputs with monetary outputs directly would eventually result in organizing the firm in profit centres which would come close to independent firms. The problem is that this is mostly impossible. The other possibility is to rely on market valuations in order to measure the value of the labour input. Clearly, market values cannot reflect the output in the context of the particular firm. But even more important, as we have seen, there are certain services that cannot be measured by markets at all.

The two aspects converge in case of one particular kind of labour which today is called ‘managerial work’, and which closely relates with entrepreneurial work. The classical Coasian approach to the ‘market vs. firm’ dichotomy posits that firms are able to conduct transactions which cannot be conducted via markets, for reasons of transaction costs. But one can think of firms also in another way, namely that they are a solution to make entrepreneurial inputs tradable. The argument runs in the following way (strongly influenced by Casson 1997). As we have seen, there are certain fundamental limits to arbitrage in markets, which are defined according to the non-tradable nature of transactional capabilities with reference to uncertain market opportunities. Now, we can define the essence of a firm as being a certain transactional regime which combines different inputs which have properties that make them difficult to measure directly via market valuation (compare Barzel 1989). The most important of these inputs is entrepreneurial work proper. Entrepreneurial work is just this, the capability to combine inputs in a way to make a firm profitable. But this implies that the firm makes those inputs tradable, as the profit of a firm is the way to measure the entrepreneurial input indirectly. This follows from the fact that the entrepreneur does not only fix the combination of inputs, but also agrees about the value of inputs which receive certain incomes, in particular wages. From this it follows that there is an inherent reason why entrepreneurs should be the owners of the firm, and hence the receivers of the residual income, that is the profit: Because this fulfils the function to make entrepreneurial inputs measurable on markets. In other words, profits measure the result of the transaction of combining all other priced inputs into one coherent whole, the firm.

I think that only this argument can explain why presumably one of the central innovations in modern capitalism was the institution of the legal person and hence of corporate actors, which includes many other institutions such as limited liability. Once a legal person can assume the role of an actor in networks, this organization can become an accounting unit keeping balances with other actors. By this, the market system develops an emergent function, namely the possibility to evaluate a non-measurable input, entrepreneurial labour, by means of profits of the corporate actor, that is a monetary magnitude. By implication, this introduced the tradability of firms, which also turns entrepreneurial work tradable. Hence, I argue that the modern firm is a specific and unique expression of the monetary economy. The firm is a solution to the problem of making non-tradable transactional capabilities tradable. These capabilities are the essence of the notion of entrepreneurship.

8.6.2. Limitations to mobility of labour and corporate governance

This view clearly reflects the fact that there is a deep connection between two essential markets in modern economies, the labour market and the capital market, that is the financial markets. This is mostly discussed in the context of the corporate governance issue, which arises when the entrepreneurial function is mostly realized by non-owners in the legal sense, that is professional managers. Again, the same argument applies here: Firms make managerial services tradable, because the market for managers suffers from severe constraints on measurement via market prices. In this context, it is essential to realize that precisely via the interaction of the labour market and the capital market, and via the corporate governance institutions and practices, the market becomes performative in another sense as discussed before. To make this point very clear, it is useful to consider the recent debates over shareholder value and related issues in improving corporate governance. This relates with the issue of the performativity of accounting systems that I discussed previously.

The shareholder value principle is related by many observers with the financialization trend in contemporary capitalism (Krippner 2005). Then, a firm corresponds to a portfolio of monetary assets, in particular equity, and owners would like to maximize the returns to these assets, but not to the firm proper; actually, the very notion of ROI can only be defined in monetary terms. The same set of monetary assets can correspond to an infinite combination of inputs into an infinite set of possible firms. Therefore, the question would be which combination is the most profitable one. The answer requires being able to measure the value of the firm, which is possible if the shares of the firm are traded on markets for equity, such as stock markets. However, once equity is traded, a new phenomenon appears: the value of the stocks as compared to the actual profitability of a company. Both are monetary quantities, but the former relates firstly, to future expectations, and secondly, is a social network market because there is fundamental uncertainty about the future value of companies. From this follows that actual profitability and market value can diverge considerably, even to the extent that the value of shares increases when losses are realized (a typical phenomenon of dotcoms is that shares can rise in value without companies even producing profits in the early years).

The fundamental problem of this construction is that it stays in tension with the principle that firms are risk transformers, that is, that they create certain income streams for the majority of employees. As it has been emphasized repeatedly in the literature, there is a considerable difference between the mobility of capital and the mobility of labour.

- Firstly, there are many constraints on the mobility of labour as compared to capital, although this is not as straightforward as it seems. In both cases there can be strong impact of regulatory conditions, such that the tradability of capital across borders, in particular, can be severely curtailed. In comparison, we know from history that under certain conditions of stress, labour can be highly mobile. One of the paradoxes of modern economic growth is that national jurisdictions tended to increase the mobility of capital but to decrease the mobility of labour via immigration controls. However, there are also principled network constraints that work for capital to a certain degree, but with emphasis for labour. We know that even international capital flows are still influenced by network features such as language and ethnicity, or, in general historical legacies (survey in Guiso et al. 2006). But in the case of labour the constraints of spatial mobility result from the fact that in modern economies, ownership to the labour services is exclusively belonging to the individual (prohibition of slavery). However, labour services cannot be dissociated from the person, so that all network constraints that operate for a person also work for labour services. Spatial mobility of persons is also constrained for other reasons, such as local identities, shared languages or certain properties of other markets, such as real estate markets. Therefore, labour markets show very different degrees of integration (compare the US and Europe).

- Secondly, the tradability of labour also depends essentially on the possibility to measure the labour output exactly. This requires a relatively high degree of context–independence of labour input in firms. Consider two different regimes. In one regime, individual labour productivity depends on the labour inputs of others in the firm, that is, there is a high level of externalities (Kremer's 1993 'O–ring' structure). Further, employees develop a large stock of knowledge specific to a firm that leverages those externalities. In this case, labour productivity will systematically differ across firms, and will depend on tenure with the firm. In the other regime, it is straightforward to measure the individual input, for example, because piece rates are implemented. There is no strong impact of the contributions of other workers to the individual contribution. Further, skills are generic and unspecific to the firm, which means that workers can easily switch between similar occupations in different firms, without any loss of embedded capabilities. Comparing the two different regimes, it is evident that in the former, the labour market will show much more long-term employment contracts and low inter–firm mobility of workers. In the second regime, the labour market will be much more fluid. To a certain degree, we could say that the second case approaches the ideal of the wage as a price on the labour market, whereas in the first scenario the wage will be disconnected from the labour market but will reflect the profitability of the firms. In the real world, the patterns will mix. For example, in many economies we observe status differences in the labour market, such as between large corporations and SME, or formal vs. informal labour markets.
- Thirdly, transactions on the labour market imply the transformation of a voluntary network relation into a coercive one. If I sell my labour service to a firm, the purpose is to subordinate my service to another person. For many reasons, this person cannot control my behaviour fully, so that there is always quality uncertainty with the labour input that is actually contributed. In particular, there is the fundamental problem that even if I sell my labour input, the fulfilment of my contractual obligation may in turn depend on the context in the firm. This problem is tricky indeed, because this does not only involve externalities and other issues mentioned previously, but even the incentive structure as such. Imagine the situation that I complain about my superior that she does not set the proper incentives which are necessary to elicit my mandated labour output.

I argue that all the solutions to these problems are performative in the strict sense. In particular, there is even an impact of economic theory on the performatives. This is most obvious in the context of corporate governance theories. Most modern corporate governance theories build on the assumptions of economic rationality and opportunism; therefore argue that strong constraints and strong pecuniary incentives are necessary to align the behaviour of managers with the interests of their owners. However, there are many organizations which are highly successful and which are sustainable on the basis of other assumptions, such as the civil service, churches or universities. The theories based on principal–agent theory directly connect with the shareholder value principle in using monetary incentives which are intended to align the incentives of managers with those of the owners, that is shareholders. Clearly, this involves another principal–agent problem, namely whether shareholders are sufficiently motivated to monitor managerial behaviour if they have the possibility to sell the shares. There are many reasons to believe that this motivation is limited, as there are the typical problems of large scale groups in terms of information externalities and free rider issues.

8.6.3. The performativity of incentive systems

Considering this, we can say that the corporate governance regime is contingent on certain combinations of networks and actors' features in the sense of distributed agency as developed in Chapters Four and Six, in particular. The principal–agent approach does not consider the possibility of systematic variations across actors in terms of their 'institutionally guided behavioural patterns'. For example, consider an agent that is highly intrinsically motivated. There are many results from psychological research that pecuniary incentive systems can even crowd out this intrinsic motivation (Frey 1997; Deci et al. 1999). Especially, incentive systems can jeopardize the willingness to cooperate (Bowles and Polonía-Reyes 2012). However, this means that the corporate governance regime that was intended to solve a perceived incentive problem actually contributes to its creation (see for example James 2005; Falk and Kosfeld 2006). This happens via two channels. Firstly, intrinsically motivated persons lose this motivation when working under this regime, but perhaps even more important, intrinsically motivated persons will not choose this segment of the labour market. That means, there is a self–selection effect through which the performativity of the entire system is supported, because only individuals with the appropriate IGPR structure will move into those career patterns. This means, on the other hand, that another model of corporate governance may change this selection process in a way that intrinsically motivated people may keep with the corporate track.

Figure 8.9 Wages as signs

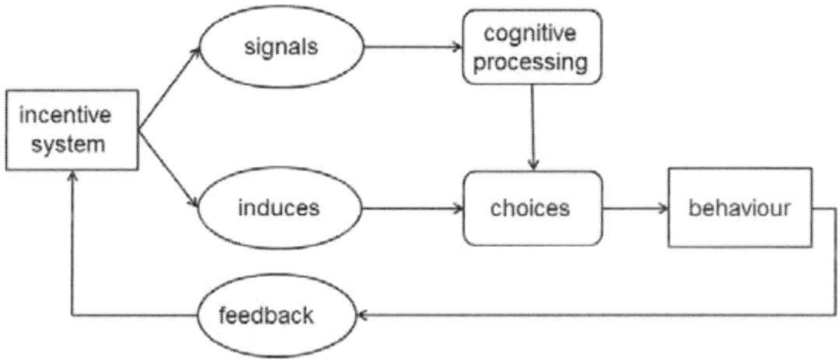

(a)

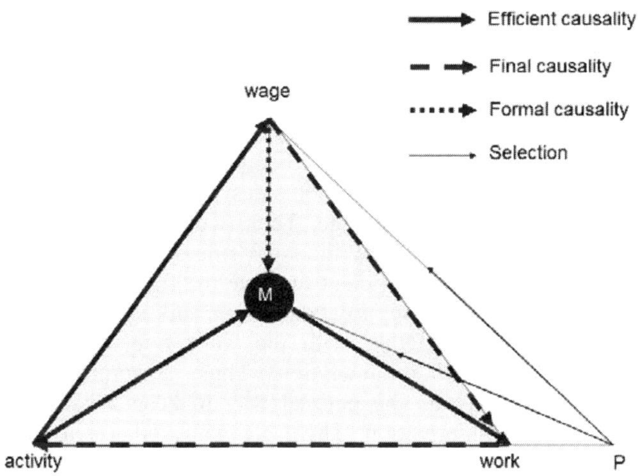

(b)

Note: Incentive systems (a) always have two different effects. One is to causally induce a particular behaviour; the other is to convey information that the designer of the system has about the environment in which it is implemented. Especially, incentive systems signal information about the types of actors in the population in which they apply. Thus, actual behaviour is triggered by the confluence of both determinants. This can be analysed semiotically (b): There is a set of activities of actors which is channelled towards the generation of work related to a particular purpose. This is induced efficient–causally by the activity, but the ultimate effect is determined by the role of the wage as a sign that enables information processing about the work environment.

These effects go back on the fact that all incentive systems operate bimodally, that is, they have effects that work via certain mechanisms in eliciting behaviour, and at the same time the incentive system is a sign that classifies those mechanisms in a particular way (figure 8.9). So, for example, if an incentive system includes strong pecuniary rewards for individuals, this works on the reward mechanisms of the human brain, as we have seen in Chapter Four, as money is a strong incentive, thus eliciting a certain behaviour. However, at the same time the incentive system is a sign that transfers information about the context of the labour contribution; in particular, this sign might signal that all members of the firm are highly opportunistic and hence need to be incentivized in this form (Sliwka 2007). Then, the incentive system might fail to elicit the required labour effort, because the motivation for opportunism is even enhanced, as a consequence of decreasing confidence into the willingness to cooperate of others. This has immediate consequences for the analysis of wages: In the context of firms, wages as signs have different functions than on labour markets. The question is how these functions are reconciled.

Akerlof and Shiller (2009: 97ff) emphasize the relationship between fairness and the labour market which is mediated via the internal organization of firms and the role of the wage. A classic is Akerlof (1982): The basic idea is that firms and workers entertain a relation of gift exchange. The firm gives a wage to the worker exceeding the prevailing market wage, which is perceived as a gift on both sides; that means, the market is supplemented by reciprocal exchange. Then, workers will feel obliged to return more effort than required by the work rules. So, the point is that the wage as a market wage is insufficient to solve the firm–internal monitoring problem. In this case, it is wrong to assume that work effort will necessarily and unequivocally vary together with the wage rate and the extent of pecuniary mechanisms of remuneration. Thus, a combination of gift exchange and wage may be the optimal way to keep a balance between extrinsic and intrinsic motivation. There are many other reasons why the wage as such may not be the proper incentive mechanism, especially in more complex tasks, which also involve multi-tasking (for a practically minded discussion, see Roberts 2004). This is particularly true, if, as we have discussed repeatedly, there are substantial positive externalities between the tasks of different people, such that the single contribution cannot be targeted unequivocally.

It is interesting to notice that in this case we have the possibility of 'counterperformativity' (MacKenzie 2006). On the one hand, the remuneration systems are performative because the relationship between intrinsic and extrinsic motivation is complex and allows for a manifold of constitutive rules, such as the emphasis on bonus systems in the context of the 'financialization' regime in recent financial capitalism. However, this does not necessarily imply that the desired effects on behaviour actually follow, because there can be negative effects, as we have seen. Counterperformativity is salient from increased frequencies of managerial misconduct in the recent years. Further, we can even show that these effects of performativity include the role of economics, as discussed in section 1. Ghoshal (2005) criticizes the American business schools and argues that those schools teach a particular economic paradigm in understanding human behaviour which contributes to the diffusion of behavioural models for which that paradigm proposes certain governance schemes to avoid the negative consequences. Thus, in my sense, business schools play an important role in the performativity of the corresponding economic system (in more detail, Herrmann-Pillath 2013).

As a result, we can state that there are systematic relations between the labour market and the capital market in two respects, namely the relationship between employees and the firm, and the corporate governance in relation to managerial work. In particular, aside from the financialization regime, regimes exist where long–term relations between asset owners and firms go together with more stable employment relations. This also affects the internal hierarchy between managers and workers, which will tend to be more participatory. This stylized comparison between two regimes owes much to the classical analysis of the 'A–firm' versus the 'J–firm' by Aoki (1988). Aoki argues that the American and the Japanese economy (until the recent 'lost decade') manifest distinct differences in the complementarity of labour and capital markets because the organization of knowledge in firms is different. This is not necessarily resulting into differences in economic performance, because there are serious problems in assessing the endogeneity of efficiency measure (compare the extensive discussion in Aoki 2001), but certainly results into differences in the material specialization patterns of different economic systems.

Interestingly, this point has also been vindicated by research in entirely different theoretical settings, such as Grossman and Maggi (2000) on international trade and specialization patterns on the country level (compare Haskel et al. 2012). The shared perspective is that there are different mappings between knowledge structures and product categories, that is the nexus between input and output markets. Compare products for which the ingenuity of single entrepreneurs and inventors is essential, and where the entire production process is highly standardized, with products which are very complex and need constant adaptations to customer needs and flexible organization of production: The two technologies have different implications for the organization of labour in the firm. In the first case, work can be highly standardized and hence, for example, can be outsourced easily, whereas the profitability of the firm depends essentially on the knowledge advantage of its leaders. The best example for this sort of firm is the US high tech industry, where firms such as Apple are actually networks of allied companies in which certain standardized production processes take place. The other regime can be found in complex investment goods industries or most advanced car production, where knowledge is more dispersed across the production processes, and competiveness relies on highly specific and complementary skills of workers. In this case, standardization of labour is less relevant, leading to patterns of organisation outlined in the main text. An excellent example for this divergence is the long run development of the German economy as compared to the American economy, where Germany developed a distinct pattern of industrial organization in which a broad educational basis of middle level managers and technicians is essential, and firms offer long-term employment perspectives, part of the model of 'Rhenish capitalism' (for an excellent historical discussion, see Abelshauser 2003, and on the general framework of management and education in Germany see Armbrüster 2005).

Aoki (1988) makes the point that is widely recognized in the 'variety of capitalism' literature that these interdependences between technology, education and firm organization directly affect the organization of capital markets, because firms of the 'J–firm' type, similar to the German type, will manifest at least implicit mechanisms of closer cooperative relations between workers and management which limit the role of arm's length capital markets in corporate governance. Instead, relational finance with banks that also accumulate more specific knowledge about the firms will be the more efficient solution. Aoki (2010) generalizes this way of thinking and argues that corporate governance and financial structure need to match with specific patterns of the division of knowledge in firms: That means, the observed institutions reflect the nature of distributed cognition across firms and industries. This argument reinforces the previous point on the performativity of incentive systems: Certain corporate governance regimes also set incentives for knowledge accumulation, which feed back on the economic performance of these regimes.

This also implies that firms and economic systems in general are rooted in certain conceptions of the identities of different actors who interact and transact, since these identities reflect the patterns of distributed cognition. For example, there are fundamental differences across different systems as far as the notion of the 'manager' is concerned (Holden 2002). In the traditional twentieth century German model most managers were industry experts, very often engineers who have a deep understanding of the technological issues. In the US American model, this applies for the new ventures as well, but less so for the sustainable operations. Managerial skills are perceived to be industry unspecific because they are seen as being related with the capability to manage the monetary side of a company. This also applies for the employees in general.

8.6.4. Fairness and wages as institutions

This leads us back to the fundamental paradox of the labour market, relinquishing control about a part of a person voluntarily. Relations between different actors in a firm are power relations involving different degrees of coercion, even though in a civilized form, though certainly including commands and other directives, and even threats to household livelihood, in the shape of lay-offs. Power relations, however, face the fundamental limitation to exert full control over labour effort. This is particularly true if labour productivity is heavily context dependent, so that a clear assignment of responsibility is not possible. This implies that the firm cannot be just interpreted as a system of implicit market exchange (the firm as a 'nexus of contracts') (for the alternative view on 'contested exchange,' see Bowles and Gintis 1993). The firm is a system of power, and as such, many non-market determinants of network interactions come into play (Marglin 1991; Van den Steen 2010 is a modern economic approach that focuses on the firm as organizational framework to establish managerial authority). It seems, however, that there is one generic conclusion that links the two domains. This is that the conjunction of voluntary and coercive actions can only lose its paradoxical nature if the firm is constructed as a cooperative venture in which the contributions of the different actors are mutually recognized not only on economic, but also ethical terms. This is why many observers of successful entrepreneurs emphasize that they do not only exercise business leadership, but also moral leadership. This is one way how ethics directly affects the operations of markets.

One dimension across which the paradoxical relationship between forced and voluntary exchange is mediated is via the notion of 'fairness'. Within the firm, the structure of wages actually is matched with a status hierarchy. As we have seen in previous chapters, status is a fundamental category in human behaviour. Firms as network configurations with power differentials establish status relations across which exchange takes place. These exchanges, however, are not market exchange by definition. Hence, it is not possible to interpret the wage that the firm pays to its employees as a direct reflection of the labour market relations. The wage regulates a specific exchange within the firm that is governed by status differences. But this wage is public in the sense of a contractual artefact, and as such it is the only wage that is observable on the market, barring constraints on the diffusion of that information. There is no other wage than the wages concluded in contractual relations between workers and firms.

So, what is the function of the wage on the labour market? I posit that the wage rate establishes reference points for signalling fairness principles across firms (in the sense of Bolton and Ockenfels 2000); this clearly establishes the wage as an institution, analogously to our previous analysis of the interest rate, but with different context and content. Within a firm, the status hierarchy defines the wage as a relational value. This means, employees consider wages in terms of the relative positions in the wage scale, and consider fairness in terms of whether the wage scales reflect the exchange relations across the status hierarchy properly. This is a major explanation for the observation in recent times that many people complained about the increasing wage gap between top level management and workers. Economists claim that this is just reflecting the dynamics of the labour market for managerial services, so cannot be seen as being 'unfair'.

However, fairness principles mainly refer to the firm–internal exchange relations, as they relate with status, and are then transferred to the assessment of similar positions across the labour market. Then, the labour market also assumes the role of a reference point for comparing firm–specific wage scales. Indeed, fairness principles also apply for the external labour market, where another kind of status hierarchy works, which focuses on skills and human capital.

Akerlof and Kranton (2001, 2005) show that these effects root in the phenomenon that I have scrutinized extensively in Chapter Four, namely human individuals have an identity (section 4.5). This identity is embedded into a network of externalities in the different groups to which the individuals belong, such that decisions and events that affect one individual will always also affect another individual. This fact is one of the most important reasons why work effort is not always an individual phenomenon, but strongly influenced by the reference groups. Groups of workers establish shared norms of appropriate work effort, which cannot be changed by an exogenous pecuniary incentive system, because deviations will affect the identity of the workers negatively. The externalities work across different groups, depending on the context. For example, people might perceive relative levels of wages across different occupational groups or across different individuals in the firm. In all these cases, perceptions of relative status can prevail over the effects on the individual position. This status hierarchy is the deeper reason for the prevalence of fairness notions in assessing the wage structure.

To abridge a complicated argument, it is highly misleading to interpret the wage as a price for labour services on the labour market. However, this does not mean that the price does not affect market–clearing. But the driving forces of establishing a certain wage as a price are not the forces of supply and demand. Once a price is established, it may clear the market or not. However, the measurement of market clearing is a problem of its own sake, because, referring to the standard supply and demand picture, a price that is not market–clearing will also affect the supply and demand schedules. For example, a high wage might attract workers to search for a job who would not wish to work at a lower price. That means, unemployment at this high wage is not simply unemployment because of the reluctance of firms to hire those workers, but also reflects the expansion of labour supply. These two quantities are impossible to distinguish at a given wage rate.

This can be analysed in the standard supply and demand diagram (figure 8.10), yielding the interesting result that labour market conditions are performative, too. This is because the effects of the wage as an institution on market clearing are mediated via the behavioural changes induced by this wage. In standard macroeconomic analysis, this refers to the distinction between 'voluntary' and 'involuntary' unemployment. If the wage rate as an institution lies above the market–clearing wage, this means that there is a number of people who would work at a lower wage, so are involuntarily unemployed. But at this wage, there is also a number of people who want to work, but would not work at the market–clearing wage. These are voluntarily unemployed. As a consequence, labour market conditions cannot be 'objectively' determined relative to a hypothetical 'equilibrium wage', as it is done by standard analysis. The labour market conditions are performative, both with relation to the aggregate level, and in relation to the role of the wage as incentive in firms.

Figure 8.10 Performativity of labour market conditions

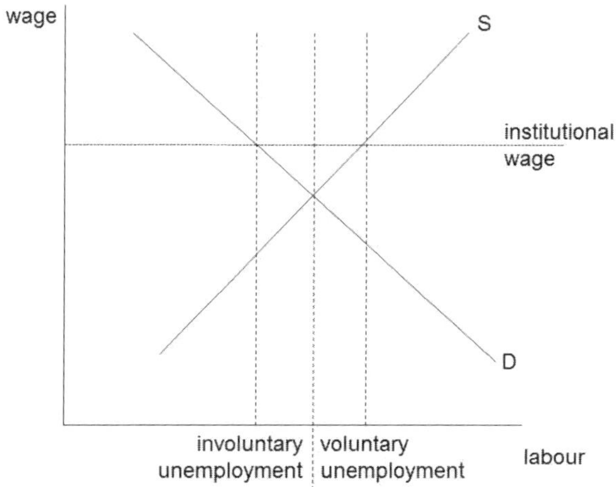

Note: In the standard supply and demand conception of market clearing, a wage rate that lies above the market clearing wage results into unemployment. However, this unemployment consists of both involuntary and voluntary unemployment; that means, there is 'overshooting' of unemployment relative to the hypothetical market–clearing wage. So, labour market conditions become performative. As the wage is an institution, there is a low probability that its exogenous determinants will drive the wage exactly to the market–clearing value.

As a result of this section, we can now state that two essential prices in the human economy related to two essential inputs of the production process, labour and capital, namely wages and interest rates, are determined exogenously in networks of interactions and have the nature of institutions. Interest rates reflect coordinated states of expectations of network actors; wages reflect fairness principles, status orders and firm–specific solutions to incentive systems in networks of human actors which manifest firms as emergent phenomena of distributed cognition. The standard supply and demand model of the labour market may apply for spot–markets of labour services in pre-industrial economies or the agricultural sector in developing economies, but certainly fails to grasp the complex conditions of firms and markets in the modern economy.

8.7. MARKETS AND GENERAL EVOLUTION

8.7.1. Money, credit and growth

So far, we have seen that the different insights gained in the previous chapters have a number of fundamental implications for the analysis of markets. In the naturalistic view, markets are artefacts with a physical structure, and all phenomena that are focused by economic analysis are physical, such as prices: A price is an observer relative fact with a material essence. This view is traced back by evolutionary analysis to the emergence of one particular artefact, money, the existence of which is the causal root of most phenomena which are deemed to be 'economic' ones with reference to the general domains of networks, institutions and technology. Although this seems to be quite obvious, the consequences for economic analysis are not yet fully explored.

One central consequence is that the direction of causal analysis in standard economic analysis needs to be reversed: Prices are not the result of economic forces that tend towards equilibrium, and hence are effects, but are causes that in turn result from a manifold of non-market forces, which can be traced back to the insights gained in the previous chapters. This is particularly true for two prices that can be duly regarded as being pivotal in modern economies, the interest rate and the wage rate. In both cases, it is misleading to approach these prices in terms of the standard supply and demand paradigm. Yet, we can certainly apply the concept of market clearing: We observe situations, in which there are no indicators of excess demand or supply, and others, where we observe them. But it is misleading, again, to assume that these forces result in the appropriate changes of the prices that would necessarily end up in 'equilibrium'. Very often, it is most reasonable to summarize the non-market forces that affect market clearing via prices as 'institutions'; so, for example, the wage rate is a complex institution that mediates the different functions of wages in different domains, such as internal organization of firms, external allocation of labour via markets, or the relative wage as indicator of status.

Now, in this naturalistic approach to markets one essential aspect is still missing that seems to be a unique feature of the modern economy, mostly dubbed 'capitalism': this is economic growth. In this final section, I am going to explore the relationship between markets and growth. The central causal intermediary is credit. The relationship between money and credit is fundamental for the possibility of sustainable growth. Here, we can establish the ultimate relationship between markets and general evolution. Historically, the emergence of modern forms of money coincided with the transition to industrialization, firstly in Britain. In fact, when I compared China and Britain in the previous chapters, I left one important part of the story out of the picture, namely that China did not continue with the institution of paper money, based on trade credit, after it had emerged for the first time in human history in the Song and Yuan periods. Economic growth in China during the last Qing dynasty was driven by the inflow of silver via the trade balance with European countries, in particular Britain. This was a genuinely macroeconomic effect, which resulted into a slow inflation and growth until the trade balance was abruptly reversed because of exploding Opium trade in the beginning of the nineteenth century. So, we can safely assume that the failure of China to industrialize was also related to the monetary fetters resulting from the absence of a modern monetary and credit system.

This example demonstrates that (modern) economic growth is fundamentally dependent on the possibility of the growth of the aggregate quantity of money via the creation of credit, which is just the expression of the growth of valued transactions in networks. If we analyse growth in terms of the growth of energetic throughputs, as it was done in Chapter Seven, this means that there is an aggregate correspondence between the evolution of the monetary economy and the workings of the MPP and MEP. This aggregate correspondence results from the fact that credit is the necessary condition for the expansion of the productive capital stock in the economy via entrepreneurial actions. The growth of the productive capital stock channels the energetic throughputs, and changes the thermodynamic conversion efficiency via technological innovation. Then, we realize that market competition reflects Lotka's principle, as it creates the selective forces which drive the entrepreneurial decisions. In other words, if we go back to the general co-evolutionary framework in figure 7.2, markets seen in terms of the entire market system are an artefact of cultural evolution which plays the essential role in establishing the peculiarly human niche created by the complex division of labour. In this niche, competitive processes unfold which follow the same evolutionary principles as general evolution, an idea that has been pursued by Evolutionary Economists from very early stages onwards (for a seminal approach, see Alchian 1977). This formal homology implies that Lotka's principle holds on different co-evolutionary levels: In general evolution, selection favours trajectories which result in increasing energetic throughputs, and in market evolution, technologies and collectives of firms evolve along trajectories that manifest the same property (compare Buenstorf 2000, though with less claims on generality).

This view has few precursors in economics, apart from ecological economics (for an overview, see van den Berg 2007). One outstanding exception is Binswanger's (2006) analysis of the 'growth spiral', which contains a number of foundational insights which I also include in my analysis. Especially, this relates with the following elements of his theory, cast into the concepts of this book:

- Firstly, money makes an essential difference in defining network relationships of exchange. All essential components of economic theories strictly spoken relate with monetary magnitudes, such as prices and price–based quantities, such as assets. As we have seen, this overturns many fundamental assumptions of economics, such as establishing the primacy of absolute prices over relative prices, and hence making the separation between the real and the monetary sphere of the economy obsolete.
- Secondly, money introduces new emergent possibilities of action, but also generates new problems to be solved in evolutionary processes. In particular, this refers to the relationship between present actions and future consequences and related actions. The existence of money implies a particular temporal sequencing of network relationships which defines basic problems of economics, such as in explaining investment. In this view, all action directed towards market opportunities is investment into uncertain future opportunities mediated by monetary relationships, in particular credit.
- Thirdly, as a result of these new phenomena, the existence of money implies a particular pattern of growth that is triggered by the profit motive which goes back on the reign of fundamental uncertainty over sequencing market actions. Economic growth happens because all actors struggle to avoid falling below a profit threshold which is reflecting the need to pay for actor's willingness to take risk.
- Fourthly, Binswanger relates this growth process with energetic throughputs as a necessary condition for enabling the material effects of profit–oriented expansion of economic opportunities. The complement of energetic throughputs is the role of creative imagination in developing new wants and new technologies via entrepreneurial action.

So, the major difference between my approach and Binswanger's is that I present a fully-fledged evolutionary analysis of these phenomena, while maintaining his economics framework, especially with reference to money and credit. In a nutshell, I put the entire naturalistic evolutionary theory of knowledge into the place which he assigns to 'imagination'. Then, the most general insight is that the process of economic growth can be directly interpreted as a manifestation of the MPP principles, and hence ultimately the MEPP. In other words, economic growth is an expression of the Second Law in open dynamical systems, and markets are certain network phenomena which enable these manifestations.

In stating this, I refer back to my original distinction between 'the market' and 'the economy'. Markets drive certain processes in the economy which reflect MPP and MEP, and ultimately are physical expressions of these principles, working in the economy in basically the same way as in the larger ecological system, that I have characterized in the concluding section of Chapter Seven (compare Annila and Salthe 2009). Hence, I neatly distinguish between 'the economy' and 'the market'. If I use the term 'market', I actually refer to 'the economy' in the standard meaning. In the evolutionary perspective, 'the economy' encompasses phenomena which go far beyond this notion. For example, 'the economy' in my sense includes all externalities in the Earth System that the economy – 'the market' in my parlance – produces.

8.7.2. Market dynamics and entropic principles

For reaching these insights, two propositions are central. The first is that markets are competitive; the dynamics of market competition corresponds to the MPP. The second is that markets build on the institution of money; money released the fetters for the MPP to work out fully in the context of a social exchange economy in continuously widening the opportunities for transactions because there is no intrinsic upper limit to hold money stocks individually. The second proposition is the precondition for the former. I interpret economic growth in terms of markets driving the physical expression of the MPP.

One interesting consequence of this view is that we do not need to distinguish between markets and the externalities caused by the markets. In the evolutionary view, human technology, as mediated via markets, is the mechanism that results into MPP, independent from the separation between internalized and externalized processes. In the physical process, technology is of course essential, since markets as such cannot produce these physical effects. So the question is how markets drive technological progress in the way that MPP is realized. The direct expression of this duality is the close correlation between urbanization as a phenomenon of network evolution and the expansion of market transactions, epitomized in the role of cities as centres of trade, reaching from trading places in early stages of human civilization to the modern financial centres. Hence, markets are physical structures in space (which was neglected by economics for long, until the revival of the 'New Economic Geography', see for example Fujita et al. 1999); the energetic transformations driven by markets happen in these physical structures. This establishes a reverse causality between market evolution and technological evolution as envisaged in Chapter Seven.

On the aggregate level, the relationship between markets and the fundamental evolutionary principles is established in a straightforward way. Technological progress and the expansion of money and credit go hand in hand in the evolution of the human economy. The intermediate mechanism is the role that the market plays in the generation of new human wants and the corresponding creation of production regimes that increase energetic throughputs. In this view, the expansion of markets into the domain of traditional technologies and social exchange is an expression of MPP on its own (such as the dissolution of traditional peasant economies into modern agriculture). Further, reflecting upon Chapter Seven, we need to recognize that the basic fact of increasing energetic throughputs holds for different production regimes, differing only in terms of the physical expression. In the regime of traditional agriculture, throughput growth mainly was channelled via population growth, this resulting into technologically stationary economies. These economies typically featured high shares of non-market exchange, such as in feudal relationships between owners and producers. With the expansion of markets concomitant to the transition from feudalism to capitalism, this system was transformed into a system featuring income growth and innovation driven by energetic throughputs, leveraged by the discovery of the uses of fossil energy.

The essential role of money is obvious once we approach the market along the lines conceived by Binswanger. Consider an entrepreneur who envisages a new product related to a perceived human want. The entrepreneur has to start production without already receiving income from the market. Therefore, she bears risk. She might need to borrow money to start production, and for this she has to pay interest. If she succeeds, she earns a profit if the profit rate is higher than the interest to be paid. In this simple system, profits are an essential condition for technological change to take place at all. In fact, we need to radicalize this view. Profits mean that the entrepreneur is able to increase her monetary wealth. Considering the emotional anchors of the institution of money, therefore the drive to innovate reflects this fundamental drive to accumulate money. So, technology transforms into a means to generate money, and only in a derivative way in a means to manifest technological functions (this is Veblen's 1914 original point). This fundamental transformation establishes the connection between markets and the MPP, because the insatiable want for money drives the process of technological innovation.

The only other condition that we need is competition. If many entrepreneurs compete, there is always a substantial risk of failure if the productivity of one firm is too low to survive under cost pressure from competition. As this information is not available ex ante, competition requires increasing competitive advantages as far as possible in order to secure a minimal level of profits. This mechanism corresponds to the MPP. In this context, it is important to realize that market competition is not driving economic efficiency in the strict sense, but maximization of relative status, along the lines of Chapter Five.

I have already discussed the role of status previously. At the current point, we can generalize over this in terms of the extension of the generic network concept of status into markets. This is the direct effect of the fact that in markets, the primordial reference for producers is other producers (White 2002). Hence, market competition manifests the Red Queen principle (see Chapter Three, section 3.5.3), as all producers compare themselves with other producers, and the improvement of one automatically deteriorates the position of the other. In this rank order, all producers perceive the continuous pressure to maximize relative status (as reflected, for example, in productivity scales) in order to keep or improve their position. More specifically, this Red Queen effect results from the deflationary effects of productivity growth via competitive investments to reap profits. Market competition creates incentives to lower costs and hence to increase profits by means of productivity increases. However, in a monetary economy this is only possible for the single entrepreneur, but not for the entire economy. Competition drives the lowering of prices that reflects the growth of productivity, and hence reduces profits for the entrepreneurs as a group. Those who cannot follow up with the productivity increase will finally not be able to cover their relatively increasing comparative level of costs. The entrepreneurs who survive under selection need to expand continuously which, under the condition of uncertainty of future technological progress, requires to take risk and hence to mobilize credit. Credit creation drives this entrepreneurial process via the renewal of profit opportunities under the expanding monetary constraints of the market. Thus, in the end the Red Queen effect leads to an on-going pressure to increase productivity. As we know from Chapter Seven, this ultimately is manifest as the increasing levels of energetic throughputs in the entire economy. In other words, markets induce a ratchet effect in the scramble for profit which induced perpetual growth, and growth is the other side of the coin of increasing energetic throughputs. This ratchet effects reflects the fundamental hypercyclic structure of the interaction between the produces and the consumer side in markets with status competition.

The role of status competition is also pivotal for growth of consumption. Status competition creates insatiable needs, as there are always ways to make a distinction towards another individual in a reference group, or in moving across reference groups (for the illuminating example of luxury cars, see Swann 2001). The simplest mechanism to achieve this is to consume goods which are scarce and rare. In traditional societies, these were mainly goods expensive to produce. This remains true today, but there is an additional mechanism: All novelties are rare in the beginning stage of their diffusion. Therefore, novelties obtain the role of status goods, thus driving the process of innovation on the consumer side (vide the Apple manias when new versions of electronic gadgets are released) (for a congenial approach, see Reinstaller and Sanditov 2005).

So, interlocking status competition on the producer and the consumer side drives the process of economic growth. With the growing money supply, and keeping the profit constraint in the average and in the long run, this finds expression in long–run growth of GDP. So, I overturn the conventional economic conception of causality: I argue that the growth of money and credit enables the working of status competition on markets, which drives the process of technological innovation, and ultimately the energetic throughputs, as we have seen in Chapter Seven. Hence, we cannot simply say that energetic throughputs drive growth, but the other way round. Growth, in turn, is not driven by given human needs, but by their endogenous expansion in an economic system that has markets at its core. I summarize this analysis in figure 8.11.

Figure 8.11 Economic growth as evolutionary process

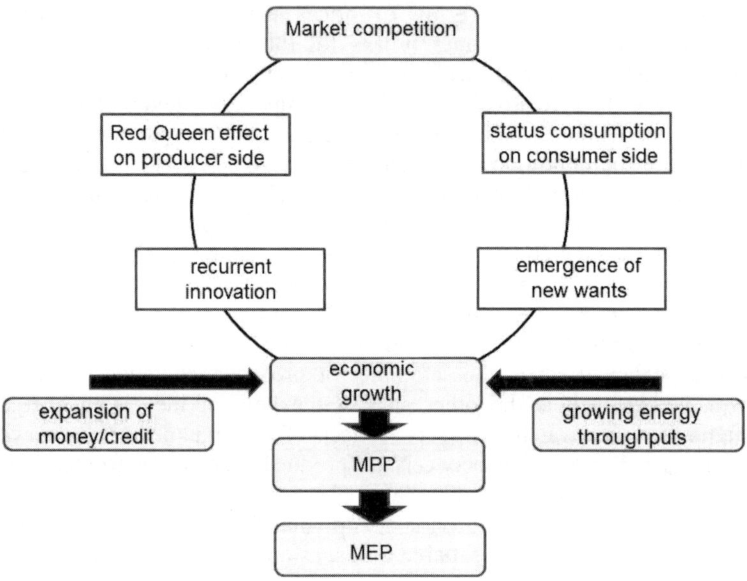

Note: The diagram shows the hypercyclic nature of economic growth in which two forms of status competition mutually leverage their effects: The Red Queen effect in producers' competition on the marketplace drives recurrent innovation, and status competition among consumers drives the emergence of new wants which provide market opportunities for innovation and vice versa. Economic growth must be enabled by the continuous expansion of money and credit necessary to maintain the entrepreneurial investment process under uncertainty, and by the growth of energy throughputs; thus, these are the two sides of a bimodal conception of growth. Growth therefore follows the fundamental evolutionary principles of MPP and MEP.

It is fascinating to observe that this view was already clearly expressed by Adam Smith who explicitly rejected the idea that markets are driven by the concern for 'utility', in the sense of the production of usable goods relative to fixed needs. Smith treated the progress of welfare in material terms as an unintended effect of status competition, and even of the ubiquity of deceit and self–deceit (compare the motto of this chapter). Another classic is Veblen (1899, 1914, 1921) who argued that markets are driven by different 'instincts', of which the desire for status is a most important one, which meets other desires, such as the desire to be efficient and skilful. Veblen believed that the two behavioural drives are actually conflicting, epitomized in the two figures of the 'engineer' and the 'captain of industry'. In market competition, the status-oriented motivation of the latter will prevail, therefore leading to losses in efficiency, but driving insatiable growth. This might entail the conclusion that markets cause over–consumption according to ecological criteria of sustainability (Arrow et al. 2004).

8.7.3. The growth of markets

This argument is not complete in order to fully understand the relationship between MPP and markets. We need to add reference to the Constructal Law. What is the most general aspect of markets in the history of human civilization? Certainly, this is the expansion of network connectivity (McNeill and McNeill 2002: 94ff, 200ff). In this sense, markets have always been present on human networks, a fact which is reflected in the diffusion of artefacts even in very early stages of civilization (McNeill and McNeill 2002: 23). However, primitive markets were sparse, such as emerging in long distance trade, and absent in local exchange relations, such as labour exchange in traditional villages. The major transition in the expansion of markets was the enabling role of money, and since then the growing importance in network interactions.

As we have seen in Chapter Six, there is one way to delimit the scope of economics in way that is congenial to its conventional approach, namely to distinguish between voluntary and forced exchange, the latter being related to violence in the most generic sense. So, the expansion of human networks has always been typically driven by both kinds of exchange, with the voluntary relationships expanding relative to the forced ones. This general idea is useful to make a difference to more specific notions of civilizational development, such as theories about major transitions for example to capitalism. I argue that these transitions refer to more specific institutional arrangements that relate power structures with all forms of exchange, including markets. Typically, this involves conceptualizations of these arrangements in terms of theories. Accordingly, the diffusion of markets in modern times was also related with the diffusion of economics as a theory, as well as certain ideologies that relate with fundamental notions of markets, such as 'liberty' epitomizing the principles of voluntary exchange.

Considering the Constructal Law, this expansion of markets can be conceptualized as the evolution of flow configurations which enhance the capacity of the economy to process matterenergy flows. The fact that markets are more effective than forced exchange relations in achieving this result can be explained by the higher degree of evolvability of markets, classically analysed in the Austrian tradition of economics. Whereas forced exchange constrains the knowledge generation process via the imposed states of subjective knowledge of certain powerful actors, markets allow for the unconstrained exploration of new opportunities by diverse groups of interacting actors, hence allow for much faster population–level knowledge generation. The symbiosis between growth and markets is reflecting this relationship. Network evolution is characterized by the transition from systems with sparse and local connectivity to systems with dense and global connectivity, and therefore also the growth of throughputs. This relationship also justifies the basic idea to measure growth in terms of GDP, as this reflects the market mediated throughputs. At the same time, this also makes clear why GDP fails to reflect adequately the effects of growth on welfare or any other direct measure of human well-being (such as in terms of 'happiness', see Chapter Four, or 'capabilities', see Chapter Five; for an overview, see Fleurbaey 2009). There are important general propositions in the Constructal Law approach which directly apply for markets, such as the need to balance efficiency and evolvability. This directly translates into the applicability of more specific concepts from general evolutionary theory, such as the ascendency measure, on markets: Market evolution typically results into the simultaneous production of information and of information capacity in terms of network overhead. In markets, 'overhead' is observable in supposedly wasteful competition, such as the regular occurrence of bad investments and entrepreneurial failure.

Interestingly, we can refer this analysis back to the Marxian idea of 'commodities'. Then, we can argue that the fundamental role of markets is to transform objects, that is resources, into 'commodities' via assigning prices to them. Hence, the price mechanism is seen as a peculiar semiotic mode in relation to the underlying physical transactions. This semiotic mode implies that certain causal mechanisms of markets govern the evolution of transactions, such as the Red Queen principle in competition. Different from the Marxian view on commodities, the evolutionary analysis refers this transformation to the general principles of MPP and ultimately MEPP. So, the triadic principle takes the position of the Marxian analysis of commodity–money transformations (figure 8.12). On the most general and abstract level, the emergence of prices is seen as a specific mechanism of formal causality that relates physical objects ('resources') with teleonomic structures of market competition. So, goods obtain the function to generate profit. However, in the evolutionary analysis this function refers to the generic MPP principle and thus drives technological evolution which determines the growth of energetic throughputs in the economy.

Figure 8.12 Commodities and MPP

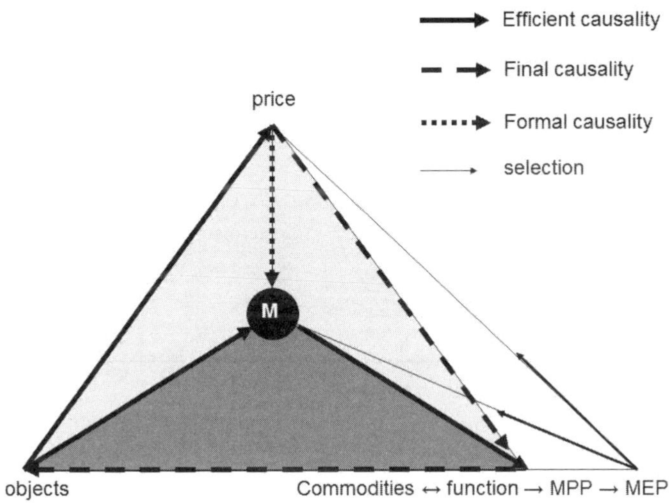

Note: Objects are transformed into commodities via the assignment of prices. Once prices are assigned, objects can become part of market dynamics, such that commodities obtain the function to generate profit, namely monetary flows, in systems were actors specialize on market opportunity. Therefore, 'commoditization' relates functions of objects with the fundamental evolutionary principles, firstly in the context of markets as human niche construction, and secondly relating growth of markets to MPP and MEPP.

This picture needs to be analysed in disaggregate terms by considering the two dimensions of compositional and subsumptive hierarchy (fig. 8.13). Then, we realize that in the compositional hierarchy, markets drive the emergence of new technological functions in the general process of energetic dissipation. These functions are embedded in larger structures which reflect MPP and MEP. In the subsumptive hierarchy, we consider nested semiotic transformations, which build on the emergence of wants and their transformation in the market context into valued opportunities for profit generation. These specific transformations are embedded into larger systemic contexts which define the scope of markets as briefly sketched in the first section.

Figure 8.13 The market system of interpretance

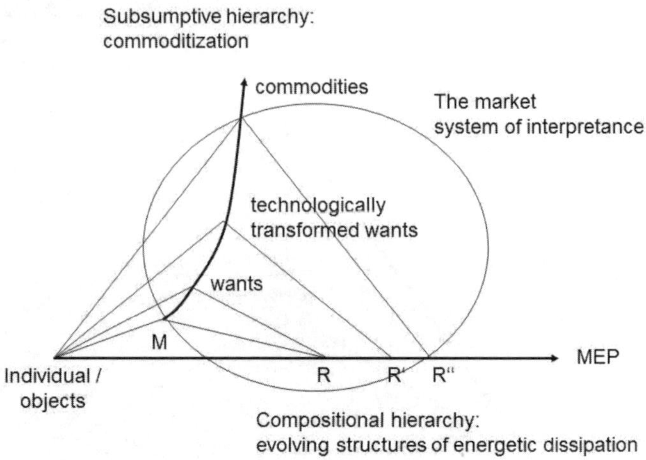

Note: This diagram conflates different levels of the market process and focuses on the matterenergy, hence technology side of market evolution; we can say that markets drive the evolution of wants in the direction of commoditization, that is wants that relate to goods that create profit opportunities on the market. This market–driven technological transformation of wants results into technological structures that speed up and enhance energy dissipation, thus ultimately manifest the MEP Principle.

One important consequence of this view is that markets drive 'commoditization' endogenously. In economics, this view is adopted by the theory of property rights (in classical treatments such as Eggertsson 1990). That means, the market system of interpretance evolves in terms of the increasing inclusiveness of markets; this happens via the institutional transformation of objects into 'commodities' which are defined via configurations of property rights. This is another expression of the performativity of markets (for the example of transforming maritime resources into commodities in this sense, see Holm and Nolde 2007). In the evolutionary approach to markets, this approach has to be seen as a special and limited view on the 'marketization' process discussed in section 1. The more fundamental transition takes place in assigning prices to certain physical items as such, thus opening the way to connecting with the general system of monetary flows in markets. The assignment of property rights is one of the most important ways to make transactions possible once the assignment of prices is enabled. This sequence of causalities is obvious if we consider the fact that societies differ in marketization across different domains of goods: For example, property rights are clearly assigned in case of human organs, but price assignments are mostly tightly constricted so that markets cannot emerge but illegally. On the other hand, prices can be assigned to pollution, but the problem is that transactions are not viable if property rights are not assigned clearly, so that markets can only emerge once new institutions such as emission rights are created. However, without enabling price assignments these markets would not emerge either.

Hence, we can make the general point that commoditization as marketization is the more fundamental process than the emergence of certain property rights regimes. Indeed, the analysis of the firm has already shown that the borderline between market transactions and non-markets interactions is fluid and both stand in a co-evolutionary relationship with each other. For example, the transition from individual rights to patents to firm rights to patents actually reduced the scope of individual property rights in favour of collective property rights represented by the legal person. This was necessary to enlarge the scope of market transactions via the creation of the possibility to evaluate the collective knowledge capital of firms in monetary terms. Similarly, the Whiggish account of the Industrial Revolution that emphasizes the role of privatization of agricultural commons in order to enhance productivity and innovation intensity does not match with the historical record which clearly shows that traditional rural communities increased productivity as well, depending on market incentives. In other words, the commoditization process was sufficient to drive agricultural changes in pre-industrial Britain, whereas the change of the property rights regime was only responding in terms of enhancing the scope of transactions over land as a resource. The same applies today in a case like China, where property rights on land are still collective. Presumably, this regime actually fosters the explosive growth of a 'capitalist' family farm economy in which the important bottleneck is the availability of more advanced TETs, such as organisational means for vertical integration (Huang et al. 2012). So, the property rights regime is a derivative of evolutionary forces that drive marketization, but it is not a prime mover.

So, we can say that economic growth is both growth driven *by* markets and growth *of* markets. This observation makes clear that 'internalization' of externalities does not imply absolute reductions of resource consumption and especially energy throughput. Internalization drives the search for efficiency gains that ultimately aim at profit generation, but also activates the hypercyclic market dynamics that ultimately results into the expansion of resource use. Therefore, markets are the institutional setting in which the evolution of technology takes place as analysed in Chapter Seven. This especially applies to the emergence and expansion of the technosphere. The technosphere is the material expression of human niche construction, which builds on distributed cognition in human networks; the evolution of distributed knowledge is institutionally enabled and channelled via markets.

References

Abbink, K., J. Brandts, B. Herrmann and H. Orzen (2010), 'Intergroup Conflict and Intra–Group Punishment in an Experimental Contest Game', *American Economic Review,* **100**(1), 420–447.

Abelshauser, Werner (2003), *Kulturkampf: Der deutsche Weg in die Neue Wirtschaft und die amerikanische Herausforderung*, Berlin: Kadmos.

Acemoglu, D. and S. Johnson, Simon (2005), 'Unbundling Institutions', *Journal of Political Economy*, **113**(5), 949–995.

Acemoglu, D., S. Johnson, Simon and J. A. Robinson, James A. (2001), 'The Colonial Origins of Comparative Development: An Empirical Investigation', *American Economic Review*, **91**(5), 1369–1401.

Acemoglu, D., S. Johnson and J. A. Robinson (2002), 'Reversal of Fortune: Geography and Institutions in the Making of the Modern World Income Distribution', *Quarterly Journal of Economics*, **117**, 1231–1294.

Ackermann, Rolf (2001), *Pfadabhängigkeit, Institutionen und Regelreform*, Tübingen: Mohr Siebeck.

Adams, F. (2003), 'The Informational Turn in Philosophy', *Minds and Machines*, **13**, 471–501.

Ainslie, George (1992), *Picoeconomics: The Strategic Interaction of Successive Motivational States within the Person*, Cambridge: Cambridge University Press.

Ainslie, George (2007), 'Thought Experiments That Explore Where Controlled Experiments Can't: The Example of Will', in Ross, Don, David Spurrett, Harold Kincaid and G. Lynn Stephens, *Distributed Cognition and the Will. Individual Volition and Social Context*, Cambridge, MA, USA: MIT Press, pp. 169–198.

Akerlof, G. A. (1970), 'The Market for "Lemons": Quality Uncertainty and the Market Mechanism', *Quarterly Journal of Economics*, **84**(3), 488–500.

Akerlof, G. A. (1982), 'Labor Contracts as Partial Gift Exchange', *Quarterly Journal of Economics*, **97**, 543–569.

Akerlof, G. A. and R. E. Kranton (2000), 'Economics and Identity', *Quarterly Journal of Economics*, **CXV**(3), 715–753.

Akerlof, G. A. and R. E. Kranton (2005), 'Identity and the Economics of Organizations', *Journal of Economic Perspectives*, **19**(1), 9–32.

Akerlof, George A. and Robert Shiller (2009), *Animal Spirits: How Human Psychology Drives the Economy, and Why It Matters for Global Capitalism*, Princeton and Oxford: Princeton University Press.

Albert, Hans (1972), *Ökonomische Ideologie und politische Theorie: Das ökonomische Argument in der ordnungspolitischen Debatte*, 2. Auflage, Göttingen: Otto Schwarz.

Albin, Peter S. (1998), *Barriers and Bounds to Rationality: Essays on Economic Complexity and Dynamics in Interactive Systems*, Princeton: Princeton University Press.

Alchian, Armen (1977), *Economic Forces at Work*, Indianapolis: Liberty Press.

Aldrich, Howard (1999), *Organizations Evolving*, London: Sage.

Aldrich, Howard et al. (2008), 'In Defence of Generalized Darwinism', *Journal of Evolutionary Economics*, **18**(5), 577–598.

Alesina, A. and E. La Ferrara (2005), 'Ethnic Diversity and Economic Performance', *Journal of Economic Literature*, **XLIII**(3), 762–800.

Alesina, Alberto and Enrico Spolaore (2003), *The Size of Nations*, Cambridge, MA, USA and London: MIT Press.

Alesina, Alberto, Paola Guiliano and Nathan Nunn (2011), *On the Origins of Gender Roles: Women and the Plough*, http://www.economics.harvard.edu/faculty/alesina/files/Plough_draft_May_2011.pdf, accessed January 25, 2013.

Alessandria, G. and J. P. Kaboski (2011), 'Pricing–to–Market and the Failure of Absolute PPP', *American Economic Journal Macroeconomics*, **3**, 91–127.

Alexander, Richard D. (1979), *Darwinism and Human Affairs*, Seattle and London: University of Washington Press.

Alexander, Richard D. (1987), *The Biology of Moral Systems*, New York: Aldine de Gruyter.

Allen, Robert C. (2009), *The British Industrial Revolution in Global Perspective*, Cambridge: Cambridge University Press.

Amir, O., D. Ariely and Z. Carmon (2008), 'The Dissociation Between Monetary Assessment and Predicted Utility', *Marketing Science*, **27**(6), 1055–1064.

Amundson, Ron (2001), 'Adaptation and Development: On the Lack of Common Ground', in Orzack, Steven Hecht and Elliott Sober (eds), *Adaptationism and Optimality*, Cambridge et al.: Cambridge University Press, pp. 303–334.

Anderlini, L. and L. Felli (1999), 'Incomplete Contracts and Complexity Costs', *Theory and Decision*, **46**, 23–50.

Anderlini, Luca and Leonardo Felli, Leonardo (1998a) *Costly Coasian Contracts*, Discussion Paper, London School of Economics and Political Science No. 362.

Anderlini, Luca and Leonardo Felli (1998b), *Costly Bargaining and Renegotiation*, Discussion Paper, London School of Economics and Political Science No. 361.

Andersen, B. (1999), 'The Hunt for S–Shaped Growth Patterns in Technological Innovation: A Patent Study', *Journal of Evolutionary Economics*, **9**(4), 487–526.

Andersen, Esben Sloth (2002), *The Tree of Industrial Life: An Approach to the Systematics and Evolution of Industry*, http://www.business.aau.dk/evolution/projects/phylo/, accessed January 24, 2013.

Andersen, Esben Sloth (2003), *The Evolving Tree of Industrial Life: An Approach to the Tranformation of European Industry*, http://www.business.aau.dk/evolution/esapapers/esa03/torino.pdf, accessed January 24, 2013.

Andersen, E. S. (2004), 'Population Thinking, Price's Equation and the Analysis of Economic Evolution', *Evolutionary and Institutional Economics Review*, **1**(1), 127–148.

Anderson, J. E. and E. van Wincoop (2004), 'Trade Costs', *Journal of Economic Literature*, **XLII**(3), 691–751.

Andrade, E. (2007), 'A Semiotic Framework for Evolutionary and Developmental Biology', *BioSystems*, **90**, 389–404.
Andreoni, J. and J. M. Rao (2011), 'The Power of Asking: How Communication Affects Selfishness, Empathy and Altruism', *Journal of Public Economics*, **95**, 513–520.
Annila, A. and E. Kuismanen (2009), 'Natural Hierarchy Emerges from Energy Dispersal', *BioSystems*, **95**, 227–233.
Annila, A. and S. N. Salthe (2009), 'Economies Evolve by Energy Dispersal', *Entropy*, 2009, **11**, 606–633.
Annila, A., S. N. Salthe (2010), 'Physical Foundations of Evolutionary Theory', *Journal of Non–Equilibrium Thermodynamics,* **35**, 301–321.
Aoki, Masahiko (1988), *Information, Incentives, and Bargaining in the Japanese Economy*, Cambridge: Cambridge University Press.
Aoki, Masahiko (1996), 'An Evolutionary Parable of the Gains from International Organizational Diversity', in Landau, Ralph, Timothy Taylor and Gavin Wright (eds), *The Mosaic of Economic Growth*, Stanford: Stanford University Press, pp. 247–263.
Aoki, Masahiko (2001), *Toward a Comparative Institutional Analysis*, Stanford: Stanford University Press.
Aoki, M. (2007), 'Endogenizing Institutions and Institutional Change', *Journal of Institutional Economics*, **3**(1), 1–31.
Aoki, M. (2011), 'Institutions as Cognitive Media between Strategic Interactions and Individual Beliefs', *Journal of Economic Behavior and Organization*, **79**, 20–34.
Aoki, Masahiko (2010), *Corporations in Evolving Diversity: Cognition, Governance, and Institutions*, Oxford: Oxford University Press.
Ariely, D. and M. I. Norton (2007), 'How Actions Create – Not Just Reveal – Preferences', *Trends in Cognitive Science*, **12**(1), 13–16.
Ariely, D. and M. I. Norton (2009), 'Conceptual Consumption', *Annual Review of Psychology*, **60**, 475–499.
Ariely, D., E. Kamenica and D. Prelec (2008), 'Man's Search for Meaning: The Case of Legos', *Journal of Economic Behavior and Organization*, **67**, 671–677.
Ariely, D., G. Loewenstein, and D. Prelec (2006), 'Tom Sawyer and the Construction of Value', *Journal of Economic Behavior and Organization*, **60**, 1–10.
Armbrüster, Thomas (2005), *Management and Organization in Germany*, Aldershot and Burlington: Ashgate.
Arrighi, Giovanni (2007), *Adam Smith in Beijing: Lineages of the Twenty–First Century*, London and New York: Verso.
Arrow, K. et al. (2004), 'Are We Consuming Too Much?', *Journal of Economic Perspectives*, **18**(3), 147–172.
Arthur, W. Brian (1988), 'Self–Reinforcing Mechanisms in Economics', in Anderson, P., K. Arrow, and D. Pines (eds), *The Economy as an Evolving Complex System*, New York: Addison–Wesley, pp. 9–31.
Arthur, W. B. (1989), 'Competing Technologies, Increasing Returns and Lock–in by Historical Events', *Economic Journal*, **99**, 116–131.
Arthur, W. Brian (2009), *The Nature of Technology: What It Is and How It Evolves*, New York: Free Press.
Arthur, W. Brian, Steven Durlauf, Steven and David Lane (eds) (1997), *The Economy as an Evolving Complex System II*, Reading: Addison–Wesley.

Atkin, Albert (2010), 'Peirce's Theory of Signs', Edward N. Zalta (ed), *The Stanford Encyclopedia of Philosophy* (Winter 2010 Edition), URL = <http://plato.stanford.edu/archives/win2010/entries/peirce–semiotics/>.

Atkins, Peter (2007), *Four Laws That Drive the Universe*, Oxford: Oxford University Press.

Aunger, Robert (ed.) (2000), *Darwinizing Culture: The Status of Memetics as a Science*, Oxford: Oxford University Press.

Aunger, Robert (2002), *The Electric Meme: A New Theory of How We Think*. New York et al.: Free Press.

Aunger, R. (2007), 'A Rigorous Periodization of 'Big' History', *Technological Forecasting and Social Change*, **74**(8), 1164–1178.

Axtell, R. (2005), 'The Complexity of Exchange', *Economic Journal*, **115**(504), F193–F210.

Ayres, Clarence E. (1944), *The Theory of Economic Progress*, Chapel Hill: University of North Carolina Press.

Ayres, Robert U. (1994), *Information, Entropy, and Progress: A New Evolutionary Paradigm*, New York: AIP Press.

Ayres, Robert U. (2005), 'Resources, Scarcity, Technology, and Growth', in Simpson, R. David, Michael A. Toman and Robert U Ayres (eds), *Scarcity and Growth Revisited. Natural Resources and the Environment in the New Millenium*, Washington: RFF Press, pp. 142–154.

Ayres, Robert U. and Leslie W. Ayres, (eds) (2002), *A Handbook of Industrial Ecology*, Cheltenham, UK and Northampton, MA, USA: Edward Elgar.

Ayres, R. U. and B. Warr, Benjamin (2003), 'Exergy, Power and Work in the US Economy', *Energy – The International Journal*, **28**, 219–273

Ayres, R. U. and B. Warr (2005), 'Accounting for Growth: The Role of Physical Work', *Structural Change and Economic Dynamics*, **16**(2), 181–209.

Ayres, Robert U. and Benjamin Warr (2009), *The Economic Growth Engine: How Energy and Work Drive Material Prosperity*, Cheltenham, UK and Northampton, MA, USA: Edward Elgar.

Baaquie, Belal A. (2004), *Quantum Finance: Path Integrals and Hamiltonians for Options and Interest Rates*, Cambridge et al.: Cambridge University Press.

Bacciagaluppi, Guido (2012), 'The Role of Decoherence in Quantum Mechanics', in Edward N. Zalta (ed),*The Stanford Encyclopedia of Philosophy* (Winter 2012 Edition), URL = <http://plato.stanford.edu/archives/win2012/entries/qm–decoherence/>.

Backhouse, R. E. and S. G. Medema (2009), 'On the Definition of Economics', *Journal of Economic Perspectives*, **23**(1), 221–233.

Baecker, Dirk (2000), *Wozu Kultur?* Berlin: Kadmos.

Baeyer, Hans Christian von (2003), *Information: The New Language of Science*, Cambridge, MA, USA and London: Harvard University Press.

Baker, W. E. (1984), 'The Social Structure of a National Securities Market', *American Journal of Sociology*, **89**(4), 775–811.

Balzer, Wolfgang (1982), 'Empirical Claims in Exchange Economics', in Wolfgang Stegmüller, Wolfgang Balzer und Wilfried Spohn (eds), *Philosophy of Economics*, Berlin, Heidelberg and New York: Springer, 16–40.

Bandiera, O. and I. Rasul (2006), 'Social Networks and Technology Adoption in Northern Mozambique', *Economic Journal*, **116**(514), 869–902.

Barabasi, Albert–László (2002), *Linked*, New York: Plume.

Barker, M. J. and R. A. Wilson (2010), 'Cohesion, Gene Flow, and the Nature of Species', *The Journal of Philosophy*, **CVII**(2), 61–79.

Barnes, Barry (1995), *The Elements of Social Theory*, Princeton: Princeton University Press.

Barney, Jay (1991), 'Firm Resources and Sustained Competitive Advantage', *Journal of Management*, **17**(1), 99–120.

Barrow, John D. (1995), 'Theories of Everything', in Cornwell, John (ed.) (1995), *Nature's Imagination. The Frontiers of Scientific Vision*, Oxford, New York and Melbourne: Oxford University Press, pp. 45–63.

Barsalou, L. W. (1999), 'Perceptual Symbol Systems', *Behavioral and the Brain Sciences*, **22**, 577–660.

Barsalou, L. W. (2008), 'Grounded Cognition', *Annual Review of Psychology*, **59**, 617–645.

Barzel, Yoram (1989), *Economic Analysis of Property Rights*, Cambridge: Cambridge University Press.

Basso, Frédéric, Laurent Guillou, and Olivier Oullier (2010), 'Embodied Entrepreneurship: A Sensory Theory of Value', in Stanton, Angela A., Mellani Day and Isabell M. Welpe (eds), *Neuroeconomics and the Firm,* Cheltenham, UK and Northampton, MA, USA: Edward Elgar, pp. 217–234.

Bateson, Gregory (1979*), Mind and Nature: A Necessary Unity*, London: Wildwood House.

Batten, David, John Casti and Roland Thord (eds) (1995), *Networks in Action: Communication, Economics and Human Knowledge*, Berlin: Springer.

Baudrillard, Jean (1970), *La Société de Consommation: Ses mythes et ses structures*, Paris: Gallimard.

Baumol, W. J. (2004), 'Red–Queen Games: Arms Races, Rule of Law and Market Economies', *Journal of Evolutionary Economics*, **14**(2), 237–248.

Beauchamp, J. P. et al. (2011), 'Molecular Genetics and Economics', *Journal of Economic Perspectives*, **25**(4), 57–82.

Bechara, A. and A. R. Damasio (2005), 'The Somatic Marker Hypothesis: A Neural Theory of Economic Decision', *Games and Economic Behavior*, **52**, 336–372.

Becker, Gary S. (1976), *The Economic Approach to Human Behavior*, Chicago: Chicago University Press.

Becker, Gary S. (1996), *Accounting for Tastes*, Cambridge, MA, USA: Harvard University Press.

Bednar, J. and S. Page (2007), 'Can Game(s) Theory Explain Culture? The Emergence of Cultural Behavior Within Multiple Games', *Rationality and Society*, **19**(1), 65–97.

Bejan, A. (2009), 'Science and Technology as Evolving Flow Architectures', *International Journal of Energy Research*, **33**, 112–125.

Bejan, A. and S. Lorente (2006), 'Constructal Theory of Generation of Configuration in Nature and Engineering', *Journal of Applied Physics*, **100**, 041301.

Bejan, A. and S. Lorente (2010), 'The Constructal Law of Design and Evolution in Nature', *Philosophical Transactions of the Royal Society B*, **365**, 1335–1347.

Ben Jacob, E., Y. Shapira and A. I. Tauber (2006), 'Seeking the Foundations of Cognition in Bacteria: From Schrödinger's Negative Entropy to Latent Information', *Physica A*, **359**, 495–524.

Bénabou, R. and J. Tirole (2002), 'Self–Confidence and Personal Motivation', *Quarterly Journal of Economics*, **117**(3), 871–915.

Bénabou, R. and J. Tirole (2004), 'Willpower and Personal Rules', *Journal of Political Economy*, **112**(4), 848–886.

Benhabib, J. and A. Bisin (2005), 'Modeling Internal Commitment Mechanisms and Self–Control: A Neuroeconomics Approach to Consumption–Saving Decisions', *Games and Economic Behaviour*, **52**: 460–492.

Bennett, Charles H. (2003), *Notes on Landauer's Principle, Reversible Computation, and Maxwell's Demon*, arXiv:physics/0210005.

Bentley, R. A. and S. J. Shennan (2003), 'Cultural Transmission and Stochastic Network Growth', *American Antiquity*, **68**(3), 459–485.

Bentley, R. A. et al. (2007), 'Regular Rates of Popular Culture Change Reflect Random Copying', *Evolution and Human Behavior*, **28**, 151–158.

Berger, Suzanne and Ronald Dore (eds) (1996), *National Diversity and Global Capitalism*, Ithaca: Cornell University Press.

Bergman, Mats and Sami Paavola (eds) (2003), *The Commens Dictionary of Peirce's Terms*, http://www.helsinki.fi/science/commens/dictionary.html, accessed January 15, 2013.

Bergstrom, T. C. (2002), 'Evolution of Social Behavior: Individual and Group Selection', *Journal of Economic Perspectives*, **16**(2), 67–88.

Bernbeck, R. (2007), 'The Rise of the State', in Bentley R. A., H.D.G. Maschner and C. Chippendale (eds), *Handbook of Archaeological Theories*, Lanham, MD: AltaMira Press, pp. 533–545.

Bernheim, B. D. (1994), 'A Theory of Conformity', *Journal of Political Economy*, **102**(5), 841–877.

Berridge, K. C. (2009), 'Liking' and 'Wanting' Food Rewards: Brain Substrates and Roles in Eating Disorders', *Physiology & Behavior*, **97**, 537–550.

Bérut, Antoine et al. (2012), 'Experimental Verification of Landauer's Principle Linking Information and Thermodynamics, *Nature*, **483**, 187–190.

Besley, T. and T. Persson (2009), 'The Origins of State Capacity: Property Rights, Taxation, and Politics', *American Economic Review*, **99**(4), 1218–1244.

Bettencourt, L. A. et al. (2007), 'Growth, Innovation, Scaling, and the Pace of Life in Cities', *Proceedings of the National Academy of Sciences*, **104**(17), 7301–7306.

Betzig, L. and S. Weber (1993), 'Polygyny in American Politics', *Politics and the Life Sciences*, **12**(1), 45–52.

Betzig, Laura (1986), *Despotism and Differential Reproduction: A Darwinian View of History*, New York: Aldine.

Betzig, Laura (2008), 'Hunting Kings', *Cross–Cultural Research*, DOI 10.1177/1069397108317488.

Beugelsdijk, S. (2006a), 'A Note on the Theory and Measurement of Trust in Explaining Differences in Economic Growth', *Cambridge Journal of Economics*, **30**, 371–387.

Beugelsdijk, S. (2006b), 'Social Capital and Growth in European Regions: An Empirical Test', *European Journal of Political Economy*, **21**, 301–324.

Beunza, Daniel and David Stark (2008), 'Tools of the Trade: The Socio–Technology of Arbitrage in a Wall Street Trading Room', in Pinch, Trevor and Richard Swedberg (eds), *Living in a Material World: Economic Sociology Meets Science and Technology Studies*, Cambridge: MIT Press, pp. 253–290.

Beunza, Daniel, Iain Hardic and Donald MacKenzie (2006), *A Price Is a Social Thing: Towards a Material Sociology of Arbitrage*, http://www.sps.ed.ac.uk/__data/assets/pdf_file/0013/3415/arbitrage.pdf

Bhagwati, Jagdish, Arvind Panagariya, and T.N. Srinivasan (1998), *Lectures on International Trade, Second Edition*, Cambridge, MA, USA: MIT Press.

Bhaskar, Roy (1989), *The Possibility of Naturalism: A Philosophical Critique of the Contemporary Human Sciences*, New York: Harvester Wheatsheaf.

Bikhchandani, S., D. Hirschleifer and I. Welch (1992), 'A Theory of Fads, Fashion, Custom, and Cultural Change as Informational Cascades', *Journal of Political Economy*, **100**(5), 992–1026.

Bikhchandani, S., D. Hirschleifer and I. Welch (1998), 'Learning From the Behavior of Others: Conformity, Fads, and Informational Cascades', *Journal of Economic Perspectives*, **12**(3), 151–170.

Binder, P.–M. (2008), 'Theories of Almost Everything', *Nature*, **455**, 884–885.

Binger, B. R. and E. Hoffman (1989), 'Institutional Persistence and Change: The Question of Efficiency', *Journal of Theoretical and Institutional Economics*, **145**, 67–84.

Binmore, Ken (1994), *Game Theory and the Social Contract Volume I: Playing Fair*, Cambridge, MA, USA and London: MIT Press.

Binmore, K. (1997), 'Rationality and Backward Induction', *Journal of Economic Methodology*, **4**(1), 23–40.

Binmore, Ken (2005), *Natural Justice*, Oxford: Oxford University Press.

Binswanger, Hans Christoph (2013), *The Growth Spiral: Money, Energy and Imagination in the Dynamics of the Market Process*, Heidelberg, New York, Dordrecht and London: Springer, revised translation of ibid. (2006): *Die Wachstumsspirale. Geld, Energie und Imagination in der Dynamik des Wachstumsprozesses*, Marburg: Metropolis.

Blackmore, Susan (2000), 'The Memes' Eye View', in Aunger, Robert (ed.), *Darwinizing Culture: The Status of Memetics as a Science*, Oxford: Oxford University Press, pp. 25–42.

Blyth, Mark (2002), *Great Transformations: Economic Ideas and Institutional Change in the Twentieth Century*, Cambridge: Cambridge University Press.

Blyth, Mark (2011), 'Ideas, Uncertainty, and Evolution', in Béland, Daniel and Robert Henry Cox (eds) (2011), *Ideas and Politics in Social Science Research*, Oxford: Oxford University Press, pp. 83–103.

Bohnet, I., B. Herrmann and R. Zeckhauser (2010), 'Trust and the Reference Points for Trustworthiness in Gulf and Western Countries', *Quarterly Journal of Economics*, **125**(2), 811–828.

Bolander, Thomas (2012), 'Self–Reference', in Edward N. Zalta (ed.), *The Stanford Encyclopedia of Philosophy* (Fall 2012 Edition), URL = <http://plato.stanford.edu/archives/fall2012/entries/self–reference/>.

Bolton, G. E. and A. Ockenfels (2000), 'ERC: A Theory of Equity, Reciprocity, and Competition', *American Economic Review*, **90**(1), 166–193.

Bonner, John Tyler (1988), *The Evolution of Complexity by Means of Natural Selection*, Princeton: Princeton University Press.

Boone, James L. (1983), 'Noble Family Structure and Expansionist Warfare in the Late Middle Ages: A Socioecological Approach', in Dyson–Hudson, Rada and Michael A. Little (eds), *Rethinking Human Adaptation: Biological and Cultural Models*, Boulder: Westview, pp. 79–96.

Born, Karl Erich (1976), *Geld und Banken im 19. und 20. Jahrhundert*, Stuttgart: Kröner.

Bowles, S. (1998), 'Endogenous Preferences: The Cultural Consequences of Markets and other Economic Institutions', *Journal of Economic Literature*, **XXXVI**, 75–111.

Bowles, Samuel (2004), *Microeconomics: Behavior, Institutions, and Evolution.* New York, Princeton and Oxford: Russell Sage and Princeton University Press.

Bowles, S. and H. Gintis (1993), 'The Revenge of Homo Economicus: Contested Exchange and the Revival of Political Economy', *Journal of Economic Perspectives,* **7**(1), 83–102.

Bowles, Samuel and Herbert Gintis (2001a), 'Community Governance: An Evolutionary Analysis', in Nicita, Antonio and Ugo Pagano (eds), *The Evolution of Economic Diversity*, London and New York: Routledge, pp. 344–367.

Bowles, Samuel and Herbert Gintis (2001b), 'Cooperation and Exclusion in Networks', in Nicita, Antonio and Ugo Pagano (eds), *The Evolution of Economic Diversity*, London and New York: Routledge, pp. 368–395.

Bowles, S., J. Choi, Jung–Kyoo and A. Hopfensitz (2003), 'The Co–Evolution of Individual Behaviors and Social Institutions', *Journal of Theoretical Biology,* **223**, 135–147.

Bowles, S. and S. Polanía–Reyes (2012), 'Economic Incentives and Social Preferences: Substitutes or Complements?', *Journal of Economic Literature*, **L**(2), 368–425.

Bowman, D. M. J. S. et al. (2009), 'Fire in the Earth System', *Science*, **324**, 481–484.

Boyd, Robert and Peter J. Richerson (1985), *Culture and the Evolutionary Process*, Chicago and London: University of Chicago Press.

Boyer, Robert (1990), *The Regulation School: A Critical Introduction*, New York: Columbia University Press.

Boyer, P. and M. B. Petersen (2012), 'The Naturalness of (many) Social Institutions: Evolved Cognition as Their Foundation', *Journal of Institutional Economics*, **8**, 1–12.

Bradie, Michael and Harms, William (2012): 'Evolutionary Epistemology', in Edward N. Zalta (ed.), *The Stanford Encyclopedia of Philosophy* (Winter 2012 Edition),
URL = <http://plato.stanford.edu/archives/win2012/entries/epistemology–evolutionary/>.

Brakel, Jaap van (2000), *Philosophy of Chemistry. Between the Manifest and the Scientific Image*, Leuven: Leuven University Press.

Brandenburger. A. (2007), 'The Power of Paradox: Some Recent Developments in Interactive Epistemology', *International Journal of Game Theory*, **35**, 465–492.

Brandon, Robert (2010), 'Natural Selection', in Edward N. Zalta (ed.), *The Stanford Encyclopedia of Philosophy* (Fall 2010 Edition), URL = <http://plato.stanford.edu/archives/fall2010/entries/natural–selection/>.

Brier, Søren (2008), *Cybersemiotics. Why Information Is Not Enough!* Toronto, Buffalo and London: University of Toronto Press.

Bringezu, Stefan and Yuichi Moriguchi (2002), 'Material Flow Analysis, in Ayres, Robert U. and Leslie W. Ayres, (eds), *A Handbook of Industrial Ecology*, Cheltenham, UK and Northampton, MA, USA: Edward Elgar, pp. 79–90.

Brocas, I. and J. D. Carrillo (2008), 'The Brain as a Hierarchical Organization', *American Economic Review*, **98**(4), 1312–1347.

Brooks, Daniel R. and E. O. Wiley (1988), *Evolution as Entropy: Toward a Unified Theory of Biology*, Chicago and London: Chicago University Press.

Brown, Joel S. (2001), 'Fit of Form and Function, Diversity of Life, and Procession of Life as an Evolutionary Game', in Orzack, Steven Hecht and Elliott Sober (eds) (2001), *Adaptationism and Optimality*, Cambridge et al.: Cambridge University Press, pp. 114–160.

Brown, K. S. et al. (2009), 'Fire as an Engineering Tool of Early Modern Humans', *Science*, **325**, 859–862.

Brown, M. and M. W. Feldman (2009), 'Sociocultural Epistasis and Cultural Exaptation in Footbinding, Marriage Form, and Religious Practices in Early 20th–century Taiwan, *Proceedings of the National Academy of Sciences*, **106**(52), 22139–22144.

Brukner, Časlav and Anton Zeilinger (2005), 'Quantum Physics as a Science of Information', in A. Elitzur, S. Dolev, and N. Kolenda (eds), *Quo Vadis Quantum Mechanics?* Berlin: Springer, pp. 47–61.

Brukner, Časlav and Zeilinger, Anton (2006), *Information and Fundamental Elements of the Structure of Quantum Theory*, arXiv:quant–ph/0212084.

Bruns, Axel (2008), *Blogs, Wikipedia, Second Life, and Beyond: From Production to Produsage*, New York: Peter Lang.

Bub, Jeffrey (2002), *Maxwell's Demon and the Thermodynamics of Computation*, arXiv:quant–ph/0203017.

Bub, Jeffrey (2006), *Quantum Information and Computation*, arXiv:quant–ph/0512125.

Buchanan, James (1969), *Cost and Choice: An Inquiry in Economic Theory*, Chicago: University of Chicago Press.

Buchanan, James M. (1979), 'A Hobbesian Interpretation of the Rawlsian Difference Principle', in Brunner, Karl (ed.), Economics & Social Institutions, Boston, The Hague and London: Martinus Nijhoff, pp. 59–78.

Buenstorf, G. (2000), 'Self–organization and Sustainability: Energetics of Evolution and Implications for Ecological Economics', *Ecological Economics*, **22**, 119–134.

Buenstorf, Guido (2004), *The Economics of Energy and the Production Process: An Evolutionary Approach*, Cheltenham, UK and Northampton, MA, USA: Edward Elgar.

Bunge, Mario (1977), *Treatise on Basic Philosophy, Volume 3. Ontology I: The Furniture of the World*, Dordrecht: Reidel.

Bunge, Mario (1979), *Treatise on Basic Philosophy, Volume 4. Ontology II: A World of Systems*, Dordrecht: Reidel.

Burch, Robert (2010), 'Charles Sanders Peirce', in Edward N. Zalta (ed.), *The Stanford Encyclopedia of Philosophy* (Fall 2010 Edition), URL = <http://plato.stanford.edu/archives/fall2010/entries/peirce/>.

Burger, J., M. Kirchner, B. Bramanti, W. Haak and M. G. Thomas (2007), 'Absence of the Lactase–persistence–associated Allele in Early Neolithic Europeans', *Proceedings of the National Academy of Sciences*, **104**(10), 3736–3741.

Burian, Richard M. (1983), '"Adaptation"', in Grene, Marjorie (ed) (1983), *Dimensions of Darwinism: Themes and Counterthemes in Twentieth–Century Evolutionary Theory*, Cambridge and Paris: Cambridge University Press and Editions de la Maison des Sciences de l'Homme, pp. 287–314.

Burkert, Walter (1996), *Creation of the Sacred: Tracks of Biology in Early Religions*, Cambridge and London: Harvard University Press.

Burt, Ronald S. (1992), *Structural Holes: The Social Structure of Competition*, Cambridge, MA, USA and London: Harvard University Press.

Burt, Ronald S. (2000), *The Network Structure of Social Capital*, http://faculty.chicagobooth.edu/ronald.burt/research/files/NSSC.pdf, accessed January 23, 2013.

Burt, Ronald S. (2002), 'The Social Capital of Structural Holes', in Guillén, Mauro F., Randall Collins, Paula England and Marshall Meyer (eds), *The New Economic Sociology: Developments in an Emerging Field*, New York: Russell Sage Foundation, pp. 148–192.

Byrne, Richard W. (1995), 'The Ape Legacy: The Evolution of Machiavellian Intelligence and Anticipatory Interactive Planning, in Goody, Esther (ed) (1995b), *Social Intelligence and Interaction: Expressions and Implications of the Social Bias in Human Intelligence*, Cambridge: Cambridge University Press, pp. 37–52.

Cai, H., Chen, Y. Chen and H. Fang (2009), 'Observational Learning: Evidence from a Randomized Natural Field Experiment', *American Economic Review*, **99**(3), 864–882.

Caldwell, B. J. (1991), 'Clarifying Popper', *Journal of Economic Literature*, **XXIX**, 1–33.

Caldwell, Bruce J. (1994), *Beyond Positivism. Economic Methodology in the Twentieth Century*, revised edition, London and New York: Routledge.

Çalışkan, Koray (2007), 'Price as a Market Device: Cotton Trading in Izmir Mercantile Exchange', in Callon, Michel, Yuval Millo and Fabian Muniesa (eds), *Market Devices*, Malden et al.: Blackwell, pp. 241–261.

Çalışkan, Koray and Michel Callon (2009), 'Economization, part 1: Shifting Attention from the Economy Towards Processes of Economization', *Economy and Society*, **38**(3), 369–398.

Çalışkan, Koray and Michel Callon (2010) 'Economization, part 2: A Research Programme for the Study of Markets', *Economy and Society*, **39**(1), 1–32.

Callon, Michel (2007), 'What Does It Mean to Say That Economics is Performative?' in MacKenzie, Donald, Fabian Muniesa and Lucia Siu (eds), *Do Economists Make Markets? On the Performativity of Economics*, Princeton and Oxford: Princeton University Press, pp. 344–357.

Callon, Michel (2008), 'Economic Markets and the Rise of Interactive Agencements: From Prosthetic Agencies to Habilitated Agencies', in Pinch, Trevor and Richard Swedberg (eds), *Living in a Material World: Economic Sociology Meets Science and Technology Studies*, Cambridge, MA, USA: MIT Press, pp. 29–56.

Callon, Michel, Yuval Millo and Fabian Muniesa (eds) (2007), *Market Devices*, Malden: Blackwell.

Calvin, William H. (1996), *The Cerebral Code: Thinking a Thought in the Mosaic of Mind*, Cambridge, MA, USA and London: MIT Press.

Calvin, W. H. (1998), 'Competing for Consciousness: A Darwinian Mechanism as an Appropriate Level of Explanation', *Journal of Consciousness Studies*, **5**(4), 389–404.

Camera, G. and M. Casari (2009), 'Cooperation among Strangers under the Shadow of the Future', *American Economic Review*, **99**(3), 979–1005.

Camerer, C. (2006), 'Wanting, Liking, and Learning: Neuroscience and Paternalism', *The University of Chicago Law Review*, **73**, 87–110.

Camerer, Colin F. (2003), *Behavioral Game Theory: Experiments in Social Interaction*, New York and Princeton: Russell Sage Foundation and Princeton University Press.

Camerer, C. (2007), 'Neuroeconomics: Using Neuroscience to Make Economic Predictions', *Economic Journal*, **117**(519), C26–C42.

Camerer, C., G. Loewenstein and D. Prelec (2005), 'Neuroeconomics: How Neuroscience Can Inform Economics', *Journal of Economic Literature*, **XLIII**, 9–64.

Campbell, Donald T. (1960), 'Blind Variation and Selective Retention in Creative Thought as in Other Knowledge Processes', reprinted 1987 in Radnitzky, Gerard and William W. Bartley III (eds), *Evolutionary Epistemology, Rationality, and the Sociology of Knowledge*, La Salle: Open Court, pp. 91–114.

Campbell, Donald T. (1974a), 'Unjustified Variation and Selective Retention in Scientific Discovery', in Ayala, Francisco J. and Theodosius Dobzhansky (eds) (1974), *Studies in the Philosophy of Biology: Reduction and Related Problems*, Berkeley and Los Angeles: University of California Press, pp. 139–163.

Candlish, Stewart and George Wrisley (2012), 'Private Language', in Edward N. Zalta (ed.), *The Stanford Encyclopedia of Philosophy* (Summer 2012 Edition), URL = <http://plato.stanford.edu/archives/sum2012/entries/private–language/>.

Carlson, W. Bernard (2000), 'Invention and Evolution: The Case of Edison's Sketches of the Telephone', Change' in Ziman, John (ed.), *Technological Innovation as an Evolutionary Process*, Cambridge: Cambridge University Press, pp. 137–158.

Carpendale, J. I. M. and C. Lewis, (2004), 'Constructing an Understanding of Mind: The Development of Children's Understanding of Mind Within Social Interaction', *Behavioral and Brain Sciences*, **27**, 79–150.

Carroll, Glenn R. and Michael T. Hannan (2000), *The Demography of Corporations and Industries*, Princeton: Princeton University Press.

Cartwright, K. V. (2008), 'Non–Calculus Derivation of the Maximum Power Transfer Theorem', *the Technology Interface*, Spring 2008, http://technologyinterface.nmsu.edu/Spring08/30_Cartwright/index.pdf.

Casson, Mark (1997), *Information and Organization: A New Perspective on the Theory of the Firm*, Oxford: Clarendon.

Cat, Jordi (2010), 'The Unity of Science', in Edward N. Zalta (ed.), *The Stanford Encyclopedia of Philosophy* (Fall 2010 Edition), URL = <http://plato.stanford.edu/archives/fall2010/entries/scientific–unity/>.

Çelen, B. and S. Kariv (2004), 'Distinguishing Informational Cascades from Herd Behavior in the Laboratory', *American Economic Review*, **94**(3), 484–498.

Chai, A. and A. Moneta (2012), 'Back to Engel? Some Evidence for the Hierarchy of Needs', *Journal of Evolutionary Economics*, **22**, 649–676.

Chaisson, Eric J. (2001), *Cosmic Evolution: The Rise of Complexity in Nature*, Cambridge, MA, USA and London: Harvard University Press.

Chaitin, Gregory J. (1995), 'Randomness in Arithmetics and the Decline and Fall of Reductionism in Pure Mathematics', in Cornwell, John (ed.), *Nature's Imagination: The Frontiers of Scientific Vision*, Oxford, New York and Melbourne: Oxford University Press, pp. 27–44.

Chaitin, Gregory J. (2005), *Metamaths: The Quest for Omega*, London: Atlantic Books.

Chao, Kang (1986), *Man and Land in China: An Economic Analysis*, Stanford: Stanford University Press.

Charness, G. and M. Sutter (2012), 'Groups Make Better Self–Interested Decisions', *Journal of Economic Perspectives*, **26**(3), 157–176.

Charness, G., L. Rigotti and A. Rustichini (2007), 'Individual Behavior and Group Membership', *American Economic Review*, **97**(4), 1340–1353.
Chavas, J.–P. and D. W. Bromley (2008), 'On the Origins and Evolving Role of Money', *Journal of Institutional and Theoretical Economics*, **164**(4), 624–651.
Chen, R. and Y. Chen (2011), 'The Potential of Social Identity for Equilibrium Selection', *American Economic Review*, **101**, 2562–2589.
Chen, Y. and S. X. Li (2009), 'Group Identity and Social Preferences', *American Economic Review*, **99**(1), 431–457.
Cimoli, M. and G. Dosi (1995), 'Technological Paradigms, Patterns of Learning and Development: An Introductory Roadmap', *Journal of Evolutionary Economics*, **5**, 243–268.
Claessen, Henri J. M., Pieter van den Velde, M. Estellie Smith (eds) (1985), *Development and Decline: The Evolution of Sociopolitical Organization*, South Hadley: Bergin and Harvey.
Clark, A. E., P. Frijters and M. A. Shields (2008), 'Relative Income, Happiness, and Utility: An Explanation for the Easterlin Paradox and Other Puzzles', *Journal of Economic Literature*, **XLVI**(1), 95–144.
Clark, Andy (2007), 'Soft Selves and Ecological Control', in Ross, Don, David Spurrett, Harold Kincaid and G. Lynn Stephens (eds), *Distributed Cognition and the Will. Individual Volition and Social Context*, Cambridge, MA, USA: MIT Press, pp. 101–122.
Clark, Andy (2011), *Supersizing the Mind: Embodiment, Action, and Cognitive Extension*, Oxford: Oxford University Press.
Clark, A. and D.J. Chalmers (1998), 'The Extended Mind', *Analysis*, **58**, 10–23.
Clark, David A. (2005), *The Capability Approach: Its Development, Critiques and Recent Advances*, GPRG–WPS–32, University of Manchester.
Clark, G. (2013), 'What Is the True Rate of Social Mobility? Evidence From the Information Content of Surnames', forthcoming, American Economic Review Papers and Proceedings, http://www.econ.ucdavis.edu/faculty/gclark/papers/Clark%20Cummins%201800–2011%20Revision2.pdf, accessed February 11, 2013.
Clark, L. (2010), 'Decision–making During Gambling: An Integration of Cognitive and Psychobiological Approaches', *Philosophical Transactions of the Royal Society B*, **365**, 319–330.
Clunas, Craig (2004), *Elegant Debts: The Social Art of Wen Zhengming*, Honululu: The University of Hawai'i Press.
Coates, J. M., M. Gurnell and Z. Sarnyai (2010), 'From Molecule to Market: Steriod Hormones and Financial Risk–Taking', *Philosophical Transactions of the Royal Society B*, **365**, 331–343.
Cohen, A. J. and G. C. Harcourt (2003), 'Whatever Happened to the Cambridge Capital Controversies?', *Journal of Economic Perspectives*, **17**(1), 199–214.
Cohen, E. G. D. (1996), *Boltzmann and Statistical Mechanics*, arXiv:cond–mat/9608054.
Cohen, J. D. (2005), 'The Vulcanization of the Human Brain: A Neural Perspective on Interactions between Cognition and Emotion', *Journal of Economic Perspectives*, **19**(4), 3–24.
Coleman, James (1990), *Foundations of Social Theory*, Cambridge, MA, USA and London: Belknap.

Collier, J. A. and C. A. Hooker (1999), 'Complexly Organized Dynamical Systems', *Open Systems and Information Dynamics*, **6**, 241–302.

Collier, John (1996), 'Causation Is the Transfer of Information', in H. Sankey (ed), *Causation, Natural Laws and Explanation*, Dordrecht: Kluwer, pp. 279–331.

Constant, Edward (2000), 'The Evolution of War and Technology', in Ziman, John (ed.), *Technological Innovation as an Evolutionary Process*, Cambridge: Cambridge University Press, pp. 281–298.

Cordes, C. (2005), 'Long–Term Tendencies in Technological Creativity – A Preference–based Approach', *Journal of Evolutionary Economics*, **15**(2), 149–168.

Cordes, C. (2006), 'Darwinism in Economics: From Analogy to Continuity', *Journal of Evolutionary Economics*, **16**(5), 529–542.

Coriat, B. and O. Weinstein, Oliver (2005), 'Patent Regimes, Firms and the Commodification of Knowledge', *Socio–Economic Review*, **10**, 267–292.

Corning, Peter A. (1983), *The Synergism Hypothesis: A Theory of Progressive Evolution*, New York: McGraw–Hill.

Corning, Peter A. (2003), *Nature's Magic. Synergy in Evolution and the Fate of Humankind*, Cambridge, UK: Cambridge University Press.

Corning, Peter A. (2005), *Holistic Darwinism: Synergy, Cybernetics, and the Bioeconomics of Evolution*, Chicago and London: Chicago University Press.

Cosmides, Leda and James Tooby (2005), 'Neurocognitive Adaptations Designed for Social Exchange', in Buss, David M. (ed.), *The Handbook of Evolutionary Psychology*, Hoboken: Wiley, pp. 584–628.

Coulson, Seana (2008), 'Metaphor Comprehension and the Brain', in Gibbs, Raymond W. (ed.), *The Cambridge Handbook of Metaphor and Thought*, New York: Cambridge University Press, pp. 177–194.

Crisafi, A. and S. Gallagher (2010), 'Hegel and the Extended Mind', *AI & Society*, **25**, 123–129.

Crutchfield, J. P. and C. R. Shalizi (1999), 'Thermodynamic Depth of Causal States: Objective Complexity via Minimal Representations', *Physical Review E*, **59**(1), 275–283.

Crutchfield, James P. / Shalizi, Cosma Rohilla (1998), *Thermodynamic Depth of Causal States: When Paddling around in Occam's Pool Shallowness is a Virtue*, arXiv:cond–math/9808147.

Crutzen, P. J. (2002), 'Geology of Mankind', *Nature*, **415**, 23.

Cubitt, R. P. and R. Sugden (2001), 'On Money Pumps', *Games and Economic Behavior*, **37**(1), 121–60.

Cubitt, R. P. and R. Sugden (2003), 'Common Knowledge, Salience and Convention: A Reconstruction of David Lewis' Game Theory', *Economics and Philosophy*, **19**, 175–210.

Cutler, D. M., E. L. Glaeser and J. M. Shapiro (2003), 'Why Have Americans Become More Obese?', *Journal of Economic Perspectives*, **17**(3), 93–118.

D'Adderio, L. (2008), 'The Performativity of Routines: Theorising the Influence of Artefacts and Distributed Agencies to Routine Dynamics', *Research Policy*, **37**, 769–789.

D'Adderio, L. (2011), 'Artifacts at the Centre of Routines: Performing the Material Turn in Routines Theory', *Journal of Institutional Economics*, **7**(2), 197–230.

Damasio, Antonio R. (1995), *Descartes' Error: Emotion, Reason and the Human Brain*, New York: G.B. Putnam's Son.

Damasio, Antonio R. (2010), *Self Comes to Mind: Constructing the Conscious Brain*, New York: Pantheon.

Danchin, É., A. Charmantier, F. A. Chanpagne, A. Mesoudi, B. Pujol and S. Blanchet (2011), 'Beyond DNA: Integrating Inclusive Inheritance Into an Extended Theory of Evolution', *Nature Reviews Genetics*, **12**, 475–486.

Dasgupta, P. (2005), 'Economics of Social Capital', *The Economic Record*, **81**(255), 2–21.

Davidson, Donald (2006), *The Essential Davidson*, Oxford: Oxford University Press.

Davies, Norman (1996), *Europe: A History*, London: Pimlico.

Davies, Paul Sheldon (2007), 'What Kind of Agent Are We? A Naturalistic Framework for the Study of Human Agency', in Ross, Don, David Spurrett, Harold Kincaid and G. Lynn Stephens (eds), *Distributed Cognition and the Will. Individual Volition and Social Context*, Cambridge, MA, USA: MIT Press, pp. 39–60.

Davis, John B. (2003), *The Theory of the Individual in Economics: Identity and Value*, London and New York: Routledge.

Davis, J. B. (2006), 'The Turn in Economics: Neoclassical Dominance to Mainstream Pluralism? *Journal of Institutional Economics*, **2**(1), 1–20.

Davis, J. B. (2007), 'Akerlof and Kranton on Identity in Economics: Inverting the Analysis', *Cambridge Journal of Economics*, 31(3), 349–362.

Davis, J. B. (2008), *Identity and Individual Economic Agents: A Narrative Approach*, ssrn.com/abstract=1151325.

Davis, John B. (2010), *Individuals and Identity in Economics*, Cambridge: Cambridge University Press.

Dawkins, Richard (1982), *The Extended Phenotype*, Oxford: Freeman.

Dawkins, Richard (1989), *The Selfish Gene*, New edition, Oxford and New York: Oxford University Press.

De Vany, Arthur and Cassey Lee (2008), *Information Cascades in Multi–Agent Models*, http://pages.stern.nyu.edu/~wgreene/entertainmentandmedia/Cascades.pdf, accessed January 23, 2013.

De Vries, Jan (2008), *The Industrious Revolution: Consumer Behavior and the Household Economy, 1650 to the Present*, Cambridge: Cambridge University Press.

Deci, E. L., R. Koestner and R. M. Ryan (1999), 'A Meta–Analytic Review of Experiments Examining the Effects of Extrinsic Rewards on Intrinsic Motivation', *Psychological Bulletin*, **125**(6), 627–668.

Del Re, G. (1998) 'Ontological Status of Molecular Structure', *HYLE – International Journal for Philosophy of Chemistry*, **4**(2), 81–103.

Delius, Juan D. (1989), 'Of Mind Memes and Brain Bugs: A Natural History of Culture', in Koch, Walter A. (ed.), *The Nature of Culture*, Bochum: Brockmeyer, pp. 26–79.

Demichelis, S. and J. W. Weibull (2008), 'Language, Meaning, and Games: A Model of Communication, Coordination, and Evolution', *American Economic Review*, **98**(4), 1292–1312.

Dennett, Daniel C. (1991), *Consciousness Explained*, Boston: Little, Brown and Company.

Dennett, Daniel C. (1995), *Darwin's Dangerous Idea: Evolution and the Meanings of Life*, New York: Simon & Schuster.

Dennett, Daniel (2009), 'Intentional Systems Theory', in McLaughlin, Brian P., Ansgar Beckermann and Sven Walter (eds), *The Oxford Handbook of Philosophy of Mind*, Oxford: Clarendon Press, pp. 339–350.

Denzau, A. T. and D. C. North (1994), 'Shared Mental Models: Ideologies and Institutions', *Kyklos,* **47**, 3–32.

Deutsch, David (1997), *The Fabric of Reality*, London: Penguin.

Dew, N., S. D. Sarasvathy and S. Venkataraman (2004), 'The Economic Implications of Exaptation', *Journal of Evolutionary Economics*, **14**(1), 69–84.

Dewar, R. C. (2009), 'Maximum Entropy Production as an Inference Algorithm that Rranslates Physical Assumptions into Macroscopic Predictions: Don't Shoot the Messenger', *Entropy*, 2009, **11**, pp. 931–944.

Dewar, R. C. (2010), 'Maximum Entropy Production and Plant Optimization Theories', *Philosophical Transactions of the Royal Society B*, **365**, 1429–1435.

Dewar, R. C. and A. Porté (2008), 'Statistical Mechanics Unifies Different Ecological Patterns', *Journal of Theoretical Biology*, **251**, 389–403.

Dewar, Roderick C. (2005), 'Maximum–Entropy Production and Non–Equilibrium Statistical Mechanics', in: Kleidon, Axel and Ralph Lorenz (eds) (2005), *Non–equilibrium Thermodynamics and the Production of Entropy: Life, Earth, and Beyond*, Heidelberg: Springer, pp. 41–55.

Di Tella, R. and R. MacCulloch (2006), 'Some Uses of Happiness Data in Economics', *Journal of Economic Perspectives*, **20**(1), 25–46.

Dickhaut, John, Sudipta Basu, Kevin McCabe, and Gregory Waymire (2009a), *NeuroAccounting Part I: The Primate Brain and Reciprocal Exchange*, ssrn.com/abstract=1336526.

Dickhaut, John, Sudipta Basu, Kevin McCabe, and Gregory Waymire (2009b): *NeuroAccounting Part II: Consilience Between Accoutning Principles and the Primate Brain*, ssrn.com/abstract=1336517.

DiMaggio, Paul (1997), 'Culture and Cognition,' *Annual Review of Sociology*, **23**, 263–287.

DiMaggio, Paul (2011), 'Cultural Networks', in Scott, John and Peter Carrington (eds), *The Sage Handbook of Social Network Analysis*, Los Angeles: Sage, pp. 286–301.

Dixit, A. K. (1997), 'Economists as Advisers to Politicians and to Society', *Economics and Politics*, **9**, 225–230.

Dixit, Avinash K. (2004), *Lawlessness and Economics: Alternative Modes of Governance*, Princeton and Oxford: Princeton University Press.

Djankov, S., E. Glaeser, R. La Porta, F. Lopez–de–Silanes and A. Shleifer (2003), 'The New Comparative Economics', *Journal of Comparative Economics*, **31**, 595–619.

Dobzhansky, Theodosius (1974), 'Chance and Creativity in Evolution', in Ayala, Francisco J. and Theodosius Dobzhansky (eds) (1974), *Studies in the Philosophy of Biology: Reduction and Related Problems*, Berkeley and Los Angeles: University of California Press, pp. 307–338.

Doing, P. (2008), 'Give me a Laboratory and I Will Raise a Discipline: The Past, Present, and Future Politics of Laboratory Studies in STS', in Hackett, Edward J., Olga Amsterdamska, Michael Lynch, Judy Wajcman, Judy (eds), *The Handbook of Science and Technology Studies*, Cambridge, MA, USA and London: MIT Press, pp. 279–297.

Dopfer, K. (2004), 'The Economic Agent as Rule Maker and Rule User: Homo Sapiens Oeconomicus', *Journal of Evolutionary Economics*, **14**(2), 177–197.

Dopfer, Kurt (2005), 'Evolutionary Economics: A Theoretical Framework', in Dopfer, Kurt (ed.) (2005), *The Evolutionary Foundations of Economics*, Cambridge, UK: Cambridge University Press, pp. 3–56.

Dosi, Giovanni (1982), Technological Paradigms and Technological Trajectories', *Research Policy*, **11**, 147–162.

Dowe, Phil (2008), 'Causal Processes', in Edward N. Zalta (ed.), *The Stanford Encyclopedia of Philosophy* (Fall 2008 Edition), URL = <http://plato.stanford.edu/archives/fall2008/entries/causation–process/>.

Downes, Stephen M. (2010), 'Heritability' in Edward N. Zalta (ed.), *The Stanford Encyclopedia of Philosophy* (Fall 2010 Edition), URL = <http://plato.stanford.edu/archives/fall2010/entries/heredity/>.

Dretske, Fred (1981), *Knowledge and the Flow of Information*, Reprint 1999, Stanford: CSLI Publications.

Dretske, Fred (1995), *Naturalizing the Mind*, Cambridge, MA, USA and London: MIT Press.

Dunbar, R. I. M. and S. Shultz, Susanne (2007), 'Understanding Primate Brain Evolution', *Philosophical Transactions of the Royal Society B*, **362**, 649–658.

Dunbar, R. I. M. (2011), 'Constraints on the Evolution of Social Institutions and Their Implications for Information Flow', *Journal of Institutional Economics*, **7**(3), 345–371.

Dunn, M. (1992), 'Firms, Markets, and Hierarchies: A Critical Appraisal of Ronald Coase's Contribution to the Explanation of the "Nature of the Firm"', ORDO, **43**, 193–204.

Durlauf, S. N. (2002), 'On the Empirics of Social Capital', *Economic Journal,* **112**, F459–F479.

Durlauf, S. N. (2012), 'Complexity, Economics, and Public Policy', *Politics, Philosophy and Economics,* **11**(1), 45–75.

Dutton, Denis (2003), 'Aesthetics and Evolutionary Psychology', in Levinson, Jerrold (ed.), *The Oxford Handbook for Aesthetics*. Oxford: Oxford University Press, pp. 693–705.

Earl, P. E. and T. Wakeley (2010), 'Alternative Perspectives on Connections in Economic Systems', *Journal of Evolutionary Economics*, **20**(2), 163–185.

Eastman, Lloyd E. (1988), *Family, Fields, and Ancestors: Constancy and Change in China's Social and Economic History*, New York and Oxford: Oxford University Press.

Edelman, Gerald M. (1987), *Neural Darwinism: The Theory of Neuronal Group Selection*, New York: Basic Books.

Edelman, Gerald M. (2006), *Second Nature: Brain Science and Human Knowledge*, New Haven and London: Yale University Press.

Edelman, Gerald M. and Gulio Tononi (1995), 'Neural Darwinism: The Brain as a Selectional System', in Cornwell, John (ed.) (1995), *Nature's Imagination: The Frontiers of Scientific Vision*, Oxford, New York and Melbourne: Oxford University Press, pp. 78–101.

Eggertsson, Thráinn (1990), *Economic Behavior and Institutions*, Cambridge: Cambridge University Press.

El–Hani, C. N., J. Queiroz and C. Emmeche (2006), 'A Semiotic Analysis of the Genetic Information System', *Semiotica*, **160**, 1–68.

Elias, Norbert (1969a/1990), *Über den Prozeß der Zivilisation: Soziogenetische und psychogenetische Untersuchungen, Erster Band: Wandlungen des Verhaltens in den weltlichen Oberschichten des Abendlandes*, Frankfurt: Suhrkamp.

Elias, Norbert (1969b/1989), *Die höfische Gesellschaft: Untersuchungen zur Soziologie des Königtums und der höfischen Aristokratie*, Frankfurt: Suhrkamp.

Elitzur, A. C. (2005), 'When Form Outlasts Its Medium: A Definition of Life Integrating Platonism and Thermodynamics', in J. Seckbach (ed.), *Life as We Know it*, Dordrecht: Kluwer Academic Publishers, pp. 607–620.

Ellikson, Robert C. (1991), *Order without Law: How Neighbours Settle Disputes,* Cambridge, MA, USA: Harvard University Press.

Ellis, George F. (2008), *On the Nature of Causation in Complex Systems*, http://www.mth.uct.ac.za/~ellis/Top–down%20Ellis.pdf (accessed January 11, 2013).

Elster, Jon (1979), *Ulysses and the Syrens: Studies in Rationality and Irrationality*, Cambridge and Paris: Cambridge University Press and Editions de la Maison des Sciences de l'Homme.

Elster, Jon, ed. (1986), *The Multiple Self*, Cambridge: Cambridge University Press.

Elster, Jon (1989a), *Nuts and Bolts for the Social Sciences*, Cambridge: Cambridge University Press.

Elster, Jon (1989b), *The Cement of Society: A Study of Social Order*, Cambridge: Cambridge University Press.

Elster, Jon (1998), 'Emotions and Economic Theory', *Journal of Economic Literature*, **XXXVI**, 47–74.

Elvin, Mark (1973), *The Pattern of the Chinese Past*, Stanford: Stanford University Press.

Elworthy, Charles (1993), *Homo Biologicus: An Evolutionary Model for the Human Sciences*, Berlin: Duncker & Humblot.

Emirbayer, Mustafa (1997), 'Manifesto for a Relational Sociology', *American Journal of Sociology*, **103**(2), 281–317.

Emmeche, C. (2002), 'The Chicken and the Orphan Egg: On the Function of Meaning and the Meaning of Function', *Sign System Studies*, **30**(1), 15–32.

Emmeche, C. and J. Hoffmeyer (1991), 'From Language to Nature – The Semiotic Metaphor in Biology', *Semiotica*, **84** (1/2), 1–42.

Epstein, Joshua M. and Robert Axtell (1996), *Growing Artificial Societies: Social Science from the Bottom Up*, Cambridge, MA, USA and London: Brookings Institution and MIT Press.

Ereshefsky, Marc (2010), 'Species', in Edward N. Zalta (ed.), *The Stanford Encyclopedia of Philosophy* (Spring 2010 Edition), URL = <http://plato.stanford.edu/archives/spr2010/entries/species/>.

Ermer, E., S. A. Guerin, L. Cosmides, J. Tooby and M. B. Miller (2006), 'Theory of Mind Broad and Narrow: Reasoning About Social Exchange Engages ToM Areas, Precautionary Reasoning Does Not', *Social Neuroscience*, **1**(3–4), 196–219.

Faber, Malte and John L. R. Proops (1998), *Evolution, Time, Production and the Environment*, Berlin, Heidelberg and New York: Springer.

Fafchamps, Marcel (2005), 'Spontaneous Market Emergence and Social Networks', in Demange, Gabrielle and Myrna Wooders (eds), *Group Formation in Economics: Networks, Clubs, and Coalitions*, Cambridge: Cambridge University Press, pp. 447–470.

Fair, D. (1979), 'Causation and the Flow of Energy', *Erkenntnis*, **14**, 219–250.

Falcon, Andrea (2012), 'Aristotle on Causality', in Edward N. Zalta (ed.) *The Stanford Encyclopedia of Philosophy* (Winter 2012 Edition), URL = <http://plato.stanford.edu/archives/win2012/entries/aristotle–causality/>.

Falk, A. and M. Kosfeld (2006), 'The Hidden Costs of Control', *American Economic Review*, **96**(5), 1611–1630.

Farrell, Joseph and Mathhew Rabin (1996), 'Cheap Talk', *Journal of Economic Perspectives*, **10**(3), 103–118.

Fath, B., B. C. Patten and J. S. Choi (2001), 'Complementarity of Ecological Goal Functions', *Journal of Theoretical Biology*, **208**, 493–506.

Fauconnier, Gilles and Mark Turner (2002), *The Way We Think: Conceptual Blending and the Mind's Hidden Complexities*, New York: Basic Books.

Fauconnier, Gilles and Mark Turner (2008), 'Rethinking Metaphor', in Gibbs, Raymond W. (ed.), *The Cambridge Handbook of Metaphor and Thought*, New York: Cambridge University Press, pp. 53–66.

Faure, David (2007), *Emperor and Ancestor: State and Lineage in South China*, Stanford: Stanford University Press.

Faye, Jan (2008), 'Copenhagen Interpretation of Quantum Mechanics', in Edward N. Zalta (ed.), *The Stanford Encyclopedia of Philosophy* (Fall 2008 Edition), URL = <http://plato.stanford.edu/archives/fall2008/entries/qm–copenhagen/>.

Feenstra, R. C., T. Yang and G. G. Hamilton (1999), 'Business Groups and Product Variety in Trade: Evidence From South Korea, Taiwan and Japan', *Journal of International Economics*, **48**, 71–100.

Feenstra, Robert C. (2004), *Advanced International Trade*, Princeton: Princeton University Press.

Fehr, E. and J. Tyran (2005), 'Individual Irrationality and Aggregate Outcomes', *Journal of Economic Perspectives*, **19**(4), 43–66.

Fehr, Ernst (2009), 'Social Preferences and the Brain', in Glimcher, Paul W., Colin F. Camerer, Ernst Fehr and Russel A. Poldrack (eds), *Neuroeconomics: Decision Making and the Brain*, Amsterdam: Elsevier, pp. 215–232.

Feldman, Marcus W. (2001), 'Biological and Cultural Evolution: Aspects of Dynamics, Statistics, and Optimization', in Nicita, Antonio and Ugo Pagano (eds), *The Evolution of Economic Diversity*, London and New York: Routledge, pp. 21–48.

Fenoaltea, Stefano (1990), 'Transaction costs, Whig history and the Common Fields, in Gustafsson, Bo (ed.), *Power and Economic Institutions: Reinterpretations in Economic History*, Aldershot: Edward Elgar, pp. 107–169.

Fernando, C., K. K. Karishma and E. Szathmáry (2008), 'Copying and Evolution of Neuronal Topology', *PloS ONE*, **3**(11), doi: 10.1371/journal.pone.003775.

Fernando, C., R. Goldstein and E. Szathmáry (2010), 'The Neuronal Replicator Hypothesis', *Neural Computation*, **22**, 2809–2857.

Fernando, Chrisantha, Eörs Szathmáry and Phil Husbands (2012), 'Selectionist and Evolutionary Approaches to Brain Function: a Critical Appraisal', *Frontiers in Computational Neuroscience*, doi: 10.3389/fncom.2012.00024

Ferrini, Cinzia (2009), 'The Challenge of Reason: From Certainty to Truth', in Westphal, Kenneth R. (ed.) (2009), *The Blackwell Guide to Hegel's Phenomenology of Spirit*, Chichester: Wiley, pp. 72–91.

Field, Alexander (2001), *Altruistically Inclined? The Behavioral Sciences, Evolutionary Theory, and the Origins of Reciprocity*, Ann Arbor: University of Michigan Press.

Findlay, Ronald and Kevin O'Rourke (2007), *Power and Plenty: Trade, War, and the World Economy in the Second Millenium*, Princeton and Oxford: Princeton University Press.

Finlay, B. L., R. B. Darlington and N. Nicastro (2001), 'Developmental Structure in Brain Evolution', *Behavioral and Brain Sciences*, **24**(2), 263–278.

Finlayson, Graham, John Halford, Neil King and John Blundell, John (2010*), Chapter 7.3: The Regulation of Food Intake in Humans*, http://www.endotext.org/obesity/obesity7.3/obesity7–3.html, accessed January 21, 2013.

Fleck, James (2000), 'Artefact ↔ Activity: The Coevolution of Artefacts, Knowledge and Organization in Technological Evolution', in Ziman, John (ed.), *Technological Innovation as an Evolutionary Process*, Cambridge: Cambridge University Press, pp. 248–266.

Fleurbaey, M. (2009), 'Beyond GDP: The Quest for a Measure of Social Welfare', *Journal of Economic Literature*, XLVII(4), 1029–1075.

Florida, Richard (2002), *The Rise of the Creative Class*, New York: Basic Books.

Floridi, Luciano (2003), Information, in Floridi, Luciano (ed) (2003), *The Blackwell Guide to the Philosophy of Computing and Information*, Oxford: Blackwell, pp. 40–61.

Flotow, Paschen von and Johannes Schmidt (2003), ‚Die "Doppelrolle des Geldes" bei Simmel und ihre Bedeutung für Ökonomie und Soziologie', in Rammstedt, Otthein (ed.), *Georg Simmels Philosophie des Geldes, Aufsätze und Materialien*, Frankfurt Suhrkamp, pp. 58–87.

Fodor, J. A. (1974), 'Special Sciences (or: The Disunity of Science as a Working Hypothesis)', *Synthese*, **28**, 97–115.

Fogassi, L. (2011), 'The Mirror Neuron System: How Cognitive Functions Emerge from Motor Organization', *Journal of Economic Behavior & Organization*, **77**(1), 66–75.

Fontana, Walter (2007), *The Topology of the Possible*, www.santafe.edu/research/publications/workingpapers/03–03–017.pdf – 2007–05–02

Fontana, Walter and Leo Buss (1996), 'The Barrier of Objects: From Dynamical Systems to Bounded Organizations', in Casti, John L. and Anders Karlqvist (eds) (1996), *Boundaries and Barrier: On the Limits of Scientific Knowledge*, Reading, Mass.: Addison–Wesley, pp. 55–115.

Foray, Dominique (2004), *Economics of Knowledge*, Cambridge and London: MIT Press.

Forsgren, Mats and Jan Johanson (eds) (1992), *Managing Networks in International Business*, Amsterdam: Gordon and Breach.

Forster, Michael N. (2008), 'Hegel and Hermeneutics', in Beiser, Frederick C. (ed) (2008), *The Cambridge Companion to Hegel and Nineteenth–Century Philosophy*, Cambridge, UK and New York: Cambridge University Press, pp. 174–203.

Foss, N. J. (1993), 'Theories of the Firm: Contractual and Competence Theories', *Journal of Evolutionary Economics*, **3**, 127–144.

Fox, Craig R. and Russell A. Poldrack (2009), 'Prospect Theory and the Brain', in Glimcher, Paul W., Colin F. Camerer, Ernst Fehr and Russel A. Poldrack (eds),

Neuroeconomics: Decision Making and the Brain, Amsterdam: Elsevier, pp. 145–174.
Foxall, G. R. (2008), 'Reward, Emotion and Consumer Choice: From Neuroeconomics to Neurophilosophy', *Journal of Consumer Behavior*, **7**, 368–396.
Frank, Robert H. (1985), *Choosing the Right Pond: Human Behavior and the Quest for Status*, New York and Oxford: Oxford University Press.
Frank, Robert H. (1988), *Passions Within Reason: The Strategic Role of Emotions*, New York and London: Norton.
Frank, Steven A. (1995a), *Foundations of Social Evolution*, Princeton: Princeton University Press.
Frank, S. A. (1995b), 'George Price's Contribution to Evolutionary Genetics', *Journal of Theoretical Biology*, **175**, 373–388.
Frank, S. A. (2009a), 'Natural Selection Maximizes Fisher Information', *Journal of Evolutionary Biology*, **22**, 231–244.
Frank, S. A. (2009b), 'The Common Patterns in Nature', *Journal of Evolutionary Biology*, **22**, 1563–1585.
Frank, S. A. (2009c), 'Evolutionary Foundations of Cooperation and Group Cohesion', in S.A. Levis (ed.), *Games, Groups, and the Global Good*, Berlin and Heidelberg: Physica.
Frank, S. A. (2011a), 'Measurement Scale in Maximum Entropy Models of Species Abundance', *Journal of Evolutionary Biology*, **24**, 485–496.
Frank, S. A. (2011b), 'Natural Selection. III. Selection versus Transmission and the Levels of Selection', *Journal of Evolutionary Biology*, **25**, 227–243.
Frank, S. A. (2012a), 'Natural Selection. IV. The Price Equation', *Journal of Evolutionary Biology*, **25**, 1002–1019.
Frank, Steven A. (2012b), 'Wright's Adaptive Landscape versus Fisher's Fundamental Theorem', in Svensson, Erik and Ryan Calsbeek (eds), *The Adaptive Landscape in Evolutionary Biology*, Oxford: Oxford University Press, pp. 41–57.
Frank, S. A. and D. E. Smith (2010), 'Measurement Invariance, Entropy, and Probability', *Entropy*, **12**, 289–303.
Frank, S. A. and D. E. Smith (2011), 'A Simple Derivation and Classification of Common Probability Distributions Based on Information Symmetry and Measurement Scale', *Journal of Evolutionary Biology*, **24**, 469–484.
Franssen, Maarten, Gert-Jan Lokhorst and Ibo van de Poel (2010), 'Philosophy of Technology', in Edward N. Zalta (ed.), *The Stanford Encyclopedia of Philosophy* (Spring 2010 Edition), URL = <http://plato.stanford.edu/archives/spr2010/entries/technology/>.
Frautschi, Steven (1988), 'Entropy in an Expanding Universe', in Weber, Bruce H., David J. Depew, and James D. Smith (eds) (1988), *Entropy, Information, and Evolution: New Perspectives on Physical and Biological Evolution*, Cambridge, MA, USA and London: MIT Press, pp. 11–22.
Freeman, Chris and Carlota Perez (1988), 'Structural Crises of Adjustment, Business Cycles and Investment Behavior', in Dosi, G., R. R. Nelson, G. Silverberg and L. Soete, L (eds) (1988), *Technical Change and Economic Theory*, London: Pinter, pp. 38–66.
Freeman, Chris and Francisco Louçã (2001), *As Time Goes By: From the Industrial Revolutions to the Information Revolution*, Oxford: Oxford University Press.

Frenken, Koen (2006), *Innovation, Evolution and Complexity Theory*, Cheltenham, UK and Northampton, MA, USA: Edward Elgar.

Frey, Bruno S. (1997), *Not Just For the Money: An Economic Theory of Personal Motivation*, Brookfield: Edward Elgar.

Frey, Bruno S. and Alois Stutzer (2002), *Happiness and Economics: How the Economy and Institutions Affect Human Well–Being*, Princeton: Princeton University Press.

Frieden, B. R. and R. A. Gatenby (2011), 'Information Dynamics in Living Systems: Prokaryotes, Eukaryotes, and Cancer', *PLoSone,* **6**(7), e22085.

Frieden, B. Roy (2004), *Science from Fisher Information: A Unification*, Cambridge, UK: Cambridge University Press.

Friedman, Milton (1953), *Essays in Positive Economics*, Chicago: Chicago University Press.

Friston, K. (2010), 'The Free–energy Principle: A Unified Brain Theory', *Nature Reviews Neuroscience*, doi: 10.1038/nrn2787.

Friston, K. J. and K. E. Stephan (2006), 'Free–energy and the Brain', *Synthese*, **159**, 417–458.

Friston, K. J., J. Daunizeau, J. Kilner, and S. J. Kiebel (2010), 'Action and Behavior: A Free–energy Formulation', *Biological Cybernetics*, doi: 10.1007/s00422–010–0364–z.

Frith, C. D. and T. Singer (2008), 'The Role of Social Cognition in Decision Making', *Philosophical Transactions of the Royal Society B*, **363**: 3975–3886.

Frith, U. and C. D. Frith (2003), 'Development and Neurophysiology of Mentalizing', *Philosophical Transactions of the Royal Society B*, **358**, 459–473.

Froot, Kenneth A., Michael Kim, Michael and Kenneth Rogoff (2001), *The Law of One Price over 700 Years*, IMF Working Paper WP 01/174.

Fuchs, Christopher A. (2002), 'Quantum Mechanics as Quantum Information (and only a little more)', arXiv:quant–ph/0205039.

Fudenberg, D. and D. K. Levine (2006), 'A Dual–Self Model of Impulse Control', *American Economic Review*, **96**(5), 1449–1477.

Fujita, Masahisa, Paul Krugman and Anthony J. Venables (1999), *The Spatial Economy: Cities, Regions, and International Trade*, Cambridge, MA, USA and London: MIT Press.

Furubotn, E. (1991), 'General Equilibrium Models, Transaction Costs, and the Concept of Efficient Allocation in a Capitalist Economy', *Journal of Institutional and Theoretical Economics*, **147**, 662–686.

Furubotn, Eirik (1998), *Economic Efficiency in a World of Frictions*, Max Planck Institut zur Erforschung von Wirtschaftssystemen, Jena, Diskussionsbeitrag 09–98.

Furubotn, Eirik, and Rudolf Richter, (1997), *Institutions and Economic Theory: An Introduction to and Assessment of the New Institutional Economics*, Ann Arbor: University of Michigan Press.

Gächter, Simon, Benedikt Herrmann and Christian Thöni (2010), *Culture and Cooperation*, CESIFO Working Paper No. 3070.

Gale, D. (1996), 'What Have We Learned From Social Learning?', *European Economic Review,* **40**, 617–628.

Gallese, V. and G. Lakoff (2005), 'The Brain's Concepts: The Role of the Sensory–Motor System in Conceptual Knowledge', *Cognitive Neuropsychology*, **22**(3 & 4), 455–479.

Garbarini, F. and M. Adenzato (2004), 'At the Root of Embodied Cognition: Cognitive Science Meets Neurophysiology', *Brain and Cognition*, **56**, 100–106.
Gardner, A. and A. Grafen (2008), 'Capturing the Superorganism: A Formal Theory of Group Adaptation', *Journal of Evolutionary Biology,* **22**(4), 659–671.
Garrett, T. J. (2011a), 'Are There Basic Physical Constraints on Future Anthropogenic Emmissions of Carbon Dioxide?' *Climatic Change,* **3**, 437–455.
Garrett, T. J. (2011b), 'No Way Out? The Double Bind in Seeking Global Prosperity and Mitigating Climate Change', *Earth System Dynamics Discussion Papers*, **2**, 315–354.
Garson, James (2012), 'Connectionism', in Edward N. Zalta (ed.), *The Stanford Encyclopedia of Philosophy* (Winter 2012 Edition), URL = <http://plato.stanford.edu/archives/win2012/entries/connectionism/>.
Gazzola, V., L. Aziz–Adeh and C. Keysers (2006), 'Empathy and the Somatotopic Auditory Mirror System in Humans', *Current Biology*, **16**, 1824–1829.
Geanakoplos, J. (1992), 'Common Knowledge', *Journal of Economic Perspectives*, **6**(4), 53–82.
Geanakoplos, John (1997), 'Promises, Promises', in Arthur, W. Brian, Steven Durlauf, Steven and David Lane (eds) (1997), *The Economy as an Evolving Complex System II*, Reading: Addison–Wesley, pp. 285–320.
Geanakoplos, John (2010), *The Leverage Cycle*, Cowles Foundation Paper No. 1304.
Geanakoplos, John (2011), *What's Missing from Macroeconomics: Endeogenous Leverage and Default*, Cowles Foundation Paper No. 1332.
Gellner, Ernest (1983), *Nations and Nationalism*, Oxford: Blackwell.
Georgescu–Roegen, Nicholas (1971), *The Entropy Law and the Economic Process*, Cambridge, MA, USA: Harvard University Press.
Georgescu–Roegen, Nicholas (1976), *Energy and Economic Myths: Institutional and Analytical Economic Essays*, New York: Pergamon.
Ghiselin, Michael T. (1997), *Metaphysics and the Origin of Species*, Buffalo, NY: SUNY Press.
Ghoshal, S. (2005), 'Bad Management Theories Are Destroying Good Management Practices', *Academy of Management Learning & Education*, **4**(1), 75–91.
Gibbon, P., J. Bair and S. Ponte (2008), 'Governing Global Value Chains: An Introduction', *Economy and Society*, **37**(3), 315–338.
Giere, Ronald N. (1990), 'Evolutionary Models of Science, in: Rescher, Nicholas (ed.), *Evolution, Cognition, and Realism*, Lanham, New York and London: University Press of America, pp. 21–32.
Giere, Ronald N. (2008), 'Cognitive Studies of Science and Technology', in Hackett, Edward J., Olga Amsterdamska, Michael Lynch, Judy Wajcman, Judy (eds), *The Handbook of Science and Technology Studies*, Cambridge and London: MIT Press, pp. 259-278.
Gigerenzer, Gerd (1996), 'Rationality: Why Social Context Matters', in Baltes, Paul B. and Ursula M. Staudinger (eds), *Interactive Minds: Life–span Perspectives on the Social Foundation of Cognition*, Cambridge: Cambridge University Press, pp. 319–346.
Gigerenzer, G. (1997), 'Bounded Rationality: Models of Fast and Frugal Inference', *Swiss Journal of Economics and Statistics*, **133**, 201–218.
Gillett, Stephen L. (2006), 'Entropy and Its Misuse, I: Energy, free and otherwise', *Ecological Economics,* **56**, 58–70.

Gintis, H. (2007), 'A Framework for the Unification of the Behavioral Sciences', *Behavioral and Brain Sciences,* **30**, 1–61.

Glaeser, Edward (2011), *Triumph of the City: How Our Greatest Invention Makes Us Richer, Smarter, Greener, Healthier, and Happier*, New York: Penguin.

Glaeser, E. L. and J. D. Gottlieb (2009), 'The Wealth of Cities: Agglomeration Economies and Spatial Equilibrium in the United States', *Journal of Economic Literature*, **XLVII**(4), 983–1028.

Glaeser, E. L., D. I. Laibson and B. Sacerdote (2002), 'An Economic Approach to Social Capital', *Economic Journal*, **112**, F437–458.

Glaeser, E. L., D. I. Laibson, J. A. Scheinkman, and C. L. Soutter, Christine, L. (2000), 'Measuring Trust', *The Quarterly Journal of Economics*, August 2000, 811–845.

Gleichmann, Peter (1977) 'Die Verhäuslichung körperlicher Verrichtungen', in Gleichmann, Peter, Johan Goudsblom and Hermann Korte (eds), *Materialien zu Norbert Elias' Zivilisationstheorie*, Frankfurt: Suhrkamp, pp. 254–279.

Glimcher, Paul W. (2009), 'Choice: Towards a Standard Back–pocket Model', in Glimcher, Paul W., Colin F. Camerer, Ernst Fehr and Russel A. Poldrack (eds) (2009), *Neuroeconomics: Decision Making and the Brain*, Amsterdam: Elsevier, pp. 503–522.

Glimcher, Paul W. (2011), *Foundations of Neuroeconomic Analysis*, Oxford and New York: Oxford University Press.

Golan, Amos (2002), 'Information and Entropy Econometrics – Editor's View', *Journal of Econometrics*, **107**, 1–15.

Goodhart, C. A. E. (1977), 'The Role, Functions and Definition of Money', in Harcourt, Geoffrey C. (ed.), *The Microfoundations of Macroeconomics*, London and Basingstoke: Macmillan, pp. 205–227.

Goody, Esther (1995a), 'Introduction: Some Implications of a Social Origin of Intelligence', in Goody, Esther (ed.), *Social Intelligence and Interaction: Expressions and Implications of the Social Bias in Human Intelligence*, Cambridge: Cambridge University Press, pp. 1–36.

Goody, Jack (1983), *The Development of the Family and Marriage in Europe*, Cambridge: Cambridge University Press.

Gould, E. D., O. Moav and A. Simhon (2008), 'The Mystery of Monogamy', *American Economic Review*, **98**(1), 333–357.

Gould, Stephen Jay (2002), *The Structure of Evolutionary Theory*, Cambridge, MA, USA and London: Belknap.

Gowdy, J. and S. Mesner (1998), 'The Evolution of Georgescu–Roegen's Bioeconomics', *Review of Social Economy*, **LVI**(2), 136–156.

Goyal, Sanjeev (2011), 'Social Networks in Economics', in Scott, John and Peter Carrington (eds), *The Sage Handbook of Social Network Analysis*, Los Angeles: Sage, pp. 67–79.

Grafen, A. (1990), 'Biological Signals as Handicaps', *Journal of Theoretical Biology*, **144**, 517–546.

Grafen, A. (2002), 'A First Formal Link between the Price Equation and an Optimization Program', *Journal of Theoretical Biology*, **217**, 75–91.

Grafen, A. (2007), 'The Formal Darwinism Project: A Mid–term Report', *Journal of Evolutionary Biology*, **20**, 1243–1254.

Grafen, A. (2008), 'The Simplest Formal Argument for Fitness Optimization', *Journal of Genetics*, **87**(4), 421–433.

Granovetter, M. (1985), 'Economic Action and Social Structure: The Problem of Embeddedness', *American Journal of Sociology*, **91**(3), 481–510.

Granovetter, Mark (2002), 'A Theoretical Agenda for Economic Sociology', in Guillén, Mauro F., Randall Collins, Paula England and Marshall Meyer (eds), *The New Economic Sociology: Developments in an Emerging Field*, New York: Russell Sage Foundation, pp. 35–60.

Granovetter, M. (2005), 'The Impact of Social Structure on Economic Outcomes', *Journal of Economic Perspectives*, **19**(1), 33–50.

Greenslade, J. V. and M. Parker (2012), 'New Insights Into Price–Setting Behavior in the UK: Introduction and Survey Results', *Economic Journal*, **122**(558), F1–F16.

Greif, A. (1993), 'Contract Enforcability and Economic Institutions in Early Trade: The Maghribi Traders' Coalition', *American Economic Review*, **83**(3), 525–548.

Greif, A. (1994), 'Cultural Beliefs and the Organization of Society: A Historical and Theoretical Reflection on Collectivist and Individualist Societies', *Journal of Political Economy*, **102**(5), 912–950.

Greif, Avner (1997), 'Cultural Beliefs as a Common Resource in an Integrating World', in Dasgupta, Partha, Karl–Göran Mäler and Alessandro Vercelli (eds), *The Economics of Transnational Commons*, Oxford: Clarendon, pp. 238–296.

Griffiths, P. E. (2001), 'Genetic Information: A Metaphor In Search of a Theory', *Philosophy of Science*, **68**, 394–412.

Grönholm, T. and A. Annila (2007), 'Natural Distribution', *Mathematical Biosciences*, **210**, 659–667.

Grossman, G. and G. Maggi (2000), 'Diversity and Trade', *American Economic Review*, **90**(5), 1255–1275.

Grossman, Herschel and M. Kim (1996), 'Predation and Production', in Garfinkel, Michelle R. and Stergios Skaperdas (eds), *The Political Economy of Conflict and Appropriation*, Cambridge: Cambridge University Press, pp. 57–71.

Gudeman, Stephen (1986), *Economics as Culture: Models and Metaphors of Livelihood*, London, Boston and Henley: Routledge and Kegan Paul.

Guillén, Mauro F., Randall Collins, Paula England and Marshall Meyer (eds) (2002), *The New Economic Sociology: Developments in an Emerging Field*, New York: Russell Sage Foundation.

Guiso, L., P. Sapienza and L. Zingales (2006), 'Does Culture Affect Economic Outcomes?', *Journal of Economic Perspectives*, **20**(2), 23–48.

Gul, F. and W. Pesendorfer (2001), 'Temptation and Self–Control', *Econometrica*, **69**, 1403–1436.

Gul, Faruk and Wolfgang Pesendorfer (2008), 'The Case for Mindless Economics', in Caplin and Andrew Schotter (eds), *The Foundations of Positive and Normative Economics*, Oxford: Oxford University Press, pp. 3–41.

Gull, S.F. (1989), *Some Misconceptions about Entropy*, http://www.ucl.ac.uk/~ucesjph/reality/entropy/text.html, accessed January 15, 2013.

Gurven, M. (2004), 'To Give and to Give Not: The Behavioral Ecology of Human Food Transfers', *Behavioral and the Brain Sciences*, **27**, 543–583.

Gustafsson, Bo (1991), 'The Rise and the Behavior of Medieeval Craft Guilds, in: Gustafsson, Bo (ed), *Power and Economic Institutions: Reinterpretations in Economic History*, Aldershot: Elgar, pp. 69–106.

Hájek, Alan (2012), 'Interpretations of Probability', in Edward N. Zalta (ed.), *The Stanford Encyclopedia of Philosophy* (Winter 2012 Edition), URL = <http://plato.stanford.edu/archives/win2012/entries/probability–interpret/>.

Haken, Hermann (1983), *Synergetics, An Introduction: Nonequilibrium Phase Transitions and Self–Organization in Physics, Chemistry, and Biology*, Berlin, Heidelberg and New York: Springer.

Hall, C., D. Lindenberger, R. Kümmel, T. Kroeger and W. Eichhorn (2001), 'The Need to Reintegrate the Natural Sciences with Economics', *BioScience*, **51**(8), 663–673.

Hallwood, C. P. (1997a), 'Competencies as Private Information: An Efficient Capital Asset Pricing Theory of the Firm', *Journal of Institutional and Theoretical Economics*, **153**, 532–544.

Hallwood, C. P. (1997b), 'Transaction Cost Theory of the (Multinational) Firm', *Journal of Institutional and Theoretical Economics*, **153**, 682–687.

Hammerstein, Peter (2001), 'Games and Markets: Economic Behavior in Humans and other Animals', in Noë, Ronald, Jan A.R.A.M. van Hooff and Peter Hammerstein (eds), *Economics in Nature: Social Dilemmas, Mate Choice and Biological Markets*, Cambridge: Cambridge University Press, pp. 1–22.

Hands, D. Wade (1993), 'Popper and Lakatos in Economic Methodology', in Mäki, Uskali, Bo Gustafsson, Bo and Christian Knudsen (eds) *Rationality, Institutions and Economic Methodology*, London and New York: Routledge, pp. 61–75.

Hannan, Michael T., László Pólos and Glenn R. Carroll, (2007), *Logics of Organization Theory: Audiences, Codes, and Ecologies*, Princeton: Princeton University Press.

Hanneman, Robert A. and Mark Riddle (2005), *Introduction to Social Network Methods*, Riverside: University of California, http://faculty.ucr.edu/~hanneman/

Hanneman, Robert A. and Mark Riddle (2011), 'Concepts and Measures for Basic Network Analysis, in Scott, John and Peter Carrington (eds), *The Sage Handbook of Social Network Analysis*, Los Angeles: Sage, pp. 340–369.

Hargreaves Heap, S. P. and D. J. Zizzo (2009), 'The Value of Groups', *American Economic Review*, **99**(1), 295–323.

Harris, Marvin (1979), *Cultural Materialism: The Struggle for a Science of Culture*, New York: Random House.

Harrison, G. W. (2008), 'Neuroeconomics: A Critical Reconsideration', *Economics & Philosophy*, **24**(3), 303–344.

Hartl, Daniel L. (2000), *A Primer of Population Genetics*, Sunderland: Sinauer.

Haskel, J., R. Z. Lawrence, E. E. Leamer and M. J. Slaughter (2012), 'Globalization and U.S. Wages: Modifying Classic Theory to Explain Recent Facts', *Journal of Economic Perspectives*, **26**(2), 119–139.

Hausman, Daniel M. (1992), *The Inexact and Separate Science of Economics*, Cambridge, UK: Cambridge University Press.

Hayek, F.A. von (1945), 'The Use of Knowledge in Society', *American Economic Review*, **XXXV**(4), 519–530.

Hayek, Friedrich August von (1952), *The Sensory Order: An Inquiry into the Foundations of Theoretical Psychology*, Chicago: University of Chicago Press.

Hayek, Friedrich August von (1967), *Studies in Philosophy, Politics, and Economics*, London: Routledge & Kegan Paul.

Hayek, Friedrich August von (1972), *Die Theorie komplexer Phänomene*, Tübingen: Mohr.

Hayek, Friedrich August von (1973), *Law, Legislation and Liberty: A New Statement of the Liberal Principles of Justice and Political Economy, Volume 1: Rules and Order*, Chicago: University of Chicago Press.

Hayek, Friedrich August von (1979), *Law, Legislation and Liberty: A New Statement of the Liberal Principles of Justice and Political Economy, Volume 3: The Political Order of a Free People*, Chicago: University of Chicago Press.

Hayek, Friedrich August von (1988), *The Fatal Conceit: The Errors of Socialism*, Chicago: University of Chicago Press.

Heath, Joseph (2011), 'Methodological Individualism', in Edward N. Zalta (ed.), *The Stanford Encyclopedia of Philosophy* (Spring 2011 Edition), URL = <http://plato.stanford.edu/archives/spr2011/entries/methodological–individualism/>.

Hegel, Georg W.F. (1807/1987), *Phänomenologie des Geistes*, Stuttgart: Reclam.

Hegselmann, Rainer (1996), 'Cellular Automata in the Social Sciences: Perspectives, Restrictions, and Artefacts', in Hegselmann, Rainer et al. (eds) (1996), *Modelling and Simulation in the Social Sciences from the Philosophy of Science Point of View*, Dordrecht: Kluwer, pp. 209–233.

Heibach, Christiane (2000), 'The Process Appears: Representation and Non–Representation in Computer–based Art, in: Roy Ascott (ed.), *Art, Technology, Consciousness – mind@large*, Bristol and Portland: intellect books, pp. 47–52.

Heilbroner, R. L. (1967), 'Do Machines Make History?' *Technology and Culture*, **8**, 335–345.

Heilbroner, Robert L. (1985), *The Nature and Logic of Capitalism*, New York and London: Norton.

Hein, G. and T. Singer (2008), 'I feel How You Feel But Not Always: The Emphatic Brain and Its Modulation', *Current Opinion in Neurobiology*, **18**, 153–158.

Helanterä, H. and T. Uller (2010), 'The Price Equation and Extended Inheritance', *Philosophy and Theory in Biology*, 2010: 2:e101.

Helpman, Elhanan (2004), *The Mystery of Economic Growth*, Cambridge, MA, USA and London: Belknap.

Henderson, J. V., A. Storeygard and D. N. Weil (2012), 'Measuring Economic Growth from Outer Space', *American Economic Review*, **102**(2), 994–1028.

Hendry, Robin F. (2006): 'Is There Downward Causation in Chemistry?', in: Baird, David, Eric Scerri and Lee McIntyre, (eds), *Philosophy of Chemistry: Synthesis of a New Discipline*, Dordrecht: Springer, pp. 173–190.

Henrich, J. et al. (2005), ''Economic Man' in Cross–cultural Perspective: Behavioral Experiments in 15 Small–Scale Societies', *Behavioral and Brain Sciences*, **28**, 795–855.

Herrmann-Pillath, C. (1990), 'Der Vergleich von Wirtschafts– und Gesellschaftssystemen: Wissenschaftsphilosophische und methodologische Überlegungen zur Zukunft eines ordnungstheoretischen Forschungsprogrammes', ORDO, **42**, 15–68.

Herrmann-Pillath, C. (1992), 'The Brain, Its Sensory Order and the Evolutionary Concept of Mind: On Hayek's Contribution to Evolutionary Epistemology', *Journal for Social and Biological Structures*, **15**(2), 145–187.

Herrmann-Pillath, C. (1993), 'New Knowledge as Creation: Notes When Reading Nietzsche on Evolution, Power and Knowledge', *Journal of Social and Evolutionary Systems*, **16**(1), 25–44.

Herrmann-Pillath, Carsten (2000), *Why there is No Such Thing Like Transaction Costs, After All*, Diskussionspapier Heft 56 der Fakultät für Wirtschaftswissenschaft der Universität Witten/Herdecke, März 2000, http://ssrn.com/abstract=949075

Herrmann-Pillath, Carsten (2001a), *Kritik der reinen Theorie des internationalen Handels, Band 1: Transaktionstheoretische Grundlagen*, Marburg: Metropolis.

Herrmann-Pillath, Carsten (2001b), 'A General Refutation of the Law of One Price as Empirical Hypothesis', *Jahrbücher für Nationalökonomie und Statistik*, **221**(1), 45–67.

Herrmann-Pillath, Carsten (2002), 'Theorie und Beobachtung im neoklassischen Wachstumsmodell', in Marco Lehmann-Waffenschmidt (ed.), *Studien zur Evolutorischen Ökonomik V*, Berlin: Duncker & Humblot, pp. 187–213.

Herrmann-Pillath, C. (2006), 'The True Story of Wine and Cloth. Building Blocks of an Evolutionary Political Economy of International Trade', *Journal of Evolutionary Economics,* **16**(4), 383–417.

Herrmann-Pillath, C. (2008), 'Deducing Principles of Economics From Ontological Constraints on Information', *Journal of Economic Issues*, **XLII**(2), 317–325.

Herrmann-Pillath, C. (2009a), 'Social Capital, Chinese Style: Individualism, Relational Collectivism and the Cultural Embeddedness of the Institutions–Performance Link', *China Economic Journal*, **2**(3), 325–350.

Herrmann-Pillath, C. (2009b),' Diversity, Identity and the Indeterminacy of the Size of Nations. A Critique of the Alesina School of Thought from the Viewpoint of Evolutionary Political Economy', *European Journal of Law and Economics*, **27**, 15–38.

Herrmann-Pillath, C. (2010), 'Entropy, Function, and Evolution: Naturalizing Peircian Semiosis', *Entropy*, **12**(2), 197–242.

Herrmann-Pillath, Carsten (2010/11), *The Economics of Identity and Creativity: A Cultural Science Approach*, St. Lucia: University of Queensland Press and New Brunswick and London: Transactions.

Herrmann-Pillath, C. (2011), 'The Evolutionary Approach to Entropy: Reconciling Georgescu–Roegen's Natural Philosophy with the Maximum Entropy Framework', *Ecological Economics*, **70**, 606–616

Herrmann-Pillath, C. (2012a), 'Towards an Externalist Neuroeconomics: Dual Selves, Signs, and Choice', *Journal of Neuroscience, Psychology and Economics*, **5**(1), 38–61.

Herrmann-Pillath, C. (2013), 'Performativity of Economic Systems: Approaches and Implications for Taxonomy', forthcoming, *Journal of Economic Methodology.*

Herrmann-Pillath, C. and I.A. Boldyrev (2012), 'Hegel's 'Objective Spirit' and the Institutional Nature of Economic Action', *Mind & Society*, DOI: 10.1007/s11299–012–0111–3.

Herrmann-Pillath, C. and S. N. Salthe (2011), 'Triadic Conceptual Structure of the Maximum Entropy Approach to Evolution', *BioSystems*, **103,** 315–330.

Hesse, Günter (1982), *Die Entstehung industrialisierter Volkswirtschaften: Ein Beitrag zur theoretischen und empirischen Analyse der langfristigen wirtschaftlichen Entwicklung*, Tübingen: Mohr Siebeck.

Hicks, John (1969), *A Theory of Economic History*, Oxford: Clarendon.

Hidalgo, César A. (2009), *The Dynamics of the Economic Complexity and the Product Space over a 42 Year Period*, CID Working Paper No. 189.

Hidalgo, C. and R. Hausman (2009), 'The Building Blocks of Economic Complexity', Proceedings of the National Academy of Science, **106**(26), 10570–10575.

Hill, K. R. et al. (2011), 'Co–Residence Patterns in Hunter–Gatherer Societies Show Unique Human Social Structure', *Science*, **331**(6022), 1286–1289.

Hippel, W. von and R. Trivers (2011), 'The Evolution and Psychology of Self–Deception', *Behavioral and the Brain Sciences*, **34**, 1–56.

Hirsch, Fred (1976), *The Social Limits to Growth*, London: Routledge & Kegan Paul.

Hirshleifer, Jack (2001), *The Dark Side of the Force: Economic Foundations of Conflict Theory*, Cambridge: Cambridge University Press.

Hodges, Richard (1982), *Dark Age Economics: The Origins of Towns and Trade AD 600–1000*, London: Duckworth.

Hodgson, G. M. (1997), 'Economics and the Return to Mecca: The Recognition of Novelty and Emergence', *Structural Change and Economic Dynamics*, **8**, 399–412.

Hodgson, G. M. (1998), 'Competence and Contract in the Theory of the Firm', *Journal of Economic Behavior & Organization*, **35**, 179–201.

Hodgson, Geoffrey M. (1999), *Evolution and Institutions: On Evolutionary Economics and the Evolution of Economics*, Cheltenham, UK and Northampton, MA, USA: Edward Elgar.

Hodgson, G. M. (2004), 'Reclaiming Habit for Institutional Economics', *Journal of Economic Psychology*, **25**, 651–660.

Hodgson, G. M. (2010), 'Choice, Habit and Evolution', *Journal of Evolutionary Economics*, **20**(1), 1–18.

Hodgson, G. M. and Knudsen, T. (2004), 'The Firm as an Interactor: Firms as Vehicles for Habits and Routines', *Journal of Evolutionary Economics*, **14**(3), 281–309.

Hodgson, G. M. and T. Knudsen (2006a), 'Dismantling Lamarckism: Why Descriptions of Socio–Econonomic Evolution as Lamarckian are Misleading', *Journal of Evolutionary Economics*, **16**(4), 343–366.

Hodgson, G. M. and T. Knudsen (2006b), 'The Nature and Units of Social Selection', *Journal of Evolutionary Economics,* **16**(5), 477–490.

Hodgson, G. M. and T. Knudsen (2007), 'Evolutionary Theorizing Beyond Lamarckism: A Reply to Richard Nelson', *Journal of Evolutionary Economics*, **17**(3), 353–360.

Hoffmeyer, Jesper (1999), *Signs of Meaning in the Universe*, Bloomington: Indiana University Press.

Hoffmeyer, J. (2000), 'The Biology of Signification', *Perspectives in Biology and Medicine*, **43**(2), 252–268.

Hoffmeyer, Jesper (2006), 'Genes, Development and Semiosis', in: Eva Neumann–Held and Christoph Rehmann–Sutter (eds), *Genes in Development: Re–reading the Molecular Paradigm*, Duke University Press: Durham and London, pp. 152–174.

Holden, Nigel (2002), *Cross–Cultural Management: A Knowledge Management Perspective*, Harlow: Financial Times Prentice Hall.

Holland, John H. (1995), *Hidden Order: How Adaptation Builds Complexity*, Reading: Addison–Wesley.

Hollis, Martin (1998), *Trust Within Reason*, Cambridge: Cambridge University Press.

Hollstein, Betina (2011), 'Qualitative Approaches', in Scott, John and Peter Carrington (eds), *The Sage Handbook of Social Network Analysis*, Los Angeles: Sage, pp. 404–417.

Holm, Peter and Kåre Nolde Nielsen (2007), 'Framing Fish, Making Markets: The Construction of Individual Transferable Quotas (ITQs)', in Callon, Michel, Yuval Millo and Fabian Muniesa (eds), *Market Devices*, Malden et al.: Blackwell, pp. 173–195.

Holz, Patrick (2012), *The Modern Firm: Towards a New Paradigm*, Marburg: Metropolis.

Hopfensitz, A. and E. Reuben (2009), 'The Importance of Emotions for the Effectiveness of Social Punishment', *Economic Journal*, **119**(540), 1534–1560.

Hopkins, E. and T. Kornienko (2004), 'Running to Keep the Same Place: Consumer Choice as a Game of Status', *American Economic Review*, **94**(4), 1085–1108.

Hordijk, W., J. Hein and M. Steel (2010), 'Autocatalytic Sets and the Origin of Life', *Entropy*, 2010, **12**, 1733–1742.

Horst, U., A. Kirman and M. Teschl (2006), *Changing Identity: The Emergence of Social Groups*, GREQAM Document de Travail 2006–51.

Houston, A. I., J. M. McNamara and M. D. Steer (2007), 'Do We Expect Natural Selection to Produce Rational Behaviour?', *Philosophical Transactions of the Royal Society B*, **362**, 1531–1543.

Hsiung, B. (1999), 'Sailing Towards the Brave New World of Zero Transaction Costs', *European Journal of Law and Economics*, **8**, 153–169.

Hsu, G. and M. T. Hannan (2005), 'Identities, Genres, and Organizational Forms', *Organization Science*, **16**(5), 474–490.

Huang, Philip C. C. (1990), *The Peasant Family and Rural Development in the Yangzi Delta, 1350–1988*, Stanford: Stanford University Press.

Huang, P. C.C. (2008), 'Centralized Minimalism: Semiformal Governance by Quasi Officials and Dispute Resolution in China', *Modern China*, **34**(1), 9–35.

Huang, P. C. C., G. Yuan and Y. Peng (2012), 'Capitalization Without Proletarianization in China's Agricultural Development', *Modern China*, **38**(2), 139–173.

Hubert, M. (2010), 'Does Neuroeconomics Give New Impetus to Economic and Consumer Research?', *Journal of Economic Psychology*, **31**, 812–817.

Hubert, M. and P. Kenning (2008), 'A Current Overview of Consumer Neuroscience', *Journal of Consumer Behavior*, **7**, 272–292.

Hull, David L. (1988), 'Interactors versus Vehicles', in Plotkin, H. C., ed. (1988), *The Role of Behavior in Evolution*, Cambridge, MA, USA and London: MIT Press, pp. 19–50.

Hull, D. L., R. E. Langman, Rodney E. and S. S. Glenn (2001), 'A General Account of Selection: Biology, Immunology and Behaviour', *Behavioral and Brain Sciences*, **24**(2), 511–573.

Hull, David and Wilkins, John S. (2008), 'Replication', in Edward N. Zalta (ed.), The Stanford Encyclopedia of Philosophy (Winter 2008 Edition), URL = <http://plato.stanford.edu/archives/win2008/entries/replication/>.

Humphrey, N. (2007), 'The Society of Selves', *Philosophical Transactions of the Royal Society B*, **362**, 745–754.

Hurley, S. (2008), 'The Shared Circuits Model: How Control, Mirroring and Simulation Can Enable Imitation, Deliberation, and Mindreading', *Behavioral and the Brain Sciences*, **31**(1), 1–21.

Hurwicz, L. (2008), 'But Who Will Guard the Guardians?', *American Economic Review*, **98**(3), 577–585.

Husserl, Edmund (1985), *Die phänomenologische Methode: Ausgewählte Texte 1*, Stuttgart: Reclam.

Hutchins, Edwin (1995), *Cognition in the Wild*, Cambridge and London: MIT Press.

Hutchins, E. (2005), 'Material Anchors for Conceptual Blends', *Journal of Pragmatics*, **37**, 1555–1577.

Hutteger, S. M. (2010), 'Generic Properties of Evolutionary Games and Adaptationism', *The Journal of Philosophy*, **CVII**(2), 80–102.

Hutter, Michael (1994), 'Communication in Economic Evolution: The Case of Money Changing the Primary Distinction: From Observer to Observation', in England, Richard W. (ed.), *Evolutionary Concepts in Contemporary Economics*, Ann Arbor: University of Michigan Press, pp. 111–138.

Ingham, Geoffrey (2000), ''Babylonian Madness': On the Historical and Sociological Origins of Money', in Smithin, John (ed.), *What Is Money?*, Abingdon and New York: Routledge, pp. 16–41.

Ingold, Tim (1986), *Evolution and Social Life*, Cambridge: Cambridge University Press.

Jablonka, Eva and Marion J. Lamb (2006), *Evolution in Four Dimensions: Genetic, Epigenetic, Behavioral and Symbolic Variation in the History of Life,* Cambridge, MA, USA and London: MIT Press.

Jackson, M. O. and B. W. Rogers (2007), 'Meeting Strangers and Friends of Friends: How Random Are Social Networks?', *American Economic Review*, **97**(3), 890–915.

James Jr., H. S. (2005), 'Why Did You Do That? A Economic Explanation of the Effect of Extrinsic Compensation on Intrinsic Motivation and Performance', *Journal of Economic Psychology*, **26**, 549–566.

Jamison, J. and J. Wegener (2010), 'Multiple Selves in Intertemporal Choice', *Journal of Economic Psychology*, **31**, 832–839.

Jaynes, E. T. (1957a), 'Information Theory and Statistical Mechanics', *The Physical Review*, **106**(4), 620–630.

Jaynes, E. T. (1957b), 'Information Theory and Statistical Mechanics II', *The Physical Review*, **108**(2), 171–190.

Jaynes, E. T. (1965), 'Gibbs vs. Boltzmann Entropies', *American Journal of Physics*, **33**(5), 391–398.

Jaynes, E. T. (1982), 'Comments on "Natural Resources: The Laws of Their Scarcity" by N. Georgescu–Roegen', http://bayes.wustl.edu/etj/articles/natural.resources.pdf, accessed January 14, 2013.

Jaynes, Edward T. (1990), 'The Second Law as Physical Fact and As Human Inference', http://bayes.wustl.edu/etj/articles/second.law.pdf, accessed January 14, 2013.

Jaynes, Edward T. (2003), *Probability Theory. The Logic of Science*, Cambridge: Cambridge University Press.

Jessop, B. and S. Oosterlynck (2008), 'Cultural Political Economy: On Making the Cultural Turn Without Falling Into Soft Economic Sociology', *Geoforum*, **39**, 1155–1169.

Ji, L., R. E. Nisbett and K. Peng (2000), 'Culture, Control, and Perception of Relationships in the Environment', *Journal of Personality and Social Psychology*, **78**(5), 943–955.

Ji, L., R. E. Nisbett and Z. Zhang (2004), 'Is It Culture or Is It Language? Examination of Language Effects in Cross–Cultural Research on Categorization', *Journal of Personality and Social Psychology*, **87**(1), 57–65.

Ji Sungchul (2012), *Molecular Theory of the Living Cell: Concepts, Molecular Mechanisms, and Biomedical Applications*, New York: Springer.

Jones, Ch. I. (2002), 'Sources of U.S. Economic Growth in a World of Ideas', *American Economic Review*, **92**(1), 220–239.

Jones, Eric L. (1988), *Growth Recurring*, Oxford: Oxford University Press.

Jones, Eric L. (2006), *Cultures Merging: An Historical and Economic Critique of Culture*, Princeton: Princeton University Press.

Kåberger, T. and B. Månsson (2001), 'Entropy and Economic Processes – Physics Perspectives', *Ecological Economics*, **36**, 165–179.

Kahnemann, D. (2003), 'Maps of Bounded Rationality: Psychology for Behavioral Economics', American Economic Review, **93**(5), 1449–1475

Kahnemann, D. and A. B. Krueger (2006), 'Developments in the Measurement of Subjective Well–Being', *Journal of Economic Perspectives*, **20**(1), 3–24.

Kahnemann, D., P. P. Wakker, and R. Sarin (1997), 'Back to Bentham? Explorations of Experienced Utility', *Quarterly Journal of Economics*, **112**, 375–405.

Kåhre, Jan (2002), *The Mathematical Theory of Information*, Boston, Dordrecht and London: Kluwer.

Karlan, D. S. (2005), 'Using Experimental Economics to Measure Social Capital and Predict Financial Decisions', *American Economic Review*, **95**(5), 1688–1699.

Karnani, M., K. Pääkkönnen and A. Annila (2009), 'The Physical Nature of Information', *Proceedings of the Royal Society A*, doi:10.1098/rspa.2009.0063.

Kauffman, Stuart A. (1993), *The Origins of Order, Self–Organization and Selection in Evolution*, New York and Oxford: Oxford University Press.

Kauffman, Stuart A. (2000), *Investigations*, Oxford: Oxford University Press.

Keen, Steve (2010), 'Solving the Paradox of Monetary Profits', *Economics: The Open–Access, Open–Assessment E–Journal*, **4**, 2010–31, doi:10.5018/economics–ejournal,ja.2010–31.

Keller, W. and C. H. Shiue (2007), 'Markets in China and Europe on the Eve of the Industrial Revolution', *American Economic Review*, **97**(4), 1189–1216.

Kennedy, Juliette (2012), 'Kurt Gödel', in Edward N. Zalta (ed.), *The Stanford Encyclopedia of Philosophy* (Winter 2012 Edition), URL = <http://plato.stanford.edu/archives/win2012/entries/goedel/>.

Kerr, B. and P. Godfrey–Smith (2008), 'Generalization of the Price Equation for Evolutionary Change', *Evolution*, **63**(2), 531–536.

Keynes, John M. (1936/1960): *The General Theory of Employment, Interest and Money*, London: Macmillan.

Khaitovitch, P. et al. (2008), 'Metabolic Changes in Schizophrenia and Human Brain Evolution', *Genome Biology*, **9**, R124.

Khalil, E. (1990), 'Entropy Law and Exhaustion of Natural Resources: Is Nicholas Georgescu–Roegen's Paradigm Defensible?', *Ecological Economics*, **2**, 163–178.

Kim, Jaegwon (2009), 'Mental Causation', in: McLaughlin, Brian P., Ansgar Beckermann and Sven Walter (eds) (2009), *The Oxford Handbook of Philosophy of Mind*, Oxford: Clarendon Press, pp. 29–53.

Kirman, A. P. (1992), 'Whom or What Does the Representative Individual Represent?', *Journal of Economic Perspectives*, **6**(2):, 117–136.

Kirman, Alan P. (2001), 'Market Organization and Individual Behavior: Evidence From Fish Markets', in Rauch, James E. and Alessandra Casella (eds) (2001), *Networks and Markets*, New York: Russell Sage Foundation, pp. 155–195.

Kirman, A. and M. Teschl (2006), 'Searching for Identity in the Capability Space', *Journal of Economic Methodology,* **13**(3), 299–325.

Kirman, A. and M. Teschl (2010), 'Selfish of Selfless? The Role of Empathy in Economics', *Philosophical Transactions of the Royal Society B,* **365**, 303–317.

Kirman, A., P. Livet and M. Teschl (2010), 'Rationality and Emotions', *Philosophical Transactions of the Royal Society B*, **365**, 215–219.

Kiwit, D. (1994), 'Zur Leistungsfähigkeit neoklassisch orientierter Transaktionskostenansätze', ORDO, **45**, 105–135.

Kleidon, A. (2009), 'Non–equilibrium Thermodynamics and Maximum Entropy Production in the Earth System: Applications and Implications', *Naturwissenschaften*, **96**, 653–677.

Kleidon, A. (2010), 'Non–equilibrium Thermodynamics, Maximum Entropy Production and Earth–system evolution', *Philosophical Transactions of the Royal Society A*, **368**, 181–196.

Kleidon, A. (2011), 'Life, Hierarchy, and the Thermodynamic Machinery of Planet Earth', *Physics of Life Reviews*, **7**, 424–460.

Kleidon, A., Y. Malhi, and P. M. Cox (2010), 'Maximum Entropy Production in Environmental and Ecological Systems', *Philosophical Transactions of the Royal Society B*, **365**, 1297–1302.

Kleidon, Axel and Ralph Lorenz (2005), 'Entropy Production in Earth System Processes', in Kleidon, Axel and Ralph Lorenz (eds) (2005), *Non–equilibrium Thermodynamics and the Production of Entropy: Life, Earth, and Beyond*, Heidelberg: Springer, pp. 1–20.

Kliemt, Hartmut (1985), *Moralische Institutionen: Empiristische Theorien ihrer Evolution*, Freiburg und München: Alber.

Kliemt, Hartmut (1986), *Antagonistische Kooperation: Elementare spieltheoretische Modelle spontaner Ordnungsentstehung*, Freiburg und München. Alber.

Knauft, B.M. (1987), 'Reconsidering Violence in Simple Human Societies: Homicide Among the Gebusi of New Guinea', *Current Anthropology*, **28**(4), 457–500.

Knoke, David and Song Yang (2008), *Social Network Analysis*, Los Angeles: Sage.

Knorr Cetina, K. and U. Bruegger (2002), 'Global Microstructures: The Virtual Societies of Financial Markets', *American Journal of Sociology*, **107**(4), 905–950.

Knudsen, Christian (1993), 'Equilibrium, Perfect Rationality and the Problem of Self–Reference in Economics', in Mäki, Uskali, Bo Gustafsson, Bo and Christian Knudsen (eds) *Rationality, Institutions and Economic Methodology*, London and New York: Routledge, 133–170.

Knudsen, T. (2002), 'Economic Selection Theory', *Journal of Evolutionary Economics*, **12**(4), 443–470.

Knudsen, T. (2004), 'General Selection Theory and Economic Evolution: The Price Equation and the Replicator/Interactor Distinction', *Journal of Economic Methodology*, **11**(2), 147–173.

Knutson, B. and P. Bossaerts (2007), 'Neural Antecedents of Financial Decisions', *The Journal of Neuroscience*, **27**(31), 8147–8177

Knutson, B. and R. Petersin (2005), 'Neurally Reconstructing Expected Utility', *Games and Economic Behavior*, **52**, 305–315.

Knutson, B. and S. Greer (2008), 'Anticipatory Affect: Neural Correlates and Consequences for Choice', *Philosophical Transactions of the Royal Society B*, doi:10.1098/rstb.2008.0155.

Knutson, B. et al. (2008), 'Neural Antecedents of the Endowment Effect', *Neuron*, **58**, 814–822.

Knutson, Brian and G. Elliott Wimmer (2007), 'Reward: Neural Circuitry for Social Valuation', in Harmon-Jones, E. and P. Winkielman (eds), *Social Neuroscience*, New York: Guilford Press, pp. 157–175.

Knutson, Brian, Mauricio Delgado, and Paul E.M. Phillips (2009), 'Representation of Subjective Value in the Striatum', in Glimcher, Paul W., Colin F. Camerer, Ernst Fehr and Russel A. Poldrack (eds) (2009), *Neuroeconomics: Decision Making and the Brain*, Amsterdam: Elsevier, pp. 389–406.

Köhler, Ulrich (1985), 'Formen des Handels aus ethnologischer Sicht', in Düwel, Klaus et al. (eds), *Untersuchungen zu Handel und Verkehr der vor– und frühgeschichtlichen Zeit in Mittel– und Nordeuropa, Teil I: Methodische Grundlagen und Darstellungen zum Handel in vorgeschichtlicher Zeit und in der Antike*, Göttingen: Vandenhoeck & Ruprecht, 13–55.

Konner, Melvin (2002), *The Tangled Wing: Biological Constraints on the Human Spirit*, 2nd Edition, New York: Henry Holt.

Koppl, R.and J. B. Rosser, Jr (2002), 'All That I Have To Say Has Already Crossed Your Mind', *Metroeconomica*, **53**, 339–360.

Kotkin, Joel (1992), *Tribes: How Race, Religion, and Identity Determine Success in the New Global Economy*, New York: Random House.

Kramer, Donald L. (2001), 'Foraging Behaviour', in Fox, Ch. W., D. A. Roff and D. J. Fairbairn (eds) (2001), *Evolutionary Ecology: Concepts and Case Studies*, Oxford: Oxford University Press, pp. 232–246.

Kranton, R. E. (1996), 'Reciprocal Exchange: A Self–Sustaining System', *American Economic Review,* **86**(4), 830–851.

Kremer, M. (1993), 'The O–Ring Theory of Economic Development', *Quarterly Journal of Economics*, **108**, 551–575.

Krippner, Greta (2005), 'The Financialization of the American Economy', *Socio–Economic Review*, **3**, 173–208.

Krugman, Paul (1991), *Geography and Trade*, Cambridge, MA, USA, London and Leuven: MIT Press and Leuven University Press.

Krugman, Paul (1996), *The Self–Organizing Economy*, Cambridge, UK and Oxford: Blackwell.

Kubon–Gilke, Gisela (1997), *Verhaltensbindung und die Evolution ökonomischer Institutionen*, Marburg: Metropolis.

Kull, Kalevi (2007), 'Biosemiotics and Biophysics – The Fundamental Approaches to the Study of Life', in Barbieri, M. (ed.), *Introduction to Biosemiotics*, New York: Springer, 167–177.

Kull, K., T. Deacon, C. Emmeche, J. Hoffmeyer and F. Stjernfelt (2009), 'Theses on Biosemiotics: Prolegomena to a Theoretical Biology', *Biological Theory*, **4**(2), 167–173.

Kümmel, Reiner (1998), *Energie und Kreativität*, Stuttgart and Leipzig: Teubner.

Küppers, Bernd–Olaf (1986), *Der Ursprung biologischer Information: Zur Naturphilosophie der Lebensentstehung*, München and Zürich: Piper.

Kuran, Timur (1995), *Private Truths, Public Lies: The Social Consequences of Preference Falsification*, Cambridge, MA, USA and London: Harvard University Press.

Kuran, Timur (2009), 'Explaining the Economic Trajectories of Civilizations: The Systemic Approach', *Journal of Economic Behavior & Organization*, **71**: 593–605.

La Porta, R., F. Lopez-de-Silvanes, A., Shleifer and R. W. Vishny (1999), 'The Quality of Government', *Journal of Law, Economics, and Organization*, **15**, 222–279.

Ladyman, James and Don Ross, with David Spurrett and John Collier (2007), *Every Thing Must Go: Metaphysics Naturalized*, Oxford: Oxford University Press.

Lahav, N., S. Nir and A. C. Elitzur (2001), 'The Emergence of Life on Earth', *Progress in Biophysics and Molecular Biology*, **75**, 75–120.

Laibson, D. (1997), 'Golden Eggs and Hyperbolic Discounting', *Quarterly Journal of Economics*, May 1997, 443–477.

Laibson, D. (2002), 'A Cue–Theory of Consumption', *The Quarterly Journal of Economics*, **116**(1), 81–119.

Lakoff, George (2008), 'The Neural Theory of Metaphor', in Gibbs, Raymond W. (ed), *The Cambridge Handbook of Metaphor and Thought*, New York: Cambridge University Press, pp. 17–38.

Landa, Janet T. (1994), *Trust, Ethnicity, and Identity: Beyond the New Institutional Economics of Ethnic Trading Networks, Contract Law, and Gift–Exchange*, Ann Arbor: Michigan University Press.

Landauer, Rolf (1961), 'Irreversibility and Heat Generation in the Computing Process' (reprint 2000), *IBM Journal of Research and Development*, **44**(1/2), 261–269.

Landes, D. S. (2006), 'Why Europe and the West? Why Not China?', *Journal of Economic Perspectives*, **20**(2), 3–22.

Landreth, A. and J. Bickle (2008), 'Neuroeconomics, Neurophysiology and the Common Currency Hypothesis', *Economics & Philosophy*, **24**(3), 419–429.

Landsberg, P.T. (1984), 'Can Entropy and "Order" Increase Together?' *Physics Letters*, **102A**,171–173.

Lane, David A. (2002), 'Complexity and Local Interactions: Towards a Theory of Industrial Districts', in Curzio, Alberto Quadrio and Marco Fortis (eds), *Complexity and Industrial Clusters: Dynamics and Models in Theory and Practice*, Heidelberg and New York: Physica, pp. 65–82.

Latour, Bruno (2005), *Reassembling the Social: An Introduction to Actor–Network.Theory*, Oxford: Oxford University Press.

Lau, Joe and Max Deutsch (2012), 'Externalism About Mental Content', Edward N. Zalta, *The Stanford Encyclopedia of Philosophy* (Winter 2012 Edition), (ed.), URL = <http://plato.stanford.edu/archives/win2012/entries/content–externalism/>.

Laughlin, Robert B. (2005), *A Different Universe. Reinventing Physics From the Bottom Down*, New York: Basic Books.

Lavis, D.A. and R.F. Streater (2002), 'Physics From Fisher Information', *Studies in the History and Philosophy of Modern Physics*, **33**, 327–343.

Lawson, C. (2008), 'An Ontology of Technology: Artifacts, Relations and Functions', *Techné*, **12**(1), 48–64.

Layzer, David (1988): Growth of Order in the Universe, in Weber, Bruce H., David J. Depew, and James D. Smith (eds) (1988), *Entropy, Information, and Evolution: New Perspectives on Physical and Biological Evolution*, Cambridge, MA, USA and London: MIT Press, pp. 23–40.

Lazaric, N. (2011), 'Organizational Routines and Cognition: An Introduction to Empirical and Analytical Contributions', *Journal of Institutional Economics*, **7**(2), 147–156.

Lea, S. G. and P. Webley (2006), 'Money As Tool, Money As Drug: The Biological Psychology of a Strong Incentive', *Behavioral and the Brain Sciences*, **29**, 161–209.

Leamer, E. E. (2007), 'A Flat World, a Level Playing Field, a Small World After All, or None of the Above? A Review of Thomas L. Friedman's The World is Flat', *Journal of Economic Literature*, **XLV**, 83–126.

Leamer, Edward E. (1992), *Testing Trade Theory*, NBER Working Paper 3957.

Leamer, Edward E. and James Levinsohn (1995), 'International Trade Theory: The Evidence', in: Grossman, Gene M. and Kenneth Rogoff (eds) (1995), *Handbook of International Economics, Vol. 3*, Amsterdam: Elsevier, pp. 1339–1394.

LeDoux, Joseph E. (1997), *The Emotional Brain: The Mysterious Underpinnings of Emotional Life*, New York: Simon & Schuster.

LeDoux, Joseph E. (2000), 'Emotion Circuits in the Brain', *Annual Review of Neuroscience*, **23**, 155–184.

Leigh Jr, E. G. (2009), 'The Group Selection Controversy', *Journal of Evolutionary Biology*, **23**, 6–19.

Leigh Jr, Egbert Giles (2001), 'Adaptation, Adaptionism, and Optimality', in Orzack, Steven Hecht and Elliott Sober (eds) (2001), *Adaptationism and Optimality*, Cambridge et al.: Cambridge University Press, pp. 358–382.

Leigh Jr., E. G. (2009), 'The Group Selection Controversy', *Journal of Evolutionary Biology*, **23**, 6–19.

Levine, Joseph (1983), 'Materialism and Qualia: The Explanatory Gap', *Pacific Philosophical Quarterly*, **64**, 354–361.

Levine, Joseph (2009), 'The Explanatory Gap, in McLaughlin, Brian P., Ansgar Beckermann and Sven Walter (eds) (2009), *The Oxford Handbook of Philosophy of Mind*, Oxford: Clarendon Press, pp. 281–291.

Levinson, Paul (1988), *Mind at Large: Knowing in the Technological Age, Research in Philosophy and Technology, Supplement 2*, Greenwich and London: JAI Press.

Lewis, Charlie and Jeremy I. M. Carpendale (2002), 'Social Cognition', in Smith P. K. and C. Hart (eds), *Blackwell Handbook of Social Cognition*, Oxford: Blackwell, pp. 375–393.

Lewis, David K. (1969), *Convention*, Cambridge, MA, USA: Harvard University Press.

Lewontin, Richard (2011), 'The Genotype/Phenotype Distinction', in Edward N. Zalta (ed.), *The Stanford Encyclopedia of Philosophy (Summer 2011 Edition)*, URL = http://plato.stanford.edu/archives/sum2011/entries/genotype–phenotype/

Libbrecht, K. G. (2005), 'The Physics of Snow Crystals', *Reports on Progress in Physics*, **68**, 855–895.

Lin, Nan (2001*), Social Capital: A Theory of Social Structure and Action*, Cambridge: Cambridge University Press.

Lindenberger, D., R. Stresing and R. Kümmel (2008), 'Cointegration of Output, Capital, Labor, and Energy', *European Physical Journal B*, **66** (2), 279–287.

List, J. A. (2006), 'The Behavioralist Meets the Market: Measuring Social Preferences and Reputation Effects in Actual Transactions', *Journal of Political Economy*, **114**(1), 1–37.

Lloyd, Elisabeth (2012), 'Units and Levels of Selection', in Edward N. Zalta (ed.), The Stanford Encyclopedia of Philosophy (Winter 2012 Edition), URL = <http://plato.stanford.edu/archives/win2012/entries/selection–units/>.

Lloyd, Seth (1999), *Universe as a Quantum Computer*, arXiv:quant–ph/9912088.

Lloyd, Seth (2000), *Ultimate Physical Limits to Computation*, arXiv:quant–ph/9908043.

Lloyd, Seth (2001), *Computational Capacity of the Universe*, arXiv:quant–ph/0110141.

Lloyd, Seth (2006), *Progamming the Universe: A Quantum Computer Scientist Takes on the Cosmos*, New York: Knopf.Lloyd, S. and H. Pagels (1988), 'Complexity as Thermodynamic Depth', *Annals of Physics*, **188**, 186–213.

Lloyd, S. and H. Pagels (1988), 'Complexity as Thermodynamic Depth', *Annals of Physics*, **188**: 186–213.

Loasby, B. (2001), 'Time, Knowledge and Evolutionary Dynamics: Why Connections Matter', *Journal of Evolutionary Economics*, **11**(4), 393–412.

Locke, J. L. and B. Bogin, (2006), 'Language and Life History: A New Perspective on the Development and Evolution of Human Language, *Behavioral and Brain Sciences*, **29**, 259–280.

Loewenstein, G. (1996), 'Out of Control: Visceral Influences on Behaviour', *Organizational Behavior and Human Decision Processes*, **65**(3), 272–292.

Lord, P. (2010), 'An Evolutionary Approach to Function', *Journal of Biomedical Semantics*, **1**(Suppl 1), 54.

Lorenz, J., H. Rauhut, F. Schweitzer and D. Helbing (2011), 'How Social Influence Can Undermine the Wisdom of Crowd Effect', *Proceedings of the National Academy of Sciences*, www.pnas.org/cgi/doi/10.1073/pnas.1008636108.

Lorenz, Konrad (1973), *Die Rückseite des Spiegels*, 9. Aufl. 1987, München: dtv.

Lorenzen, Mark (2007), 'Localized Learning and Social Capital, in Rutten, Roel and Frans Boekema (eds), *The Learning Region: Foundations, State of the Art, Future*, Cheltenham, UK and Northampton, MA, USA: Edward Elgar, pp. 206–230.

Lösch, August (1945/1962), *Die räumliche Ordnung der Wirtschaft*, Stuttgart: Gustav Fischer.

Lotka, A. (1922a), 'Contribution to the Energetics of Evolution', *Proceedings of the National Academy of Sciences*, **8**, 147–151.

Lotka, A. (1922b), 'Natural Selection as a Physical Principle', *Proceedings of the National Academy of Sciences,* **8**, 151–154.

Lotka, A. (1945), 'The Law of Evolution as a Maximal Principle', *Human Biology*, **17**(3): 167–194, reprint in: Schweitzer, Frank and Gerald Silverberg (ed) (1998), *Evolution und Selbstorganisation in der Ökonomie, Selbstorganisation, Jahrbuch für Komplexität in den Natur–, Sozial– und Geisteswissenschaften*, Band 9, Berlin: Duncker & Humblot, pp. 443–465.

Lotman, Juri (2005), 'On the Semiosphere', *Sign System Studies*, **33**(1), 205–229.

Lovelock, J. E. (1990), *Hands up for the Gaia Hypothesis*, *Nature*, **344** (6262), 100–102.

Lovelock, J. E. and L. Margulis (1974), 'Atmospheric Homeostasis For and By the Biosphere: The Gaia Hypothesis', *Tellus*, **26**(1–2), 2–10.

Lozada, Gabriel A. (2006), 'Entropy, Free Energy, Work, and other Thermodynamic Variables in Economics', *Ecological Economics*, **56**, 71–78.
Lucas, J. R. (1961), 'Minds, Machines, and Gödel', *Philosophy*, **XXXVI**, 112–127.
Luchini, S. and M. Teschl (2004), 'Is There Personal Identity in Economics?' *Ethics and Economics*, **3**(1), https://papyrus.bib.umontreal.ca/jspui/bitstream/1866/3328/1/2005v3n1_LUCHINI_ET_TESCHL.pdf, accessed January 22, 2013.
Luhmann, Niklas (1984), *Soziale Systeme: Grundriß einer allgemeinen Theorie*, Frankfurt: Suhrkamp.
Lumsden, Charles and Edward O. Wilson (1981), *Genes, Mind and Culture: The Coevolutionary Process*, Cambridge, MA, USA and London: Harvard University Press.
Lycan, William G. (1999), *Philosophy of Language: An Introductory Text*, London and New York: Routledge.
Ma Debin (2012), 'Rock, Scissors, Paper: The Problem of Incentives and Information in the Traditional Chinese State and the Origin of the Great Divergence', in Aoki, Masahiko, Timur Kuran and Gérard Roland (eds), *Institutions and Comparative Economic Development*, IEA Conference Volume 150/1, London: Palgrave Macmillan.
Macdonald, Graham and David Papineau (2006), 'Introduction: Prospects and Problems for Teleosemantics', in Macdonald, Graham and David Papineau (eds), *Teleosemantics: New Philosophical Essays*, Oxford and New York: Oxford University Press, pp. 1–22.
MacFarlane, Alan and Sarah Harrison (2000), 'Technological Evolution and Involution: A Preliminary Comparison of Europe and Japan', in Ziman, John (ed.), *Technological Innovation as an Evolutionary Process*, Cambridge: Cambridge University Press, pp. 77–90.
MacKenzie, Donald (2006), *An Engine, Not a Camera: How Financial Models Shape Markets*, Cambridge and London: MIT Press.
MacKenzie, Donald (2007), 'Is Economics Performative? Option Theory and the Construction of Derivatives Market's, in MacKenzie, Donald, Fabian Muniesa and Lucia Siu (eds), *Do Economists Make Markets? On the Performativity of Economics*, Princeton and Oxford: Princeton University Press, pp. 54–86.
Mailath, G. J., A. Postlewaite and L. Samuelson (2004), 'Sunk Investments Lead to Unpredictable Prices', *American Economic Review*, **94**(4), 896–918.
Mäkelä, T. and Annila, A. (2010), 'Natural Patterns of Energy Dispersal', *Physics of Life Reviews*, **7**, 477–498.
Malerba, F., R. R. Nelson, L. Orsenigo and S. Winter (2007), 'Demand, Innovation, and the Dynamics of Market Structure: The Role of Experimental Users and Diverse Preferences', *Journal of Evolutionary Economics*, **17**(4), 371–400.
Malinas, Gary and Bigelow, John (2012), 'Simpson's Paradox', in: Edward N. Zalta (ed.), The Stanford Encyclopedia of Philosophy (Winter 2012 Edition), URL = <http://plato.stanford.edu/archives/win2012/entries/paradox–simpson/>.
Mandelbrot, Benoit and Richard L. Hudson (2008), *The (Mis)Behavior of Markets: A Fractal View of Risk, Ruin and Reward*, London: Profile Books.
Mann, Michael (1986), *The Sources of Social Power, Vol. I: A History of Power From the Beginning to A.D. 1760*, Cambridge: Cambridge University Press.
Mantzavinos, Chrysostomos (2001), *Individuals, Institutions, and Markets*, Cambridge: Cambridge University Press.

Mantzavinos, Chrysostomos (2005), *Naturalistic Hermeneutics*, Cambridge: Cambridge University Press.

Marglin, Stephen A. (1991), 'Understanding Capitalism: Control versus Efficiency', in Gustafsson, Bo (ed), *Power and Economic Institutions: Reinterpretations in Economic History*, Aldershot: Elgar, pp. 225–252.

Margulis, Lynn (1999), *Symbiotic Planet: A New Look At Evolution*, Houston: Basic Books.

Markose, S. M. (2005), 'Computability and Evolutionary Complexity: Markets as Complex Adaptive Systems (CAS), *Economic Journal*, **115**(504), F159–F193.

Markose, Sheri (1998), The Liar Strategy and Surprises: So What Is the Lucas Critique? A New Perspective From Computation Theory, http://privatewww.essex.ac.uk/~scher/markets_as_complex_adaptive_syst.htm, accessed January 24, 2013.

Maroney, Owen (2009), 'Information Processing and Thermodynamic Entropy', in Edward N. Zalta (ed*.), The Stanford Encyclopedia of Philosophy* (Fall 2009 Edition), URL = <http://plato.stanford.edu/archives/fall2009/entries/information–entropy/>.

Marshall, Alfred (1890), *The Principles of Economics*, London: Macmillan.

Martyushev, L. M. and V. D. Seleznev, V.D. (2006), 'Maximum Entropy Production Principle in Physics, Chemistry and Biology', *Physics Reports*, **426**, 1–45.

Matsumoto, David and Hyi Sung Hwang (2011), 'Culture, Emotion, and Expression', in Gelfland, Michele J., Chi–yue Chiu and Ying–yi Hong (eds), *Advances in Culture and Psychology, Volume One*, Oxford and New York: Oxford University Press, pp. 53–98.

Matthen, Mohan (2006), 'Teleosemantics and the Consumer, in Macdonald, Graham and David Papineau (eds), *Teleosemantics: New Philosophical Essays*, Oxford and New York: Oxford University Press, pp. 146–166.

Maynard Smith, J. (2000), 'The Concept of Information in Biology', *Philosophy of Science*, **67**(2), 177–194.

Maynard Smith, John and Eörs Szathmáry (1995), *The Major Transitions in Evolution*, Oxford and New York: Freeman.

Mayr, Ernst (1982), *The Growth of Biological Thought: Diversity, Evolution, and Inheritance*, Cambridge, MA, USA and London: Belknap.

McCarthy, I. (2005), 'Towards a Phylogenetic Reconstruction of Organizational Life', *Journal of Bioeconomics*, **7**, 271–307.

McCarthy, I., K. Ridgway, M. Leseure and N. Fieller (2000), 'Organisational Diver–sity, Evolution and Cladistic Classifications', *Omega*, **28**, 77–95.

McCloskey, Donald N. (1994), *Knowledge and Persuasion in Economics*, Cambridge: Cambridge University Press.

McClure, S. M. et al. (2004), 'Neural Correlates of Behavioral Preference for Culturally Familiar Drinks', *Neuron*, **44**, 379–387.

McClure, S. M., K. M. Ericson, D. I. Laibson, G. Loewenstein, and J. D. Cohen (2007), 'Time Discounting for Primary Rewards', *The Journal of Neuroscience*, **27**(21), 5796–5804.

McDermott, R., J. H. Fowler and O. Smirnov (2008), 'On the Evolutionary Origin of Prospect Theory Preferences', *The Journal of Politics*, **70**(2), 335–350.

McGill, B. J. (2010), 'Towards a Unification of Unified Theories of Biodiversity, Ecology Letters', **13**, 627–642.

McLaren, J. (1997), 'Size, Sunk Cost, and Judge Bowker's Objection to Free Trade', *American Economic Review*, **87**(3), 400–420.
McNeill, J. R. and William H. McNeill (2003), *The Human Web: A Bird's–eye View of World History*, New York and London: Norton.
Mehta, Jal (2011), 'The Varied Roles of Ideas in Politics: From "Whether" to "How"', in Béland, Daniel and Robert Henry Cox (eds), *Ideas and Politics in Social Science Research*, Oxford: Oxford University Press, pp. 23–46.
Menary, R. (2007), 'Writing as Thinking', *Language Sciences*, **29**, 621–632.
Mengel, F. (2009), 'Conformism and Cooperation in a Local Interaction Model', *Journal of Evolutionary Economics*, **19**(3), 397–416.
Menger, Carl (1892), 'On the Origins of Money', *Economic Journal*, **2**, 239–55, http://socserv.mcmaster.ca/econ/ugcm/3ll3/menger/money.txt
Mercer, J. (2010), 'Emotional Beliefs', *International Organization*, **64**, 1–31.
Mesoudi, A. (2011), 'Culture and the Darwinian Renaissance in the Social Sciences and Humanities', *Journal of Evolutionary Psychology,* 2011, 1–16, DOI: 10.1556/JEP.9.2011.29.1.
Mesoudi, A. and M. J. O'Brien (2008), The Cultural Transmission of Great Basin Projectile Point Technology II: An Agent–based Computer Simulation, *American Antiquity*, **73**(4), 627–644.
Metcalfe, J. Stanley (1998), *Evolutionary Economics and Creative Destruction*, London and New York: Routledge.
Metcalfe, J. S. (2000), 'Consumption, Preferences, and the Evolutionary Agenda', *Journal of Evolutionary Economics*, **11**(1), 37–58.
Metcalfe, J. Stanley (2001), 'Evolutionary Approaches to Population Thinking and the Problem of Growth and Development', in Dopfer, Kurt (ed.) (2001), *Evolutionary Economics. Program and Scope*, Boston, Dordrecht and London: Kluwer, pp. 141–164.
Metcalfe, J. S. (2002), 'Knowledge of Growth and the Growth of Knowledge', *Journal of Evolutionary Economics*, **12**(1–2), 3–16.
Metcalfe, J. Stanley (2009), *Technology and Economic Theory*, Papers on Economics & Evolution ,0909, MPI Jena.
Meysman, F. J. R. and S. Bruers (2010), 'Ecosystem Functioning and Maximum Entropy Production: A Quantitative Test of Hypotheses', *Philosophical Transactions of the Royal Society B*, **365**, 1405–1416.
Michaelean, K. (2011), 'Thermodynamic Dissipation Theory for the Origin of Life', *Earth System Dynamics,* **2**, 37–51.
Michalopoulos, S. (2012), 'The Origins of Ethnolinguistic Diversity', *American Economic Review*, **102**(4), 1508–1539.
Mick, D. G. (1986), 'Consumer Research and Semiotics: Exploring the Morphology of Signs, Symbols, and Significance', *Journal of Consumer Research*, **13**, 196–213.
Mick, D. G., J. E. Burroughs, P. Hetzel and M. Y. Brannen (2004), 'Pursuing the Meaning of Meaning in the Commercial World: An International Review of Marketing and Consumer Research Founded in Semiotics', *Semiotica*, **152**(1/4): 1–74.
Mijovic–Prelec, D. and D. Prelec (2010), 'Self–Deception and Self–signalling: A Model and Experimental Evidence', *Philosophical Transactions of the Royal Society B*, **365**, 227–240.

Miller, John H. and Scott E. Page (2007), *Complex Adaptive Systems: An Introduction to Computational Models of Social Life*, Princeton: Princeton University Press.

Millikan, Ruth (1989), 'Biosemantics', *Journal of Philosophy*, **86**, 281–297.

Millikan, Ruth (2005), *Language: A Biological Model*, Oxford: Clarendon.

Millikan, Ruth G. (2009), 'Biosemantics', in: McLaughlin, Brian P., Ansgar Beckermann and Sven Walter (eds), *The Oxford Handbook of Philosophy of Mind*, Oxford: Clarendon Press, pp. 394–406.

Millo, Yuval (2007), 'Making Things Deliverable: The Origins of Index–Based Derivatives', in Callon, Michel, Yuval Millo and Fabian Muniesa (eds), *Market Devices*, Malden et al.: Blackwell, pp. 196–214.

Minsky, Hyman P. (1982), *Can 'It' Happen Again: Essays on Instability and Finance*, Armong, NY: Sharpe.

Minsky, Marvin (1986), *The Society of Minds*, New York: Simon & Schuster.

Mirowski, Philip (1988), *Against Mechanism: Protecting Economics Against Science*, Totowa: Rowman & Littlefield.

Mirowski, P. and K. Somefun (1998), 'Markets as Evolving Computational Entities', *Journal of Evolutionary Economics*, **8**(4), 329–357.

Mische, Ann (2011), 'Relational Sociology, Culture, and Agency', in Scott, John and Peter Carrington (eds), *The Sage Handbook of Social Network Analysis*, Los Angeles: Sage, pp. 80–98.

Mises, Ludwig von (1949), *Human Action: A Treatise on Economics*, Yale: Yale University Press.

Mitcham, Carl (1994), *Thinking Through Technology: The Path Between Engineering and Philosophy*, Chicago and London: University of Chicago Press.

Moav, O. and Z. Neeman (2012), 'Saving Rates and Poverty: The Role of Conspicuous Consumption and Human Capital', *Economic Journal*, **122**, 933–956.

Mohr, J. W. and H. C. White (2008), 'How to Model an Institution', *Theory and Society*, **37**, 485–521.

Mohr, John W. and Craig Rawlings (2012), 'Four Ways to Measure Culture: Social Science, Hermeneutics, and the Cultural Turn', in Alexander, Jeffrey, Ronald Jacobs and Philip Smith (eds), *The Oxford Handbook of Cultural Sociology*, Oxford: Oxford University Press. pp. 70–113.

Mokyr, J. (1998), 'Induced Technical Innovation and Medical History: An Evolutionary Approach', *Journal of Evolutionary Economics*, **8**(2), 119–138.

Mokyr, Joel (2000), 'Evolutionary Phenomena in Technological Change' in Ziman, John (ed), *Technological Innovation as an Evolutionary Process*, Cambridge: Cambridge University Press, pp. 52–65.

Moll, H. and M. Tomasello (2007), 'Cooperation and Human Cognition: The Vygotskian Intelligence Hypothesis', *Philosophical Transactions of the Royal Society B*, **362**, 639–648.

Molnar–Szakacs, I. (2011), 'From Actions to Empathy and Morality – A Neural Perspective', *Journal of Economic Behavior & Organization*, **77**, 76–85.

Monthoux, Pierre Guillet de (2003), 'Monetarisierung und Organisation, eine Geschichte des imaginären Geldes für Erwachsene', in Rammstedt, Otthein (ed.), *Georg Simmels Philosophie des Geldes, Aufsätze und Materialien*, Frankfurt Suhrkamp, pp. 88–114.

Morewedge, C. K., Y. E. Huh and J. Vosgerau (2010), 'Thought for Food: Imagined Consumption Reduces Actual Consumption', *Science*, **330**, 1530–1533.
Moriguchi, Yuichi (2002), 'Material Flow Analysis and Industrial Ecology Studies in Japan', in Ayres, Robert U.and Leslie W. Ayres, (eds), *A Handbook of Industrial Ecology*, Cheltenham, UK and Northampton, MA, USA: Edward Elgar, pp. 301–310.
Moyar, Dean (2008), 'Self–completing Alienation: Hegel's Argument for Transparent Conditions of Free Agency', in Moyar, Dean and Michael Quante (eds), *Hegel's Phenomenology of Spirit: A Critical Guide*, Cambridge: Cambridge University Press, pp. 150–172.
Munz, Peter (1993), *Philosophical Darwinism: On the Origin of Knowledge by Means of Natural Selection*, London and New York: Routledge.
Murphy, D. J. and C. A. S. Hall. (2010), 'Year in Review – EROI or Energy Return on (Energy) Invested', *Annals of the New York Academy of Sciences*, **1185**, 102–118.
Myerson, Roger B. (2008a), *Fundamental Theory of Institutions: A Lecture in Honor of Leo Hurwicz*, http://home.uchicago.edu/~rmyerson/research/hurwicz.pdf, accessed January 23, 2013.
Myerson, Roger B. (2008b), 'The Autocrat's Credibility Problem and the Foundations of the Constitutional State', *American Political Science Review*, **102**(1), 125–139.
Neander, Karen (2006), 'Content for Cognitive Science', in Macdonald, Graham and David Papineau (eds) (2006), *Teleosemantics: New Philosophical Essays*, Oxford and New York: Oxford University Press, pp. 167–194.
Neander, Karen (2012): 'Teleological Theories of Mental Content', in Edward N. Zalta (ed.), *The Stanford Encyclopedia of Philosophy* (Spring 2012 Edition), URL = <http://plato.stanford.edu/archives/spr2012/entries/content–teleological/>.
Negishi, Takashi (1979), *Microeconomic Foundations of Keynesian Macroeconomics*, Amsterdam, New York and Oxford: North–Holland.
Nelson, Michael (2012) 'Existence', in Edward N. Zalta (ed.), *The Stanford Encyclopedia of Philosophy* (Winter 2012 Edition), URL = <http://plato.stanford.edu/archives/win2012/entries/existence/>.
Nelson, R. R. (1995), 'Recent Evolutionary Theorizing About Economic Change', *Journal of Economic Literature*, **XXXIII**, 48–90.
Nelson, R. R. (2006), 'Evolutionary Social Science and Universal Darwinism', *Journal of Evolutionary Economics*, **16**(5), 491–510.
Nelson, R. R. and D. Consoli (2010), 'An Evolutionary Theory of Household Consumption Behavior', *Journal of Evolutionary Economics*, **20**(5), 665–688.
Nelson, R. R. (2013), 'Demand, Supply, and their Interactions on Markets, as Seen from the Perspective of Evolutionary Economic Theory', *Journal of Evolutionary Economics*, **23**(1), 17–38.
Nelson, Richard R. and Sidney G. Winter (1982), *An Evolutionary Theory of Economic Change*, Cambridge, MA, USA and London: Belknap.
Netzer, Nick (2009), 'Evolution of Time Preferences and Attitudes Towards Risk', *American Economic Review*, **99**(3), 937–955.
Neumärker, B. (2007), 'Neuroeconomics and the Economic Logic of Behaviour', *Analyse & Kritik*, **29**, 60–85.
Newman, Mark E. J. (2003), *The Structure and Function of Complex Networks*, arXiv:cond–mat/0303516.

Newman, Mark E. J. (2006), *Power Laws, Pareto Distributions and Zipfs's Law*, arXiv:cond–mat/0412004v3.
Newman, Mark E. J. (2010), *Networks: An Introduction*, Oxford: Oxford University Press.
Nisbett, Robert (2003), *The Geography of Thought: How Asians and Westerners Think Differently...and Why*, New York: Free Press.
Niven, R. K. (2010), 'Minimization of a Free–energy–like Potential for Non–Equilibrium Flow Systems as Steady State', *Philosophical Transactions of the Royal Society B*, **365**, 1323–1331.
Noë, Ronald, Jan A.R.A.M. van Hooff and Peter Hammerstein (eds) (2001), *Economics in Nature: Social Dilemmas, Mate Choice and Biological Markets*, Cambridge et al.: Cambridge University Press.
Nooteboom, Bart (2002), Trust: Forms, Foundations, Functions, Failures and Figures, Cheltenham, UK and Northampton, MA, USA: Edward Elgar.
Nooteboom, B. ed. (2006), 'Simmel's Treatise on the Triad (1908)', *Journal of Institutional Economics*, **2**(3), 365–383.
North, D. C. and J. J. Wallis, (1994), 'Integrating Institutional Change and Technical Change in Economic History: A Transaction Cost Approach', *Journal of Theoretical and Institutional Economics*, **150**, 609–623.
North, D. C., J. J. Wallis and B. R. Weingast, (2009), *Violence and Social Orders: A Conceptual Framework for Interpreting Recorded Human History*, Cambridge: Cambridge University Press.
North, Douglass C. (1981), *Structure and Change in Economic History*, New York: Norton.
North, Douglass C. (1990), *Institutions, Institutional Change, and Economic Performance*, Cambridge: Cambridge University Press.
North, Douglass C. (2005), *Understanding the Process of Economic Change*, Princeton and Oxford: Princeton University Press.
O'Flaherty, B. and J. Bhagwati (1997), 'Will Free Trade With Political Science Put Normative Economists Out of Work?' *Economics and Politics*, **9**(3), 207–219.
Odling-Smee, F. John, Kevin N. Laland, and Marcus W. Feldman (2003), *Niche Construction: The Neglected Process in Evolution*, Princeton: Princeton University Press.
Odling-Smee, F.J. (1988), 'Niche–Constructing Phenotypes', in Plotkin, H. C. (ed), *The Role of Behavior in Evolution*, Cambridge, MA, USA and London: MIT Press, pp. 73–132.
Odum, Howard T. (2007), *Environment, Power, and Society for the Twenty–First Century: The Hierarchy of Energy*, New York: Columbia University Press.
Ofek, Haim (2001), *Second Nature: Economic Origins of Human Evolution*, Cambridge: Cambridge University Press.
Oullier, O. and F. Basso (2010), 'Embodied Economics: How Bodily Information Shapes the Social Coordination Dynamics of Decision–making', *Philosophical Transactions of the Royal Society B*, **365**, 291–301.
Oullier, O. and J. A. S. Kelso (2009), 'Social Coordination, from the Perspective of Coordination Dynamics', in Meyers, R.A. (ed.), *Encyclopedia of Complexity and Systems Sciences*, Berlin: Springer.
Oullier, O., A. P. Kirman, Alan P. and J. A. S. Kelso (2008), 'The Coordination Dynamics of Economic Decision Making: A Multilevel Approach to Social

Neuroeconomics', *IEEE Transactions on Neural Systems and Rehabilitation Engineering*, **16**(6), 557–571.

Oyama, Susan (2000), *Evolution's Eye: A Systems View of the Biology–Culture Divide*, Durham and London, Duke University Press.

Oyama, Susan (2001), *The Ontogeny of Information: Developmental Systems and Evolution*, Durham and London: Duke University Press.

Padgett, John F. (1997), 'The Emergence of Simple Ecologies of Skills: A Hypercycle Approach to Economic Organization', in Arthur, W. Brian, Steven Durlauf, Steven and David Lane (eds) *The Economy as an Evolving Complex System II*, Reading: Addison–Wesley, pp. 199–221.

Padgett, John F. (2006), *Organizational Genesis in Florentine History: Four Multiple Network–processes*, https://webshare.uchicago.edu/users/jpadgett/Public/papers/unpublished/Four.Org .Genesis.mechanisms.pdf, accessed January 24, 2013.

Padgett, J. F. and P. D. McLean (2006), 'Organizational Invention and Elite Transformation: The Birth of the Partnership Systems in Renaissance Florence', *American Journal of Sociology*, **111**(5), 1463–1568.

Padgett, J. F., D. Lee, and N. Collier, Nieck (2003), 'Economic Production as Chemistry', *Industrial and Corporate Change*, **12**(4), 843–877.

Page, Scott E. (2007), *The Difference: How the Power of Diversity Creates Better Groups, Firms, Schools, and Societies*, Princeton: Princeton University Press.

Papillloud, Christian (2003a), 'Wert', in Rammstedt, Otthein (ed), *Georg Simmels Philosophie des Geldes, Aufsätze und Materialien*, Frankfurt Suhrkamp, pp.168–178.

Papilloud, Christian (2003b), 'Tausch. Autopsie eines soziologischen Typus', in Rammstedt, Otthein (ed.), *Georg Simmels Philosophie des Geldes, Aufsätze und Materialien*, Frankfurt Suhrkamp, pp. 158–167.

Papilloud, Christian and Cécile Rol (2003), 'Lebenstil', in Rammstedt, Otthein (ed), *Georg Simmels Philosophie des Geldes, Aufsätze und Materialien*, Frankfurt Suhrkamp, pp. 179–190.

Papineau, David (2009a), 'The Causal Closure of the Physical and Naturalism', in McLaughlin, Brian P., Ansgar Beckermann and Sven Walter (eds) (2009), *The Oxford Handbook of Philosophy of Mind*, Oxford: Clarendon Press, pp. 53–65.

Papineau, David (2009b), 'Naturalism', in Edward N. Zalta (ed.) *The Stanford Encyclopedia of Philosophy* (Spring 2009 Edition), URL = http://plato.stanford.edu/archives/spr2009/entries/naturalism/

Pasinetti, Luigi L. (1981), *Structural Change and Economic Growth: A Theoretical Essay on the Dynamics of the Wealth of Nations*, Cambridge: Cambridge University Press.

Pasinetti, Luigi L. (1993), *Structural Economic Dynamics: A Theory of the Economic Consequences of Human Learning*, Cambridge: Cambridge University Press.

Pecher, Diane and Rolf A. Zwaan, (eds) (2005), *Grounding Cognition. The Role of Perception and Action in Memory, Language and Thinking*, Cambridge: Cambridge University Press.

Peirce, Charles Sanders (1992), *The Essential Peirce. Selected Philosophical Writings, Volume 1 (1867–1893)*, eds. Nathan Houser and Christian Kloesel, Bloomington and Indianapolis: Indiana University Press.

Peirce, Charles Sanders (1998), *The Essential Peirce. Selected Philosophical Writings, Volume 2 (1893–1913)*, eds. Peirce Edition Project, Bloomington and Indianapolis: Indiana University Press.

Penrose, Roger (1989), *The Emperor's New Mind. Concerning Computers, Minds, and the Laws of Physics*, Oxford: Oxford University Press.

Penrose, Roger (1995), 'Must Mathematical Physics Be Reductionist? in Cornwell, John (ed.) (1995), *Nature's Imagination: The Frontiers of Scientific Vision*, Oxford, New York and Melbourne: Oxford University Press, pp. 12–26.

Penrose, Roger (2004), *The Road to Reality: A Complete Guide to the Laws of the Universe*, New York: Knopf.

Pérez–Lombard, L., J. Ortiz and C. Pout (2008), 'A Review on Buildings Energy Consumption Information', *Energy and Buildings*, **40**, 394–398.

Perlman, Mark (2009), 'Changing the Mission of Theories of Teleology: DOs and DON'Ts for Thinking About Function', in Krohs, Ulrich and Peter Kroes (eds), *Functions in Biological and Artifical Worlds*, Cambridge: MIT Press, pp. 17–35.

Perry, J. and A. Nölke (2006), 'The Political Economy of International Accounting Standards', *Review of International Political Economy*, **13**(4), 559–586.

Petroski, Henry (1994), *The Evolution of Useful Things*, New York: Vintage Books.

Petroski, Henry (1996), *Invention by Design: How Engineers Get From Thought to Think*, Cambridge, MA, USA and London: Harvard University Press.

Pham, M. T. (2004), 'The Logic of Feeling', *Journal of Consumer Psychology*, **14**(4), 360–369.

Pham, M. T. (2007), 'Emotion and Rationality: A Critical Review and Interpretation of Empirical Evidence', *Review of General Psychology*, **11**(2), 155–176.

Phelps, Elisabeth A. (2009), 'The Study of Emotion in Neuroeconomics', in: Glimcher, Paul W., Colin F. Camerer, Ernst Fehr and Russel A. Poldrack (eds), *Neuroeconomics: Decision Making and the Brain*, Amsterdam: Elsevier, pp. 233–250.spiral

Piaget, Jean (1975), *L'Équilibration des Structures Cognitives: Problème Central du Développement*, Paris: Presses Universitaires de France.

Pieper, Annemarie (1974), Individuum, in Hermann Krings, Hans Michael Baumgartner und Christoph Wild (ed.), *Handbuch philosophischer Grundbegriffe*, München: Kösel, pp. 728–737.

Pinker, Steven (2007), *The Stuff of Thought: Language as a Window into Human Nature*, New York: Penguin.

Pinker, Steven (2011), *The Better Angels of Our Nature: The Decline of Violence in History and Its Causes*, London: Penguin.

Plassmann, H., T. Ambler, S. Braeutigam, and P. Kenning (2007), 'What Can Advertisers Learn From Neuroscience?' *International Journal of Advertising*, **26**(2), 151–175.

Platteau, J.-P. (1994), 'Behind the Market Stage Where Real Societies Exist – Part I: The Role of Public and Private Order Institutions', and 'Part II: The Role of Moral Norms', *Journal of Development Studies* **30**(3 + 4), 533–577, 753–817.

Plott, Charles R. and Vernon L. Smith (2008), 'Markets', in Plott, Charles R. and Vernon L. Smith (eds), *Handbook of Experimental Economics Results, Volume 1*, Amsterdam: North–Holland.

Podolny, J. M. (1993), 'A Status–based Model of Market Competition', *American Journal of Sociology*, **98**(4), 829–872.

Podolny, Joel M. (2005), *Status Signals: A Sociological Study of Market Competition*, Princeton and Oxford: Princeton University Press.

Pomeranz, Kenneth (2000), *The Great Divergence: China, Europe, and the Making of the Modern World Economy*, Princeton and Oxford: Princeton University Press.

Popitz, Heinrich (1985), *Phänomene der Macht*, Tübingen: Mohr Siebeck.
Popper, Karl R. (1935), *Logik der Forschung*, Achte Auflage 1984, Tübingen: Mohr Siebeck.
Popper, Karl R. (1945), *The Open Society and Its Enemies*, London: Routledge.
Popper, Karl R. (1972), *Objective Knowledge. An Evolutionary Approach*, Oxford: Clarendon.
Popper, Karl R. (1982), *The Open Universe. An Argument for Indeterminism*, London: Hutchinson.
Popper, Karl R. (1983), *Realism and the Aim of Science*, London: Hutchinson.
Post, John F. (1987), 'Paradox in Critical Rationalism and Related Theories', in Radnitzky, Gerard and William W. Bartley III (eds) (1987), *Evolutionary Epistemology, Rationality, and the Sociology of Knowledge*, La Salle: Open Court, pp. 217–252.
Potts, J. (2001), 'Knowledge and Markets', *Journal of Evolutionary Economics*, **11**(4), 413–432.
Potts, J., S. Cunningham, J. Hartley, and P. Ormerod (2008), 'Social Network Markets: A New Definition of the Creative Industries', *Journal of Cultural Economics*, **32**(3), 167–185.
Potts, Jason (2000), *The New Evolutionary Microeconomics: Complexity, Competence and Adaptive Behavior*, Cheltenham, UK and Northampton, MA, USA: Edward Elgar.
Preda, Alex (2005), 'The Investor as a Cultural Figure of Global Capitalism', in Knorr Cetina, Karin and Alex Preda (eds) (2005), *The Sociology of Financial Markets*, Oxford: Oxford University Press, pp. 141–162.
Preda, Alex (2008a), 'STS and Social Studies on Finance', Hackett, Edward J., Olga Amsterdamska, Michael Lynch, Judy Wajcman, Judy (eds), *The Handbook of Science and Technology Studies*, Cambridge and London: MIT Press, pp. 901–920.
Preda, Alex (2008b), 'Technology, Agency, and Financial Price Data', in Pinch, Trevor and Richard Swedberg (eds), *Living in a Material World: Economic Sociology Meets Science and Technology Studies*, Cambridge: MIT Press, pp. 217–254.
Price, Carolyn (2006), 'Fearing Fluffy: The Content of an Emotional Appraisal', in Macdonald, Graham and David Papineau (eds), *Teleosemantics: New Philosophical Essays*, Oxford and New York: Oxford University Press, pp. 208–228.
Price, R. G. (1973), 'The Nature of Selection', reprinted 1995 in *Journal of Theoretical Biology*, **175**, 389–396.
Pryor, Frederic L. (1977), *The Origins of the Economy: A Comparative Study of Distribution in Primitive and Peasant Societies*, New York: Academic Press.
Pueyo, S., F. He and T. Zillio (2007), 'The Maximum Entropy Formalism and the Idiosyncratic Theory of Biodiversity', *Ecology Letters*, **10**, 1017–1028.
Putnam, Robert (2000), *Bowling Alone: The Collapse and Revival of American Community*, New York: Simon & Schuster.
Radnitzky, Gerard and Peter Bernholz, Peter (eds) (1987), *Economic Imperialism. The Economic Approach Applied Outside the Field of Economics*, New York: Paragon.
Raine, Alan, John Foster, and Jason Potts (2006), 'The New Entropy Law and the Economic Process', *Ecological Complexity,* **3**, 354–360.

Rammstedt, Otthein (2003), 'Wert, Geld und Individualität', in Rammstedt, Otthein (ed.), *Georg Simmels Philosophie des Geldes, Aufsätze und Materialien*, Frankfurt Suhrkamp, pp. 27–44.

Ramsey, Jeffrey L. (2000), 'Realism, Essentialism, and Intrinsic Properties: The Case of Molecular Shape', in Bhushan, Nalini and Stuart Rosenfeld (eds), *Of Minds and Molecules: New Philosophical Perspectives on Chemistry*, New York: Oxford University Press, pp. 117–128.

Rappaport, Roy A. (1979), *Ecology, Meaning, and Religion*, Richmond: North Atlantic Books.

Rauch, J. E. (2001), 'Business and Social Networks in International Trade', *Journal of Economic Literature*, **XXXIX**, 1177–1203.

Rauch, James E. and Gary G. Hamilton (2001), 'Networks and Markets: Concepts for Bridging Disciplines', in Rauch, James E. and Alessandra Casella (eds), *Networks and Markets*, New York: Russell Sage Foundation, pp. 1–29.

Redding, Paul (2008), 'The Independence and Dependence of Self–Consciousness: The Dialectic of Lord and Bondsman in Hegel's Phenomenology of Spirit', in Beiser, Frederick C. (ed.) (2008), *The Cambridge Companion to Hegel and Nineteenth–Century Philosophy*, Cambridge, UK and New York: Cambridge University Press, pp. 94–110.

Redish, A. D., S. Jensen and A. Johnson (2008), 'A Unified Framework for Addiction: Vulnerabilities in the Decision Process', *Behavioral and Brain Sciences*, **31**, 415–487.

Redman, Deborah A. (1993), *Economics and the Philosophy of Science*, New York and Oxford: Oxford University Press.

Reimann, M. and A. Bechara (2010), 'The Somatic Marker Hypothesis as a Neurological Theory of Decision–Making: Review, Conceptual Comparisons, and Future Neuroeconomics Research', *Journal of Economic Psychology*, **31**, 767–776.

Reinstaller, A. and B. Sanditov (2005), 'Social Structure and Consumption: On the Diffusion of Consumer Good Innovation', *Journal of Evolutionary Economics*, **15**, 505–531.

Rendell, L. et al. (2010), 'Why Copy Others? Insights from the Social Learning Strategies Tournament', *Science*, **328**, 208–213.

Rescher, Nicholas (1999), *The Limits of Science*, Pittsburgh: Pittsburgh University Press.

Richerson, Peter J. and Robert Boyd (2005), *Not By Genes Alone: How Culture Transformed Human Evolution*. Chicago: University of Chicago Press.

Richerson, P. J., R. Boyd and J. Henrich (2010), 'Gene–Culture Coevolution in the Age of Genomics', *Proceedings of the National Academy of Sciences*, **107**(suppl. 2), 8985–8992.

Richter, Rudolf (1987), *Geldtheorie: Vorlesung auf der Grundlage der Allgemeinen Gleichgewichtstheorie und der Institutionenökonomik*, Berlin, Heidelberg and New York: Springer.

Riedl, Rupert (1983), The Role of Morphology in the Theory of Evolution, in Grene, Marjorie (ed.), *Dimensions of Darwinism: Themes and Counterthemes in Twentieth Century Evolutionary Theory*, Cambridge and Paris: Cambridge University Press and Editions de la Maison des Sciences de l'Homme, pp. 205–240.

Rindos, David (1984), *The Origins of Agriculture: An Evolutionary Perspective*, New York: Academic Press.

Rindos, David (1985), 'Darwinian Selection, Symbolic Variation, and the Evolution of Culture', *Current Anthropology*, **26**(1), 65–88.

Rindos, David (1986), 'The Evolution of the Capacity for Culture: Sociobiology, Structuralism, and Cultural Selectionism', *Current Anthropology*, **27**(4), 315–332.

Ring, Peter Smith (1996), *Networked Organization: A Resource Based Perspective*, Uppsala: Acta Universitatis Upsaliensis.

Rizvi, S. A. T. (2006), 'The Sonnenschein–Mantel–Debreu Results after Thirty Years', *History of Political Economy*, **38**, 228–245.

Robb, David and John Heil (2009): 'Mental Causation', in Edward N. Zalta (ed), The *Stanford Encyclopedia of Philosophy* (Summer 2009 Edition), URL = <http://plato.stanford.edu/archives/sum2009/entries/mental–causation/>.

Robbins, Lionel (1945), *An Essay on the Nature and Significance of Economic Science*, London: Macmillan.

Roberts, John (2004), *The Modern Firm: Organizational Design for Performance and Growth*, Oxford: Oxford University Press.

Robinson, A. and C. Southgate (2010), 'A General Definition of Interpretation and Its Application to Origin of Life Research', *Biology and Philosophy*, **25**, 163-181.

Robson, Arthur J. (2001), 'The Biological Basis of Economic Behaviour', *Journal of Economic Literature*, **XXXIV**, 11–33.

Robson, A. J. (2002), 'Evolution and Human Nature', *Journal of Economic Perspectives*, **16**(2), 89–106.

Robson, A. J. (2005), 'Complex Evolutionary Systems and the Red Queen', *Economic Journal*, **115**, F211–F224.

Robson, A. J. and H. S. Kaplan (2003), 'The Evolution of Human Life Expectancy and Intelligence in Hunter–Gatherer Economies', *American Economic Review*, **93**(1), 150–169.

Robson, Arthur J. and Larry Samuelson, Larry (2010), 'The Evolutionary Foundations of Preferences', in Benhabib, Jess, Matthew Jackson and Alberto Bisin (eds), *Handbook of Social Economics*, Amsterdam: North–Holland, pp. 221–310.

Roehner, Bertrand (2002), *Patterns of Speculation. A Study in Observational Econophysics*, Cambridge, UK: Cambridge University Press.

Roff, Derek A. (2001), 'Age and Size at Maturity', in Fox, Ch. W., D. A. Roff and D. J. Fairbairn (eds) (2001), *Evolutionary Ecology: Concepts and Case Studies*, Oxford: Oxford University Press, pp. 99–112.

Rogers, D. S. and P. R. Ehrlich (2008), 'Natural Selection and Cultural Rates of Change', *Proceedings of the National Academy of Sciences*, **105**(9), 3416–3420.

Rosenberg, Alexander and , Frederic Bouchard (2010), 'Fitness', in Edward N. Zalta (ed.), *The Stanford Encyclopedia of Philosophy* (Fall 2010 Edition), URL = <http://plato.stanford.edu/archives/fall2010/entries/fitness/>.

Ross, Don (2005), *Economic Theory and Cognitive Science: Microexplanations*, Cambridge, MA, USA and London: MIT Press.

Ross, Don (2007a), *The Economic Agent: Not Human, But Important,* http://www.uab.edu/philosophy/faculty/ross/The–economic–agent–Not–human–but–important.htm

Ross, D. (2007b), 'H. sapiens as Ecologically Special: What Does Language Contribute?' *Language Studies*, **29**, 710–731.

Ross, D. (2008), 'Two Styles of Neuroeconomics', *Economics & Philosophy*, **24**, 473–483.
Ross, Don (2012), 'Neuroeconomics and Economic Methodology', in Davis, John B. and D. Wade Hands (eds), *The Elgar Companion to Recent Economic Methodology*, Cheltenham, UK and Northampton, MA, USA: Edward Elgar, pp. 61–93.
Ross, Don, Carla Sharp, Rudy E. Vuchinich and David Spurrett (2008), *Midbrain Mutiny: The Picoeconomics and Neuroeconomics of Disordered Gambling*, Cambridge, MA, USA MIT Press.
Roth, A. E. (2008), 'What Have We Learned From Market Design?', *Economic Journal*, **118**, 285–310.
Roth, Gerhard (1992), 'Kognition: Die Entstehung von Bedeutung im Gehirn', in Krohn, Wolfgang and Günter Küppers (ed.), *Emergenz: Die Entstehung von Ordnung, Organisation und Bedeutung*, Frankfurt: Suhrkamp, pp. 104–133.
Rubinstein, Ariel (2000), *Economics and Language: Five Essays*, Cambridge et al.: Cambridge University Press.
Rubinstein, A. (2008), 'Comments on Neuroeconomics', *Economics & Philosophy*, **24**, 485–494.
Ruprecht, W. (2005), 'The Historical Development of the Consumption of Sweeteners – A Learning Approach', *Journal of Evolutionary Economics*, **15**, 247–272.
Ruth, Matthias (2005), 'Insight from Thermodynamics for the Analysis of Economic Processes', in Kleidon, Axel and Ralph Lorenz (eds), *Non–equilibrium Thermodynamics and the Production of Entropy: Life, Earth, and Beyond*, Heidelberg: Springer, pp. 243–254.
Ryder, D. (2004), 'SINBAD Neurosemantics: A Theory of Mental Representations', *Mind & Language*, **19**(2), 211–240.
Ryder, Dan (2006), 'On Thinking of Kinds: A Neuroscientific Perspective', in Macdonald, Graham and David Papineau (eds), *Teleosemantics. New Philosophical Essays*, Oxford and New York: Oxford University Press, pp. 115–145.
Ryle, Gilbert (1949), *The Concept of Mind*, Chicago: Chicago University Press.
Saad, Gad (2007), *The Evolutionary Bases of Consumption*, New York: Lawrence Erlbaum.
Sacks, Oliver (1995), 'A New Vision of Mind', in Cornwell, John (ed.) (1995), *Nature's Imagination: The Frontiers of Scientific Vision*, Oxford, New York and Melbourne: Oxford University Press, pp. 101–122.
Safarzyńska, K. and J. C. J. C. van den Berg (2010), 'Evolutionary Models in Economics: A Survey of Methods and Building Blocks', *Journal of Evolutionary Economics*, **20**(3), 329–374.
Sahlins, Marshall (1976), *Culture and Practical Reason*, Chicago: University of Chicago Press.
Salter, Frank (2003), *On Genetic Interests: Family, Ethnicity and Humanity in an Age of Mass Migration*, Frankfurt am Main: Peter Lang
Salthe, Stanley N. (1986), *Evolving Hierarchical Systems: Their Structure and Representation*, New York: Columbia University Press.
Salthe, Stanley N. (1993), *Development and Evolution: Complexity and Change in Biology*, Cambridge, MA, USA: MIT Press.

Salthe, S.N. (2002), 'Summary of the Principles of Hierarchy Theory, *General Systems Bulletin*, **31**, 13-17.
Salthe, S.N. (2007), 'The Natural Philosophy of Work', *Entropy*, 2007, **9**, 83–99.
Salthe, Stanley N. (2009), 'The System of Interpretance: Meaning as Finality', *Biosemiotics*, **1**, 285–294.
Samuelson, L. (2004), 'Modeling Knowledge in Economic Analysis', *Journal of Economic Literature*, **XLII**(2), 367–404.
Sandberg, M. (2007), 'The Evolution of IT Innovations in Swedish Organizations: A Darwinian Critique of 'Lamarckian' Institutional Economics', *Journal of Evolutionary Economics*, **17**, 1–23.
Santos, L. R. and M. K. Chen, (2009), 'The Evolution of Rational and Irrational Economic Behavior: Evidence and Insight from a Non-human Primate Species', in Glimcher, Paul W., Colin F. Camerer, Ernst Fehr and Russel A. Poldrack (eds), *Neuroeconomics: Decision Making and the Brain*, Amsterdam: Elsevier, pp. 81–94.
Sartorius, Christian (2003), *An Evolutionary Approach to Social Welfare*, London and New York: Routledge.
Saviotti, P. P. (2001), 'Variety, Growth, and Demand', *Journal of Evolutionary Economics*, **11**(1), 119–142.
Saviotti, Pier Paolo (1996), *Technological Evolution, Variety and the Economy*, Cheltenham: Elgar.
Schantz, Richard (2004), 'Introduction', in Schantz, Richard (ed.), *The Externalist Challenge*, Berlin: de Gruyter, pp. 1–36.
Schelling, Thomas C. (1978), *Micromotives and Macrobehavior*, New York and London: Norton.
Schlicht, Ekkehard (1998), *On Custom in the Economy*, Oxford: Clarendon.
Schluchter, Wolfgang (1979), *Die Entwicklung des okzidentalen Rationalismus: Eine Analyse von Max Webers Gesellschaftsgeschichte*, Tübingen: Mohr Siebeck.
Schmidt, Vivienne A. (2008), 'Discursive Institutionalism: The Explanatory Power of Ideas and Discourse', *Annual Review of Political Science*, **11**, 303–326.
Schmidt, Vivienne A. (2011), 'Reconciling Ideas and Institutions Through Discursive Institutionalism', in Béland, Daniel and Robert Henry Cox (eds), *Ideas and Politics in Social Science Research*, Oxford: Oxford University Press, pp. 47–65.
Schneider, Dieter (1986), 'Die Erklärung hierarchischer Unternehmensorganisation aus der Unternehmerfunktion im Wettbewerb: Anfänge einer institutionellen Marktprozeßtheorie?', in Leipold, Helmut und Alfred Schüller (eds), *Zur Interdependenz von Unternehmens– und Wirtschaftsordnung*, Stuttgart and New York: G. Fischer, pp. 67–94.
Schneider, Harold K. (1974), *Economic Man: The Anthropology of Economics*, New York: Free Press.
Schot, J. and F. W. Geels (2007), 'Niches in Evolutionary Theories of Technical Change: A Critical Survey in the Literature', *Journal of Evolutionary Economics*, **17**(5), 605–621.
Schotter, Andrew (1982), *The Economic Theory of Social Institutions*, Cambridge: Cambridge University Press.
Schrödinger, Erwin (1944), *What Is Life? The Physical Aspect of the Living Cell,* Cambridge: Cambridge University Press.

Schüller, Alfred (1983), 'Property Rights, Theorie der Firma und wettbewerbliches Marktsystem', in Schüller, Alfred (ed.), *Property rights und ökonomische Theorie*, München: Vahlen, pp. 145–184.

Schultz, Wolfram (2009), 'Midbrain Dopamine Neurons: A Retina of the Reward System?', in Glimcher, Paul W., Colin F. Camerer, Ernst Fehr and Russel A. Poldrack (eds), *Neuroeconomics: Decision Making and the Brain*, Amsterdam: Elsevier, pp. 323–329.

Schweitzer, Thomas (1996), *Muster sozialer Ordnung: Netzwerkanalyse als Fundament der Sozialethnologie*, Berlin: Reimer.

Sciubba, E. (2011), 'What Did Lotka Really Say? A Critical Assessment of the "Maximum Power Principle"', *Ecological Modelling*, **222**, 1347–1353.

Scott, John (2011), 'Social Physics and Social Networks', in Scott, John and Peter Carrington (eds), *The Sage Handbook of Social Network Analysis*, Los Angeles: Sage, pp. 55–66.

Seabright, Paul (2004), *The Company of Stangers: A Natural History of Economic Life*, Princeton: Princeton University Press.

Seager, William and Sean Allen–Hermanson (2012), 'Panpsychism', in Edward N. Zalta (ed.), *The Stanford Encyclopedia of Philosophy* (Winter 2012 Edition), URL = <http://plato.stanford.edu/archives/win2012/entries/panpsychism/>.

Searle, J. R. (2005), 'What Is an Institution?', *Journal of Institutional Economics* **1**(1), 1–22.

Searle, John R. (1995), *The Construction of Social Reality*, New York: Free Press.

Searle, John R. (2010), *Making the Social World: The Structure of Human Civilization*, Oxford: Oxford University Press.

Sen, Armatya (1984), *Commodities and Capabilities*, reprint 1999, New Dehli: Oxford University Press.

Sen, A. (1995), 'Rationality and Social Choice', *American Economic Review*, **85**(1), 1–24.

Sen, Amartya (2002), *Rationality and Freedom*, Cambridge and London: Belknap.

Sen, Amartya (2007), *Identity and Violence: The Illusion of Destiny*, London: Penguin.

Sen, Armatya (2009), *The Idea of Justice*, Cambridge: Belknap.

Shackle, G. L. S. (1972), *Epistemics & Economics: A Critique of Economic Doctrines*, Cambridge: Cambridge University Press.

Shafir, E., P. Diamond and A. Tversky (1997), 'Money Illusion', *Quarterly Journal of Economics*, **CXII**(2), 341–374.

Shapin, Steven (2008), 'Science and the Modern World', in Hackett, Edward J., Olga Amsterdamska, Michael Lynch, Judy Wajcman, Judy (eds), *The Handbook of Science and Technology Studies*, Cambridge and London: MIT Press, pp. 433–448.

Shavitt, Sharon, Carlos J. Torelli, Carlos J. and Hila Riemer (2011), 'Horizontal and Vertical Individualism and Collectivism: Implications for Understanding Psychological Process', in Gelfland, Michele J., Chi-yue Chiu and Ying-yi Hong (eds), *Advances in Culture and Psychology, Volume One*, Oxford and New York: Oxford University Press, pp. 309–350.

Shennan, S. (2008), 'Canoes and Cultural Evolution', *Proceedings of the National Academy of Sciences*, **105**(9), 3175–3176.

Short, Thomas L. (2007), *Peirce's Theory of Signs*, Cambridge, UK and New York: Cambridge University Press.

Simmel, Georg (1907), *Philosophie des Geldes*, second edition, reprint 2009, Cologne: Anaconda.
Simon, Herbert A. (1996), *The Sciences of the Artificial*, Third Edition, Cambridge, MA, USA: MIT Press.
Singer, Tania (2009), 'Understanding Others: Brain Mechanisms of Theory of Mind and Empathy', in Glimcher, Paul W., Colin F. Camerer, Ernst Fehr and Russel A. Poldrack (eds), *Neuroeconomics: Decision Making and the Brain*, Amsterdam: Elsevier, pp. 251–268.
Singer, T. and C. Lamm (2009), 'The Social Neuroscience of Empathy', *Annals of the New York Academy of Sciences*, **1156**, 81–96.
Singer, Wolf (2002), *Der Beobachter im Gehirn: Essays zur Hirnforschung*, Frankfurt: Suhrkamp.
Skaperdas, S. (1992), 'Cooperation, Conflict, and Power in the Absence of Property Rights', *American Economic Review*, **82**(4), 720–739.
Skinner, G. W. (1964/65), 'Marketing and Social Structure in Rural China', *Journal of Asian Studies*, **24**, 3–43, 195–228, 363–399.
Sklar, Lawrence (2009), 'Philosophy of Statistical Mechanics', Edward N. Zalta (ed.) *The Stanford Encyclopedia of Philosophy* (Summer 2009 Edition), URL = <http://plato.stanford.edu/archives/sum2009/entries/statphys–statmech/>.
Skyrms, Brian (1996), *Evolution of the Social Contract*, Cambridge: Cambridge University Press.
Skyrms, Brian (2004), *The Stag Hunt and the Evolution of Social Structure*, Cambridge: Cambridge University Press.
Skyrms, Brian (2010), *Signals: Evolution, Learning, & Information*, Oxford: Oxford University Press.
Sliwka, D. (2007), 'Trust as a Signal of a Social Norm and the Hidden Costs of Incentive Schemes', *American Economic Review*, **97**(3), 999–1012.
Smil, Vaclav (1999), *Energies: An Illustrated Guide to the Biosphere and Civilization*, Cambridge, MA, USA and London: MIT Press.
Smil, Vaclav (2003), *The Earth's Biosphere: Evolution, Dynamics, and Change*, Cambridge, MA, USA and London: MIT Press.
Smil, Vaclav (2008), *Energy in Nature and Society: General Energetics of Complex Systems*, Cambridge, MA, USA and London: MIT Press.
Smit, J.P., F. Buekens and S. du Plessis (2011), 'What is Money? An Alternative to Searle's Institutional Facts', *Economics & Philosophy*, **27**(1), 1–22.
Smith, Adam (1759/1976), *The Theory of Moral Sentiments*, Oxford: Oxford University Press.
Smith, K. and J. Dickhaut (2005), 'Economics and Emotion: Institutions Matter', *Games and Economic Behavior*, **52**, 316–335.
Smith, Peter B. and Michael Harris Bond (1993), *Social Psychology across Cultures: Analysis and Perspectives*, New York and London: Harvester Wheatsheaf.
Smith, V. L. (2003), 'Constructivist and Ecological Rationality in Economics', *The American Economic Review*, **93**(3), 465–508.
Smolin, Lee (1997), *The Life of the Cosmos*, Oxford and New York: Oxford University Press.
Smolin, Lee (2006), *The Trouble With Physic: The Rise of String Theory, the Fall of a Science, and What Comes Next*, New York: Houghton Mifflin.
Smolin, Lee (2007), *Scientific Alternatives to the Anthropic Principle*, arXiv:hep–th/0407213.

Snowdon, Brian, Howard Vane and Peter Wynarczyk (1994), *A Modern Guide to Macroeconomics: An Introduction to Competing Schools of Thought*, Cheltenham: Edward Elgar.
Sobal, J. and B. Wansink (2007), 'Kitchenscapes, Tablescapes, Platescapes, and Foodscapes: Influences of Microscale Built Environments on Food Intake', *Environment and Behavior*, **39**(1), 124–142.
Sobel, Joel (2002), 'Can We Trust Social Capital?', *Journal of Economic Literature*, **40**, 139–154.
Sober, Elliott and David Sloan Wilson (1998), *Unto Others: The Evolution and Psychology of Un–selfish Behavior*, Cambridge, MA, USA and London: Harvard University Press.
Solow, Robert M. (2000), 'Notes on Social Capital and Economic Performance', in Dasgupta, Partha and Ismail Serageldin (eds), *Social Capital: A Multifaceted Perspective*, Washington: World Bank, pp. 6–10.
Sommers, Tamler (2007), 'The Illusion of Freedom Evolves', in Ross, Don, David Spurrett, Harold Kincaid and G. Lynn Stephens (eds) (2007), *Distributed Cognition and the Will. Individual Volition and Social Context*, Cambridge, MA, USA: MIT Press, pp. 61–76.
Sorrell, S. (2009), 'Jevon's Paradox Revisited: The Evidence for Backfire From Improved Energy Efficiency', *Energy Policy*, **37**, 1456–1469.
Sorrell, S., J. Dimitropoulos, and M. Sommerville (2009), 'Empirical Estimates of the Direct Rebound Effect: A Review', *Energy Policy,* **37**, 1356–1371.
Sperber, Dan (2011), 'A Naturalistic Ontology for Mechanistic Explanations in the Social Sciences', in Demeulenaere, Pierre (ed.), *Analytical Sociology and Social Mechanisms*, Cambridge: Cambridge University Press), pp. 64–77.
Sperber, Dan and Deidre Wilson (2008), 'A Deflationary Account of Metaphor', in Gibbs, Raymond W. (ed.), *The Cambridge Handbook of Metaphor and Thought*, New York: Cambridge University Press, pp. 84–105.
Spolaore, E. and R. Wacziarg (2009), 'The Diffusion of Development', *The Quarterly Journal of Economics*, May 2009, 469–529.
Sprevak, M. (2009), 'Extended Cognition and Functionalism', *Journal of Philosophy*, **CVI**(9), 503–527.
Stadler, B. M. R., P. F. Stadler, G. P. Wagner, and W. Fontana (2001), 'The Topology of the Possible: Formal Spaces Underlying Patterns of Evolutionary Change', *Journal of Theoretical Biology*, **213**, 241–274.
Stankiewicz, Rikard (2000), 'The Concept of "Design Space"', in Ziman, John (ed), *Technological Innovation as an Evolutionary Process*, Cambridge: Cambridge University Press, pp. 234–247.
Steckel, R. H. (2008), 'Biological Measures of the Standard of Living', *Journal of Economic Perspectives*, **22**(1), 129–152.
Steele, G. R. (2002), 'Hayek's Sensory Order', *Theory & Psychology*, **12**(3), 387–409.
Stegmüller, Wolfgang (1973), *Probleme und Resultate der Wissenschaftstheorie und der Analytischen Philosophie, Band II: Theorie und Erfahrung, Zweiter Teilband: Theoriestrukturen und Theoriendynamik*, Berlin und Heidelberg: Springer.
Stegmüller, Wolfgang (1983), *Probleme und Resultate der Wissenschaftstheorie und der Analytischen Philosophie, Band I: Erklärung, Begründung, Kausalität*, Berlin und Heidelberg: Springer.

Stegmüller, Wolfgang (1986), *Probleme und Resultate der Wissenschaftstheorie und der Analytischen Philosophie, Band II: Theorie und Erfahrung, Dritter Teilband: Die Entwicklung des neuen Strukturalismus seit 1973*, Berlin und Heidelberg: Springer.

Stekeler-Weihofer, Pirmin (2011), 'Intuition, Understanding, and the Human Form of Life', in Ikäheimo, Heikki and Arto Laitinen (eds), *Recognition and Social Ontology*, Leiden, Boston: Brill, pp. 117–144.

Stephens, David W. and John R. Krebs (1987), *Foraging Theory*, Princeton: Princeton University Press.

Sterelny, Kim (2004), 'Externalism, Epistemic Artefacts and The Extended Mind', in Schantz, Richard (ed.), *The Externalist Challenge*, Berlin: de Gruyter, pp. 239–254.

Sterelny, K. (2005), 'Made By Each Other: Organisms and Their Environment', *Biology and Philosophy*, **20**(1), 21–36.

Sterelny, Kim (2006), 'Language, Modularity, and Evolution', in Macdonald, Graham and David Papineau (eds), *Teleosemantics: New Philosophical Essays*, Oxford and New York: Oxford University Press, pp. 23–41.

Stern, Robert (2008), 'Hegel's Idealism', in Beiser, Frederick C. (ed.) (2008), *The Cambridge Companion to Hegel and Nineteenth–Century Philosophy*, Cambridge, UK and New York: Cambridge University Press, pp. 135–173.

Stiglitz, Joseph and Bruce Greenwald (2003), *Towards a New Paradigm in Monetary Economics*, Cambridge: Cambridge University Press.

Storper, M. (1995), 'The Resurgence of Regional Economies, Ten Years Later: The Region as a Nexus of Untraded Interdependencies', *European Urban and Regional Studies*, **2**(3), 191–221.

Strange, Susan (1994), *States and Markets*, Second Edition, London and New York: Pinter.

Strassert, Gunter (2002), 'Physical Input–Output Accounting', in Ayres, Robert U.and Leslie W. Ayres, (eds), *A Handbook of Industrial Ecology*, Cheltenham, UK and Northampton, MA, USA: Edward Elgar, pp. 102–113.

Strauss, Claudia and Naomi Quinn (1997), *A Cognitive Theory of Cultural Meaning*, Cambridge: Cambridge University Press.

Streit, Manfred and Gerhard Wegner (1993), 'Information, Transaction, and Catallaxy: Reflections on Some Key Concepts of Evolutionary Market Theory', in Witt, Ulrich (ed.), *Evolutionary Economics*, Aldershot: Edward Elgar, pp. 125–149.

Strumsky, Deborah, José Lobo and Sander van der Leeuw (2011), *Measuring the Importance of Reusing, Recombining and Creating Technologies in the Process of Invention*, Santa Fé Institute Working Paper http://www.santafe.edu/media/workingpapers/11–02–003.pdf.

Stützel, Wolfgang (1953/1979), *Paradoxa der Geld– und Konkurrenzwirtschaft*, Neudruck Aalen: Scentia.

Stützel, Wolfgang (1958/1978), *Volkswirtschaftliche Saldenmechanik: Ein Beitrag zur Geldtheorie*, Tübingen: Mohr Siebeck.

Sugden, R. (2000), 'Team Preferences', *Economics and Philosophy*, **16**, 175–204.

Sugden, R. (2001), 'The Evolutionary Turn in Game Theory', *Journal of Economic Methodology*, **8**(1), 113–130.

Sugden, R. (2002), 'Beyond Sympathy and Empathy: Adam Smith's Concept of Fellow–Feeling', *Economics and Philosophy*, **18**, 63–87.

Sugden, R.(2004), 'The Opportunity Criterion: Consumer Sovereignty without the Assumption of Coherent Preferences', *American Economic Review*, **94**(4), 1014–33.

Sugden, Robert (2011), 'Salience, Inductive Reasoning and the Emergence of Conventions', *Journal of Economic Behavior and Organization*, **79**, 35–47.

Susskind, Leonard (2006), *The Cosmic Landscape: String Theory and the Illusion of Intelligent Design*, New York and Boston: Little, Brown and Company.

Sutton, D. S. (2007), 'Ritual, Cultural Standardization, and Orthopraxy in China: Reconsidering James L. Watson's Ideas', *Modern China*, **33**(1), 3–21.

Swallow, D. M. (2003), 'Genetics of Lactase Persistence and Lactose Intolerance', *Annual Review of Genetics*, **37**, 197–219, doi:10.1146/annurev.genet.37.110801.143820.

Swann, G.M. Peter (2000), *The Economics of Standardization*, Final Report for Standards and Technical Regulations Directorate, Department of Trade and Industry, Manchester Business School, http://www.bis.gov.uk/files/file11312.pdf, accessed January 24, 2013.

Swann, G. M. P. (2001), 'The Demand for Distinction and the Evolution of the Prestige Car', *Journal of Evolutionary Economics*, **11**(1), 59–76.

Swann, G.M. Peter (2010), *The Economics of Standardization: An Update*, Report for the UK Department of Business, Skills and Innovation, http://www.bis.gov.uk/assets/biscore/innovation/docs/e/10–1135–economics–of–standardization–update.pdf, accessed January 24, 2013.

Swedberg, Richard (2008), 'The Centrality of Materiality: Economic Theorizing from Xenophon to Home Economics and Beyond', in Pinch, Trevor and Richard Swedberg (eds), *Living in a Material World: Economic Sociology Meets Science and Technology Studies*, Cambridge: MIT Press, pp. 57–88.

Tabellini, G. (2008), 'Institutions and Culture', *Journal of the European Economic Association*, **6**(2-3), 255–294.

Taylor, Charles M. (1985), 'Hegel's Philosophy of Mind', in: Charles Taylor, *Human Agency and Language, Philosophical Papers*, Cambridge: Cambridge University Press, pp. 77–96.

Taylor, Charles (1989), *Sources of the Self: The Making of Modern Identity*, Cambridge, MA, USA: Harvard University Press.

Taylor, Michael (1987), *The Possibility of Cooperation*, Cambridge: Cambridge University Press.

Teubner, Gunther (1990), 'Hyperzyklus in Recht und Organisation: Zum Verhältnis von Selbstbeobachtung, Selbstkonstitution und Autopoiese', in Krohn, Wolfgang and Günter Küppers (ed.) (1992), *Selbstorganisation: Aspekte einer wissenschaftlichen Revolution*, Braunschweig and Wiesbaden: Vieweg, pp. 231–264.

Thaler, R. H. (1994), *Quasi–Rational Economics*, New York: Russell Sage.

Thomas, R. Roosevelt jr. (1991), *Beyond Race and Gender: Unleashing the Power of Your Total Work Force by Managing Diversity*, New York: Amacom.

Tilly, Charles (ed.) (1975), *The Formation of National States in Western Europe*, Princeton: Princeton University Press.

Tilly, Charles (1990), *Coercion, Capital, and European States, AD 990–1992*, Cambridge and Oxford: Blackwell.

Todd, P. M. and G. Gigerenzer (2003), 'Bounding Rationality to the World', *Journal of Economic Psychology*, **24**, 143–165.

Tomasello, M. and M. Carpenter (2007), 'Shared Intentionality', *Developmental Science*, **10**(1), 121–125.

Tomasello, M., M. Carpenter, J. Call, T. Behne and H. Moll, (2005), Understanding and Sharing Intentions: The Origin of Cultural Cognition, *Behavioral and Brain Sciences*, **28**, 675–735.

Tomasello, Michael (2008), *Origins of Human Communication*, Cambridge and London: MIT Press.

Tooby, John and Leda Cosmides (2005), 'Conceptual Foundations of Evolutionary Psychology', in Buss, David M. (ed.), *The Handbook of Evolutionary Psychology*, Hoboken: Wiley, pp. 5–67.

Trepel, C., C. R. Fox and R. A. Poldrack (2005), 'Prospect Theory on the Brain? Toward a Cognitive Neuroscience of Decision Under Risk', *Cognitive Brain Research*, **23**, 34–50.

Trivers, Robert (1985*), Social Evolution*. Menlo Park: Benjamin/Cummings.

Tuckett, David (2009), *Addressing the Psychology of Financial Markets*, Institute for Public Policy Research, May 2009.

Tuisku, P., T. K. Pernu and A. Annila (2009), 'In the Light of Time', *Proceedings of the Royal Society A*, **465**, 1173–1198.

Tuomela, R. (2011), 'Searle's New Construction of Social Reality', *Analysis Reviews* **71**(4), 707–719.

Tuomela, Raimo (1995), *The Importance of Us: A Philosophical Study of Basic Social Notions*, Stanford: Stanford University Press.

Tuomela, Raimo (2007), *The Philosophy of Sociality*, Oxford: Oxford University Press.

Turnbull, David (2000), 'Gothic Tales of Spandrels, Hooks and Monsters: Complexity, Multiplicity and Association in the Explanation of Technological Change', in Ziman, John (ed.), *Technological Innovation as an Evolutionary Process*, Cambridge: Cambridge University Press, pp. 101–117.

Turner, Mark (2008), 'Frame Blending', in Rema Rossini Favretti (ed.) (2008), *Frames, Corpora, and Knowledge Representation*, Bologna: Bologna University Press, pp. 13–32.

Tylecote, Andrew (1992), *The Long Wave in the World Economy: The Present Crisis in Historical Perspective*, London and New York: Routledge.

Uffink, Jos (2001), 'Bluff Your Way in the Second Law of Thermodynamics', *Studies in History and Philosophy of Modern Physics*, **32**, 305–394.

Ulanowicz, R. E., S. J. Goerner, B. Lietaer and R. Gomez (2009), 'Quantifying Sustainability: Resilience, Efficiency and the Return of Information Theory', *Ecological Complexity*, **6**(2009), 27–36.

Ulanowicz, Robert E. (1997), *Ecology, the Ascendent Perspective*, New York: Columbia University Press.

Vallino, J. J. (2010), 'Ecosystem Biogeochemistry Considered as a Distributed Metabolic Network Ordered by Maximum Entropy Production', *Philosophical Transactions of the Royal Society B*, **365**, 1417–1427.

Van den Steen, Eric (2010), 'Interpersonal Authority in a Theory of the Firm', *American Economic Review*, **100**(1), 466–490.

Van den Berg, J. C. J. M. (2007), 'Evolutionary Thinking in Environmental Economics', **17**(5), 521–550.

Van Gulik, Robert (2009), 'Functionalism', in McLaughlin, Brian P., Ansgar Beckermann and Sven Walter (eds) (2009), *The Oxford Handbook of Philosophy of Mind*, Oxford: Clarendon Press, pp. 128–151.

Van Veelen, M. and A. Hopfensitz (2007), 'In Love and War: Altruism, Norm Formation, and Two Different Types of Group Selection', *Journal of Theoretical Biology*, **249**, 667–680.

Veblen, Thorstein (1899/1965), *The Theory of the Leisure Class*, New York: Kelley.

Veblen, Thorstein (1914/1990), *The Instinct of Workmanship and the State of Industrial Arts*, New Brunswick and London: Transaction.

Veblen, Thorstein (1921), *The Engineers and the Price System*, reprint 1983, New Brunswick: Transaction.

Vehkavaara, T. (2002), 'Why and How to Naturalize Semiotic Concepts for Biosemiotics', *Sign System Studies,* **30**(1), 293–313.

Vemulapalli, G. K. (2006), 'Physics in the Crucible of Chemistry: Ontological Boundaries and Epistemological Blueprints', in Baird, David, Eric Scerri and Lee McIntyre (eds), *Philosophy of Chemistry: Synthesis of a New Discipline*, Dordrecht: Springer, pp. 191–206.

Vermeij, Geerat J. (2004), *Nature: An Economic History*, Princeton and Oxford: Princeton University Press.

Vermeij, G. J. (2009), 'Comparative Economics: Evolution and the Modern Economy', *Journal of Bioeconomics*, **11**, 105–134.

Vickers, John (2012), 'The Problem of Induction', in Edward N. Zalta (ed.), *The Stanford Encyclopedia of Philosophy* (Winter 2012 Edition), URL = <http://plato.stanford.edu/archives/win2012/entries/induction–problem/>.

Virgo, N. (2010), 'From Maximum Entropy to Maximum Entropy Production: A New Approach', *Entropy* 2010, **12**, 107–126.

Volk, T. and O. Pauluis (2010), 'It Is Not the Entropy You Produce, Rather, How You Produce It', *Philosophical Transactions of the Royal Society B*, **365**, 1317–1322.

Volkenstein, Mikhail V. (2009), *Entropy and Information*, Basel, Boston and Berlin: Birkhäuser.

Vromen, Jack J. (2001), 'The Human Agent in Evolutionary Economics', in Laurent, John and John Nightingale (eds), *Darwinism and Evolutionary Economics*, Cheltenham, UK and Northampton, MA, USA: Edward Elgar, pp. 184–208.

Vromen, J. J. (2006), 'Routines, Genes and Program–Based Behaviour', *Journal of Evolutionary Economics*, **16**(5), 543–560.

Vromen, J. J. (2011), 'Routines as Multilevel Mechanisms', *Journal of Institutional Economics,* **7**(2), 175–196.

Wagner, D., S. Dal Cin, J. D. Sargent, W. M. Kelley and T. F. Heatherton (2011), 'Spontaneous Action Representation in Smokers when Watching Movie Characters Smoke', *Journal of Neuroscience*, **31**(3), 894–898.

Wallerstein, Immanuel (1974), *The Modern World System: Capitalist Agriculture and the Origins of the Modern World–Economy in the Sixteenth Century*, New York and London: Academic Press.

Walsh, Adrian and Tony Lynch (2008), *The Morality of Money: An Exploration in Analytic Philosophy*, Houndsmills and New York: Palgrave Macmillan.

Wang Ning (2003), *Measuring Transaction Costs: An Incomplete Survey*, Ronald Coase Institute Working Paper 2.

Wargo, Donald T., Norman A. Baglini and Katherine A. Nelson (2010), 'The New Millenium's First Global Financial Crisis: The Neuroeconomics of Greed, Self–interest, Deception, False Trust, Overconfidence and Risk Perception', in: Stanton, Angela A., Mellani Day and Isabell M. Welpe (eds), *Neuroeconomics and the Firm*, Cheltenham, UK and Northampton, MA, USA: Edward Elgar, pp. 78–100.

Warr, B., H. Schandl and R. U. Ayres, Robert U. (2008), 'Long Term Trends in Resource Exergy Consumption and Useful Work Supplies in the UK, 1900 to 2000', *Ecological Economics*, **68**, 126–140.

Watts, Duncan (1999), *Small Worlds: The Dynamics of Networks Between Order and Randomness*, Princeton: Princeton University Press.

Weber, B., A. Rangel, M. Wibral and A. Falk, Armin (2009), 'The Medial Prefrontal Cortex Exhibits Money Illusion', *Proceedings of the National Academy of Sciences*, **106**(13), 5025–5028.

Weber, Max (1922), *Wirtschaft und Gesellschaft*, Studienausgabe 8. Auflage, 1985, Tübingen: Mohr Siebeck.

Wegner, Daniel M. and Betsy Sparrow (2007), 'The Puzzle of Coaction', in Ross, Don, David Spurrett, Harold Kincaid and G. Lynn Stephens (eds) (2007), *Distributed Cognition and the Will. Individual Volition and Social Context*, Cambridge, MA, USA: MIT Press, pp. 17–38.

Weintraub, E. Roy (1979), *Microfoundations: The Compatibility of Microeconomics and Macroeconomics*, Cambridge: Cambridge University Press.

Weitzman, M. L. (1998), 'Recombinant Growth', *The Quarterly Journal of Economics*, **CXIII**(2), 331–360.

Weizsäcker, Carl Christian von (2011), *Staatliches Gewaltmonopol, Staatsverschuldung und individuelle Vorsorge*, Walter–Adolf–Jöhr–Vorlesung 2011, Universität St. Gallen, Volkswirtschaftliche Beiträge 13, August 2011.

Wesseling, Ewald (1991), *Individuum und Information. Die Erfassung von Information und Wissen in ökonomischen Handlungstheorien*, Tübingen: Mohr.

West, G. B. and J. H. Brown (2005), 'The Origin of Allometric Scaling Laws in Biology From Genomes to Ecosystems: Towards a Quantitative Unifying Theory of Biological Structure and Organization', *The Journal of Experimental Biology*, **208**, 1575-1592.

West, G. B., J. H. Brown and B. J. Enquist (1997), 'A General Model for the Origin of Allometric Scaling Laws in Biology', *Science*, **276**, 122-126.

West, Robert (2006), *Theory of Addiction*, Oxford: Blackwell and Addiction Press.

West, S. A., A. S. Griffin, and A. Gardner (2007), 'Social Semantics: Altruism, Cooperation, Mutualism, Strong Reciprocity and Group Selection', *Journal of Evolutionary Biology*, **20**, 415–432.

Westphal, Kenneth R. (2008), 'Philosophizing about Nature: Hegel's Philosophical Project, in Beiser, Frederick C. (ed.) (2008), *The Cambridge Companion to Hegel and Nineteenth–Century Philosophy*, Cambridge, UK and New York: Cambridge University Press, pp. 281–311.

White, Colin (1987), *Russia and America: The Roots of Economic Divergence*, London, New York and Sydney: Croom Helm.

White, Douglas R. (2011), 'Kinship, Class, and Community', in Scott, John and Peter Carrington (eds), *The Sage Handbook of Social Network Analysis*, Los Angeles: Sage, pp. 129–147.

White, H. (1981), 'Where Do Markets Come From?', *American Journal of Sociology*, **82**, 517–547.
White, Harrison (2002), *Markets from Networks: Socioeconomic Models of Production*, Princeton: Princeton University Press.
White, Harrison C. (2008), *Identity & Control: How Social Formations Emerge*, Princeton: Princeton University Press.
Whitfield, J. (2005), 'Order Out of Chaos', *Nature*, **436**, 905–907.
Whitfield, J. (2007), 'Survival of the Likeliest?', *PloS Biology*, **5**(5), 962–965.
Wichardt, P. C. (2008), 'Identity and Why We Cooperate With Those We Do', *Journal of Economic Psychology*, **29**, 127–139.
Wicker, Bruno et al. (2003), 'Both of Us Disgusted in My Insula: The Common Neural Basis of Seeing and feeling Disgust', *Neuron*, **40**, 655–664.
Wilcox, K., B. Vallen, L. Block and G. J. Fitzsimons (2009), 'Vicarious Goal Fulfilment: When the Mere Presence of a Healthy Option Leads to an Ironically Indulgent Decision', *Journal of Consumer Research*, **36**, 380–393.
Wilkinson, Nick and Matthias Klaes (2012), *An Introduction to Behavioral Economics*, 2nd edition, Houndmills, Basingstoke: Palgrave Macmillan.
Williamson, Oliver (1985), *The Economic Institutions of Capitalism*, New York: The Free Press.
Wilson, Edward O. (1998), *Consilience. The Unity of Knowledge*, London: Abacus.
Wilson, Robert A. (2004), *Boundaries of the Mind. The Individual in the Fragile Sciences: Cognition*, Cambridge, UK: Cambridge University Press.
Windrum, P., C. Diaz and D. Filiou (2009), 'Exploring the Relationship between Technical and Service Characteristics', *Journal of Evolutionary Economics*, **19**(4), 567–588.
Witt, U. (1992), 'The Endogenous Public Choice Theorist', *Public Choice*, **73**, 117–129.
Witt, U. (2000), 'Learning to Consume – A Theory of Wants and the Growth of Demand', *Journal of Evolutionary Economics*, **11**(1), 23–36.
Witt, Ulrich (2003*), The Evolving Economy. Essays on the Evolutionary Approach to Economics*, Cheltenham, UK and Northampton, MA, USA: Edward Elgar.
Witt, U. (2005), '"Production" in Nature and Production in the Economy – Second Thoughts About Some Basic Economic Concepts', *Structural Change and Economic Dynamics*, **16**, 165–179.
Witt, U. (2008), 'What Is Specific about Evolutionary Economics?', *Journal of Evolutionary Economics*, **18**(5), 547–576.
Witt, U. (2009), 'Propositions about Novelty', *Journal of Economic Behavior & Organization*, **70**, 311–320.
Witt, U. (2010), 'Symbolic Consumption and the Social Construction of Product Characteristics', *Structural Change and Economic Dynamics*, **21**(1), 17–25.
Witt, U. and T. Brenner (2008), 'Output Dynamics, Flow Equilibria and Structural Change – A Prolegomenon to Evolutionary Macroeconomics', *Journal of Evolutionary Economics*, **18**(2), 249–260.
Wittgenstein, Ludwig (1958), *Philosophical Investigations*, Oxford: Basil Blackwell.
Wolfram, Stephen (2002), *A New Kind of Science*, Champaign, IL: Wolfram Media.
Wolpert, David H. (2001), 'Computational Capabilities of Physical Systems', *Physical Review E*, **65**, 016128.
Wolpert, David H. (2008), *Physical Limits to Inference*, arXiv:0708.1362v2.

Woodford, M. (2010), 'Financial Intermediation and Macroeconomic Analysis', *Journal of Economic Perspectives*, **24**(4), 21–44.

Woodward, James (2003), *Making Things Happen. A Theory of Causal Explanation*, Oxford: Oxford University Press.

Woolcock, M. (1998), 'Social Capital and Economic Development: Toward a Theoretical Synthesis and Policy Framework', *Theory and Society*, **27**, 151–208.

World Bank (2008), *Commission on Growth and Development: The Growth Report, Strategies for Sustained Growth and Inclusive Development*, Washington: World Bank.

World Trade Organization (2008), *World Trade Report 2008: Trade in a Globalizing World*, http://www.wto.org/english/res_e/booksp_e/anrep_e/world_trade_report08_e.pdf.

Wrangham, R. and N. Conklin–Brittain (2003), 'Cooking As a Biological Trait', *Comparative Biochemistry and Physiology Part A*, **136**, 35–46.

Wrangham, R. W. et al. (1999), 'The Raw and the Stolen: Cooking and the Ecology of Human Origins', *Current Anthropology*, **40**(5), 567–594.

Wright, L. (1973), 'Functions', *Philosophical Review*, **82**, 139–168.

Wuketits, Franz (1987), 'Evolution als Systemprozeß: Die Systemtheorie der Evolution', in Siewing, Rolf (ed.), *Evolution. Bedingungen – Resultate – Konsequenzen*, Stuttgart/New York: Gustav Fischer, pp. 453–474.

Wyatt, Sally (2008), 'Technological Determinism Is Dead: Long Live Technological Determininism', in Hackett, Edward J., Olga Amsterdamska, Michael Lynch, Judy Wajcman, Judy (eds), *The Handbook of Science and Technology Studies*, Cambridge and London: MIT Press, pp. 166–180.

Yamagishi, Toshio (2012), 'Micro–Macro Dynamics of the Cultural Construction of Reality. A Niche Construction Approach to Culture', in Gelfland, Michele J., Chi-yue Chiu and Ying-yi Hong (eds), *Advances in Culture and Psychology, Volume One*, Oxford and New York: Oxford University Press, pp. 251–308.

Yoo, Julie (2009), 'Anomalous Monism', in: McLaughlin, Brian P., Ansgar Beckermann and Sven Walter (eds) (2009), *The Oxford Handbook of Philosophy of Mind*, Oxford: Clarendon Press, pp. 95–109.

Young, H. Peyton (1998), *Individual Strategy and Social Structure*, Princeton: Princeton University Press.

Young, J. J. (2001), 'Risk(ing) Metaphors', *Critical Perspectives on Accounting*, **12**, 607–625.

Zahavi, Amotz and Avishag Zahavi (1997), *The Handicap Principle: A Missing Piece of Darwin's Puzzle*, New York and Oxford: Oxford University Press.

Zak, P. J. (2011), 'The Physiology of Moral Sentiments', *Journal of Economic Behavior & Organization*, **77**, 53–65.

Zalasiewicz, J., M. Williams et al. (2008), 'Are We Now Living in the Anthropocene?', *GSA Today*, **18**(2), 4–8.

Zaloom, C. (2003), 'Ambiguous Numbers: Trading Technologies and Interpretation in Financial Markets', *American Ethnologist*, **30**(2), 258–272.

Zaloom, C. (2004), 'The Productive Life of Risk', *Current Anthropology*, **19**(3), 365–391.

Zeh, H. Dieter (2005), *Entropie*, Frankfurt: Fischer.

Zehe, E., T. Blume and G. Blöschl (2010), 'The Principle of 'Maximum Energy Dissipation': A Novel Thermodynamic Perspective on Rapid Water Flows in

Connected Soil Structures', *Philosophical Transactions of the Royal Society B*, **365**, 1377–1386.

Zeidler, P. (2000), 'The Epistemological Status of Theoretical Models of Molecular Structure', *HYLE – International Journal for Philosophy of Chemistry,* **6**(1), 17–34.

Zeilinger, Anton (1996), *On the Interpretation and Philosophical Foundation of Quantum Mechanics*, http://www.quantum.at/fileadmin/zeilinger/philosoph.pdf, accessed January 11, 2013.

Zeilinger, Anton (1999), 'A Foundational Principle for Quantum Mechanics', *Foundations of Physics*, **29**(4), 631–643.

Zelin, M. (2009), 'The Firm in Early Modern China', *Journal of Economic Behavior & Organization*, **71**, 623–637.

Zhirnov, V. V. and D. J. C. Herr (2001), 'New Frontiers: Self–Assembly and Nanoelectronics', *Computer*, **34**(1), 34–43.

Zurek, W.H. (1989a), 'Algorithmic Randomness and Physical Entropy', *Physical Review A,* **40**(8), 4731–4751.

Zurek, W.H. (1989b), 'Thermodynamic Costs of Computation, Algorithmic Complexity and the Information Metric', *Nature*, **341**, 119–124.

Zweynert, Joachim (2011), 'Shock Therapy and the Transfer of Institutions: The New Debate and Some Lessons from the Post–1806 Reforms in Prussia and in Southwestern Germany, *Constitutional Political Economy*, **22**, 122–140.

Index